NBER Macroeconomics Annual 2004

NBER Macroeconomics Annual 2004

Editors
Mark Gertler and
Kenneth Rogoff

The MIT Press
Cambridge, Massachusetts
London, England

NBER/Macroeconomics Annual, Number 19, 2004
ISSN: 0889-3365
ISBN: Hardcover 0-262-07263-7
ISBN: Paperback 0-262-57229-X

Published annually by The MIT Press, Cambridge, Massachusetts 02142-1407

Standing orders/subscriptions are available. Inquiries, and changes to subscriptions and addresses should be addressed to MIT Press Standing Order Department/BB, Five Cambridge Center, Cambridge, MA 02142-1407, phone 617-258-1581, fax 617-253-1709, email standing-orders@mitpress.mit.edu

In the United Kingdom, continental Europe, and the Middle East and Africa, send single copy and back volume orders to: The MIT Press Ltd., Fitzroy House, 11 Chenies Street, London WC1E 7ET England, phone 44-020-7306-0603, fax 44-020-7306-0604, email info@hup-MITpress.co.uk, website http://mitpress.mit.edu

In the United States and for all other countries, send single copy and back volume orders to: The MIT Press c/o Triliteral, 100 Maple Ridge Drive, Cumberland, RI 02864, phone 1-800-405-1619 (U.S. and Canada) or 401-658-4226, fax 1-800-406-9145 (U.S. and Canada) or 401-531-2801, email mitpress-orders@mit.edu, website http://mitpress.mit.edu

This book was set in Palatino on 3B2 by Asco Typesetters, Hong Kong, and was printed and bound in the United States of America.

10 9 8 7 6 5 4 3 2 1

Contents

Relation of the Directors to the Work and Publications of the NBER

1. The object of the NBER is to ascertain and present to the economics profession, and to the public more generally, important economic facts and their interpretation in a scientific manner without policy recommendations. The Board of Directors is charged with the responsibility of ensuring that the work of the NBER is carried on in strict conformity with this object.

2. The President shall establish an internal review process to ensure that book manuscripts proposed for publication DO NOT contain policy recommendations. This shall apply both to the proceedings of conferences and to manuscripts by a single author or by one or more co-authors but shall not apply to authors of comments at NBER conferences who are not NBER affiliates.

3. No book manuscript reporting research shall be published by the NBER until the President has sent to each member of the Board a notice that a manuscript is recommended for publication and that in the President's opinion it is suitable for publication in accordance with the above principles of the NBER. Such notification will include a table of contents and an abstract or summary of the manuscript's content, a list of contributors if applicable, and a response form for use by Directors who desire a copy of the manuscript for review. Each manuscript shall contain a summary drawing attention to the nature and treatment of the problem studied and the main conclusions reached.

4. No volume shall be published until forty-five days have elapsed from the above notification of intention to publish it. During this period a copy shall be sent to any Director requesting it, and if any Director objects to publication on the grounds that the manuscript contains policy recommendations, the objection will be presented to the author(s) or editor(s). In case of dispute, all members of the Board shall

be notified, and the President shall appoint an ad hoc committee of the Board to decide the matter; thirty days additional shall be granted for this purpose.

5. The President shall present annually to the Board a report describing the internal manuscript review process, any objections made by Directors before publication or by anyone after publication, any disputes about such matters, and how they were handled.

6. Publications of the NBER issued for informational purposes concerning the work of the Bureau, or issued to inform the public of the activities at the Bureau, including but not limited to the NBER Digest and Reporter, shall be consistent with the object stated in paragraph 1. They shall contain a specific disclaimer noting that they have not passed through the review procedures required in this resolution. The Executive Committee of the Board is charged with the review of all such publications from time to time.

7. NBER working papers and manuscripts distributed on the Bureau's web site are not deemed to be publications for the purpose of this resolution, but they shall be consistent with the object stated in paragraph 1. Working papers shall contain a specific disclaimer noting that they have not passed through the review procedures required in this resolution. The NBER's web site shall contain a similar disclaimer. The President shall establish an internal review process to ensure that the working papers and the web site do not contain policy recommendations, and shall report annually to the Board on this process and any concerns raised in connection with it.

8. Unless otherwise determined by the Board or exempted by the terms of paragraphs 6 and 7, a copy of this resolution shall be printed in each NBER publication as described in paragraph 2 above.

Editorial, NBER Macroeconomics Annual 2004

In 2004, as the world continues its steady emergence from the global slowdown, several questions loom over the policy world: the aggressive countercyclical U.S. fiscal policy was clearly a significant factor in softening the global recession. But if the federal government continues to pile up large deficits, what will be the long-term effect on U.S. and global interest rates? As the world looks ahead to the day when Alan Greenspan is no longer chair of the Federal Reserve Board, can economic science offer an algorithm for capturing the Fed's complex nuanced readings of the economy? And how important is monetary policy anyway? Is the world driven by Schumpeterian technology shocks more than financial factors, and as prices and wages become more flexible, is monetary policy becoming more impotent? As is well known to long-time readers of the NBER *Macroeconomics Annual*, there is an intense debate among academic macroeconomists about the role of real factors, as opposed to Keynesian demand shocks, in driving business cycles. What about emerging markets and developing countries, many of whom experienced severe macroeconomic distress during the downturn, with seemingly very little scope for countercyclical policy? Is there anything they can do now, during the upturn, to prepare for the inevitable next slowdown? This volume of the NBER *Macroeconomics Annual* features a range of papers by leading researchers aimed at providing coherent and informative answers to these important questions.

Eric M. Engen and R. Glenn Hubbard's paper, "Federal Government Debt and Interest Rates," reveals a truly remarkable emerging empirical consensus on the effects of budget deficits on interest rates. It is especially remarkable given the empirical controversy that has dogged the field for many years in the wake of Robert Barro's classic paper suggesting that the baseline effect ought to be zero. The "NBER

Macroeconomics Annual consensus" estimates appear to be that a \$110 billion increase in government debt (equal to 1% of GDP) raises real U.S. interest rates by approximately 3.5 basis points, and reduces the U.S. \$30 trillion capital stock by approximately .4%, or \$120 billion. Engen and Hubbard's critical survey of the literature appears to support this conclusion, as does the new theoretical and empirical research they present here. Given the wide range of perspectives provided by authors and discussants, and the lack of any previous recognized consensus in the literature, the consensus produced here is notable. Thus, a back-of-the-envelope calculation suggests that if cumulative deficits had been \$2 trillion lower over the first four years of the Bush administration (where Hubbard served from 2000–2002 as chair of the Council of Economic Advisers), real interest rates would be approximately 70 basis points lower than they are today. The consensus breaks down, however, when it comes to extrapolating welfare effects. Just because the change in interest rates is modest does not mean that the cumulative loss in output—coming from having a capital stock that may remain over \$1 trillion lower for a sustained period—is necessarily small. Though the welfare analysis does not end in a clear consensus, the reader should find the debate highly illuminating, both in showing the key policy questions and the direction of future research.

It is widely recognized that the United States Federal Reserve staff's Greenbook forecasts of growth and inflation—on which Federal Open Market Committee interest rate decisions are based—far outperform what can be achieved mechanically with any standard econometric model based on publicly available information. In an extremely ambitious exercise, Domenico Giannone, Lucrezia Reichlin, and Luca Sala attempt to find a way to match Greenbook forecasts, using reasonably straightforward econometric methods and, more important, real-time data, that is, data that was actually available at the time the Greenbook was published rather than later revised data. Interestingly, they find that for a panel of Greenbook forecasts dating from 1970–1996, the bulk of the dynamics of inflation and output, as well as Greenbook forecasts of these same variables, can be explained by two shocks, one nominal and one real. Output appears to be driven mainly by the real shock and inflation by the nominal shock. This finding, if it stands up to later challenges, including points raised by their discussants, suggests that the stochastic dimension of the U.S. economy is relatively small, in turn implying that relatively simple rules (e.g., Taylor rules) can potentially be very effective. Indeed, their findings suggest that one may well be able to find other relatively simple rules that outperform the Taylor rule since by tracking any forecastable measure of real activity and price dynamics, the central bank can effectively track all the macroeconomic fundamentals of an economy.

Jordi Galí and Pau Rabanal's paper, "Technology Shocks and Aggregate Fluctuations: How Well Does the Real Business Cycle Model Fit Postwar U.S. Data?" extends a significant recent literature (including several early papers by Galí) that poses a challenge to the Kydland–Prescott real business cycle view of the world. The authors' answer to the rhetorical question posed in their paper is, quite simply, no. Their claim, simply put, is that technology shocks cannot explain 75% of output volatility as Prescott claimed, but rather one-third or less, with preference shocks (demand shocks) being far more important, and accounting for well over half the variance of output. To arrive at their conclusion, Galí and Rabanal rely primarily on a direct econometric estimation rather than on calibration and matching of variances, as in conventional real business cycle analyses. Galí and Rabanal argue that, even if technological shocks *were* more important than their estimates suggest, the most important variety is likely to be sector-specific rather than the kind of aggregate production shocks emphasized in the RBC model. Galí and Rabanal's conclusions, while exceptionally stark, are not totally at odds with recent perspectives in the literature. Robert Lucas's famous monetary neutrality result in 1972, while leading much of the profession to temporarily abandon Keynesian-style sticky-price and sticky-wage models for almost two decades, no longer seems as compelling in an era where businesspeople and investors hang on every word uttered by central bank officials. Nevertheless, the question for researchers now is whether the pendulum has now swung back too far in the other direction. Certainly, both the discussants in our volume think so, including Valerie Ramey and, even more so, Ellen R. McGrattan. The discussants make a spirited attempt to show that Galí and Rabanal take their rejection of RBC models too far. This is clearly the kind of fundamental methodological issue the *Macroeconomics Annual* was created to deal with, and we anticipate further discussions in later issues.

Paul Gomme, Richard Rogerson, Peter Rupert, and Randall Wright, in their paper "The Business Cycle and the Life Cycle," also attempt to cast doubt on the growing consensus that nominal wage and price rigidities must play a central role in business cycles. The essence of their claim is that real business cycles do a decent job in accounting for employment fluctuations among 45- to 64-year-old workers, and without resorting to the extreme labor supply elasticities that have undermined the credibility of most previous RBC models of labor market cycles. Their life-cycle RBC model confronts problems only in explaining employment fluctuations among the younger group. Their paper, which is innovative both methodologically (in its treatment of the life cycle in an RBC context) and in terms of the micro data set they use, would appear to develop a new stylized fact that both sides of the debate must seek to explain. Can the answer be that, for older workers, it is easier for employers to vary other parameters of the employment contract (pensions, health care, etc.) than for younger workers, making the constraints of nominal wage contracting less severe? Or do young workers have much higher employment volatility due to union seniority rules, greater matching problems, or other issues? This paper, together with Robert Shimer's 1998 NBER *Macroeconomics Annual* paper on cohort effects and employment fluctuations, show that the representative agent model may be highly misleading when it comes to understanding business and employment cycles.

In their paper "When It Rains, It Pours: Procyclical Capital Flows and Macroeconomic Policies," Graciela L. Kaminsky, Carmen M. Reinhart, and Carlos A. Végh systematically tackle the question of whether macroeconomic policy is really more procyclical in developing countries, and why. Gavin and Perotti had written on this very same topic eight years ago for the *Macroeconomics Annual*, though their paper did not cover developing countries; Kaminsky, Reinhart, and Végh appear to be the first to do so. Also, Gavin and Perotti looked only at fiscal policy and not monetary policy. Consistent with conventional wisdom, they find that fiscal policy is procyclical in developing countries, and highly positively correlated with the capital inflow cycle. For monetary policy, policy is highly procyclical for developing countries that are emerging markets, that is, countries that have significant access to, and engagement with, international capital markets. One interesting nuance that comes out of the monetary policy analysis is that developing countries with more flexible exchange rate systems appear to have more countercyclical monetary policy than do countries with inflexible exchange rates. The authors also show that fiscal policy is less universally countercyclical in Organization for Economic Cooperation and Development (OECD) countries than is commonly supposed. In particular, countries like Belgium and Italy, with extremely high public debts exceeding over 100% of gross domestic product (GDP), find it difficult to conduct countercyclical policy, perhaps for similar reasons as those for developing countries: they would like to run bigger deficits during recessions, but with cumulated past debts already extremely high, they would have to face a very high interest rate penalty. This point was highlighted by Roberto Rigobon in his discussion. Gita Gopinath, in her discussion, argued that the significant component of the different fiscal policy and capital flow cycles one sees in OECD countries versus emerging markets comes from the fact that output shocks are much more transitory in the former group. For emerging markets, the cycle is the trend, so that sharp responses are rational. Her analysis, of course, raises the question of whether emerging market government policy is partly responsible for the apparent unit root nature of output in those countries, as Kaminsky, Reinhart, and Végh suggest.

Finally, David K. Backus, Bryan R. Routledge, and Stanley E. Zin provide an extremely user-friendly guide to "Exotic Preferences for Macroeconomists." Over the past twenty years, problems such as the equity premium puzzle, the generation of adequate persistence in standard macroeconomic simulation models, and the inability to explain saving behavior adequately have driven macroeconomists to search for richer varieties of preferences on which to base the microeconomic foundations of their models. Under the label *exotic*, the authors include departures from expected utility, nonlinear aggregators of preferences over time, hyperbolic discounting, and other frameworks. They illustrate the models in the context of a variety of problems, including asset pricing, portfolio allocation, consumption, and saving. Backus, Routledge, and Zin's clear and elegant exposition of alternative preference structures should make their application less daunting to macroeconomists who are considering trying out these new tools.

The authors would like to take this opportunity to thank Martin Feldstein and the National Bureau of Economic Research for its continued support of the NBER *Macroeconomics Annual* and its associated conference; the NBER's conference staff, especially Rob Shannon, for excellent logistical support; and the National Science Foundation for financial assistance. Jane Trahan did a superb job in helping to edit and produce the manuscript. We also appreciate the assistance of Marisa Dinkin. Finally, Julen Esteban-Pretel did an excellent job as a conference rapporteur and editorial assistant for this volume.

Mark Gertler and Kenneth Rogoff

Abstracts

"When It Rains, It Pours: Procyclical Capital Flows and Macroeconomic Policies"
GRACIELA L. KAMINSKY, CARMEN M. REINHART, AND CARLOS A. VÉGH

Based on a sample of 104 countries, we document four key stylized facts regarding the interaction among capital flows, fiscal policy, and monetary policy. First, net capital inflows are procyclical (i.e., external borrowing increases in good times and falls in bad times) in most Organization for Economic Cooperation and Development (OECD) and developing countries. The procyclicality of net capital inflows is particularly strong for middle-high-income countries (emerging markets). Second, fiscal policy is procyclical (i.e., government spending increases in good times and falls in bad times) for the majority of developing countries. Third, for emerging markets, monetary policy appears to be procyclical (i.e., policy rates are lowered in good times and raised in bad times). Fourth, in developing countries—and particularly for emerging markets—periods of capital inflows are associated with expansionary macroeconomic policies and periods of capital outflows with contractionary macroeconomic policies. In such countries, therefore, when it rains, it does indeed pour.

"Federal Government Debt and Interest Rates"
ERIC M. ENGEN AND R. GLENN HUBBARD

Does government debt affect interest rates? Despite a substantial body of empirical analysis, the answer based on the past two decades of research is mixed. While many studies suggest, at most, a single-digit rise in the interest rate when government debt increases by 1% of gross domestic product (GDP), others estimate either much larger effects or find no effect. Comparing results across studies is complicated by differences in economic models, definitions of government debt and interest rates, econometric approaches, and sources of data.

Using a standard set of data and a simple analytical framework, we reconsider and add to empirical evidence about the effect of federal government debt and interest rates. We begin by deriving analytically the effect of government debt on the real interest rate and find that an increase in government debt equivalent to 1% of GDP would be predicted to increase the real interest rate by about two to three basis points. While some existing studies estimate effects in this range, others find larger effects. In almost all cases, these larger estimates come from specifications relating federal deficits (as opposed to debt) and the level of interest rates or from specifications not controlling adequately for macroeconomic influences on interest rates that might be correlated with deficits.

We present our own empirical analysis in two parts. First, we examine a variety of conventional reduced-form specifications linking interest rates and government debt and other variables. In particular, we provide estimates for three types of specifications to permit comparisons among different approaches taken in previous research; we estimate the effect of an expected, or projected, measure of federal government debt on a forward-looking measure of the real interest rate; an expected, or projected, measure of federal government debt on a current measure of the real interest rate; and a current measure of federal government debt on a current measure of the real interest rate. Most of the statistically significant estimated effects are consistent with the prediction of the simple analytical calculation. Second, we provide evidence using vector autoregression analysis. In general, these results are similar to those found in our reduced-form econometric analysis and are consistent with the analytical calculations.

Taken together, the bulk of our empirical results suggests that an increase in federal government debt equivalent to 1% of GDP, all else being equal, would be expected to increase the long-term real rate of interest by about three basis points (though one specification suggests a larger impact), while some estimates are not statistically significantly different from zero. By presenting a range of results with the same data, we illustrate the dependence of estimation on specification and definition differences.

"Monetary Policy in Real Time"
DOMENICO GIANNONE, LUCREZIA REICHLIN, AND LUCA SALA

We analyze the panel of the Greenbook forecasts (sample 1970–1996) and a large panel of monthly variables for the United States (sample 1970–2003) and show that the bulk of dynamics of both the variables and their forecasts is explained by two shocks. A two-factor model that exploits, in real time, information on many time series to extract a two-dimensional signal produces a degree of forecasting accuracy of the federal funds rate similar to that of the markets and, for output and inflation, similar to that of the Greenbook forecasts. This leads us to conclude that the stochastic dimension of the U.S. economy is two. We also show that dimension two is generated by a real and nominal shock, with output mainly driven by the real shock, and inflation mainly driven by the nominal shock. The implication is that, by tracking any forecastable measure of real activity and price dynamics, the central bank can track all fundamental dynamics in the economy.

"Technology Shocks and Aggregate Fluctuations: How Well Does the Real Business Cycle Model Fit Postwar U.S. Data?"
JORDI GALÍ AND PAU RABANAL

Our answer: not so well. We reach that conclusion after reviewing recent research on the role of technology as a source of economic fluctuations. The bulk of the evidence suggests a limited role for aggregate technology shocks, pointing instead to demand factors as the main force behind the strong positive comovement between output and labor input measures.

"Exotic Preferences for Macroeconomists"
DAVID K. BACKUS, BRYAN R. ROUTLEDGE, AND STANLEY E. ZIN

We provide a user's guide to exotic preferences: nonlinear time aggregators, departures from expected utility, preferences over time with known and unknown probabilities, risk-sensitive and robust control, hyperbolic discounting, and preferences over sets (temptations). We apply each to a number of classic problems in macroeconomics and finance, including consumption and saving, portfolio choice, asset pricing, and Pareto optimal allocations.

"The Business Cycle and the Life Cycle"
PAUL GOMME, RICHARD ROGERSON, PETER RUPERT, AND RANDALL WRIGHT

Our paper documents the differences in the variability of hours worked over the business cycle across several demographic groups and shows that these differences are large. We argue that understanding these differences should be useful in understanding the forces that account for aggregate fluctuations in hours worked. In particular, it is well known that standard models of the business cycle driven by technology shocks do not account for all of the variability in hours of work. This raises the following question: To what extent can the forces in this model account for the differences across demographic groups? We explore this in the context of hours fluctuations by age groups by formulating and analyzing a stochastic overlapping generations model. Our analysis shows that the model does a good job of accounting for hours fluctuations for prime-age workers but not for young or old workers. We conclude that a key issue is to understand why fluctuations for young and old workers are so much larger.

When It Rains, It Pours: Procyclical Capital Flows and Macroeconomic Policies

Graciela L. Kaminsky,
Carmen M. Reinhart, and
Carlos A. Végh
George Washington University and NBER; University of Maryland, College Park and NBER; and UCLA and NBER

1. Introduction

Any expert on financial crises in emerging markets could cite ample anecdotal evidence to support the view that macroeconomic policies are highly procyclical, at least in moments of extreme duress. At the time that economic activity is contracting (often markedly) amidst a crisis, the fiscal authority cuts budgets deficits while the central bank raises interest rates—possibly exacerbating the economic contraction. Procyclical policies, however, do not appear to be limited to crisis periods in many developing countries. In fact, the roots of most of the debt crises in emerging markets are all too often found in governments that go through bouts of high spending and borrowing when the times are favorable and international capital is plentiful.[1]

Gavin and Perotti (1997) first called attention to the phenomenon of procyclical fiscal policy by showing that fiscal policy in Latin America tends to be expansionary in good times and contractionary in bad times. Talvi and Végh (2000) argued that, far from being a phenomenon peculiar to Latin America, procyclical fiscal policy seems to be the norm in the developing world just as fiscal policy is acyclical in the advanced economies. Using a different econometric approach, Braun (2001) reaches a similar conclusion for developing countries, though he finds evidence that fiscal policy is countercyclical in OECD countries. Lane (2003) also provides evidence on the procyclical nature of fiscal policy in developing countries compared to OECD countries.

Several explanations have been advanced to explain the procyclical nature of fiscal policy in developing countries compared to industrial countries. Gavin and Perotti (1997), among others, have argued that developing countries face credit constraints that prevent them from borrowing in bad times. Hence, they are "forced" to repay in bad times, which requires a contractionary fiscal policy. In contrast, Tornell and Lane (1999) develop a political economy model in which competition for a common pool of funds among different units (ministries, provinces) leads to the so-called voracity effect, whereby expenditure could actually exceed a given windfall. Taking as given such a political distortion, Talvi and Végh (2000) show how policymakers would find it optimal to run smaller primary surpluses in good times by increasing government spending and reducing tax rates. Last, Riascos and Végh (2003) show how incomplete markets could explain procyclical fiscal policy as the outcome of a Ramsey problem without having to impose any additional frictions.

In terms of monetary policy, the impression certainly exists that developing countries often tighten the monetary strings in bad times (see Lane, 2003), but systematic empirical work is scant.[2] This is probably due to the notorious difficulties (present even for advanced countries) in empirically characterizing the stance of monetary policy.[3]

Relying on data for 104 countries for the period 1960–2003, this paper revisits the evidence on the procyclical nature of fiscal policy and, as far as we know, presents a first systematic effort to document empirically the cyclical properties of monetary policy in developing countries. It departs from earlier efforts investigating fiscal policy cycles in several dimensions. First, it provides an analytical framework for interpreting the behavior of a broad variety of fiscal indicators, which leads to a reinterpretation of some earlier results in the literature. Second, it analyzes countries grouped by income levels to capture the fact that while wealthier countries have continuous access to international capital markets, low-income countries are almost exclusively shut out at all times, and middle-income countries have a precarious and volatile relationship with international capital. Third, it examines closely the interaction among the business cycle, international capital flows, and macroeconomic policy.[4] Our premise is that the capital flow cycle is tied to the business cycle and may even influence macroeconomic policies, particularly in middle income countries. Fourth, it offers an eclectic approach toward defining good and bad times and measuring the stance of fiscal and monetary policy by employing a broad range of indicators. Fifth, it disaggregates the sample along a variety of dimensions, by (1) differentiating crises episodes from tranquil periods, (2) treating the more rigid exchange rate arrangements separately from the more flexible ones, and (3) comparing earlier and more recent periods to assess whether the degree of capital market integration has altered cyclical patterns and relationships. Last, the analysis offers more comprehensive country coverage than earlier efforts.

The paper proceeds as follows. The next section discusses the underlying conceptual framework used to interpret the data on capital flows and fiscal and monetary policy, and describes the approach followed to define business cycles. Section 3 presents a broad view of our main findings; Section 4 provides greater detail on the main stylized facts by grouping countries according to income per-capita levels, type of exchange rate arrangement, and other relevant subsamples. Section 5 contains concluding remarks.

2. Conceptual Framework

This section lays out the conceptual framework used to interpret our empirical findings in the following sections. Specifically, we will discuss how to think about the cyclical properties of capital flows, fiscal policy, and monetary policy. A thorough reading of the blossoming literature on the cyclical nature of policy in developing countries reveals a somewhat loose approach to defining basic concepts, which often renders the discussion rather imprecise. For instance, countercyclical fiscal policy is often defined as running fiscal deficits in bad times and surpluses in good times (i.e., as a positive correlation between changes in output and changes in the fiscal balance). As we will argue, however, this is an unfortunate way of defining the concept since running a fiscal deficit in bad times may be consistent with rather different approaches to fiscal stabilization. In the same vein, considering fiscal variables as a proportion of GDP—as is most often done in this literature—could yield misleading results since the cyclical stance of fiscal policy may be dominated by the cyclical behavior of output.

In light of these critical conceptual issues—and at the risk of perhaps appearing sometimes obvious—we will be very specific as to how we define countercyclicality, procyclicality, and acyclicality.

2.1 *Capital Flows*

We define the cyclical properties of capital flows as follows (Table 1):

1. Capital flows into a country are said to be countercyclical when the correlation between the cyclical components of net capital inflows and

Table 1
Capital flows: theoretical correlations with the business cycle

	Net capital inflows	Net capital inflows/GDP
Countercyclical	–	–
Procyclical	+	–/0/+
Acyclical	0	–

output is negative. In other words, the economy borrows from abroad in bad times (i.e., capital flows in) and lends/repays in good times (i.e., capital flows out).

2. Capital flows are procyclical when the correlation between the cyclical components of net capital inflows and output is positive. The economy thus borrows from abroad in good times (i.e., capital flows in) and lends/repays in bad times (i.e., capital flows out).

3. Capital flows are acyclical when the correlation between the cyclical components of net capital inflows and output is not statistically significant. The pattern of international borrowing and lending is thus not systematically related to the business cycle.

While this may appear self-evident, the mapping between the cyclical properties of net capital inflows as a share of GDP (a commonly used measure) and the business cycle is not clear cut. As the second column of Table 1 indicates, in the case of countercyclical capital inflows, this ratio should also have a negative correlation with output since in good (bad) times, net capital inflows fall (increase) and GDP increases (fall). In the case of procyclical net capital inflows, however, this ratio could have any sign since in good (bad) times, net capital inflows increase (fall) and GDP also increases (falls). In the acyclical case, the behavior of the ratio is dominated by the changes in GDP and therefore has a negative correlation. Thus, the ratio of net capital inflows to GDP will only provide an unambiguous indication of the cyclicality of net capital inflows if it has a positive sign (or is zero) in which case it would be indicating procylical capital flows. If it has a negative sign, however, it does not allow us to discriminate among the three cyclical patterns.

Our definition of the cyclical properties of capital flows thus focuses on whether capital flows tend to reinforce or stabilize the business cycle. To fix ideas, consider the standard endowment model of a small open economy (with no money). In the absence of any intertemporal distortion, households want to keep consumption flat over time. Thus, in response to a temporary negative endowment shock, the economy borrows from abroad to sustain the permanent level of consumption. During good times, the economy repays its debt. Saving is thus positively correlated with the business cycle. Hence, in the standard model with no investment, capital inflows are countercyclical and tend to stabilize the cycle. Naturally, the counterpart of countercyclical borrowing in the standard real model is a procyclical current account.

Conversely, if the economy borrowed during good times and lent during bad times, capital flows would be procyclical because they would tend to reinforce the business cycle. In this case, the counterpart would be a countercyclical current account. Plausible theoretical explanations for procyclical capital flows include the following. First, suppose that physical capital is added to the basic model described above and that the business cycle is driven by productivity shocks. Then, a temporary and positive productivity shock would lead to an increase in saving (for the consumption smoothing motives described above) and to an increase in investment (as the return on capital has increased). If the investment effect dominates, then borrowing would be procyclical because the need to finance profitable investment more than offsets the saving effect.

A second explanation—particularly relevant for emerging countries—would result from intertemporal distortions in consumption imposed by temporary policies (like inflation stabilization programs or temporary liberalization policies; see Calvo, 1987; Calvo and Végh, 1999). An unintended consequence of such temporary policies is to make consumption relatively cheaper during good times (by reducing the effective price of consumption), thus leading to a consumption boom that is financed by borrowing from abroad. In this case, saving falls in good times, which renders capital flows procyclical.[5]

A third possibility—also relevant for emerging countries—is that the availability of international capital varies with the business cycle. If foreign investors respond to the evidence of an improving local economy by bidding down country risk premiums (perhaps encouraged by low interest rates at financial centers), residents of the small economy may view this as a temporary opportunity to finance consumption cheaply and therefore dissave.[6] We should remember that the consumption booms financed by capital inflows in many emerging market economies in the first part of the 1990s were seen at the time as an example of the capital inflow problem, as in Calvo, Leiderman, and Reinhart (1993, 1994).

Finally, notice that, in practice, movements in international reserves could break the link between procyclical borrowing and current account deficits (or countercyclical borrowing and current account surpluses) that would arise in the basic real intertemporal model. Indeed, recall the basic balance of payments accounting identity:

Change in international reserves

$$= \textit{current account balance} + \textit{capital account balance}$$

Hence, positive net capital inflows (a capital account surplus) would not necessarily be associated with a negative current account balance if international reserves were increasing. Therefore, the cyclical properties of the current account are an imperfect indicator of those of capital flows.

2.2 *Fiscal Policy*

Since the concept of policy cyclicality is important to the extent that it can help us understand or guide actual policy, it makes sense to define policy cyclicality in terms of policy instruments as opposed to outcomes (i.e., endogenous variables). Hence, we will define the cyclicality of fiscal policy in terms of government spending (g) and tax rates (τ) (instead of defining it in terms of, say, the fiscal balance or tax revenues). Given this definition, we will then examine the cyclical implications for important endogenous variables such as the primary fiscal balance, tax revenues, and fiscal variables as a proportion of GDP. We define fiscal policy cyclicality as follows (see Table 2):

1. A countercyclical fiscal policy involves lower (higher) government spending and higher (lower) tax rates in good (bad) times. We call

Table 2
Fiscal indicators: theoretical correlations with the business cycle

	g	τ	Tax revenues	Primary balance	g/GDP	Tax revenues/ GDP	Primary balance/ GDP
Countercyclical	−	+	+	+	−	−/0/+	−/0/+
Procyclical	+	−	−/0/+	−/0/+	−/0/+	−/0/+	−/0/+
Acyclical	0	0	+	+	−	−/0/+	−/0/+

such a policy countercyclical because it would tend to stabilize the business cycle (i.e., fiscal policy is contractionary in good times and expansionary in bad times).

2. A procyclical fiscal policy involves higher (lower) government spending and lower (higher) tax rates in good (bad) times. We call such a policy procyclical because it tends to reinforce the business cycle (i.e., fiscal policy is expansionary in good times and contractionary in bad times).[7]

3. An acyclical fiscal policy involves constant government spending and constant tax rates over the cycle (or more precisely, for the case of a stochastic world, government spending and tax rates do not vary systematically with the business cycle). We call such a policy acyclical because it neither reinforces nor stabilizes the business cycle.

The correlations implied by these definitions are shown in the first two columns of Table 2.

We next turn to the implications of these cyclical definitions of fiscal policy for the behavior of tax revenues, the primary fiscal balance, and government expenditure, tax revenues, and primary balance as a proportion of GDP.[8] In doing so, we will make use of the following two definitions:

Tax revenues $=$ *tax rate* $\times$ *tax base*

Primary balance $=$ *tax revenues* $-$ *government expenditures*

(excluding interest payments)

Consider first an acyclical fiscal policy. Since the tax rate is constant over the cycle and the tax base increases in good times and falls in bad times, tax revenues will have a positive correlation with the business cycle. This, in turn, implies that the primary balance will also be positively correlated with the cycle. The ratio of government expenditure (net of interest payments) to GDP will be negatively correlated with the cycle because government expenditure does not vary and, by definition, GDP is high (low) in good (bad) times. Given that tax revenues are higher (lower) in good (bad) times, the correlation of the ratio of tax revenues to GDP with the cycle is ambiguous (i.e., it could be positive, zero, or negative, as indicated in Table 2). As a result, the correlation of the primary balance as a proportion of GDP with the cycle will also be ambiguous.

Consider procyclical fiscal policy. Since by definition the tax rate goes down (up) in good (bad) times but the tax base moves in the opposite direction, the correlation of tax revenues with the cycle is ambiguous. Since *g* goes up in good times, the correlation of g/GDP can, in principle, take on any value. Given the ambiguous cyclical behavior of tax revenues, the cyclical behavior of tax revenues as a proportion of GDP is also ambiguous. The behavior of the primary balance as a proportion of GDP will also be ambiguous.

Last, consider countercyclical fiscal policy. By definition, tax rates are high in good times and low in bad times, which implies that tax revenues vary positively with the cycle. The same is true of the primary balance since tax revenues increase (fall) and government spending falls (increases) in good (bad) times. The ratio g/GDP will vary negatively with the cycle because g falls (increases) in good (bad) times. Since tax revenues increase in good times, the behavior of tax revenues as a proportion of GDP will be ambiguous and, hence, so will be the behavior of the primary balance as a proportion of GDP.

Several important observations follow from Table 2 regarding the usefulness of different indicators in discriminating among the three cases:

1. From a theoretical point of view, the best indicators to look at would be government spending and tax rates. By definition, these indicators would clearly discriminate among the three cases. As Table 2 makes clear, no other indicator has such discriminatory power. In practice, however, there is no systematic data on tax rates (other than perhaps the inflation tax rate), leaving us with government spending as the best indicator.

2. The cyclical behavior of tax revenues will be useful only to the extent that it has a negative or zero correlation with the business cycle. This would be an unambiguous indication that fiscal policy is procyclical. It would signal a case in which the degree of procyclicality is so extreme that in, say, bad times, the rise in tax rates is so pronounced that it either matches or dominates the fall in the tax base.

3. The cyclical behavior of the primary balance will be useful only to the extent that it has a negative or zero correlation with the business cycle. This would be an unambiguous indication that fiscal policy is procyclical. It would indicate a case in which, in good times, the rise in government spending either matches or more than offsets a possible increase in tax revenues or a case in which a fall in tax revenues in

good times reinforces the effect of higher government spending on the primary balance. Given our definition of fiscal policy cyclicality, it would be incorrect to infer that a primary deficit in bad times signals countercyclical fiscal policy. A primary deficit in bad times is, in principle, consistent with any of three cases.[9]

4. The cyclical behavior of the primary balance as a proportion of GDP will never provide an unambiguous reading of the cyclical stance of fiscal policy. Most of the literature (Gavin and Perotti, 1997; Braun, 2001; Dixon, 2003; Lane, 2003a; and Calderon and Schmidt-Hebbel, 2003) has drawn conclusions from looking at this indicator. For instance, Gavin and Perotti (1997) find that the response of the fiscal surplus as a proportion of GDP to a one-percentage-point increase in the rate of output growth is not statistically different from zero in Latin America and take this as an indication of procyclical fiscal policy. Calderon and Schmidt-Hebbel (2003), in contrast, find a negative effect of the output gap on deviations of the fiscal balance from its sample mean and interpret this as countercyclical fiscal policy. Given our definitions, however, one would not be able to draw either conclusion (as the last column of Table 2 makes clear).

5. The cyclical behavior of the ratio g/GDP will be useful only to the extent that it has a positive or zero correlation with the business cycle. This would be an unambiguous indication that fiscal policy is procyclical. In other words, finding that this ratio is negatively correlated with the cycle does not allow us to discriminate among the three cases. Once again, this suggests caution in interpreting some of the existing literature that relies on this indicator for drawing conclusions.

6. Last, the cyclical behavior of the ratio of tax revenues to GDP will not be particularly useful in telling us about the cyclical properties of fiscal policy since its theoretical behavior is ambiguous in all three cases.

In sum, our discussion suggests that extreme caution should be exercised in drawing conclusions on policy cyclicality based either on the primary balance or on the primary balance, government spending, and tax revenues as a proportion of GDP. In light of this, we will rely only on indicators that, given our definition of procyclicality, provide an unambiguous measure of the stance of fiscal policy: government spending and—as a proxy for a tax rate—the inflation tax rate.[10]

From a theoretical point of view, various models could rationalize different stances of fiscal policy over the business cycle. Countercyclical fiscal policy could be rationalized by resorting to a traditional Keynesian model (in old or new clothes) with an objective function that penalizes deviations of output from trend since an increase (reduction) in government spending and/or a reduction (increase) in tax rates would expand (contract) output. An acyclical fiscal policy could be rationalized by neoclassical models of optimal fiscal policy that call for roughly constant tax rates over the business cycle (see Chari and Kehoe, 1999). If government spending is endogeneized (by, say, providing direct utility), it would optimally behave in a similar way to private consumption and hence would be acyclical in the presence of complete markets (Riascos and Végh, 2003). Procyclical fiscal policy could be rationalized by resorting to political distortions (Tornell and Lane, 1999; Talvi and Végh, 2000), borrowing constraints (Gavin and Perotti, 1997; Aizeman, Gavin, and Hausmann, 1996), or incomplete markets (Riascos and Végh, 2003).

2.3 *Monetary Policy*

Performing the same conceptual exercise for monetary policy is much more difficult because (1) monetary policy instruments may depend on the existing exchange rate regime and (2) establishing outcomes (i.e., determining the behavior of endogenous variables) requires the use of some (implicit) model.

For our purposes, it is enough to define two exchange rate regimes: fixed or predetermined exchange rates and flexible exchange rates (which we define as including any regime in which the exchange rate is allowed some flexibility). By definition, flexible exchange rate regimes include relatively clean floats (which are rare) and dirty floats (a more common type, as documented in Reinhart and Rogoff, 2004).

Under certain assumptions, a common policy instrument across these two different regimes would be a short-term interest rate. The most prominent example is the federal funds rate in the United States, an overnight interbank interest rate that constitutes the Federal Reserve's main policy target. From a theoretical point of view, under flexible exchange rates, monetary policy can certainly be thought of in terms of some short-term interest rate since changes in the money supply will directly influence interest rates. Under fixed or predetermined exchange rates, the only assumption needed for a short-term interest rate to also be thought of as a policy instrument is that some imperfect substitution exist between domestic and foreign assets (see Flood and

Table 3
Monetary indicators: theoretical correlations with the business cycle

	Short-term interest rate	Rate of growth of central bank domestic credit	Real money balances (M1 and M2)	Real interest rate
Countercyclical	+	−	−/0/+	−/0/+
Procyclical	−	+	+	−
Acyclical	0	0	+	−

Jeanne, 2000; Lahiri and Végh, 2003). In fact, it is common practice for central banks to raise some short-term interest rate to defend a fixed exchange rate.

In principle, then, observing the correlation between a policy-controlled short-term interest rate and the business cycle would indicate whether monetary policy is countercyclical (the interest rate is raised in good times and reduced in bad times, implying a positive correlation), procyclical (the interest rate is reduced in good times and increased in bad times, implying a negative correlation), or acyclical (the interest rate is not systematically used over the business cycle, implying no correlation), as indicated in Table 3.

The expected correlations with other monetary variables are more complex. In the absence of an active interest rate policy, we expect real money balances (in terms of any monetary aggregate) to be high in good times and low in bad times (i.e., positively correlated with the business cycle), and real interest rates to be lower in good times and high in bad times (i.e., negatively correlated with the cycle).[11] A procyclical interest rate policy would reinforce this cyclical pattern.[12] A countercyclical interest rate policy would in principle call for lower real money balances and higher real interest rates relative to the benchmark of no activist policy. In principle, this leaning-against-the wind policy could be so effective as to render the correlation between real money balances and output zero or even negative, and the correlation between real interest rates and the cycle zero or even positive (as indicated in Table 3). In sum—and as Table 3 makes clear—the cyclical behavior of real money balances and real interest rates will only be informative in a subset of cases:

1. A negative or zero correlation between (the cyclical components of) real money balances and output would indicate countercyclical

monetary policy. In this case, real money balances would fall in good times and rise in bad times. In contrast, a positive correlation is, in principle, consistent with any monetary policy stance.

2. A positive or zero correlation between (the cyclical components of) the real interest rate and output would indicate countercyclical monetary policy. In this case, policy countercyclicality is so extreme that real interest rates increase in good times and fall in bad times. In contrast, a negative correlation is, in principle, consistent with any monetary policy stance.

In practice, however, even large databases typically carry information on overnight or very short-term interest rates for only a small number of countries. Hence, the interest rates that one observes in practice are of longer maturities and thus include an endogenous cyclical component (for instance, the changes in inflationary expectations, term premiums, or risk premiums over the cycle). To the extent that the inflation rate tends to have a small positive correlation with the business cycle in industrial countries and a negative correlation with the business cycle in developing countries, there will be a bias toward concluding that monetary policy is countercyclical in industrial countries and procyclical in developing countries. To reduce this bias, we will choose interbank/overnight rates whenever possible.

A second policy instrument under either regime is the rate of growth of the central bank's domestic credit. Naturally, how much a given change in domestic credit will affect the monetary base and hence interest rates will depend on the particular exchange rate regime. Under predetermined exchange rates and perfect substitution between domestic and foreign assets, the monetary approach to the balance of payments tells us that the change in domestic credit will be exactly undone by an opposite change in reserves. Under imperfect substitution between domestic and foreign assets, however, an increase in domestic credit will have some effect on the monetary base. The same is true under a dirty floating regime, because the change in reserves will not fully offset the change in domestic credit.

In this context, a countercyclical monetary policy would imply reducing the rate of domestic credit growth during good times, and vice versa (i.e., a negative correlation). A procyclical monetary policy would imply increasing the rate of domestic credit growth during good times, and vice versa (i.e., a positive correlation). An acyclical policy would not systematically vary the rate of growth of domestic

Table 4
Taylor rules

Nature of monetary policy	Expected sign on β_2
Countercyclical	+ and significant
Procyclical	− and significant
Acyclical	Insignificant

credit over the business cycle.[13] Of course, changes in domestic credit growth can be seen as the counterpart of movements in short-term interest rates, with a reduction (an increase) in domestic credit growth leading to an increase (reduction) in short-term interest rates.

In addition to computing the correlations indicated in Table 3, we will attempt to establish whether monetary policy is procyclical, acyclical, or countercyclical by estimating Taylor rules for every country for which data are available (see Taylor, 1993). Following Clarida, Galí, and Gertler (1999), our specification takes the form:

$$i_t = \alpha + \beta_1(\pi_t - \underline{\pi}) + \beta_2 y_t^c, \qquad (1)$$

where i_t is a policy-controlled short-term interest rate; $\pi_t - \underline{\pi}$ captures deviations of actual inflation from its sample average, $\underline{\pi}$, and y_t^c is the output gap, measured as the cyclical component of output (i.e., actual output minus trend) divided by actual output. The coefficient β_2 in equation (1) would indicate the stance of monetary policy over the business cycle (see Table 4) over and above the monetary authority's concerns about inflation, which are captured by the coefficient β_1.

Several remarks are in order regarding equation (1). First, we are assuming that current inflation is a good predictor of future inflation. Second, we are assuming that the mean inflation rate is a good representation of some implicit/explicit inflation target on the basis that central banks deliver on average the inflation rate that they desire. Third, given potential endogeneity problems, the relation captured in equation (1) is probably best interpreted as a long-run cointegrating relationship. Fourth, since our estimation will be based on annual data, equation (1) does not incorporate the possibility of gradual adjustments of the nominal interest rate to some target interest rate. Fifth, by estimating equation (1), we certainly do not mean to imply that every country in our sample has followed some type of Taylor rule throughout the sample. Rather, we see it as a potentially useful way of characterizing the correlation between a short-term interest rate and the output gap once one controls for the monetary authority's implicit or explicit inflation target.

By now, numerous studies have estimated Taylor rules, though most are limited to developed countries. For example, for the United States, Japan, and Germany, Clarida, Galí and Gertler (1997) report that, in the post-1979 period, the inflation coefficient is significantly above 1 (indicating that in response to a rise in expected inflation, central banks raised nominal rates enough to raise real rates) and the coefficient on the output gap is significantly positive except for the United States. In other words—and using the terminology spelled out in Table 4—since 1979 Japan and Germany have pursued countercyclical monetary policy (lowering interest rates in bad times and increasing them in good times), but monetary policy in the United States has been acyclical. In the pre-1979 period, however, the Federal Reserve also pursued countercyclical monetary policy (see Clarida, Gertler, and Galí, 1999). For Peru, Moron and Castro (2000) use the change in the monetary base as the dependent variable and add an additional term involving the deviation of the real exchange rate from trend; they find that monetary policy is countercyclical. For Chile, Corbo (2000) finds that monetary policy does not respond to output (i.e., is acyclical).

In terms of the theoretical literature, there has been extensive work on how to theoretically derive Taylor-type rules in the context of Keynesian models (see, for example, Clarida, Gertler, and Galí, 1999). This literature would rationalize countercyclical monetary policy on the basis that increases (decreases) in the output gap call for higher (lower) short-term interest rates to reduce (boost) aggregate demand. Acyclical monetary policy could be rationalized in terms of neoclassical models of optimal monetary policy which call for keeping the nominal interest rate close to zero (see Chari and Kehoe, 1999). Collection costs for conventional taxes could optimally explain a positive—but still constant over the cycle—level of nominal interest rates (see Calvo and Végh, 1999 and the references therein). Some of the stories put forward to explain procyclical fiscal policy mentioned above could also be used to explain procyclical monetary policy if the nominal interest rate is part of the policy set available to the Ramsey planner. Nonfiscal-based explanations for procyclical monetary policy might include the need for defending the domestic currency under flexible exchange rates (Lahiri and Végh, 2004)—which in bad times would call for higher interest rates to prevent the domestic currency from depreciating further—and models in which higher interest rates may provide a signal of the policymaker's intentions (see Drazen, 2000). In these models, establishing credibility in bad times may call for higher interest rates.

2.4 *Measuring Good and Bad Times*

Not all advanced economies have as clearly defined business cycle turning points as those established by the National Bureau of Economic Research (NBER) for the United States. For developing economies, where quarterly data for the national income accounts is at best recent and most often nonexistent, even less is known about economic fluctuations and points of inflexion. Thus, to pursue our goal of assessing the cyclical stance of capital flows and macroeconomic policies, we must develop some criterion that breaks down economic conditions into good and bad times. Taking an eclectic approach to sort out this issue, we will follow three different techniques: a nonparametric approach and two filtering techniques commonly used in the literature.

The nonparametric approach consists in dividing the sample into episodes where annual real GDP growth is above the median (good times) and those times where growth falls below the median (bad times). The relevant median or cutoff point is calculated on a country-by-country basis. We then compute the amplitude of the cycle in different variables by comparing the behavior of the variable in question in good and bad times. We should notice that, although growth below the median need not signal a recession, restricting the definition of recession to involve only periods where GDP growth is negative is too narrow a definition of bad times for countries with rapid population growth (which encompasses the majority of our sample), or rapid productivity growth, or countries that have seldom experienced a recession by NBER standards. This approach is appealing because it is nonparametric and free from the usual estimation problems that arise when all the variables in question are potentially endogenous.

The other two approaches consist of decomposing each time series into its stochastic trend and cyclical component using two popular filters—the ubiquitous Hodrick-Prescott (HP) filter and the bandpass filter developed in Baxter and King (1999). After decomposing each series into its trend and cyclical component, we report a variety of pairwise correlations among the cyclical components of GDP, net capital inflows, and fiscal and monetary indicators for each of the four income groups. These correlations are used to establish contemporaneous comovements, but a fruitful area for future research would be to analyze potential temporal causal patterns.

3. The Big Picture

This section presents a visual overview of the main stylized facts that we have uncovered, leaving the more detailed analysis of the results for the following sections.[14] Our aim here is to contrast OECD and developing (i.e., non-OECD) countries, and synthesize our findings in terms of key stylized facts. It is worth stressing that we are not trying to identify underlying structural parameters or shocks that may give rise to these empirical regularities, but merely trying to uncover reduced-form correlations hidden in the data. Our findings can be summarized in terms of four stylized facts.

Stylized fact 1. Net capital inflows are procyclical in most OECD and developing countries.

This is illustrated in Figure 1, which plots the correlation between the cyclical components of net capital inflows and GDP. As the plot makes clear, most countries exhibit a positive correlation, indicating that countries tend to borrow in good times and repay in bad times.

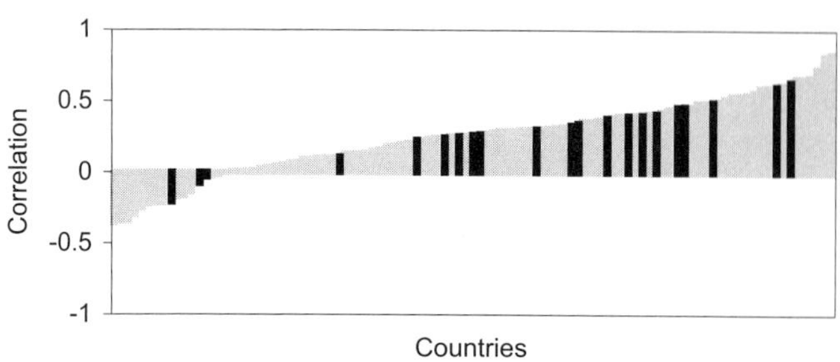

Figure 1
Country correlations between the cyclical components of net capital inflows and real GDP, 1960–2003
Notes: Dark bars are OECD countries and light ones are non-OECD countries. The cyclical components have been estimated using the Hodrick-Prescott filter. A positive correlation indicates procyclical capital flows.
Source: IMF, *World Economic Outlook*.

Stylized fact 2. With regard to fiscal policy, OECD countries are, by and large, either countercyclical or acyclical. In sharp contrast, developing countries are predominantly procyclical.

Figures 2 through 4 illustrate this critical difference in fiscal policy between advanced and developing economies. Figure 2 plots the correlation between the cyclical components of real GDP and real government spending. As is clear from the graph, most OECD countries have a negative correlation, while most developing countries have a positive correlation. Figure 3 plots the difference between the percentage change in real government spending when GDP growth is above the median (good times) and when it is below the median (bad times). This provides a measure of the *amplitude* of the fiscal policy cycle: large negative numbers suggest that the growth in real government spending is markedly higher in bad times (and thus policy is strongly countercyclical), while large positive numbers indicate that the growth in real government spending is markedly lower in bad times (and thus policy is strongly procyclical). In our sample, the most extreme case of procyclicality is given by Liberia, where the growth in real government spending is 32.4 percentage points higher in good times compared to bad times. The most extreme cases of countercyclicality are Sudan and Denmark, where real government spending growth is over 7 percentage points lower during expansions. In addition to a more volatile cycle—and as Aguiar and Gopinath (2004) show for some of the larger emerging markets—the trend component of output is itself highly

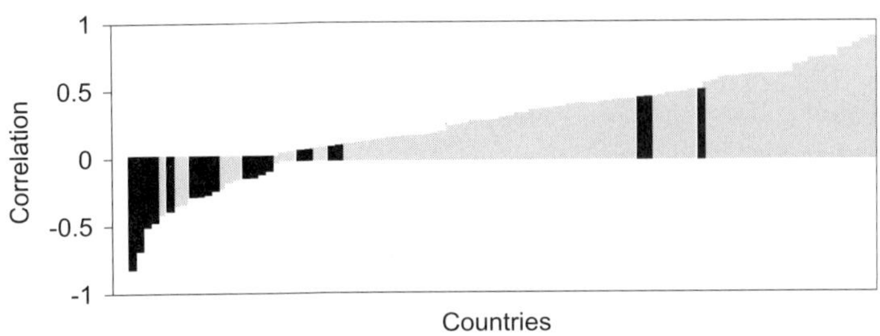

Figure 2
Country correlations between the cyclical components of real government expenditure and real GDP, 1960–2003
Notes: Dark bars are OECD countries and light ones are non-OECD countries. The cyclical components have been estimated using the Hodrick-Prescott filter. A positive correlation indicates procyclical fiscal policy. Real government expenditure is defined as central government expenditure deflated by the GDP deflator.
Source: IMF, *World Economic Outlook.*

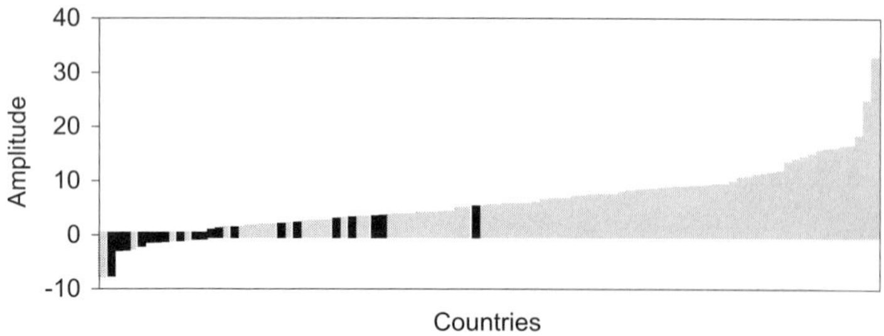

Figure 3
Amplitude of the fiscal policy cycle, 1960–2003
Notes: Dark bars are OECD countries and light ones are non-OECD countries. The amplitude of the fiscal policy cycle is captured by the difference (in percentage points) between the growth of real government expenditure in good times and bad times. Real government expenditure is defined as central government expenditure deflated by the GDP deflator. Good (bad) times are defined as those years in which GDP growth is above (below) the median. A positive correlation indicates procyclical fiscal policy.
Source: IMF, *World Economic Outlook.*

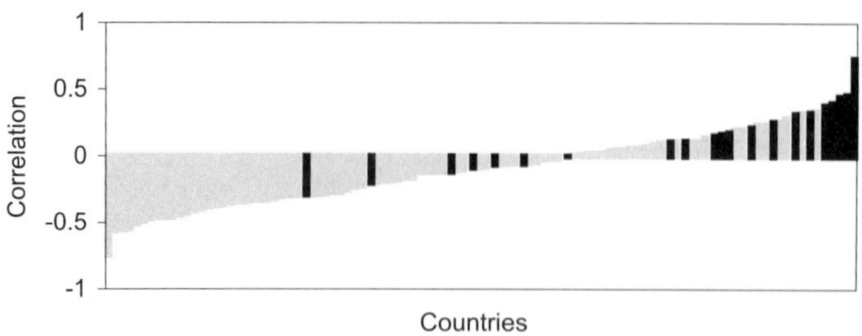

Figure 4
Country correlations between the cyclical components of the inflation tax and real GDP, 1960–2003
Notes: Dark bars are OECD countries and light ones are non-OECD countries. The cyclical components have been estimated using the Hodrick-Prescott filter. A positive correlation indicates countercyclical fiscal policy.
Sources: IMF, *World Economic Outlook* and *International Financial Statistics.*

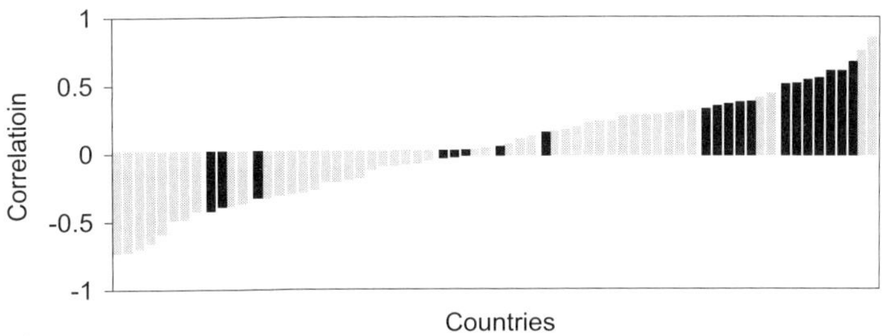

Figure 5
Country correlations between the cyclical components of the nominal lending interest rate and real GDP, 1960–2003
Notes: Dark bars are OECD countries and light ones are non-OECD countries. The cyclical components have been estimated using the Hodrick-Prescott filter. A positive correlation indicates countercyclical monetary policy.
Sources: IMF, *World Economic Outlook* and *International Financial Statistics.*

volatile, which would also be captured in this measure of amplitude. Finally, Figure 4 plots the correlation between the cyclical components of output and the inflation tax. A negative correlation indicates procyclical fiscal policy because it implies that the inflation tax rate is lower in good times. Figure 4 makes clear that most OECD countries exhibit a positive correlation (countercyclical policy) while most developing countries exhibit a negative correlation (procyclical policy).

Stylized fact 3. With regard to monetary policy, most OECD countries are countercyclical, while developing countries are mostly procyclical or acyclical.

This is illustrated in Figure 5 for nominal lending rates. This holds for other nominal interest rates (including various measures of policy rates), as described in the next section. We plot the lending rate because it is highly correlated with the policy rates but offers more comprehensive data coverage.

Stylized fact 4. In developing countries, the capital flow cycle and the macroeconomic policy cycle reinforce each other (we dub this positive relationship as the "when it rains, it pours" phenomenon).

Put differently, macroeconomic policies are expansionary when capital is flowing in, and they are contractionary when capital is flowing out. This is illustrated in Figures 6 through 8. Figure 6 shows that most developing countries exhibit a positive correlation between the cyclical

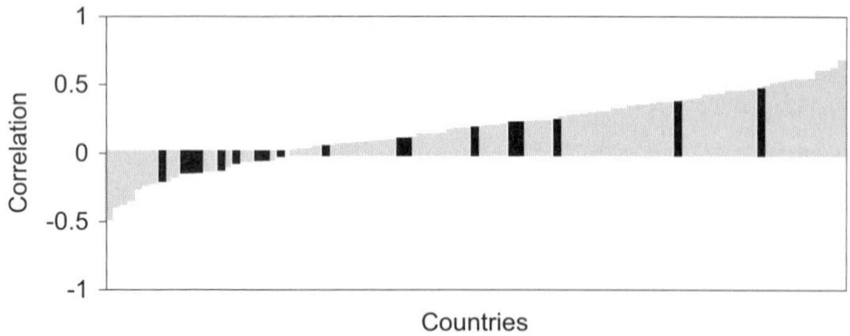

Figure 6
Country correlations between the cyclical components of real government expenditure and net capital inflows, 1960–2003
Notes: Dark bars are OECD countries and light ones are non-OECD countries. The cyclical components have been estimated using the Hodrick-Prescott filter. Real government expenditure is defined as central government expenditure deflated by the GDP deflator.
Source: IMF, *World Economic Outlook.*

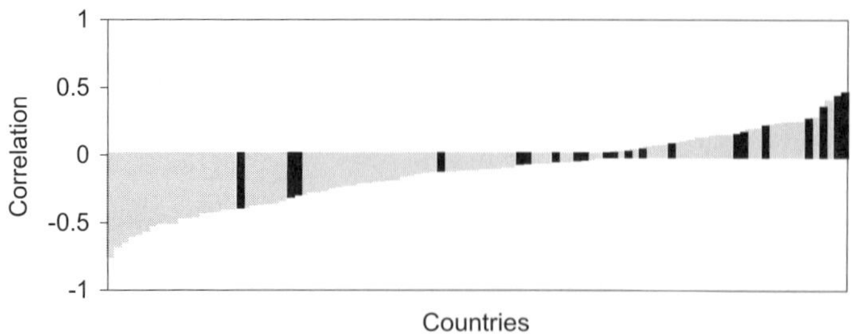

Figure 7
Country correlations between the cyclical components of the inflation tax and net capital inflows
Notes: Dark bars are OECD countries and light ones are non-OECD countries. The cyclical components have been estimated using the Hodrick-Prescott filter.
Source: IMF, *World Economic Outlook.*

components of government spending and net capital inflows, but there does not seem to be an overall pattern for OECD countries. In the same vein, Figure 7 shows that in developing countries, the correlation between the cyclical components of net capital inflows and the inflation tax is mostly negative, while no pattern is apparent for OECD countries. Last, Figure 8 shows a predominance of negative correlations between the cyclical components of net capital inflows and the nominal lending rate for developing countries, suggesting that the capital flow and the monetary policy cycle reinforce each other. The opposite appears to be true for OECD countries.

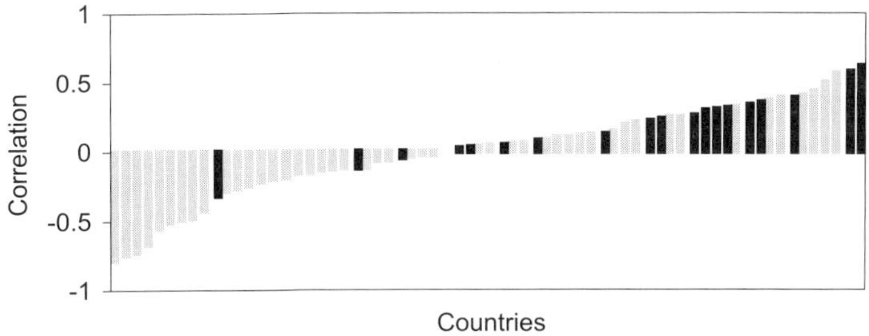

Figure 8
Country correlations between the cyclical components of the nominal lending interest rate and net capital inflows, 1960–2003
Notes: Dark bars are OECD countries and light ones are non-OECD countries. The cyclical components have been estimated using the Hodrick-Prescott filter.
Source: IMF, *World Economic Outlook.*

4. Further Evidence on Business, Capital Flows, and Policy Cycles

This section examines the four stylized facts presented in the preceding section in greater depth by looking at alternative definitions of monetary and fiscal policy; using different methods to define the cyclical patterns in economic activity, international capital flows, and macroeconomic policies; and splitting the sample along several dimensions. In particular—and as discussed in Section 2—we will use three different approaches to define good and bad times: a nonparametric approach that allows us to quantify the *amplitude* of the cycles and two more standard filtering techniques (the Hodrick-Prescott filter and the bandpass filter).

4.1 Capital Flows

Tables 5 through 7 present additional evidence on *stylized fact 1* (i.e., net capital inflows are procyclical in most OECD and developing countries). Table 5 shows that net capital inflows as a proportion of GDP tend to be larger in good times than in bad times for all groups of countries, which indicates procyclical net capital inflows. (Recall from Table 1 that a positive correlation between capital inflows as a proportion of GDP and real GDP implies procyclical net capital inflows).[15,16] The decline in capital inflows as a proportion of GDP in bad times is largest for the middle-high income economies (1.4 percent of GDP). This should come as no surprise because this group of countries is

Table 5
Amplitude of the capital flow cycle

	Net capital inflows/GDP		
Countries	Good times (1)	Bad times (2)	Amplitude (1) – (2)
OECD	0.5	0.4	0.1
Middle-high income	4.4	3.0	1.4
Middle-low income	4.2	3.0	1.2
Low income	3.9	3.6	0.3

Notes: Capital inflows/GDP is expressed in percentage terms. Good (bad) times are defined as those years in which GDP growth is above (below) the median.
Source: IMF, *World Economic Outlook.*

Table 6
International credit ratings

	Institutional investor ratings		
Countries	Good times (1)	Bad times (2)	Amplitude (1) – (2)
OECD	78.5	78.4	0.1
Middle-high income	42.2	40.4	1.8
Middle-low income	32.9	30.8	2.1
Low income	24.2	24.2	0.0

Good (bad) times are defined as those years in which GDP growth is above (below) the median.
Sources: *Institutional Investor* and IMF, *World Economic Outlook.*

Table 7
International credit ratings and real GDP: descriptive statistics

	Countries			
Statistics	OECD	Middle-high income	Middle-low income	Low income
	Institutional Investor Index: 1979–2003			
Coefficient of variation	0.06	0.22	0.23	0.18
Mean	79.9	41.5	32.0	21.8
	Real GDP Growth: 1960–2003			
Coefficient of variation	0.80	1.20	1.20	1.60
Mean	3.90	4.90	4.70	3.30

Sources: *Institutional Investor* and IMF, *World Economic Outlook.*

Table 8
Correlations between the cyclical components of net capital inflows and real GDP

Countries	Correlations	
	HP filter	Bandpass filter
OECD	0.30*	0.25*
Middle-high income	0.35*	0.26*
Middle-low income	0.24*	0.20*
Low income	0.16*	0.10*

Note: An asterisk denotes statistical significance at the 10 percent level.
Sources: IMF, *International Financial Statistics* and *World Economic Outlook.*

noted for having on-and-off access to international private capital markets, partly due to a history of serial default.[17]

The behavior of international credit ratings, such as the Institutional Investor Index (III), also provides insights on capital market access.[18] As discussed in Reinhart, Rogoff, and Savastano (2003), at very low ratings (the low-income countries), the probability of default is sufficiently high that countries are entirely shut out of international private capital markets, while ratings at the high end of the spectrum are a sign of uninterrupted market access. These observations are borne out in Tables 6 and 7. Table 6 shows that there is essentially no difference in credit ratings during good and bad times for the wealthy OECD economies and the low-income countries. The largest difference in ratings across good and bad times is for the middle-income countries, where ratings are procyclical (i.e., high in good times and low in bad times).

This U-shaped pattern is also evident in the volatility of the credit ratings. Table 7 presents basic descriptive statistics for growth and the Institutional Investor ratings. Not surprisingly, ratings are far more stable for OECD economies (the coefficient of variation is 0.06), but so is growth, with a coefficient of variation of 0.8. Despite the fact that output is the most volatile for the group of low-income economies (with a coefficient of variation is 1.6, or twice the level of the OECD group), its international ratings (0.18) are more stable than those of middle-income countries (with coefficients of variation of 0.22 and 0.23).

Finally, Table 8 presents correlations (using our two different filters) between the cyclical components of real GDP and net capital inflows.[19] The correlations are positive and significant for all four groups of

Table 9
Amplitude of the fiscal policy cycle

Fiscal indicators	Increase in the fiscal indicator: Good times (1)	Bad times (2)	Amplitude (1) − (2)
	OECD countries		
Central government:			
Expenditure (WEO)	3.4	3.1	0.3
Current expenditure minus interest payments	4.2	2.8	1.4
Expenditure on goods and services	3.0	2.0	1.0
Expenditure on wages and salaries	2.6	1.3	1.3
General or consolidated government:			
Expenditure (WEO)	3.6	3.2	0.4
Current expenditure minus interest payments	4.1	3.5	0.6
Inflation tax, $\pi/(1+\pi)$	4.5	5.4	−0.9
	Middle-high-income countries		
Central government:			
Expenditure (WEO)	8.1	0.0	8.1
Current expenditure minus interest payments	9.6	−0.1	9.7
Expenditure on goods and services	8.1	−0.3	8.4
Expenditure on wages and salaries	8.3	0.4	7.9
General or consolidated government:			
Expenditure (WEO)	6.9	−0.1	7.0
Current expenditure minus interest payments	7.6	1.8	5.8
Inflation tax, $\pi/(1+\pi)$	10.9	13.1	−2.2
	Middle-low-income countries		
Central government:			
Expenditure (WEO)	6.7	2.7	4.0
Current expenditure minus interest payments	9.3	3.1	6.2
Expenditure on goods and services	9.7	3.6	6.1
Expenditure on wages and salaries	8.9	4.2	4.7
General or consolidated government:			
Expenditure (WEO)	6.4	2.5	3.9
Current expenditure minus interest payments	8.5	−2.1	10.6
Inflation tax, $\pi/(1+\pi)$	8.7	10.1	−1.4
	Low-income countries		
Central government:			
Expenditure (WEO)	8.3	−0.2	8.5
Current expenditure minus interest payments	5.0	0.5	4.5
Expenditure on goods and services	5.1	0.6	4.5
Expenditure on wages and salaries	4.0	0.8	3.2

Table 9
(continued)

General or consolidated government:			
Expenditure (WEO)	7.3	−0.5	7.8
Current expenditure minus interest payments	5.7	−0.4	6.1
Inflation tax, $\pi/(1+\pi)$	9.4	12.4	−3.0

Notes: All data are from International Monetary Fund, *Government Financial Statistics*, unless otherwise noted. The increase for the fiscal spending indicators is the average annual real rate of growth expressed in percentage terms. The inflation tax figure is multiplied by one hundred. The increase in the inflation tax denotes the average change in this indicator. Good (bad) times are defined as those years with GDP growth above (below) the median.
Sources: IMF, *Government Financial Statistics* and *World Economic Outlook* (WEO).

countries and for both filters. Not surprisingly, the correlations are the highest for OECD and middle-high income countries and the lowest for low-income countries. These results thus strongly support the idea that capital inflows are indeed procyclical for both industrial and developing countries.

4.2 *Fiscal Policy*

With regard to *Stylized fact 2* (i.e., fiscal policy in OECD countries is, by and large, either countercyclical or acyclical, while in developing countries fiscal policy is predominantly procyclical), Table 9 provides a measure of the amplitude of the fiscal policy cycle by showing—for six different measures of government spending—the difference between the change in real government spending when GDP growth is above the median and when it is below the median. Under this definition, a positive amplitude indicates procyclical government spending. The inflation tax is also included as the remaining fiscal indicator, with a negative amplitude denoting a procyclical tax rate. As argued in Section 2, government spending and the inflation tax rate provide the best indicators to look at in terms of their ability to discriminate among different cyclical policy stances (recall Table 3). Other indicators—such as fiscal balances or tax revenues—convey less information.

The striking aspect of Table 9 is that, as shown in the last column, the amplitude of the fiscal spending cycle for non-OECD countries is considerably large for all measures of government spending. This suggests that, in particular for the two middle income groups, fiscal policy is not only procyclical, but markedly so. In contrast, while positive, the analogous figures for OECD countries are quite small, suggesting, on average, an acyclical fiscal policy.

Based on the country-by-country computations of the amplitude of the fiscal spending cycle underlying Table 9 (which are illustrated in Figure 3), the conclusion that non-OECD countries are predominantly procyclical is overwhelming. For instance, for real central government expenditure, 94 percent of low-income countries exhibit a positive amplitude. For middle-low income countries this figure is 91 percent. Every single country in the middle-high income category registers as procyclical. In contrast, when it comes to OECD countries, an even split exists between procyclical and countercyclical countries.

Turning to the inflation tax rate, $\pi/(1+\pi)$, it registers as procyclical in all of the four groups. The amplitude is the largest for the low-income group (3 percentage points) and the smallest for OECD countries (0.9 percentage point).[20] Not surprisingly, the increase in the inflation tax rate is the highest during recessions (13.1 percent) for the middle-high-income countries (which include chronic high inflation countries like Argentina, Brazil, and Uruguay) and lowest for the OECD, at 5.4 percent.

Table 10 presents the pairwise correlations for the expenditure measures shown in Table 9 as well as for the inflation tax rate. With regard to the correlations between the cyclical components of GDP and government expenditure, the most salient feature of the results presented in Table 10 is that for the three developing country groups, all of the 36 correlations reported in the table (18 correlations per filter) are positive regardless of the expenditure series used or the type of filter. By contrast, all of the 12 correlations reported for the OECD are negative (though low). This is not to say that the relationship between the fiscal expenditure and business cycle is an extremely tight one; several entries in Table 10 show low correlations that are not significantly differently from zero—consistent with an acyclical pattern as defined in Table 2. When one examines these results, however, it becomes evident that for non-OECD countries (at least according to this exercise), fiscal policy is squarely procyclical.[21]

In terms of the inflation tax, the results for both filters coincide; the correlation between the cyclical components of GDP and the inflation tax is positive and significant for OECD countries (indicating countercyclical fiscal policy) and negative and significant for all groups of developing countries (indicating procyclical fiscal policy).

Table 10 also presents evidence on the relationship between capital inflows and fiscal policy. Our premise is that the capital flow cycle may affect macroeconomic policies in developing countries, particularly in the highly volatile economies that comprise the middle-high-income countries. To this end, we report the correlations (using both the HP and bandpass filters) of the cyclical components of the fiscal variables and net capital inflows. Remarkably, all but one of the 36 correlations (18 per filter) for non-OECD countries are positive with 21 of them being significantly different from zero. This provides clear support for the idea that the fiscal spending cycle is positively linked to the capital flow cycle (*stylized fact 4*.) The evidence is particularly strong for middle-high-income countries (with 10 out of the 12 positive correlations being significant). We do not pretend, of course, to draw inferences on causality from pairwise correlations, but it is not unreasonable to expect that a plausible causal relationship may run from capital flows to fiscal spending—an issue that clearly warrants further study. More surprising is the evidence suggesting that the relationship between the fiscal spending cycle and capital flows is also important for low income countries (most of which have little access to international capital markets). It may be fruitful to explore to what extent this result may come from links between cycles in commodity prices and government expenditure.[22] In sharp contrast to developing countries, the correlations for OECD countries are—with only one exception—never significantly different from zero, which suggests that there is no link between the capital flow cycle and fiscal spending.

Table 10 also indicates that the inflation tax is significantly and negatively correlated with the capital flow cycle for all developing countries (and both filters). Our conjecture is that inflation provides a form of alternative financing when international capital market conditions deteriorate. For OECD countries, this correlation is not significantly different from zero.

4.3 *Monetary Policy*

To document *stylized fact 3* (i.e., monetary policy is countercyclical in most OECD countries while it is mostly procyclical in developing ones), we perform the same kind of exercises carried out for the fiscal indicators, but we also estimate variants of the Taylor rule, as

Table 10
Correlations between fiscal policy, real GDP, and net capital inflows

Countries	Central government: Expenditure	Central government: Expenditure minus interest payments	Central government: Expenditure on goods and services	Central government: Expenditure on wages and salaries	General government expenditure	Consolidated government expenditure minus interest payments	Inflation tax
HP Filter							
Correlation with real GDP							
OECD	−0.13*	−0.05	−0.06	−0.15*	−0.06	−0.07	0.16*
Middle-high income	0.38*	0.10	0.08	0.01	0.43*	0.10	−0.15*
Middle-low income	0.22*	0.13	0.07	0.03	0.20*	0.12	−0.09*
Low income	0.38*	0.24*	0.54*	0.59*	0.37*	0.17*	−0.20*
Correlation with net capital inflows							
OECD	0.03	0.05	0.04	0.04	0.09	0.03	0.04
Middle-high income	0.25*	0.22*	0.28*	0.27*	0.25*	0.20*	−0.31*
Middle-low income	0.16*	0.11	0.13	0.12	0.18*	0.13	−0.14*
Low income	0.20*	0.05	0.20	0.37	0.24*	−0.16	−0.09*
Bandpass filter							
Correlation with real GDP							
OECD	−0.05	−0.15*	−0.11	−0.20*	−0.02	−0.12	0.15*
Middle-high income	0.53*	0.19*	0.23*	0.13	0.44*	0.23*	−0.13*
Middle-low income	0.29*	0.29*	0.26*	0.23*	0.23*	0.23*	−0.10*
Low income	0.46*	0.42*	0.53*	0.59*	0.34*	0.32*	−0.16*

			Correlation with net capital inflows				
OECD	0.07	0.08	0.05	0.04	0.14*	0.00	0.02
Middle-high income	0.19*	0.12	0.28*	0.25*	0.16*	0.09	−0.25*
Middle-low income	0.14*	0.08	0.05	0.10	0.16*	0.11	−0.10*
Low income	0.19*	0.25*	0.27*	0.39*	0.22*	0.13	−0.07*

Notes: An asterisk denotes statistical significance at the 10 percent level.
Source: IMF, *World Economic Outlook*.

Table 11
Amplitude of the monetary policy cycle

Interest rate	Increases in nominal interest rates: Good times (1)	Bad times (2)	Amplitude (1) – (2)
		OECD countries	
Interbank rate	0.3	−0.7	1.0
Treasury bill rate	0.2	−0.4	0.6
Discount rate	0.5	−0.5	1.0
Lending rate	0.0	−0.3	0.3
Deposit rate	0.1	−0.3	0.4
		Middle-high-income countries	
Interbank rate*	−2.2	2.3	−4.5
Treasury bill rate	−2.6	−1.5	−1.1
Discount rate	−1.5	2.7	−4.2
Lending rate	−4.0	2.1	−6.1
Deposit rate*	0.7	1.0	−0.3
		Middle-low-income countries	
Interbank rate	−0.8	−0.1	−0.7
Treasury bill rate	−0.7	1.1	−1.8
Discount rate	0.5	0.5	0.0
Lending rate	−1.0	0.4	−1.4
Deposit rate	−0.5	−0.5	0.0
		Low-income-countries	
Interbank rate	−1.3	1.5	−2.8
Treasury bill rate	−1.0	0.5	−1.5
Discount rate*	−0.8	0.2	−1.0
Lending rate	−4.7	0.2	−4.9
Deposit rate*	−1.6	0.2	−1.8

Notes: Increases in interest rates are defined as the average annual change in interest rates (with interest rates expressed in percentage points). Good (bad) times are defined as those years with GDP growth above (below) the median.
*The median is reported in lieu of the average because the average is distorted by one or more very high inflation (or hyperinflation) episodes.
Sources: IMF, *World Economic Outlook* and *International Financial Statistics*.

described in Section 2. Table 11 presents the same exercise performed in Table 9 for the five nominal interest rate series used in this study. As discussed in Section 2, a short-term policy instrument, such as the interbank rate (or in some countries the T-bill or discount rate), is the best indicator of the stance of monetary policy. In this case, a negative amplitude denotes procyclical monetary policy. The difference between the OECD countries and the other groups is striking. For the OECD countries, interest rates decline in recessions and increase in expansions (for example, the interbank interest rate falls on average 0.7 percent or 70 basis points during recessions). In sharp contrast, in non-OECD countries, most of the nominal interest rates decline in expansions and increase in recessions (for instance, interbank rates in middle-high-income countries rise by 2.3 percent or 230 basis points in recessions). Thus, the pattern for the non-OECD group is broadly indicative of procyclical monetary policy.[23]

Table 12 presents the correlations of the cyclical components of real GDP, capital inflows, and the five nominal interest rates introduced in Table 11. In terms of the cyclical stance of monetary policy, the evidence seems the most compelling for OECD countries (countercyclical monetary policy), where all 10 correlations are positive and seven significantly so. There is also evidence to suggest procyclical monetary policy in middle-high-income countries (all ten correlations are negative and four significantly so). The evidence is more mixed for the other two groups of countries where the lack of statistical significance partly reflects the fact that they have relative shorter time series on interest rates.[24]

Turning to the correlations between net capital inflows and interest rates in Table 12, the evidence is strongest again for the OECD countries (with all 10 correlations significantly positive), clearly indicating that higher interest rates are associated with capital inflows. For middle-high-income countries, 8 out of the 10 correlations are negative but not significantly different from zero (again, shorter time series are an important drawback). Still, we take this as suggestive evidence of the when-it-rains-it-pours syndrome.

Given the notorious difficulties (present even for advanced countries such as the United States) in empirically characterizing the stance of monetary policy, we performed a complementary exercise as a robustness check for all income groups. Specifically, we estimated the Taylor rule specified in Section 2. Table 13 reports the results for the three

Table 12
Correlations between monetary policy, real GDP, and net capital inflows

Countries	Nominal interest rates Interbank	T-bill	Discount	Lending	Deposit
			HP filter		
			Correlation with real GDP		
OECD	0.28*	0.39*	0.37*	0.23*	0.21*
Middle-high income	−0.24*	−0.09	−0.02	−0.24*	−0.21*
Middle-low income	0.02	0.00	0.04	0.07	0.01
Low income	−0.12	−0.02	0.04	−0.02	−0.10
			Correlation with net capital inflows		
OECD	0.14*	0.25*	0.20*	0.19*	0.11*
Middle-high income	−0.11	−0.24	0.11	−0.13	−0.09
Middle-low income	0.04	0.03	0.07	0.05	0.00
Low income	0.01	0.06	0.03	−0.11	0.05
			Bandpass filter		
			Correlation with real GDP		
OECD	0.12	0.13*	0.23*	0.01	0.06
Middle-high income	−0.23	−0.14	−0.10	−0.10	−0.13*
Middle-low income	0.19*	0.00	−0.03	0.03	−0.03
Low income	−0.09	−0.04	−0.07	−0.07	−0.08
			Correlation with net capital inflows		
OECD	0.16*	0.28*	0.19*	0.16*	0.13*
Middle-high income	−0.05	−0.17	0.08	−0.18	−0.11
Middle-low income	0.30*	−0.03	0.11	0.00	−0.07
Low income	0.12	0.07	0.02	−0.11	0.04

Notes: An asterisk denotes statistical significance at the 10 percent level.
Sources: IMF, *World Economic Outlook* and *International Financial Statistics.*

nominal interest rates that are, at least in principle, more likely to serve as policy instruments (interbank, T-bill, and discount.) Recalling that countercyclical policy requires a positive and significant β_2, the main results are as follows.[25] First, monetary policy in OECD countries appears to be countercyclical (as captured by positive and significant coefficients in two out of the three specifications). Second, there is some evidence of monetary policy procyclicality in middle-income countries (as captured by the negative and significant coefficients for the T-bill regressions). This overall message is thus broadly consistent with that of Tables 11 and 12.

Table 13
Taylor rules

Regression $i_t = \alpha + \beta_1(\pi_t - \underline{\pi}) + \beta_2 y_t^c + u_t$
i_t = Short term interest rate. Definitions of the rates are given below
$\pi_t - \underline{\pi}$ = Inflation rate minus sample mean
y_t^c = Cyclical component of real GDP (HP filter) divided by actual output

Dependent variable (number of observations)	β_1	β_2	R^2
		OECD countries	
Interbank rate (663)	0.56*	0.02	0.27
T-bill rate (503)	0.60*	0.12*	0.39
Discount rate (758)	0.49*	0.15*	0.25
		Middle-high income countries	
Interbank rate (187)	4.84*	−0.31	0.48
T-bill rate (152)	0.32*	−0.12*	0.04
Discount rate (413)	0.43*	−0.11	0.01
		Middle-low income countries	
Interbank rate (250)	0.81*	−0.19	0.34
T-bill rate (218)	0.44*	−0.27*	0.11
Discount rate (686)	1.21*	0.26	0.42
		Low income countries	
Interbank rate (282)	0.38*	0.18*	0.09
T-bill rate (258)	0.29*	0.11	0.17
Discount rate (951)	6.03*	1.59	0.22

Notes: The equations have been estimated using panel data with fixed effects.
*Denotes significance at the 10 percent level.
Sources: IMF, *World Economic Outlook* and *International Financial Statistics*.

4.4 Exchange Rate Arrangements, Capital Market Integration, and Crises

In the remainder of this section, we divide the sample along three different dimensions to assess whether our results are affected by the degree of capital mobility in the world economy, the existing exchange rate regime, and the presence of crises. First, to examine whether the increased capital account integration of the more recent past has affected the cyclical patterns of the variables of interest, we split our sample into two subperiods (1960–1979 and 1980–2003) and performed all the exercises described earlier in this section. Second, we break up the sample according to a rough measure of the de facto degree of exchange rate flexibility. Last, we split the sample into currency crisis periods and tranquil periods. This enables us to ascertain whether our results on procyclicality are driven to some extent by the more extreme crises episodes. The results for each of these partitions—which are presented in Table 14—will be discussed in turn.[26]

4.4.1 1960–1979 Versus 1980–2003

The four main results that emerge from dividing the sample into 1960–1979 and 1980–2003 are the following. First, capital flows are consistently procyclical in both periods, with the correlation increasing in the latter period for middle-high-income countries. Second, the cyclical stance of government spending does not appear to change across periods for non-OECD countries (i.e., fiscal policy is procyclical in both periods) but OECD countries appear to have been acyclical in the pre-1980 period and turn countercyclical in the post-1980 period. Third, the inflation tax appears to be essentially acyclical in the pre-1980 period only to turn significantly countercyclical for OECD countries and procyclical for the rest of the groups in the post-1980 period. Fourth, monetary policy seems to have switched from acyclical to countercyclical for OECD countries. Lack of data for developing countries precludes a comparison with the earlier period.

4.4.2 Fixed Versus Flexible Exchange Rates

This partition assesses whether the cyclical patterns in net capital inflows and macroeconomic policies differ across exchange-rate regimes (broadly defined). To this effect, we split the sample into three groups (a coarser version of the five-way de facto classification in Reinhart and Rogoff, 2004). The fixed-exchange-rate group comprises the exchange rate regimes labeled 1 and 2 (pegs and crawling pegs) in the five-way classification just mentioned. The flexible-exchange-rate group comprises categories 3 (managed floating) and 4 (freely floating). Those labeled freely falling by the Reinhart and Rogoff classification (category 5) were excluded from the analysis altogether.

The main results to come out of this exercise are as follows. First, there are no discernible differences in the correlations between net capital inflows and real GDP cycles across the two groups. Second, no differences are detected either for government spending. Third, the inflation tax appears to be more countercyclical for OECD countries and more procyclical for non-OECD countries in flexible regimes. Last, monetary policy is more countercyclical for the OECD group under flexible rates.

Table 14
Cyclical characteristics of net capital inflows, fiscal policy, and monetary policy

	Correlation with real GDP							
			Fiscal policy				Monetary policy	
Countries	Net capital inflows		Central government expenditure		Inflation tax		Lending rate	
	Pre-1980	Post-1980	Pre-1980	Post-1980	Pre-1980	Post-1980	Pre-1980	Post-1980
OECD	n/a	0.38*	−0.19	−0.14*	0.11	0.22*	0.04	0.25*
Middle-high income	0.25*	0.38*	0.43*	0.33*	−0.04	−0.16*	n/a	−0.23*
Middle-low income	0.28*	0.26*	0.39*	0.19*	−0.01	−0.12*	n/a	0.03
Low income	0.20*	0.17*	0.43*	0.38*	−0.08	−0.23*	n/a	0.03
	Fix	Flex	Fix	Flex	Fix	Flex	Fix	Flex
OECD	0.35*	0.40*	−0.09	−0.19	0.11	0.26*	0.13	0.38*
Middle-high income	0.39*	0.35*	0.39*	0.22*	−0.15*	−0.26*	−0.12	−0.06
Middle-low income	0.21*	0.34*	0.24*	0.31*	0.04	−0.15*	0.06	0.29*
Low income	0.27*	0.20*	0.40*	0.28*	−0.13*	−0.21*	−0.01	0.01
	Crisis	Tranquil	Crisis	Tranquil	Crisis	Tranquil	Crisis	Tranquil
OECD	n/a	0.37*	n/a	−0.13*	n/a	0.17*	n/a	0.23*
Middle-high income	0.56*	0.36*	0.38*	0.41*	−0.41*	−0.14*	n/a	−0.22*
Middle-low income	0.57*	0.28*	0.05	0.24*	−0.15	−0.06*	n/a	0.08
Low income	0.14	0.14*	0.30*	0.32*	−0.09	−0.09*	n/a	−0.06

Notes: All correlations were computed using the HP filter. Pre-1980: Includes observations from 1960 to 1979. Post-1980: Includes observations from 1980 to 2003. Fix: Includes years with pegs and crawling pegs. Flex: Includes years with managed floating and freely floating. Crisis: Includes years with a 25 percent or higher monthly depreciation that is at least 10 percent higher than the previous month's depreciation as well as the two years following the devaluation. Tranquil: Includes years not defined as crisis years. An asterisk denotes statistical significance at the 10 percent level.
Sources: IMF, *World Economic Outlook* and *International Financial Statistics*.

4.4.3 Crisis Versus Tranquil Periods

We define currency crashes as referring to a 25 percent or higher monthly depreciation that is at least 10 percent higher than the previous month's depreciation. Those years (as well as the two years following the crisis) are treated separately from tranquil periods. The idea is to check whether our main results are driven by the presence of crises. Table 14 suggests that this is definitely not the case. Indeed, our results appear to hold also as strongly—if not more—in tranquil times. We thus conclude that the paper's message does not depend on our having crises periods in our sample.

5. Concluding Remarks

We have studied the cyclical properties of capital flows and fiscal and monetary policies for 104 countries for the period 1960–2003. Much more analysis needs to be undertaken to refine our understanding of the links among the business cycle, capital flows, and macroeconomic policies, particularly across such a heterogeneous group of countries and circumstances (and especially in light of endemic data limitations). With these considerations in mind, our main findings can be summarized as follows:

1. Net capital inflows are procyclical in most OECD and developing countries.

2. Fiscal policy is procyclical for most developing countries and markedly so in middle-high income countries.

3. Though highly preliminary, we find some evidence of monetary policy procyclicality in developing countries, particularly for the middle-high-income countries. There is also some evidence of countercyclical monetary policy for the OECD countries.

4. For developing countries—and particularly for middle-high-income countries—the capital flow cycle and the macroeconomic cycle reinforce each other (the when-it-rains-it-pours syndrome).

From a policy point of view, the implications of our findings appear to be of great practical importance. While macroeconomic policies in OECD countries seem to be aimed mostly at stabilizing the business cycle (or, at the very least, remaining neutral), macroeconomic policies in developing countries seem mostly to reinforce the business cycle, turning sunny days into scorching infernos and rainy days into torrential downpours. While there may be a variety of frictions explaining this phenomenon (for instance, political distortions, weak institutions, and capital market imperfections), the inescapable conclusion is that developing countries—and in particular emerging countries—need to find mechanisms that would enable macro policies to be conducted in a neutral or stabilizing way. In fact, evidence suggests that emerging countries with a reputation of highly skilled policymaking (the case of Chile immediately comes to mind) are able to graduate from the procyclical gang and conduct neutral/countercyclical fiscal policies (see Calderon and Schmidt-Hebbel, 2003). In the particular case of Chile, the adoption of fiscal rules specifically designed to encourage public saving in good times may have helped in this endeavor.

Table 15
Data sources

Indicator	Source
1. External	
Financial account (net capital inflows)	IMF, *World Economic Outlook* (WEO)
Institutional Investor Ratings	*Institutional Investor*
2. Fiscal	
Central government:	
Expenditure	IMF, WEO
Current expenditure, current expenditure minus interest payments, expenditure on goods and services, expenditure on wages and salaries	IMF, *Government Financial Statistics* (GFS)
General or consolidated government:	
Expenditure	IMF, WEO
Current expenditure, current expenditure minus interest payments, expenditure on goods and services, expenditure on wages and salaries	IMF, GFS
Inflation tax, $\pi/(1+\pi)$	IMF, *International Financial Statistics* (IFS)
3. Monetary	
Domestic credit, M0, M1, M2, interbank rate, treasury bill rate, discount rate, lending rate, deposit rate	IMF, IFS
4. Other	
Real GDP	IMF, WEO
GDP deflator	IMF, WEO
Consumer price index	IMF, IFS

Note: WEO uses the concept of central and general government expenditure, while GFS uses central government budgetary accounts and consolidated government accounts.

Table 16
Countries in the sample

Low-income countries (40)	Middle-low-income countries (25)	Middle-high-income countries (18)	OECD countries (21)
Angola	Algeria	Argentina	Australia
Bangladesh	Bolivia	Botswana	Austria
Benin	Cape Verde	Brazil	Belgium
Burma (now Myanmar)	China	Chile	Canada
Cambodia	Colombia	Costa Rica	Denmark
Cameroon	Dominican Republic	Gabon	Finland
Central African Republic	Ecuador	Korea, Republic of	France
Chad	Egypt	Lebanon	Germany
Comoros	El Salvador	Malaysia	Greece
Congo (Republic of)	Guatemala	Mauritius	Japan
Côte d'Ivoire	Honduras	Mexico	Ireland
The Gambia	Iran	Oman	Italy
Ghana	Iraq	Panama	Netherlands
Haiti	Jamaica	Saudi Arabia	New Zealand
India	Jordan	Seychelles	Norway
Indonesia	Morocco	Trinidad and Tobago	Portugal
Kenya	Paraguay	Uruguay	Spain
Laos	Peru	Venezuela	Sweden
Liberia	Philippines		Switzerland
Madagascar	South Africa		United Kingdom
Mali	Sri Lanka		United States
Mauritania	Syria		
Mongolia	Thailand		
Mozambique	Tunisia		
Nepal	Turkey		
Nicaragua			
Niger			
Nigeria			
Pakistan			
Rwanda			
Senegal			
Sierra Leone			
Sudan			
Tanzania			
Togo			
Uganda			
Vietnam			
Yemen			
Zambia			
Zimbabwe			

Note: The total number of countries is 104. Iceland and Luxembourg are not included in our sample of OECD countries and Korea is included in the middle-high income countries.

Finally, it is worth emphasizing that our empirical objective has consisted in computing reduced-form correlations in the data (in the spirit of the real business cycle literature) and *not* in identifying policy rules or structural parameters. The types of friction that one would need to introduce into general equilibrium models to explain the when-it-rains-it-pours syndrome identified in this paper should be the subject of further research. In sum, we hope that the empirical regularities identified in this paper will stimulate theoreticians to reconsider existing models that may be at odds with the facts and empiricists to revisit the data with more refined techniques.

6. Appendix

Table 15 shows the data sources for our data set. Table 16 lists the countries included in our study.

Notes

Kaminsky was visiting the International Monetary Fund (IMF) Institute and Végh was Senior Resident Scholar at the IMF's Research Department when this paper was written. They both gratefully acknowledge the IMF's hospitality. Kaminsky and Végh also wish to thank the Institute of Public Policy at George Washington University and the UCLA Senate, respectively, for financial support. The authors wish to thank Peter Benczur, Mark Gertler, Gita Gopinath, Ayhan Kose, Pablo Lopez Murphy, Attila Raftai, Raghu Rajan, Alessandro Rebucci, Vincent R. Reinhart, Roberto Rigobon, Kenneth S. Rogoff, Evan Tanner, and Guillermo Tolosa for useful comments and suggestions and Eric Bang and especially Ioannis Tokatlidis for excellent research assistance. This paper was prepared for the NBER's nineteenth conference on Macroeconomics, organized by Mark Gertler and Kenneth S. Rogoff. The views expressed here are the authors' own and not those of the IMF.

1. See Reinhart, Rogoff, and Savastano (2003) for an analysis of borrowing/default cycles.

2. Of course if bad times are defined exclusively as currency or banking crises, then there is a small but growing theoretical literature on monetary policy in general and interest rate defenses in particular. See, for instance, Aghion, Bacchetta, and Banerjee (2001) and Lahiri and Végh (2003). The empirical evidence in this area is, however, rather inconclusive.

3. For a discussion of some of the challenges in estimating monetary policy rules for industrial countries, see Clarida, Galí, and Gertler (1999).

4. Throughout this paper, business cycle refers to the real gross domestic product (GDP) cycle.

5. Lane and Tornell (1998) offer some empirical evidence to show that saving in Latin American countries has often been countercyclical (i.e., saving falls in good times, and vice versa).

6. Section 4 presents evidence in support of this hypothesis. See also Neumeyer and Perri (2004), who examine the importance of country risk in driving the business cycle in emerging economies.

7. It is important to notice that, under this definition, a procyclical fiscal policy implies a *negative* correlation between tax rates and output over the business cycle. Our terminology thus differs from the one in the real business cycle literature in which any variable positively (negatively) correlated with the output cycle is referred to as procyclical (countercyclical).

8. It is worth emphasizing that, in deriving the theoretical correlations below, the only assumption made is that the tax base (output or consumption) is high in good times and low in bad times. This is true by definition in the case of output and amply documented for the case of consumption. Aside from this basic assumption, what follows is an accounting exercise that is independent of any particular model.

9. By the same token, it would also seem unwise to define procyclical fiscal policy as a negative correlation between output and the fiscal balance (as is sometimes done in the literature) since a zero or even positive correlation could also be consistent with procyclical fiscal policy, as defined above.

10. We are, of course, fully aware that there is certainly no consensus on whether the inflation tax should be thought of as just another tax. While the theoretical basis for doing so goes back to Phelps (1973) and has been greatly refined ever since (see, for example, Chari and Kehoe, 1999), the empirical implications of inflation as an optimal tax have received mixed support. See Calvo and Végh (1999) for a discussion.

11. A negative correlation between real interest rates and output would arise in a standard endowment economy model (i.e., a model with exogenous output) in which high real interest rates today signal today's scarcity of goods relative to tomorrow. In a production economy driven by technology shocks, however, this relationship could have the opposite sign. In addition, demand shocks, in and of themselves, would lead to higher real interest rates in good times and vice versa. Given these different possibilities, any inferences drawn on the cyclical stance of monetary policy from the behavior of real interest rates should be treated with extreme caution.

12. If, as part of a procyclical monetary policy, policymakers lowered reserve requirements, this should lead to even higher real money balances.

13. In practice, however, using domestic credit to measure the stance of monetary policy is greatly complicated by the fact that inflation (especially in developing countries) tends to be high and variable. Hence, a large growth rate does not always reflect expansionary policies. For this reason, in the empirical section, we will restrict our attention to short-term nominal interest rates as a policy instrument.

14. Our data set covers 104 countries for the period 1960–2003 (the starting date for each series varies across countries and indicators). See Table 14 for data sources and Table 15 for the list of countries (both tables are in the appendix).

15. Based on data for 33 poor countries over a 25-year period, Pallage and Robe (2001) conclude that foreign aid has also been procyclical, which is consistent with our overall message.

16. We also found that for both groups of middle-income countries, the current account deficit is larger in good times than in bad times, which is consistent with procyclical capital flows.

17. See Reinhart, Rogoff, and Savastano (2003).

18. The Institutional Investor Index (III) ratings, which are compiled twice a year, are based on information provided by economists and sovereign risk analysts at leading global banks and securities firms. The ratings grade each country on a scale from 0 to 100, with a rating of 100 given to countries perceived as having the lowest chance of defaulting on government debt obligations.

19. Tables 8, 10, 12, and 14 report the average country correlation for the indicated group of countries. We use a standard t-test to ascertain where the average is significantly different from 0.

20. Figures on the inflation tax are multiplied by 100.

21. In terms of the country-by-country computations underlying Table 10, it is worth noting that for, say, real central government expenditure, 91 percent of the correlations for developing countries are positive (indicating procyclical fiscal policy), whereas 65 percent of the correlations for OECD countries are negative (indicating countercyclical fiscal policy), as illustrated in Figure 2.

22. In this regard, see Cuddington (1989).

23. Appendix Tables 3 and 4 in the working paper version of this paper show results analogous to those in Table 11 for real interest rates and real monetary aggregates, respectively. Broadly speaking, real rates for OECD countries show a positive correlation with the cycle (i.e., they generally rise in good times and fall in bad times). This is, in principle, consistent with countercyclical monetary policy (recall Table 3). In contrast, for middle-high and middle-low-income countries, real interest rates appear to be negatively correlated with the cycle. These results are consistent with those reported in Neumeyer and Perri (2004). The results for low-income countries are harder to interpret as they are more similar to those for OECD countries. The results for real money balances in Appendix Table 4 are in line with our priors—with real money balances rising more in good times than in bad times. This positive correlation, however, does not allow us to draw any inference on the stance of monetary policy (recall Table 3).

24. It is important to warn the reader that the data on interest rates for non-OECD countries is spotty and rather incomplete. Our results should thus be interpreted with caution and as merely suggestive.

25. As an aside, notice that the coefficient on the inflation gap is always positive and significant.

26. To conserve on space, Table 14 presents results for only one measure of government spending and one interest rate using the HP filter. The remaining results are available upon request from the authors.

References

Aghion, Phillipe, Philippe Bacchetta, and Abhijit Banerjee. (2001). Currency crises and monetary policy in an economy with credit constraints. *European Economic Review* 45:1121–1150.

Aguiar, Mark, and Gita Gopinath. (2004). Emerging market business cycles: The cycle is the trend. University of Chicago. Mimeo.

Aizenman, Joshua, Michael Gavin, and Ricardo Hausmann. (1996). Optimal tax policy with endogenous borrowing constraints. NBER Working Paper No. 5558.

Baxter, Marianne, and Robert G. King. (1999). Measuring business cycles: Approximate bandpass filters for economic time series. *Review of Economics and Statistics* 81:575–593.

Braun, Miguel. (2001). Why is fiscal policy procyclical in developing countries? Harvard University. Mimeo.

Calderon, Cesar, and Klaus Schmidt-Hebbel. (2003). Macroeconomic policies and performance in Latin America. *Journal of International Money and Finance* 22:895–923.

Calvo, Guillermo A. (1987). On the costs of temporary policy. *Journal of Development Economics* 27:245–262.

Calvo, Guillermo A., Leonardo Leiderman, and Carmen M. Reinhart. (1993). Capital inflows and real exchange rate appreciation in Latin America: The role of external factors. *IMF Staff Papers* 40:108–151.

Calvo, Guillermo A., Leonardo Leiderman, and Carmen M. Reinhart. (1994). The capital inflows problem: Concepts and issues. *Contemporary Economic Policy* XII:54–66.

Calvo, Guillermo A., and Carlos A. Végh. (1999). Inflation stabilization and BOP crises in developing countries. In *Handbook of Macroeconomics*, Volume C, John Taylor and Michael Woodford (eds.). Amsterdam: North Holland, 1531–1614.

Chari, V. V., and Patrick Kehoe. (1999). Optimal fiscal and monetary policy. NBER Working Papers No. 6891.

Clarida, Richard, Jordi Galí, and Mark Gertler. (1997). Monetary policy rules in practice: Some international evidence. NBER Working Paper No. 6254.

Clarida, Richard, Jordi Galí, and Mark Gertler. (1999). The science of monetary policy: A new Keynesian perspective. *Journal of Economic Literature* 37:1161–1707.

Corbo, Vittorio. (2000). Monetary policy in Latin America in the 90s. Central Bank of Chile Working Paper No. 78.

Cuddington, John. (1989). Commodity export booms in developing countries. *The World Bank Research Observer* 4(2, July):143–165.

Dixon, Jay. (2003). Voracity, Volatility, and Growth. University of California at Los Angeles. Mimeo.

Drazen, Alan. (2000). Interest rate and borrowing defense against speculative attack. *Carnegie-Rochester Series on Public Policy* 53:303–348.

Flood, Robert P., and Olivier Jeanne. (2000). An interest rate defense of a fixed exchange rate? IMF Working Paper No. 00/159.

Gavin, Michael, and Roberto Perotti. (1997). Fiscal policy in Latin America. *NBER Macroeconomics Annual*. Cambridge, Mass.: MIT Press, pp. 11–61.

Lahiri, Amartya, and Carlos A. Végh. (2003). Delaying the inevitable: Interest rate defense and BOP crises. *Journal of Political Economy* 111:404–424.

Lahiri, Amartya, and Carlos A. Végh. (2004). On the non-monotonic relation between interest rates and the exchange rate. New York Fed and UCLA. Mimeo.

Lane, Philip. (2003). Business cycles and macroeconomic policy in emerging market economies. Trinity College, Dublin. Mimeo.

Lane, Philip, and Aaron Tornell. (1998). Why aren't Latin American savings rates procyclical? *Journal of Development Economics* 57:185–200.

Moron, Eduardo, and Juan Francisco Castro. (2000). Uncovering central bank's monetary policy objective: Going beyond the fear of floating. Universidad del Pacifico. Mimeo.

Neumeyer, Pablo A., and Fabrizio Perri. (2004). Business cycles in emerging economies: The role of interest rates. NBER Working Paper No. 10837.

Pallage, Stephane, and Michel A. Robe. (2001). Foreign aid and the business cycle. *Review of International Economics* 9:637–668.

Phelps, Edmund. (1973). Inflation in the theory of public finance. *Swedish Journal of Economics* 75:67–82.

Reinhart, Carmen M., and Kenneth S. Rogoff. (2004). The modern history of exchange rate arrangements: A reinterpretation. *Quarterly Journal of Economics* CXIX(1):1–48.

Reinhart, Carmen M., Kenneth S. Rogoff, and Miguel A. Savastano. (2003). Debt intolerance. In *Brookings Papers on Economic Activity*, William Brainard and George Perry (eds.), Vol. 1, pp. 1–74.

Riascos, Alvaro, and Carlos A. Végh. (2003). Procyclical fiscal policy in developing countries: The role of incomplete markets. UCLA and Banco Republica, Colombia. Mimeo.

Talvi, Ernesto, and Carlos A. Végh. (2000). Tax base variability and procyclical fiscal policy. NBER Working Paper No. 7499.

Taylor, John. (1993). Discretion versus policy rules in practice. *Carnegie-Rochester Conference Series on Public Policy* 39:195–214.

Tornell, Aaron, and Philip Lane. (1999). The voracity effect. *American Economic Review* 89:22–46.

Comment

Gita Gopinath
University of Chicago and
NBER

This paper is an extremely nice effort at documenting and contrasting certain features of the business cycle for a large set of countries. The authors focus on the cyclical properties of capital flows, fiscal policy, and monetary policy. They contrast the behavior of these variables across groups of countries defined to be OECD, middle-high, middle-low, and low-income countries. The middle-high-income countries are the so-called emerging markets (EM). Based on their analysis, the authors identify a striking feature that appears to characterize EMs. That is, in good times (when output is above trend), EMs receive above-average levels of capital flow from the rest of the world at the same time as fiscal and monetary policies are strongly expansionary. This feature, which the authors describe as when it rains, it pours, is either not true or less true of other countries in the sample. We are then presented with a seemingly unique feature of EMs that seeks an explanation. This paper is a nice source for facts on EMs that will discipline future theoretical research and call for further empirical research on the facts themselves.

In my comments, I will briefly examine and summarize the evidence and then proceed to present a perspective on emerging markets that will help us in interpreting the facts. My main comment will be to emphasize that what we call the business cycle in an EM is very different from the cycle in a developed economy. In the case of the latter, we typically think of the output process as characterized by a fairly stable trend and transitory fluctuations around this trend. In the case of EMs, in contrast, the trend is highly volatile and this dominates the volatility of transitory shocks. This characterization captures the frequent switches in regimes that EMs endure, often associated with clearly defined changes in government policy, including dramatic changes in monetary, fiscal, and trade policies. There is a large literature on the political economy of emerging markets in general, and the tensions behind the sporadic appearance of progrowth regimes in particular, that is consistent with a volatile trend (see, for example, Dornbusch and Edwards, 1991). Once we recognize this difference in the business cycle, several features of the data that this paper documents appear to be less puzzling. It also informs our inference of causation between variables. Most of my comments arise from work I have done jointly with Mark Aguiar (Aguiar and Gopinath, 2004a; Aguiar and Gopinath, 2004b).

1. Empirical Findings

The main empirical findings are the following. First, capital flows into developing countries tend to be more strongly procyclical than in the case of OECD countries. Second, several measures of government fiscal policy appear to be markedly procyclical in developing countries compared to OECD countries. Ideally, one would like to examine *jointly* several measures of fiscal policy to examine the stance of fiscal policy. It is possible, for instance, that even if income tax rates stay unchanged, governments might try harder to fight tax evasion in good times (as a part of reform), implying a tighter fiscal policy. The only tax measure the authors employ is the inflation tax rate, mainly restricted by data availability. A fruitful exercise will be to put together evidence on other measures of taxation and alternate fiscal instruments.

The third finding is that in the case of EMs, the fiscal spending cycle is positively linked to the capital flow cycle. However, the magnitude of these correlations appear to be sensitive to the filtering procedure used and in some cases are quite small. The last finding relates to monetary policy. As the authors acknowledge, measuring the policy component of monetary aggregates is a tricky problem. The evidence that the authors find is that short-term interest rates are negatively correlated with the business cycle in EMs. This contrasts with interest rates in OECD countries, which are positively correlated with the cycle. The behavior of domestic interest rates in EMs is strikingly similar to the behavior of interest rates at which EMs borrow from the rest of the world. Neumeyer and Perri (2004) document a strong negative correlation between interest rates on dollar-denominated debt and the business cycle in EMs. This behavior of interest rates is consistent with the market response to changing default probabilities over the business cycle. I will say more about this later. The main point, however, is that for the evidence on monetary policy more empirical work must be done to provide conclusive evidence on the stance of monetary policy.

2. Emerging Market Business Cycles: The Cycle Is the Trend

The question of what is the business cycle in emerging markets is explored here. A standard representation of the production function is

$$Y_t = e^{z_t} K_t^{\alpha} (\Gamma_t L_t)^{(1-\alpha)}$$

where K_t is the level of the capital stock and L_t is the labor input. The variable z_t represents transitory shocks to productivity and follows an AR(1) process.

$$z_t = \rho_z z_{t-1} + \varepsilon_t^z$$

$\varepsilon_t^z \sim N(0, \sigma_z^2)$, $|\rho_z| < 1$. Γ_t represents the stochastic trend productivity; g_t is the growth rate of trend output.

$$\Gamma_t = g_t \Gamma_{t-1}$$

$$\ln(g_t) = (1 - \rho_g) \ln(\mu_g) + \rho_g \ln(g_{t-1}) + \varepsilon_t^g$$

$\varepsilon_t^g \sim N(0, \sigma_g^2)$, $|\rho_g| < 1$.

In Aguiar and Gopinath (2004b), we document that the ratio of volatility of trend shocks to level shocks, (σ_g/σ_z), is higher in an EM, such as Mexico, compared to a developed small open economy such as Canada. That is, unlike developed markets, fluctuations at business cycle frequencies in EMs are driven primarily by trend shocks as opposed to transitory level shocks. Figure 1 plots log GDP for three small open economies (SOE)—Canada, Mexico, and Argentina. The plot for each economy includes the log level of GDP (where we have extracted any significant seasonal component) and the stochastic trend. The latter was calculated using the methodology of King, Plosser, Stock, and Watson (1991). To be precise, the trend is obtained by setting the transitory shocks to zero and feeding only the permanent shock through the system. This should not be confused with equating the trend to the random walk component à la Beveridge and Nelson (1981). Casual observation of the plots suggests that Canada, our benchmark developed SOE, experiences relatively small fluctuations around a stable trend. On the other hand, Mexico and particularly Argentina display a volatile trend that mirrors movements in GDP at

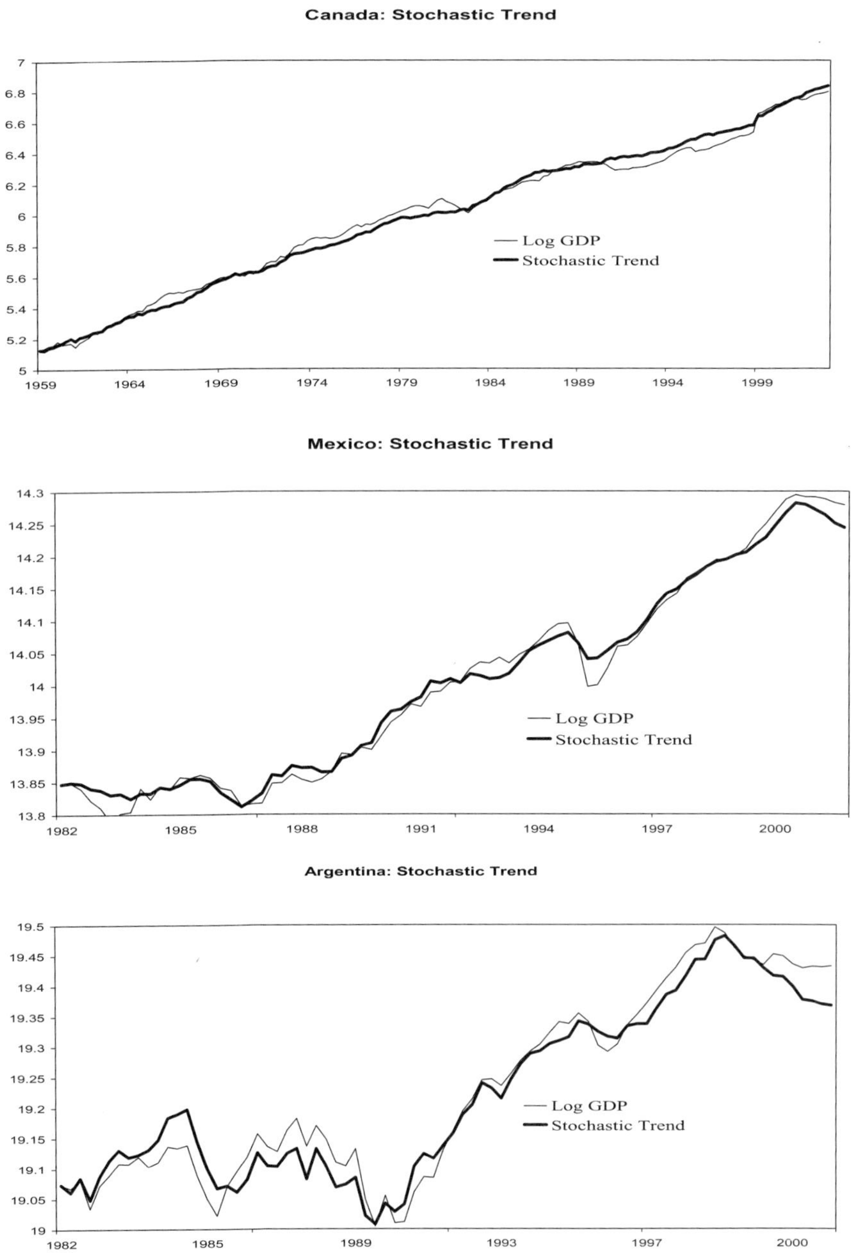

Figure 1
Stochastic trends estimated using the KPSW (1991) methodology

high frequencies. We find that at business-cycle frequencies (12 quarters), the fraction of output variance explained by permanent shocks in the case of Canada is around 50%, while the same number for Mexico is 82%, supporting the view that the cycle is the trend for these markets.

3. Capital Flows, Interest Rates, and Macroeconomic Policies

The first empirical finding in the paper that capital flows (current accounts) are more strongly procyclical (countercyclical) in EMs is then a natural implication of a standard real business cycle model wherein the stochastic trend is the main shock. The current account (negative of capital flows) is the difference between national saving and national investment. In response to a positive transitory shock to productivity (z), investment rises. All else being equal, this will cause the current account to worsen. In response to a transitory shock, however, savings also rise since agents wish to smooth consumption. The savings effect then counters the investment effect and the current account is less countercyclical or acyclical. For developed markets, where we view the trend to be stable, one would expect little cyclicality of the current account. On the other hand, the response to a positive trend shock, g, will be for savings to fall on impact. Agents experience higher income following this shock but expect income to increase even more in the future (as they enter a new growth regime). Consequently, savings will fall on impact. Now, the current account will be more strongly countercyclical, as the authors find in this paper for EMs. Figure 2 plots the current account against the standard deviation of the growth rate of real GDP for 28 small open economies. There is a clear negative relation between the trade balance (as a ratio of GDP) and the volatility of the growth rate. Countries with more volatile growth rates (in the group of middle- and high-income small open economies), the EMs, tend to have more countercyclical trade balances.

Our view on the role of the trend in EMs also resonates in evidence that this paper documents on the behavior of international credit ratings in Tables 6 and 7. The authors find that it is precisely the middle-income countries that experience the biggest swings in ratings across good and bad states of nature. Since credit ratings incorporate the probability of default, a switch from a high-growth regime to a low-growth regime will have dramatic negative effects on the countries'

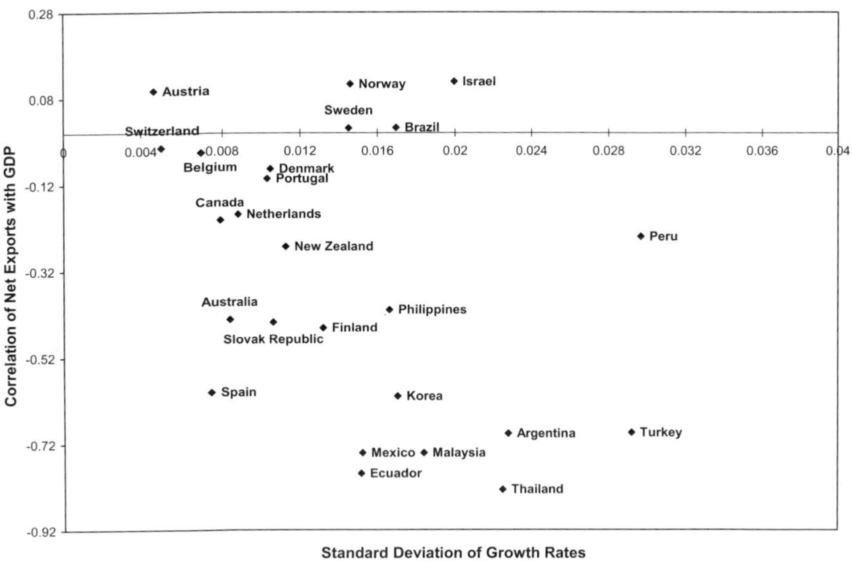

Figure 2

ability to repay and consequently should affect ratings more substantially compared to transitory shocks.

The question then is, What underlies the regime switches we observe in EMs? One can argue for the role of government policy here. Argentina's adoption of the currency board at the start of 1990 that brought an end to years of hyperinflation in the economy is one such regime switch. In this case, interpreting any causal link running from capital flows to fiscal policy becomes tricky. The finding that inflation tax rates are countercyclical (Table 9) could precisely be the regime change that then attracts capital flows into the economy. The negative correlation between capital flows and inflation tax for EMs is consistent with this. Other forms of regime switches involve privatizations and nationalizations that can dramatically affect productivity. For instance, Restuccia and Schmitz (2004) provide evidence of a 50% drop in productivity in the petroleum industry in Venezuela within five years of its nationalization in 1975. Similarly, Schmitz and Teixeira (2004) document almost a doubling of productivity in the Brazilian iron-ore industry following its privatization in 1991.

Last, I will comment on the countercyclicality of interest rates and the positive correlation between interest rates and the current account.

As mentioned earlier, strong evidence suggests the countercyclicality of dollar interest rates at which EMs borrow from the rest of the world. This same literature documents that dollar interest rates and the current account are positively correlated. That is, EMs borrow more in good times and at lower interest rates. In Aguiar and Gopinath (2004a), we describe a model of sovereign default and show that this relation among interest rates, current account, and GDP follows directly when an economy is subject to trend shocks. Put simply, in a high-growth regime, agents wish to borrow (as they face an upward-sloping income profile). All else being equal, this should raise interest rates because higher levels of debt raise the probability of default. In an economy subject to trend shocks, however, the positive trend shock has the effect of lowering interest rates at all levels of debt. Consequently, it is possible that the economy pays a lower interest rate on its borrowing. We show that this is a more likely scenario in an economy subject primarily to trend shocks as opposed to transitory shocks around a stable trend.

To conclude, this paper presents us with interesting business-cycle features of EMs that tend to contrast with the experience of developed markets. While this paper significantly enhances our knowledge of the fiscal and monetary cycles in countries, more empirical work remains to be done in further documenting these facts. In interpreting these facts, it is important to bear in mind that the underlying income process in EMs and developed markets are quite different. Once this is taken into account, contrasting features of EMs appear to be less puzzling.

References

Aguiar, Mark, and Gita Gopinath. (2004a). Defaultable debt, interest rates and the current account. NBER Working Paper No. 10731.

Aguiar, Mark, and Gita Gopinath. (2004b). Emerging market business cycles: The cycle is the trend. NBER Working Paper No. 10734.

Beveridge, Stephen, and Charles R. Nelson. (1981). A new approach to decomposition of economic time series into permanent and transitory components with particular attention to the measurement of the business cycle. *Journal of Monetary Economics* 7:151–174.

Dornbusch, Rudiger, and Sebastian Edwards. (1991). Macroeconomics of Populism in Latin America. NBER Conference Report, University of Chicago Press, Chicago and London.

King, Robert, Charles Plosser, James Stock, and Mark Watson. (1991). Stochastic trends and economic fluctuations. *American Economic Review* 81(4):819–840.

Neumeyer, Andy, and Fabrizio Perri. (2004). Emerging market business cycles: The role of interest rates. NBER Working Paper No. 10387.

Restuccia, Diego, and Schmitz, James. (2004). Nationalization's impact on output and productivity: The case of Venezuelan minerals. Federal Reserve Bank of Minneapolis Working Paper.

Schmitz, James, and Arilton Teixeira. (2004). Privatization's impact on private productivity: The case of Brazilian iron ore. Staff Reports No. 337, Federal Reserve Bank of Minneapolis.

Comment

Roberto Rigobon
Sloan School of Management,
MIT and NBER

1. Introduction

The classical literature points to countercyclical policy responses as means to moderate the cost of business cycles. While the prescription of the theory is clear, this behavior is rarely observed in practice. Kaminsky, Reinhart, and Végh's (KRV) paper documents, quite convincingly, that emerging markets suffer from acute procyclical policies—hence their title "When It Rains, It Pours." Although this behavior had been highlighted before in the case of fiscal policy, KRV extend the years, number of countries, and variables included in the analysis, and they find, overwhelmingly, that procyclical behavior is a generalized feature of emerging markets. An important contribution of KRV is the analysis of which macroeconomic indicators are appropriate to the measurement of the procyclical behavior. However, is the procyclical behavior a reflection of different shocks hitting the economies, or is it the outcome of wrong choices by policymakers? If it is the first, then it is unclear why we should care about procyclicality. Nevertheless, if it is the second, then something could—or should—be done.

The preliminary evidence shown in these comments is that most of the differences across countries is due to the dissimilar shocks hitting them and not to their diverse responses to the same shocks. In other words, emerging markets are more procyclical because they are usually hit by shocks that create positive comovement among the variables of interest.

These comments are organized as follows. First, I reproduce the stylized facts in KRV (using their data) but presenting the results in a different fashion. Second, I try to address the reasons behind the procyclical behavior. I explore first the issues of endogeneity and then the more general problem of the different mixture of shocks. Finally, I present some concluding remarks.

2. Procyclical Policies

Although KRV study several dimensions of procyclical policy—monetary, fiscal, etc.—in these comments, I concentrate entirely on fiscal policy, and in particular on real expenditures. This is a small part of the analysis performed by KRV, but I believe it is enough to provide the intuition, and highlight the issues, that I would like to concentrate on.

Standard macroeconomic theory implies that government consumption should be smoothed through the business cycle to lessen the severity of the macroeconomic fluctuations. In this sense, therefore, it should be expected that fiscal policies follow a countercyclical pattern. A closer look at the data suggests that reality is far from this theoretical paradigm.

Using yearly data on real gross domestic product (GDP) and real total expenditures for more than 100 countries from 1960s to today (same data as KRV), I computed the correlation between output and total expenditures country by country. In the original version of KRV, they mostly concentrated on the average of such correlation, which is what most of the literature does. To clarify the points behind my discussion, I have preferred to look at the estimate country by country, sorting the data from the lowest to the largest coefficient.[1] The results are shown in Figure 1. The countries in light gray are the developed economies, while the countries in dark gray are the developing countries.

As can be seen, not all developed economies have a negative correlation, although they are mostly located on the left side of the graph. Indeed, if we were to compute the average correlation in the sample, we would find that it is easy to accept the hypothesis that the correlation of developed countries is statistically smaller than that of developing countries. This is exactly what KRV do.

This result is also confirmed if, instead of using the level of expenditure, I compute the correlation of output and expenditure share (defined as the total expenditures as a percentage of GDP). In this case, the pattern is not exactly the same, but the final message is identical. In Figure 2, the same figure as before is reproduced, but expenditure shares are used instead of total expenditures. Again, developed economies are mostly located in the left part of the figure, suggesting

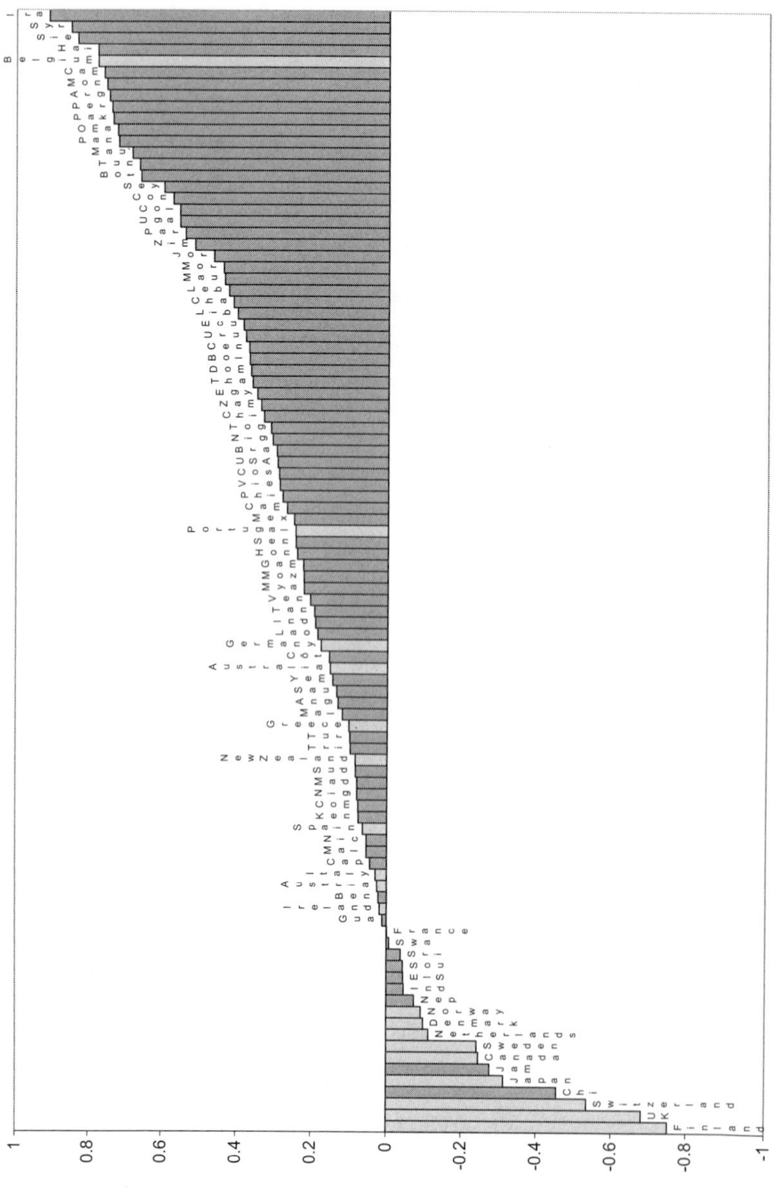

Figure 1
Simple correlation: output and total expenditures

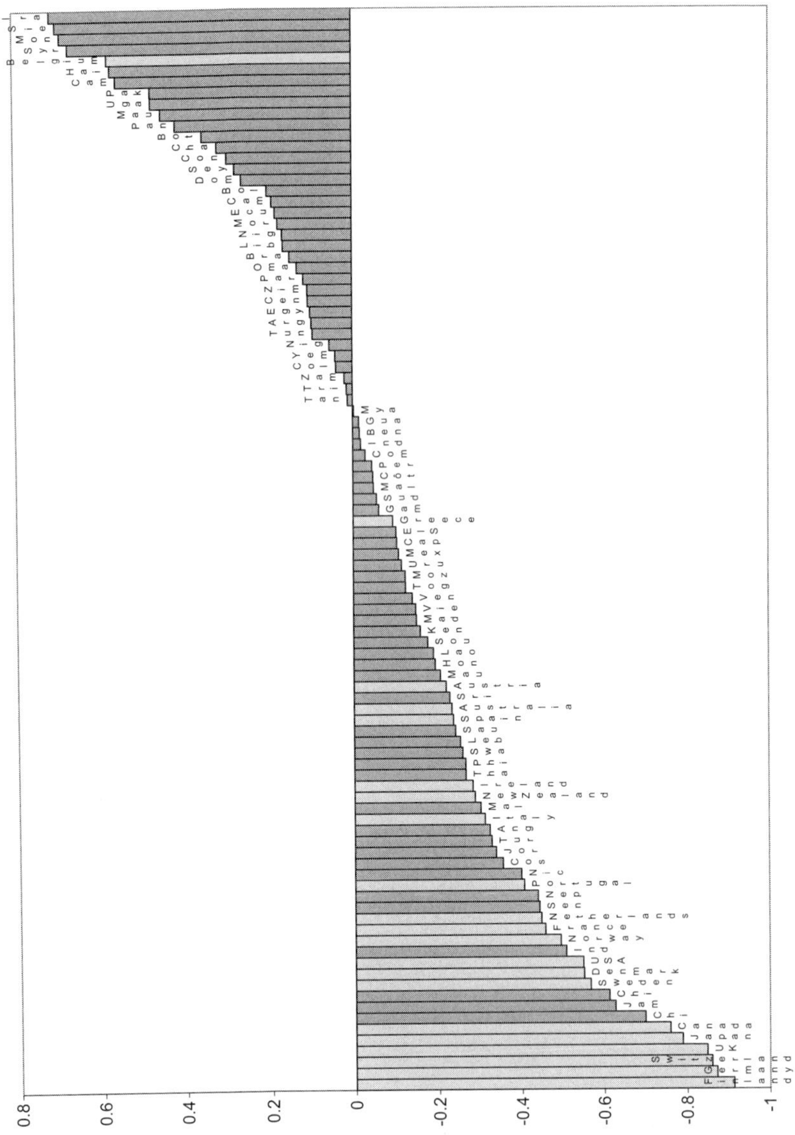

Figure 2
Simple correlation: output and expenditure share

that their fiscal policies are less procyclical than those in developing countries.

This pattern is so strong that it is found not only in correlations—as has been done here and in KRV—but it is also found using other measures of comovement. For example, estimating the simple regression $g_t = \alpha y_t + \varepsilon_t$ country by country and plotting the OLS coefficients produces exactly the same pattern. Figure 3 presents the results. As can be seen, the pattern across all three figures is almost identical. Developed economies are always located to the left of the figure, regardless of how the comovement is computed. These figures confirm what KRV find formally in the comparisons of simple correlations across groups.

3. What Does This Mean?

3.1 *Endogeneity*

It is important to clarify that even though the correlations have different signs, it does not imply that countries react differently to output shocks, which is usually the claim in the literature. In other words, this pattern of correlations can be explained either because the endogenous response of fiscal policy to output shocks is different between developed and developing countries, or because the shocks that hit these economies are by themselves dissimilar. Although, this point should be trivial, unfortunately, most of the empirical literature favors the first interpretation and gives little attention to the second.[2] Starting from the original contribution by Gavin and Perotti (1997), the literature is mostly devoted to the argument that the *coefficients* in the policy reaction functions of developing economies are *different* from those of developed economies. Assume that equation (1) represents the fiscal policy reaction function. Then the discussion of procyclicality centers around the signs of the coefficient α.

$$g_t = \alpha y_t + \varepsilon_t \tag{1}$$

The claim—or implicit argument—is that developed economies have countercyclical policies, i.e., α is negative, while developing economies have procyclical policies and α is negative.

Certainly this has been underscored in the literature. First, the voracity effect of Lane and Tornell (1996) is one of the theories in which the difference between emerging and developed economies is in the

Figure 3
OLS coefficient country by country

sign of the coefficients. In this case, the political process does not allow for savings to take place during booms; therefore, fiscal policy moves with external shocks or output. Second, the theory based on credit-constrained governments indicates that a positive correlation exists between expenditures and output because during booms, the constraint is relaxed. As before, this theory has a direct implication on the size and sign of the coefficients in equation (1).

Although a different sign on the coefficients is a distinct possibility, this is not the conclusion that should be extracted from the evidence. Not at all! For example, regarding the relationship between fiscal expenditures and output, it can be claimed that equation (1) is only one side of the economy. It describes the decision of the fiscal authority in reaction to a transitory movement of output, and the residuals of that equation represent the fiscal shocks to which the economy is subjected. However, it should also be clear that an output equation, where fiscal expenditures affect output, exists as well:

$$y_t = \beta g_t + \eta_t \tag{2}$$

The residuals in equation (2) represent, for instance, productivity shocks. We have plenty of evidence that $\beta > 0$.

If these two equations describe the economy, it should be obvious that it is possible to obtain very different correlations even though the parameters remain the same. In other words, it is possible that a country could have a positive correlation between fiscal expenditures and output, even with $\alpha < 0$. The reason is simply because that country could be subjected to mostly fiscal shocks. A simple exploration of these two equations provides a clearer view of the importance of the relative variances as a source of the counter- and procyclical policies in developed and emerging markets. Equations (1) and (2) imply a reduced form given by

$$g_t = \frac{1}{1 - \alpha\beta}(\varepsilon_t + \alpha\eta_t)$$

$$y_t = \frac{1}{1 - \alpha\beta}(\beta\varepsilon_t + \eta_t)$$

If $\beta > 0$ and $\alpha < 0$, then the productivity shocks create negative correlations, while the fiscal shocks produce positive correlations.

Can the different variance of the shocks be the explanation of the observed pattern of correlations in the data? To evaluate the importance of this explanation, we must solve the problem of endogeneity. Nevertheless, without further assumptions, the problem cannot be solved. However, there is a proxy. We can compute the relative variances of expenditures and output, and compare them. Under the assumption that the absolute value of both coefficients is smaller than 1, then a higher ratio of volatility of fiscal shocks to productivity shocks should be accompanied by a larger ratio between the variances of expenditures to output.

I show this ratio in Figure 4. I computed the proportion between output volatility and expenditures volatility. The conjecture is that countries subject to larger productivity shocks will experience negative correlations between expenditures and output, while countries that experience primarily fiscal shocks will have positive correlations. As can be seen in Figure 4, developed economies have variance-of-output to variance-of-expenditure ratios that are much larger than those in developing countries.[3] This is in line with the conjecture that countries with negative correlation experience it because they are subject to a higher share of output shocks than are those that have positive correlations.

This is the ratio of the endogenous variables and not the ratio of the variances of the structural shocks. To answer the question fully, further analysis and the resolution of the simultaneous equations problem are required. One alternative is to find an instrument to estimate equation (1) properly. To be valid, however, this instrument has to be correlated with output but not with government expenditures. Few variables indeed satisfy these requirements. Two come to mind: terms of trade (TOT) and output of major trading partners.

Both variables are subject to critique. On the one hand, TOT might enter the expenditure equation directly, making it a bad instrument. The reason is that several countries in the sample are heavy commodity exporters, and a sizable proportion of the government revenues come from that sector. In those circumstances, an improvement in the TOT increases government revenues and likely will increase expenditures as well. TOT has been weakly correlated historically with output; hence, even if it does not enter the expenditure equation, it still suffers from the weak instruments problem. On the other hand, the output of major trading partners term has its own problems. First, the relationship between the output of trading partners and domestic output is unclear. It depends on the degree of substitubility of the exports and on the elasticity of exports to foreign demand. There is no reason why

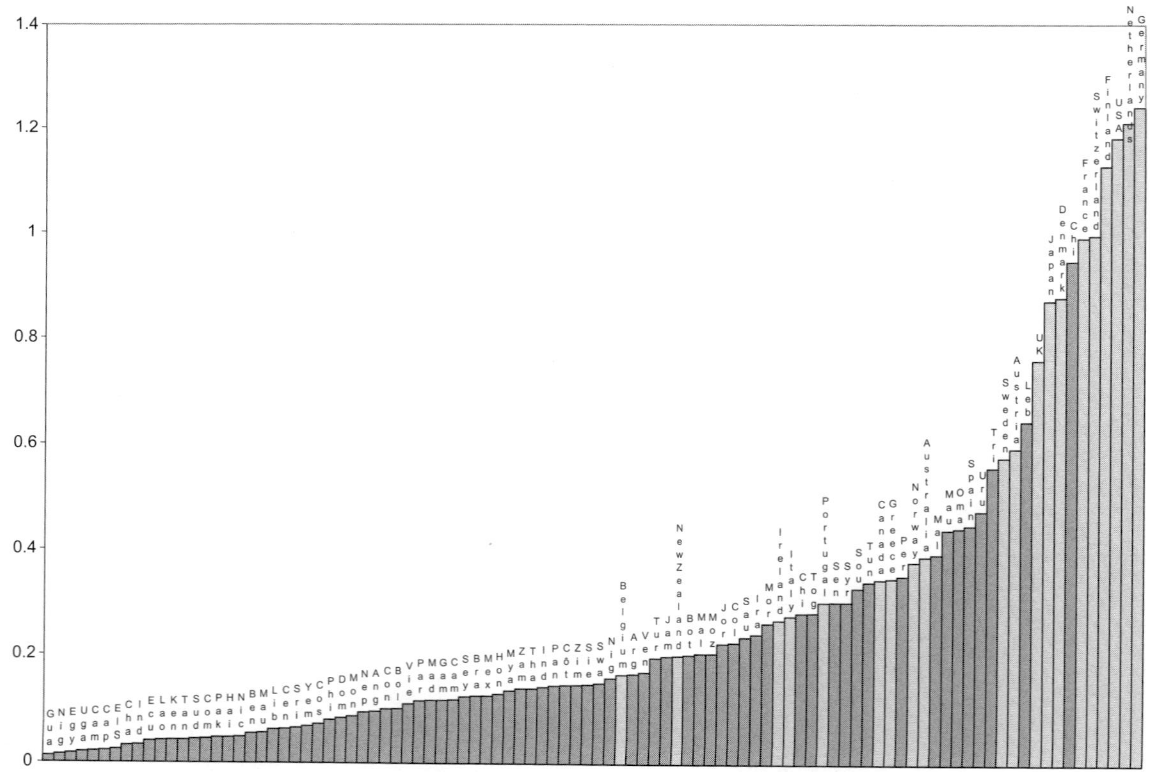

Figure 4
Variance of output divided by variance of expenditures

these effects should be the same across countries; not even their signs should be the same. In the end, assuming that the model has constant coefficients will make the variable a weak instrument.

Galí and Perotti (2004) have studied the implications of using output from trading partners as an instrument. They indeed find that most of the differences in correlations are due to changes in the mixture of shocks and not to different coefficients. They study only European countries, and we expect them to be similar to start with; thus, their results cannot be extrapolated to the rest of the world. Nevertheless, they are suggestive.

In this section, I concentrate on the TOT. As I have already mentioned it is a weak instrument and therefore the results should be taken cautiously. Estimating equation (1) using the TOT as instrument and sorting the coefficients, we find that there is no pattern between the coefficients and the countries. Figure 5 presents the results. Notice that the developed countries (the light gray bars) are spread all over, and the pattern we found in previous exercises is lost.

This evidence suggests that the difference across the two groups—developing versus developed countries—is mainly in the relative variance of the shocks and not in the average coefficients. Indeed, the hypothesis that the average coefficients in the instrumental variables estimation are different across the two groups cannot be rejected.

3.2 *Latent Factors*

In the previous subsection, I concentrated entirely on the problem of simultaneous equations. However, this should be only a small part of the problem, assuming that only two types of shocks are hitting the economy: productivity and fiscal. In reality, expenditures and output are driven by a much more complex set of factors that can affect positive comovement. In this section, I explore a different model. I allow for several factors explaining output and expenditures. The model is as follows:

$$g_t = \sum_{i=1}^{n} \gamma_i z_{i,t} - \sum_{i=n+1}^{m} \gamma_i z_{i,t}$$

$$y_t = \sum_{i=1}^{n} z_{i,t} + \sum_{i=n+1}^{m} z_{i,t}$$

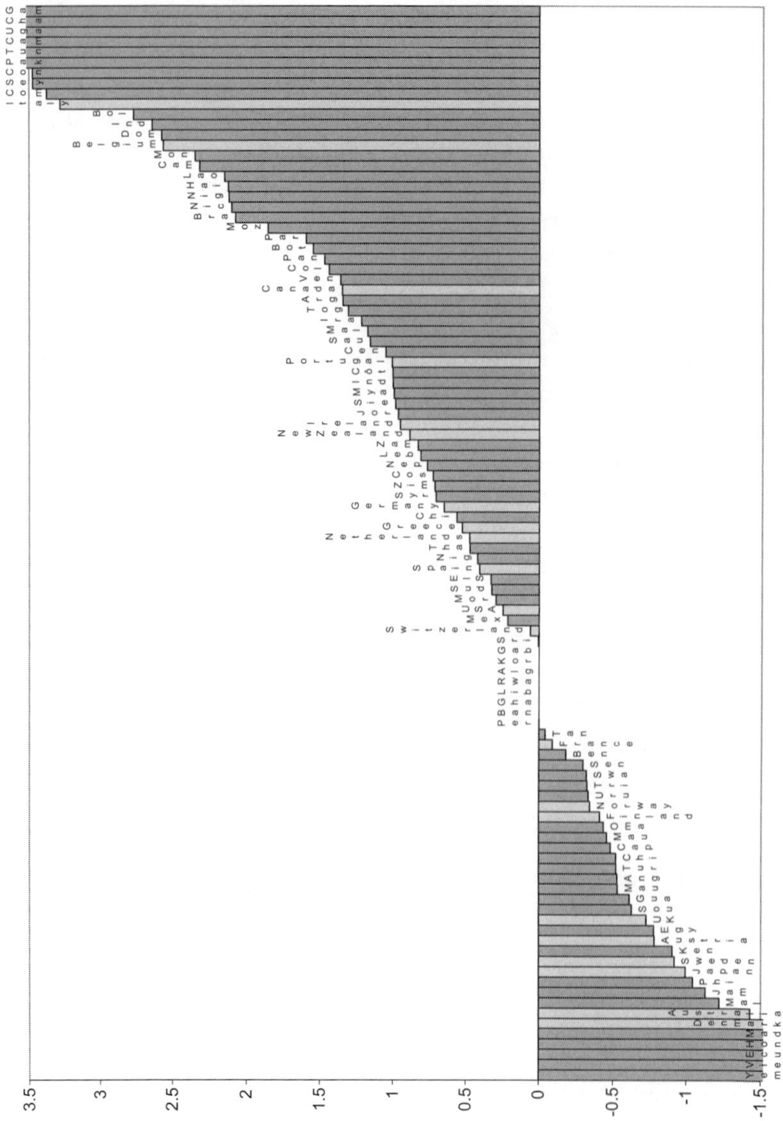

Figure 5
IV estimates using TOT

where all $\gamma > 0$ and it has been assumed that expenditure and output are driven by m different shocks. The first n creates positive comovement, and the later ones create a negative correlation. Notice that this model encompasses the simultaneous equation model discussed before. The questions we are interested are twofold: can we explain the different patterns of correlations across countries by appealing only to the heteroskedasticity of the shocks and keeping the coefficients constant among the two groups of countries? And if not, how different are the coefficients?

In order to answer these questions, we are forced to make strong assumptions. The model, as it is, is not identified. I will make the following assumptions: (1) four groups of countries (as in KRV) are ordered by their degree of development; (2) the countries in each of the groups share the same coefficients, but I allow the coefficients to be different across groups; (3) heteroskedasticity exists in the data; and (4) within each group, all latent factors affect positively or negatively the same coefficient.

The first two assumptions are relatively uncontroversial. The first one is the dimension we are interest in studying. The second one is implicitly assuming that we should concentrate on the average coefficient within each group. The third assumption is easily checked in the data and therefore we will do so. The fourth assumption, on the other hand, is perhaps the strongest one. It is indeed assuming that the model to be estimated is the following:

$$g_t = \tilde{\gamma}_1 \sum_{i=1}^{n} z_{i,t} - \tilde{\gamma}_2 \sum_{i=n+1}^{m} z_{i,t}$$

$$y_t = \sum_{i=1}^{n} z_{i,t} + \sum_{i=n+1}^{m} z_{i,t}$$

In other words, to be able to estimate this model, we have to summarize all the factors that create positive comovement within one single factor, as well as collapsing the factors that create negative comovement in a single factor. Therefore, the changes in the coefficients are part of the residuals of each of these equations. The model to be estimated is then:

$$g_t = \tilde{\gamma}_1 \sum_{i=1}^{n} z_{i,t} - \tilde{\gamma}_2 \sum_{i=n+1}^{m} z_{i,t} + \varepsilon_{g,t}$$

$$y_t = \sum_{i=1}^{n} z_{i,t} + \sum_{i=n+1}^{m} z_{i,t}$$

$$\varepsilon_{g,t} = \sum_{i=1}^{n} (\gamma_i - \tilde{\gamma}_1) z_{i,t} - \sum_{i=n+1}^{m} (\gamma_i - \tilde{\gamma}_2) z_{i,t}$$

If we assume that $(\gamma_i - \tilde{\gamma}_1)$ and $(\gamma_i - \tilde{\gamma}_2)$ are orthogonal to the factors, then we can estimate the model using identification through heteroskedasticity.[4] The idea of the procedure is to use the heteroskedasticity in the data to generate enough equations to solve the problem of identification.

The idea is that we have to estimate:

$$q_t = \gamma_1 \varepsilon_t - \gamma_2 \eta_t$$

$$y_t = \varepsilon_t + \eta_t$$

where, ε_t and η_t are the factors in the previous equations. In this model, the only statistic we can compute from the sample is the covariance matrix of the observable variables. However, this covariance matrix is explained by four unknowns: γ_1, γ_2, and the variances of ε_t and η_t. This is the standard identification problem in simultaneous equations—there are fewer equations (moments in this case) than the number of unknowns. Algebraically, the covariance matrix of the reduced form is:

$$\Omega = \begin{bmatrix} \gamma_1^2 \sigma_\varepsilon^2 + \gamma_2^2 \sigma_\eta^2 & \gamma_1 \sigma_\varepsilon^2 - \gamma_2 \sigma_\eta^2 \\ & \sigma_\varepsilon^2 + \sigma_\eta^2 \end{bmatrix}$$

where the lefthand side can be estimated in the data, and in the righthand side we have the theoretical moments. Assume that the data can be split in two sets according to the heteroskedasticity of the residuals, i.e., that the residuals in these two sets have different variances. Remember that in the original model, we have already stipulated that the coefficients are the same across all observations. In these two subsamples, we can estimate two variance-covariance matrices:

$$\Omega_1 = \begin{bmatrix} \gamma_1^2 \sigma_{\varepsilon,1}^2 + \gamma_2^2 \sigma_{\eta,1}^2 & \gamma_1 \sigma_{\varepsilon,1}^2 - \gamma_2 \sigma_{\eta,1}^2 \\ & \sigma_{\varepsilon,1}^2 + \sigma_{\eta,1}^2 \end{bmatrix}$$

$$\Omega_2 = \begin{bmatrix} \gamma_1^2 \sigma_{\varepsilon,2}^2 + \gamma_2^2 \sigma_{\eta,2}^2 & \gamma_1 \sigma_{\varepsilon,2}^2 - \gamma_2 \sigma_{\eta,2}^2 \\ & \sigma_{\varepsilon,2}^2 + \sigma_{\eta,2}^2 \end{bmatrix}$$

This implies that now six moments can be estimated in the sample, which are explained by six coefficients: the two parameters of interest and four variances. Notice that there are as many equations as there are unknowns. In the standard literature on system of equations, this means that the system satisfies the *order* conditions. To solve the problem fully then, we have to verify that the six equations are linearly independent—which is known as the *rank* condition. Under our assumptions, we know that both coefficients of interest are positive. Obviously, the estimation requires the existence of heteroskedasticity. The sufficient conditions are discussed in Sentana and Fiorentini (2001) and Rigobon (2003a).

The countries were divided in the four groups studied by KRV. The idea is to estimate the coefficient for each group and then compare the coefficients. One advantage of the methodology is that the coefficients *and*, but also the variances are estimated, and hence a comparison between the relative variances of the groups can be performed.

When the groups were split, group 1 did not exhibit enough heteroskedasticity to be estimated. Instead of pooling the countries into group 2—which clearly is a possibility—I decided just to drop the countries because this will make for a better comparison with the paper. The results from the estimation are as follows:

Groups		2	3	4
γ^1	Point	1.159	1.170	1.064
	Standard deviation	0.169	0.173	0.151
γ^2	Point	0.832	0.828	0.732
	Standard deviation	0.193	0.189	0.548

The first set of rows shows the coefficient for the factors that create positive comovement. The first row is the point estimate, and the second row is the standard deviation. As can be seen, for groups 2, 3, and 4, the point estimates are very well estimated (the t-stats are large for all of them), but the point estimates are close among the groups. Indeed, we cannot reject the hypothesis that they are the same. Group 4 (the developed economies) has a smaller coefficient, but the difference is not statistically significant.

The second set of rows estimates the coefficient on the factor that creates negative comovement. As before, the first row is the point estimate, and the second row is the standard deviation. The estimates are also precise, although the coefficient on group 4 is not statistically significant. As in the case of the previous coefficient, it is impossible to reject the hypothesis that the coefficients are the same across groups.

This evidence should suggest that the reason for the different correlations in the sample is mainly due to changes in the relative importance of the shocks. Indeed, comparing the ratio of positive to negative shocks across the sample, we find that in group 4, the shocks that create positive comovement have a variance that is 2.08 times larger than negative comovement factors. However, groups 2 and 3 have a relative variance of 4.47 and 4.55, respectively, indicating that the sources of positive comovement are clearly more important in groups 2 and 3 than in developed countries.

Last, as a source of additional evidence that the relative variance is what explains the pattern of correlations observed in the data, let me compute the correlation in developed countries (only) using rolling windows of 10 years. These correlations are shown in Figure 6. As can be seen, the time-series variation of the correlations is as strong as the cross-country variation we have shown before. If we were to ask ourselves what explains the changing pattern of correlations in the time series, we would say that different variances are at stake. Indeed, this would be the first choice. And if this is the first choice for the time series, why have we neglected it as the first choice for the cross-section?

4. Conclusion

Clear evidence supports the strong procyclical behavior in fiscal and monetary policy in emerging markets. This is confirmed in KRV, and I can substantiate it with another 100 regressions. The purpose of KRV is to document these facts, and they have done a superb job. On the other hand, the purpose of this comment has been to indicate or guide toward possible explanations behind those facts. Are emerging markets more procyclical because their economies are subject to a different mixture of shocks, or because they react differently to them?

The preliminary evidence in this paper (which coincides with Galí and Perotti, 2004) is that the most important source of the differences is in the variances and not the coefficients. Obviously, in the process I have made a lot of sometimes unreasonable assumptions. Future research should be devoted to study these aspects further.

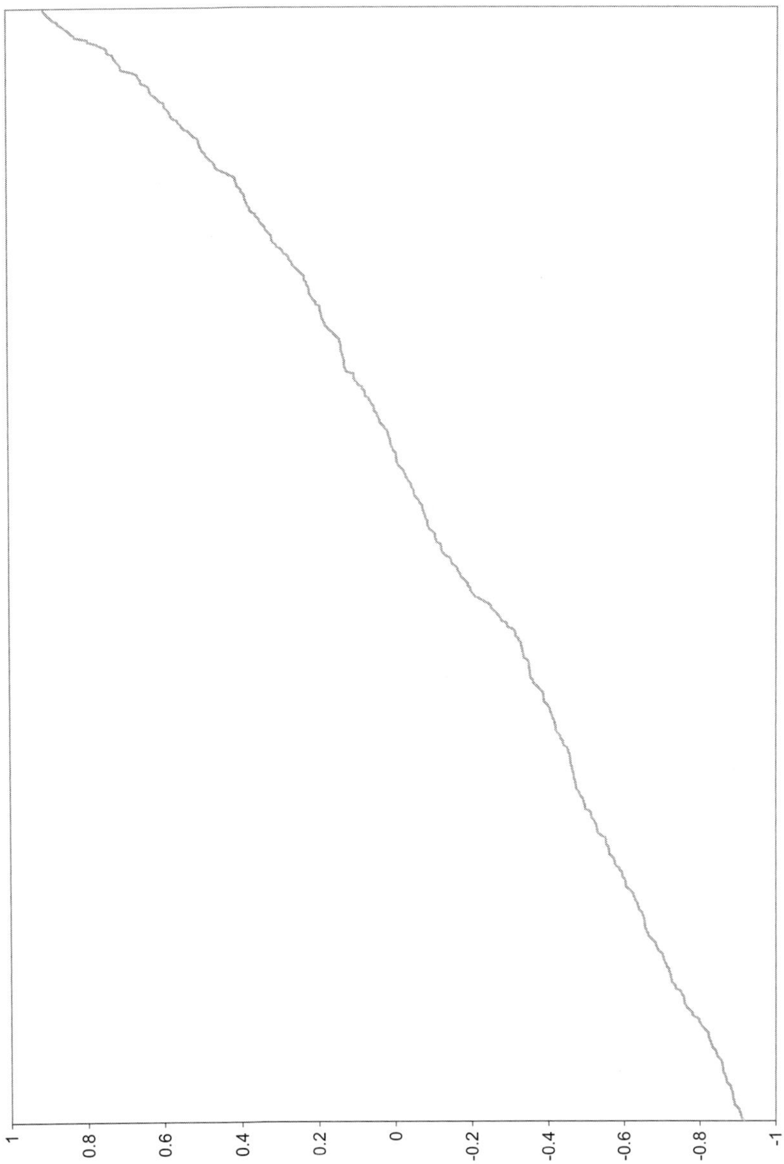

Figure 6
Rolling correlation on developed countries

Notes

1. Indeed, Section 4 in the paper now has adopted this procedure to highlight the patterns in the data.

2. There are some notable exceptions, such as Galí and Perotti (2004), which indeed make this exact same point within the procyclical policies of European countries.

3. Indeed, Galí and Perotti (2004) make a similar point for the case of European countries.

4. For the theoretical derivations, see Rigobon (2003a), Sentana (1992), and Sentana and Fiorentini (2001). Applications where the heteroskedasticity is modeled as a GARCH process are found in Caporale et al. (2002a), Rigobon (2002b), Rigobon and Sack (2003b). Applications where the heteroskedasticity is described by regimes shifts are found in Rigobon (2002a, 2003b), Rigobon and Sack (2003a), and Caporale et al. (2002b). Applications to event study estimation are developed by Rigobon and Sack (2002) and Evans and Lyons (2003). Finally, several application to panel data can be found in the literature. Hogan and Rigobon (2002) apply the method to a very large panel data to estimate the returns to education. Rigobon and Rodrik (2004) study instead the impact of institution on income, and how the different types of institutions are affected by income levels and the degree of openness of the country. Klein and Vella (2003) also use heteroskedasticity to estimate the returns to education. Broda and Weinstein (2003) use the inequality constraints, together with the heteroskedasticity, to estimate the elasticities of substitution in models of trade to evaluate the gains from variety. Pattillo, Poirson, and Ricci (2003) use the identification through heteroskedasicity method to identify the impact of external debt on growth. Hviding, Nowak, and Ricci (2003) investigate the impact of official reserves on exchange-rate volatility. Lee, Ricci, and Rigobon (2004) estimate the impact of openness on growth.

References

Broda, C., and D. Weinstein. (2003). Globalization and the gains from variety. Columbia University. Mimeo.

Caporale, G. M., A. Cipollini, and P. Demetriades. (2002a). Monetary policy and the exchange rate during the Asian crisis: Identification through heteroskedasticity. CEMFE. Mimeo.

Caporale, G. M., A. Cipollini, and N. Spagnolo. (2002b). Testing for contagion: A conditional correlation analysis. CEMFE. Mimeo.

Evans, M., and R. Lyons. (2003). How is macro news transmitted to exchange rates? NBER Working Paper No. 9433.

Galí, Jordi, and Roberto Perotti. (2004). Fiscal policy and monetary integration in Europe. *Economic Policy*, forthcoming.

Gavin, Michael, and Roberto Perrotti. (1997). Fiscal policy in Latin America. In *NBER Macroeconomics Annual 1997*, B. Bernanke and J. Rotemberg (eds.). Cambridge, MA: MIT Press, pp. 11–71.

Hogan, V., and R. Rigobon. (2002). Using unobserved supply shocks to estimate the returns to education. MIT. Mimeo.

Hviding, K., M. Nowak, and L. A. Ricci. (2003). Can higher reserves help reduce exchange rate Volatility? IMF. Mimeo.

Klein, R., and F. Vella. (2003). Identification and estimation of the triangular simultaneous equations model in the absence of exclusion restrictions through the presence of heteroskedasticity. Rutgers. Mimeo.

Lane, Phillip, and Aaron Tornell. (1996). Power, growth, and the voracity effect. *Journal of Economic Growth* XX:217–245.

Lee, Ha Yan, Luca Ricci, and Roberto Rigobon. (2004). Once again, is openness good for growth? *Journal of Development Economics*, forthcoming.

Pattillo, C., H. Poirson, and L. A. Ricci. (2003). The channels through which external debt affects growth. *Brookings Trade Forum*, pp. 229–258.

Rigobon, R. (2002a). Contagion: How to measure it? In *Preventing Currency Crises in Emerging Markets*, Sebastian Edwards and Jeffrey Frankel (eds.). Chicago, IL: University Chicago Press, pp. 269–334.

Rigobon, R. (2002b). The curse of noninvestment grade countries. *Journal of Development Economics* 69(2):423–449.

Rigobon, R. (2003a). Identification through heteroskedasticity. *Review of Economics and Statistics*, forthcoming.

Rigobon, R., and D. Rodrik. (2004). Rule of law, democracy, openness, and income: Estimating the interrelationships. MIT. Mimeo.

Rigobon, R., and B. Sack. (2002). The impact of monetary policy on asset prices. *Journal of Monetary Economics*, forthcoming.

Rigobon, R., and B. Sack. (2003a). Measuring the reaction of monetary policy to the stock market. *Quarterly Journal of Economics* 118(2):639–669.

Rigobon, R., and B. Sack. (2003b). Spillovers across U.S. financial markets. MIT. Mimeo.

Sentana, E. (1992). Identification of multivariate conditionally heteroskedastic factor models. LSE. FMG Discussion Paper, 139.

Sentana, E., and G. Fiorentini. (2001). Identification, estimation and testing of conditional heteroskedastic factor models. *Journal of Econometrics*, 102(2):143–164.

Discussion

Several of the participants commented on Roberto Rigobon's point regarding the distinction between the endogenous and exogenous components of fiscal policy. Jordi Galí pointed out that one instrument that had proven useful in estimating these fiscal policy rules was the gross domestic product (GDP) of a large trading partner because it is not correlated to domestic fiscal shocks and there is some common component in the cycle. Galí remarked that in a recent paper he co-authored with Roberto Perotti, the use of this instrument showed that most of the acyclical or procyclical behavior responded to the exogenous component, while the endogenous component was largely countercyclical. Alan Stockman added that it was important to look at the GDP of a country in relation to the GDP of the world and of its trading partners rather than at the GDP alone. Michael Woodford said that if one looked at permanent innovation in real GDP and assumed that exogenous changes responded necessarily to something other than monetary or fiscal policy, one could determine to what extent the correlation was in fact due to endogenous responses of monetary or fiscal policy to the level of real activity. He believed that by using this instrument, one could conclude that developing countries had a procyclical policy.

Mark Gertler also agreed with Rigobon that it was important to distinguish between impulse and propagation, but he expressed reservations in considering that big fiscal adjustments were purely exogenous. He believed that important fiscal adjustments did not take place for reasons completely unrelated to what was happening in the economy, and he said that it would be interesting to consider the institutions of these countries. As an example, he cited the exchange regime and the importance of distinguishing between fixed and floating regimes to analyze policy responses. If a country were on a fixed regime, it would not be able to use monetary policy and this might be one factor leading to a big fiscal adjustment.

The participants also commented on the differences between the policies of developed and developing countries. David Backus disagreed with the suggestion that there was a need to look at the recent period as different from the 1970s, and rather we could look as far back as the data could go to show that developed countries in the nineteenth century had more volatility in output and much more countercyclical net exports. He suggested analyzing the fiscal policy behavior of these countries then and looking for similarities with developing countries today. Harald Uhlig suggested looking at the different roles of government in OECD countries and emerging market economies. While Rigobon's argument could lead to the conclusion that governments used fiscal policy as a stabilizer—in other words, that a government spent more on unemployment during a recession, for example—governments in emerging market economies had to spend on building infrastructure such as roads, telephone systems, new buildings, etc.

Fabrizio Perri suggested that in counties such as Argentina, procyclical fiscal policies might respond to the fact that these countries needed to attract capital flows. During a financial crisis, these flows dry out, and countries cut government expenditures because it is the only way to attract capital. The fact that they had limited access to capital markets might be part of the driving force of fiscal reactions to cyclical variations.

In response to the comments, Carmen Reinhart welcomed the suggestion of a break in the recent period as very useful and acknowledged that although the authors were constrained in their data, they were aware of the differences before and after financial liberalization periods. She said that they were very confident that the only thing that came close to identifying a more structured approach was their estimation of the Taylor rules. She recognized that they were aware that on the fiscal side, they had only come to establish a set of correlations and did not really address what types of shocks were driving these correlations. She disagreed with Rigobon on the need to look for a three-way relationship that included capital flows when trying to identify the shocks. She argued that they did not consider capital flows to be exogenous. In the paper, it was explained how capital flows could be driven by exogenous shocks and affected by factors such as exchange rates, among others.

Reinhart acknowledged that finding an appropriate instrument was a major challenge. She also explained that at this stage, they did not intend to estimate policy feedback rules, which she believed was the next step, but rather to establish the striking differences.

Federal Government Debt and Interest Rates

Eric M. Engen and R. Glenn Hubbard
American Enterprise Institute; and Columbia University and NBER

1. Introduction

The recent resurgence of federal government budget deficits has rekindled debates about the effects of government debt on interest rates. While the effects of government debt on the economy can operate through a number of different channels, many of the recent concerns about federal borrowing have focused on the potential interest rate effect. Higher interest rates caused by expanding government debt can reduce investment, inhibit interest-sensitive durable consumption expenditures, and decrease the value of assets held by households, thus indirectly dampening consumption expenditures through a wealth effect. The magnitude of these potential adverse consequences depends on the degree to which federal debt actually raises interest rates.

While analysis of the effects of government debt on interest rates has been ongoing for more than two decades, there is little empirical consensus about the magnitude of the effect, and the difference in views held on this issue can be quite stark. While some economists believe there is a significant, large positive effect of government debt on interest rates, others interpret the evidence as suggesting that there is no effect on interest rates. Both economic theory and empirical analysis of the relationship between debt and interest rates have proved inconclusive.

We review the state of the debate over the effects of government debt on interest rates and provide some additional perspectives not covered in other reviews. We also present some new empirical evidence on this relationship. The paper is organized as follows. In the second section, we discuss the potential theoretical effects of government debt on interest rates, and we provide what we think are some important guidelines for interpreting empirical analysis of this issue. In the third section, we look at some basic empirical facts about federal government debt and interest rates, review recent econometric analysis of the interaction of federal government debt and interest rates, and introduce some new analysis of this relationship. Finally, in the last section, we summarize our conclusions and briefly discuss the potential effects of government debt on the economy in general.

2. Theory: How Might Government Debt Affect Interest Rates?

A standard benchmark for understanding and calibrating the potential effect of changes in government debt on interest rates is a standard model based on an aggregate production function for the economy in which government debt replaces, or crowds out, productive physical capital.[1] In brief, this model has the interest rate (r) determined by the marginal product of capital (MPK), which would increase if capital (K) were decreased, or crowded out, by government debt (D). With a Cobb-Douglas production function:

$$Y = AK^{\alpha}L^{(1-\alpha)}$$

where L denotes labor units, A is the coefficient for multifactor productivity, and α is the coefficient on capital in the production function, then the total return to capital in the economy ($MPK^{*}K$) as a share of output (Y) equals α:

$$\alpha = (MPK \times K)/Y$$

This implies that the interest rate is determined by:

$$r = MPK = \alpha \times (Y/K) = \alpha \times A \times (L/K)^{1-\alpha}$$

If government debt completely crowds out capital, so that:

$$\partial K/\partial D = -1$$

then an exogenous increase in government debt (holding other factors constant) causes the interest rate to increase:

$$\partial r/\partial D = (\partial r/\partial K)(\partial K/\partial D) = \alpha(1-\alpha)(Y/K^2) > 0$$

because $0 < \alpha < 1$ and Y and K are positive.

In this theoretical framework, which is commonly used to describe the potential effects of government debt on interest rates, are several important implications for empirical analysis of those effects. First, the *level* of the interest rate is determined by the level of the capital stock and thus by the *level* of government debt. The *change* in the interest rate is affected by the government budget deficit, which is essentially equal to the *change* in government debt. Empirical estimates of the effect on interest rates tend to differ markedly depending on whether the deficit or debt is used (as we show later), and most empirical work uses a specification different from that implied by this economic model; that is, the deficit is regressed on the level of the interest rate.

A model that suggests that deficits affect the level of the interest rate is a Keynesian *IS-LM* framework where deficits increase the interest rate not only because debt may crowd out capital but also because deficits stimulate aggregate demand and raise output. However, an increase in interest rates in the short run from stimulus of aggregate demand is a quite different effect than an increase in long-run interest rates owing to government debt crowding out private capital. As discussed by Bernheim (1987), it is quite difficult (requiring numerous assumptions about various elasticities) to construct a natural Keynesian benchmark for quantifying the short-term stimulus from deficits and the long-term crowding out of capital in trying to parse out the effect of government deficits on interest rates.

Second, factors other than government debt can influence the determination of interest rates in credit markets. For example, in a growing economy, the monetary authority will purchase some government debt to expand the money supply and try to keep prices relatively constant.[2] Government debt held by the central bank does not crowd out private capital formation, but many empirical studies of federal government debt and interest rates ignore central bank purchases of government debt.

More difficult econometric problems are posed by the fact that other potentially important but endogenous factors are involved in the supply and demand of loanable funds in credit markets. In addition to public-sector debt, private-sector debt incurred to increase consumption also could potentially crowd out capital formation. Typically, measures of private-sector debt or borrowing are not included in empirical studies of government debt. In a variant of a neoclassical model of the economy that implies Ricardian equivalence, increases in government debt (holding government consumption outlays and marginal tax rates constant) are offset by increases in private saving, and thus the capital stock is not altered by government debt and the interest rate does not rise.[3] Private-sector saving is usually not included in empirical analyses of government debt and the interest rate. Also, in an economy that is part of a global capital market, increases in government debt can be offset by increases in foreign-sector lending. Many empirical analyses of government debt and interest rates do not account for foreign-sector lending and purchases of U.S. Treasury securities.

Finally, the interest rate is also affected by other general macroeconomic factors besides capital that influence output (Y); in the simple model here, that includes labor and multifactor productivity. Thus, there is usually some accounting for general macroeconomic factors that can affect the performance of the economy in empirical analyses of the effect of government debt on interest rates.

Certain assumptions—Ricardian equivalence or perfectly open international capital markets in which foreign saving flows in to finance domestic government borrowing—provide one benchmark for the potential effect of government debt on the interest rate. In these scenarios, government debt does not crowd out capital (i.e., $\partial K/\partial D = 0$) and thus has no effect on the interest rate. For the alternative crowding-out hypothesis (i.e., $-1 \leq \partial K/\partial D < 0$), the production-function framework presented above can provide a range of plausible calculations of the potential increase in interest rates from an increase in the government debt.

By taking logs of the interest rate equation above, differentiating, and noting that *dlnx* is approximately equal to the percentage change (%Δ) in x yields:

$$\%\Delta r = \%\Delta Y - \%\Delta K = (\alpha - 1)(\%\Delta K) + (1 - \alpha)\%\Delta L$$

Because labor input is typically held constant (i.e., $\%\Delta L = 0$) in the debt-crowd-out experiment,

$$\%\Delta r = (\alpha - 1)(\%\Delta K)$$

For the purpose of calculating a benchmark, we assume that the capital share of output is $\alpha = \frac{1}{3}$, which is approximately equal to its historical value in the United States. National accounts data suggests that the marginal product of capital is about 10 percent. The value of U.S. private fixed assets (less consumer durables) is about $31 trillion.[4] Thus, an increase in government debt of 1% of gross domestic product (GDP)—equal to about $110 billion—would reduce the capital stock by 0.36 percent, assuming that there is no offset to the increase in federal debt from increased domestic saving or inflows of foreign saving

Table 1
Changes in federal government debt and interest rates: calculations from an economic model of crowding out

Increase in federal debt (% of GDP)	Change in interest rates (basis points)		
	No offset $\partial K/\partial D = -1$ (1)	20% offset $\partial K/\partial D = -0.8$ (2)	40% offset $\partial K/\partial D = -0.6$ (3)
(1) 1 percent	2.4	1.9	1.4
(2) 5 percent	11.8	9.5	7.1
(3) 10 percent	23.7	18.9	14.2
Eliminate federal debt			
(4) $4 trillion	−86	−69	−52

(i.e., $\partial K/\partial D = -1$). Multiplying this percentage decline by -0.67 (which is equal to $\alpha - 1$, where $\alpha = 0.33$) implies an increase in the marginal product of capital of 0.24 percent. The resulting increase in interest rates is 2.4 basis points, as shown in the first column of Table 1. Similarly, a government surplus of 1% of GDP would be expected to decrease interest rates 2.4 basis points.

If the increase in federal debt were larger—5% of GDP—then interest rates are calculated to rise by 11.8 basis points, as the second row of the first column in Table 1 shows. This effect could be the result of an increase in federal debt in a single year, or the result of a persistent increase in federal debt (i.e., a persistent deficit) of 1% of GDP per year over five years. An increase in the federal debt of 10% of GDP—again, the result of a one-time increase or the consequence of a persistent increase in federal debt of 1% of GDP per year over ten years—would increase interest rates by 23.7 basis points.[5]

Currently, total federal debt held by the public is about $4 trillion, or 12.9% of the $31 trillion private capital stock. Holding other factors constant, eliminating the federal debt (measured in this way) entirely and assuming it would increase the private capital stock on a one-for-one basis imply a decrease in interest rates of 86 basis points, as shown in the fourth row of the first column.

The calculations in the first column of Table 1 assume no offset from increased private saving or capital inflows from abroad, which is not consistent with the U.S. economic experience. As shown in the second column, if, for example, 20% of the increase in government debt is offset by these factors (i.e., $\partial K/\partial D = -0.8$), then a $110 billion (1% of GDP) increase in federal government debt would reduce the U.S.

capital stock by \$88 billion, or about 0.28%. This implies an increase in the marginal product of capital of 0.19%, so the resulting increase in interest rates is about 1.9 basis points. An increase in federal debt of 5% of GDP—or a \$550 billion increase in government debt—would increase the interest rate by 9.5 basis points. Alternatively, totally eliminating the federal debt is calculated to reduce interest rates by about 69 basis points. Assuming a larger but plausible offset to increases in federal debt from domestic and/or foreign saving of 40% (i.e., $\partial K/\partial D = -0.6$),[6] suggests that even an increase in federal debt equal to 10% of GDP would increase interest rates by only 14 basis points. Under this scenario, eliminating the federal debt would lower interest rates a little over 50 basis points.

These calculations provide a reasonable benchmark for evaluating the traditional crowding-out effect on interest rates of an exogenous increase in government debt, holding other factors constant. Given the size of deficits and surpluses seen in the United States, these effects are more subdued than one might think given some of the commentary on federal deficits and interests rates. However, because other factors that influence interest rates are not constant, changes in government debt are influenced by both exogenous and endogenous factors, and the likely interest rate effects of changes in federal government debt consistent with historical U.S. experience may be in the range of single-digit basis points, this poses a particular burden on empirical analysis to estimate these effects with less-than-perfect data and econometric techniques.

3. Empirical Evidence: Is There a Clear Answer?

Because economic theory is not conclusive in determining whether federal government debt raises interest rates, and if it does, by how much, this issue must ultimately be addressed by empirical analysis. However, model-based calculations of the potential effects of government debt on interest rates are instructive and provide some benchmarks to help assess empirical estimates of this relationship. Before turning to econometric analysis of the possible effects of federal government debt on interest rates in the United States, we first examine some basic empirical facts about government debt, interest rates, and other related factors in the U.S. economy. These facts illustrate some of the difficulties posed for econometric analysis.

3.1 *Some Basic Facts*

Over the past half-century, U.S. federal government debt held by the public as a percentage of GDP has fluctuated from a high of about 60% of GDP to a low of around 25% of GDP in the mid-1970s, as shown in Figure 1.[7] While federal debt climbed during the 1980s and early 1990s to almost 50% of GDP, it declined thereafter and still remains below 40% of GDP despite its recent upturn.

Federal borrowing, or the yearly change in federal debt, as a percentage of GDP has averaged about 2% over the past fifty years, and has fluctuated from peaks around 5% of GDP to the retirement of debt equal to about 3% of GDP in 2000, as shown in Figure 2.[8] Not surprisingly, federal borrowing tended to rise shortly after the recession episodes in 1974–1975, 1980–1981, 1990–1991, and 2001.

One of the primary concerns about federal debt is its potential to crowd out the formation of capital in the economy. Figure 3 shows federal government debt as a percentage of the U.S. private capital stock.[9] Federal government debt is currently equal to about 13% of the private capital stock, which provides an upper bound on the amount of capital that federal debt could have directly crowded out.

The federal government is not the only borrower in U.S. credit markets, and indeed it is not the largest. Figure 4 shows that federal

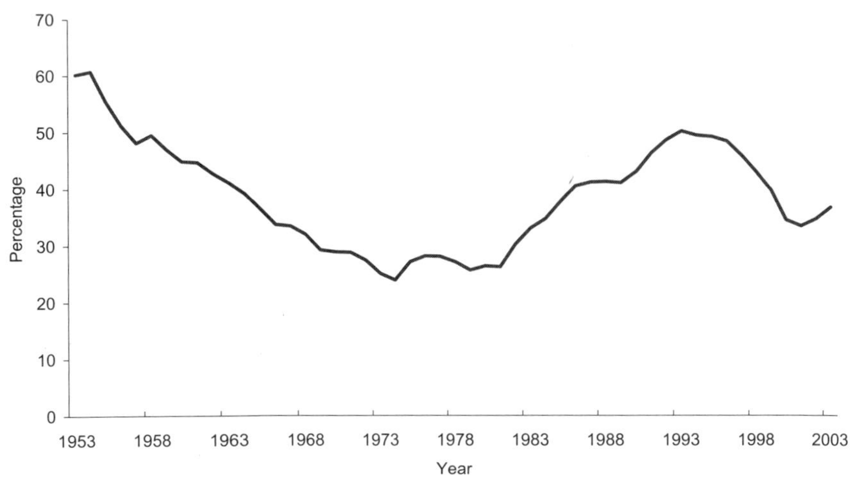

Figure 1
U.S. federal government debt held by the public as a percentage of GDP

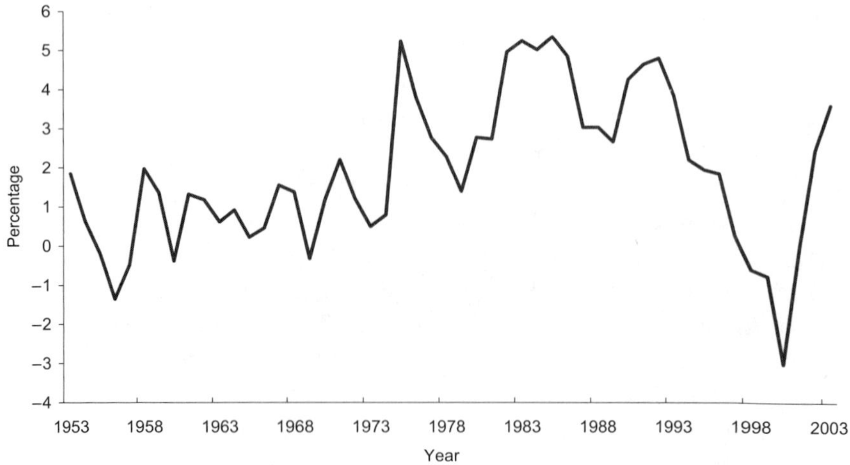

Figure 2
U.S. federal government borrowing as a percentage of GDP

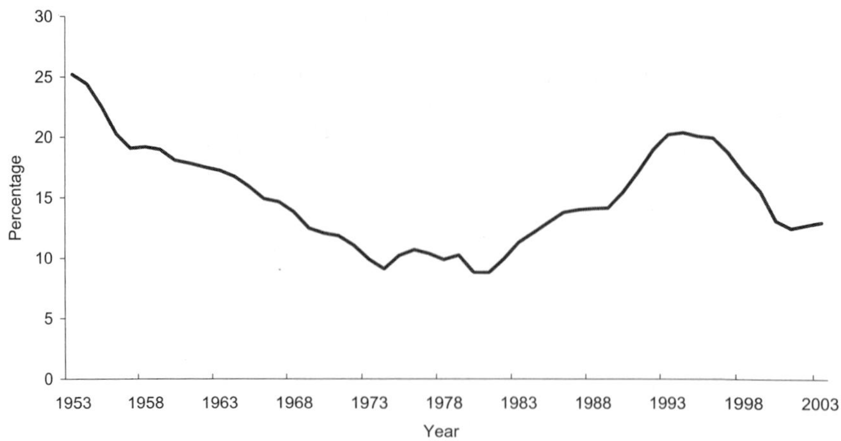

Figure 3
U.S. federal government debt held by the public as a percentage of U.S. private capital stock

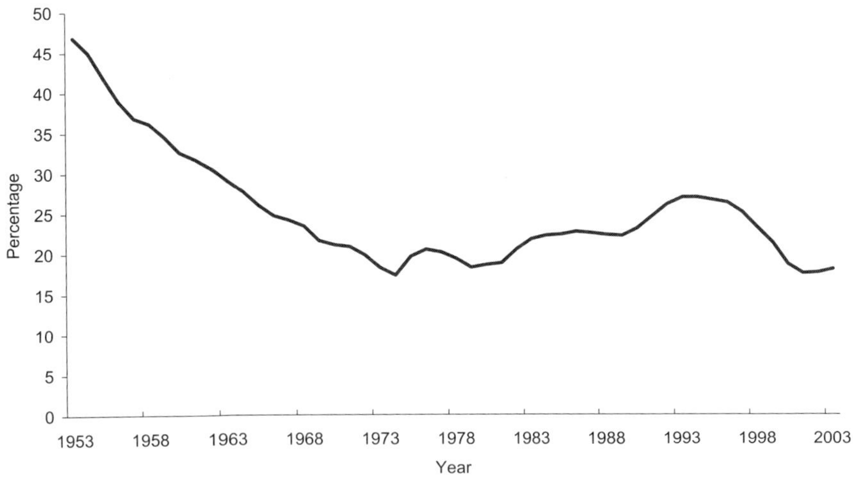

Figure 4
U.S. federal government debt held by the public as a percentage of total U.S. domestic nonfinancial debt

government debt as a share of total U.S. domestic (nonfinancial) debt has declined significantly since 1953, and it currently is less than 20% of total debt.[10] Figure 5 shows annual federal borrowing relative to total domestic U.S. borrowing. Federal government borrowing currently claims about one-fifth of the total funds loaned in U.S. credit markets. As global capital markets have become more integrated over time, the relevant size of the loanable funds market in which federal government debt interacts is much larger than the size of just the U.S. credit market, and thus these two figures overstate the relative size of federal debt and borrowing in the pool of available loanable funds. We return to this point below.

The debt incurred by the household, business, and state and local government sectors has been consistently larger than that incurred by the federal government over the past fifty years; it has also grown at a faster rate. Figure 6 shows U.S. domestic nonfederal (nonfinancial) debt as a percentage of GDP. Currently standing at approximately 160% of GDP, domestic nonfederal debt is about four times as large as federal government debt. Figure 7 presents annual nonfederal borrowing as a percentage of GDP; such borrowing has consistently been greater than federal borrowing over the past fifty years, except during the credit crunch of the early 1990s.

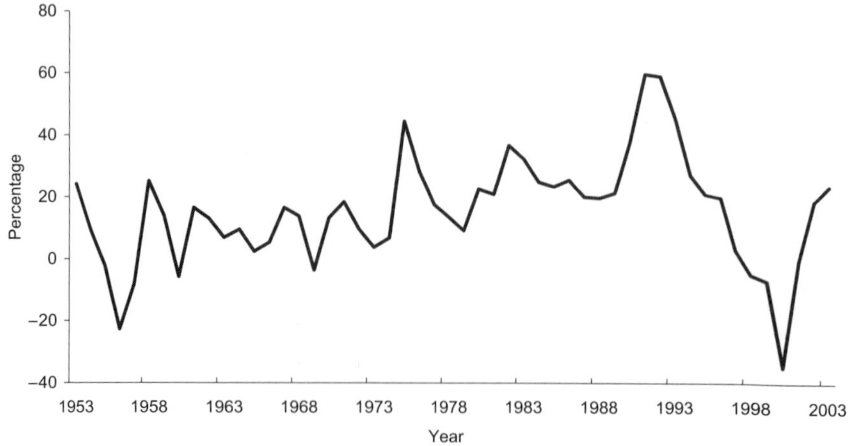

Figure 5
U.S. federal government borrowing as a percentage of total U.S. domestic nonfinancial borrowing

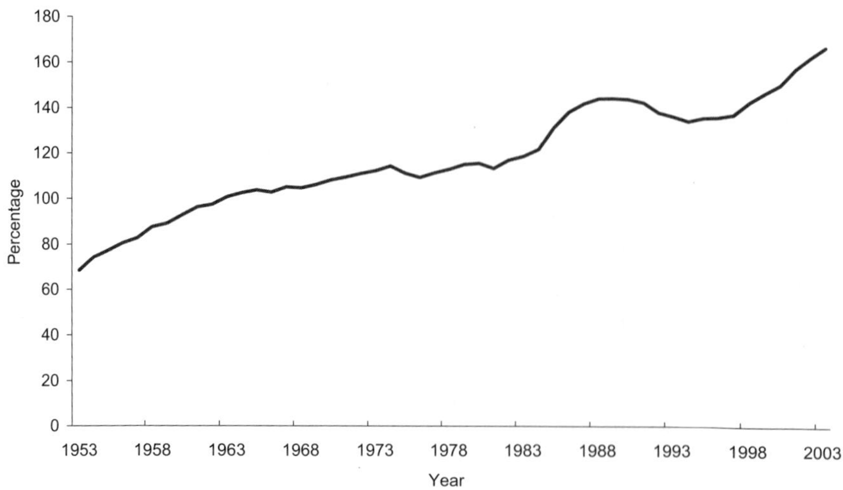

Figure 6
U.S. domestic nonfinancial, nonfederal debt as a percentage of GDP

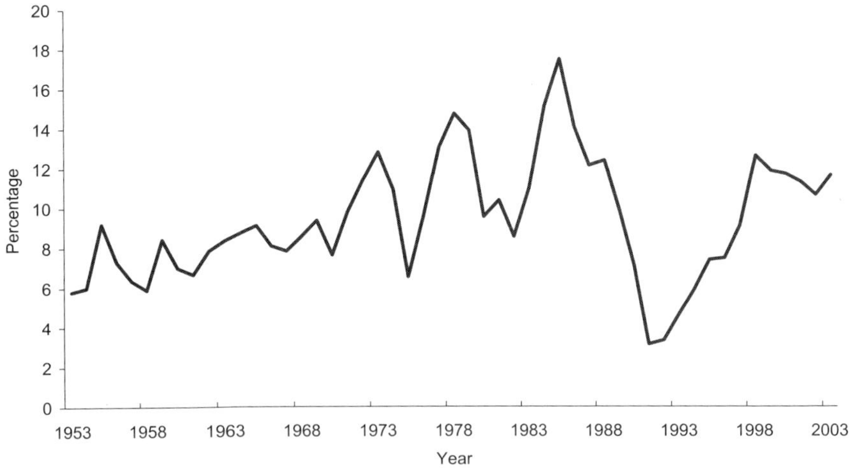

Figure 7
U.S. domestic nonfinancial, nonfederal borrowing as a percentage of GDP

Foreign saving is an ever-more important source of funds to U.S. credit markets, one that could also potentially influence the effect of federal government debt on interest rates. Indeed, foreign funds have been used increasingly to purchase U.S. federal government debt. As shown in Figure 8, while foreign holdings of U.S. Treasury securities were less than 5% of total outstanding federal debt just over 30 years ago, foreign purchases of Treasury securities have increased dramatically since then, and foreigners currently hold a little more than one-third of total federal debt.[11] Note that the recent surge in foreign holdings of U.S. Treasury securities is not unprecedented; both the early 1970s and the mid-1990s were periods when foreigners significantly increased their holdings of Treasury instruments.

Domestic private savers and foreign savers are not the only sectors that hold debt issued to the public by the federal government. As the U.S. monetary authority, the Federal Reserve also holds Treasury securities, using them to conduct monetary policy. The Federal Reserve currently holds about 15% of outstanding Treasury securities, up from around 10% about a decade ago, as Figure 9 shows. In a growing economy, the Federal Reserve must consistently acquire some Treasury securities in open-market operations to expand the money supply and prevent deflation, as we noted in the previous section. Treasury debt purchased by the Federal Reserve to increase the money supply may

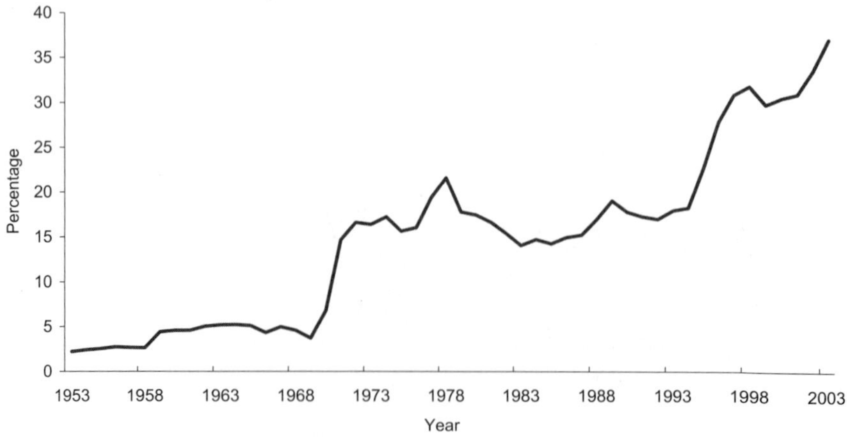

Figure 8
Foreign holdings of U.S. Treasury securities as a percentage of total U.S. Treasury securities outstanding

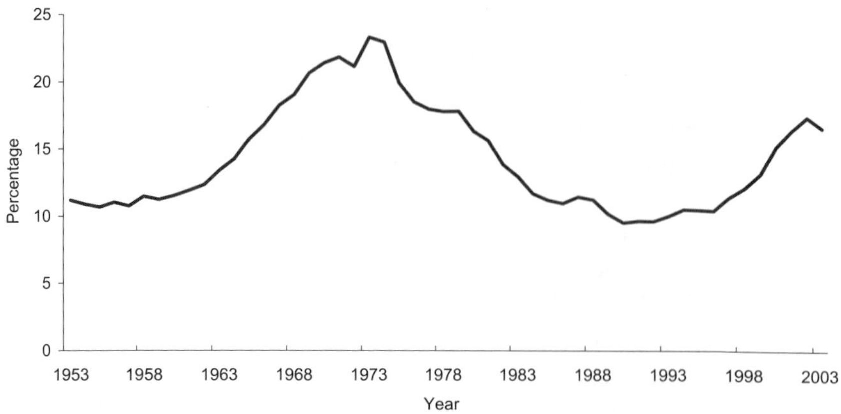

Figure 9
Federal Reserve holdings of U.S. Treasury securities as a percentage of total U.S. Treasury securities outstanding

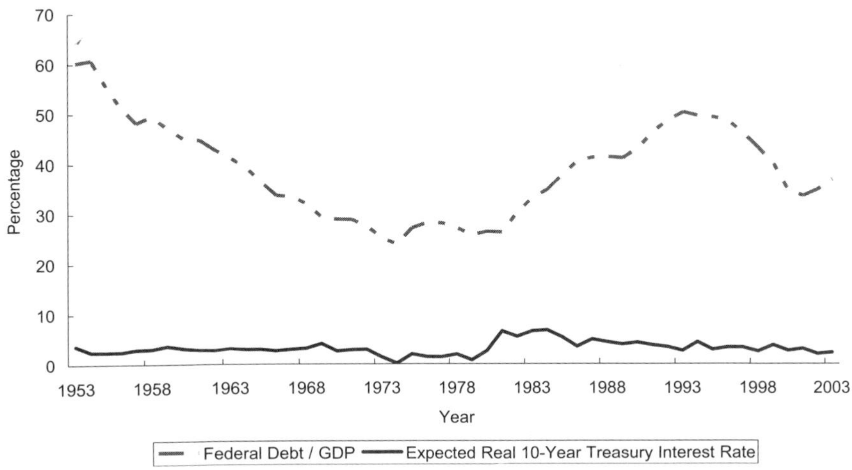

Figure 10
U.S. federal government debt held by the public as a percentage of GDP and real 10-year Treasury interest rate

not have the same effect of crowding out private capital formation as does federal debt purchased by the private sector.

Financing decisions of the federal government along with those of private-sector borrowers, state and local government borrowers, domestic and foreign savers, and the Federal Reserve all interact in the U.S. and international credit market to influence interest rates on U.S. Treasury debt and other debt. To get a sense of what effect U.S. federal government debt has had on interest rates, it is instructive to look at the historical evolution in federal debt (relative to GDP) compared to interest rates over the past fifty years. Figure 10 shows U.S. federal government debt held by the public as a percentage of GDP and a measure of the real interest rate on ten-year Treasury securities.[12] While federal debt relative to GDP has varied substantially, the real interest rate has been less variable and is currently equal to its average value over the past fifty years of about 3%. Indeed, the simple correlation between the stock of federal debt and this measure of the real interest rate over the entire period shown is only 0.15. Over the twenty-year period from the early 1950s to the early 1970s—when federal debt decreased by 50% relative to the size of the economy—the real interest rate remained relatively constant. The real interest rate did rise in the early 1980s, coincident with an increase in federal debt, but the real interest rate then declined and remained quite

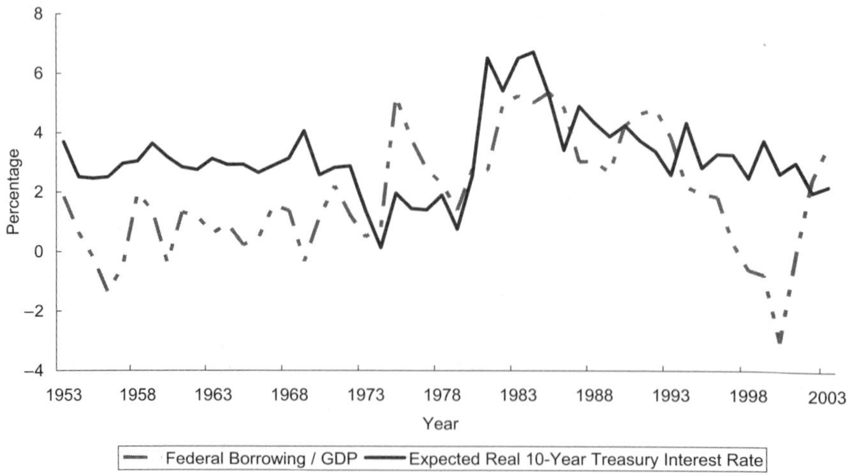

Figure 11
U.S. federal government borrowing as a percentage of GDP and real 10-year Treasury interest rate

steady even as federal debt continued to grow in the 1980s and early 1990s, and then fell in the late 1990s.

Figure 11 shows annual federal government borrowing as a percentage of GDP relative to the real rate on ten-year Treasury securities. Here, the correlation between federal government borrowing and the real interest rate is 0.39, higher than that between federal government debt and the real interest rate, but still modest. As we noted earlier, a simple economic model of crowding-out implies that federal government borrowing, which is equal to the change in federal government debt, is related to the change in the real interest rate rather than the level of the real interest rate, as shown in Figure 11. Figure 12 plots federal government borrowing (as a percentage of GDP) relative to the change in the real ten-year Treasury rate. The correlation between federal borrowing and the change in the real interest rate is 0.06, much smaller than the correlation between federal borrowing and the level of the real interest rate.

In addition to the concern that federal government debt might crowd out private capital formation by causing real interest rates to rise, federal government debt may also bring the temptation to monetize the debt, causing inflation. The presentation in Figure 13 of data for federal government debt (as a percentage of GDP) and both the expected

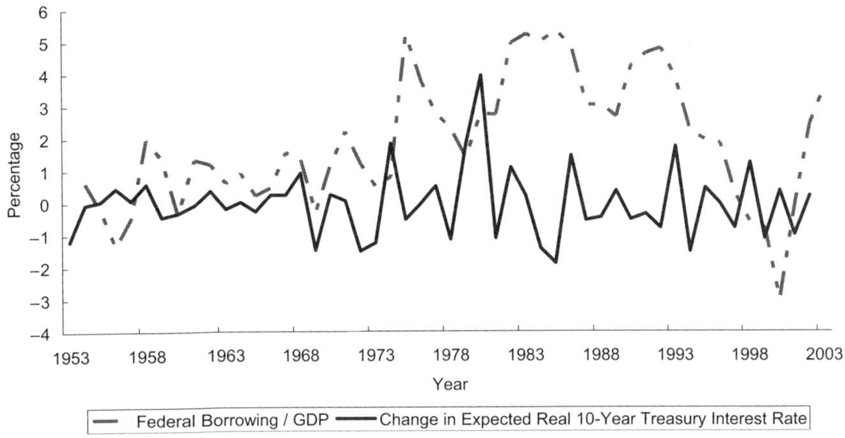

Figure 12
U.S. federal government borrowing as a percentage of GDP and the change in the real 10-year Treasury interest rate

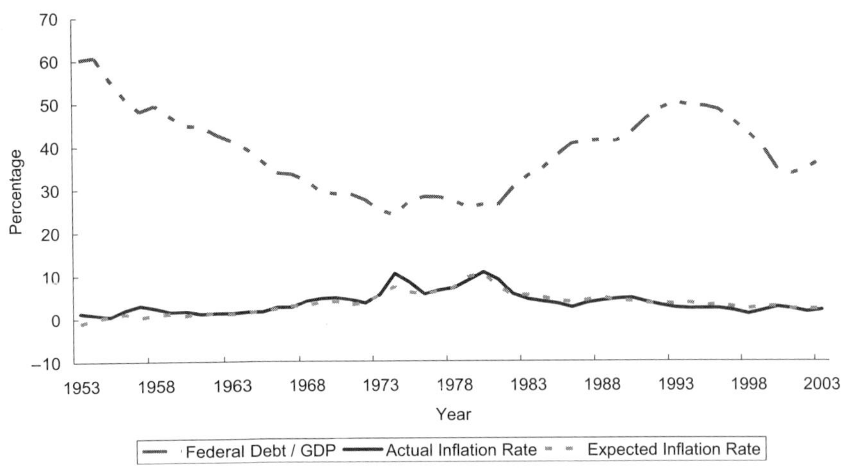

Figure 13
U.S. federal government debt held by the public as a percentage of GDP and the actual and expected inflation rate

inflation rate and the inflation rate shows that this concern has not been a problem in the United States over the past fifty years.[13] The correlation between federal government debt and the actual inflation rate is −0.71 over this period (and is similar for the expected inflation rate); inflation peaked when the federal debt relative to GDP was at its lowest points and declined as federal debt grew in the 1980s.

Returning to the potential effects of government debt on real interest rates, it is also useful to examine the difference in real interest rates between the United States and other major industrial economies. If international capital markets were not well integrated, then real interest rates might vary according to differences in government debt and borrowing patterns. Alternatively, if credit markets were integrated in the global economy, then real interest rates might be expected to be more similar across these different economies. Figure 14 presents real interest rates on ten-year government securities for the United States, Canada, France, Germany, Italy, Japan, and the United Kingdom since 1990.[14] Over this period real interest rates have generally declined, and currently there is much less dispersion in these real interest rates than there was in the early 1990s. Italy has the lowest real interest rate—just below 2%—while Germany has the highest at just under 4%. However, the current government financial positions of these countries are quite different. While Japan currently has a stock of government debt

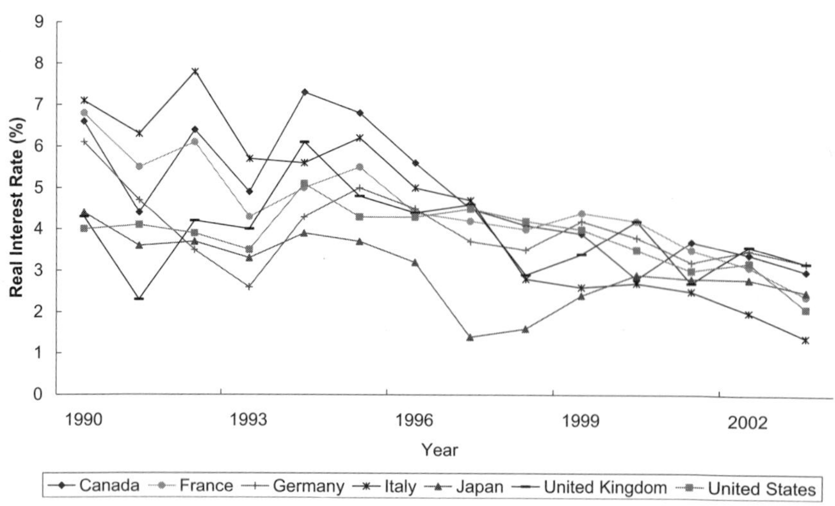

Figure 14
Real interest rates on 10-year government bonds for major advanced economies

of more than 70% of GDP, and an annual budget deficit of about 7% of its GDP, its real interest rate is almost the same as the United States and France, both of which have stocks of government debt and flow deficits (both relative to GDP) about half the size of those in Japan. Italy, currently with the lowest real interest rate, has a ratio of government debt to GDP of more than 90%, the highest in this group of economies. The United Kingdom currently has a deficit to GDP ratio of 1.5%, and Canada has a government surplus of almost 1%, but real interest rates in those countries are somewhat higher than in the United States. The similarity of real interest rates across these countries, despite having very different government borrowing needs, suggests that global credit markets are fairly integrated, so that the pool of loanable funds that any government may draw from substantially exceeds funds in the domestic credit market alone.

Several basic points summarize our assessment of these data on U.S. federal government debt and interest rates. First, the federal government is not the largest borrower in the U.S. domestic credit market, and the stock of outstanding federal debt has generally remained under 25% of total U.S. domestic debt for the past 30 years. Second, there is strong evidence that global credit markets have become increasingly integrated, so the relative role of U.S. federal government borrowing in the relevant international market for loanable funds is even smaller than in the domestic credit market. Third, the simple bivariate correlation between federal government debt and real interest rates in the United States has been quite weak over the past fifty years, so a strong positive relationship between federal government debt and real interest rates is not obvious. Of course, more rigorous econometric analysis of this relationship is necessary before a more definitive conclusion can be drawn.

3.2 *Review of Previous Studies*

Several different surveys over the past twenty years have evaluated the empirical literature on the relationship between federal government debt and interest rates: Barth, Iden, and Russek (1984); Bernheim (1987, 1989); Barro (1989); Barth, Iden, Russek, and Wohar (1991); Seater (1993); Elmendorf and Mankiw (1999); and Gale and Orszag (2002, 2003), for example. Despite the volume of work, no universal consensus has emerged. For example, Barth, Iden, Russek, and Wohar (1991), referring also to their earlier review, write:

> There was not then and there is not now a clear consensus on whether there is a statistically and economically significant relationship between government deficits and interest rates ... Since the available evidence on the effects of deficits is mixed, one cannot say with complete confidence that budget deficits raise interest rates and reduce saving and capital formation. But, equally important, one cannot say that they do not have these effects.

In their surveys of studies of Ricardian equivalence, Bernheim (1987, 1989) and Seater (1993) enumerate problems with tests of this hypothesis performed by examining the relationship between federal government debt and deficits with interest rates. Bernheim (1989) concludes that: "[I]t is easy to cite a large number of studies that support any conceivable position." However, in the end, Seater generally finds more overall support for the Ricardian equivalence hypothesis, which implies that federal government debt has no effect on interest rates, than does Bernheim, who argues that the Ricardian equivalence hypothesis should be rejected, which would make a positive relationship between federal government debt and interest rates more likely. Barro (1989) takes a similar position as Seater, concluding: "Overall, the empirical results on interest rates support the Ricardian view. Given these findings, it is remarkable that most macroeconomists remain confident that budget deficits raise interest rates."

In discussing empirical research on federal government debt and interest rates, Elmendorf and Mankiw (1999) state that "it is worth noting that this literature has typically supported the Ricardian view that budget deficits have no effect on interest rates." However, they go on to evaluate this evidence, writing: "Our view is that this literature, like the literature regarding the effect of fiscal policy on consumption, is ultimately not very informative. Examined carefully, the results are simply too hard to swallow...." Gale and Orszag (2002), in their survey of the economic effects of federal government debt, also acknowledge that "the evidence from the literature as a whole is mixed" but go on to conclude:

> Closer examination of the literature, however, suggests the findings may not be as ambiguous as they initially appear. Indeed, studies that (properly) incorporate deficit expectations in addition to current deficits tend to find economically and statistically significant connections between anticipated deficits and current long-term interest rates.

Thus, while surveys of the empirical literature on federal government debt and interest rates note the wide range of results reported in different studies, interpretations and assessments of these mixed empirical results still differ. While we do not evaluate every empirical paper that has been written on the relationship between federal government debt and interest rates, we will offer an assessment of the existing literature, focusing primarily on more recent papers.

Many studies analyzing the effects of U.S. federal government debt or deficits on U.S. interest rates do not incorporate the potential effects of the fact that international financial markets are increasingly integrated. To account for this, Barro and Sala-i-Martin (1990) and Barro (1991) provide estimates of the effects that economic, fiscal, and monetary policy variables have on expected real world interest rates across ten major developed economies, including the United States. They use a structural approach where the world interest rate is determined by investment demand and desired saving. While they conclude that current government debt or deficits do not play an important role in the determination of real expected interest rates in these countries, their empirical analysis does not use expected future government deficits or debt.

Cohen and Garnier (1991) use forecasts of federal deficits for the United States provided by the Office of Management and Budget (OMB), and in additional analysis they also investigate the effects of forecasts of general government deficits made by the Organization for Economic Cooperation and Development (OECD) on interest rates across the G7 countries. Their analysis yields mixed results. For the United States, they generally do not find significant effects of the current deficit or expected deficits on interest rates, although they do find a significant statistical relationship between OMB deficit forecast *revisions* and interest rates in the United States. Their estimates imply that an upward revision in OMB's federal deficit forecast of one percentage point of GDP could increase real interest rates by about 80 to100 basis points. However, the theoretical calculations that we presented earlier raise the question of whether this result is economically plausible. In their analysis of the G7 countries, they find no evidence of a positive and significant relationship between home-country current debt or deficits and current interest rates, similar to Barro and Sala-i-Martin (1990) and Barro (1991), and they find that one-year-ahead forecasts of home-country government deficits by the OECD tend to have a significant *negative* effect on nominal short-term interest rates, in contrast to the prediction of the government deficit crowding-out hypothesis. However, one-year-ahead forecasts of other-country government deficits by the OECD tend to have a significant effect on home-country nominal short-term interest rates in the direction consistent with the government deficit crowding-out hypothesis, and also imply that credit markets across these countries are integrated.

Cebula and Koch (1989) explore the effect of the current U.S. federal government deficit, split into its cyclical and structural components, on both ten-year Treasury yields and corporate bond yields, while also controlling for foreign capital inflows. Their results imply that positive foreign capital inflows significantly lower both Treasury and corporate rates, consistent with integrated global credit markets, and significantly reduce the estimated effect of structural government deficits on interest rates. They find a statistically insignificant effect of the structural federal government deficit on Treasury yields but report a statistically significant effect of the structural federal government deficit on corporate bond yields, implying that the structural federal government deficit affects the yield spread between corporate and Treasury rates. It is not obvious why structural federal government deficits should affect the corporate-to-Treasury-yield spread. In contrast, Laubach (2003) reports that, based on regression analysis, he finds no evidence that yield spreads between corporate bonds and Treasuries, adjusted for cyclical variation, are systematically related to projected deficit-to-GDP ratios. Thus, the fact that Cebula and Koch (1989) are using current federal deficits in their analysis instead of expected federal deficits may be contributing to their result.[15]

Elmendorf (1993) analyzes the effect of expected federal government deficits on Treasury yields using a private-sector forecast of the federal government deficit from Data Resources, Inc. (DRI) instead of federal government deficit projections made by the OMB or the Congressional Budget Office (CBO). Presumably, the DRI deficit forecast incorporates expectations of fiscal policy changes that are not part of CBO and OMB projections and thus may be a more accurate reflection of financial market participants' expectations of future federal government deficits. Regression results show that the DRI forecasts of federal government deficits have significant and large (and statistically significant) positive effects on medium-term (three- or five-year) Treasury yields—an increase in the expected deficit of 1% of GDP is estimated to increase medium-term Treasury rates by more than 40 basis points—but have a smaller and statistically insignificant effect on a long-term (20-year) Treasury rate. If federal government borrowing is crowding out private capital formation, then one would expect to find a larger impact on long-term interest rates than on shorter-term interest rates.

Kitchen (2002) examines the effects of the CBO's current standardized federal government deficit measure—which adjusts the actual deficit for business-cycle effects and other (usually) one-time budget effects—on the spread between the three-month Treasury yield and longer-term Treasury rates, rather than the level of Treasury rates. In a parsimonious specification controlling only for inflation and the difference between actual GDP and the CBO's measure of potential GDP, he estimates that a 1% increase in the current standardized federal government deficit (relative to GDP) increases the spread between the ten-year Treasury rate and the three-month Treasury rate by 42 basis points. This estimate is much larger than the benchmark calculations from our simple economic framework presented above. Kitchen also uses a regression specification—effectively regressing the level of the interest rate on the federal deficit—that is not implied by the model. Also, because the estimates are based on *current* measures of interest rates and the federal deficit, it is not obvious whether the influence of other economic factors that might affect the interest rate, but are not included in his parsimonious regression specification, is affecting the estimate of the effect of federal deficits.

Laubach (2003) estimates the effect of five-year-ahead projections by the CBO of federal government debt or deficits on the five-year-ahead real ten-year Treasury yield. The purpose for using five-year-ahead interest rates and debt or deficit projections is to try to omit any effects of current economic conditions from measuring the effects of federal government deficits on the interest rate. He finds that a one-percentage-point (relative to GDP) increase in the measure of the expected federal government deficit increases the forward-looking ten-year Treasury rate by 28 basis points. However, when Laubach estimates an econometric specification that uses expected federal government debt instead of the deficit (which, in contrast to using a deficit measure, is a specification consistent with a standard economic model of crowding-out), he estimates that a one-percentage-point increase in the expected debt-GDP ratio increases the forward-looking ten-year Treasury rate by only five basis points—an estimate close to the benchmark calculations we presented previously. Thus, these results illustrate that whether an interest rate measure is regressed on the federal government deficit or on the federal government debt can yield markedly different implications for the magnitude of the associated interest rate effect.

Laubach suggests that the difference in these results can be reconciled by the fact that federal budget deficits tend to be serially correlated in historical U.S. data, and thus financial market participants may expect an increase in the federal government deficit to be persistent, and in turn there is a larger increase in interest rates.[16] However, federal government debt is also serially correlated in U.S. data. This is not surprising because federal government debt ($DEBT_t$) at the end of time period t is the sum of the federal budget deficit ($DEFICIT_t$) during time period t and federal government debt at the end of the prior period, $t-1$:

$$DEBT_t = DEFICIT_t + DEBT_{t-1}$$

If financial market participants expect an increase in federal government deficits to be persistent, then they should also expect increases in federal government debt to be persistent, so it is not clear that this explanation reconciles the difference in the estimated interest rate effects when using federal deficits instead of federal debt. Indeed, current (end-of-period) debt contains information not only about the current deficit but also captures all information about previous government borrowing, and thus is a better measure to evaluate the effect of government borrowing on the *level* of the interest rate, as suggested in our theoretical discussion above. The *change* in government debt, or the deficit, would be expected to affect the *change* in the real interest rate, not necessarily the level of the interest rate, but that is not the econometric specification used by Laubach. We return to this point in our empirical work below.

Miller and Russek (1996) show that different econometric approaches can yield different conclusions about the effect of federal government deficits on interest rates. While their conventional estimates of reduced-form specifications indicate that increases in the current real per-capita deficit increases current nominal Treasury rates (although it is difficult to interpret the magnitude of this effect from their reported regression results), using vector autoregression (VAR) methods yields mixed results about this relationship.[17]

Evans and Marshall (2002) use a VAR framework to investigate the macroeconomic determinants of the variability in the nominal Treasury yield curve. They find that general macroeconomic shocks account for most of the variability in nominal Treasury yields, with fiscal policy shocks generally having mixed effects. Their measure of fiscal deficit shocks—derived from Blanchard and Perotti (2000)—does not significantly explain nominal Treasury yield variability. However, they do find that the measure of military buildup shocks suggested by Ramey and Shapiro (1998) tends to increase nominal Treasury rates.

Another approach to looking at the effects of federal government deficits on interest rates has been to focus on media-reported budget news. If news concerning federal government deficits occasionally leads to significant movements in bond market prices, then standard time-series techniques may have little power to identify these occasional, possibly nonlinear events. Previous economic research that has analyzed the effects of news announcements about federal government deficits on interest rates (Wachtel and Young, 1987; Thorbecke, 1993; Quigley and Porter-Hudak, 1994; Kitchen, 1996), have generally found only small or transitory effects. Elmendorf (1996) found that higher expected federal deficits and government spending tended to raise interest rates, but his methodology does not provide evidence of the magnitude of the effect.

Calomiris, Engen, Hassett, and Hubbard (2003) add to this analysis of the effects of federal budget news on interest rates in two ways. First, they estimated the extent to which monthly deviations of private-sector consensus forecasts of the federal government budget balance from actual monthly Treasury budget balance reports, along with deviations in consensus forecasts and actual reports on other macroeconomic variables, predict movements in interest rates. They found that stronger than expected reports on many macroeconomic factors (such as the employment situation, industrial production, and retail sales, for example) tended to increase interest rates, but actual deviations from expected monthly federal government budget deficits had no statistically significant effect on interest rates. Second, they collected historical data on large daily movements in interest rates and catalog the economic news that occurred on these days. Typically, the days with large interest rate movements are associated with general economic news rather than with federal budget news, and the movement in interest rates is consistent with what economic theory would suggest; that is, news that suggests more robust economic growth is associated with increases in interest rates. Both of these approaches yielded little evidence that unexpected news about the federal budget situation had significant effects on interest rates.

Evaluating the effects of government debt on interest rates is difficult given the lack of consensus on the appropriate underlying economic model of how federal debt or deficits and interest rates should interact. Variable definitions and other features of the data and econometric methodology vary across these studies, making comparisons difficult. As with most of the earlier reviews of the economic literature on federal debt, deficits, and interest rates, our view is that the existing evidence is quite mixed. Some studies find positive effects of federal deficits on interest rates; others do not. Even among the studies that do find a positive effect of deficits on interest rates, the magnitude of the effect on interest rates is still uncertain. However, looking systematically at the influence of different econometric specifications, different measures of federal government debt or deficits, different measures of the interest rate, and different econometric methodologies, the estimated effect of federal government debt on interest rates should provide some insight into this issue.

3.3 *Empirical Analysis of the Federal Debt and Interest Rates*

We now provide some new empirical evidence on the potential effects of federal government debt on interest rates. Consistent with most prior analysis, we initially examine this relationship by estimating a reduced-form equation:

$$i_t = \beta_0 + \beta_1 d_t + \Gamma Z + \varepsilon_t$$

where i_t is a measure of the interest rate (in time period t), d_t is a measure of federal government debt, and Z is a vector of other relevant variables that may influence interest rates. The effect of federal government debt on the interest rate is described by the estimate of the coefficient, β_1.

The specification of the interest rate variable, i, and the federal government debt variable, d, in the reduced-form equation can take different forms. As we noted earlier, the hypothesis that federal government debt might crowd out private capital formation and thus raise long-term real interest rates is typically based on a simple economic model as we presented above.[18] This model implies that:

1. The *level* of the real interest rate, i, is related to the *level*, or stock, of federal government debt, d, or

2. The *change* in the real interest rate, Δi, is related to the *change* in federal government debt, Δd, which is equal to federal government borrowing, or the deficit.

We estimate this reduced-form equation using both of these specifications for i and d. Although not consistent with the specifications for i

and *d* implied by an economic model of crowding-out, we also estimate this reduced-form equation using a third specification, in which:

3. The level of the real interest rate, *i*, is regressed on federal government borrowing (or the deficit), Δd.

A number of prior studies have used this third specification, and it is informative to compare the results from using this specification with those that employ the previous two specifications, even though it is not consistent with a simple crowding-out model. Economic theory suggests that it is the total *stock* of government debt that is the most relevant for explaining the *level* of the interest rate, not just the one-period change in government debt.

Another important issue for specifying *i* and *d* is whether these are *forward-looking*, or expected, measures of real interest rates and federal government debt, or whether they are *current* measures of these variables. Previous studies have varied in whether forward-looking or current measures of interest rates and federal government debt were used in their analysis. To compare how these different specifications for *i* and *d* affect estimates of the relationship between these two variables, we provide estimates for three different types of specifications. In particular, we estimate:

1. The effect of an expected, or projected, measure of federal government debt on a forward-looking measure of the real interest rate;
2. The effect of an expected, or projected, measure of federal government debt on a current measure of the real interest rate; and
3. The effect of a current measure of federal government debt on a current measure of the real interest rate.

A number of other economic variables should be included in the vector *Z* because they presumably also influence the determination of the real interest, *i*, and excluding them could bias the estimate of the coefficient β_1. As we noted in the earlier section discussing the potential theoretical effect of federal government debt on interest rates, it is important to account for general macroeconomic factors that can affect the performance of the economy. Accordingly, in the vector *Z*, we include the growth rate in real GDP, which is a variable usually included in these types of regressions.[19] The analysis by Barro and Sala-i-Martin (1990) and Barro (1991) finds that real oil prices are also an important exogenous macroeconomic variable that can affect real interest rates, so we include a measure of real oil prices in the vector *Z*.[20]

Laubach (2003) observes that in a Ramsey model of economic growth, where the preferences of a representative household are incorporated with a production function similar to the one we presented in Section 2 above, the real interest rate, r, is determined by:

$$r = \sigma g + \theta$$

where σ is the coefficient of relative risk aversion for the representative household in the model, g is the growth rate of technology, and θ is the rate of time preference for the representative household. He estimates that a measure of the equity premium—used as a proxy for risk aversion—is an important factor affecting real interest rates, so we include it in the vector Z.[21] If relative risk aversion declines, then households may be more willing to purchase equities than debt instruments, thereby leading to a rise in the interest rate.

Fiscal policies other than federal government debt may also affect real interest rates. Ramey and Shapiro (1998) and Evans and Marshall (2002) find that exogenous defense spending shocks—measured by Ramey and Shapiro as a dummy variable denoting the time period in which a significant military buildup begins—tend to increase interest rates.[22] This effect is consistent with the theoretical implication of an exogenous increase in government consumption in a neoclassical model even if the Ricardian equivalence hypothesis is operative.[23] Therefore, we include a variable to capture exogenous defense spending shocks in the vector Z.[24]

While conducting monetary policy, the Federal Reserve regularly purchases U.S. Treasury securities as the economy grows, which may reduce the impact of federal government debt on the real interest rate. Thus, we include a variable measuring the purchase of U.S. Treasury securities by the Federal Reserve, relative to GDP, in our specification of the regression equation.[25]

To summarize, in vector Z of the regression equation, we include the following variables:

1. The rate of growth in real GDP.
2. The real domestic crude oil price.
3. A measure of the equity premium (as a proxy for risk aversion).
4. A dummy variable for military buildups.
5. Federal Reserve purchases of U.S. Treasury securities.

We now turn to our empirical results.[26]

3.3.1 Forward-Looking Interest Rates and Federal Government Debt

The only previous study of which we are aware that analyzes the effect of forward-looking projections of federal government debt on a forward-looking measure of the real interest rate is Laubach (2003). The purpose for using these forward-looking measures is to attempt to omit any effects of current economic conditions and policies from the empirical estimate of the effect of federal government debt on interest rates.

Laubach constructs data from 1976 through 2003 on nominal ten-year Treasury rates expected to prevail five years ahead and then subtracts a series of inflation expectations taken from the Federal Reserve's econometric model of the United States. These data on real five-year-ahead ten-year Treasury yields are calculated to coincide with the CBO's five-year-ahead projections of federal government debt and deficits, relative to GDP, released in its annual *Economic and Budget Outlook*.[27] In this section, we use these measures of the forward-looking real interest rate and forward-looking federal government debt in our analysis. We also use the CBO's five-year ahead projection of real GDP growth rate. The other variables correspond to the time period just preceding the release of the CBO's annual report.

In the first column of Table 2, we report coefficient estimates for regressions of the real five-year-ahead ten-year Treasury yield on the five-year projection of federal government debt along with the other variables. The results imply that a one-percentage-point (relative to GDP) increase in the CBO's five-year-ahead projection of federal government debt increases the real five-year-ahead ten-year Treasury yield by a little less than three basis points, and the estimate is statistically significantly different from zero.[28] This estimate is also consistent with the theoretical calculations presented in Table 1. The estimated coefficients on all of the other variables have the expected sign and are statistically significant from zero, except for the insignificant coefficient estimate on the projected real GDP growth rate.[29]

Coefficient estimates obtained by regressing the *change* in the real five-year-ahead ten-year Treasury yield on the CBO's five-year-ahead projection of the federal government deficit (relative to GDP) and the other variables are reported in the second column of Table 2. The results imply that a one-percentage-point (relative to GDP) increase in CBO's five-year-ahead projection of the federal government deficit increases the change in the real five-year-ahead ten-year Treasury yield

Table 2
Regression results for real five-year-ahead ten-year Treasury rate and CBO five-year-ahead federal debt or deficit projections (1976–2003)

	Dependent variable		
	(1) Level of Treasury rate	(2) Change in Treasury rate	(3) Level of Treasury rate
Federal debt/GDP	0.028 (0.011)*	—	—
Federal deficit/GDP	—	0.030 (0.053)	0.185 (0.066)*
Real GDP growth rate	−0.014 (0.284)	—	0.029 (0.279)
Change in real GDP growth rate	—	−0.851 (0.246)	—
Real oil price	0.059 (0.014)*	—	0.049 (0.021)*
Change in real oil price	—	0.028 (0.018)	—
Equity premium	−0.269 (0.134)*	—	−0.279 (0.105)*
Change in equity premium	—	−0.332 (0.164)*	—
Defense shock	1.398 (0.568)*	1.822 (0.210)*	1.087 (0.492)*
Federal Reserve Treasury holdings	−0.410 (0.197)*		
Federal Reserve Treasury purchases	—	−0.810 (0.570)	−0.521 (0.629)
Constant	4.136 (1.448)*	0.108 (0.231)	3.299 (0.501)*
Adjusted R-squared	0.69	0.32	0.69
DW statistic	2.52	2.90	2.39
N	28	28	28

Note: Newey-West standard errors in parentheses.
*Coefficient estimate significant at 10% level.

by about three basis points, but the estimate is not statistically significantly different from zero.

In the third column, the regression results suggest that a one-percentage-point (relative to GDP) increase in the CBO's five-year-ahead projection of the federal government deficit increases the real five-year-ahead ten-year Treasury yield by about 18 basis points, and the estimate is statistically significantly different from zero.[30] As we noted earlier, however, this specification is not consistent with one implied by an economic model of crowding out, so interpreting this result is difficult. The *stock* of federal debt is most relevant for determining the level of the interest rate, and the deficit, which represents only the most recent period's *change in the debt*, does not contain all relevant information—specifically, prior accumulated federal debt—contained in the measure of total federal debt. However, because the CBO's projections of federal deficits (as a percentage of GDP) are closely correlated with their projections of federal debt (as a percentage of GDP)—the correlation coefficient between these two series is 0.89 over the sample period—then the coefficient estimate on the smaller deficit component also picks up the effect of prior accumulated government debt, and the coefficient estimate is larger than when total government debt is used.

The results in Table 2 indicate that the estimated effect of projected federal government debt or deficits on a forward-looking measure of the real interest rate depends to a large degree on the specification. The estimates for the two specifications consistent with the analytical model of crowding out presented earlier imply that an increase in federal government debt of 1% of GDP raises the real interest rate by, at most, about three basis points.

3.3.2 Current Interest Rates and Expected Federal Government Debt

In this section, we employ a measure of the *current* real ten-year Treasury yield in our analysis while all of the other variables remain the same, as in the previous section. The nominal ten-year Treasury yields over the months that the CBO projections were released were then adjusted for expected inflation to construct the current real interest rates used in this section of our analysis.[31]

The first column of Table 3 reports the coefficient estimates when regressing the level of the real ten-year Treasury yield on the five-year-ahead projection of federal government debt (relative to GDP) made

Table 3
Regression results for current real ten-year Treasury rate and CBO five-year-ahead federal debt or deficit projections (1976–2003)

	Dependent variable		
	(1) Level of Treasury rate	(2) Change in Treasury rate	(3) Level of Treasury rate
Federal debt/GDP	0.033 (0.013)*	—	—
Federal deficit/GDP	—	0.034 (0.068)	0.236 (0.064)*
Real GDP growth rate	−0.373 (0.291)	—	−0.266 (0.347)
Change in real GDP growth rate	—	−0.607 (0.417)	—
Real oil price	0.091 (0.014)*	—	0.081 (0.024)*
Change in real oil price	—	0.064 (0.051)	—
Equity premium	−0.376 (0.134)*	—	−0.389 (0.145)*
Change in equity premium	—	−0.472 (0.189)*	—
Defense shock	0.440 (0.380)	0.665 (1.046)	0.047 (0.469)
Federal Reserve Treasury holdings	−0.668 (0.260)*		
Federal Reserve Treasury purchases	—	−0.485 (0.726)	−1.064 (0.587)*
Constant	5.058 (1.94)*	0.105 (0.260)	3.119 (0.634)*
Adjusted R-squared	0.86	0.42	0.86
DW statistic	1.68	2.90	1.68
N	28	28	28

Note: Newey-West standard errors in parentheses.
*Coefficient estimate significant at 10% level.

by the CBO, along with the other explanatory variables. The estimates imply that a one-percentage-point increase in the expected federal government debt-to-GDP ratio increases the current real ten-year Treasury yield by a little more than three basis points and is statistically significantly different from zero. This estimate is about one-half of one basis point larger than when the forward-looking real ten-year Treasury yield was used in the specification reported in the first column of Table 2.

The coefficient estimates for the specification regressing the change in the current real ten-year Treasury yield on the CBO's five-year-ahead projection of the federal government deficit (relative to GDP), along with the other variables, are reported in the second column of Table 3. Similar to the estimate in the first column, the estimated coefficient on the projected deficit variable implies that a one-percentage-point increase in the CBO's projection of the federal government deficit (relative to GDP) increases the current real ten-year Treasury yield by about three basis points, but here this estimate is not statistically significantly different from zero. In contrast, when instead the *level* of the current real ten-year Treasury yield is regressed on the CBO's projection of the federal government deficit, the estimated relationship suggests that increasing the expected federal deficit-to-GDP ratio by one percentage point causes the current real ten-year Treasury yield to increase by almost 24 basis points. While this estimate is statistically significant from zero, it is far larger than the benchmark calculations presented in Table 1, and it is also about five basis points larger than the corresponding estimate in Table 2, in which the forward-looking measure of the real ten-year yield was used. As discussed previously, however, this specification is not consistent with an economic model of crowding out. The coefficient estimate on the deficit is larger because it also incorporates the effect of prior accumulated federal government debt that is included in the total federal debt variable in the first column but is not included when using just the deficit measure in the third column.

The results in Table 3 indicate that the estimated effect of projected federal government debt or deficits on a current measure of the real interest rate is only a bit larger than those in which the forward-looking measure of the real interest rate was employed in estimating the results in Table 2. However, the forward-looking measure of the real interest rate may be a better measure for trying to separate the effect of current economic conditions on the interest rate and isolate the effect of expected federal government debt on real interest rates.

As before, the estimated results also depend to a great degree on the specification of the regression equation. The coefficient estimates derived using the two specifications of real interest rates consistent with an economic model of crowding out—the first two columns—imply that federal government debt may have a statistically significant effect on the level of real interest rates (or not, as shown in second column), but if so, the effect—about 3 basis points for an increase in the debt of 1% of GDP—is consistent with benchmark calculations presented earlier.

3.3.3 Current Interest Rates and Current Federal Government Debt

While using expected measures of interest rates and federal debt is a much more theoretically appealing approach to estimating the relationship between these variables, many previous studies have used only current measures of federal debt and interest rates. Thus, it is informative to estimate the effects of *current* federal debt on *current* real ten-year Treasury yields to compare the results to those of the prior sections.

To do so, we replace the data for the CBO's annual projections of federal government debt and deficits with data on current federal government debt and borrowing.[32] We also replace the CBO's projections for the rate of growth in real GDP with current real GDP growth rates. The current real ten-year Treasury yield measure reflects the prevailing rate at the end of each year and is constructed the same as in the prior section.[33] All of the other variables are the same as in the previous analysis.

As we show in the first column of Table 4, when using current federal government debt (relative to GDP) and a measure of the current real ten-year Treasury yield, the regression results imply that a one-percentage-point increase in the federal debt–GDP ratio is estimated to increase the real ten-year Treasury rate by a little less than five basis points, but the coefficient estimate is not statistically significantly different from zero.[34] The second column reports estimates for the regression equation where the change in the real ten-year Treasury yield is regressed on federal borrowing. The results imply that a one-percentage-point increase in federal government borrowing (relative to GDP) increases real ten-year Treasury rates by seven basis points, but again this estimate is not statistically significantly different from zero.

Alternatively, if the level of the real ten-year Treasury yield is regressed on this measure of federal government borrowing, the

Table 4
Regression results for current real ten-year Treasury rate and current federal debt or borrowing (1953–2003)

	Dependent variable		
	(1) Level of Treasury rate	(2) Change in Treasury rate	(3) Level of Treasury rate
Federal debt/GDP	0.047 (0.036)	—	—
Federal deficit/GDP	—	0.071 (0.066)	0.091 (0.107)
Real GDP growth rate	0.102 (0.049)*	—	0.112 (0.040)*
Change in real GDP growth rate	—	0.100 (0.035)*	—
Real oil price	0.101 (0.043)*	—	0.099 (0.039)*
Change in real oil price	—	0.115 (0.042)*	—
Equity premium	−0.224 (0.297)	—	−0.135 (0.286)
Change in equity premium	—	−0.091 (0.302)	—
Defense shock	−0.425 (0.349)	−0.195 (0.412)	−0.515 (0.321)
Federal Reserve Treasury holdings	−0.401 (0.525)		
Federal Reserve Treasury purchases	—	0.259 (0.544)	0.500 (0.496)
Constant	1.976 (4.407)	−0.263 (0.192)	1.017 (1.084)
AR(1)	0.521 (0.128)*		
Adjusted R-squared	0.60	0.21	0.59
DW statistic	2.02	2.56	2.13
N	50	50	50

Note: Newey-West standard errors in parentheses.
*Coefficient estimate significant at 10% level.

coefficient estimates shown in the third column imply that a one-percentage-point increase in the federal government borrowing–GDP ratio increases the real ten-year Treasury rate by about nine basis points, although this effect is not statistically significantly different from zero, as it is in the first two specifications. This estimate of the empirical relationship between federal government borrowing and the level of the real ten-year Treasury yield in Table 4 is markedly smaller than the corresponding estimates in Tables 2 and 3, which used forward-looking measures of federal government borrowing and the real interest rate. Unlike the strong positive correlation between the CBO's projected measures of federal debt and the deficit, there is not a positive correlation between actual federal debt and borrowing (both measured as a percentage of GDP); the correlation coefficient is −0.13 for these two series.

3.3.4 Vector Autoregressions

An alternative approach to the reduced-form equation estimation used in our analysis above is to estimate the relationship between federal government debt, or federal government borrowing, and the level of the real ten-year Treasury rate in a VAR framework. This methodology has been used in a number of empirical studies on the relationship between federal government debt and borrowing.

In estimating the VARs, we use the same data as those in the first and third columns of Tables 2 through 4; thus, we analyze the effect of a measure of the federal debt on the level of the interest rate and the effect of a measure of the federal deficit on the level of the interest rate. A useful way to analyze the results of the VAR estimates is to look at the impulse responses generated from these estimates. The corresponding impulse responses stemming from VAR estimates using projected federal government debt and the five-year ahead measure of the ten-year real Treasury rate are shown in Figure 15, and Figure 16 shows the impulse responses when the projected federal government deficits (instead of debt) is used in the VAR. The ordering of the variables used to generate these impulse responses is the same as the order of the charts in each figure: real oil prices, military buildup shocks, Treasury security holdings (or purchases) by the Federal Reserve, projected federal government debt (or deficits), the equity premium, and the projected real GDP growth rate. The charts of the impulse responses also include the plus or minus two standard-error (SE) bands, using Monte Carlo standard errors.

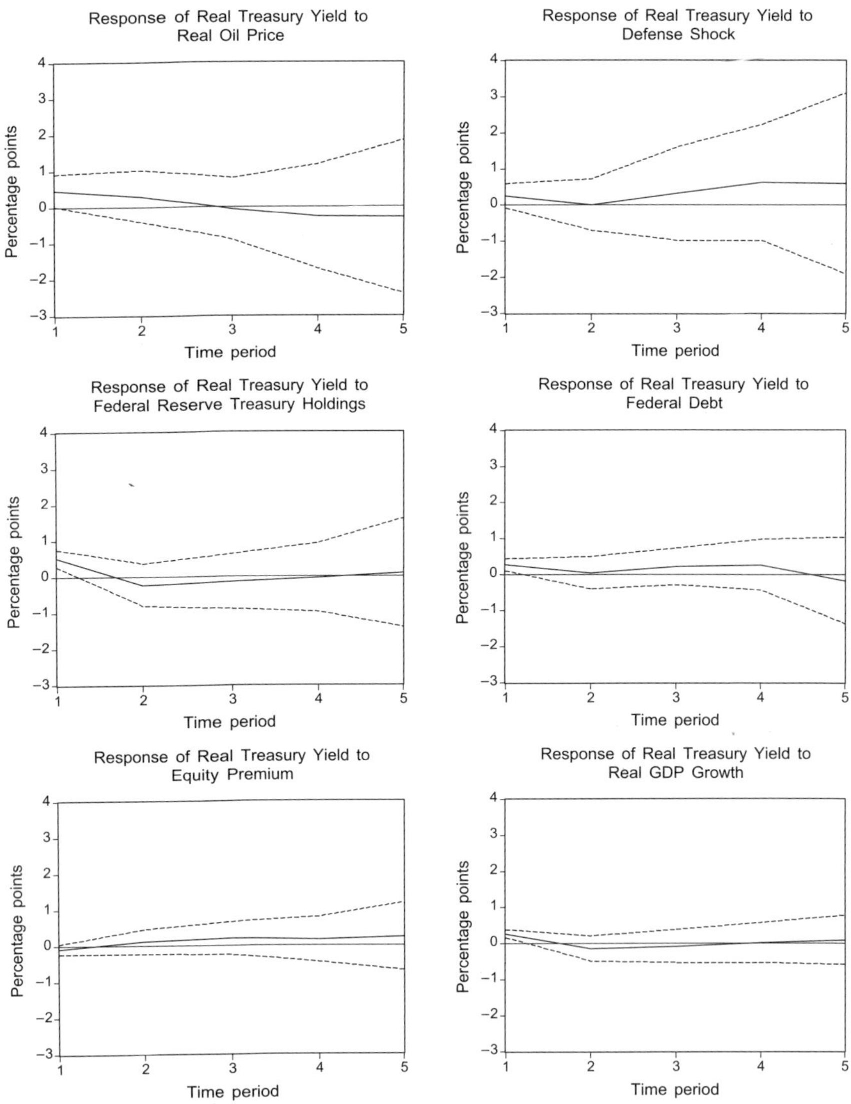

Figure 15
Effects of macroeconomic and projected debt variables on forward-looking real Treasury rate, VAR analysis (Response to Cholesky One S.D. Innovations $\pm$ 2 SE)

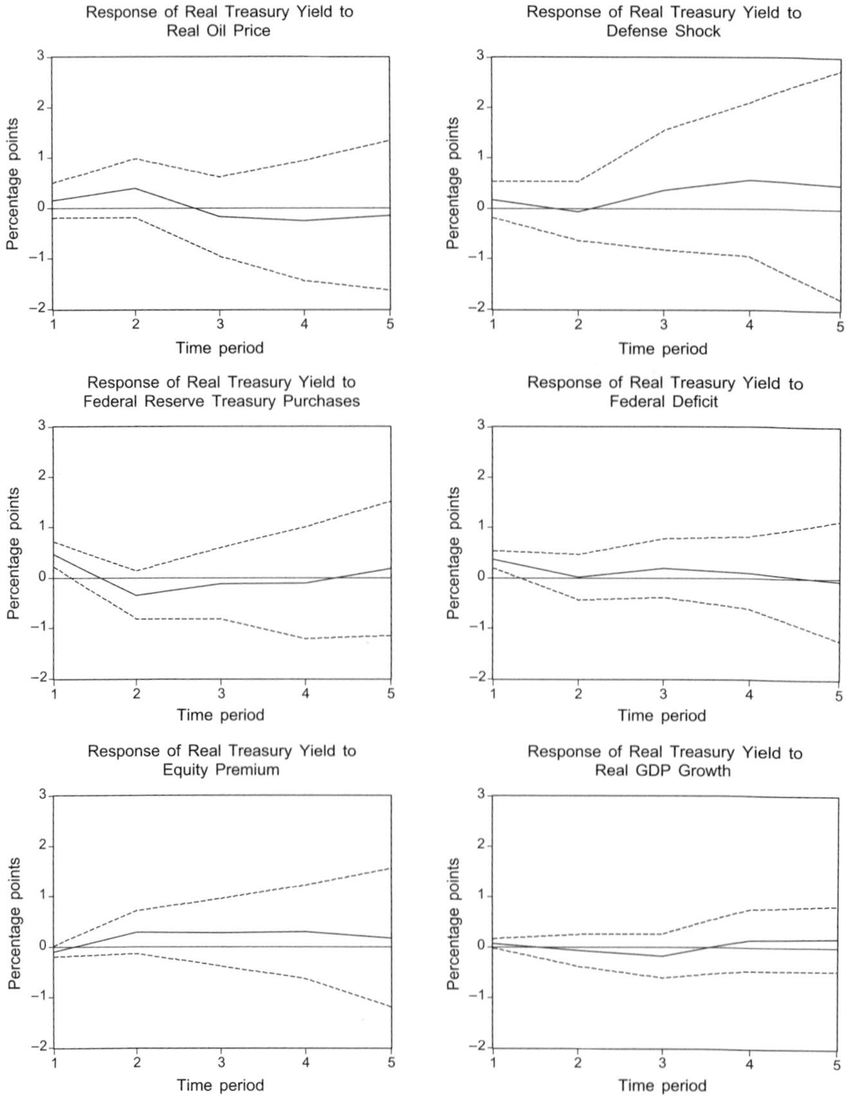

Figure 16
Effects of macroeconomic and projected deficit variables on forward-looking real Treasury rate, VAR analysis (Response to Cholesky One S.D. Innovations $\pm$ 2 SE)

In Figure 15, the second chart from the top on the right side shows the response of the five-year-ahead real ten-year Treasury rate from a one standard deviation shock to projected federal government debt. The response of the forward-looking measure of the real interest rate to an increase in projected federal debt (relative to GDP) is positive and statistically significant in the first period. A one-standard-deviation shock in the projected federal debt–GDP ratio, which is equal to 16.3%, is estimated to increase the forward-looking real interest rate by 26.6 basis points. Thus, this estimate implies that an increase in federal debt equal to 1% of GDP causes the real interest rate to increase by about $1\frac{1}{2}$ basis point, which is somewhat smaller than the corresponding estimate from the reduced form regression results in Table 2 but is still consistent with the theoretical calculations presented in Table 1. As shown in the corresponding variance decomposition presented in Table 5, only 10% of the variation in the forward-looking measure of the real interest rate is due to the innovation in projected federal debt.

Figure 16 shows the impulse responses from the VAR estimates when the projected federal government deficit (relative to GDP) is used instead of federal government debt. An increase in the projected federal government deficit is estimated here to have a positive effect on the five-year-ahead measure of the real ten-year Treasury yield and is statistically significantly different from zero in the first period. A one standard deviation shock in the projected federal deficit–GDP ratio, which is equal to 3%, is estimated to increase the forward-looking real interest rate by 36.6 basis points. Thus, this estimate implies that an increase in the federal deficit equal to 1% of GDP causes the real interest rate to increase by about 12 basis points, which is somewhat smaller than the corresponding estimate from the reduced-form regression results in Table 2. As shown in the corresponding variance decomposition presented in Table 6, about 28 percent of the variation in the forward-looking measure of the real interest rate is due to the innovation in projected federal deficit. However, this specification is not consistent with our analytical model of crowding out, and the estimated effect is much larger than the benchmark calculations presented in Table 1. The estimated effect of the projected deficit is also larger than the effect of the projected federal debt, as in the reduced-form regression estimates in Table 2, but as explained above, this is because the projected deficit variable is strongly correlated with the projected debt variable, and the deficit variable does not include the relevant information on prior accumulated federal debt.

Table 5
Variance decomposition of five-year-ahead, ten-year Treasury rate (Corresponds to impulse responses in Figure 15)

Period	S.E.	Oil price	Defense shock	Federal Reserve Treasury holdings	Projected federal debt	Equity premium	Projected real GDP growth	Forward-looking real Treasury yield
1	4.50	30.26	8.27	36.82	10.05	1.39	9.65	3.56
		(16.28)	(10.13)	(12.60)	(6.09)	(1.67)	(4.16)	(1.24)
2	6.29	33.78	6.62	35.73	8.23	2.32	10.29	3.02
		(16.22)	(9.52)	(12.95)	(5.70)	(5.20)	(5.25)	(1.41)
3	6.88	27.45	14.04	30.73	10.81	5.12	8.99	2.87
		(14.29)	(17.39)	(12.22)	(6.91)	(5.15)	(4.53)	(2.06)
4	7.60	23.22	32.01	20.53	11.14	4.91	5.97	2.21
		(15.33)	(16.17)	(12.13)	(5.91)	(4.48)	(4.29)	(1.71)
5	8.41	21.58	40.13	15.83	9.86	6.12	4.80	1.68
		(13.77)	(17.43)	(12.84)	(6.40)	(4.61)	(4.42)	(1.47)

Cholesky ordering: oil price, defense shock, Federal Reserve Treasury holdings, projected federal debt, equity premium, projected real GDP growth, forward-looking real Treasury yield.
Standard errors: Monte Carlo (100 repetitions).

Table 6
Variance decomposition of five-year-ahead, ten-year Treasury rate (Corresponds to impulse responses in Figure 16)

Period	S.E.	Oil price	Defense shock	Federal Reserve Treasury purchases	Projected federal deficit	Equity premium	Projected real GDP growth	Forward-looking real Treasury yield
1	3.88	4.79	6.11	45.68	28.35	1.92	1.04	12.10
		(8.77)	(8.29)	(14.05)	(10.09)	(2.20)	(1.85)	(4.74)
2	7.04	21.32	3.92	39.76	16.01	10.98	1.18	6.82
		(13.70)	(8.13)	(10.23)	(6.91)	(9.70)	(3.24)	(3.12)
3	7.77	17.95	13.98	29.91	14.71	14.67	3.63	5.14
		(12.79)	(14.57)	(9.84)	(7.73)	(8.30)	(3.56)	(3.15)
4	8.27	16.22	29.02	21.39	10.77	15.30	3.67	3.63
		(12.30)	(17.78)	(9.35)	(6.76)	(8.53)	(2.79)	(2.70)
5	8.91	14.51	35.21	19.29	9.07	14.21	4.51	3.20
		(12.40)	(17.08)	(8.11)	(8.79)	(7.94)	(3.86)	(2.83)

Cholesky ordering: oil price, defense shock, Federal Reserve Treasury purchases, projected federal deficit, equity premium, projected real GDP growth, forward-looking real Treasury yield.
Standard errors: Monte Carlo (100 repetitions).

Figures 17 and 18 show the impulse responses of the current real ten-year Treasury rate to innovations in the projected measures of federal debt and deficits along with our other explanatory variables. The second chart from the top on the right side of Figure 17 shows the impulse response of the current real ten-year Treasury rate from a one standard deviation shock to projected federal government debt. The projected federal debt is estimated to have a positive and statistically significant effect on the current real interest rate. A one standard deviation shock in the projected federal debt–GDP ratio (equal to 16.3%) is estimated to increase the current real interest rate by 40 basis points. Thus, this estimate implies that an increase in federal debt equal to 1% of GDP causes the current real interest rate to increase by about $2\frac{1}{2}$ basis points. This estimate is somewhat smaller than the corresponding estimate from the reduced form regression results in Table 3, but it is still consistent with the theoretical calculations presented in Table 1. As shown in the corresponding variance decomposition presented in Table 7, about 37% of the variation in the current real interest rate is due to the innovation in projected federal debt.

As shown in Figure 18 and Table 8, the effect of the projected federal deficit on the current real interest rate is positive but not statistically significantly different from zero, in contrast to both the results in Figure 16, when the forward-looking measure of the real interest rate was used, and the corresponding estimate from the reduced-form regression results in Table 3. Figure 19 and Table 9, and Figure 20 and Table 10, also show that innovations in the current federal debt, or current federal borrowing, have effects on the current real interest rate that are not statistically significantly different from zero. These results are similar to the corresponding estimates shown in Table 4 for our reduced-form regression analysis.

In general, our analysis of the effect of federal government debt on the real interest rate using VAR analysis is fairly similar to the results we find from our reduced-form regression estimates. Projected measures of the federal debt tend to have a statistically significant, positive effect on forward-looking or current real interest rates; an increase in the projected federal debt equal to 1% of GDP is estimated to increase the real interest rate by about two to three basis points. However, current measures of the federal debt do not have a statistically significant effect on current real interest rates.

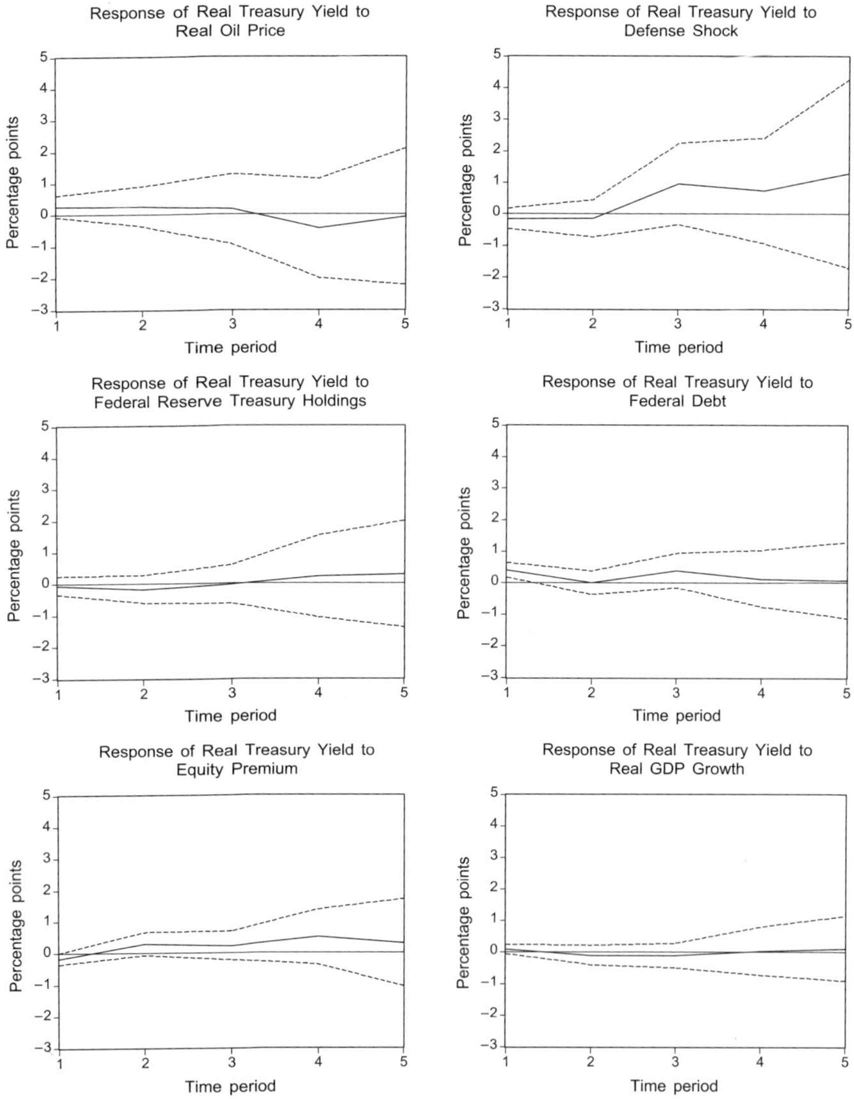

Figure 17

Effects of macroeconomic and projected debt variables on current real Treasury rate, VAR analysis (Response to Cholesky One S.D. Innovations $\pm$ 2 SE)

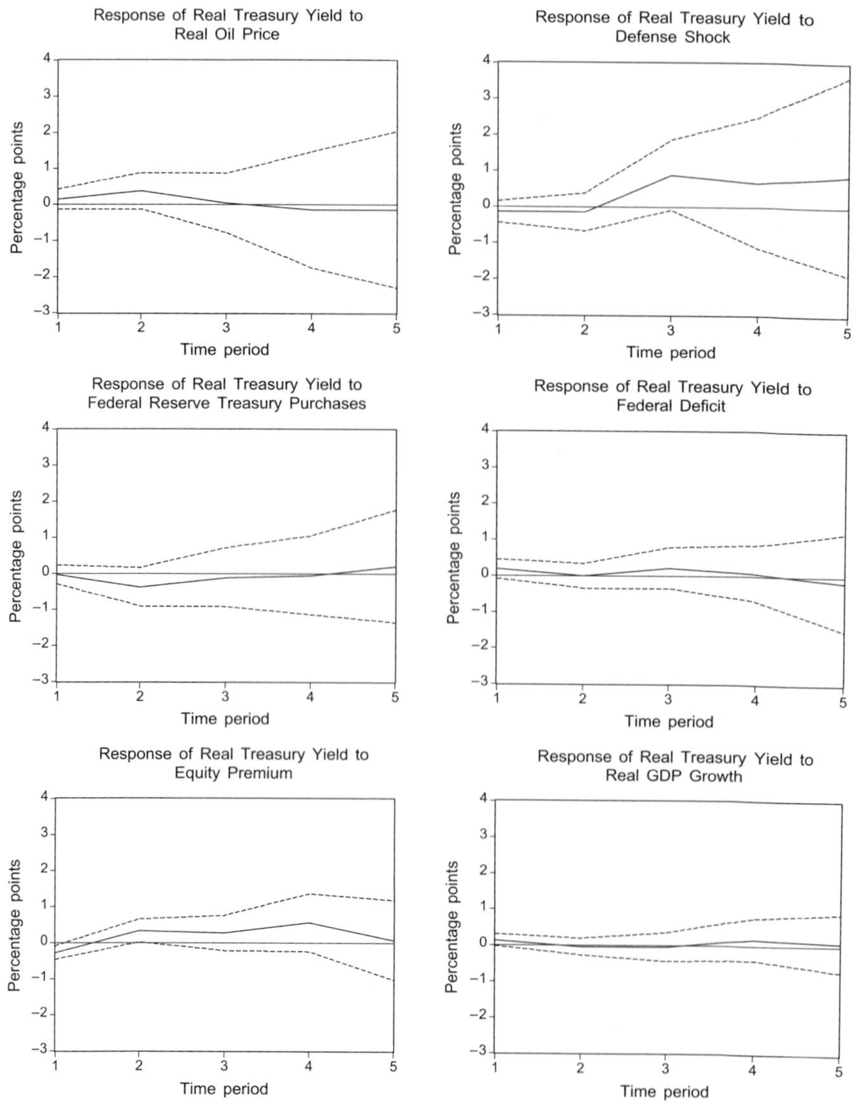

Figure 18
Effects of macroeconomic and projected deficit variables on current real Treasury rate, VAR analysis (Response to Cholesky One S.D. Innovations $\pm$ 2 SE)

Table 7
Variance decomposition of current ten-year Treasury rate (Corresponds to impulse responses in Figure 17)

Period	S.E.	Oil price	Defense shock	Federal Reserve Treasury holdings	Projected federal debt	Equity premium	Projected real GDP growth	Current real Treasury yield
1	5.12	16.84	5.67	0.65	37.42	7.09	1.91	30.41
		(13.88)	(7.98)	(5.39)	(13.96)	(7.63)	(3.29)	(10.28)
2	6.44	21.01	7.02	4.91	24.25	17.08	2.93	22.78
		(15.97)	(9.09)	(8.29)	(9.60)	(9.87)	(3.81)	(7.90)
3	6.94	9.10	52.38	1.81	16.84	9.07	1.78	9.02
		(16.54)	(19.78)	(6.64)	(8.12)	(5.77)	(3.55)	(4.74)
4	8.22	12.44	51.65	2.73	11.20	14.34	1.15	6.50
		(15.49)	(17.04)	(6.06)	(7.59)	(8.71)	(3.61)	(3.77)
5	9.48	7.54	64.47	3.40	6.80	10.53	0.92	6.34
		(13.49)	(16.53)	(5.53)	(6.74)	(7.03)	(3.86)	(4.78)

Cholesky ordering: oil price, defense shock, Federal Reserve Treasury holdings, projected federal debt, equity premium, projected real GDP growth, current real Treasury yield.
Standard errors: Monte Carlo (100 repetitions).

Table 8
Variance decomposition of current ten-year Treasury rate (Corresponds to impulse responses in Figure 18)

Period	S.E.	Oil price	Defense shock	Federal Reserve Treasury purchases	Projected federal deficit	Equity premium	Projected real GDP growth	Current real Treasury yield
1	4.30	5.80	7.29	0.34	10.26	24.80	5.29	46.21
		(10.18)	(8.22)	(4.69)	(8.45)	(11.53)	(5.69)	(10.96)
2	7.11	20.56	6.40	20.19	4.31	24.55	2.54	21.45
		(17.06)	(7.52)	(12.98)	(6.25)	(10.04)	(3.40)	(6.19)
3	8.00	9.35	49.35	9.98	4.51	15.37	1.34	10.10
		(14.16)	(19.53)	(9.32)	(5.68)	(7.67)	(3.24)	(3.87)
4	8.33	7.27	50.87	6.90	3.26	22.84	2.03	6.83
		(11.94)	(17.68)	(10.14)	(5.51)	(9.76)	(3.57)	(3.77)
5	8.92	5.99	59.25	6.19	3.26	16.84	1.68	6.79
		(12.05)	(15.99)	(9.99)	(7.92)	(7.07)	(3.02)	(3.39)

Cholesky ordering: oil price, defense shock, Federal Reserve Treasury purchases, projected federal deficit, equity premium, projected real GDP growth, current real Treasury yield.
Standard errors: Monte Carlo (100 repetitions).

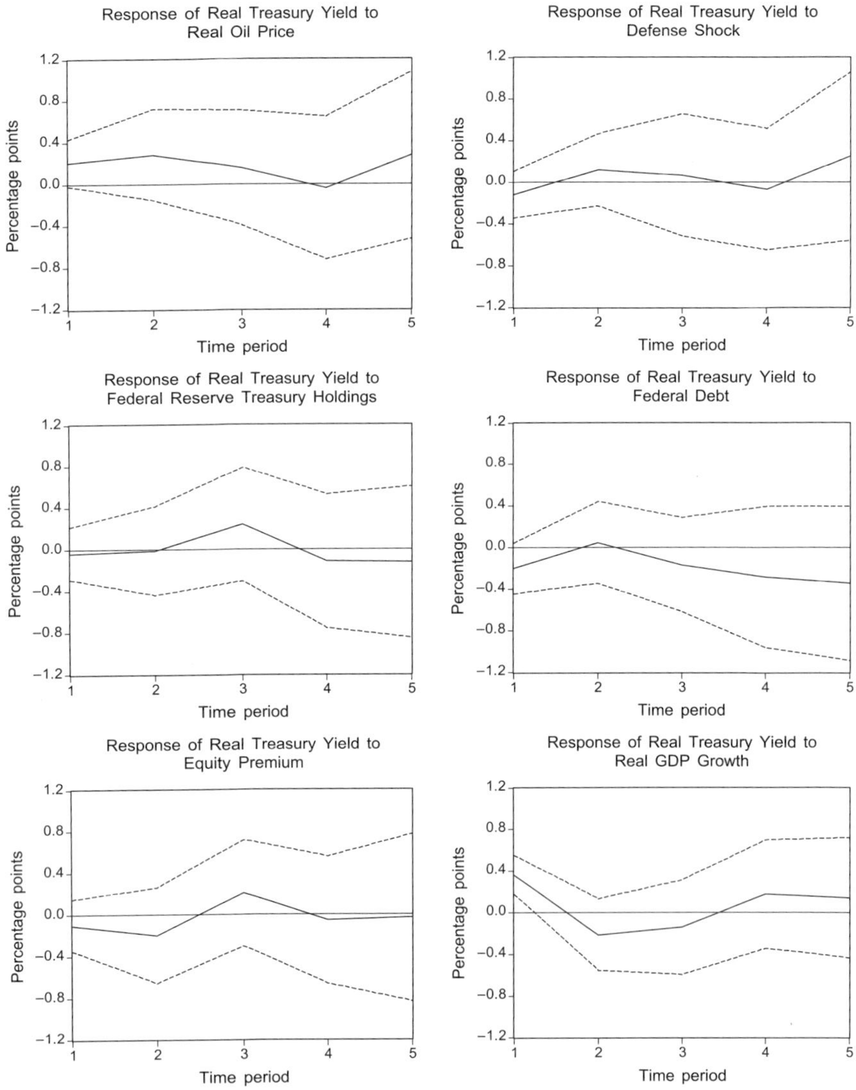

Figure 19
Effects of macroeconomic and current debt variables on current real Treasury rate, VAR analysis (Response to Cholesky One S.D. Innovations $\pm$ 2 SE)

Table 9
Variance decomposition of current ten-year Treasury rate (Corresponds to impulse responses in Figure 19)

Period	S.E.	Oil price	Defense shock	Federal Reserve Treasury holdings	Federal debt	Equity premium	Real GDP growth	Current real Treasury yield
1	4.23	7.15	2.41	0.25	6.86	1.78	22.09	59.46
		(6.31)	(5.06)	(2.86)	(6.77)	(3.38)	(8.97)	(11.45)
2	5.42	15.57	3.65	0.22	5.45	6.49	22.48	46.14
		(9.37)	(6.83)	(5.41)	(5.97)	(7.38)	(9.03)	(10.54)
3	6.54	15.25	3.44	6.12	7.39	9.71	20.44	37.66
		(10.19)	(5.76)	(8.93)	(6.68)	(8.27)	(7.87)	(9.73)
4	7.39	13.10	3.33	6.42	13.60	8.53	20.14	34.87
		(10.33)	(6.76)	(8.63)	(8.01)	(8.11)	(7.14)	(7.93)
5	8.10	15.49	6.91	6.18	19.09	6.78	17.23	28.33
		(9.79)	(8.92)	(7.84)	(8.46)	(8.13)	(7.00)	(6.50)

Cholesky ordering: oil price, defense shock, Federal Reserve Treasury holdings, federal debt, equity premium, real GDP growth, current real Treasury yield.
Standard errors: Monte Carlo (100 repetitions).

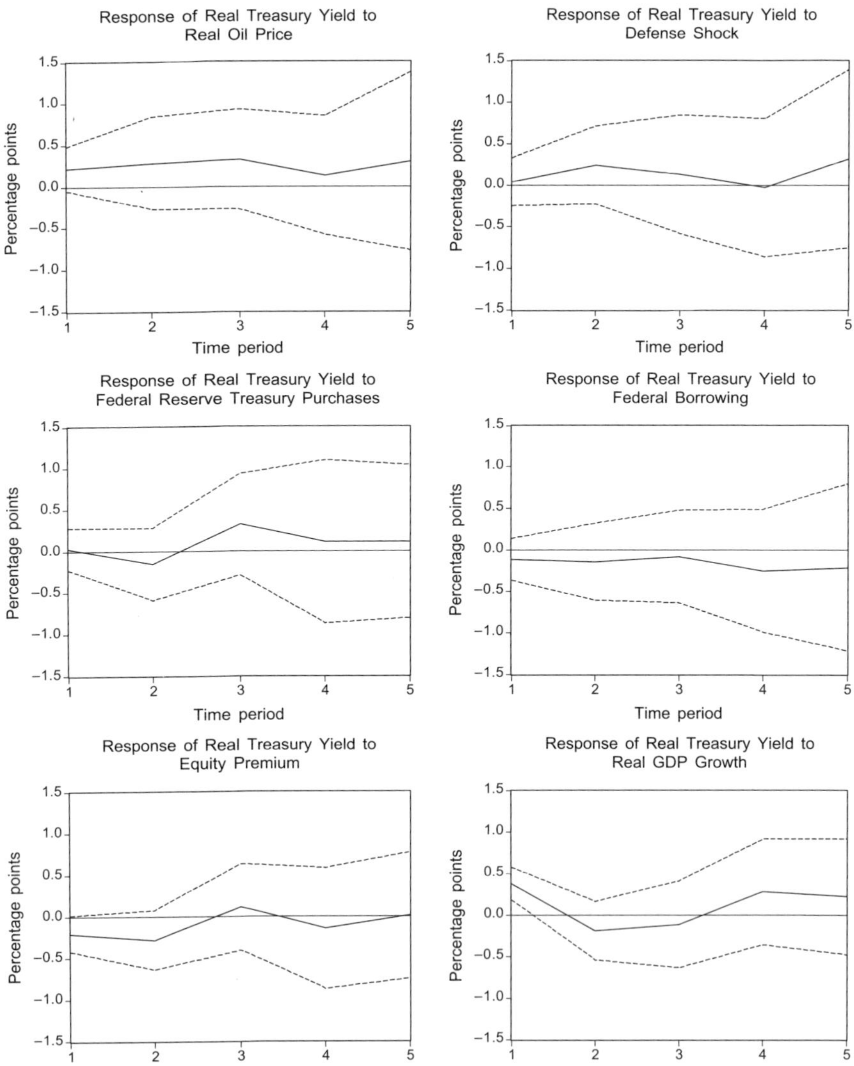

Figure 20
Effects of macroeconomic and current deficit variables on current real Treasury rate, VAR analysis (Response to Cholesky One S.D. Innovations $\pm$ 2 SE)

Table 10
Variance decomposition of current ten-year Treasury rate (Corresponds to impulse responses in Figure 20)

Period	S.E.	Oil price	Defense shock	Federal Reserve Treasury purchases	Federal borrowing	Equity premium	Real GDP growth	Current real Treasury yield
1	4.72	7.17	0.25	0.12	2.07	6.70	22.07	61.62
		(7.85)	(3.39)	(3.71)	(3.68)	(7.05)	(8.69)	(9.88)
2	6.19	12.99	6.32	2.60	3.63	13.04	18.56	42.86
		(11.01)	(7.94)	(6.52)	(6.43)	(9.31)	(6.87)	(9.35)
3	6.99	18.71	6.27	10.46	3.43	11.25	15.69	34.20
		(12.79)	(9.39)	(8.00)	(6.46)	(7.06)	(6.07)	(7.79)
4	7.47	16.51	5.22	9.41	7.17	10.73	18.05	32.91
		(11.29)	(8.63)	(9.13)	(7.70)	(6.40)	(6.16)	(7.16)
5	7.82	18.65	9.94	8.52	8.52	8.91	17.70	27.76
		(11.13)	(11.15)	(8.25)	(7.50)	(6.39)	(6.91)	(6.37)

Cholesky ordering: oil price, defense shock, Federal Reserve Treasury purchases, federal borrowing, equity premium, real GDP growth, current real Treasury yield.
Standard errors: Monte Carlo (100 repetitions).

4. Conclusion

As we noted at the outset, the recent reemergence of U.S. federal government budget deficits has focused attention on an old question: Does government debt affect interest rates? Despite a substantial body of empirical analysis, the answer based on the past two decades of research is mixed. While some studies suggest a small increase in the real interest rate when federal debt increases, others estimate large effects, and some studies find no statistically significant interest rate effect. Comparing results across studies is complicated by differences in economic models, definitions of government debt and interest rates, econometric approaches, sources of data, and rhetoric.

Using a standard set of data and a simple economic framework, we reconsider and add to empirical evidence on the effect of federal government debt and interest rates. We begin by deriving analytically the effect of government debt on the real interest rate and conclude that an increase in government debt equivalent to 1% of GDP would likely increase the real interest rate by about two to three basis points. While some existing studies estimate effects in this range, others find larger effects. In almost all cases, larger estimates come from specifications relating federal deficits (as opposed to debt) and the level interest rates (as opposed to changes in interest rates).

We present our own empirical analysis in two parts. First, we examine a variety of conventional reduced-form specifications linking interest rates and government debt and other variables. In particular, we provide estimates for three types of specifications to permit comparisons among different approaches taken in previous research; we estimate the effect of (1) an expected, or projected, measure of federal government debt on a forward-looking measure of the real interest rate; (2) an expected, or projected, measure of federal government debt on a current measure of the real interest rate; and (3) a current measure of federal government debt on a current measure of the real interest rate. Most of the statistically significant estimated effects are consistent with the prediction of our economic model calculations. Second, we provide evidence using vector autoregression analysis. In general, these results are similar to those found in our reduced-form econometric analysis and are consistent with the analytical calculations.

Taken together, the bulk of our empirical results suggest that an increase in federal government debt equivalent to 1% of GDP, all else being equal, is likely to increase the long-term real rate of interest by about three basis points, while some estimates are not statistically significantly different from zero. By presenting a range of results with the same data, we illustrate the dependence of estimation on specification and definition differences.

This paper is deliberately narrow in its scope; our focus, as the paper's title suggests, is only on the interest rate effects of government debt. The effect of debt and deficits on interest rates has been the focus of much of the recent and previous policy discussions concerning the effects of government borrowing on investment and economic activity. However, we do believe that other effects of federal debt and deficits on economic factors other than interest rates are important topics for analysis. We have not investigated the degree to which federal borrowing might be offset by private domestic saving or inflows of foreign saving or both. These factors interact with federal borrowing in ways that may have similar effects on interest rates but different effects on the overall economy.[35]

Our findings should not be construed as implying that deficits don't matter. Substantially larger, persistent, and unsustainable levels of government debt can eventually put increasing strains on the available domestic and foreign sources of loanable funds, and they can represent a large transfer of wealth to finance current generations' consumption from future generations, which much eventually pay down federal debt to a sustainable level. Holding the path of noninterest government outlays constant, deficits represent higher future tax burdens to cover both these outlays plus interest expenses associated with the debt, which have adverse consequences for economic growth. In the United States at the present time, unfunded implicit obligations associated with the Social Security and Medicare programs are particularly of concern.[36]

Notes

An earlier draft of this paper was prepared for presentation at the NBER Macroeconomics Annual Conference in Cambridge, MA, April 2–3, 2004. We thank Bill Gale, Mark Gertler, Kevin Hassett, Thomas Laubach, Jonathan Parker, Ken Rogoff, Matthew Shapiro, and NBER conference participants for helpful comments, and Anne Moore for providing excellent research assistance with this paper.

1. See Ball and Mankiw (1995), Elmendorf and Mankiw (1999), and Council of Economic Advisers (2003).

2. See McCallum (1984) for more discussion of this issue.

3. See Bernheim (1987), Barro (1989), and Seater (1993) for discussions of the Ricardian equivalence hypothesis.

4. We calculate the private capital stock using data in the Federal Reserve's flow of funds accounts on the fixed assets of the household, business, farm (excluding farmland, which is not included in the accounts), and nonprofit sectors of the economy. This measure does not include stocks of consumer durables or business inventories. This measure understates the size of the total capital stock in the United States that could potentially be affected by federal government debt since it does not include the capital of state and local governments, and thus somewhat overstates the potential percentage change in interest rates from federal government debt crowding out capital formation in other sectors of the economy.

5. *Expectations* of future government borrowing are not part of the simple framework presented here. But it is probably a reasonable benchmark to assume that the expected crowding-out effect on current interest rates from expected future federal borrowing is similar in magnitude to the calculations presented here; i.e., if borrowing is expected to be higher by 1 percent of GDP in each of the next ten years, then the current real interest rate may be expected to be about 24 basis points higher. However, Cohen and Follette (2003) have shown that budget deficit forecasts beyond one year are typically very poor, primarily owing to the difficulty in forecasting federal tax receipts. See also Congressional Budget Office (2004) for a discussion about the difficulty of forecasting federal budget deficits.

6. This is a measure of the degree of offset to federal government borrowing that is consistent with a discussion in Council of Economic Advisers (1994), for example.

7. Data on federal government debt held by the public are from the Federal Reserve's flow of fund accounts, and includes federal debt held by the Federal Reserve. This measure of federal government debt does not, of course, include the implicit unfunded liabilities associated with the Social Security and Medicare programs. Data for GDP are from the national income and product accounts produced by the Bureau of Economic Analysis.

8. Federal borrowing here is the net issuance of new federal debt, as measured by the Federal Reserve's flow of funds accounts, and thus is not exactly equal to the federal unified federal budget deficit, though it is closely correlated with it. However, it is a measure that captures better the potential effects of federal borrowing in credit markets.

9. This measure of the U.S. private capital stock is constructed with data from the Federal Reserve's flow of fund accounts, as we described in footnote 4.

10. We constructed data for U.S. domestic (nonfinancial) debt and borrowing used in Figures 4 through 7 from the Federal Reserve's flow of funds accounts.

11. Data on U.S. Treasury security holdings shown in Figures 9 and 10 are from the Federal Reserve's flow of funds accounts.

12. Data on nominal ten-year Treasury yields are from the Federal Reserve. The real interest rate is computed by subtracting the average expected inflation rate for the consumer price index (CPI) from the Livingston Survey compiled by the Federal Reserve Bank in Philadelphia.

13. The expected inflation rate is the same measure from the Livingston Survey used to construct the real interest rate in the previous charts. The actual rate of inflation is

measured by the growth rate in the price index for personal consumption expenditures in the national income and product accounts.

14. These measures of the real interest rate are constructed using data from the Organization for Economic Cooperation and Development (OECD) for nominal ten-year government bond yields and the actual rate of growth in the price index for personal consumption expenditures in each country's national income accounts. To our knowledge, measures of expected inflation for each country are not readily available.

15. In a subsequent paper by Cebula and Koch (1994), again investigating the effects of current federal government deficits and capital inflows on corporate yields, they do not separate the deficit into its structural and cyclical components and do not report results of the effects of deficits and capital inflows on Treasury yields. Given the results of their 1989 analysis, these are significant omissions, so it is not clear how to interpret their findings of a positive effect of government deficits on corporate yields in their 1994 paper.

16. In related research, Auerbach (2003) and Bohn (1998) note that U.S. fiscal policy appears responsive to fiscal conditions so that spending is reduced and/or taxes are raised when federal debt and deficits increase.

17. In related analysis, Miller and Russek (1991) use Granger-causality tests to assess the relationship between federal government deficits and long-term Treasury rates. They find bidirectional causality between current real per-capita federal government deficits (or current real per-capita federal debt) and long-term interest rates. Again, however, it is difficult to interpret the magnitude of the effect on interest rates from their results.

18. We focus on the effect of federal government debt on a measure of the real, long-term interest rate because that is the measure of the interest rate most likely to be affected by federal government debt if it is crowded out by private capital formation. Accordingly, we use a measure of the ten-year Treasury yield, adjusted for expected inflation, for our analysis.

19. Data for the growth rate of real GDP are available in the national income and product accounts produced by the Bureau of Economic Analysis (BEA).

20. Data for inflation-adjusted domestic crude oil prices in the United States are obtained from the Department of Energy. Barro and Sala-i-Martin (1990) and Barro (1991) find that an increase in the real price of oil tends to increase the real interest rate presumably because the resulting decline in investment demand is dominated by the fall in desired saving.

21. As in Laubach (2003), we calculate the equity premium as dividend income from the national income and product accounts, as a percentage of the market value of corporate equities held by households in the Federal Reserve's flow of fund accounts, plus the trend growth rate in real GDP, minus the real ten-year Treasury yield.

22. See Cohen and Follette (2003) and Eichenbaum and Fisher (2004) for more discussion about exogenous defense spending shocks.

23. See, for example, Bernheim (1987), Barro (1989), and Seater (1993). Baxter and King (1993) show that in a neoclassical model, however, the interest rate may increase only in the short run but be unchanged in the long run.

24. The time periods denoted in this dummy variable as significant military buildups include the beginning of the Vietnam war buildup in 1965 and the Carter–Reagan military buildup beginning in 1980, as in Ramey and Shapiro (1998), and we add the beginning of

the military buildup for the war in Afghanistan and Iraq in 2002, as in Eichenbaum and Fisher (2004).

25. This variable is constructed using data on Federal Reserve purchases of U.S. Treasury securities from the Federal Reserve's flow of funds accounts expressed as a ratio to GDP from the national income and product accounts.

26. We do not include additional variables to capture other demands on loanable funds (such as private-sector debt) and sources of loanable funds (such as domestic and foreign saving) because of significant potential endogenity problems.

27. We thank Thomas Laubach for making these data on forward-looking real interest rates available to us; see Laubach (2003) for more details on the calculation of these data. The data do not go back earlier than 1976 because the CBO has been in existence only since the mid-1970s.

28. If we estimate the more parsimonious regression specification of Laubach (2003)—which includes only the projected federal debt, projected real GDP growth, and the equity premium—then the results imply that a one-percentage-point (relative to GDP) increase in the CBO's five-year-ahead projection of the federal debt increases the real five-year-ahead ten-year Treasury yield by a bit more than five basis points, which replicates his estimate. This estimate is more than two basis points larger than when the larger set of other explanatory variables is used, as in the first column of Table 2, suggesting that part of Laubach's estimated effect of projected debt reflected inadequate control for other current macroeconomic factors that determine the real interest rate. Thus, the operating assumption that using forward-looking measures of federal government debt and interest rates omits any effects of current economic conditions and policies from the empirical estimate appears to be invalid.

29. If the oil price, defense shock, and Federal Reserve Treasury holding variables are not included, as in Laubach, then the coefficient on the projected real GDP growth rate variable is estimated with the expected sign (positive) and is statistically significant from zero.

30. If the set of independent variables includes only the projected federal deficit, projected real GDP growth, and the equity premium, as in Laubach (2003), then the regression results imply that a one-percentage-point (relative to GDP) increase in the CBO's five-year-ahead projection of federal deficit increases the real five-year-ahead ten-year Treasury yield by 28 basis points, which replicates his estimate. This estimate is almost ten basis points larger than when the larger set of other explanatory variables is used in the third column of Table 2.

31. We obtained data for the nominal ten-year Treasury from the Federal Reserve Board, and the data for average inflation expectations from the Livingston Survey maintained by the Federal Reserve Bank of Philadelphia.

32. These data are from the Federal Reserve Board's flow of funds accounts. Because the time period of the data is not limited by the availability of the CBO projections, we extend the data back to 1953.

33. The timing is adjusted slightly so that it reflects the prevailing interest rate at the end of the year (December) rather than the month when the CBO projections are released (which is typically in the following month of January).

34. Preliminary estimates of this equation revealed the presence of serially correlated errors, so the regression results reported here are for estimates with an AR(1) corrected specification of the residuals.

35. Recent federal income tax reductions have also rekindled interest in the impact of deficits on consumption. Shapiro and Slemrod (2003) and Johnson, Parker, and Souleles (2004) investigate the impact of deficit-increasing tax reductions on household consumption.

36. See Congressional Budget Office (2003) and Gokhale and Smetters (2003), for example, for recent discussions of the potentially large unfunded obligations associated with these entitlement programs.

References

Auerbach, Alan J. (2003). Fiscal policy, past, and present. National Bureau of Economic Research. Working Paper No. 10023. October.

Ball, Laurence, and N. Gregory Mankiw. (1995). What do budget deficits do? *Proceedings*, Federal Reserve Bank of Kansas City, pp. 95–149.

Barro, Robert J. (1989). The neoclassical approach to fiscal policy. In *Modern Business Cycle Theory*, Robert J. Barro (ed.). Cambridge, MA: Harvard University Press, pp. 178–235.

Barro, Robert J. (1992). World interest rates and investment. *Scandinavian Journal of Economics* 34(2):323–342.

Barro, Robert J., and Xavier Sala-i-Martin. (1990). World real interest rates. In *NBER Macroeconomics Annual*, O. J. Blanchard and S. Fischer, (eds.). Cambridge, MA: MIT Press.

Barth, James R., George Iden, and Frank S. Russek. (1984). Do federal deficits really matter? *Contemporary Policy Issues* 3(1, Fall):79–95.

Barth, James R., George Iden, Frank S. Russek, and Mark Wohar. (1991). The effects of federal budget deficits on interest rates and the composition of domestic output. In *The Great Fiscal Experiment*, Rudolph G. Penner (ed.). Washington, DC: The Urban Institute Press, pp. 71–141.

Baxter, Marianne, and Robert G. King. (1993). Fiscal policy in general equilibrium. *American Economic Review* 83(3, June):315–334.

Bernheim, B. Douglas. (1987). Ricardian equivalence: An evaluation of theory and evidence. In *NBER Macroeconomics Annual*, Stanley Fischer (ed.). Cambridge: MIT Press, pp. 263–304.

Bernheim, B. Douglas. (1989). A neoclassical perspective on budget deficits. *Journal of Economic Perspectives* 3(2, Spring):55–72.

Blanchard, Olivier J., and Roberto Perotti. (2000). An empirical characterization of the dynamic effects of changes in government spending and taxes on output. MIT. Mimeo.

Bohn, Henning. (1998). The behavior of U.S. public debt and deficits. *Quarterly Journal of Economics* 113(3, August):949–963.

Calomiris, Charles, Eric M. Engen, Kevin Hassett, and R. Glenn Hubbard. (2003). Do budget deficit announcements move interest rates? American Enterprise Institute and Columbia University. Mimeo. December.

Cebula, Richard J., and James V. Koch. (1989). An empirical note on deficits, interest rates, and international capital flows. *Quarterly Review of Economics and Business* 29(3, Autumn):121–127.

Cebula, Richard J., and James V. Koch. (1994). Federal budget deficits, interest rates, and international capital flows: A further note. *Quarterly Review of Economics and Finance* 34(1, Spring):117–120.

Cohen, Darrel, and Glenn Follette. (2003). Forecasting exogenous fiscal variables in the United States. Board of Governors of the Federal Reserve System. Finance and Economics Discussion Series 2003-59. November.

Cohen, Darrel, and Olivier Garnier. (1991). The impact of forecasts of budget deficits on interest rates in the United States and other G7 countries. Board of Governors of the Federal Reserve System. Mimeo.

Congressional Budget Office. (2003). The long-term budget outlook. December.

Congressional Budget Office. (2004). The uncertainty of budget projections: A discussion of data and methods. April.

Council of Economic Advisers. (1994). *Economic Report of the President*. Washington, DC: U.S. Government Printing Office.

Council of Economic Advisers. (2003). *Economic Report of the President*. Washington, DC: U.S. Government Printing Office.

Eichenbaum, Martin, and Jonas Fisher. (2004). Fiscal policy in the aftermath of 9/11. National Bureau of Economic Research. Working Paper No. 10430. April.

Elmendorf, Douglas W. (1993). Actual budget deficit expectations and interest rates. Harvard University. Mimeo. March.

Elmendorf, Douglas W. (1996). The effect of deficit-reduction laws on real interest rates. Board of Governors of the Federal Reserve System. Mimeo. October.

Elmendorf, Douglas W., and N. Gregory Mankiw. (1999). Government debt. In *Handbook of Macroeconomics*, John B. Taylor and Michael Woodford (eds.). Amsterdam: Elsevier Science, Chapter 25.

Evans, Charles L., and David Marshall. (2002). Economic determinants of the nominal Treasury yield curve. Federal Reserve Bank of Chicago. Working Paper No. 2001-16 (revised).

Gale, William G., and Peter Orszag. (2002). The economic effects of long-term fiscal discipline. Urban Institute-Brookings Institution Tax Policy Center. Discussion Paper. December.

Gale, William G., and Peter Orszag. (2003). Economic effects of sustained budget deficits. *National Tax Journal* 56(3, September):463–485.

Gokhale, Jagadeesh, and Kent Smetters. (2003). *Fiscal and Generational Imbalances: New Budget Measures for New Budget Priorities*. Washington, DC: AEI Press.

Johnson, David S., Jonathan A. Parker, and Nicholas S. Souleles. (2004). The response of consumer spending to the randomized income tax rebates of 2001. Bureau of Labor Statistics, Princeton University, and University of Pennsylvania. Mimeo. February.

Kitchen, John. (1996). Domestic and international financial market responses to federal deficit announcements. *Journal of International Money and Finance* 15(2):239–254.

Kitchen, John. (2002). A note on interest rates and structural budget deficits. U.S. Congress, House of Representatives, Budget Committee. Mimeo. October.

Laubach, Thomas. (2003). New evidence on the interest rate effects of budget deficits and debt. Board of Governors of the Federal Reserve System. Finance and Economics Discussion Series 2003-12. May.

McCallum, Bennett. (1984). Are bond-financed deficits inflationary? A Ricardian analysis. *Journal of Political Economy* 92(1):123–135.

Miller, Stephen M., and Frank S. Russek. (1991). The temporal causality between fiscal deficits and interest rates. *Contemporary Policy Issues* 9(July):12–23.

Miller, Stephen M., and Frank S. Russek. (1996). Do federal deficits affect interest rates? Evidence from three econometric methods. *Journal of Macroeconomics* 18(3, Summer):403–428.

Quigley, Michael Regan, and Susan Porter-Hudak. (1994). A new approach in analyzing the effect of deficit announcements on interest rates. *Journal of Money, Credit, and Banking* (26, November):894–902.

Ramey, Valerie A., and Matthew D. Shapiro. (1998). Costly capital reallocation and the effects of government spending. *Carnegie Rochester Conference Series on Public Policy* (48, June):145–194.

Seater, John J. (1993). Ricardian equivalence. *Journal of Economic Literature* (31, March):142–190.

Shapiro, Matthew D., and Joel Slemrod. (2003). Did the 2001 tax rebate stimulate spending? Evidence from taxpayer surveys. In *Tax Policy and the Economy 17*, James Poterba (ed.). Cambridge, MA: MIT Press.

Thorbecke, Willem. (1993). Why deficit news affects interest rates. *Journal of Policy Modeling* (15, February):1–11.

Wachtel, Paul, and John Young. (1987). Deficit announcements and interest rates. *American Economic Review* 77(December):1007–1022.

Comment

Jonathan A. Parker
Princeton University and
NBER

1. Introduction

This article addresses a timely question of significant import for today's policymakers: What is the effect of government debt on interest rates? The article measures how much larger real interest rates have been when the federal government has run large deficits or had a large debt.

The received wisdom on this topic is given by the following quote from the 2003 Economic Report of the President:

> [T]he marginal product of capital rises by 0.67 percent when the capital stock falls by 1.0 percent ... one dollar of debt reduces the capital stock by about 60 cents.... A conservative rule of thumb based on this relationship is that interest rates rise by about 3 basis points for every additional $200 billion in government debt (Council of Economic Advisers, 2003, pp. 57–58).

R. Glen Hubbard was of course the chair of the Council of Economic Advisers when this report was written. And the rule of thumb in this quote is a useful guide for policymakers because it makes the point that government debt can raise interest rates and reduce private investment and economic growth. Thus, the benefits of any policy that increases debt should be weighed against these costs.

As the paper describes, the received wisdom comes in part from the analysis of a Cobb-Douglas production function in which output (Y) is produced from capital (K) and labor (N) with capital share of about a third, denoted α. Cost minimization by firms implies that:

$$r = \frac{\partial}{\partial K}F(K/N) = A\alpha k^{\alpha-1} \tag{1}$$

where A is the level of technology and k is the capital labor ratio. The authors take the net return on private capital to be 10%.[1] Differentiating both sides of equation (1) with respect to the level of government debt (D), the change in the real interest rate for a change in debt is:

$$\frac{dr}{dD} = \left(\frac{\partial K}{\partial D}\frac{\partial}{\partial K} + \frac{\partial N}{\partial D}\frac{\partial}{\partial N}\right)\frac{\partial}{\partial K}F(K/N)$$

If $dN = 0$, multiplying both sides by Y gives:

$$\frac{dr}{dD/Y} = A\alpha(\alpha - 1)k^{\alpha-2}y\frac{\partial K}{\partial D} = (\alpha - 1)r\frac{y}{k}\frac{\partial K}{\partial D} \simeq -2.2\left(\frac{\partial K}{\partial D}\right)\%$$

So if we assume, as above, that $\partial K/\partial D = -0.6$, then a 1% change in the debt to GDP ratio leads to a 0.013% change in the real interest rate. This is small relative to the volatility of the real interest rate. For a change in debt of $4 trillion, or 40% of Y, which is both about the current level of federal debt and about how much the Congressional Budget Office's forecast of debt 10 years in the future has increased from January 2001 to the present, the real interest rate is predicted to change by just over 0.5%.

From this exercise, the authors take three points: if debt crowds out capital, it raises the real interest rate; the level of debt determines the level of the real interest rate; and the magnitude of the effect is small.

All the empirical findings of the paper are consistent with Figures 11 and 12. There is a small but significant correlation between debt and real interest rates. And there is a larger and significant relationship between deficits and real interest rates. The former finding is consistent with a slightly larger effect than implied by the above rule of thumb. The regressions suggest that a 1% increase in D/Y is associated with a 0.03 percentage point increase in r. The latter—the larger relationship between deficits and interest rates—supports, informally at least, a significant short-term Keynensian effect of deficits: deficits increase the demand for goods and raise interest rates.

According to my reading of the literature and this paper, these findings are robust and correct. To reverse them would require cruel and unusual treatment of the data. The balance of my discussion therefore focusses on interpretation.

I make two points. First, we are less concerned with the effect of debt on interest rates than the effect on capital or other measures of future well-being. The curvature of the production function, which the authors use to argue that the interest rate effect should be small, also implies that there are large effects of debt on capital for only small interest rate movements. Second, the effect of debt on interest rates is determined by the structure of the economy and by the tax and spending policies pursued in response to debt. In terms of understanding the causal effect of tax and spending policies on the capital stock and interest rates, at best the deficit and debt are noisy regressors. At worst, they are concepts without economic content.

2. Do We Care About the Effect on Interest Rates?

Only indirectly. We care directly about the effect of debt on real variables and outcomes, which can be large even when the effect on interest rates is small.

In extreme, there can be no effect of debt on real rates, and yet debt might significantly depress economic activity. Thus, small interest rate effects do not imply small welfare costs of debt.

For example, the capital–labor ratio determines wages as well as the return to capital according to $w = f(k) - rf'(k)$. If a policy that increases debt also lowers labor supply or the accumulation of human capital, then the policy can have no effect on real rates and yet decrease output. As another example, if production has features of learning by doing or if there are human capital spillovers, so that the aggregate production function has the *AK* structure, then policy choices that increase debt and decrease capital will not change the interest rate even though they may have detrimental effects on output and economic growth. Finally, the United States is a reasonably open economy, and so capital inflows offset government debt. In extreme, a policy that increases debt can have no effect on the interest rate or the capital stock but can significantly reduce the future income of households.

Even assuming away movements in labor, taking as given the Cobb-Douglas production function, and assuming no capital inflows, the curvature of the production function, which the authors use to argue that the interest rate effect should be small, also implies that there are large effects of debt on capital and output for only small interest rate movements. Above, I calculated what the rule of thumb implies about the effect of the current federal debt on interest rates. We can also calculate the effect on output. The production function implies that we can write:

$$\frac{dY}{dD} = \frac{\partial}{\partial K}F(K/N)\frac{\partial K}{\partial D} = r\frac{\partial K}{\partial D}$$

The current debt is roughly \$4 trillion, which is roughly \$13,000 per person. For $\partial K/\partial D = -0.60$, output declines by about \$1,000/year/person given marginal product of capital of 10%.

Finally, the same point can be made in reverse: policies that lead to large debt can be quite beneficial, regardless of their effect on the real interest rate. It is possible that some policies that raise the debt also have benefits that outweighed the costs of the debt. While more debt is bad because it requires lower spending on public goods and services or higher levels of distortionary taxation, there can be benefits from the tax cuts or spending increases that caused the increase in debt. And the benefits of a policy can outweigh the costs of raising debt. Depending on your politics, think Head Start, defense spending, or investment tax credits. What matters in each case is not the effect on interest rates, but the benefits and costs—inclusive of debt—that the policy causes.

3. Do We Care About the Effect of Debt?

We certainly care about the impact of any policy, as just noted. But the definition of debt is arbitrary. I make this point first in the context of measurement, using the example of the liabilities of the Social Security system. Then I argue that economic theory is not even clear about what debt is.[2]

Consider the U.S. Social Security and Medicare System (SSMS). Households pay into the system and are promised in return a pension and health insurance when they retire. The government could set aside contributions and use them to fund the future benefits of the contributors. But it has not and does not, so that current benefits are paid from current contributions.[3] Thus, the government has a commitment to pay resources to future retirees and does not have the assets to cover these future liabilities.

Compare these promises made by the SSMS to government debt. Debt is a commitment by the government to pay resources to bondholders, and the government does not have the assets to cover these future liabilities. Thus, the liabilities of the SSMS are just like debt, with the one exception that the government does not count these liabilities as debt.

Is this a purely academic point? Not at all. The implicit liabilities in the SSMS are larger than the current federal debt. And Figure 1 shows that at current benefit rates, the SSMS annual benefits are expected to increase dramatically. If the tax system remains stable, SSMS expenses

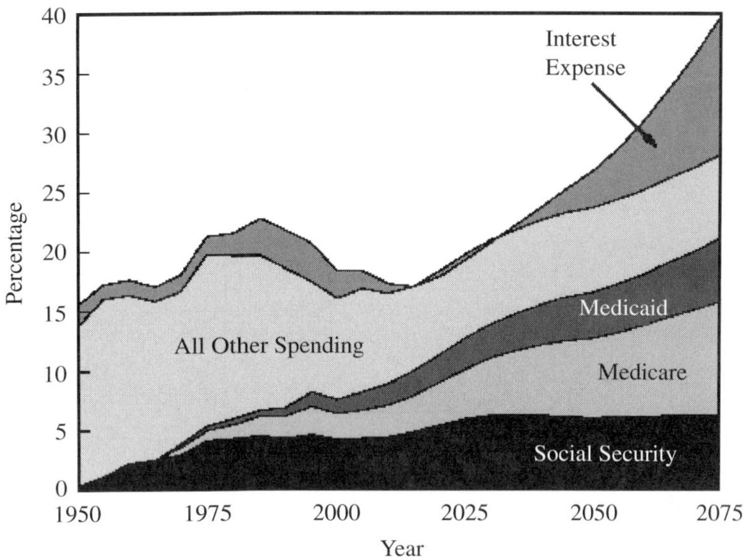

Figure 1
Federal outlays by type; as a percentage of GDP
Source: Congressional Budget Office (2002).

and interest on the official debt would exceed total federal government revenues in fifty years (Figures 1 and 2). Including SSMS liabilities in debt measures would not only increase the official debt but would make it vary quite differently. The official debt is a political construction, not an economic concept, and it can be radically changed by a change of definition. This issue presents a significant problem for empirical work based on the official measure of debt.

Further, this issue—that the definition of debt is arbitrary—really means that to measure the effect of a policy on interest rates correctly requires a model of the future path of distortions and benefits of any policy. This requires many more assumptions about the structure of the economy than we can confidently make—making the case that historical correlations as studied by this paper are useful. But the main ingredients at least are clear, and the parameter that the paper estimates is an amalgam of these ingredients.

The correlation between debt and interest rates is determined by whether debt changes due to changes in government spending, lump-sum taxation, or distortionary taxation. As a basic example, consider deterministic variation in government defense purchases in a Ricardian

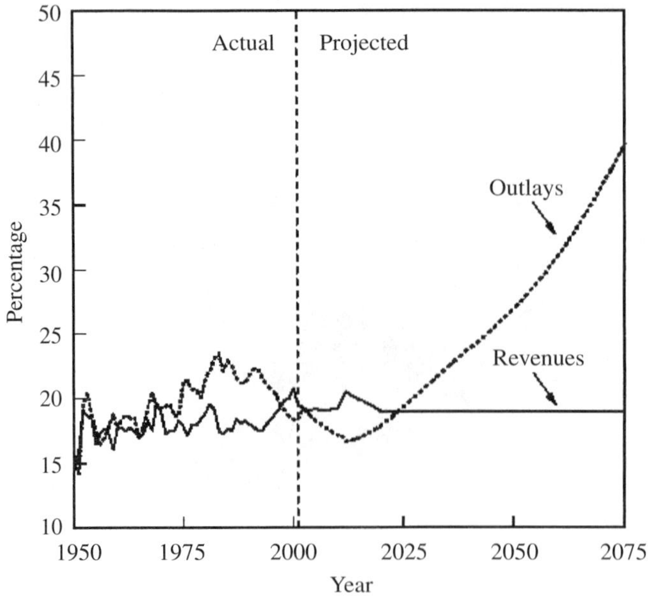

Figure 2
Federal revenues and outlays as a percentage of GDP
Source: Congressional Budget Office (2002).

economy with a fixed level of taxation. When government spending is high, deficits are high and the debt level rises, and there is high demand for goods today relative to goods tomorrow so that the real interest rate is high. But the debt is completely irrelevant for the capital stock and the prevailing interest rate. If instead debt were being raised and lowered by fluctuations in lump-sum taxes with a constant level of government spending, we would observe no correlation between interest rates and debt (ceteris paribus) because the interest rate would be constant (at least on the balanced growth path).

More generally how is debt reduced? Bohn (1991) shows that historically just under two-thirds of the U.S. debt has been eliminated by reductions in government spending (as a share of gross domestic product [GDP]) instead of increases in taxes. Thus, interest rates are raised by high debt because government spending is expected to be lower in the future and because taxes are expected to be higher.

Finally, the correlation between debt and interest rates depends on how distortionary taxes are. Other things being equal, the presence of less distortionary taxes makes fluctuations in debt less likely to affect the return on capital. An extreme example is the opportunity—readily available right now in the United States—to default on the debt. On the other hand, if all taxes were extremely distortionary, then debt could crowd out capital more than one for one if high debt meant that taxes had to be raised.

4. Conclusion: What Is Debt?

Consider a variant of the neoclassical model due to McGrattan and Prescott (2001), in which a price-taking representative household maximizes the present discounted value of utility from consumption (C) and leisure (l):

$$Max \sum_t \beta^t U(C_t, l_t)$$

subject to an intertemporal budget constraint:

$$\sum_t R_{0,t}\{C_t + V_t(s_{t+1} - s_t)\} = \sum_t R_{0,t}\{(1 - \tau_{div})d_t s_t + (1 - \tau_{per})(w_t N_t + INT_t) + T_t\}$$

where β is the discount factor, $R_{0,t}$ is the gross real interest rate—the price of output at time t relative to time 0, V_t is the value of a share of the capital stock, s_t is the number of shares the household owns, τ_{div} is the tax rate on dividends, d_t is the dividends per share, τ_{per} is the personal income tax rate, w_t is the wage rate, INT_t is interest on government debt, and T_t are lump-sum transfers from the government to the household. We assume that $U(C_t, l_t)$ is of the King-Plosser-Rebelo class of utility functions so that permanent changes in after-tax wages have no impact on labor supply (N).

Firms maximize the present discounted value of dividends, where dividends are the profits of the firm after corporate taxes:

$$d_t = (1 - \tau_{corp})\{f(K_t, N_t) - w_t N_t - \delta K_t\} - K_{t+1} + K_t$$

where τ_{corp} is the corporate tax rate; we assume that capital depreciates at rate δ. Finally, markets clear:

$$l_t + N_t = 1$$

$$C_t + (K_{t+1} - (1 - \delta)K_t) + G_t = F(K_t, N_t)$$

Let the economy start in steady state with fixed tax rates and debt $= 0$, such that the intertemporal budget constraint of the government is met. And, as in the United States, let the consumption share of output be greater than the labor share, so that net payments from firms to households are positive.

Consider a shock that raises debt (or consider two otherwise identical economies with different initial levels of debt). Does debt raise interest rates and crowd out capital? Not necessarily. The following three policies to balance the budget at $t = 0$ do not affect the time path of $\{Y, C, K\}$:

1. A permanent increase in τ_{div}
2. A permanent cut in transfers
3. A one-time cut in entitlements: eliminate payments to bondholders

Under scenarios 1 and 2, the debt remains high for some time and is slowly reduced. Under scenario 3, the debt is eliminated at time zero (this policy can also be called seigniorage). Thus, among these policies, neither the debt shock nor the level of debt has any effect on the real outcomes of the economy.[4]

These claims follow almost directly from the following three equilibrium conditions (see also Bradford, 1981):

$$R_{t,t+1}^{-1} = \frac{V_{t+1} + (1 - \tau_{div})d_{t+1}}{V_t}$$

$$R_{t,t+1}^{-1} = (1 - \tau_{corp})(F_1(K_t, N_t) - \delta) + 1$$

$$R_{t,t+1}^{-1} = \beta \frac{u_{1,t+1}}{u_{1,t}}$$

The third pins down $R_{t,t+1}^{-1}$ as a function of the discount rate. The second gives the capital–labor ratio as a function of τ_{corp} and $R_{t,t+1}^{-1}$. And the first gives the value of the capital stock as a function of $R_{t,t+1}^{-1}$ and d_t, which in turn is given by the fixed steady-state level of N, τ_{corp} and the already pinned down capital–labor ratio.

When are interest rates affected? The second equilibrium condition shows that debt would lead to an increase in the interest rate if households expected an increase in τ_{corp} to balance the budget. The interest rate—the rate of return to capital—is reduced by the corporate tax rate. In steady state, the capital stock is lower the higher τ_{corp}.

So what is debt? Debt is only a plan to take money from some people and give it to some people, sometimes even the same people. And the plan can be abandoned. There is nothing in tastes or technology that requires debt in the present to have any impact on the economy. But the interesting point for economic theory is that it seems to.

Notes

1. In this discussion, all percentages are given at annual rates and all interest rates are real.

2. Kotlikoff (2002) presents the general argument in the context of an overlapping generations model.

3. There is a modest surplus in the current Social Security trust fund, it is held in Treasury bonds.

4. It is also the case here that permanent changes in τ_{pers} are nondistortionary. But if we modeled human capital accumulation, then taxes on labor income would be capital taxes and so would be distortionary.

References

Bohn, Henning. (1991). Budget balance through revenue or spending adjustments? *Journal of Monetary Economics* 27:333–359.

Bradford, David F. (1981). The incidence and allocation effects of a tax on corporate distributions. *Journal of Public Economics* 15:1–22.

Congressional Budget Office. (2002). A 125-year picture of the federal government's share of the economy, 1950 to 2075. *Long-Range Fiscal Policy Brief*, No. 1 (June) (See: http://www.cbo.gov/showdoc.cfm?index=3521&sequence=0).

Council of Economic Advisers. (2003). *Economic Report of the President*. Washington, DC: Government Printing Office.

Kotlikoff, Laurence J. (2002). Generational Policy. In *Handbook of Public Economics*, Volume 4, A. J. Auerbach and M. Feldstein (eds.).

McGrattan, Ellen, and Edward Prescott. (2001). Taxes, regulations, and asset prices. NBER Working Paper No. 8623.

Comment

Matthew D. Shapiro
University of Michigan and NBER

Are cookies fattening? For every 2,850 calories one eats in excess of the steady-state caloric requirement for maintaining weight, one gains a pound. Suppose a cookie has 100 calories. So eating a cookie, all other things being equal, leads to a weight gain of 0.035 pound, a positive but small effect on weight. The 0.035 is the marginal effect of a cookie on weight. Engen and Hubbard's aim in this paper is to estimate a similar parameter, the marginal effect of federal debt on long-term interest rates. They survey the evidence and present new empirical estimates and theoretical calculations. Based on their analysis, they conclude, according to their preferred metric, that increasing the ratio of federal debt to GDP by 1 percentage point will increase long-term real interest rates by 0.035 percentage point, or 3.5 basis points. Hence, they characterize their results as showing that the marginal effect of federal debt on long-term interest rates is small but positive.

There is little to quarrel with in this estimate. It is in line with results found in a recent, careful study by Thomas Laubach (2003) of the Federal Reserve Board. Nonetheless, the paper does not tell the full story about the impact of federal debt on the interest rates and the economy in general. The main message of the paper is that changes in the federal debt have statistically significant but very small effects on real interest rates and, by extension, to the real economy. Though the authors are careful not to say so explicitly, the implication is that the public and policymakers should not be unduly concerned about the recent and projected increases in federal debt since 2001. Notwithstanding qualifications inserted in the paper, by focusing on the marginal effect of increasing debt, they leave the impression that the effects of federal debt are so small that the recent and persistent fiscal imbalances—from the tax cuts in each of the last three years, the slowdown in economic growth, the increase in military spending after 9/11, and the general abandonment of fiscal restraint in the rest of the budget (e.g., the agriculture bill of 2001 and the Medicare prescription drug bill)—are of no concern, at least insofar as they might affect borrowing costs and therefore investment. Likewise, the paper could be read to imply that the substantial progress made in reducing deficits and debt during the 1990s was of little consequence for economic performance.

What does the positive but small effect identified by Engen and Hubbard imply in practice about the effect of federal borrowing on interest rates? To answer this question, I return to my question, "Are cookies fattening?" As I already noted, if I eat a cookie, I gain 0.035 pound. That is only a very small fraction of my body weight, so I might conclude that cookies are not fattening. Yet eating one cookie is not really the issue if I am trying to watch my weight. My experience with cookies suggests that the right question is, What if I eat a cookie a day for a year in addition to my normal caloric intake? In that case, I will gain 365 times 0.035 pounds per day, which equals 12.8 pounds in a year. If I do this for 10 years.... Well, let's not go there. Based on these considerations, I would say that cookies are fattening.

Federal deficits have a similar implication for the federal debt as eating cookies does for weigh gain. They are persistent, so nibbles tend to cumulate. Consider the increase in the debt/GDP ratio in the 1980s. It rose from roughly one-quarter to one-half of GDP, an increase of 25 percentage points. As Benjamin Friedman notes, using the preferred estimate of Engen and Hubbard, this would increase long-term real interest rates by 25 times 3.5 basis points, which equals 87.5 basis points. Such an increase in interest rates will have major implications for the accumulation of capital and housing, for financial markets, and for the cost of financing the federal debt. With current policy, we appear to be repeating the experiment of the 1980s, that is, cutting taxes, increasing defense spending, and not restraining nondefense spending. The authors' estimates thus imply that current policy will lead to a noticeable, sustained increase in real interest rates.

Engen and Hubbard's estimates for the effect of borrowing on interest rates are very close to those found in several recent papers that carefully study the relationship between interest rates and federal borrowing. In particular, estimates by Thomas Laubach (2003) of the Federal Reserve Board point to only slightly higher marginal effects of debt on real long-term interest rates. Laubach finds large effects on interest rates of a percentage point increase in the *deficit*/GDP ratio, results that Engen and Hubbard confirm in their regressions. Engen and Hubbard downplay these larger point estimates, however, for the deficit. Yet as the authors hint in their discussion of the evidence, the big coefficient on the deficit is not inconsistent with the smaller coefficient on the debt. Deficits are persistent, so a current deficit implies increases for the debt in the medium run. Taking into account the persistence of the deficit and the difference in units, the estimates based on deficits and debt tell similar stories.

So the estimates presented by Engen and Hubbard are in line with those found in the literature. Why then do the Fed and the Brookings Institution agree that the recent shift in fiscal policy pushed long-term rates up by 50 to 100 basis points (see Gale and Potter, 2002), which is surely a substantial number that has noticeable real effects? As Gale and Orszag (2003) observe, this magnitude of increase in borrowing costs more relative to the offsets in the reductions in marginal rates in the 2001 bill in the cost of capital. What accounts for the difference in interpretation of the evidence is Engen and Hubbard's focus on percentage point movements in the debt/GDP ratio and inferred moves in the capital/GDP ratio, both of which are very misleading. I will show you this by taking the ingredients of Engen and Hubbard's analysis and embedding it in the Solow growth model, which for this application is a good approximation to what one would find with a dynamic general equilibrium (DGE) model. Using the Solow model will link the analysis to the national saving and investment rates, which are a better way to understand and quantify the economics rather than debt per se.

In implementing these calculations, I will embrace the details of Engen and Hubbard's analysis. I agree with them that modeling the saving rate is a good way to summarize the effects on capital accumulation of changes in government saving, even if the changes in national saving are not identical to the changes in government saving. That is, a 1% increase in the federal deficit might reduce national saving by less than 1% because of foreign capital flows or Ricardian increases in private saving. The current paper does not have anything new to say about these effects. To approximate them, consider, a 2 percentage point drop in national saving, which may arise, for example, from a 4 percentage point drop in federal saving that is partially offset by an increase in private saving. The purpose of using the Solow model is to get the stock-flow identities right and to calculate the dynamic general equilibrium effects of the change in the capital stock from the change in saving.

Let me start by considering steady-state changes in the saving rate. The Solow model is so familiar that I will not rehearse its equations for you. Let me tell you, however, what parameter values I use. The growth rate ($n + g$) is 4% per year, the rate of depreciation (δ) is 4% per year, the investment rate (s) is 20% of income, and the capital share (α) is 0.33. These parameters are totally conventional. The warranted growth rate of 4%, 1% for labor force, and 3% for technology is in line with most estimates. The depreciation rate of 4% matches Bureau of Economic Analysis (BEA) aggregates for the total net capital stock. (Like Engen and Hubbard, this capital stock and depreciation rate includes residential and nonresidential structures as well as business equipment.) The investment rate is a little high, but call me an optimist. These parameters loosely replicate U.S. aggregates. That is, they generate a capital/output ratio of 2.5 and a gross marginal product of capital of 13.2%. The capital/output ratio in the data is 2.7. The MPK of 13.2 is in line with estimates of the pretax gross return to capital.[1]

Now let's run several policy experiments through the Solow model. Consider economies where the steady-state saving rate (taken equal to the investment rate) was lower by 1, 2, or 4 percentage points. Table 1 shows the steady-state effects of these changes in the saving rate. Such permanent reductions of the saving rate have very large effects on the steady-state marginal product of capital (these are percentage points, not basis points) and on the capital stock itself. For a 1% permanent cut in the saving rate, the marginal product would increase 70 basis points and the capital stock would fall 7.4%. Because of diminishing marginal product of capital, the effects of larger drops in saving are more than proportional. These effects are very large and would correspond to significant decreases in consumption per capita on a permanent basis, though there would be increases in consumption along the transition path. In thinking about the prospect of fiscal deficits for the

Table 1
Steady-state effect of changing savings on MPK: Solow model

Change in savings rate (fraction)	Change in MPK (percentage points)	Change in K (percent)
−0.01	0.7	−7.4
−0.02	1.5	−14.6
−0.04	3.3	−28.4

Table 2
Steady-state effect of changing savings on MPK: Solow model

Change in savings rate (fraction)	Change in MPK (percentage points)	Change in K (percent)
−0.00036	0.024	−0.27
−0.00134	0.090	−1.0
−0.00200	0.135	−1.5

distant future, these calculations give an estimate of the permanent effects.

Why are Engen and Hubbard less concerned? First, their static, partial equilibrium calculation significantly understates the steady-state effects. Second, the perturbations they consider lead to only very small changes in national saving in a steady-state analysis. Let me illustrate these points by asking what change in saving in steady state would generate results that Engen and Hubbard highlight. First, what change in saving would generate the steady-state change in MPK of 2.4 basis points that they feature in their discussion? This calculation is shown in Table 2. To get this change, the saving rate would have to fall by 36/100,000. First, this is a very small change in the saving rate. Second, note that the capital stock does not fall by nearly 1%. To get the capital stock to fall by 1%, the drop in the saving rate must be larger, 136/100,000, but still very small. Finally, to get the capital/output ratio to fall by 1%, the saving rate has to fall by 2/1,000. This is the experiment that Engen and Hubbard have in mind in column 1 of Table 1. Note two points. First, again this drop in the capital stock is generated by a very small decline in saving. Second, dynamic general equilibrium effects of this drop leading to a 1% drop in the K/Y ratio lead to a 13.5 basis point increase in the MPK, not a 2.4 increase.

Now the steady-state calculations of the Solow model likely overstate the effect of fiscal deficits because they are based on permanent changes in national saving and investment. Also, they refer to effects long in the future that may have little relevance even for current long-term interest rates. I will address both these points later in this discussion by considering the dynamic response to a realistic path of deficits in the Solow model. Nonetheless, these calculations are the right theoretical benchmark for starting the discussion of persistent federal dissaving and tell a much different story from that of the authors' static calculations.

Before returning to the dynamic general equilibrium impact of a realistic path for deficits, let me raise some additional issues about the paper. There are other factors, hard to control for in regressions that affect the relationship between debt or deficits and interest rates. One of the most important ones is monetary policy. Much *Macroeconomics Annual* ink has been spilled in the past and will continue to be spilled in the future about how monetary policy affects the real interest rate. But it is pretty clear that when the Fed changes nominal short rates, the real short rate moves almost one for one. And these changes in the short rates have a surprisingly strong impact on longer-term rates. Hence, whether the Fed is accommodating a fiscal expansion or leaning against it will have a significant effect on the interest rate/deficit linkage. The Fed will behave differently given different circumstances, so this effect is not systematic. For example, in 1993, we had tightening fiscal policy and accommodative monetary policy. In 2003, we had loosening fiscal policy and accommodative monetary policy. Perhaps these effects could be controlled for in the regressions by including a variable that indicated the deviation of the federal funds rate from its long-term target. Doing so would be hard, however, because it is hard to imagine a variable that is more endogenous. Nonetheless, the point that the stance of monetary policy has an important impact on the real rate and that monetary policy and fiscal policy are not unrelated should not be lost.

The long-term stance of monetary policy is also important for fiscal policy and its link to the real interest rate. Around the world, it is fairly clear the central banks have new and firm commitments to low inflation. For fiscal policy, this means that there is little prospect for inflating away accumulated debt in the future. This places an added constraint on fiscal authorities such that, if we are to stay out of scary regions predicted by the fiscal theory of the price level, the fiscal balance must be achieved in the future by raising taxes or lowering spending.

This point about monetary policy disciplining fiscal policy leads to a more general point about deficits: they might be persistent, but they are not permanent. Though the debt/GDP ratio in the United States has some important low-frequency swings, it has stayed under control because we have been willing to pay off the debt we have accumulated by fighting wars and have corrected previous fiscal imbalances. For example, a combination of higher tax rates and stronger-then-expected economic growth during the Clinton administration brought the debt/

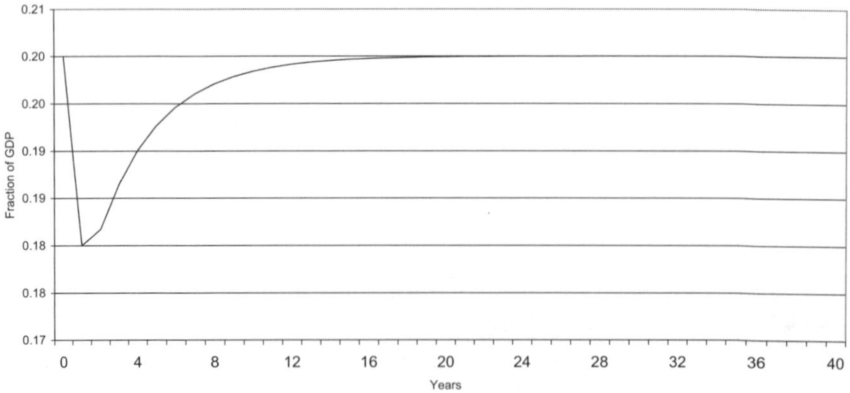

Figure 1
Dynamics of a shock to savings

GDP ratio down (see figures in the paper). It has started to rise again since 2001, but if previous experience repeats itself, some future administration will tackle the fiscal imbalances that we see currently. At some point, presumably when the economy is stronger, political attention will shift to the deficit, as it did in the mid-1980s to 1990s.

Or maybe not. If it becomes clear that the nation does not have the will to pay its bills over the long haul, interest rates are likely to rise sharply. With the looming liabilities associated with the aging of the population, it is an open question how this will play out. But for now, financial markets are telling us that they do expect the fiscal problems to be addressed.

The data bear out the point that the deficits are persistent but not permanent. Using quarterly data, I estimated a simple AR(4) model of the deficit/GDP ratio. Figure 1 presents the dynamic response to a 0.02 of GDP drop in federal saving. (Controlling for the cycle does not affect the picture much.) This shows persistent deficits, but deficits that correct themselves over a decade or so. (These estimates perhaps somewhat understate the persistence of deficits because I have not corrected the AR coefficients for the downward bias. The largest quarterly autoregressive root is 0.93.) Hence, the time series evidence is consistent with a view that deficits, though persistent, are not permanent. What if we run this path through the Solow model? I think it corresponds well to what might be expected from the current fiscal imbalances. The impulse is a drop in saving of 0.02 of GDP. This is less than half the

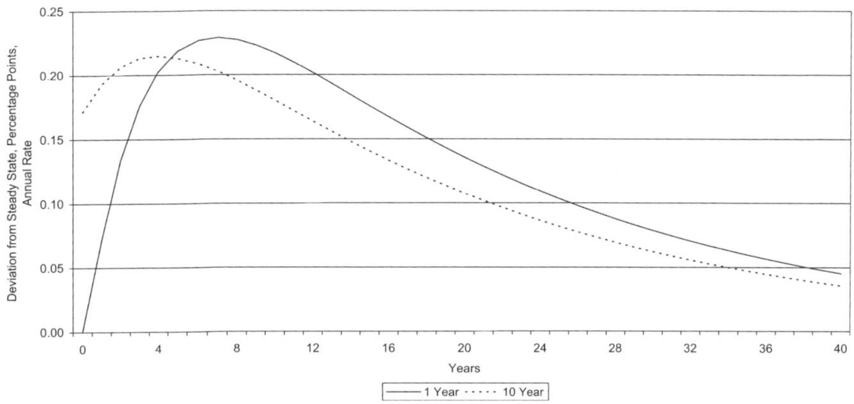

Figure 2
Response of MPK to shock to savings, Solow model

size of current deficits, so it allows for some private response to damp the effect of the deficit on national saving.

Figure 2 shows the MPK implications for this dynamic change in the saving rate in Figure 1. The solid line is the one-period MPK. The dashed line is the 10-year forward average—a simple way to approximate the 10-year interest rate that is featured in the paper. These calculations show that the 10-year rate increases by about 17 basis points on impact. The capital stock is maximally affected in year 8; the 10-year rate peaks somewhat earlier at about an increase of 22 basis points.

Note how much smaller these effects are than a permanent reduction in the saving rate shown in Table 2. That deficits typically self-correct substantially damps their effect. Yet I view the simulation in Figure 2 as somewhat conservative. It assumes that fiscal discipline will be restored at the historical rate. Given that there is no prospect in the near run for cutting spending, especially with growing national security concerns, and little willingness either to pay for our increased defense, increased drug benefits, or future liability to retirees, a more realistic path of deficits would show higher interest rates.

Finally, I want to conclude by saying that the tight focus on the link between interest rates and federal saving of this paper misses the larger picture. First, even if there were no interest rate effects (e.g., because foreigners elastically supplied saving to finance our deficit), these loans will have to be repaid. We are simply borrowing from the future. Engen and Hubbard know this point well. That they do not make it, however, testifies to the very narrow focus of this paper and its very narrow implications for the economic effects of debt.

Second, calculations based on the Cobb-Douglas production function and disembodied technology, such as those presented in the paper and I have mirrored, probably understate the cost of squeezing current investment. If there are growth rate effects of capital accumulation, or technology is embodied in new capital, the cost of deferring investment could be very much higher than in standard estimates.

Note

1. The empirical analysis of the paper concerns the Treasury bond rate, which is riskless except for inflation risk. The theoretical model of the paper and this comment concerns the return to capital, which earns a substantial risk premium. An implicit assumption of the paper is that changes in the capital/output ratio in the range considered do not affect the risk premium, so that changes in marginal product of capital map one-for-one into the interest rate.

References

Gale, William G., and Peter Orszag. (2003). Economic effects of sustained budget deficits. *National Tax Journal* 56(3, September):463–485.

Gale, William G., and Samara R. Potter. (2002). An economic evaluation of the Economic Growth and Tax Relief Reconciliation Act of 2001. *National Tax Journal* 55(1, March):133–186.

Laubach, Thomas. (2003). New evidence on the interest rate effects of budget deficits and debt. Board of Governors of the Federal Reserve System. Finance and Economics Discussion Series 2003-12. May.

Discussion

In response to the discussants' comments, R. Glenn Hubbard emphasized that the paper he and Engen wrote was not about the effects on interest rates or on the economy, and that it was never their intention for anybody to infer that a small effect on interest rates was a small effect on the economy. In his intervention, Engen also said that the paper was only about government debt and interest rates, and he acknowledged that there might be other important economic effects but that they were not the topic of this work. He remarked that Jonathan Parker's comment on national income, consumption, and wealth was very interesting and that they would consider using them, but that it was not the subject they were trying to address in their paper. Hubbard then said, and Engen later agreed, that the relation of government spending versus taxation was very important and that one would expect that in almost any model an increase in government spending would raise the real interest rate. However, in a period when military shocks dominate fiscal positions, government spending would give little information about deficit shock. He quoted a work by Evans and Marshall in which they made the argument that tax shocks or deficit shocks did not appear to have much impact; the impact was coming from military spending. Hubbard also acknowledged that the point about incentive effects was very important because some tax changes had stronger incentive effects than others.

Eric M. Engen addressed the issue raised by both discussants that when there are savings inflows, interest may not change at that time but it will have to be paid some time in the future. Engen pointed out that while that was true and was normally regarded as a bad outcome, people often missed the fact that players in the economy, policymakers, and society itself had decided to make an intertemporal tradeoff. They enjoyed higher levels of consumption today for lower levels of income later.

Engen went on to say that he and Hubbard wanted to work more on identifying the expectations of the market and economic agents about what policymakers were going to do in the future. This was complicated, however, starting with the decision about which indicators to use and how to build those expectations into a simple reduced form of regression or some kind of vector autoregression (VAR) framework.

Several of the participants raised the issue of the proportion of government debt that was in the hands of foreigners. Graciela Kaminsky was impressed by the increase from basically zero to about 35% of the debt. She believed this was a reflection of the differences between globalization in the 1950s and globalization in the 1990s and could explain significantly the structural stability on the regressions that were estimated in the paper. Kaminsky also said that it might be interesting to look at the different effects in the earlier and later parts of the sample on the current account and whether deficits were likely to be financed by the rest of the world. The authors responded to this issue that although it would be interesting to determine this and they actually tried it, their sample size was too small and only spanned from 1976 to 2003. Engen added that precisely because of sample-size issues, they had added foreign purchases of Treasuries as one of their macro variables to try to control for the differences over time in the longer regressions. He also pointed out that most of the integration has taken place in a short period of time and that led to small-sample-size issues.

On the other hand, Robert Gordon did not consider there to be a break in the post–World War II period. According to him, the deficit–gross domestic product (GDP) ratio consistently decreased up until the early 1980s, only to rise during the Reagan–Bush period (which for him runs from 1982 to 2000) and then decline again. Gordon was also concerned about whether foreigners would finance the U.S. debt forever. He pointed out the fact that every year the United States had net international liabilities equal to 25% of GDP, and yet it had negative net investment income in the current account. According to Gordon, this responded to the fact that foreigners invested in low-yield government debt. Stephen Cecchetti also commented on the large proportion of debt owned by foreigners but warned about the fact that this only reflected official holdings and that private holdings might not be as easy to identify. He said that if a private brokerage firm such as Merrill Lynch were to be holding U.S. Treasuries for a foreign investor, this would appear as domestic holdings.

Kenneth Rogoff and Cecchetti both commented on the variations in debt and deficits across countries, and the similarities in interest rates. Rogoff believed that the similarities in interest rates responded to highly integrated global capital markets, and the fact that this accounted for only one-quarter of global GDP led to the expectation of a small interest rate effect. On the other hand, Cecchetti did not believe that interest rates were similar at all despite the relatively high correlation in the sample. He cited differences of between 2 and 4 percentage points, which he considered quite large on a medium-term interest rate. Engen responded that this is true if one looked at the most-current rates, but that if one looked at different countries and their fiscal positions, it would become evident that some of the countries with the worst fiscal positions, like Japan, were at the low end of that range and some of the better ones were at the high end. One had to look beyond real interest rates and see that some of the discrepancy did not seem to correlate with their fiscal positions.

Rogoff and Benjamin Friedman commented on the issue of whether the effects of interest rates are small or large. Rogoff agreed with the discussants that there seemed to be a legacy of the Barro debt neutrality regressions in which interest rates were small and therefore it did not really matter that much. However, the calibrations in the paper showed that this was wrong and that in fact one could get fairly large welfare effects from small interest rate effects. He recommended that the authors could say that their calibration showed that even though deficits could be catastrophic, this would not come up in interest rates, instead of simply stating in the paper they were not claiming deficits were bad. Friedman was concerned with the definition of a small effect and a large one. The authors, he said, presented their base case as a 1% increase in the debt ratio, and that did not seem to be a lot. However, he cited the example of the Reagan–Bush Sr. period, in which the debt–GDP ratio was raised by 20 to 25%, and if one were to multiply this by 3.5 basis points, one would obtain an increase of between 70 and 80 basis points, which was very large for U.S. real interest rates. This would be an example of why it could not really be said that the paper was purely about real interest rates and not about the effect of the capital stock because *small* and *large* were relative terms. If one were to look at the effect on the capital stock, and the analysis was grounded in a production function with little curvature, small changes in rates would become large. He recommended eliminating the adjectives *small* and *large* to add credibility to the paper. Engen responded to this issue by saying that they presented the result as one percentage point in the debt–GDP ratio for purposes of comparability with other studies that present it in the same way.

Friedman also considered it odd that the regressors in Tables 2, 3, and 4 included the flow of removal of securities from the market by either foreigners or the domestic central bank as purchases and did not include the flow of the Treasury's putting new securities in the market. Engen responded that they had tried to simplify so they would have less changes and that two of the specifications were changes in debt, so classifying them as purchases was appropriate. If they had been classified as holdings, the estimated effect of federal debt on the interest rate would remain unchanged. However, he acknowledged the need for greater consistency. Hubbard added that he agreed that it was silly to hide behind interest rates and that the point of the discussion should be future tax burdens.

Valerie Ramey questioned the reference to the neoclassical model in the paper because it departed significantly from what she believed the neoclassical model to be. She said that what mattered were government purchases, not how they were financed, even if they were financed with distortionary taxes. There should not be a permanent effect in real interest rates even with a permanent increase in government purchases. When government purchases increase, there is a negative wealth effect that leads to a decrease in leisure, which in turn leads to an increase in the marginal product of capital and higher interest rates in the short run and an increase in capital stock that responds to an increase in government spending. Eventually, interest rates would go back to their steady state. She then said that work carried out by Matthew Shapiro and herself supported this with empirical evidence, and she recommended a more developed model in which transition dynamics were included in addition to the steady state.

Fumio Hayashi wanted to know if the authors were drawing from the Investment-Saving/Liquidity of Money (IS/LM) model used for the Congressional Budget Office (CBO) forecasts, which assumed the effect of deficits on interest rates in their regression of interest rates on the CBO forecasts of debts and deficits. Eric Engen responded that the CBO makes projections of debt and deficit, but the forward-looking interest rates were different. They were a constructed five-year-ahead measure of the ten-year Treasury rates. He explained that the CBO did not use that forecast for interest rates and that the problem might arise if the markets were really taking the CBO projections of debt and deficit seriously, in which case those projections might be determining interest rates.

Monetary Policy in Real Time

Domenico Giannone, Lucrezia Reichlin, and Luca Sala
ECARES, Université Libre de Bruxelles; ECARES, Université Libre de Bruxelles, and CEPR; and IGIER and Universitá Bocconi

1. Introduction

It is widely recognized that the job of a central banker is a hard one because of the uncertainty under which policy decisions have to be made. There is uncertainty about the current state of the economy due to delays with which statistics are released and to the preliminary nature of the first releases, uncertainty about the nature of exogenous shocks, and uncertainty about the model (i.e., about the mechanisms that govern the interactions among policy, private-sector expectations, and economic performance).

Facing the complex problem of conducting policy under uncertainty, however, the central banker seems to respond systematically to (possibly filtered) output and inflation (Taylor, 1993, 1999; Clarida, Galí, and Gertler, 2000). Although the exact form of this rule has been the subject of debate, and although real-time estimates differ from the simple ex-post Taylor fit (e.g., Orphanides et al., 2000; Orphanides, 2001, 2003; Rudebusch, 2002), Taylor rules, defined in the broad sense, have been found to be a good characterization of monetary policy in the medium run.

This paper asks whether this finding reflects the conduct of monetary policy or the structure of the U.S. economy. We argue that the simplicity of the empirical monetary policy rule is a consequence of the simplicity of the U.S. economy and that a simple rule would have emerged, in ex-post analysis, even if policy had responded to variables other than output and inflation. From a real-time perspective, on the other hand, a rule in terms of forecastable contemporaneous and future output and inflation is observationally equivalent to a rule that responds to large movements in all real and nominal variables.

Simplicity, we find, takes three forms. First, only two shocks drive the U.S. macroeconomy. These shocks explain the fundamental business-cycle behavior of all key variables and, in particular, of the federal funds rate, inflation, and output.

Second, the two orthogonal shocks can be robustly identified as generating, respectively, medium- and long-run output dynamics and medium- and long-run inflation dynamics. Medium- and long-term inflation and output, therefore, capture well the two-dimensional space generated by the two shocks.

Third, once we extract from our series the medium- and long-run signal, we find that the leading-lagging structure linking gross domestic product (GDP) to other real variables is very simple and there is a lot of synchronization within the real bloc. The same is true for inflation and the nominal bloc.

Because two shocks explain the fundamental movements of the macroeconomy, and as long as the Fed responds systematically to these fundamental movements, the estimated rule would result in some version of the Taylor rule, i.e., as a function linking the federal funds rate to some transformation of output and inflation. Since the two large shocks are nominal and real and they generate a simple dynamics in the responses of, respectively, nominal and real variables, the transformation (the filters on output and inflation) has to be simple.

Simplicity is a consequence of the nature of the U.S. economy and does not necessarily reflect simple policy. Our claims about simplicity are based on the analysis of two panels of time series starting in 1970: the panel of the Greenbooks forecasts, i.e., the forecasts prepared by the Fed's staff to inform the Federal Open Market Committee (FOMC) meetings (available up to 1996), and a panel of 200 time series that roughly corresponds to what is used by the Fed in its short-term forecasting exercise (up to 2003).

We bring several pieces of evidence.

For both panels, two principal components explain more than 60% of the total variance and over 70% of the variance of key variables, such as the federal funds rate, output, industrial production, inflation measures (these percentages are even higher at medium- and long-run frequencies). This is not a surprising result, given strong comovements between economic variables (see, for example, Sargent and Sims, 1977; Stock and Watson, 2002; Giannone, Reichlin, and Sala, 2002; and Uhlig, 2003). It suggests that the stochastic dimension of the U.S. economy is two.

This finding is confirmed by a real-time forecasting exercise. The projection on two factors extracted from our large panel produces forecasts of the GDP growth rate and inflation comparable with the Greenbook forecasts and a forecast of the federal funds rate up to two quarters ahead, which is in line with that of the future market. Our analysis extends the forecasting exercise conducted in Bernanke and Boivin (2003) and Stock and Watson (1999) and brings new interpretation. Our forecast exercise mimics the real-time analysis conducted by the Fed in the sense that we use (as much as possible) sequential information sets that were available historically. (On the concept of real-time analysis, see Diebold and Rudebusch, 1991; Croushore and Stark, 1999; and Orphanides, 2001.) Since it is widely recognized that the Greenbook forecasts and future market forecasts are hard to beat, this is a remarkable result.

The good forecasting performance of the two-shocks model suggests that the role for judgmental action is small and that the Fed, on average, disregards movements that are idiosyncratic and not too correlated with the fundamental changes in the economy. Of course, the Fed may have reasons to respond, at particular times, to idiosyncratic events. However, if the Fed responded often to particular episodes generating idiosyncratic dynamics on exchange rate or financial markets, for example, our forecast based on two factors would be much poorer.

Finally, the ex-ante and ex-post structural analysis of shocks and propagation mechanisms, based on a novel identification procedure that exploits the cross-sectional information in our large panel, unravels common characteristics of the nominal and real side of the economy and indicates that the bulk of the dynamics of real variables is explained by the same shock, while nominal variables, at medium-long-run frequencies, are mainly explained by a shock orthogonal to it. The ex-ante analysis focuses on particular historical events of large inflation and output movements (recessions), which are the episodes in which the Fed moves aggressively and are therefore the more informative.

Our results suggest that a rule in terms of two variables is not identified uniquely. This might be bad news for econometricians, but it is good news for real-time monetary policy because, by tracking any forecastable measure of real activity and price dynamics, it does not leave out any other dimension of the fundamentals.

Finally, an implication of our result of near-orthogonality of output and inflation is that, while the dimension of the economy is two, the dimension of the policy problem is one. Although we cannot rule out that this dichotomy may itself be the result of monetary policy, it is quite striking that real-nominal orthogonality is also a feature of the Fed's model that produces the Greenbooks forecasts. If this were really an exogenous feature of the economy, we would conclude not only that the U.S. economy is simple, but also that the job of the central banker is easier than one may think!

The paper is organized as follows. Section 2 investigates the question on the number of shocks in the U.S. economy analyzing both the panel of the Greenbook forecasts and a large panel of monthly time series on about 200 monthly variables since 1970. Section 3 studies the response of the federal funds rate to the exogenous shocks while Section 5 draw implications on the form of the policy function. Section 6 concludes.

2. The Dimension of the Greenbook Model and of the U.S. Economy

Macroeconomic variables comove, especially at business-cycle frequencies and in the long run. This implies that the multivariate dynamics of a large set of macroeconomic variables is driven by few large shocks. This feature might be obscured by short-run dynamics, typically reflecting measurement errors, poorly correlated across variables, and by the fact that the dynamics are not perfectly synchronized across time series, but they can be recovered by simple statistical methods. The degree of comovement can be measured by the percentage of the variance captured by the first few dynamic principal components or by checking the goodness of fit of the projection of the variables of interest onto principal components. Since macroeconomic series are autocorrelated, what we are interested in is the approximate *dynamic rank*, i.e., the approximate rank of the spectral density of the panel. Principal components computed from the latter are linear combinations of present, past, and future observations rather than contemporaneous standard principal components (see Brillinger, 1981; Forni et al., 2000).

Here we are dealing with two panels. First, a panel of about 200 series of monthly variables (only GDP and GDP deflator are quarterly), whose structure is illustrated by Table 1. (The appendixes provide a more detailed description of the data and of data transformations.)

Table 1
Structure of the panel

Category	# series	Category	# series
Industrial production	21	Wages	10
Capacity utilization	8	Import and export	3
Labor markets	32	Surveys	12
Consumption spending	13	Money and loans	16
Inventories and orders	15	Prices	28
Financial markets	16	Miscellaneous	6
Interest rates	10		

Surveys, industrial production series, labor market variables, and a number of other series labeled as miscellaneous are typically the variables used by the Fed to nowcast and forecast GDP. We have added prices and monetary and financial data (including exchange rates) to cover the nominal side of the economy.

Our second panel is that of fifteen selected variables from the Greenbook forecasts.[1] This is a subsample of the forecasts prepared by the board of governors at the Federal Reserve for the meetings of the FOMC. They are published in correspondence with the dates of the meetings (roughly every six weeks) and refer to quarterly data. Because Greenbook's forecasts are made publicly available with a five-year delay, our data set ends in 1996. We consider meetings closer to the middle of each quarter (four releases out of eight) and have selected the fifteen variables for which forecasts are available since 1978 and are reported up to four quarters ahead. This panel mainly contains forecasts of real variables, with less than a third representing nominal variables. To understand the structure of our data sets, let us define $z_{t|v}$ as the vector of the Greenbook forecasts computed at time v for observations at time $t = v-2, v-1, v, v+1, \ldots, v+4$. If $t > v$, we have the forecasts; for $t = v$, we have the nowcasts; for $t < v$, the backcasts. For example, at $t = v-1$, we have the first release of GDP and the final estimate of employment.

The same indexes can be used for the vintages of the panel of the 200 time series; let us define it as $x_{t|v}$.

Let us first consider the panel $x_{t|v}$, with $v = 2003Q4$. This is the last available vintage on the 200 time series.

To study the degree of collinearity in the panel, we compute, for each element $x_{it\,|\,v}$, $i = 1, \ldots, n$, and for each $q = 1, 2, \ldots, n$, the q

Table 2
Percentage of variance explained by the first five dynamic principal components on $x_{t\,|\,2003Q4}$, selected variables

	$q = 1$	$q = 2$	$q = 3$	$q = 4$	$q = 5$
Average	0.49	0.63	0.71	0.77	0.82
Real GDP	0.63	0.74	0.77	0.83	0.86
Sales	0.71	0.77	0.83	0.86	0.88
Personal consumption expenditures	0.47	0.63	0.71	0.76	0.82
Services	0.41	0.55	0.61	0.66	0.74
Construction	0.48	0.61	0.70	0.76	0.82
Employment	0.85	0.91	0.93	0.95	0.95
Industrial production index	0.88	0.93	0.94	0.95	0.96
Capacity utilization rate	0.89	0.93	0.94	0.95	0.96
GDP implicit deflator	0.44	0.71	0.79	0.83	0.87
CPI	0.55	0.76	0.85	0.89	0.92
Wages	0.21	0.45	0.57	0.68	0.73
FFR	0.57	0.72	0.78	0.82	0.87

dimensional linear combination of present, past, and future observations $k_q(L)x_{t|v}$ such that the following mean squared error is minimized:

$$\text{MSE}_i(q) = \text{E}\{x_{it\,|\,v} - \text{Proj}[x_{it\,|\,v}\,|\,k_q(L)x_{t|v}]\}^2$$

This quantity will give us, for each variable, the variance explained by the q dynamic principal components (DPC). The average of these quantities over $i, 1/n\sum_i \text{MSE}_i(q)$, gives us the variance explained for the whole panel (see Brillinger, 1981).

We are interested in how close the dynamic covariance of the panel (spectral density) is to rank two. If it were reasonably close, this would imply that the projection of the variables onto the first two dynamic principal components will give a good fit and that two macroeconomic shocks generate most of the dynamics of the variables.

Table 2 reports the results for some selected variables (for $t = v$) and the results for the sum of the mean squared errors over all variables and for principal components[2] (with $q = 1, 2, \ldots, 5$). Two principal components explain more than 60% of the variance of each selected variable and of the whole panel. Key macroeconomic variables such as GDP, industrial production, employment, price indexes, and the federal funds rate show percentages way above the average, implying that they strongly comove with the rest of the economy.

Table 3
Percentage of variance explained by the first five dynamic principal components on $z_{t|v}$

	Number of DPC				
	$q=1$	$q=2$	$q=3$	$q=4$	$q=5$
$t=v-2$	0.49	0.69	0.80	0.86	0.91
$t=v-1$	0.53	0.72	0.82	0.87	0.91
$t=v$	0.53	0.74	0.84	0.89	0.93
$t=v+1$	0.54	0.77	0.86	0.92	0.95
$t=v+2$	0.54	0.77	0.87	0.92	0.95
$t=v+3$	0.57	0.79	0.88	0.92	0.95
$t=v+4$	0.53	0.77	0.87	0.92	0.95

If variables comove, the same must be true, in general, for the forecasts, even if model misspecification could induce decorrelation in some cases. Tables 3 and 4 report results describing the degree of comovements in the panel of the Greenbook forecasts for different horizons.

The principal component analysis of the Greenbook forecasts shows that the percentage of the variance explained by two principal components is larger than for the panel of the observations. This is not surprising because forecasting implies smoothing idiosyncratic dynamics that are typically highly volatile and unforecastable.

These results tell us that, to understand macroeconomic dynamics, we need to study the effect of few shocks only. Few shocks also explain the dynamics of the Greenbook forecasts.

More formal statistical analysis, along the lines of Forni et al. (2000) could be used to select the number of pervasive shocks for these panels. In this paper, however, since our goal is to understand the empirical success of the Taylor rule, which is expressed in term of two variables, we will follow a different route: fix the dimension of the economy at $q=2$ and, having made this choice, study the forecasting performance and structural impulse responses with a two-shocks model.[3]

In their seminal paper, Sargent and Sims (1977) used a panel of eleven monthly time series from 1950 to 1970 for the U.S. economy. They obtained a result similar to what we found in this paper and in Giannone, Reichlin, and Sala (2002) for a large panel of U.S. quarterly data from 1982 to 2001. The two-shocks finding appears to be a robust result, at least for the U.S. economy.

Table 4
Percentage of variance explained by the first two dynamic principal components on $z_{t|v}$, selected variables

	$t = v - 2$	$t = v - 1$	$t = v$	$t = v + 1$	$t = v + 2$	$t = v + 3$	$t = v + 4$
Real GDP	0.84	0.85	0.85	0.88	0.88	0.86	0.84
Final sales	0.72	0.75	0.84	0.83	0.78	0.83	0.81
Personal consumption expenditures	0.75	0.76	0.63	0.75	0.82	0.84	0.85
Services	0.38	0.70	0.59	0.58	0.64	0.67	0.68
Business fixed inventory	0.57	0.72	0.70	0.69	0.58	0.68	0.71
Residential structures	0.73	0.72	0.74	0.74	0.66	0.64	0.64
Government consumption and investment	0.28	0.34	0.36	0.42	0.50	0.41	0.32
Unemployment rate	0.74	0.74	0.76	0.77	0.78	0.87	0.87
Industrial production index	0.76	0.71	0.72	0.80	0.85	0.86	0.84
Capacity utilization rate	0.74	0.75	0.83	0.85	0.79	0.85	0.83
GDP implicit deflator	0.82	0.81	0.85	0.87	0.92	0.92	0.93
CPI	0.74	0.74	0.81	0.90	0.90	0.85	0.92
Output per hour	0.68	0.75	0.68	0.77	0.76	0.79	0.61
Compensation per hour	0.73	0.72	0.81	0.78	0.82	0.86	0.85
Unit labor cost	0.85	0.78	0.88	0.88	0.88	0.89	0.92

2.1 *Forecasting Output, Inflation, and the Federal Funds Rate with Two Factors Extracted from Many Time Series*

The descriptive analysis above suggests that output variables, aggregate price indexes, and the federal funds rate exhibit a higher than average degree of commonality: more than 70% of the variance of these variables can be explained by a projection on two aggregates.[4] This in turn suggests that a models with two shocks should be empirically successful in explaining the federal funds rate.

In this section, we will produce forecasts of the federal funds rate using two orthogonal aggregate shocks extracted from our panel. We take the results of this forecast as a benchmark, i.e., the best we can obtain from a projection on a two-dimensional span. We expect to obtain results reasonably close to those of the private-market forecasts (the futures).

The same strategy will be used to forecast output and inflation. Given our results on the dimension of the Greenbook forecasts, we expect to obtain results similar to those reported in the Greenbook.

The forecasting exercise is a pseudo real-time experiment in which we try to mimic as closely as possible the real-time analysis performed by the Fed when forecasting, at each period of time, on the basis of different vintages of data sets.[5] The experiment is real time because we consider the releases on GDP and GDP deflator specific to each vintage and because each vintage has missing data information at the end of the sample reflecting the calendar of data releases. This allows us to reproduce, each month within the quarter, the typical end of the sample unbalance faced by the Fed; due to the lack of synchronization of these releases, missing data are more or less numerous depending on the series considered. The experiment is pseudo because we do not have real-time information for variables other than GDP and GDP deflator.[6]

For each variable of interest, we write the forecast (or the nowcast) as:

$$x_{it\,|\,v}^{*} = \text{Proj}[x_{it\,|\,v} \,|\, \overline{span}(u_{t-k}, k \geq 0)]$$

where $u_t = [u_{1t}\ u_{2t}]'$ is the two-dimensional vector of the common shocks (normalized to be orthogonal white noise) estimated from the following model on the vector $x_{t|v}$ of the variables of the panel:

$$x_{t|v} = \Lambda F_t + \xi_{t|v}$$

$$F_t = AF_{t-1} + Bu_t$$

where F_t is the $r \times 1$ $(r \geq 2)$ vector of the static factors, $\Lambda = [\Lambda_1', \ldots, \Lambda_n']'$ is the $n \times r$ matrix of the loadings, B is a $r \times q$ matrix, and $\xi_{t|v}$ is the n-dimensional stationary vector process of the idiosyncratic component with covariance matrix $\mathrm{E}(\xi_{t|v}\xi_{t|v}') = \Psi$. We assume that the idiosyncratic components are weakly cross-correlated.[7]

Having set the dimension of u_t to be two, we identify the dimension of F_t, r, by statistical criteria.[8] Notice that, while the dimension of u_t identifies the stochastic dimension of the economy (the number of common shocks), the dimension of $F_t(r)$, depends on the heterogeneity of the lag structure of the propagation mechanisms of those shocks. Typically, in a dynamic economy, $r > q$.

It is important to note that, to be able to express our forecasting equation in terms of a one-sided filter on the two-dimensional vector of the common shocks, we assume implicitly that they can be recovered from the past of F_t of dim $r > q$ (see Remark 4 in Appendix 6.1). This assumption is reasonable, provided that there are enough leading variables in the panel and that r is sufficiently large (see Forni et al., 2003). Under this assumption, we can write the model for x_t as:

$$x_{it\,|\,v} = C_i(L)u_t + \xi_{t|v} = c_{i1}(L)u_{1t} + c_{i2}(L)u_{2t} + \xi_{t|v} \tag{1}$$

where $C_i(L) = \Lambda_i(I_r - AL)^{-1}B$ is the impulse response function of the ith variable to the common shocks.

The appendixes detail the estimation procedure. Let us outline it here. In the first step, we use principal components to estimate the parameters of the factor model $\hat{\Lambda}, \hat{A}, \hat{B}$, and $\hat{\Psi}$; in the second step, we use these estimates and the data $(x_{1|v}, x_{2|v}, \ldots, x_{v|v})$ to apply the Kalman filter on the state-space model to obtain:

$$\hat{F}_t = \mathrm{Proj}[F_t \,|\, x_{1|v}, \ldots, x_{v|v}], \qquad t = 0, 1, \ldots, v + h$$

and $\hat{u}_t$. Notice that all these estimates depend on the vintage v, but we have dropped the subscript for notational simplicity.

Once we have the nowcast and the forecast of the factors, we can construct the nowcast and forecast of the variables.[9] Notice that this forecasting method disregards the idiosyncratic component of each variable. The intuition is that the idiosyncratic element captures that part of the dynamics that is unforecastable because it is mostly explained by high-frequency variations that reflect measurement error or variable-specific dynamics.

Our objectives are the nowcasts and forecasts of the annualized quarterly growth rate of GDP, the annual rate of change of the GDP deflator, and the quarterly average of the federal funds rate.

We adapt this framework to estimate the factors on the basis of the incomplete data set, i.e., a data set that, as we have described, is some missing values corresponding to data not yet released. We write the model as:

$$\tilde{x}_{t|v} = \Lambda F_t + \xi_{t|v}$$

$$F_t = AF_{t-1} + Bu_t$$

where

$$\begin{aligned} E(\xi^2_{it\,|\,v}) = \tilde{\psi}_{it\,|\,v} &= \psi_i && \text{if } x_{it\,|\,v} \text{ is available} \\ &= \infty && \text{if } x_{it\,|\,v} \text{ is not available} \end{aligned}$$

$$\begin{aligned} \tilde{x}_{it\,|\,v} &= x_{it\,|\,v} && \text{if } x_{it\,|\,v} \text{ is available} \\ &= 0 && \text{if } x_{it\,|\,v} \text{ is not available} \end{aligned}$$

Notice that imposing $\psi_{it\,|\,v} = \infty$ when $x_{it\,|\,v}$ is missing implies that the filter will put no weight to the missing variable in the computation of the factors at time t.

The forecasts are computed each month, using the data available up to the first Friday. The parameters of the model are estimated using data up to the last date when the balanced panel is available.

In the estimation of the factor model, we use quarterly differences of the annual GDP deflator inflation and the quarterly differences of the federal funds rate, so we recover the levels of both variables by using the last available values. Our forecasts are compared with:

1. The Greenbook forecast for (quarterly) inflation and output (roughly corresponding to the second month of the quarter—four releases out of eight).

2. The survey of professional forecasts for quarterly output and inflation (released in the middle of the second month).

3. The futures on the federal funds rate (aggregate monthly forecast to obtain quarterly forecast—take the forecast first day of the first month).

4. The random walk forecast, only for inflation and the federal funds rate, where we assume that the forecast at all the horizons is given by

Table 5
Forecast comparison: root mean squared errors (RMSE)

	Quarters ahead ($h = t - v$)				
	0	1	2	3	4
GDP growth rate					
GB/2-shocks	1.09	1.03	1.00	0.88	0.86
Naive/2-shocks	1.23	1.02	0.98	0.94	0.93
SPF/2-shocks	1.14	1.00	0.99	0.99	1.01
2-shocks	1.83	2.21	2.30	2.39	2.43
Annual GDP deflator inflation					
GB/2-shocks	0.96	0.79	0.89	0.95	1.23
Random walk (RW)/2-shocks	1.05	1.10	1.15	1.20	1.22
SPF/2-shocks	0.99	0.92	0.98	1.17	1.27
2-shocks	0.30	0.40	0.48	0.55	0.60
Federal funds rate					
RW/2-shocks	1.23	1.17	—	—	—
Futures/2-shocks	0.47	0.76	—	—	—
2-shocks	0.41	0.79	—	—	—

the last available number of the federal funds rate and inflation at the date in which the forcast is taken.[10] For the GDP growth rate, we construct a naive forecasts that predicts a constant growth rate equal to the average growth rate over the sample 1970:1–1988:12 to have a measure of overall forecastability.

Table 5 reports root mean squared errors (RMSE) of the three variables relative to our model (forecasts produced during the second month of the quarter) and the ratio of the RMSE by the survey of professional forecasters (SPF) conducted by the Federal Reserve Bank of Philadelphia, the Greenbook (GB), and the future markets with respect to our model. The forecasts are performed using the whole sample but are reported only since 1989, when we start having information on the future market forecasts. Notice that Greenbook forecasts are available to the public only up to 1996. The table shows the following features:

- Our forecasts on inflation and output are overall very close to the Greenbook forecasts, with our model doing better in the short-run for output and in the long-run for inflation. Notice also that the factor model does relatively well for the nowcast of output, where there is predictability, and for inflation at the longer horizons, which are those relevant for policy.

• For inflation, the factor model outperforms the random walk benchmark, suggesting that there is forecastability in inflation four quarters ahead. At that horizon, the Greenbook has similar performance to the random walk, as noticed by Atkeson and Ohanian (2001). In general, the factor model outperforms the SPF's, while it is close to the Greenbook forecasts.

• The random walk does poorly for the federal funds rate, and the market's forecast is best. The two-factors model does well, however, at horizon two. As many have observed (e.g., Evans, 1998), it is very hard for a statistical, automatic model to beat the markets at the short horizon since those forecasts incorporate information such as the dates of the meetings, the chair's last speech, and institutional events, to which models cannot adapt. As we will see below, however, our performance is close to the market's when the Fed moves its instrument a lot, especially during recessions. In general, the forecasting performance of the two-factor model is far superior to the one based on a Taylor rule using Greenbook's inflation forecasts and real-time output gap estimates. Altough that model achieves a good in-sample fit, it does very poorly in forecasting (see, for example, Rudebusch, 2001; Soderlind, Soderstrom, and Vredin, 2003).

Overall, these results tell us that a simple linear two-factors model does well at mimicking the behavior of the Fed. Notice that this analysis qualifies results by Bernanke and Boivin (2003) and Stock and Watson (1999), which found that taking into account information on many variables helps forecasting. Our results confirm that finding and show that two shocks (dynamic factors) are sufficient to obtain it.

The analysis of forecasting performance over time sheds some further light on the federal funds rate behavior. Figures 1 to 3 illustrate forecast errors squared (panel A) and forecasts (panel B) for output at a zero-quarter horizon (nowcast), inflation at a one-year horizon, and the federal funds rate at a one-quarter horizon and for different forecasting models.

Let us make the following observations:

• The two-factors model does very well in forecasting output, especially during recessions, when all variables comove strongly. This is not surprising since it exploits optimally collinearity in the data. On average, we are close to the Greenbooks. Note that we identified the beginning of the last recession (first quarter of negative growth) one

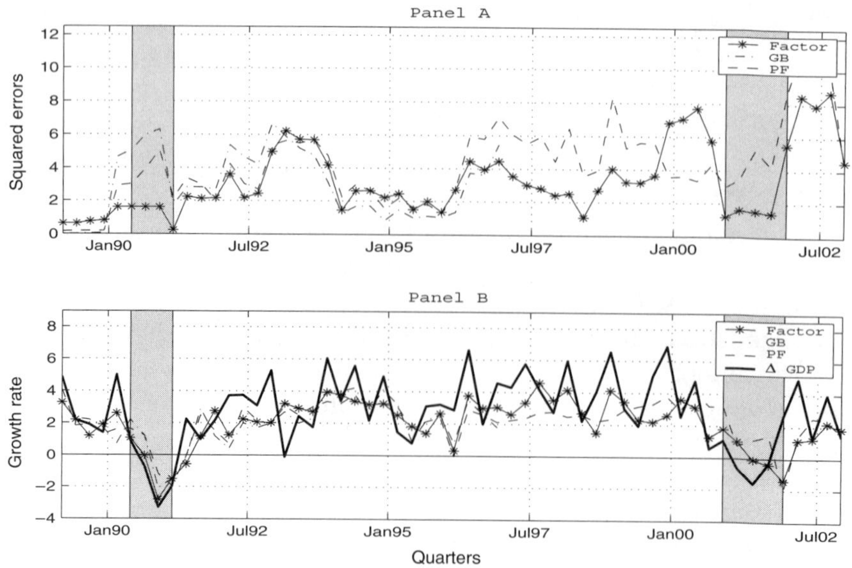

Figure 1
Forecasting GDP growth rate

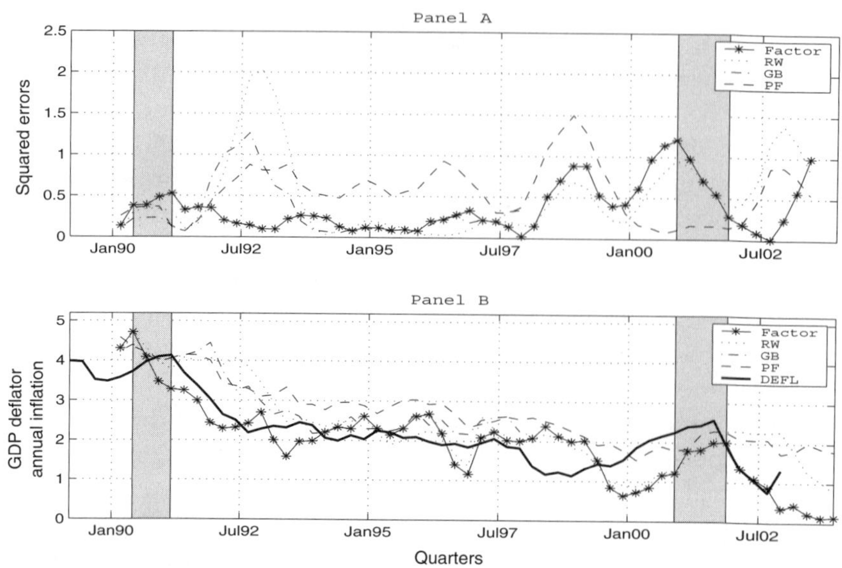

Figure 2
Forecasting inflation

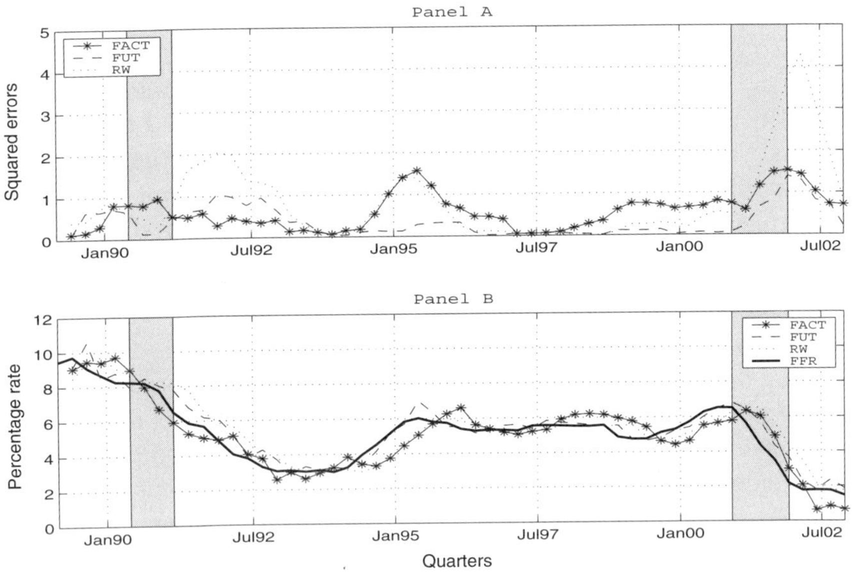

Figure 3
Tracking Greenspan

quarter after it occurred, while the SPF identified the peak when the recession had already ended.

• Concerning inflation, the two-factor model does well in detecting the decline that followed the 1990 recession. In addition, unlike the SPF, the model does not overestimate inflation in the 1990s (overprediction of inflation during this period has been noted by Brayton, Roberts, and Williams, 1999; Rudebusch, 2001), but it misses the upsurge of inflation in the late 1990s. Finally, it identifies well the last decline in inflation.

• For the federal funds rate, the factor model does well when it does well in predicting output and inflation and during recessions, when the Fed moves a lot. In particular, our model does well during the fall of the federal funds rate at the beginning of the 1990s because it can capture both the decline of output during the recession and the decline of inflation that occurred when the recession ended. The factor model can predict the monetary easing started in 2001, when it also predicts in a timely way the 2001 recession and the decline of inflation started in the second half of 2001. On the other hand, the two-factors forecast performs poorly during the preemptive strike against inflation in 1994, when the Fed responded not only to its own predictions of inflation but also to market expectations (see Goodfriend, 2002) and during the monetary tightening that started in the late 1990s. That episode is associated with an increase in inflation that was not predicted by the two shocks. Finally, the two-shocks model does not predict the cut in the federal funds rate in the second half of 1998, which was not justified in terms of shocks on inflation and real activity but rather as a response to the financial market turbulence associated with the Russian crisis. This is an example of judgmental policy that cannot be incorporated in simple rules. (On this point, see Svensson (2003).)

What do the results of the forecasting exercise tell us about monetary policy in real time? The key message is that a two-shocks model does well in forecasting output and inflation even when compared with tough benchmarks such as the SPF and the Greenbook. This brings additional support to our claim that the relevant dimension of the U.S. economy is two. Second, the model produces a good forecast of the policy instrument, suggesting that it captures some essential elements of the forecasting model of the Fed and its reaction function. What are these elements? The first, as already observed, is the reduced dimension. The second is the particular version of output and inflation to which policy responds. We turn to this analysis in the next section.

3. The Dimension of the Policy Problem

3.1 *What are the Two Large Shocks?*

This section moves to the structural interpretation. If the stochastic dimension is two, two large shocks must drive the economy. Can we identify them?

Let us define the forecast errors from the Greenbook model as:

$$z_{it+h\,|\,t+1} - z_{it+h\,|\,t} = e_{it}^{h}$$

where $h = -1, 0, 1, \ldots, 4$. For $h = -1$ and $h = 0$, we have errors on revisions, while for $h = 1, \ldots, 4$ we have errors from the Fed's model.

Figure 4 plots errors for inflation against those for output at different values of h. Visual inspection of the figure suggests no clear pattern of correlation. Indeed, our calculations show that only a few of them are significantly different than zero, and very little survives once the recession of the mid-1970s is taken out of the sample. This suggests that the

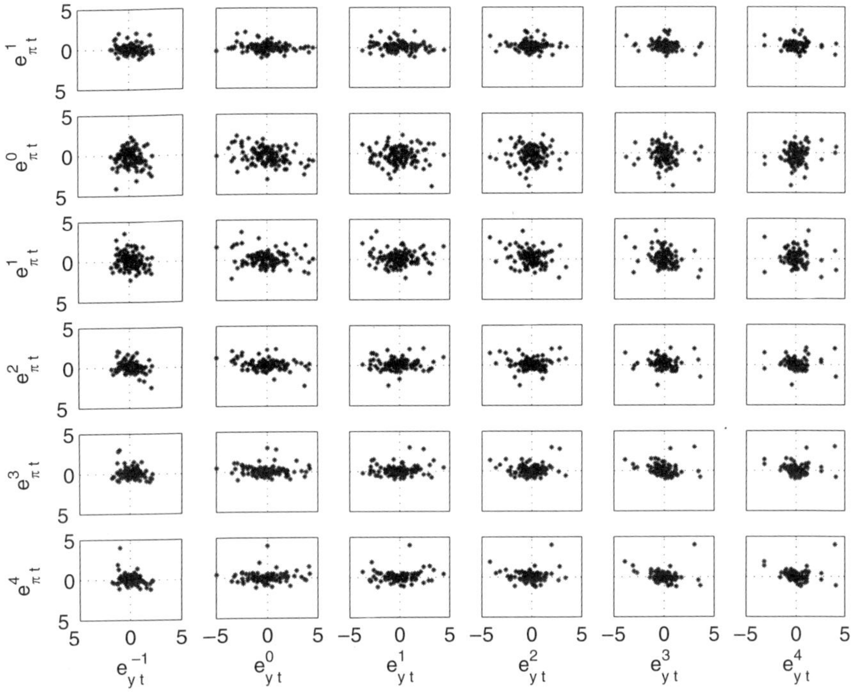

Figure 4
Correlation of inflation and output, Greenbook forecast errors

uncertainty about inflation originates from sources that are weakly correlated with the sources of uncertainty about real activity. In other words, the inflation and output shocks faced by the Fed are not much correlated. This is in line with the results reported by Romer and Romer (1994), who found that the ability of the Fed to predict output is not related to its ability to forecast inflation.

How strong is the correlation between nominal and real variables induced by the two shocks? If it is weak, then there must be a real shock explaining the bulk of GDP dynamics, and a nominal shock explaining the bulk of inflation dynamics. To investigate this point, we compute ex-post and real-time impulse response functions to orthogonalized shocks extracted from our panel of observations. We will start by reporting ex-post estimates (i.e., estimates on revised data for the whole sample). We will move to the ex-ante real-time analysis in the next subsection.

For the ex-post exercise, we proceed as follows. We identify the real shock as the one that explains the maximum variance of the

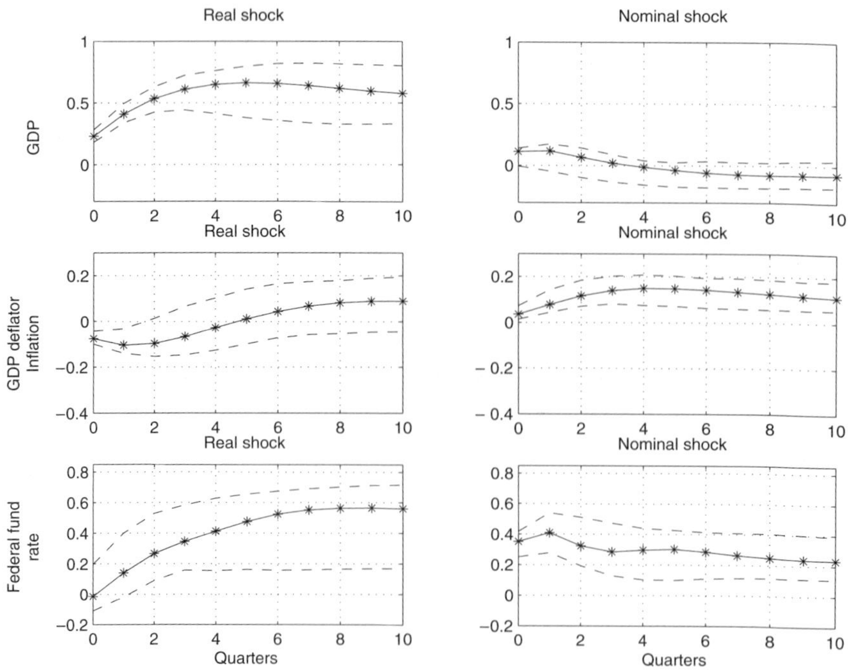

Figure 5
Impulse response functions

real variables in the panel. We propose that the following quantity is maximized:

$$\frac{\sum_{i \in J_R} \sum_{h=0}^{\infty} (c_{i1}^h)^2}{\sum_{i \in J_R} \sum_{h=0}^{\infty} (c_{i1}^h)^2 + \sum_{i \in J_R} \sum_{h=0}^{\infty} (c_{i2}^h)^2}$$

where J_R is the set containing the positions of the real variables in the panel. This identification procedure allows us to exploit information on the multivariate dynamics of the panel and to extract a shock that has its main effect on the real sector of the economy so that we can label it real. The other shock is labeled as nominal. Figure 5 illustrates impulse response functions for GDP, the federal funds rate, and inflation to the real and nominal shocks,[11] while Figure 6 reports ex-post conditional histories.[12]

A few comments are in order:

- The shape of the responses of the federal funds rate and output to the real shock are very similar, with the federal funds rate lagging GDP. In

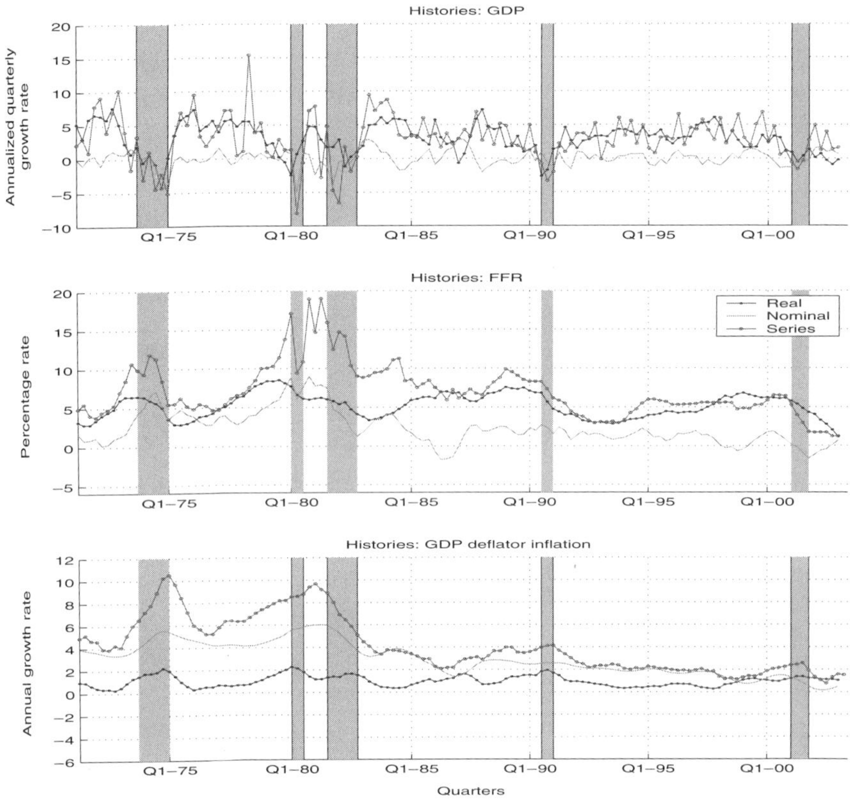

Figure 6
Inflation, output, and the federal funds rate: realizations and conditional histories

response to the nominal shock, the federal funds rate leads inflation and it responds more than one to one.

• Even though this is not the focus of the paper, note that neither of the two shocks can be identified as a monetary policy shock. This is justified by two findings: one of the two shocks is permanent on output, the second moves inflation and the federal funds rate in the same direction. For further analysis on this point, see our earlier work in Giannone, Reichlin, and Sala (2002).

• GDP is driven mainly by the real shock, the deflator is driven mainly by the nominal shock, and the federal funds rate is driven by both.

• The real component explains a big part of recessions, in particular in the early 1990s. Since the dynamics of output associated to the nominal shock is small, the Phillips curve relation is weak.

- The sums of the conditional histories, for each variable, are their corresponding common component (the components driven by the two common shocks). We can infer from figure 6 that they represent a smoothed version of the variable, which tracks quite well medium-term dynamics.

Essentially, the federal funds rate responds vigorously to both shocks. At first sight, this is not surprising since they are the large shocks affecting output, and inflation and output and inflation are the variables usually considered as objectives of monetary policy. We will show in Section 4 that the previous statement can be generalized: to the extent that there are only two shocks in the economy, any couple of uncorrelated variables can be used to explain the movements in the federal funds rate.

As a robustness check, we also follow the more traditional strategy (see Blanchard and Quah, 1989) of assuming that there exists a transitory and a permanent shock on output. We impose the restriction that the long-run multiplier on the transitory shocks on output is equal to zero, i.e., that $c_{y,2}(1) = 0$ in equation (1).

Impulse response function and conditional histories from the two identification schemes give almost identical results. As expected, the permanent shock is almost identical to the real shock, while the transitory is identical to the nominal (we do not report results for this identification here; they are available on request).

3.2 *Real-Time Analysis of the Shocks*

Shocks in real time are conditional forecast errors derived from the real-time forecasting exercise. We can build on the forecasting exercise of the previous section to produce impulse response functions of the common shocks derived from the conditional real-time forecasts. Let us define:

$$w_{it}(T_1, T_2) = x^*_{it\,|\,T_2} - x^*_{it\,|\,T_1}, \qquad T_2 > T_1$$

as the difference of the path for the common component of variable x_{it}, defined as x^*_{it} estimated at time T_2, and the path that was expected at time T_1. These quantities should be understood as weighted realizations of shocks that occurred between time T_1 and T_2, where the weights depend on the propagation mechanism of the shocks.[13] If a certain type of disturbance has been prevalent between T_1 and T_2, then

$w_{it}(T_1, T_2)$ will reflect the series-specific propagation mechanism and the realizations of such disturbance.

More precisely, for $t > T_1$, $w_{it}(T_1, T_2)$ is an estimate of:

$$d_{i1}(L)u_{1,T_1+1} + d_{i2}(L)u_{2,T_1+1} + \cdots + d_{i1}(L)u_{1,T_2} + d_{i2}(L)u_{2,T_2}$$

A particular case is $t > T_1 + 1$, when $w_{it}(T_1, T_1 + 1)$ is an estimate of the impulse response function weighted by the realization of the shock at time $T_1 + 1$, i.e., $d_1(L)u_{1,T_1+1} + d_2(L)u_{1,T_1+1}$.

For example, suppose that T_1 is the first quarter of 2001, the last peak announced by the National Bureau of Economic Research (NBER), and that T_2 is the fourth quarter of 2001, the corresponding trough. Then $w_{it}(Q1.01, Q4.01)$ measures the convolution of the propagation mechanism for the variable x_{it} with the shocks that have generated the recession.

Forecast errors conditional on the permanent shocks can be obtained by shutting down the transitory shocks. The same can be done for the transitory shocks.

We report selected episodes: the two recessions in our sample and two episodes of inflation scares. From left to right, the plots in Figures 7 and 8 must be read as unconditional impulses on output, the federal funds rate, and inflation, and impulses conditional on the permanent shock for the same variables and impulses conditional on the transitory shock, respectively.

Here is what emerges from the analysis:

- *Recessions*

1. *1990Q3–1991Q1.* The interest rate reacts to the decline in output with a lag, but very aggressively. Very little happens to inflation because the recession is almost entirely driven by the real shock. The interest rate therefore reacts to the real shock and not to the nominal.
2. *2001Q1–2001Q4.* The real shock is also the driving force for this recession. Inflation dynamics is driven by the nominal shock. Inflation continues to decline conditionally on that shock, even after the recovery has started. The federal funds rate moves aggressively with output during the recession, moving before inflation declines.

- *Inflation scares*

1. *1993Q4–1995Q2.* The upsurge of inflation is driven entirely by the nominal component, which also drives output upward. This is a case in which there is a Phillips relation. As we have seen from the ex-post conditional histories, a Phillips relation emerges conditionally only to

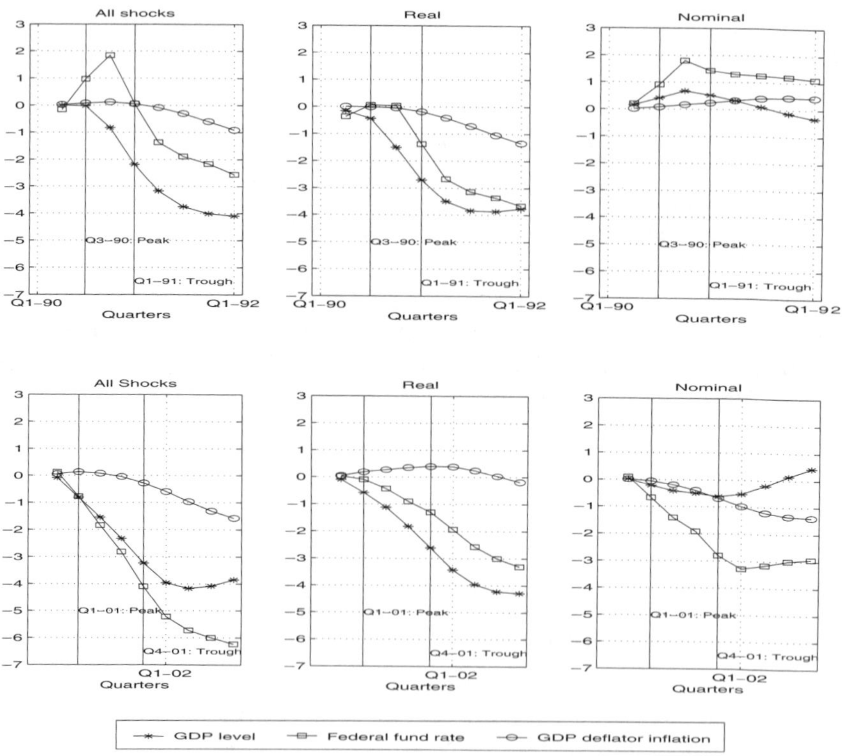

Figure 7
Recessions

the nominal shock, i.e., conditionally on the small shock on output. In this episode, the federal funds rate moves with output and leads inflation.

2. *1999Q2–2000Q3*. Inflation moves up with the nominal shock and so does output. The federal funds rate moves upward aggressively with inflation.

The picture emerging from the ex-ante, real-time analysis is similar to what emerged from the ex-post analysis: the real shock affects output but not inflation, the nominal shock affects inflation but not output.

Notice that inflation moves very little during recessions. Facing large movements, the Fed reacts aggressively either to inflation or to output. What is most important, as noticed by Romer and Romer (1994), is that large movements in inflation and large movements in output are largely independent from one another.

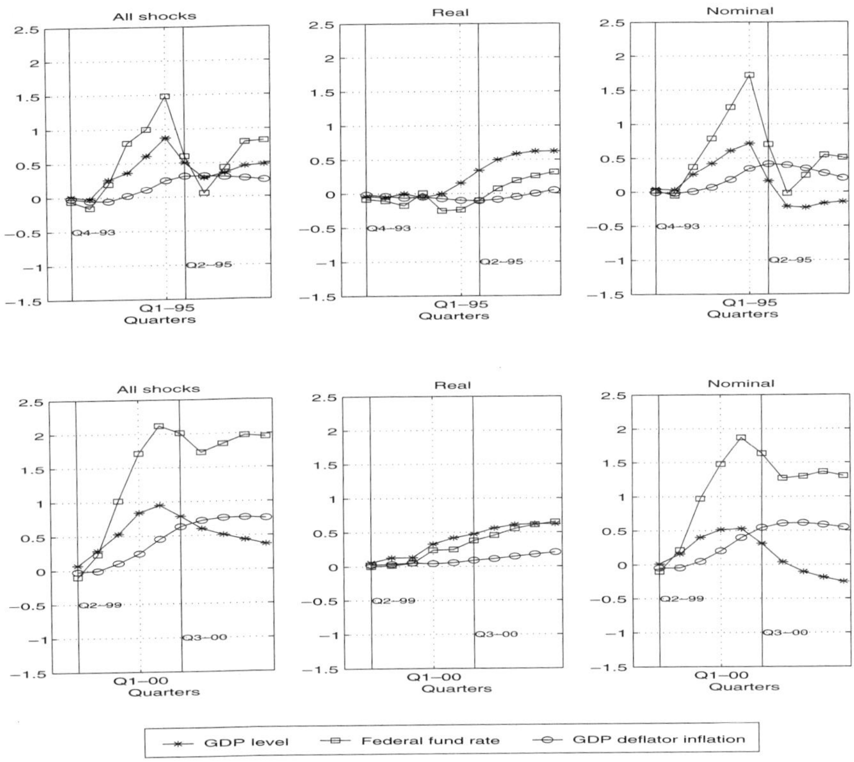

Figure 8
Inflation scares

4. Taylor Rules: Discussion

As we have seen, the fundamental business-cycle dynamics of the U.S. economy is driven by two shocks. We have seen from the historical account of the forecasting performance of the two-shocks model that the responses of the federal funds rate to nonfundamental fluctuations, i.e., to those fluctuations driven by shocks other than the two large common ones we have identified, are not systematic. In our frame work, they are captured by the idiosyncratic component that is a white noise in first difference.[14]

It is then easy to see that, even if the Fed reacted, in addition to output and inflation, to other variables driven by the fundamentals, their inclusion in the federal funds rate equation would not improve the fit. This policy would be observationally equivalent to a systematic policy reacting to inflation and output only. Inflation and output, as we have seen, are indeed highly correlated with, respectively, the nominal and real part of the economy and they are nearly orthogonal at business-cycle frequencies, so they capture well the two-dimensional space generated by the two fundamental shocks.

Ex-post estimates of the Taylor rule point at a simple function: the Taylor rule is a simple contemporaneous relation between the federal funds rate and the output gap and inflation. Does such simplicity reflect the simplicity of the Federal Reserve policy or the fact that real and nominal variables react similarly to, respectively, the real and nominal shocks?

To investigate this issue we have run two sets of regressions.

First, we have regressed the component of the federal funds rate generated by the real shock on the components of all real variables generated by the real shock (cumulated). Second, we have regressed the component of the federal funds rate generated by the nominal shock on the components of all nominal variables generated by the nominal shock (cumulated).

We have obtained two sets of fits—nominal and real—and constructed 10% lower and upper bands by excluding, at each t, the 20% of extreme points (10% lower and 10% upper). The upper quadrant of Figure 9 reports the bands as well as the projection of the federal funds rate on GDP and the federal funds rate conditional on the real shock that we have reported earlier (see Figure 6). The lower quadrant does the same for the nominal case.

Figure 9 shows a striking similarity of shapes within the real and nominal group. Not only do the lower and upper bounds move in the same direction, but both the projection of the federal funds rate on real GDP, conditional on the real shock, and the projection of the federal funds rate on the deflator, conditional on the nominal shock, are within the bands. Considering that the variables analyzed are quite different, this is indeed a strong result. The U.S. economy is simple not only because it is mainly driven by two shocks, but also because the responses of real variables to the real shock are similar and so are the responses of nominal variables to the nominal shock.

Obviously variables are not completely synchronized, and some leading-lagging relations can be identified.[15] The lower bound curve leads the upper bound curve. The projection on GDP leads the real component of the federal funds rate, which implies that the latter leads GDP (real variables). On the contrary, from the lower quadrant, we can see that the conditional federal funds rate leads inflation (nominal vari-

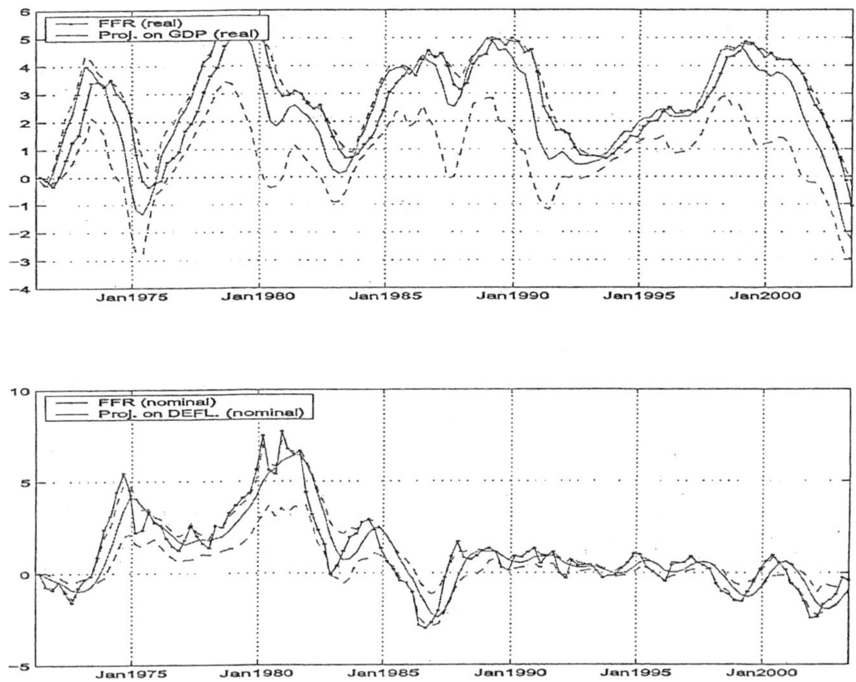

Figure 9
Taylor fits

ables) and crosses often the lower bound. The fact that the federal funds rate is lagging with respect to real variables might be a consequence of the fact that information about the real side of the economy is less timely than financial or price information.

From an ex-ante perspective, one possible interpretation of our results is that the Fed, instead of tracking two particular variables such as a version of measured output gap and inflation, follows a robust policy, moving when all real variables (and among them GDP) move and all nominal variables (and among them the inflation rate) move.

In real time, the exercise of nowcasting and forecasting by the Fed essentially amounts to smoothing out short-run dynamics and unforecastable idiosyncratic variance from output and inflation, making use of information contained in a large cosssection of data and exploiting their comovements as well as their historical leading and lagging relations. This applies specific filters to output and inflation. Our analysis suggests also that the filters are two-sided and that this is a consequence of the fact that the variables, although rather synchronized, are

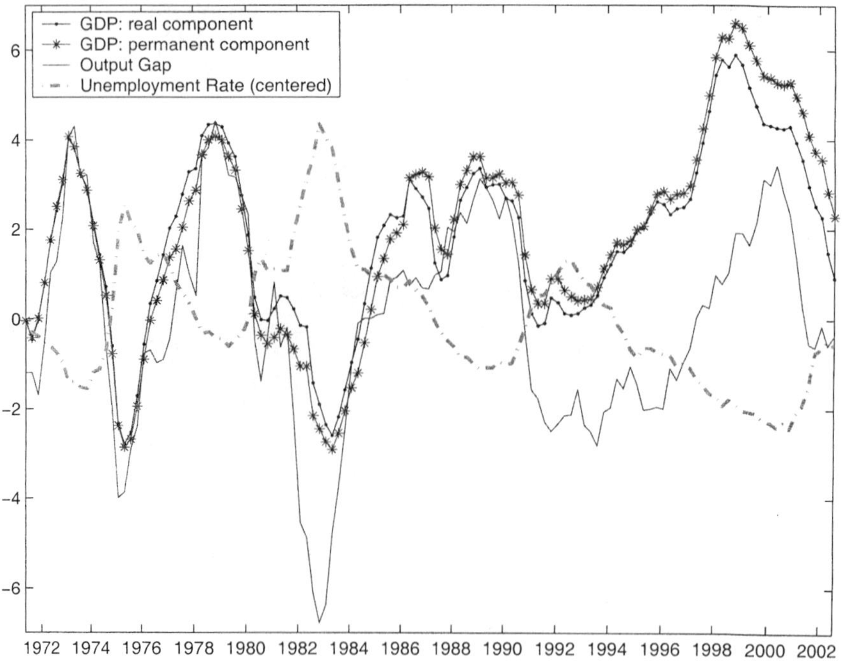

Figure 10
The output gap (centered), unemployment rate, the permanent component of output, output generated by the real shock

not perfectly aligned and that the leading ones are used to nowcast and forecast inflation and output.

We can also ask how the output variable we have used relates to current measures of the output gap. We have seen that we can interpret the large shock on output as either a real shock or as the shock generating long-run movements in output. However, Figure 10 shows that not only the output component generated by the real shock and the long-run component are empirically very close to one another, but (more disturbingly) that the output gap measured as the Hodrick-Prescott filter on output and the (centered) unemployment rate are both strongly correlated with those two components. The correlation, with the exception of the mid-1990s, is striking.

This suggests that a major aspect of uncertainty faced by the central bank is the lack of knowledge on whether shocks affecting the economy are of long or short duration. As we have seen, output growth at horizons longer than two quarters is unforecastable. This implies that it is hard to measure the long-run effect of the shocks and, as a consequence, to distinguish between the output gap and long-run component of output. Although the permanent component contains, by construction, the zero frequency (long-run) component, its measure is strongly correlated with detrended output. The unemployment rate, on the other hand, is very persistent and its natural level is badly measured (see also Staiger, Stock, and Watson [1997] and Orphanides and Van Norden [2002] for the consequences of this observation on real-time monetary policy). This obviously leads to a problem of interpretation on what the Fed does. Does it follow the permanent component of output, the output gap, or simply the forecastable component of output growth?

Finally, let us notice that our model is estimated in difference form, which implies that the nonsystematc component of the policy equation has a unit root. This is a consequence of the fact that the real interest rate is very persistent (see, for example, Rudebusch, 2001). Since the federal funds rate, inflation, and output either have a unit root or are close to the unit root case, in real-time, their level is difficult to forecast. A rule in first differences is easier to implement (see also Orphanides, 2003). However, with a first difference specification, we cannot learn anything about important issues such as the level of the natural rate of interest or the natural rate of unemployment.

5. Conclusions and Some Caveats

The message of this paper can be summarized as follows. The complex dynamic interaction among many macroeconomic variables in the U.S. economy can be captured by two aggregates. The bulk of medium- and long-run dynamics of output is explained by one shock that has similar effects on all real variables and the bulk of medium- and long-run dynamics of inflation by a shock, orthogonal to it, that has a similar effect on all nominal variables. The federal funds rate, by responding to the two large shocks, can track the fundamental dynamics of both output and inflation, i.e., the dynamic correlated with the whole economy and that it is forecastable. Occasionally, the Fed may decide to monitor special events, such as exchange rate crises or surges in inflationary expectations from the private sector that are not correlated with its own forecasts of the fundamentals, but this judgmental part of policy seems to be small.

The consequence of these results is that the simple Taylor rule found to fit U.S. data so well may be interpreted as the ex-post result of a policy that ex-ante, responds vigorously when all real variables *or* all nominal variables move together. The weak trade-off between output and inflation and between output and inflation in the Greenbook forecasts suggest that inflation scares and recession scares can be addressed as distinct stabilization problems.

The main purpose of our analysis has been to identify the history of U.S. monetary policy in the last twenty years and point out problems of interpretation of results from existing studies. From a real-time perspective, it is important to understand what the Fed has done, given uncertainty about the current and future state of the economy and the delays in data releases. We have seen that output growth is unforecastable at long horizons, which makes any rule based on the identification of the long run on output or its residual unreliable. Inflation, on the other hand, is more forecastable at longer horizons. In both cases, the forecastable component is one that correlates with the rest of the economy. A normative implication is that a robust rule should not depend on idiosyncratic movements of specific variables but rather move when all real or nominal variables move. One possible interpretation of this finding, is that the Fed, indeed, follows this type of rule. This conjecture is supported, in particular, by the fact that we replicate well the policy behavior during recessions. These situations are also those in which the Fed has been successful in reacting promptly to output decline.

There are other important aspects of the monetary policy debate where our analysis is not informative. Although we can say something about what the Fed has done, we cannot quantify the effect of monetary policy on the economy. For example, the finding on the weakness of the Phillips curve trade-off might be an effect of successful policy. Such analysis would require the specification of a structural model. At this stage, however, structural models have not produced forecasting results that even come close to those produced by the Greenbooks and by the markets.

6. Appendixes

6.1 Econometrics

Consider the model:

$$x_t = \Lambda F_t + \xi_t$$

$$F_t = AF_{t-1} + Bu_t$$

$u_t \sim WN(0, I_q)$

$\mathrm{E}(\xi_t \xi_t') = \Psi$

where

F_t is the $r \times 1$ $(r \geq 2)$ vector of the static factors

$\Lambda = [\Lambda_1', \ldots, \Lambda_n']'$ is the $n \times r$ matrix of the loadings

B is a $r \times q$ matrix of full rank q

A is an $r \times r$ matrix and all roots of $\det(\mathrm{I_r} - \mathrm{Az})$ lie outside the unit circle

ξ_t is the n-dimensional stationary linear process

We make two assumptions.

1. Common factors are pervasive:

$$\liminf_{n\to\infty}\left(\frac{1}{n}\Lambda'\Lambda\right) > 0$$

2. Idiosyncratic factors are nonpervasive:

$$\lim_{n\to\infty}\frac{1}{n}\left(\max_{v'v=1} v'\Psi v\right) = 0$$

Consider the following estimator of the common factors:

$$(\tilde{F}_t, \hat{\Lambda}) = \arg\min_{F_t, \Lambda}\sum_{t=1}^{T}\sum_{i=1}^{n}(x_{it} - \Lambda_i F_t)^2$$

Define the sample covariance matrix of the observable (x_t):

$$S = \frac{1}{T}\sum_{t=1}^{T} x_t x_t'$$

Denote by D the $r \times r$ diagonal matrix with diagonal elements given by the largest r eigenvalues of S and by V the $n \times r$ matrix of the corresponding eigenvectors subject to the normalization $V'V = I_r$. We estimate the factors as:

$\tilde{F}_t = V'\bar{x}_t$

The factor loadings, $\hat{\Lambda}$, and the covariance matrix of the idiosyncratic components, $\hat{\Psi}$, are estimated by regressing the variables on the estimated factors:

$$\hat{\Lambda} = \sum_{t=1}^{T} x_t \tilde{F}_t' \left(\sum_{t=1}^{T} \tilde{F}_t \tilde{F}_t' \right)^{-1} = V$$

and:

$$\hat{\Psi} = S - VDV'$$

The other parameters are estimated by running a VAR on the estimated factors, specifically:

$$\hat{A} = \sum_{t=2}^{T} \tilde{F}_t \tilde{F}_{t-1}' \left(\sum_{t=2}^{T} \tilde{F}_{t-1} \tilde{F}_{t-1}' \right)^{-1}$$

$$\hat{\Sigma} = \frac{1}{T-1} \sum_{t=2}^{T} \tilde{F}_t \tilde{F}_t' - \hat{A} \left(\frac{1}{T-1} \sum_{t=2}^{T} \tilde{F}_{t-1} \tilde{F}_{t-1}' \right) \hat{A}'$$

Define P as the $q \times q$ diagonal matrix, with the entries given by the largest q eigenvalues of $\hat{\Sigma}$, and by M the $r \times q$ matrix of the corresponding eigenvectors:

$$\hat{B} = MP^{1/2}$$

The estimates $\hat{\Lambda}, \hat{\Psi}, \hat{A}, \hat{B}$ can be shown to be consistent as $n, T \rightarrow \infty$ (Forni et al., 2003).

Having obtained the estimates of the parameters of the factor model, the factors are reestimated as:

$$\hat{F}_t = \text{Proj}[F_t \mid x_1, \ldots, x_T], \qquad t = 0, 1, \ldots, t+h$$

by applying the Kalman filter to the following state-space representation obtained by replacing estimated parameters in the factor representation:

$$x_t = \hat{\Lambda} F_t + \xi_t$$

$$F_t = \hat{A} F_{t-1} + \hat{B} u_t$$

$$u_t \sim WN(0, I_q)$$

$$\mathrm{E}(\xi_t \xi_{tv}') = \text{diag } \hat{\Psi}$$

and $\hat{u}_t = P^{-1/2} M' (\hat{F}_t - A\hat{F}_{t-1})$.

Remark 1 When applying the Kalman filter, we set to zero the off-diagonal elements of the estimated covariance matrix of the idiosyncratic since they are poorly estimated if n, the dimension of the panel, is large. However, assumptions A1 and A2 ensure that even under such restriction the factors can be consistently estimated.

Remark 2 The estimates of the factors in the second step are more efficient since the Kalman filter performs the best linear projection on the present and past observations.

Remark 3 In practice, the procedure outlined above is applied to standardized data, and then the sample mean and the sample standard deviation are reattributed accordingly.

Remark 4 Since the r-dimensional factors F_t are assumed to have a VAR representation, the q common shocks are fundamental; i.e., they can be recovered from the present and past of the r factors. Notice that, since $r \gg q$, our assumption is weaker than the assumption of the fundamental nature of the q-dimensional common shocks u_t with respect to any two of the factors, or any couple of common components. In particular, the common shocks u_t are in general a function not only of the present and past but also of the future of any couple of common components (see Forni et al., 2003).

6.2 *The Dataset*

Series:	Transformation	Variance explained by DPC 1	2	3
1 Index of IP: total	3	0.88	0.93	0.94
2 Index of IP: final products and non-industrial supplies	3	0.83	0.90	0.92
3 Index of IP: final products	3	0.78	0.86	0.89
4 Index of IP: consumer goods	3	0.70	0.79	0.83
5 Index of IP: durable consumer goods	3	0.73	0.80	0.83
6 Index of IP: nondurable consumer goods	3	0.33	0.47	0.59
7 Index of IP: business equipment	3	0.75	0.81	0.84
8 Index of IP: materials	3	0.84	0.89	0.93
9 Index of IP: materials, nonenergy, durables	3	0.79	0.85	0.90

(continued)

Series:		Transformation	Variance explained by DPC 1	2	3
10	Index of IP: materials, nonenergy, nondurables	3	0.78	0.82	0.85
11	Index of IP: mfg	3	0.87	0.92	0.94
12	Index of IP: mfg, durables	3	0.83	0.88	0.92
13	Index of IP: mfg, nondurables	3	0.67	0.73	0.80
14	Index of IP: mining	3	0.21	0.54	0.64
15	Index of IP: utilities	3	0.12	0.27	0.45
16	Index of IP: energy, total	3	0.24	0.45	0.57
17	Index of IP: nonenergy, total	3	0.89	0.93	0.95
18	Index of IP: motor vehicles and parts (MVP)	3	0.44	0.55	0.62
19	Index of IP: computers, comm. equip., and semiconductors (CCS)	3	0.35	0.47	0.58
20	Index of IP: nonenergy excl CCS	3	0.90	0.93	0.94
21	Index of IP: nonenergy excl CCS and MVP	3	0.89	0.92	0.93
22	Capacity utilization: total	2	0.89	0.93	0.94
23	Capacity utilization: mfg	2	0.90	0.93	0.94
24	Capacity utilization: mfg, durables	2	0.87	0.91	0.93
25	Capacity utilization: mfg, nondurables	2	0.78	0.83	0.86
26	Capacity utilization: mining	2	0.25	0.56	0.65
27	Capacity utilization: utilities	2	0.20	0.32	0.50
28	Capacity utilization: computers, comm. equip., and semiconductors	2	0.45	0.56	0.61
29	Capacity utilization: mfg excl CCS	2	0.90	0.93	0.94
30	Purchasing Managers Index (PMI)	0	0.86	0.88	0.90
31	ISM mfg index: production	0	0.83	0.87	0.89
32	Index of help-wanted advertising	3	0.77	0.83	0.87
33	No. of unemployed in the civ. labor force (CLF)	3	0.74	0.82	0.85
34	CLF employed: total	3	0.72	0.76	0.82
35	CLF employed: nonagricultural industries	3	0.70	0.74	0.80
36	Mean duration of unemployment	3	0.60	0.67	0.71
37	Persons unemployed less than 5 weeks	3	0.48	0.56	0.64
38	Persons unemployed 5 to 14 weeks	3	0.68	0.74	0.78
39	Persons unemployed 15 to 26 weeks	3	0.63	0.73	0.77
40	Persons unemployed 15+ weeks	3	0.70	0.77	0.80
41	Avg weekly initial claims	3	0.72	0.81	0.83

(continued)

Series:	Transformation	Variance explained by DPC 1	2	3
42 Employment on nonag payrolls: total	3	0.85	0.91	0.93
43 Employment on nonag payrolls: total private	3	0.85	0.92	0.93
44 Employment on nonag payrolls: goods-producing	3	0.87	0.93	0.94
45 Employment on nonag payrolls: mining	3	0.21	0.46	0.54
46 Employment on nonag payrolls: construction	3	0.61	0.72	0.78
47 Employment on nonag payrolls: manufacturing	3	0.85	0.92	0.93
48 Employment on nonag payrolls: manufacturing, durables	3	0.86	0.92	0.93
49 Employment on nonag payrolls: manufacturing, nondurables	3	0.68	0.78	0.83
50 Employment on nonag payrolls: service-producing	3	0.70	0.76	0.84
51 Employment on nonag payrolls: utilities	3	0.08	0.21	0.59
52 Employment on nonag payrolls: retail trade	3	0.59	0.67	0.78
53 Employment on nonag payrolls: wholesale trade	3	0.66	0.78	0.83
54 Employment on nonag payrolls: financial activities	3	0.31	0.32	0.52
55 Employment on nonag payrolls: professional and business services	3	0.51	0.65	0.71
56 Employment on nonag payrolls: education and health services	3	0.19	0.26	0.42
57 Employment on nonag payrolls: lesiure and hospitality	3	0.39	0.48	0.57
58 Employment on nonag payrolls: other services	3	0.32	0.39	0.59
59 Employment on nonag payrolls: government	3	0.25	0.36	0.45
60 Avg weekly hrs. of production or nonsupervisory workers ("PNW"): total private	3	0.49	0.61	0.65
61 Avg weekly hrs of PNW: mfg	3	0.57	0.65	0.70
62 Avg weekly overtime hrs of PNW: mfg	3	0.65	0.70	0.74
63 ISM mfg index: employment	3	0.70	0.77	0.80

(continued)

Series:	Transformation	Variance explained by DPC 1	2	3
64 Sales: mfg and trade—total (mil of chained 96$)	3	0.71	0.77	0.83
65 Sales: mfg and trade—mfg, total (mil of chained 96$)	3	0.76	0.82	0.87
66 Sales: mfg and trade—merchant wholesale (mil of chained 96$)	3	0.53	0.60	0.70
67 Sales: mfg and trade—retail trade (mil of chained 96$)	3	0.33	0.47	0.58
68 Personal cons. expenditure: total (bil of chained 96$)	3	0.47	0.63	0.71
69 Personal cons. expenditure: durables (bil of chained 96$)	3	0.36	0.53	0.62
70 Personal cons. expenditure: nondurables (bil of chained 96$)	3	0.30	0.48	0.56
71 Personal cons. expenditure: services (bil of chained 96$)	3	0.41	0.55	0.61
72 Personal cons. expenditure: durables—MVP—new autos (bil of chained 96$)	3	0.19	0.42	0.57
73 Privately-owned housing, started: total (thous)	3	0.53	0.62	0.71
74 New privately-owned housing authorized: total (thous)	3	0.55	0.65	0.73
75 New 1-family houses sold: total (thous)	3	0.42	0.52	0.62
76 New 1-family houses—months supply at current rate	3	0.34	0.43	0.55
77 New 1-family houses for sale at end of period (thous)	3	0.46	0.51	0.57
78 Mobile homes—mfg shipments (thous)	3	0.45	0.55	0.61
79 Construction put in place: total (in mil of 96$) (1)	3	0.48	0.61	0.71
80 Construction put in place: private (in mil of 96$)	3	0.56	0.65	0.74
81 Inventories: mfg and trade: total (mil of chained 96$)	3	0.65	0.70	0.76
82 Inventories: mfg and trade: mfg (mil of chained 96$)	3	0.59	0.68	0.72
83 Inventories: mfg and trade: mfg, durables (mil of chained 96$)	3	0.59	0.67	0.71
84 Inventories: mfg and trade: mfg, nondurables (mil of chained 96$)	3	0.36	0.47	0.55
85 Inventories: mfg and trade: merchant wholesale (mil of chained 96$)	3	0.30	0.39	0.49

(continued)

Series:	Transformation	Variance explained by DPC 1	2	3
86 Inventories: mfg and trade: retail trade (mil of chained 96$)	3	0.48	0.61	0.67
87 ISM mfg index: inventories	0	0.74	0.79	0.86
88 ISM mfg index: new orders	0	0.84	0.86	0.87
89 ISM mfg index: suppliers deliveries	0	0.64	0.72	0.78
90 Mfg new orders: all mfg industries (in mil of current $)	3	0.67	0.76	0.84
91 Mfg new orders: mfg indusries with unfilled orders (in mil of current $)	3	0.45	0.54	0.63
92 Mfg new orders: durables (in mil of current $)	3	0.65	0.74	0.79
93 Mfg new orders: nondurables (in mil of current $)	3	0.43	0.61	0.73
94 Mfg new orders: nondefense capital goods (in mil of current $)	3	0.36	0.48	0.57
95 Mfg unfilled orders: all mfg industries (in mil of current $)	3	0.55	0.62	0.72
96 NYSE composite index	3	0.27	0.41	0.51
97 S&P composite	3	0.26	0.41	0.50
98 S&P P/E ratio	3	0.44	0.56	0.63
99 Nominal effective exchange rate	3	0.15	0.37	0.46
100 Spot Euro/US (2)	3	0.15	0.39	0.48
101 Spot SZ/US	3	0.15	0.36	0.47
102 Spot Japan/US	3	0.17	0.32	0.43
103 Spot UK/US	3	0.11	0.28	0.40
104 Commercial paper outstanding (in mil of current $)	3	0.41	0.49	0.56
105 Interest rate: federal funds rate	2	0.57	0.72	0.78
106 Interest rate: U.S. 3-mo Treasury (sec. market)	2	0.53	0.73	0.79
107 Interest rate: U.S. 6-mo Treasury (sec. market)	2	0.51	0.73	0.79
108 Interest rate: 1-year Treasury (constant maturity)	2	0.48	0.72	0.78
109 Interest rate: 5-year Treasury (constant maturity)	2	0.39	0.65	0.75
110 Interest rate: 7-year Treasury (constant maturity)	2	0.37	0.63	0.75
111 Interest rate: 10-year Treasury (constant maturity)	2	0.33	0.61	0.74
112 Bond yield: Moodys AAA corporate	2	0.36	0.59	0.71

(continued)

Series:	Transformation	Variance explained by DPC 1	2	3
113 Bond yield: Moodys BAA corporate	2	0.30	0.54	0.69
114 M1 (in bil of current $)	3	0.15	0.30	0.51
115 M2 (in bil of current $)	3	0.17	0.26	0.59
116 M3 (in bil of current $)	3	0.07	0.19	0.52
117 Monetary base, adjusted for reserve requirement (rr) changes (bil of $)	3	0.09	0.24	0.36
118 Depository institutions reserves: total (adj for rr changes)	3	0.09	0.24	0.43
119 Depository institutions: nonborrowed (adj for rr changes)	3	0.17	0.30	0.47
120 Loans and securities at all commercial banks: total (in mil of current $)	3	0.30	0.38	0.58
121 Loans and securities at all comm banks: securities, total (in mil of $)	3	0.31	0.39	0.47
122 Loans and securities at all comm banks: securities, U.S. govt (in mil of $)	3	0.46	0.53	0.61
123 Loans and securities at all comm banks: real estate loans (in mil of $)	3	0.41	0.51	0.60
124 Loans and securities at all comm banks: comm and Indus loans (in mil of $)	3	0.39	0.47	0.59
125 Loans and securities at all comm banks: consumer loans (in mil of $)	3	0.44	0.49	0.62
126 Delinquency rate on bank-held consumer installment loans (3)	3	0.18	0.28	0.39
127 PPI: finished goods (1982 = 100 for all PPI data)	4	0.34	0.67	0.75
128 PPI: finished consumer goods	4	0.29	0.62	0.71
129 PPI: intermediate materials	4	0.50	0.72	0.80
130 PPI: crude materials	4	0.15	0.33	0.43
131 PPI: finished goods excl food	4	0.40	0.66	0.78
132 Index of sensitive materials prices	4	0.53	0.60	0.67
133 CPI: all items (urban)	4	0.55	0.76	0.85
134 CPI: food and beverages	4	0.31	0.52	0.61
135 CPI: housing	4	0.55	0.69	0.78
136 CPI: apparel	4	0.20	0.43	0.52
137 CPI: transportation	4	0.30	0.49	0.68
138 CPI: medical care	4	0.51	0.66	0.70
139 CPI: commodities	4	0.33	0.63	0.76
140 CPI: commodities, durables	4	0.25	0.54	0.63
141 CPI: services	4	0.51	0.67	0.75

(continued)

Series:	Transformation	Variance explained by DPC 1	2	3
142 CPI: all items less food	4	0.51	0.70	0.82
143 CPI: all items less shelter	4	0.43	0.72	0.82
144 CPI: all items less medical care	4	0.53	0.75	0.84
145 CPI: all items less food and energy	4	0.57	0.74	0.81
146 Price of gold ($/oz) on the London market (recorded in the p.m.)	4	0.14	0.54	0.64
147 PCE chain weight price index: total	4	0.45	0.77	0.85
148 PCE prices: total excl food and energy	4	0.37	0.66	0.72
149 PCE prices: durables	4	0.28	0.54	0.65
150 PCE prices: nondurables	4	0.37	0.65	0.78
151 PCE prices: services	4	0.28	0.52	0.60
152 Avg hourly earnings: total nonagricultural (in current $)	4	0.21	0.45	0.57
153 Avg hourly earnings: construction (in current $)	4	0.22	0.45	0.55
154 Avg hourly earnings: mfg (in current $)	4	0.16	0.42	0.58
155 Avg hourly earnings: finance, insurance, and real estate (in current $)	4	0.16	0.40	0.55
156 Avg hourly earnings: professional and business services (in current $)	4	0.23	0.35	0.51
157 Avg hourly earnings: education and health services (in current $)	4	0.25	0.38	0.49
158 Avg hourly earnings: other services (in current $)	4	0.22	0.36	0.50
159 Total merchandise exports (FAS value) (in mil of $)	3	0.34	0.50	0.60
160 Total merchandise imports (CIF value) (in mil of $) (NSA)	3	0.43	0.57	0.66
161 Total merchandise imports (customs value) (in mil of $)	3	0.35	0.46	0.54
162 Philadelphia Fed business outlook: general activity (5)	0	0.76	0.83	0.86
163 Outlook: new orders	0	0.70	0.77	0.81
164 Outlook: shipments	0	0.68	0.73	0.78
165 Outlook: inventories	0	0.50	0.59	0.64
166 Outlook: unfilled orders	0	0.73	0.76	0.79
167 Outlook: prices paid	0	0.40	0.65	0.82
168 Outlook: prices received	0	0.40	0.62	0.82
169 Outlook employment	0	0.77	0.81	0.84
170 Outlook: work hours	0	0.72	0.76	0.81

(continued)

Series:	Transfor-mation	Variance explained by DPC 1	2	3
171 Federal govt deficit or surplus (in mil of current $)	0	0.08	0.17	0.27
172 Real GDP	3	0.63	0.74	0.77
173 GDP deflator	4	0.44	0.71	0.79

0: no transformation. X_t
1: logarithm. $\log(X_t)$
2: quarterly differences. $(1 - L^3)X_t$
3: quarterly growth rates. $400(1 - L^3)\log(X_t)$
4: quarterly difference of yearly growth rates. $(1 - L^3)(1 - L^{12})\log(X_t)$

Notes

We thank the Division of Monetary Affairs of the Federal Reserve Board for hosting this project and providing partial funding. In particular, we are indebted to David Small for helpful suggestions and Ryan Michaels for helping in the construction of the data set. Thanks are also due to Athanasios Orphanides, Barbara Rossi, Philippe Weil, and Mike Woodford as well as our discussants, Harald Uhlig and Mark Watson, and to participants at the NBER Macroeconomic Annual 2004 conference.

1. Greenbook data can be obtained from the Web site of the Philadelphia Fed: www.phil.frb.org/econ/forecast/greenbookdatasets.html.

2. These estimates are computed on data aggregated at the quarterly level.

3. For the project at the Board of Governors of the Federal Reserve, on which the present paper is based, we have used a formal analysis to select q and found it to be 2.

4. This percentage is above 80% if we concentrate on business-cycle frequencies.

5. Real-time data, organized in vintages, have been obtained from the Philadelphia Fed Web site: www.phil.frb.org/econ/forecast/reaindex.html.

6. The fact that we use revised data should not affect our results because revision errors are typically series specific and hence have negligible effects when we extract the two common factors. The robustness of the pseudo real-time exercise has been demonstrated by Bernanke and Boivin (2003).

7. For a definition of identification conditions and other technical aspects of the model, see Forni, Hallin, Lippi, and Reichlin (2002); Stock and Watson (2002).

8. We apply the criterion of Bai and Ng (2000) for the sample 1970:1–1988:12. This criterion is very sensible to different specifications of the penalty term but suggests a quite large value of r. We select $r = 10$ and find that results are robust over larger values. This is explained by the fact that the methodology is robust if we select a static rank higher than the true one, provided that the dynamic rank, q, is well specified. On this point, see Forni, Giannone, Lippi, and Reichlin (2004).

9. The Kalman filter step improves on the principal component estimator proposed by Stock and Watson (2002) by allowing us to take into explicit account the dynamics of the

panel. An alternative strategy, in the frequency domain, is that followed by Forni, Hallin, Lippi, and Reichlin (2002).

10. As for the factor model, we use the real-time series of the GDP deflator.

11. Confidence intervals have been computed by bootstrap methods, as we did in Giannone, Reichlin, and Sala (2002) and as in Forni et al. (2003).

12. The mean has been attributed to the two conditional histories according to the long-run variance decomposition. For GDP, this corresponds to 1 to the real shock and 0 to the nominal; for the federal funds rate, .67 and .33, respectively; for the deflator, .8 and .2, respectively.

13. To isolate the effects of the shocks from the difference arising from the estimation of the parameters, we estimate the model at time T_1 and keep the same parameters to compute the signal at time T_2.

14. The Ljung-Box Q-statistic at lag 1 on the idiosyncratic components of the fedral funds rate is 1.2, with a p-value of 0.27. The statistic is also not significant for a higher lag.

15. This is not a surprising result since, if all real variables had contemporaneous conditional dynamics and so did nominal variables, we would have found the dynamic rank to be equal to the static rank, i.e., $r = q$.

References

Atekeson, A., and L. E. Ohanian. (2001). Are Phillips curves useful for forecasting inflation? *Federal Reserve Bank of Minneapolis Quarterly Review* 25:2–11.

Bai, J., and S. Ng. (2000). Determining the number of factors in approximate factor models. *Econometrica* 70:191–221.

Bernanke, B. S., and J. Boivin. (2003). Monetary policy in a data rich environment. *Journal of Monetary Economics* 50:525–546.

Blanchard, O. J., and D. Quah. (1989). The dynamic effects of aggregate demand and supply disturbances. *American Economic Review* 79:654–673.

Brayton, F., J. M. Roberts, and J. C. Williams. (1999). What's happened to the Phillips curve? *Board of Governors of the Federal Reserve, Finance and Economics Discussion Series* 1999/49.

Brillinger, D. R. (1981). *Time Series: Data Analysis and Theory*. San Francisco: Holden-Day.

Clarida, R., J. Galí, and M. Gertler. (2000). Monetary policy rules and macroeconomic stability: Evidence and some theory. *Quarterly Journal of Economics* 115:147–180.

Croushore, D., and T. Stark. (1999). A real-time data set for macroeconomists: Does the data vintage matter? *Review of Economics and Statistics*, forthcoming.

Diebold, F. X., and G. Rudebusch. (1991). Forecasting output with the composite leading index: A real-time analysis. *Journal of the American Statistical Association* 86:603–610.

Evans, C. L. (1998). Real-time Taylor rules and the federal funds futures market. *Chicago Fed Economic Perspectives* 2.

Forni, M., D. Giannone, M. Lippi, and L. Reichlin. (2004). Opening the black box: Identifying shocks and propagation mechanisms in VAR and factor models. www.dynfactors.org.

Forni, M., M. Hallin, M. Lippi, and L. Reichlin. (2000). The generalized factor model: Identification and estimation. *The Review of Economics and Statistics* 82:540–554.

Forni, M., M. Hallin, M. Lippi, and L. Reichlin. (2002). The generalized dynamic factor model: One-sided estimation and forecasting. CEPR Working Paper No. 3432.

Giannone, D., L. Reichlin, and L. Sala. (2002). Tracking Greenspan: Systematic and unsystematic monetary policy revisited. CEPR Working Paper No. 3550.

Goodfriend, M. (2002). The phases of U.S. monetary policy: 1987 to 2001. *Economic Quarterly*. Federal Reserve Bank of Richmond.

Orphanides, A. (2001). Monetary policy rules based on real-time data. *American Economic Review* 91:964–985.

Orphanides, A. (2003). Historical monetary policy analysis and the Taylor rule. *Journal of Monetary Economics* 50:983–1022.

Orphanides, A., R. D. Porter, D. L. Reifschneider, R. J. Tetlow, and F. Finan. (2000). Errors in the measurement of the output gap and the design of monetary policy. *Journal of Economics and Business* 52:117–141.

Orphanides, A., and S. Van Norden. (2002). The unreliability of output gap estimates in real time. *The Review of Economics and Statistics* 84:569–583.

Romer, C., and David H. Romer. (1994). What ends recessions? *NBER Macroeconomics Annual* 9:13–57.

Rudebusch, G. D. (2001). Term structure evidence on interest rate smoothing and monetary policy inertia. *Journal of Monetary Economics* 49:1161–1187.

Rudebusch, G. (2002). Assessing nominal income rules for monetary policy with model and data uncertainty. *Economic Journal* 12:402–432.

Sargent, T. J., and C. A. Sims. (1977). Business cycle modelling without pretending to have much *a priori* economic theory. In *New Methods in Business Research*, C. Sims (ed.). Minneapolis: Federal Reserve Bank of Minneapolis.

Soderlind, P., U. Soderstrom, and A. Vredin. (2003). Taylor rules and the predictability of interest rates. Sveriges Riksbank Workin Paper Series No. 247.

Staiger, D., J. H. Stock, and M. W. Watson. (1997). The NAIRU, unemployment, and monetary policy. *Journal of Economic Perspectives* 11:33–49.

Stock, J. H., and M. W. Watson. (1999). Forecasting inflation. *Journal of Monetary Economics* 44:293–335.

Stock, J. H., and M. W. Watson. (2002). Macroeconomic forecasting using diffusion indexes. *Journal of Business and Economic Statistics* 40:147–162.

Svensson, L. E. O. (2003). What is wrong with Taylor rules? Using judgment in monetary policy through targeting rules. *Journal of Economic Literature* 41:426–477.

Taylor, J. B. (1993). Discretion versus policy rules in practice. *Carnegie-Rochester Conference Series on Public Policy* 39:195–214.

Taylor, J. B. (1999). Monetary policy rules. Chicago, IL: University of Chicago Press.

Uhlig, H. (2003). What moves real GDP? Humboldt University. Unpublished Manuscript.

Comment

Harald Uhlig
Humboldt University, CentER,
Bundesbank, and CEPR

This paper holds an enticing promise. Start from the observation that Taylor rules work well to explain the observed paths for the federal funds rate. Add to that the insight of recent research on macroeconomic factors, that a large share of the movements in the main aggregates of the economy can be explained by only a few, perhaps two, fundamental forces or shocks; see, for example, Forni et al. (2000), Stock and Watson (2002), Uhlig (2003), and the paper at hand. Consider that it may be more appealing to state Taylor rules in terms of forecasts of the output gap and inflation rate, and note that macroeconomic factor models are good for providing forecasts. Then you get the promise that this paper holds: to understand monetary policy choices or to conduct monetary policy, pay attention to the macroeconomic factors and the two key shocks driving their movements.

This promise is enticing, because monetary policy needs to make its choices in a "data-rich environment" (Bernanke and Boivin, 2003). Ordinarily, one would need to pay attention to each bit of the plethora of information in the many time series observable by the policymaker and consider how to react to it. Similarly, analysts of monetary policy need to sift through the many influences on monetary policy to see why and when interest rates move. But equipped with the factor analysis in this paper, one can reduce and organize this wealth of information into a few key shocks only, which then warrant most of the attention. The rest is idiosynchratic noise, which one should not ignore entirely but which is of small residual importance. The techniques in the paper at hand show how to construct the relevant factors and to assess their impact on the key macroeconomic aggregate in real time, i.e., in terms of the data available to policymakers at decision time.

This discussion is organized around this promise. I agree that the factor model works remarkably well for forecasting inflation, output growth, and the federal funds rate. I also agree that the main macroeconomic aggregates seem to be driven to a considerable degree by two shocks only: this indeed is an important insight. But I caution against the promise described above, which a reader of Giannone, Reichlin, and Sala's paper might take away all too easily as the implied conclusion. To show why I think this promise is problematic, I shall ask and answer three questions.

1. Do Taylor Rules Fit Because of Dimension Two?

Figure 1 shows a simple benchmark Taylor rule, estimated by regressing the federal funds rate on a constant, lagged inflation and the deviation of lagged log gross domestic product (GDP) from its five-year moving average (as a crude measure of the output gap), using quarterly data from 1971 to 2001. The R^2 is 0.60.

Gianonne, Reichlin, and Sala (GRS) view these regressors as well as the federal funds rate as part of a panel x_t of macroeconomic time series, driven by ten macroeconomic factors F_t, which in turn are driven by two shocks u_t, plus noise ξ_t:

$$x_t = \Lambda F_t + \xi_t$$

$$F_t = AF_{t-1} + Bu_t$$

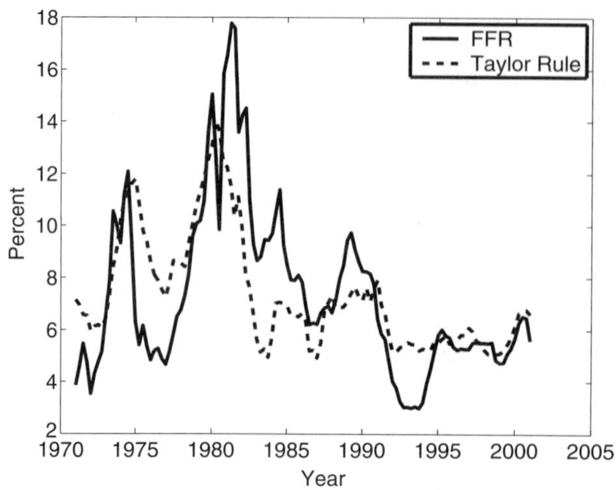

Figure 1
Taylor Rule, estimated with lagged CPI inflation and lagged log GDP minus its five-year moving average, quarterly data

Hence, the static dimension is ten, whereas the dynamic dimension is two. With this, instead of regressing the federal funds rate r_t on some measure of the output gap g_t and inflation π_t, it would seem to be more direct to regress the federal funds rate on the factors F_t, in particular as one can thereby avoid the noise component ξ_t in the regressors.

But in contrast to what one may be led to believe by GRS, this does not improve matters. First, while the original Taylor rule gets by with just two regressors, the first two factors alone provide a pretty bad fit (the R^2 is just 0.07), and even with all ten factors, the picture does not look great. See Figure 2: the R^2 increases to just 0.20.

Part of the reason for the bad fit seems to be that the factors are calculated with, for example, the first differences of interest rates, so they may be more informative about changes in the federal funds rate than its level. Thus, Figure 3 uses both the factors as well as their cumulative sums as regressors. This does not change the dynamic dimension since the two-dimensional shock vector u_t still suffices to explain also the evolution of the cumulative sums, but it does double the number of regressors. With two factors (and thus four regressors), one obtains an R^2 of 0.74, while with all ten factors (and thus twenty regressors), R^2 is 0.94, and one obtains nearly perfect fit. Of course, with twenty regressors, this may not be very surprising. Note that my results here are consistent with the results of Table 2 in their paper, where, for example, the first two dynamic principal components can explain 72% of the variance of the first difference of the federal funds rate, and additional regressors would presumably be needed also to get the level of the federal funds rate right. My results are also consistent with Section

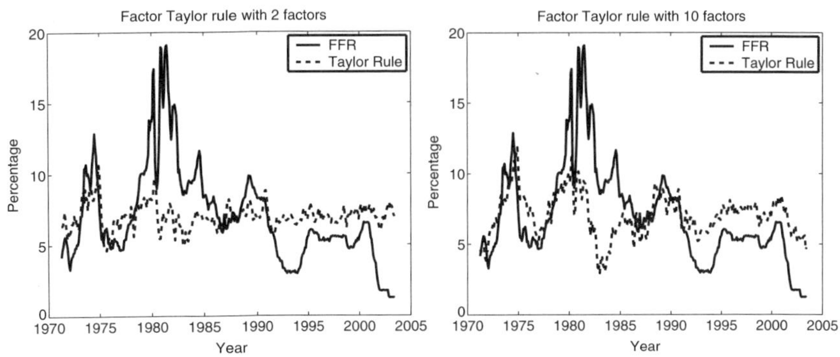

Figure 2
Taylor Rule, estimated with the first two respectively all ten factors

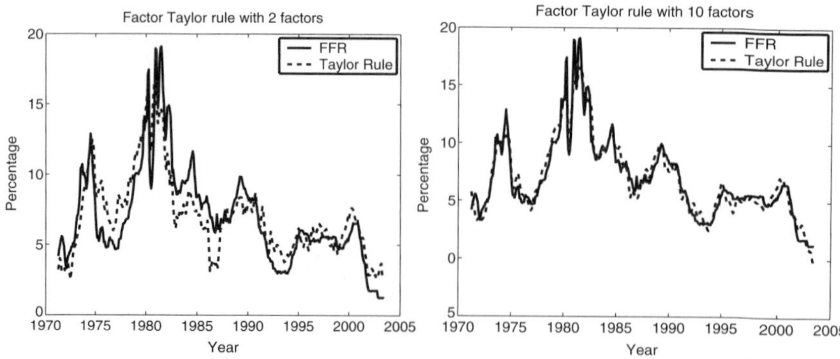

Figure 3
Taylor Rule, estimated with the first two respectively all ten factors plus their cumulative sums

4 of GRS, which concentrates not on the original federal funds rate series, but on that part of the federal funds rate series that can be explained with the real or the nominal factors, discarding the possibly more important noise of the federal funds rate factor regression.

What the exercise above shows is that a two-dimensional shock u_t does not imply at all that a Taylor rule with two regressors closely related to these u_t will fit well. Since F_t is ten-dimensional, and is thus recording lagged u_t's as well, it would in fact be surprising if all this rather complicated dynamics of the two underlying shocks could be folded into just two macroeconomic time series, output and inflation. So the fact that the original Taylor rule fits so well may have little to do with the issue that the dynamic dimension of the economy is two. Instead, it is plausible that something else is going on: simple Taylor rules fit well because monetary policy cares about the output gap and inflation. Typical theoretical derivations of optimal monetary policy often have that feature; see, for example, Woodford, 2003 (And if not, one could try to identify those macroeconomic aggregates that the monetary policymaker cares about: it is these aggregates, not the factors, that should show up in Taylor rules of well-chosen monetary policy). Thus, there is a good chance that the noise component ξ_t in the output gap and inflation is of similar or even greater importance for monetary policy than the movements of the underlying factors. The two-factor model in turn also fits reasonably well because two factors suffice to fit the bulk of the cyclical dynamics in output and inflation. However, since the noise part ξ_t is missing in the factor model, the fit is worse.

To illuminate this, consider the original Taylor rule:

$$r_t = \alpha + \beta g_t + \gamma \pi_t + \varepsilon_t$$

and suppose that the output gap g_t and inflation π_t have a particularly simple dependence on two factors, which in turn have a particularly simple dynamic structure:

$$g_t = \lambda_g F_{1t} + \xi_{gt}$$

$$\pi_t = \lambda_\pi F_{2t} + \xi_{\pi t}$$

$$F_{1t} = u_{1t}$$

$$F_{2t} = u_{2t}$$

Assume that all innovations $\varepsilon_t, u_{1t}, u_{2t}, \xi_{gt}$, and $\xi_{\pi t}$ have zero mean and are mutually orthogonal. If the Taylor rule is recalculated using the factors, one obtains:

$$r_t = \alpha + (\beta \lambda_g) F_{1t} + (\gamma \lambda_\pi) F_{2t} + v_t$$

where

$$v_t = \beta \xi_{gt} + \gamma \xi_{\pi t} + \varepsilon_t$$

has a higher variance than ε_t, and the fit is therefore worse than the original Taylor rule. If the factors even have a dynamic structure, for example:

$$F_{1t} = a_1 F_{1,t-1} + u_{1t}$$

$$F_{2t} = a_2 F_{2,t-1} + u_{2t}$$

the best-fitting factor Taylor rule would now be:

$$r_t = \alpha + (\beta \lambda_g) F_{1t} - (a_1 \beta \lambda_g) F_{1,t-1} + (\gamma \lambda_\pi) F_{2t} - (a_2 \gamma \lambda_\pi) F_{2,t-1} + v_t$$

The fit is just as bad as for the factor Taylor rule in the simple specification above, but now four rather than two regressors are required in the factor Taylor rule, just to keep up with the original specification.

These arguments (plus the arguments in the third section below) provide good intuition for the findings above. In sum, a two-factor Taylor rule *does* work. But it is worse, not better, than the original output-gap-and-inflation Taylor rule. It is the original Taylor rule that captures the essence of the underlying economic logic, and the factor model just happens to provide a statistically good fit, not the other way around, as GRS may lead a reader to believe.

The key assumption in the arguments above is the orthogonality of ε_t to ξ_{gt} and $\xi_{\pi t}$. If it was the case, for example, that v_t is orthogonal to ξ_{gt} and $\xi_{\pi t}$ in the simple specification above, with:

$$\varepsilon_t = v_t - (\beta \xi_{gt} + \gamma \xi_{\pi t})$$

then obviously the factor Taylor rule would fit better. One way to interpret GRS is that they take this perspective and not the perspective of the preceding argument. To check which perspective is appropriate, one needs to investigate why the Fed deviates from the Taylor rule, i.e., to explain the movements in ε_t. Let me turn to this issue now.

2. Why Does the Fed Deviate from the Taylor Rule?

There is another reason to be interested in explaining the movements in the residual of the original Taylor rule, even if one buys into the argument by GRS, that simple Taylor rules work because the economy is two-dimensional. If all we get out is another Taylor rule, have we really learned much? Central bankers often assert that their job is considerably more complicated than just running a Taylor rule. Whether this is just a self-serving claim (or worse the result of faulty monetary policy analysis) or whether their job is really considerably more complex shall not be the issue discussed here (although I do believe the latter to be the case). Rather, we do observe empirically that gaps remain between actual federal funds rate choices and those implied by Taylor rules (see, for example, Figure 1). So the interesting issue is, What explains these deviations from the Taylor rule, and can the macroeconomic factors help to resolve these issues?

To answer this question, I have done the following. I calculate the Taylor rule residual as in Figure 1 but based on data from 1955 to 2001. I fit a Bayesian vector autoregression (VAR) in this residual as well as PPI inflation, industrial production, hours worked, capacity utilization, private investment, and labor productivity in manufacturing, using quarterly data from 1973 to 2001 and two lags. The goal shall be to explain as much as possible of the movement in the Taylor rule residual with as few different types of shocks as possible. Thus, in the seven-dimensional space of the one-step-ahead prediction errors, I find those two dimensions that explain most of the sum of the k-step ahead prediction revision variances for the Taylor rule residual. I explain the details of this methodology in Uhlig (2003), and they are similar to the

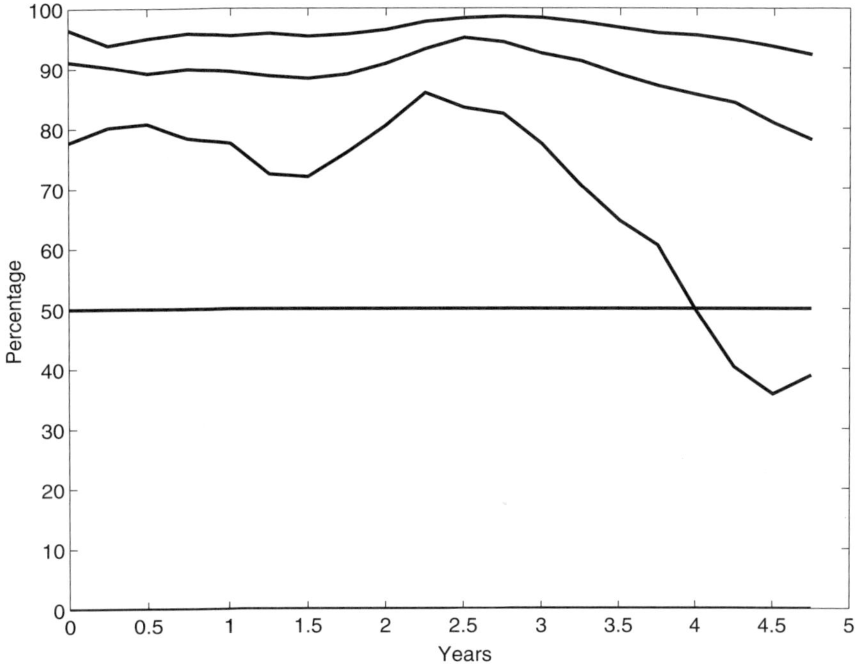

Figure 4
Fraction of the variance of the *k*-step ahead forecast revision for the Taylor rule residual, explained by two shocks in the seven-variable VAR with other economic variables

construction in GRS, Section 3.1, when they construct shocks to "explain the maximum of the variance of real variables in panel."

I find the following. Two shocks can explain around 90% of the variance of the *k*-step-ahead prediction revision variance for all horizons *k* between 0 and five years (see Figure 4). The impulse response of the Taylor rule residual to the first shock is fairly persistent (see Figure 5) and coincides with movements of labor productivity in manufacturing in the opposite direction (see Figure 6). This suggests that the deviation here could be explained by a more subtle measurement of the output gap: the Fed sets interests rates higher than would be implied by the line calculated in Figure 1 because it sees output not supported by corresponding gains in productivity. And indeed, industrial production changes course from an initial expansion to a contraction within two years. The second shock looks like a quickly reverted error in interest rate policy (see Figure 7).

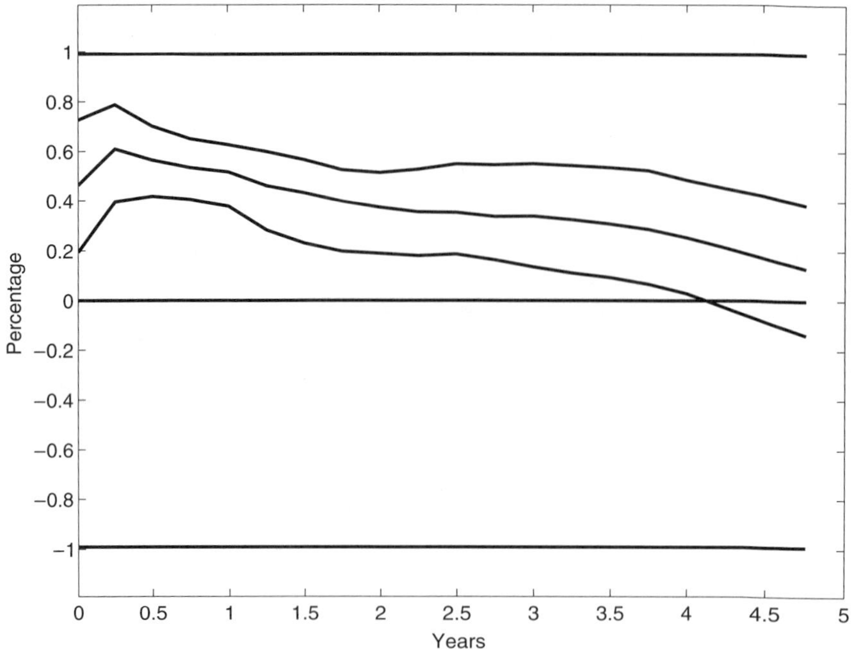

Figure 5
Impulse response of the Taylor rule residual to the first shock, $\theta = 0$

One can redo the same exercise using the ten factors in the VAR instead of the economic variables listed above. To obtain impulse responses for these variables, they can in turn be regressed on the VAR series and their innovations, plus their own lags. The results are now much less clear cut. First, the fraction of variance explained for the Taylor rule residual is not quite as high (see Figure 8). The impulse response of the Taylor rule residual to the first shock in Figure 9 seems to be in between the more persistent response of Figure 5 and the quick-error-reversal response in Figure 7. And the implied impulse responses of industrial production and productivity do not tell a clear-cut story (see Figure 10): industrial production has no clearly signed response, while productivity keeps expanding gradually.

This clinches the point made above: for monetary policy, the noise component of some key economic variables may be more important than the stochastic disturbances to the factors. The factors paint too coarse a picture to be a sufficiently precise guide to monetary policy or its analysis.

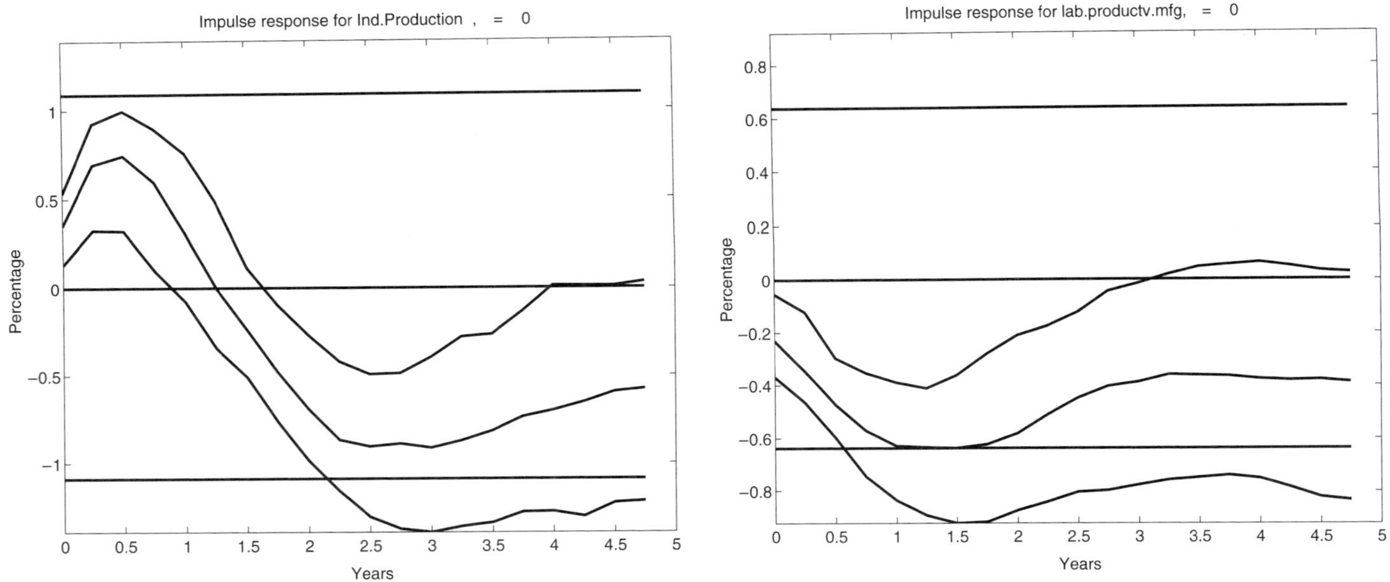

Figure 6
Impulse response of industrial production and labor productivity in manufacturing to the first shock, $\theta = 0$

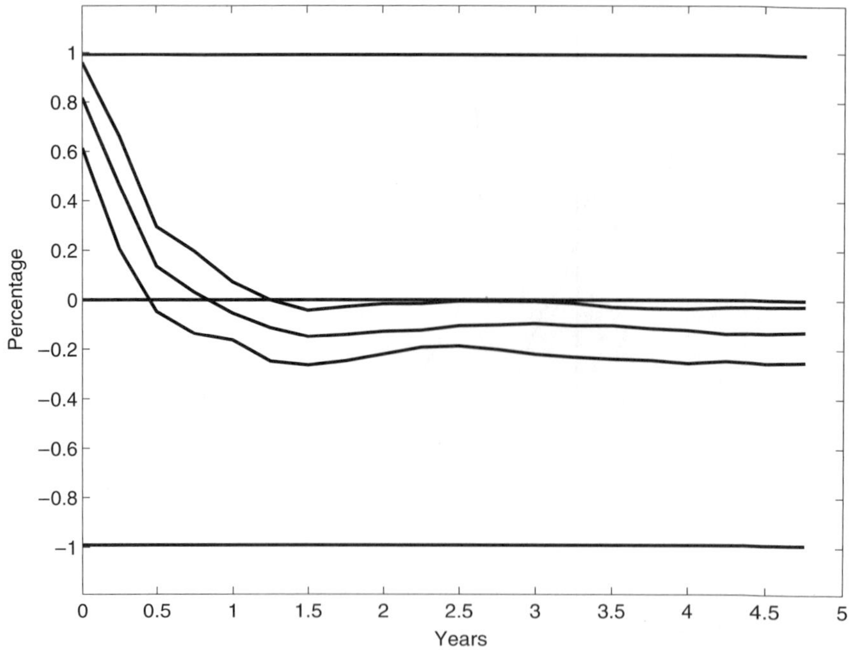

Figure 7
Impulse response of the Taylor rule residual to the second shock, $\theta = 90$

3. Do We Need to Worry About Causality?

At this point, a skeptical reader might point out that this discussion began with calculating factor Taylor rules with ten factors and their partial sums, and that they provided a nearly perfect fit. Shouldn't this be good news for an analysis of monetary policy, based on macroeconomic factors? But aside from factors capturing the economically relevant variables—the output gap and inflation—there is another reason that the Taylor rule estimated with all ten factors and their cumulative sums should fit well. The ten factors are the leading ten principal components of the variance-covariance matrix of a panel of macroeconomic time series. According to Table 1 in GRS, a substantial fraction of the variables included in the panel are closely related to monetary policy or are likely to react sensitively to changes in the federal funds rate. For example, the variables labeled as "financial markets," "interest rates," and "money and loans" count for 22% of the entire panel and probably an even higher fraction of the total variance. Since variance

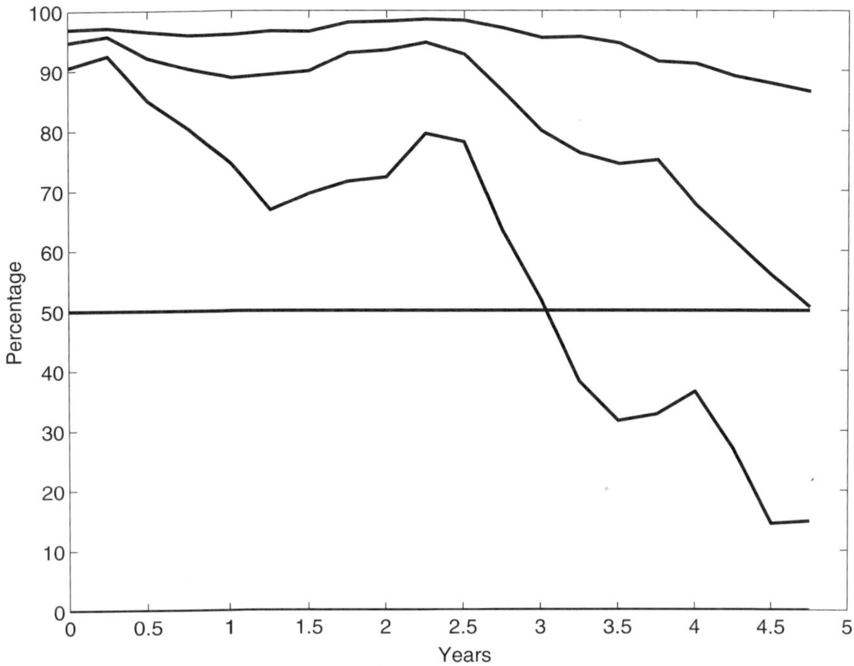

Figure 8
Fraction of the variance of the *k*-step ahead forecast revision for the Taylor rule residual, explained by two shocks in the eleven-variable VAR with ten factors

matters for the calculation of the principal components, the influence of these variables is likely to be even larger than 22%. So there is a sense in which the factor Taylor rules above or, likewise, the fraction of the variance in the federal funds rate explained by the factors as stated in the paper, are just regressions of the federal funds rate on itself.

Whether or not this is a problem hinges on whether or not one believes some monetary policy shocks are not explained by economic fundamentals. If there are none or if they are negligible, then the information contained in the movements of financial market variables just reflects the underlying economic fundamentals, and this appears to be the position the paper implicitly takes. Indeed, the paper gives an economic interpretation to the two shocks and views them as untainted by monetary policy shocks. A substantial fraction of the VAR literature on monetary policy can be read as supportive of this position.

On the other hand, if there are sizable monetary policy shocks, then the principal component shocks identified in the paper are likely to be

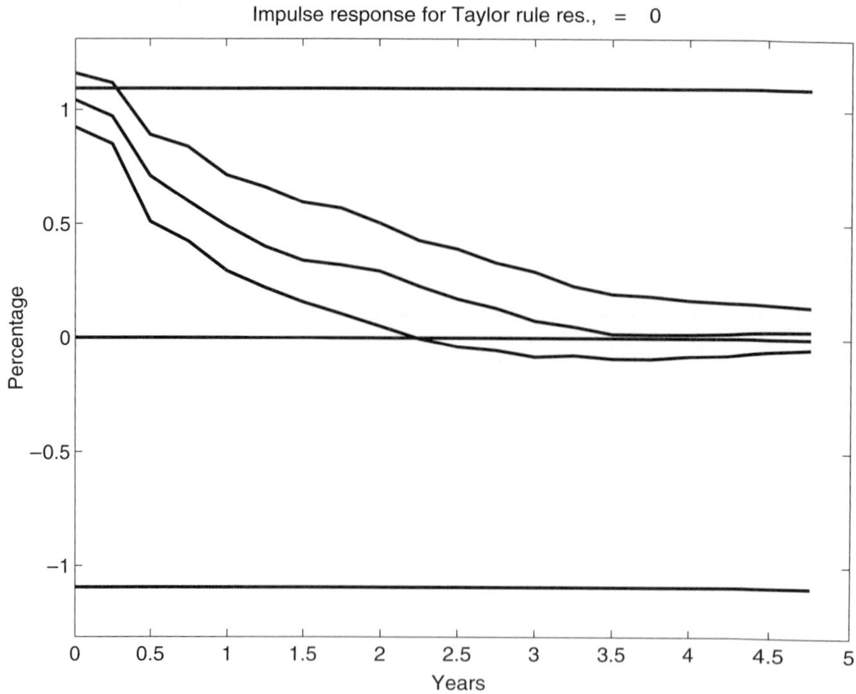

Figure 9
Impulse response of the Taylor rule residual to the first shock in the eleven-variable VAR with factors, $\theta = 0$

at least partly tainted by monetary policy shocks, or even to represent the monetary policy shocks themselves (when using some linear combination of the factor shocks). The 22% of the variables closely related or reacting sensitively to the federal funds rate then move in reaction to monetary policy choices, or even anticipate them, due to speeches, information released between federal open market committee (FOMC) meetings, etc., and so will the extracted factors. Even using factors extracted from data available before the FOMC meeting may just recover market expectations and echoes of previous Fed announcements. Analyzing the movements of the extracted factors thus will not be helpful for choosing interest rates or understanding these choices.

Another way to see this is to think about the information contained in futures. Table 5 in GRS shows that the root mean square error (RMSE) for futures/2-shocks is 0.47 for lead 0 and 0.76 for lead 1, so in terms of fitting monetary policy choices, one would do even better

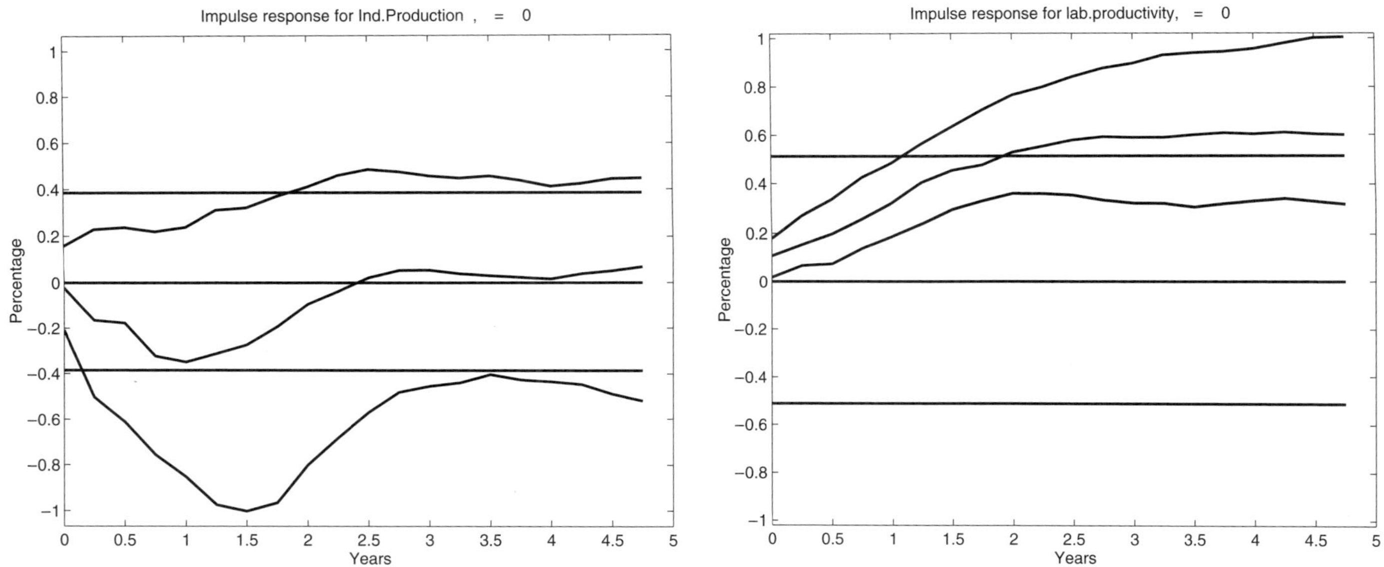

Figure 10
Implied impulse response of industrial production and labor productivity in manufacturing to the first shock in the eleven-variable VAR with factors, $\theta = 0$

with data on futures than with data on factors. But that does not imply that the Fed should follow what futures markets expect it to do nor is this of helpful guidance to the Fed; the futures presumably simply fit so well because they pay close attention to signals coming from the Fed about what it plans to do in the future, not the other way around. Thus, similarly, if the extracted factors contain market expectations about Fed policy, then the forecasts constructed with these factors for inflation and output growth rates are the resulting inflation rates and output growth rates, if the Fed fulfills these expectations. This is useful for monetary policy; for example, the Fed then can and should ask if it wants to deviate from these on-the-equilibrium-path expectations. But that does not answer the question about where these expectations came from in the first place.

So if there are monetary policy shocks, then one would ideally seek to find factors and factor innovations which are causal to Fed choices and Fed announcements, both for conducting policy as well as for understanding Fed choices. This gets us into the usual VAR identification debates. This debate is assumed away in this paper by implicitly assuming that monetary policy shocks are too small or matter too little to be of relevance to the extracted factors.

4. Conclusion

Current thinking about monetary policy (as in Woodford [2003], for example) focuses on the output gap, inflation rates, and their forecasts and relates them to choices of the interest rate. Perhaps it is sensible and possible to write down theories in which the relevant economic variables for conducting monetary policy are factors or in which the right measure of the output gap corresponds to what GRS have captured with their factors. But a priori, I remain skeptical. What matters to monetary policy are rather specific variables and their rather specific own dynamics: the macroeconomic factors can be somewhat but not sufficiently informative about them. The noise component does matter.

Thus, I view the methodology provided by GRS mainly as a method to provide the Fed with on-the-equilibrium-path forecasts of output, inflation, and interest rates, i.e., as a forecast of the economy, provided the Fed follow market expectations. Where these expectations come from or what the fundamental forces are to which the Fed reacts requires additional substantive identifying assumptions (like the absence of monetary policy shocks), which one ought to be careful in making.

Despite all these skeptical remarks and despite the obligation of the discussant to describe what he or she disagrees with, it is also important to emphasize where the agreements are and to point out the achievements of GRS. Their paper has convincingly demonstrated that two shocks capture the main dynamics of a large number of macroeconomic aggregates. This is interesting and it is an important base on which to build macroeconomic theories, which emphasize few, not many, driving forces. GRS have also shown that interesting things can be done with these factors. I share their view that there is much more of a dichotomy between the real and the nominal side of the economy than is often believed, and that it may be feasible for monetary policy to concentrate on fighting inflation without having to worry too much about the real side of the economy. Excessive worries about real effects were the original reason that the Volcker disinflation came so late. The real impact of the disinflation turned out to be smaller than many anticipated (see the discussion in Cogley and Sargent, 2004). Excessive worries sometimes dominate monetary policy discussions also, especially in policy circles outside central banks. It is remarkably hard to justify these worries with a proper analysis of the data, as I have found in my own work (see Uhlig, 2004), and as GRS have also shown in their paper. It is time to use data rather than just conventional wisdom as a guide to monetary policy analysis and to take these results seriously.

References

Bernanke, B. S., and Boivin, J. (2003). Monetary policy in a data rich environment. *Journal of Monetary Economics* 50:525–546.

Cogley, T., and Sargent, T. (2004). The conquest of U.S. inflation: Learning and robustness to model uncertainty. New York University. Unpublished Manuscript.

Forni, M., M. Hallin, M. Lippi, and L. Reichlin. (2000). The generalized factor model: Identification and estimation. *The Review of Economics and Statistics* 82:540–554.

Stock, J. H., and M. W. Watson. (2002). Macroeconomic forecasting using diffusion indexes. *Journal of Business and Economic Statistics* 40:147–162.

Uhlig, H. (2003). What moves real GDP? Humboldt University. Unpublished Manuscript.

Uhlig, H. (2004). What are the effects of monetary policy on output? Results from an agnostic identification procedure. *Journal of Monetary Economics*, forthcoming.

Woodford, M. (2003). *Interest and prices: Foundations of a theory of monetary policy*. Princeton, NJ: Princeton University Press.

Comment

Mark W. Watson
Princeton University and NBER

1. Introduction

This paper considers three questions. How many shocks are needed to explain the comovement of variables in the macroeconomy? What are these common shocks? And what are the implications of these findings for empirical characterizations of monetary policy rules?

The paper argues that very few shocks—only two—are needed. The authors arrive at this conclusion using three complimentary exercises. First, they apply large-*n* dynamic factor analysis methods to a data set that includes 200 representative macroeconomic time series over the 1970–2003 time period. A distributed lag of two shocks (the equivalent of two dynamic factors) explains a large fraction of the common variance in these series. Second, they apply similar methods to a panel of forecasts of fifteen important variables from the Fed's Greenbook over the 1978–1996 period. Again, it seems that much of the variance in these forecasts is explained by two shocks. Finally, the 2-shock/200-variable model is used to construct pseudo-real-time forecasts of the growth rate of real gross domestic product (GDP), the growth rate of the GDP deflator, and the federal funds interest rate over the 1989–2003 time period. Short-run forecasts based on the two-factor model perform well.

The authors identify the shocks as real and nominal. Real variables are driven by the real shock, inflation is driven by the nominal shock, and both shocks are important for the federal funds rate. These results, the authors argue, provide a mechanical explanation for why the Taylor rule provides a good description of the federal funds rate. The federal funds rate depends on two shocks, output growth is related to one of the shocks, inflation is related to the other; thus, a regression of the federal funds on output growth and inflation fits the data well.

In my comments, I will address each of these points. First, I will review empirical results from the 1970s on the fit of the two-factor model to see how the results have changed over time. Remarkably, the empirical results from the 1970s are nearly identical to the results found in this paper. Second, in some parts of the paper, the authors argue that inflation is driven by the nominal shock, output is driven by the real shock, and the two shocks are uncorrelated. This implies that movements in output and inflation are uncorrelated, a result that appears at odds with a large literature that documents a positive correlation between movements in output and inflation (the Phillips correlation). I will present results that reconcile the paper's finding of a weak correlation between output and inflation, with a larger and stable Phillips correlation. Finally, I offer a few remarks about the paper's two-factor explanation for the fit of the Taylor rule.

2. Can the U.S. Macroeconomy Be Summarized by Two Factors? A View from the 1970s

Rigorous statistical analysis of multifactor models in macroeconomics started with the work of Sargent and Sims (1977) and Geweke (1977). Indeed, Sargent and Sims considered many of the same empirical questions addressed in this paper, albeit with somewhat different methods and data. They used small-*n* frequency domain factor analysis and U.S. macroeconomic data from 1950–1970, while this paper uses large-*n* factor methods and data from 1970–2003. A comparison of the results in the two papers provides an assessment of the robustness of the results to the sample period and statistical method.

Table 1 shows the results from both papers on the fit of the two-factor model. The results are strikingly similar. One factor explains much of the variance of the real variables. The second factor adds little additional explanatory power for the real series. In contrast, nominal prices require two factors. In both papers, retail sales have more idiosynchratic variability than the other real series and only a small fraction of the variability of M1 is explained by the two factors. The only major difference between the two sets of results is for sensitive materials prices, a result that is not surprising given the dramatic swings in this series that occurred in the sample period used by Giannone, Reichlin, and Sala. In summary, the good fit of the two-factor model seems a remarkably stable feature of the postwar U.S. data.

Table 1
Fraction of variance explained by one- and two-factor models

	Sargent and Sims[1]		Giannone, Reichlin, and Sala[2]	
Series	1 factor	2 factors	1 factor	2 factors
Average weekly hours	0.77	0.80	0.49	0.61
Layoffs	0.83	0.85	0.72	0.82
Employment	0.86	0.88	0.85	0.91
Unemployment	0.77	0.85	0.74	0.82
Industrial production	0.94	0.94	0.88	0.93
Retail sales	0.46	0.69	0.33	0.47
New orders durables	0.67	0.86	0.65	0.74
Sensitive material prices	0.19	0.74	0.53	0.60
Wholesale prices	0.20	0.69	0.34	0.67
M1	0.16	0.20	0.15	0.30

1. From Table 21 of Sargent and Sims (1977).
2. From Appendix 6.2.

3. What Happened to the Phillips Correlation?

The positive correlation between real activity and inflation is one of the most well-known stylized facts in macroeconomics. Yet this correlation is not apparent in the scatter plots in Figure 4 of the paper, and the paper argues that output and inflation are largely reflections of independent sources of variability. Has the Phillips correlation vanished, or is it somehow masked in the factor model? The answer to both questions is no. Rather, many of the results in this paper highlight correlation over high frequencies (where the correlation is weak) instead of business-cycle frequencies (where the correlation is stronger).

In the spirit of the paper's analysis, I have constructed an estimate of the real factor and an estimate of the inflation factor. For the real factor, I use the XCI described in Stock and Watson (1989), which is a weighted average of the logarithm of real personal income, industrial production, manufacturing and trade sales, and employment. For the inflation factor I use a simple average of the inflation rates of the consumer price index, the producer price index, and the price deflator for personal consumption expenditures.

Figure 1 shows an estimate of the coherence between the two factors estimated using monthly data from 1960–2003.[1] Recall that the coherence is a frequency domain of correlation (adjusted for phase shifts),

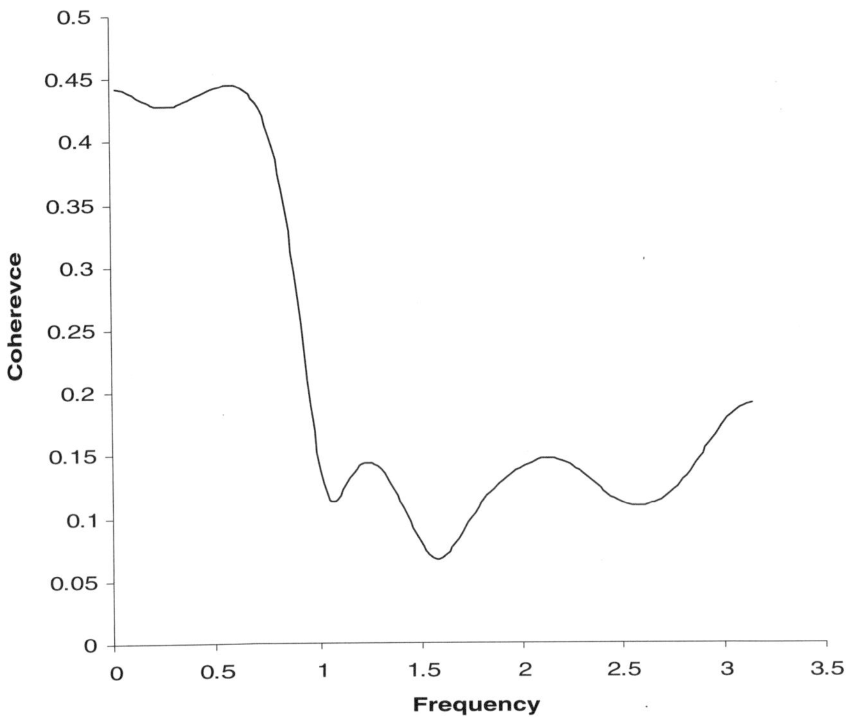

Figure 1
Coherence of output and inflation factors

so that, roughly speaking, the figure shows the correlation of the series over different frequencies. The coherence is approximately 0.45 for frequencies lower than 0.50 (periods longer than 12 months), but it is only 0.10 for frequencies higher than 1.0 (periods shorter than 6 months). Evidently, the series are very weakly correlated at high frequencies, but the correlation is substantially larger over business-cycle frequencies.

Figure 2 tells a similar story using the correlation of forecast errors constructed from a bivariate VAR of the two factors. Correlations are small for short horizons (less than 6 months), but they increase to values larger than 0.35 for horizons longer than 18 months.

Figures 1 and 2 show results for the 1960–2003 sample period, but similar results are obtained over the 1989–2003 period, the pseudo-out-of-sample period considered in this paper. Table 2 summarizes the results.

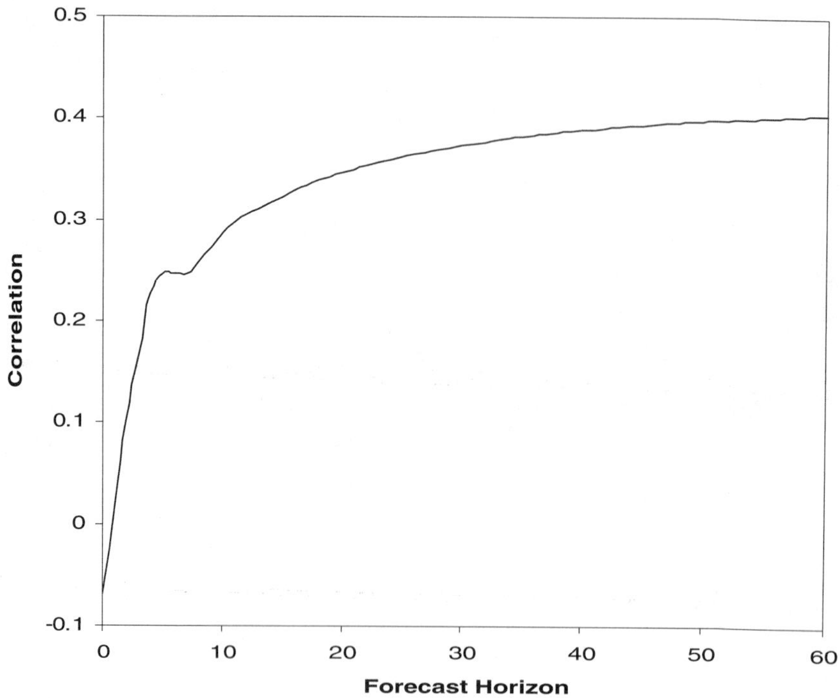

Figure 2
Correlation of output and inflation factor forecast errors

Table 2
Coherence and forecast error correlations

	Average coherence for periods		Correlation of forecast errors for forecast horizon			
Sample period	≤6	≥12	3	12	24	48
1960–2003	0.13	0.43	0.10	0.30	0.36	0.40
1989–2003	0.23	0.44	0.08	0.19	0.27	0.34

Note: These results are computed from estimated VAR(6) models using monthly data.

4. Using the Two-Factor Model to Rationalize the Fit of the Taylor Rule

If the two-factor model is correct, then the federal funds rate depends on two factors. The real factor is reflected in GDP, the nominal factor is reflected in inflation; thus, as the paper argues, it is reasonable that a Taylor rule specification should fit the data well. Yet the story is little more complicated. GDP growth and inflation are imperfect indicators of the underlying factors. The logic of the factor model then says that including (potentially many) other variables in the regression may significantly improve the fit of the Taylor rule because these additional variables help the regression estimate the factors. Indeed, this logic suggests that a better way to study the monetary policy rule is to use factor models like those developed in this paper and in the complimentary analysis in Bernanke and Boivin (2003) and Giannone, Reichlin, and Sala (2002).

Note

1. The coherence was estimated from a VAR(6) model estimated from the first differences of the two factors. Similar results were found using different lag lengths in the VAR.

References

Bernanke, B. S., and J. Boivin. (2003). Monetary policy in a data-rich environment. *Journal of Monetary Economics* 50:3.

Geweke, J. (1977). The dynamic factor analysis of economic time series. In *Latent Variables in Socio-Economic Models*, D. J. Aigner and A. S. Goldberger (eds.). Amsterdam: North Holland, pp. 365–383.

Giannone, D., L. Reichlin, and L. Sala. (2002). Tracking Greenspan: Systematic and unsystematic monetary policy revisited. ECARES, Universite Libre de Bruxelles, Manuscript.

Sargent, T. J., and C. A. Sims. (1977). Business cycle modeling without pretending to have too much a-priori economic theory. In *New Methods in Business Cycle Research*, C. Sims et al. (eds.). Minneapolis: Federal Reserve Bank of Minneapolis.

Stock, J. H., and M. W. Watson. (1989). New indexes of coincident and leading economic indicators. *NBER Macroeconomics Annual* 4:351–393.

Discussion

Lucrezia Reichlin commented on Harald Uhlig's discussion and pointed out that, as shown in his example, not any two aggregates were going to give as good a fit as output and inflation did in the Taylor rule. Inflation and output, she claimed, are very collinear with the rest of the economy and that was why one gets very good forecasting results by projecting on two shocks. She also believed that her forecasting results were very impressive since nobody in the vector autoregression (VAR) literature had gotten close to such results.

Reichlin also responded to Uhlig's concern about the fact that the authors mainly looked at the systematic part and not at the residuals. She said that their empirical work showed that the residual part, the nonsystematic part, was very small, which does not mean that the Federal Reserve always followed systematic output and inflation, as was seen in her example of the Russian crisis episode, but that on average one could explain the bulk of its actions by looking at the systematic part.

There was some discussion among the participants about Uhlig's reservations about the Phillips curve models. Michael Woodford stated that simple models of the Phillips curve relationship, even the ones that did not have any kind of important disturbances to them, were not going to imply that an increase in real activity should lead to the same increase in inflation. According to Woodford, the authors showed that there was a first type of shock that permanently increased real GDP and had little effect on inflation. If one interpreted that permanent increase in real GDP as also a productivity-driven increase in GDP, then one should not expect much effect on inflation. Then there was a second shock that had a big effect on inflation and could be interpreted as a disturbance orthogonal to a technology shock, which had a temporary effect both on the real activity and on inflation, which in turn was what a Phillips curve relationship implied.

Mark Gertler commented that in his opinion Uhlig's point was that even if one had a Phillips curve, the actual reduced-form correlation between output and inflation depended on how well the central bank was performing. He added that one might want to split the sample and look at pre- and post-1979, since in his view if the central bank was doing well, as was the case of the Federal Reserve from the mid-1990s, then the economy might not look very different from what a real business cycle model, with some qualifications, would predict. Reichlin remarked that although the lags in the Phillips curve might be coming from the effect of policy, and one way to tackle this problem was to look at subsamples, she believed that their forecasting results showed that if one ran the model through the whole period, on average, one tracked the federal funds rate well.

Several discussants expressed their view on the number of shocks needed to characterize the economy. Robert Gordon said that in his opinion the economy was characterized by three factors, although they could be reduced to two. The three original factors were the real factor, used also by the authors, that we observed in the form of the negative correlation between unemployment and output; nominal inflation, which was driven by the growth of money; and the supply shocks, which were used to solve the dilemma that sometimes output was negatively correlated with inflation, as in the case of an increase in oil prices, and other times this correlation was positive, as occurred when the economy was hit by a pure monetary shock as in the German hyperinflation. But if one used a simple model with a vertical long-run Phillips curve, a short-run positively sloped Phillips curve on the output-inflation space, a negatively sloped demand curve, and finally a policy response, then two shocks, demand and supply shocks, were enough to obtain the responses the authors were looking for. According to Matthew Shapiro, two real shocks were needed to fit most of the data. He argued that there were short-term productivity shocks and there were other shocks that moved the trend, either the growth rate of productivity or the NAIRU, and if one implemented a Taylor rule, one had to keep track of both the timeless and the time-variant parts of unemployment, so he wondered how the authors could get such good results with only one real shock. Reichlin answered these comments by saying that they had run different specifications of the model, with two and three shocks, and found that the third shock was very small. She added that from the forecasting results they had shown, one did not seem to need a third shock to improve the forecasting of the model.

Jean Boivin stated that in one of his papers they found that to be able to track well the dynamic response of the economy, as the one obtained in a VAR setup, more than two factors were necessary. He then wondered about the size of the residuals in the policy rules of the authors and if the key for the difference in their results could be found there. Reichlin replied that she did not think that their results contradicted his since what she and her co-authors were saying was that, given that the dimension was roughly two, then the Taylor rule should be a good fit. This did not mean, she added, that one could not improve the Taylor rule, which could be done by writing the Taylor rule in terms of shocks, although in that case one might run into invertibility problems, as Mark Watson pointed out. Concerning the size of the residuals, she commented that when looking at the federal funds rate in first differences, medium-run frequencies, one could explain 80% of the variation, which meant that 20% of the variation was what they called unsystematic behavior and this led them to think that there was no other dimension.

Technology Shocks and Aggregate Fluctuations: How Well Does the Real Business Cycle Model Fit Postwar U.S. Data?

Jordi Galí and Pau Rabanal
CREI, UPF, CEPR, and NBER; and International Monetary Fund

1. Introduction

Since the seminal work of Kydland and Prescott (1982) and Prescott (1986b), proponents of the real business cycle (RBC) paradigm have claimed a central role for exogenous variations in technology as a source of economic fluctuations in industrialized economies. Those fluctuations have been interpreted by RBC economists as the equilibrium response to exogenous variations in technology, in an environment with perfect competition and intertemporally optimizing agents, and in which the role of nominal frictions and monetary policy is, at most, secondary.

Behind the claims of RBC theory lies what must have been one of the most revolutionary findings in postwar macroeconomics: a calibrated version of the neoclassical growth model augmented with a consumption-leisure choice, and with stochastic changes in total factor productivity as the only driving force, seems to account for the bulk of economic fluctuations in the postwar U.S. economy. In practice, "accounting for observed fluctuations" has meant that calibrated RBC models match pretty well the patterns of unconditional second moments of a number of macroeconomic time series, including their relative standard deviations and correlations. Such findings led Prescott to claim "that technology shocks account for more than half the fluctuations in the postwar period, with a best point estimate near 75 percent."[1] Similarly, in two recent assessments of the road traveled and the lessons learned by RBC theory after more than a decade, Cooley and Prescott (1995) could confidently claim that "it makes sense to think of fluctuations as caused by shocks to productivity," while King and Rebelo (1999) concluded that "[the] main criticisms levied against first-generation real business cycle models have been largely overcome."

While most macroeconomists have recognized the methodological impact of the RBC research program and have adopted its modeling tools, other important, more substantive elements of that program have been challenged in recent years. First, and in accordance with the widely acknowledged importance of monetary policy in industrialized economies, the bulk of the profession has gradually moved away from real models (or their near-equivalent frictionless monetary models) when trying to understand short-run macroeconomic phenomena. Second, and most important for the purposes of this paper, the view of technological change as a central force behind cyclical fluctuations has been called into question. In the present paper, we focus on the latter development by providing an overview of the literature that has challenged the central role of technology in business cycles.

A defining feature of the literature reviewed here lies in its search for evidence on the role of technology that is more direct than just checking whether any given model driven by technology shocks, and more or less plausibly calibrated, can generate the key features of the business cycle. In particular, we discuss efforts to identify and estimate the *empirical* effects of exogenous changes in technology on different macroeconomic variables, and to evaluate quantitatively the contribution of those changes to business-cycle fluctuations.

Much of that literature (and, hence, much of the present paper) focuses on one central, uncontroversial feature of the business cycle in industrialized economies, namely, the strong positive comovement between output and labor input measures. That comovement is illustrated graphically in Figure 1, which displays the quarterly time series for hours and output in the U.S. nonfarm business sector over the period 1948:1–2002:4. In both cases, the original series has been transformed using the bandpass filter developed in Baxter and King (1999), calibrated to remove fluctuations of periodicity outside an interval between 6 and 32 quarters. As in Stock and Watson (1999), we interpret the resulting series as reflecting fluctuations associated with business cycles.

As is well known, the basic RBC model can generate fluctuations in labor input and output of magnitude, persistence, and degree of comovement *roughly* similar to the series displayed in Figure 1. As shown in King and Rebelo (1999), when the actual sequence of technology shocks (proxied by the estimated disturbances of an autoregres-

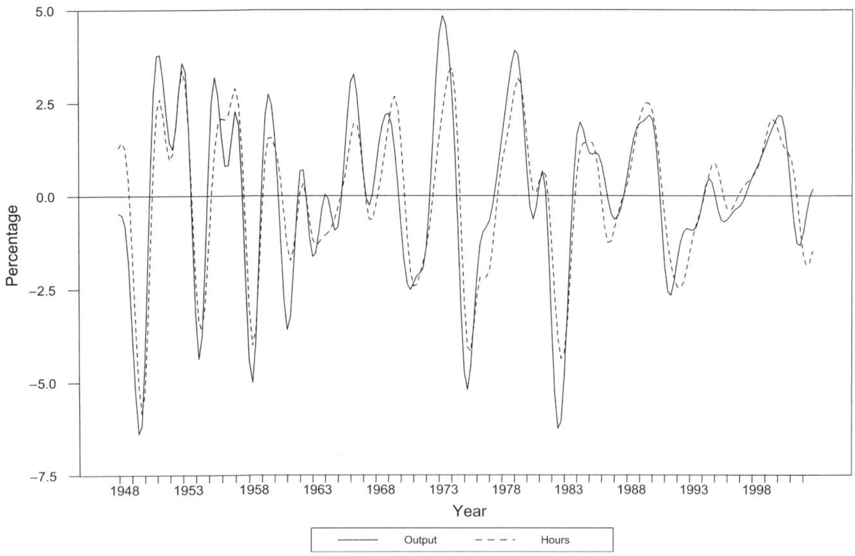

Figure 1
Business-cycle fluctuations in output and hours

sive (AR) process for the Solow residual) is fed as an input into the model, the resulting equilibrium paths of output and labor input track surprisingly well the observed historical patterns of those variables; the latter exercise can be viewed as a more stringent test of the RBC model than the usual moment-matching.

The literature reviewed in the present paper asks very different questions, however: What have been the effects of technology shocks in the postwar U.S. economy? How do they differ from the predictions of standard RBC models? What is their contribution to business-cycle fluctuations? What features must be incorporated in business-cycle models to account for the observed effects? The remainder of this paper describes the tentative (and sometimes contradictory) answers that the efforts of a growing number of researchers have yielded. Some of that research has exploited the natural role of technological change as a source of permanent changes in labor productivity to identify technology shocks using structural vector autoregressions (VARs); other authors have instead relied on more direct measures of technological change and examined their comovements with a variety of macro variables. It is not easy to summarize in a few words the wealth of existing evidence nor to agree on some definite conclusions of a literature that is still very much ongoing. Nevertheless, it is safe to state that the bulk of the evidence reviewed in the present paper provides little support for the initial claims of the RBC literature on the central role of technological change as a source of business cycles.

The remainder of the paper is organized as follows. Section 2 reviews some of the early papers that questioned the importance of technology shocks and presents some of the basic evidence regarding the effects of those shocks. Section 3 discusses a number of criticisms and possible pitfalls of that literature. Section 4 presents the case for the existence of nominal frictions as an explanation of the estimated effects of technology shocks. Section 5 summarizes some of the real explanations for the same effects found in the literature. Section 6 lays out and analyzes an estimated dynamic stochastic general equilibrium (DSGE) model that incorporates both nominal and real frictions, and evaluates their respective roles. Section 7 concludes.

2. Estimating the Effects of Technology Shocks

In Galí (1999), the effects of technology shocks were identified and estimated using a structural VAR approach. In its simplest specification, to which we restrict our analysis here, the empirical model uses information on two variables: output and labor input, which we denote respectively by y_t and n_t, both expressed in logs. Those variables are used to construct a series for (log) labor productivity, $x_t \equiv y_t - n_t$. In what follows, the latter is assumed to be integrated of order one (in a way consistent with the evidence reported below). Fluctuations in labor productivity growth (Δx_t) and in some stationary transformation of labor input $(\hat{n}_t)$ are assumed to be a consequence of two types of shocks hitting the economy and propagating their effects over time. Formally, the following moving average (MA) representation is assumed:

$$\begin{bmatrix} \Delta x_t \\ \hat{n}_t \end{bmatrix} = \begin{bmatrix} C^{11}(L) & C^{12}(L) \\ C^{21}(L) & C^{22}(L) \end{bmatrix} \begin{bmatrix} \varepsilon_t^z \\ \varepsilon_t^d \end{bmatrix} \equiv C(L)\varepsilon_t \tag{1}$$

where ε_t^z and ε_t^d are serially uncorrelated, mutually orthogonal structural disturbances whose variance is normalized to unity. The polynomial $|C(z)|$ is assumed to have all its roots outside the unit circle. Estimates of the distributed lag polynomials $C^{ij}(L)$ are obtained by a suitable transformation of the estimated reduced form VAR for $[\Delta x_t, \hat{n}_t]$ after imposing the long-run identifying restriction $C^{12}(1) = 0$.[2] That restriction effectively defines $\{\varepsilon_t^z\}$ and $\{\varepsilon_t^d\}$ as shocks *with* and *without* a *permanent* effect on labor productivity, respectively. On the basis of some of the steady-state restrictions shared by a broad range of macro models (and further discussed below), Galí (1999) proposes to interpret permanent shocks to productivity $\{\varepsilon_t^z\}$ as *technology shocks.* On the other hand, transitory shocks $\{\varepsilon_t^d\}$ can potentially capture a variety of driving forces behind output and labor input fluctuations that would not be expected to have permanent effects on labor productivity. The latter include shocks that could have a permanent effect on output (but not on labor productivity), but which are nontechnological in nature, as would be the case for some permanent shocks to preferences or government purchases, among others.[3] As discussed below, they could in principle capture *transitory* technology shocks as well.

2.1 *Revisiting the Basic Evidence on the Effects of Technology Shocks*

Next, we revisit and update the basic evidence on the effects of technology shocks reported in Galí (1999). Our baseline empirical analysis uses quarterly U.S. data for the period 1948:I–2002:IV. Our source is the Haver USECON database, for which we list the associated mnemonics. Our series for output corresponds to nonfarm business-sector output (LXNFO). Our baseline labor input series is hours of all persons in the nonfarm business sector (LXNFH). Below we often express the output and hours series in per-capita terms, using a measure of civilian noninstitutional population aged 16 and over (LNN).

Our baseline estimates are based on a specification of hours in first-differences; i.e., we set $\hat{n}_t = \Delta n_t$. That choice seems consistent with the outcome of Augmented Dickey-Fuller (ADF) tests applied to the hours series, which do not reject the null of a unit root in the level of hours at a 10% significance level, against the alternative of stationarity around a linear deterministic trend. On the other hand, the null of a unit root in the first-differenced series is rejected at a level of less than 1%.[4] In a way consistent with the previous result, a Kwiatkowski et al. (1992) (KPSS) test applied to n_t rejects the stationarity null with a significance level below 1%, while failing to reject the same null when applied to Δn_t. In addition, the same battery of ADF and KPSS tests applied to our x_t and Δx_t series support the existence of a unit root in labor productivity, a necessary condition for the identification strategy based on long-run restrictions employed here. Both observations suggest the

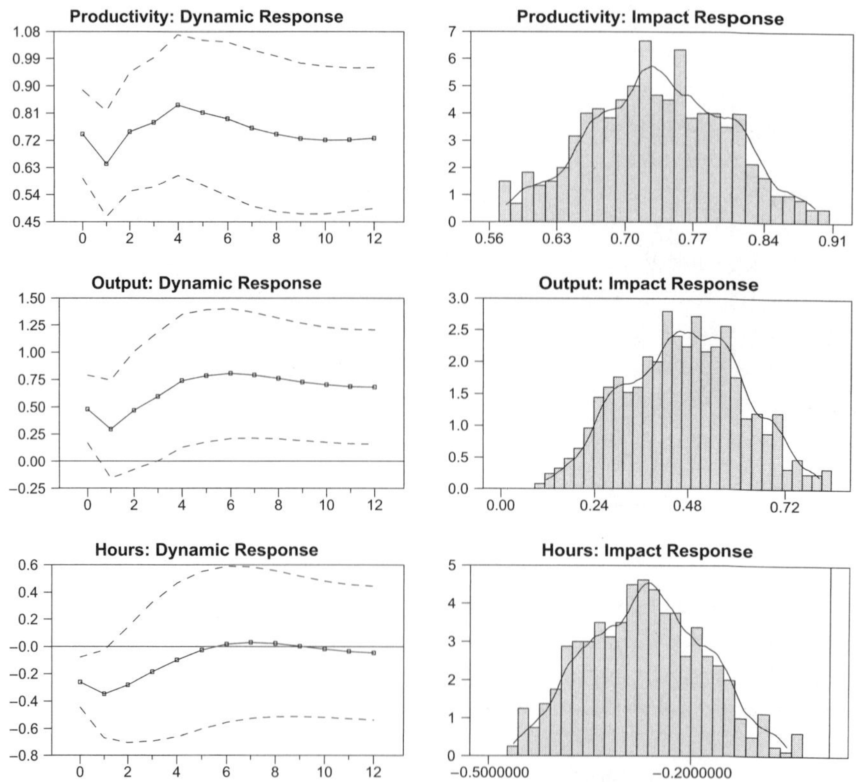

Figure 2
The estimated effects of technology shocks (*Difference specification, 1948:01–2002:04*)

specification and estimation of a VAR for $[\Delta x_t, \Delta n_t]$. Henceforth, we refer to the latter as the *difference* specification.

Figure 2 displays the estimated effects of a positive technology shock, of a size normalized to one standard deviation. The graphs on the left show the dynamic responses of labor productivity, output, and hours, together with (±) two standard error bands.[5] The corresponding graphs on the right show the simulated distribution of each variable's response *on impact*. As in Galí (1999), the estimates point to a significant and persistent decline in hours after a technology shock that raises labor productivity permanently.[6] The point estimates suggest that hours do eventually return to their original level (or close to it), but not until more than a year later. Along with that pattern of hours, we observe a positive but muted initial response of output in the face of a positive technology shock.

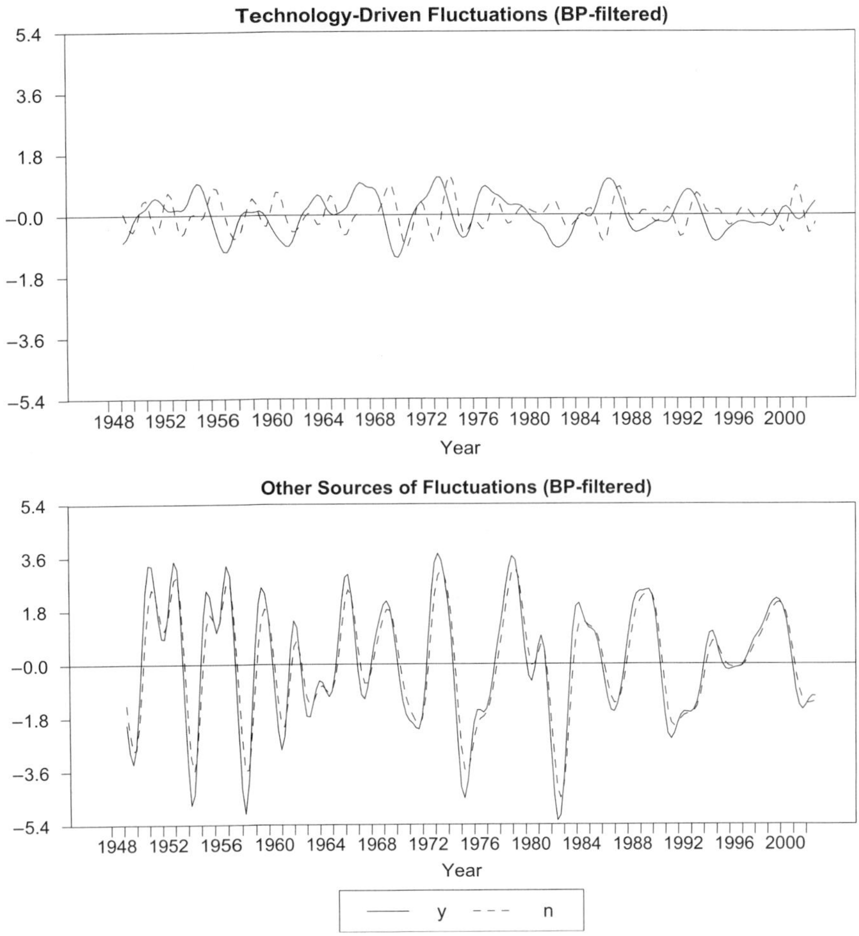

Figure 3
Sources of U.S. business cycle fluctuations (*Difference specification, sample period: 1948:01–2002:04*)

The estimated responses to a technology shock displayed in Figure 2 contrast starkly with the predictions of a standard calibrated RBC model, which would predict a positive comovement among the three variables plotted in the figure in response to that shock.[7]

Not surprisingly, the previous estimates have dramatic implications regarding the sources of the business-cycle fluctuations in output and hours displayed in Figure 1. This is illustrated in Figure 3, which displays the estimated business-cycle components of the historical series for output and hours associated with technology and nontechnology shocks. In both cases, the estimated components of the (log) levels of productivity and hours have been detrended using the same bandpass filter underlying the series plotted in Figure 1. As in Galí (1999), the picture that emerges is very clear: fluctuations in hours and output driven by technology shocks account for a small fraction of the variance of those variables at business-cycle frequencies: 5 and 7%, respectively. The comovement at business-cycle frequencies between output and hours resulting from technology shocks is shown to be essentially zero (the correlation is −0.08), in contrast with the high positive comovement observed in the data (0.88). Clearly, the pattern of technology-driven fluctuations, as identified in our structural VAR, shows little resemblance to the conventional business-cycle fluctuations displayed in Figure 1.

The picture changes dramatically if we turn our attention to the estimated fluctuations of output and hours driven by shocks with no permanent effects on productivity (displayed in the bottom graph). Those shocks account for 95 and 93% of the variance of the business-cycle component of hours and output, respectively. In addition, they generate a nearly perfect correlation (0.96) between the same variables. In contrast with its technology-driven counterpart, this component of output and hours fluctuations displays a far more recognizable business-cycle pattern.

A possible criticism to the above empirical framework is the assumption of only two driving forces underlying the fluctuations in hours and labor productivity. As discussed in Blanchard and Quah (1989), ignoring some relevant shocks may lead to a significant distortion in the estimated impulse responses. Galí (1999) addresses that issue by estimating a five-variable VAR (including time series on real balances, interest rates, and inflation). That framework allows for as many as four shocks with no permanent effects on productivity, and for which no separate identification is attempted. The estimates generated by that higher-dimensional model regarding the effects of technology shocks are very similar to the ones reported above, suggesting that the focus on only two shocks may not be restrictive for the issue at hand.[8]

2.2 *Related Empirical Work*

The empirical connection between technological change and business-cycle fluctuations has been the focus of a rapidly expanding literature.

Next, we briefly discuss some recent papers that provide evidence on the effects of technology shocks, and that reach conclusions similar to Galí (1999), while using a different data set or empirical approach. We leave for later a discussion of the papers whose findings relate more specifically to the content of other sections, including those that question the evidence reported above.

An early contribution is given by the relatively unknown paper by Blanchard, Solow, and Wilson (1995). That paper already spells out some of the key arguments found in the subsequent literature. In particular, it stresses the need to sort out the component of productivity associated with exogenous technological change from the component that varies in response to other shocks that may affect the capital-labor ratio. They adopt a simple instrumental variables approach, with a number of demand-side variables assumed to be orthogonal to exogenous technological change used as instruments for employment growth or the change in unemployment in a regression that features productivity growth as a dependent variable. The fitted residual in that regression is interpreted as a proxy for technology-driven changes in productivity. When they regress the change in unemployment on the filtered productivity growth variable, they obtain a positive coefficient; i.e., an (exogenous) increase in productivity drives the unemployment rate up. A dynamic specification of that regression implies that such an effect lasts for about three quarters, after which unemployment starts to fall and returns rapidly to its original value.

As mentioned in Galí (1999, footnote 19) and stressed by Valerie Ramey (2005) in her comment about this paper (also in this volume), the finding of a decline in hours (or an increase in unemployment) in response to a positive technology shock could also have been detected by an attentive reader in a number of earlier VAR papers, though that finding generally goes unnoticed or is described as puzzling. Blanchard and Quah (1989) and Blanchard (1989) are exceptions because they provide some explicit discussion of the finding, which they interpret as consistent with a traditional Keynesian model "in which increases in productivity ... may well increase unemployment in the short run if aggregate demand does not increase enough to maintain employment."[9]

The work of Basu, Fernald, and Kimball (1999) deserves special attention here, given its focus and the similarity of its findings to those in Galí (1999) despite the use of an unrelated methodology. Basu, Fernald, and Kimball (BFK) use a sophisticated growth accounting methodology allowing for increasing returns, imperfect competition, variable factor utilization, and sectoral compositional effects to uncover a time series for aggregate technological change in the postwar U.S. economy. Their approach, combining elements of earlier work by Hall (1990) and Basu and Kimball (1997), among others, can be viewed as an attempt to cleanse the Solow residual (Solow, 1957) of its widely acknowledged measurement error resulting from the strong assumptions underlying its derivation. Estimates of the response of the economy to innovations in their measure of technological change point to a sharp short-run decline in the use of inputs (including labor) when technology improves, with output showing no significant change (with point estimates suggesting a small decline). After that short-run impact, both variables gradually adjust upward, with labor input returning to its original level and with output reaching a permanently higher plateau several years after the shock.

Kiley (1997) applies the structural VAR framework in Galí (1999) to data from two-digit manufacturing industries. While he does not report impulse responses, he finds that technology shocks induce a negative correlation between employment and output growth in 12 of the 17 industries considered. When he estimates an analogous conditional correlation for employment and productivity growth, he obtains a negative value for 15 out of 17 industries. Francis (2001) conducts a similar analysis, though he attempts to identify industry-specific technology shocks by including a measure of aggregate technology, which is assumed to be exogenous to each of the industries considered. He finds that, for the vast majority of industries, a sectoral labor input measure declines in response to a positive industry-specific technology shock. Using data from a large panel of 458 manufacturing industries and 35 sectors, Franco and Philippon (2004) estimate a structural VAR with three shocks: technology shocks (with permanent effects on industry productivity), composition shocks (with permanent effects on the industry share in total output), and transitory shocks. They find that technology shocks (1) generate a negative comovement between output and hours within each industry, and (2) are almost uncorrelated across industries. Thus, they conclude that technology shocks can account for only a small fraction of the variance of aggregate hours and output (with two-thirds of the latter accounted for by transitory shocks).

Shea (1998) uses a structural VAR approach to model the connection between changes in measures of technological innovation (research and development [R&D] and number of patent applications) and subsequent changes in total factor productivity (TFP) and hired inputs, using industry-level data. For most specifications and industries, he finds that an innovation in the technology indicator does not cause any significant change in TFP but tends to increase labor inputs in the short run. While not much stressed by Shea, however, one of the findings in his paper is particularly relevant for our purposes: in the few VAR specifications for which a significant increase in TFP is detected in response to a positive innovation in the technology indicator, inputs—including labor—are shown to respond in the direction opposite to the movement in TFP, a finding in line with the evidence above.[10]

Francis and Ramey (2003a) extend the analysis in Galí (1999) in several dimensions. The first modification they consider consists in augmenting the baseline VAR (specified in first differences) with a capital tax rate measure to sort out the effects of technology shocks from those of permanent changes in tax rates (more below). Second, they identify technology shocks as those with permanent effects on real wages (as opposed to labor productivity) and/or no long-run effects on hours, both equally robust predictions of a broad class of models that satisfy a balance growth property. Those alternative identifying restrictions are not rejected when combined into a unified (overidentified) model. Francis and Ramey show that both the model augmented with capital tax rates and the model with alternative identifying restrictions (considered separately or jointly) imply impulse responses to a technology shock similar to those in Galí (1999) and, in particular, a drop in hours in response to a positive technology shock.

Francis, Owyang, and Theodorou (2003) use a variant of the sign restriction algorithm of Uhlig (1999) and show that the finding of a negative response of hours to a positive technology shock is robust to replacing the restriction on the asymptotic effect of that shock with one imposing a positive response of productivity at a horizon of ten years after the shock.

A number of recent papers have provided related evidence based on non-U.S. aggregate data. In Galí (1999), the structural VAR framework discussed above is also applied to the remaining G7 countries (Canada, the United Kingdom, France, Germany, Italy, and Japan). He uncovers a negative response of employment to a positive technology shock in all countries, with the exception of Japan. Galí (1999) also points out some differences in those estimates relative to those obtained for the United States: in particular, the (negative) employment response to a positive technology shocks in Germany, the United Kingdom, and Italy appears to be larger and more persistent, which could be interpreted as evidence of hysteresis in European labor markets. Very similar qualitative results for the Euro area as a whole can also be found in Galí (2004), which applies the same empirical framework to the quarterly data set that has recently been available. In particular, technology shocks are found to account for only 5% and 9% of the variance of the business-cycle component of euro area employment and output, respectively, with the corresponding correlation between their technology-driven components being −0.67). Francis and Ramey (2003b) estimate a structural VAR with long-run identifying restrictions using long-term U.K. annual time series tracing back to the nineteenth century; they find robust evidence of a negative short-run impact of technology shocks on labor in every subsample.[11] Finally, Carlsson (2000) develops a variant of the empirical framework in BFK (1999) and Burnside et al. (1995) to construct a time series for technological change, and applies it to a sample of Swedish two-digit manufacturing industries. Most prominently, he finds that positive shocks to technology have, on impact, a contractionary effect on hours and a nonexpansionary effect on output, as in BFK (1999).

2.3 *Implications*

The implications of the evidence discussed above for business-cycle analysis and modeling are manifold. Most significantly, those findings reject a key prediction of the standard RBC paradigm, namely, the positive comovement of output, labor input, and productivity in response to technology shocks. That positive comovement is the single main feature of that model that accounts for its ability to generate fluctuations that resemble business cycles. Hence, taken at face value, the evidence above rejects in an unambiguous fashion the empirical relevance of the standard RBC model. It does so in two dimensions. First, it shows that a key feature of the economy's response to aggregate technology shocks predicted by calibrated RBC models cannot be found in the data. Second, and to the extent that one takes the positive comovement between measures of output and labor input as a defining characteristic of the business cycle, it follows as a corollary that technology shocks cannot be a quantitatively important (and, even less, a dominant) source of observed aggregate fluctuations. While the latter implication is particularly damning for RBC theory, given its traditional emphasis on aggregate technology variations as a source of business cycles, its relevance is independent of one's preferred macroeconomic paradigm.

3. Possible Pitfalls in the Estimation of the Effects of Technology Shocks

This section has two main objectives. First, we try to address a question that is often raised regarding the empirical approach used in Galí (1999): to what extent can we be confident in the economic interpretation given to the identified shocks and, in particular, in the mapping between technology shocks and the nonstationary component of labor productivity? We provide some evidence below that makes us feel quite comfortable about that interpretation. Second, we describe and address some of the econometric issues that Christiano, Eichenbaum, and Vigfusson (2003) have raised and that focus on the appropriate specification of hours (levels or first differences). Finally, we discuss a paper by Fisher (2003) that distinguishes between two types of technology shocks: neutral and investment-specific.

3.1 *Are Long-Run Restrictions Useful in Identifying Technology Shocks?*

The approach to identification proposed in Galí (1999) relies on the assumption that only (permanent) technology shocks can have a permanent effect on (average) labor productivity. That assumption can be argued to hold under relatively weak conditions, satisfied by the bulk of business-cycle models currently used by macroeconomists. To review the basic argument, consider an economy whose technology can be described by an aggregate production function:[12]

$$Y_t = F(K_t, A_t N_t) \tag{2}$$

where Y denotes output, K is the capital stock, N is labor input and A is an index of technology. Under the assumption that F is homogeneous of degree 1, we have:

$$\frac{Y_t}{N_t} = A_t F_k(k_t, 1) \tag{3}$$

where $k_t \equiv K_t/(A_t N_t)$ is the ratio of capital to labor (expressed in efficiency units). For a large class of models characterized by an underlying balanced growth path, the marginal product of capital F_k must satisfy, along that path, a condition of the form:

$$(1-\tau)F_k(k, 1) = (1+\mu)\left(\rho + \delta + \frac{\gamma}{\sigma}\right) \tag{4}$$

where μ is the price markup, τ is a tax on capital income, ρ is the time discount rate, δ is the depreciation rate, σ is the intertemporal elasticity of substitution, and γ is the average growth rate of (per-capita) consumption and output. Under the assumption of decreasing returns to capital, it follows from equation (4) that the capital labor ratio k will be stationary (and will thus fluctuate around a constant mean) as long as all the previous parameters are constant (or stationary). In that case, equation (3) implies that only shocks that have a permanent effect on the technology parameter A can be a source of the unit root in labor productivity, thus providing the theoretical underpinning for the identification scheme in Galí (1999).

How plausible are the assumptions underlying that identification scheme? Preference or technology parameters like ρ, δ, σ, and γ are generally assumed to be constant in most examples and applications found in the business-cycle literature. The price markup μ is more likely to vary over time, possibly as a result of some embedded price rigidities; in the latter case, however, it is likely to remain stationary, fluctuating around its desired or optimal level. In the event that desired markups (or the preference and technology parameters listed above) are nonstationary, the latter would more likely take the form of some smooth function of time, which should be reflected in the deterministic component of labor productivity, but not in its fluctuations at cyclical frequencies.[13] Finally, notice that the previous approach to identification of technology shocks requires that (1) F_k be decreasing, so that k is uniquely pinned down by equation (4), and (2) that the technology process $\{A_t\}$ is exogenous (at least with respect to the business cycle). The previous assumptions have been commonly adopted by business-cycle modelers.[14]

3.1.1 Do Capital Income Tax Shocks Explain Permanent Changes in Labor Productivity?

The previous argument is much less appealing, however, when applied to the capital income tax rate. As Uhlig (2004) and others have pointed out, the assumption of a stationary capital income tax rate may be unwarranted, given the behavior of measures for that variable over the postwar period. This is illustrated in Figure 4, which displays two alternative measures of the capital income tax rate in the United States. Figure 4.A displays a quarterly series for the average capital income tax rate constructed by Jones (2002) for the period 1958:I–1997:IV. Figure 4.B shows an annual measure of the average marginal capital income tax rate constructed by Ellen McGrattan for the period 1958–1992 and that corresponds to an updated version of the one used in McGrattan (1994).[15] Henceforth we denote those series by τ_t^J and τ_t^M, respectively. Both series display an apparent nonstationary behavior, with highly persistent fluctuations. This is confirmed by a battery of ADF tests, which fail to reject the null hypothesis of a unit root in both series, at conventional significance levels.

As shown in Figures 4.C and 4.D, which display the same series in first differences, the presence of sizable short-run variations in those measures of capital taxes could hardly be captured by means of some deterministic or smooth function of time (their standard deviations being 0.79% for the quarterly Jones series, and 2.4% for the annual McGrattan series). In fact, in both cases, that first-differenced series $\Delta\tau_t$ shows no significant autocorrelation, suggesting that a random walk process can approximate the pattern of capital income tax rates pretty well.

The previous evidence, combined with the theoretical analysis above, points to a potential caveat in the identification approach followed in Galí (1999): the shocks with permanent effects on productivity estimated therein could be capturing the effects of permanent changes in tax rates (as opposed to those of genuine technology shocks). That mislabeling could potentially account for the empirical findings reported above.

Francis and Ramey (2003a) attempt to overcome that potential shortcoming by augmenting the VAR with a capital tax rate variable, in addition to labor productivity and hours. As mentioned above, the introduction of the tax variable is shown not to have any significant influence on the findings: positive technology shocks still lead to short-run declines in labor.

Here, we revisit the hypothesis of a tax rate shock mistaken for a technology shock by looking for evidence of some comovement between (1) the permanent shock ε_t^z estimated using the structural VAR discussed in Section 2, and (2) each of the two capital tax series, in first-differences. Given the absence of significant autocorrelation in $\Delta\tau_t^J$ and $\Delta\tau_t^M$, we interpret each of those series as (alternative) proxies for the shocks to the capital income tax rate. Also, when using the McGrattan series, we annualize the permanent shock series obtained from the quarterly VAR by averaging the shocks corresponding to each natural year.

The resulting evidence can be summarized as follows. First, innovations to the capital income tax rate show a near-zero correlation with

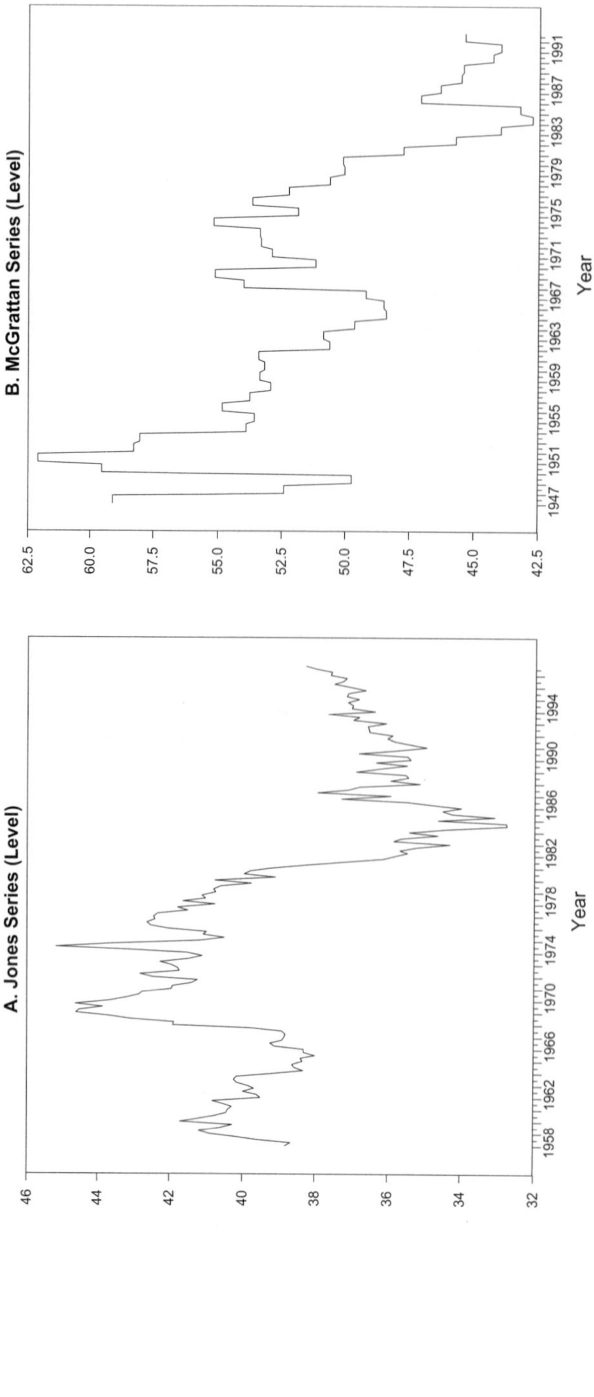

Figure 4
Capital income tax rates

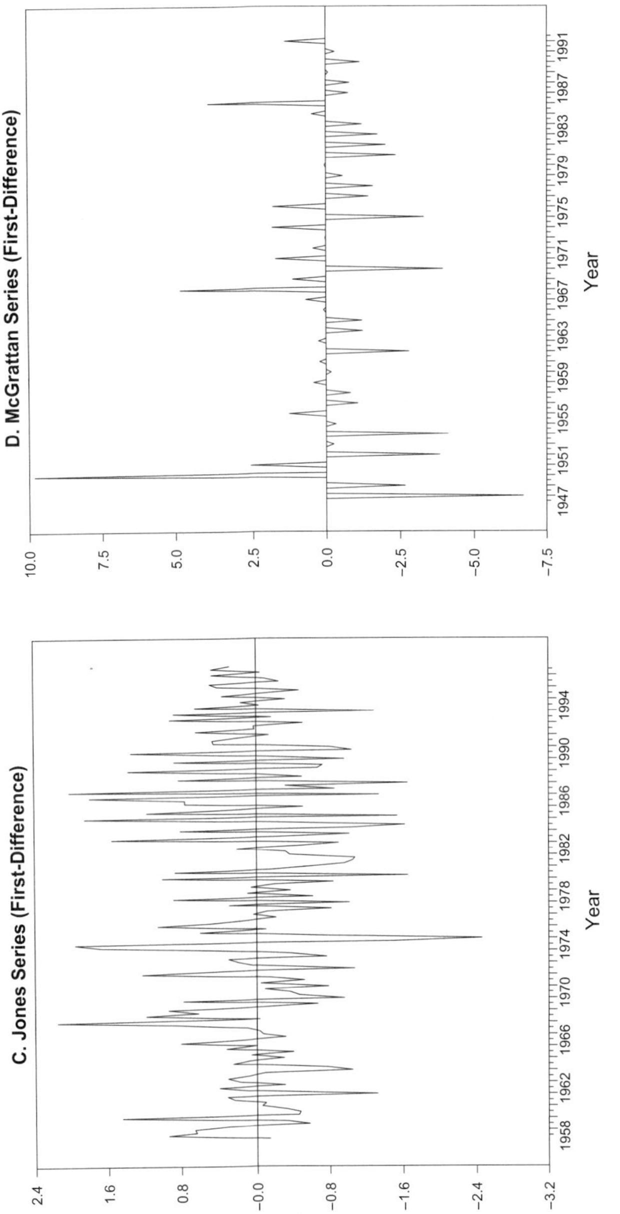

Figure 4
(continued)

the permanent shocks from the VAR. More precisely, our estimates of $corr(\Delta\tau_t^J, \varepsilon_t^z)$ and $corr(\Delta\tau_t^M, \varepsilon_t^z)$ are, respectively, −0.06 and 0.12, neither of which is significant at conventional levels. Thus, it is highly unlikely that the permanent VAR shocks may be capturing exogenous shocks to capital taxes.

Second, an ordinary least squares (OLS) regression of the Jones tax series $\Delta\tau_t^J$ on current and lagged values of ε_t^z yields jointly insignificant coefficient estimates: the p-value is 0.54 when four lags are included, 0.21 when we include eight lags. A similar result obtains when we regress the McGrattan tax series $\Delta\tau_t^M$ on current and several lags of ε_t^z, with the p-value for the null of zero coefficients being 0.68 when four lags are included (0.34 when we use 8 lags). Since the sequence of those coefficients corresponds to the estimated impulse response of capital taxes to the permanent VAR shock, the previous evidence suggests that the estimated effects of the permanent VAR shocks are unlikely to be capturing the impact of a possible endogenous response in capital taxes to whatever exogenous shock underlies the estimated permanent VAR shock.

We conclude from the previous exercises that there is no support for the hypothesis that the permanent shocks to labor productivity, interpreted in Galí (1999) as technology shocks, could be instead capturing changes in capital income taxes.[16]

3.1.2 Do Permanent Shocks to Labor Productivity Capture Variations in Technology?

Having all but ruled out variations in capital taxes as a significant factor behind the unit root in labor productivity, we present next some evidence that favors the interpretation of the VAR permanent shock as a shift to aggregate technology. We also provide some evidence against the hypothesis that transitory variations in technology may be a significant force behind the shocks identified as transitory shocks, a hypothesis that cannot be ruled out on purely theoretical grounds.

Francis and Ramey (2003a) test a weak form of the hypothesis of permanent shocks as technology shocks by looking for evidence of Granger-causality among several indicators that are viewed as independent of technology on one hand, and the VAR-based technology shock on the other. The indicators include the Romer and Romer (1989) monetary shock dummy, the Hoover and Perez (1994) oil shock dummies, Ramey and Shapiro's (1998) military buildup dates, and the federal funds rate. Francis and Ramey show that none of them have a significant predictive power for the estimated technology shock.

Here, we provide a more direct assessment by using the measure of aggregate technological change obtained by Basu, Fernald, and Kimball (1999).[17] As discussed earlier, those authors constructed that series using an approach unrelated to ours. The BFK variable measures the annual rate of technological change in the U.S. nonfarm private business sector. The series has an annual frequency and covers the period 1950–1989. Our objective here is to assess the plausibility of the technology-related interpretation of the VAR shocks obtained above by examining their correlation with the BFK measure. Given the differences in frequencies we annualize both the permanent and transitory shock series obtained from the quarterly VAR by averaging the shocks corresponding to each natural year.

The main results can be summarized as follows. First, the correlation between the VAR-based permanent shock and the BFK measure of technological change is positive and significant at the 5% level, with a point estimate of 0.45. The existence of a positive contemporaneous comovement is apparent in Figure 5, which displays the estimated VAR permanent shock together with the BFK measure (both series have been normalized to have zero mean and unit variance, for ease of comparison).

Second, the correlation between our estimated VAR transitory shock and the BFK series is slightly negative, though insignificantly different from zero (the point estimate is −0.04). The bottom graph of Figure 5, which displays both series, illustrates the absence of any obvious comovement between the two.

Finally, and given that the BFK series is mildly serially correlated, we have also run a simple OLS regression of the (normalized) BFK variable on its own lag, and the contemporaneous estimates of the permanent and transitory shocks from the VAR. The estimated equation, with t-statistics in brackets, is given by:

$$BFK_t = \underset{(1.85)}{0.29}\, BFK_{t-1} + \underset{(2.16)}{0.67}\, \varepsilon_t^z - \underset{(-1.11)}{0.32}\, \varepsilon_t^d$$

which reinforces the findings obtained from the simple contemporaneous correlations.

In summary, the results from the above empirical analysis suggest that the VAR-based permanent shocks may indeed be capturing exogenous variations in technology, in a way consistent with the

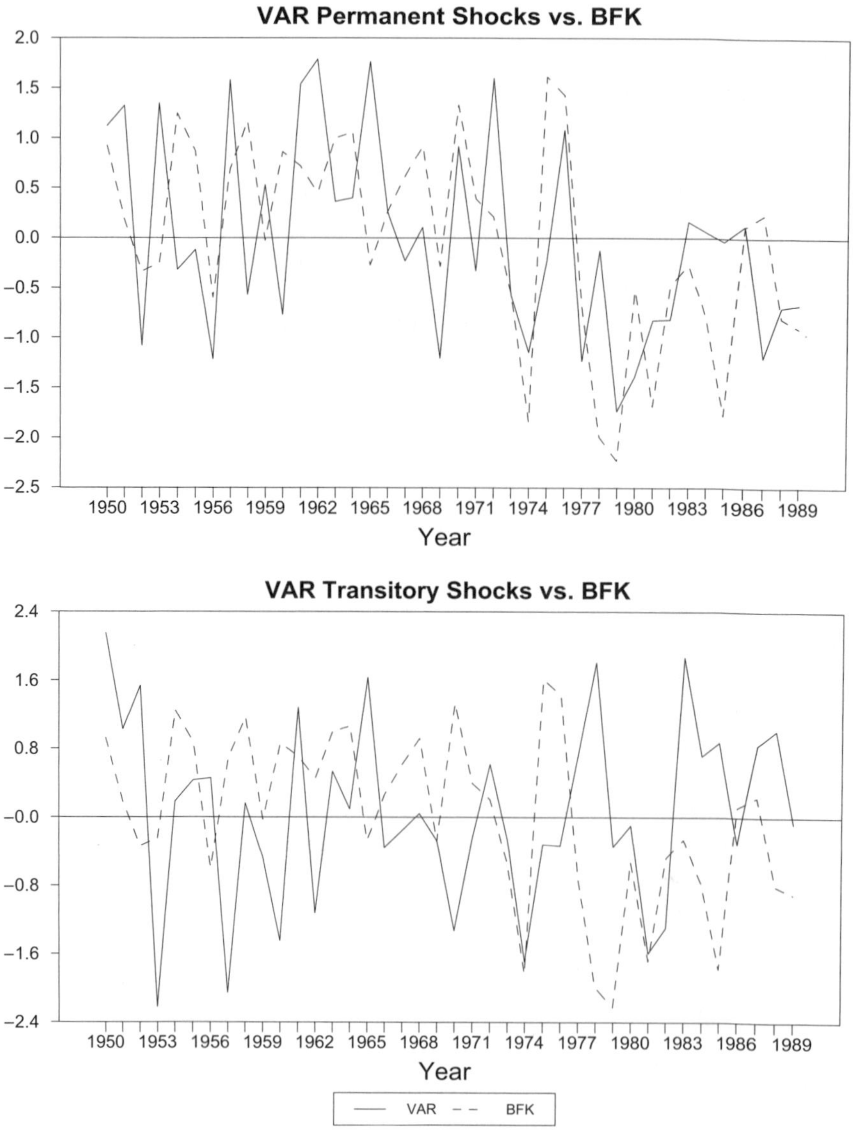

Figure 5
Technology shocks: VAR versus BFK

interpretation made in Galí (1999). In addition, we cannot find evidence supporting the view that the VAR transitory shocks—which were shown in Section 2 to be the main source of business-cycle fluctuations in hours and output—may be related to changes in technology.

3.2 *Robustness to Alternative VAR Specifications*

Christiano, Eichenbaum, and Vigfusson (2003) have questioned some of the VAR-based evidence regarding the effects of technology shocks found in Galí (1999) and Francis and Ramey (2003a), on the basis of their lack of robustness to the transformation of labor input used. In particular, Christiano, Eichenbaum, and Vigfusson (CEV) argue that first-differencing the (log) of per-capita hours may distort the sign of the estimated response of that variable to a technology shock, if that variable is truly stationary. Specifically, their findings—based on a bivariate VAR model in which (per-capita) hours are specified in levels ($\hat{n}_t = n_t$)—imply that output, hours, and productivity all rise in response to a positive technology shock. On the other hand, when they use a difference specification, they obtain results similar to the ones reported above, i.e., a negative comovement between output (or productivity) and hours in response to technology shocks. Perhaps most interesting, CEV discuss the extent to which the findings obtained under the level specification can be accounted for under the assumption that the difference specification is the correct one, and vice versa. Given identical priors over the two specifications, that encompassing analysis leads them to conclude that the odds in favor of the level specification relative to the difference specification are about 2 to 1.[18] CEV obtain similar results when incorporating additional variables in the VAR.

Our own estimates of the dynamic responses to a technology shock when we specify (per-capita) hours in levels do indeed point to some qualitative differences. In particular, the point estimate of the impact response of hours worked to a positive technology is now positive, though very small. In contrast with the findings in CEV, that impact effect and indeed the entire dynamic response of hours is not significantly different from zero. The sign of the point estimates is sufficient, however, to generate a positive correlation (0.88) between output and hours conditional on the technology shock. As reported in the second row of Table 1, under the level specification, technology shocks still account for a (relatively) small fraction of the variance of output and

Table 1
The effects of technology shocks on output and hours in the nonfarm business sector

	Contribution to		Conditional	Impact on n and y	
	var(y)	var(n)	corr(y, n)	Sign	Significance
Per-capita hours					
Difference	0.07	0.05	−0.08	−/+	Yes/yes
Level	0.37	0.11	0.80	+/+	No/yes
Detrended	0.07	0.05	−0.11	−/+	Yes/yes
Total hours					
Difference	0.06	0.06	−0.03	−/+	Yes/yes
Level	0.10	0.36	0.80	−/−	Yes/no
Detrended	0.15	0.36	0.80	−/0	Yes/no

hours at business-cycle frequencies (37 and 11%, respectively), though that fraction is larger than the one implied by the difference specification estimates.[19]

While we find the encompassing approach adopted by CEV enlightening, their strategy of pairwise comparisons with uniform priors (which mechanically assigns a $\frac{1}{2}$ prior to the level specification) may lead to some bias in the conclusions. In particular, a simple look at a plot of the time series for (log) per-capita hours worked in the United States over the postwar period, displayed in Figure 6, is not suggestive of stationarity, at least in the absence of any further transformation. In particular, and in agreement with the ADF and KPSS tests reported above, the series seems perfectly consistent with a unit root process, though possibly not a pure random walk. On the basis of a cursory look at the same plot, and assuming that one wishes to maintain the assumption of a stationary process for the stochastic component of (log) per-capita hours, a quadratic function of time would appear to be a more plausible characterization of the trend than just the constant implicit in CEV's analysis. In fact, an OLS regression of that variable on a constant, time and time squared, yields a highly significant coefficient associated with both time variables. A test of a unit root on the residual from that regression fails to reject that hypothesis, while the KPSS does not reject the null of stationarity, at a 5% significance level in both cases.[20] Figure 6 displays the fitted quadratic trend and the associated residual, illustrating graphically that point. When we re-estimate the dynamic responses to a technology shock using detrended (log) per-capita hours, we find again a decline in hours in

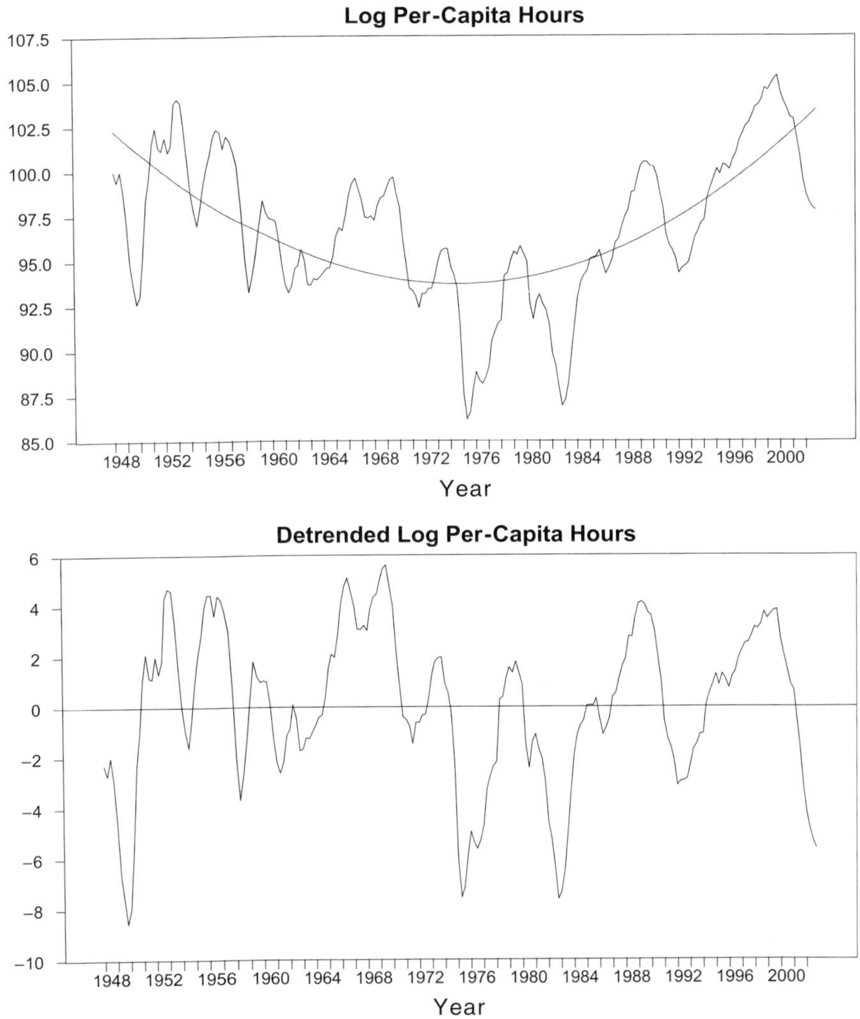

Figure 6
Hours worked, 1948–2002

response to a positive technology shock, and a slightly negative (−0.11) conditional correlation between the business-cycle components of output and hours. In addition, the estimated contribution of technology shocks to the variance of output and hours is very small (7 and 5%, essentially the same as under difference specification; see Table 1).[21]

To assess further the robustness of the above results, we have also conducted the same analysis using a specification of the VAR using an alternative measure of labor input, namely, (log) *total hours*, without a normalization by working-age population. As it should be clear from the discussion in Section 3.1, the identification strategy proposed in Galí (1999) and implemented here should be valid independent of whether labor input is measured in per-capita terms since labor productivity in invariant to that normalization.[22] The second panel in Table 1 summarizes the results corresponding to three alternative transformations considered (first differences, levels, quadratic detrending). In the three cases, a positive technology shock is estimated to have a strong and statistically significant negative impact on hours worked, at least in the short run. Under the level and detrended transformations, that negative response of hours is sufficiently strong to pull down output in the short run, despite the increase in productivity. Note, however, that the estimated decline in output is not significant in either case.[23] The estimated contribution of technology shocks to the variance of the business-cycle component of output and hours is small in all cases, with the largest share being 36% of the variance of hours, obtained under the level and detrended specifications.

As an additional check on the robustness of our findings, we have also estimated all the model specifications discussed above using employment as labor input measure (instead of hours), and real GDP as an output measure. A summary of our results for the six specifications considered using employment and GDP can be found in Table 2. The results under this specification are much more uniform: independent of the transformation of employment used, our estimates point to a decline in that variable in the short run in response to a positive technology shock, as well as a very limited contribution of technology shocks to the variance of GDP and employment. We should stress that we obtained those findings even when we specify employment rate in levels, even though the short-run decline in employment is not statistically significant in that case. In summary, the previous robustness exercise based on postwar U.S. data has shown that, for all but one of the transformations of hours used, we uncover a decline in labor input

Table 2
The effects of technology shocks on GDP and employment

	Contribution to		Conditional	Impact on n and y	
	var(y)	var(n)	corr(y, n)	Sign	Significance
Employment rate					
Difference	0.31	0.04	0.40	−/+	Yes/yes
Level	0.03	0.19	−0.30	−/+	Yes/no
Detrended	0.15	0.04	−0.43	−/+	Yes/yes
Total employment					
Difference	0.21	0.03	−0.40	−/+	Yes/yes
Level	0.09	0.08	−0.72	−/+	Yes/yes
Detrended	0.09	0.09	−0.68	−/+	Yes/no

in response to a positive technology shock, in a way consistent with the literature reviewed in Section 2. The exception corresponds to the level specification of per-capita hours, but even in that case the estimated positive response of hours does not appear to be significant. In most cases, the contribution of technology shocks to the variance of the cyclical component of output and hours is very small, and always below 40%. Finally, and possibly with the exception mentioned above, the pattern of comovement of output and hours at business-cycle frequencies resulting from technology shocks fails to resemble the one associated with postwar U.S. business cycles.

Fernald (2004) makes an important contribution to the debate by uncovering the most likely source of the discrepancy of the estimates when hours are introduced in levels. In particular, he shows the existence of a low-frequency correlation between labor productivity growth and per-capita hours. As illustrated through a number of simulations, the presence of such a correlation, while unrelated to the higher-frequency phenomena of interest, can distort significantly the estimated short-run responses. Fernald illustrates that point most forcefully by re-estimating the structural VAR in its levels specification (as in CEV), though allowing for two (statistically significant) trend breaks in labor productivity (in 1973:I and 1997:II): the implied impulse responses point to a significant decline in hours in response to a technology shock, a result that also obtains when the difference specification is used.

Additional evidence on the implications of alternative transformations of hours using annual time series spanning more than a century is provided by Francis and Ramey (2003b). Their findings based on U.S. data point to considerable sensitivity of the estimates across subsample periods and the choice of transformation for hours. To assess the validity of the different specifications, they look at their implications for the persistence of the productivity response to a nontechnology shock, the plausibility of the patterns of estimated technology shocks, as well as the predictability of the latter (the Hall-Evans test). On the basis of that analysis, they conclude that first-differenced and, to a lesser extent, quadratically detrended hours yields are the most plausible specification. Francis and Ramey show that in their data, those two preferred specifications generate a short-run negative comovement between hours and output in response to a shock that has a permanent effect on technology in the postwar period. In the pre–World War II period, however, the difference specification yields an increase in hours in response to a shock that raises productivity permanently. On the other hand, when they repeat the exercise using U.K. data (and a difference specification), they find a clear negative comovement of employment and output both in the pre–World War II and postwar sample periods.[24]

In light of those results and the findings in the literature discussed above, we conclude that there is no clear evidence favoring a conventional RBC interpretation of economic fluctuations as being largely driven by technology shocks, at least when the latter take the form assumed in the standard one-sector RBC model. Next, we consider how the previous assessment is affected once we allow for technology shocks that are investment-specific.

3.3 *Investment-Specific Technology Shocks*

In a series of papers, Greenwood, Hercowitz, and Huffman (1988), and Greenwood, Hercowitz, and Krusell (1997, 2000) put forward and analyze a version of an RBC model in which the main source of technological change is specific to the investment sector. In the proposed framework, and in contrast with the standard RBC model, a technology shock does not have any immediate impact on the production function. Instead, it affects the rate of transformation between current consumption and productive capital in the future. Thus, any effects on current output must be the result of the ability of that shock in eliciting a change in the quantity of input services hired by firms. Greenwood, Hercowitz, and Krusell (GHK) motivate the interest in studying the potential role of investment-specific technology shocks by pointing to the large variations in measures of the relative price of new equipment constructed by Gordon (1990), both over the long-run as well as at business-cycle frequencies. In particular, GHK (2000) analyze a calibrated model in which investment-specific technology shocks are the only driving force. They conclude that the latter can account for about 30% of U.S. output fluctuations, a relatively modest figure compared to the claim of the earlier RBC literature regarding the contribution of aggregate, sector-neutral technology shocks in calibrated versions of one-sector RBC models.

Fisher (2003) revisits the evidence on the effects of technology shocks and their role in the U.S. business cycle and uses an empirical framework that allows for separately identified sector-neutral and investment-specific technology shocks (which, following Fisher, we refer to, respectively, as N-shocks and I-shocks). In a way consistent with the identification scheme proposed in Galí (1999), both types of technology shocks are allowed to have a permanent effect on labor productivity (in contrast with nontechnology shocks). In a way consistent with the GHK framework, only investment-specific technology shocks are allowed to affect permanently the relative price of new investment goods. Using times series for labor productivity, per-capita hours, and the price of equipment (as a ratio to the consumption goods deflator) constructed by Cummins and Violante (2002), Fisher estimates impulse responses to the two types of shocks and their relative contribution to business-cycle fluctuations. We have conducted a similar exercise and have summarized some of the findings in Table 3.[25] For each type of technology shock and specification, the table reports its contribution to the variance of the business-cycle component of output and hours, as well as the implied conditional correlation between those two variables.

The top panel in Table 3 corresponds to three specifications using per-capita hours worked, the labor input variable to which Fisher (2003) restricts his analysis. Not surprisingly, our results essentially replicate some of his findings. In particular, we see that under the three transformations of labor input measures considered, N-shocks are estimated to have a negligible contribution to the variance of output and hours at business-cycle frequencies, and to generate a very low correlation between those two variables.

The results for I-shocks are different in at least two respects. First, and as stressed in Fisher (2003), I-shocks generate a high positive

Table 3
Investment-specific technology shocks: the Fisher model

	Contribution of N-shocks to:			Contribution of I-shocks to:		
	var(y)	var(n)	corr(y, n)	var(y)	var(n)	corr(y, n)
Per-capita hours						
Difference	0.06	0.06	−0.09	0.22	0.19	0.94
Level	0.12	0.02	0.16	0.62	0.60	0.96
Detrended	0.08	0.07	−0.03	0.10	0.09	0.94
Total hours						
Difference	0.07	0.06	0.05	0.16	0.14	0.94
Level	0.05	0.15	0.33	0.82	0.78	0.97
Detrended	0.10	0.28	0.62	0.09	0.08	0.93
Employment rate						
Difference	0.21	0.05	0.08	0.19	0.13	0.93
Level	0.08	0.08	−0.32	0.86	0.89	0.95
Detrended	0.06	0.17	−0.11	0.12	0.10	0.92
Total employment						
Difference	0.19	0.06	−0.05	0.10	0.06	0.90
Level	0.04	0.16	−0.25	0.64	0.52	0.96
Detrended	0.04	0.20	0.05	0.12	0.09	0.90

correlation between output and hours. The last column of Table 3 tells us that such a result holds for all labor input measures and transformations considered. As argued in the introduction, that property must be satisfied by any shock that plays a central role as a source of business cycles. Of course, this is a necessary, not a sufficient, condition. Whether the contribution of I-shocks to business-cycle fluctuations is large or not depends once again on the transformation of labor input used. Table 3 shows that when that variable is specified in levels, it accounts for more than half of the variance of output and hours at business-cycle frequencies, a result that appears to be independent of the specific labor input measure used. On the other hand, when hours or employment are specified in first differences or are quadratically detrended, the contribution becomes much smaller and always remains below one-fourth.

What do we conclude from this exercise? First of all, the evidence does not speak with a single voice: whether technology shocks are given a prominent role or not as a source of business cycles depends on the transformation of the labor input measure used in the analysis.

Perhaps more interesting, the analysis of the previous empirical model makes it clear that if some form of technological change plays a significant role as a source of economic fluctuations, it is not likely to be of the aggregate, sector-neutral kind that the early RBC literature emphasized, but of the investment-specific kind stressed in GHK (2000). Finally, and leaving aside the controversial question of the importance of technology shocks, the previous findings, as well as those in Fisher (2003), raise a most interesting issue: why do I-shocks appear to generate the sort of strong positive comovement between output and labour input measures that characterizes business cycles, while that property is conspicuously absent when we consider N-shocks? Below we attempt to provide a partial explanation for this seeming paradox.

4. Explaining the Effects of Technology Shocks

In this section, we briefly discuss some of the economic explanations for the anomalous response of labor input measures to technology shocks. As a matter of simple accounting, firms' use of inputs (and labor, in particular) will decline in response to a positive technology shock only if they choose (at least on average) to adjust their level of output less than proportionally to the increase in total factor productivity. Roughly speaking, we can think of two broad classes of factors that are absent in the standard RBC model and that could potentially generate that result. The first class involves the presence of nominal frictions, combined with certain monetary policies. The second set of explanations is unrelated to the existence of nominal frictions, so we refer to it as real explanations. We discuss them in turn next.

4.1 *The Role of Nominal Frictions*

A possible explanation for the negative response of labor to a technology shock, put forward both in Galí (1999) and BFK (1999), relies on the presence of nominal rigidities. As a matter of principle, nominal rigidities should not, *in themselves*, necessarily be a source of the observed employment response. Nevertheless, when prices are not fully flexible, the equilibrium response of employment (or, for that matter, of any other endogenous variable) to any real shock (including a technology shock) is *not* invariant to the monetary policy rule in place; in particular, it will be shaped by how the monetary authority reacts to the shock under consideration.[26] Different monetary policy rules will thus imply different equilibrium responses of output and employment to a technology shock, ceteris paribus.

Galí (1999) provided some intuition behind that result by focusing on a stylized model economy in which the relationship $y_t = m_t - p_t$ holds in equilibrium,[27] firms set prices in advance (implying a predetermined price level), and the central bank follows a simple money-supply rule. It is easy to see that, in that context, employment will experience a short-run decline in response to positive technology shocks, unless the central bank endogenously expands the money supply (at least) in proportion to the increase in productivity. Galí (2003) shows that the previous finding generalizes (for a broad range of parameter values) to an economy with staggered price setting, and a more realistic interest elasticity of money demand, but still an exogenous money supply. In that case, even though all firms will experience a decline in their marginal cost, only a fraction of them will adjust their prices downward in the short run. Accordingly, the aggregate price level will decline, and real balances and aggregate demand will rise. Yet when the fraction of firms adjusting prices is sufficiently small, the implied increase in aggregate demand will be less than proportional to the increase in productivity. That, in turn, induces a decline in aggregate employment.

Many economists have criticized the previous argument on the grounds that it relied on a specific and unrealistic assumption regarding how monetary policy is conducted, namely, that of a money-based rule (e.g., Dotsey, 2002). In the next subsection, we address that criticism by analyzing the effects of technology shocks in the context of a simple illustrative model with a more plausible staggered price-setting structure, and a monetary policy characterized by an interest rate rule similar to the one proposed by Taylor (1993). The model is simple enough to generate closed-form expressions for the responses of output and employment to variations in technology, thus allowing us to illustrate the main factors shaping that response and thus generating a negative comovement between the two variables.

4.1.1 A Simple Illustrative Model

The model we use to illustrate the role of nominal rigidities and monetary policy in shaping the effects of technology shocks is a standard new Keynesian framework with staggered price setting à la Calvo (1983). Its equilibrium dynamics can be summarized as follows. On the demand side, output is determined by a forward-looking IS-type equation:

$$y_t = E_t\{y_{t+1}\} - \sigma(r_t - E_t\{\pi_{t+1}\}) \tag{5}$$

where y_t denotes (log) output, r_t is the nominal interest rate, and $\pi_t \equiv p_t - p_{t-1}$ denotes the rate of inflation between $t-1$ and t. The parameter σ can be broadly interpreted as a measure of the sensitivity of aggregate demand to changes in interest rates and thus of the effectiveness of monetary policy.

Inflation evolves according to a forward-looking new Keynesian Phillips curve:

$$\pi_t = \beta E_t\{\pi_{t+1}\} + \kappa(y_t - \bar{y}_t) \tag{6}$$

where $\bar{y}_t$ is the natural level of output (or potential output), defined as the one that would prevail in the absence of nominal frictions. The variable $\bar{y}_t$ can also be interpreted as the equilibrium output generated by some background real business-cycle model driven by technology. The previous equation can be derived from the aggregation of optimal price-setting decisions by firms subject to price adjustment constraints à la Calvo (1983). In that context, coefficient κ is inversely related to the degree of price stickiness: stronger nominal rigidities imply a smaller response of inflation to any *given* sequence of output gaps.

For simplicity, we assume that exogenous random variations in productivity are the only source of fluctuations in the economy and hence the determinants of potential output. Accordingly, we postulate the following reduced-form expression for potential output:[28]

$$\bar{y}_t = \bar{\psi}_y a_t \tag{7}$$

where a_t represents an exogenous technology parameter. The latter is assumed to follow an AR(1) process $a_t = \rho_a a_{t-1} + \varepsilon_t$, where $\rho_a \in [0, 1]$. Notice that under the assumption of an aggregate production function of the form $y_t = a_t + (1-\alpha)n_t$, we can derive the following expression for the natural level of employment $\bar{n}_t$:

$$\bar{n}_t = \bar{\psi}_n a_t$$

where $\bar{\psi}_n \equiv (\bar{\psi}_y - 1)/(1-\alpha)$. Since we want to think of the previous conditions as a reduced-form representation of the equilibrium of a standard calibrated RBC model (without having to specify its details), it is natural to assume $\bar{\psi}_y \geq 1$ (and hence $\bar{\psi}_n > 0$). In that case, a positive technology shock generates an increase in both output and employment, as generally implied by the RBC models under conventional calibrations. It is precisely this property that makes it possible for any technology-driven RBC model to generate equilibrium fluctuations that replicate some key features of observed business cycles, including a positive comovement of output and employment.[29]

In that context, a natural question is, To what extent is the comovement of output and employment in response to technology shocks found in the evidence described above the result of the way monetary policy has been conducted in the United States and other industrialized economies? To illustrate that point, we use the simple model above and derive the implications for the effects of technology shocks of having the central bank follow an interest rate rule of the form:

$$r_t = \phi_\pi \pi_t + \phi_y y_t \tag{8}$$

A rule similar to equation (8) has been proposed by Taylor (1993) and others as a good characterization of monetary policy in the United States and other industrialized economies in recent decades. Notice that, as in Taylor, we assume that the monetary authority responds to output (or its deviations from trend), and not to the output gap. We view this as a more realistic description of actual policies (which emphasize output stabilization) and consistent with the fact that the concept of potential output used here, while necessary to construct any measure of the output gap, cannot be observed by the policymaker.[30]

Combining equation (8) with equilibrium conditions in equations (5) and (6), we can derive the following closed-form expression for equilibrium output:

$$\begin{aligned} y_t &= \Theta \bar{\psi}_y a_t \\ &\equiv \psi_y a_t \end{aligned}$$

where

$$\Theta \equiv \frac{\kappa(\phi_\pi - \rho_a)}{(1 - \beta\rho_a)[\sigma^{-1}(1 - \rho_a) + \phi_y] + \kappa(\phi_\pi - \rho_a)}$$

Notice that under the (weak) assumption that $\phi_\pi > \rho_a$, we have $0 < \Theta \leq 1$. The fact that Θ is greater than 0 guarantees that a positive (negative) technology shock raises (lowers) output, as in the standard RBC model. On the other hand, $\Theta \leq 1$ implies that:

$$\psi_y \leq \bar{\psi}_y$$

i.e., in the presence of nominal frictions, the size of response of output to a technology shock, ψ_y, is bounded above by that implied by the corresponding RBC model ($\bar{\psi}_y$) when the central bank follows the rule in equation (8). Hence, the combination of sticky prices and a Taylor rule will tend to overstabilize the output fluctuation resulting from technology shocks. We can interpret parameter Θ as an index of *effective policy accommodation,* i.e., one that measures the extent to which the Taylor rule in equation (8) accommodates the changes in potential output resulting from variations in technology shocks, given the persistence of the latter and the rest of the parameters describing the economy. Notice that the index of effective policy accommodation Θ is increasing in the size of the inflation coefficient in the Taylor rule (ϕ_π), and in the effectiveness of interest changes (as reflected by σ). It is also positively related to κ (and hence inversely related to the degree of price stickiness). On the other hand, it is inversely related to the size of the output coefficient in the Taylor rule (ϕ_y).

Let us now turn to the equilibrium response of employment to a technology shock, which is given by:

$$n_t = \left(\frac{\Theta \bar{\psi}_y - 1}{1 - \alpha} \right) a_t$$

$$\equiv \psi_n a_t$$

Notice that, in a way analogous to the output case, we have $\psi_n \leq \bar{\psi}_n$. In other words, the size of the employment response to a (positive) technology shock in the presence of nominal frictions is bounded above by the size of the response generated by the underlying frictionless RBC model. It is clear that the impact of a technology shock on employment may be positive or negative, depending on the configuration of parameter values.

We can get a sense for the likely sign and plausible magnitude for ψ_n by using conventional values used in calibration exercises in the literature involving similar models. Thus, Rotemberg and Woodford's (1999) estimates, based on the response to monetary policy shocks, imply a value of 0.024 for κ. A unit value is often used as an upper bound for σ. Taylor's widely used values for ϕ_π and ϕ_y are 1.5 and 0.5, respectively. In standard RBC calibrations, the assumption $\rho_a = 0.95$ is often made. Finally, we can set $\beta = 0.99$ and $\alpha = \frac{1}{3}$, two values that are not controversial. Under those assumptions, we obtain a value for Θ of 0.28. The latter figure points to a relatively low degree of effective policy accommodation.

Using a standard calibrated RBC model, Campbell (1994) obtains a range of values for $\bar{\psi}_y$ between 1 and 2.7, depending on the persistence of the shock and the elasticity of the labor supply. In particular, given a unit labor supply elasticity and a 0.95 autocorrelation in the technology process, he obtains an elasticity $\bar{\psi}_y$ of 1.45, which we adopt as our benchmark value.[31] When we combine the latter with our calibrated value for Θ computed, we obtain an implied benchmark elasticity of employment ψ_n equal to -0.87.

The previous calibration exercise, while admittedly quick and loose, illustrates that condition $\psi_n < 0$ is likely to hold under a broad range of reasonable parameter values. Under those circumstances, and subject to the caveat implied by the simplicity of the model and the characterization of monetary policy, it is hard to interpret the negative comovement between output and employment observed in the data as a puzzle, as it has often been done.[32]

In his seminal paper, Prescott (1986b) concluded his description of the predictions of the RBC paradigm by stating: "In other words [RBC] theory predicts what is observed. Indeed, if the economy did not display the business cycle phenomena, there would be a puzzle." In light of the analysis above, perhaps we should think of turning Prescott's dictum over its head, and argue instead that if, as a result of technology variations, the economy did indeed display the typical positive comovement between output and employment that characterizes the business cycle, then there would be a puzzle!

4.1.2 Nominal Rigidities and the Effects of Investment-Specific Technology Shocks

The logic behind the impact of nominal rigidities on the effects of conventional aggregate, sector-neutral technology shocks, on which the previous discussion focuses, would also seem consistent with the estimated effects of investment-specific technology shocks, as reported in Fisher (2003) and discussed in Section 3 above. The argument can be made most clearly in the context of a sticky-price version of a model like that in the GHK (2000) model. Once again, let us say for simplicity that the relationship $y_t = m_t - p_t$ holds in equilibrium, and that both m_t and p_t are pre-determined relative to the shock. In that case, firms will want to produce the same quantity of the good but, in contrast with the case of neutral technology shocks, to do so they will need to employ the same level of inputs since the efficiency of the latter has not been affected (only newly purchased capital goods will enhance that productivity in the future). That property of I-shocks is illustrated in Smets and Wouters (2003a) in the context of a much richer DSGE model. In particular, those authors show that even in the presence of the substantial price and wage rigidities estimated for the U.S. economy, a positive I-shock causes output and labor input to increase simultaneously, in a way consistent with the Fisher (2003) VAR evidence. In fact, as shown in Smets and Wouters (2003a), the qualitative pattern of the joint response of output and hours to an I-shock is not affected much when they simulate the model with all nominal rigidities turned off.

4.1.3 Evidence on the Role of Nominal Rigidities

A number of recent papers have provided evidence, often indirect, on the possible role of nominal rigidities as a source of the gap between the estimated responses of output and labor input measures to a technology shock and the corresponding predictions of an RBC model. Next, we briefly describe a sample of those papers.

Models with nominal rigidities imply that the response of the economy to a technology shock (or to any other shock, for that matter) will generally depend on the endogenous response of the monetary authority and should thus not be invariant to the monetary policy regime in place. Galí, López-Salido, and Vallés (2003) exploit that implication and try to uncover any differences in the estimated response to an identified technology shock across subsample periods. Building on the literature that points to significant differences in the conduct of monetary policy between the pre-Volcker and the Volcker–Greenspan periods, they estimate a four-variable structural VAR with a long-run restriction as in Galí (1999) for each of those subsample periods. Their evidence points to significant differences in the estimated responses to a technology shock. In particular, they show that the decline in hours in response to a positive technology shock is much more pronounced in the pre-Volcker period and is hardly significant in the Volcker–Greenspan. That evidence is consistent with the idea that monetary policy in the latter period has focused more on the stabilization of inflation and not so much on the stabilization of economic activity.[33]

Some evidence at the micro-level is provided by Marchetti and Nucci (2004), who exploit a detailed data set containing information on output, inputs, and price-setting practices for a large panel of Italian manufacturing firms. Using a modified Solow residual approach, they construct a time series for total factor productivity at the firm level, and estimate the responses of a number of firm-specific variables to an innovation in the corresponding technology measure. Among other findings, they provide evidence of a negative impact effect of a technology shock on labor input. Most interesting is that Marchetti and Nucci also exploit firm-specific information regarding the frequency of price adjustments. They split the sample of firms according to the frequency of their price revisions: flexible-price firms (adjust prices every three months or more often) and sticky-price firms (adjusting every six months or less often). They find that the negative response of employment to a positive technology shock is larger (and significant) in the case of sticky-price firms, and much weaker (and statistically insignificant) for flexible-price firms. That evidence suggests that nominal rigidities may be one of the factors underlying the estimated effects of technology shocks.[34]

4.2 *Real Explanations*

Several authors have proposed explanations for the evidence described in Section 2 that do not rely on the presence of nominal rigidities. Such real explanations generally involve some modification of the standard RBC model. Next, we briefly describe some of those explanations.

Francis and Ramey (2003a) propose two modifications of an otherwise standard RBC model that can potentially account for the negative comovement of output and hours in response to a technology shock. The first model incorporates habit formation in consumption and capital adjustment costs. As shown in Francis and Ramey, a calibrated version of that model can account for many of the estimated effects of technology shocks. In particular, the response to a permanent improvement in technology of consumption, investment, and output is more sluggish than in the standard model with no habits or capital adjustment costs. If that dampening effect is sufficiently strong, the increase in output may be smaller than the increase in productivity itself, thus causing a reduction in hours. The latter decline is consistent with the optimal decision of households to consume more leisure (despite the higher wage) as a consequence of a dominant income effect.[35] A similar mechanism underlies the modification of the basic RBC model proposed by Wen (2001), who assumes a utility function with a subsistence level of consumption (equivalent to a constant habit).

The second modification of the RBC model proposed by Francis and Ramey (2003a) hinges on the assumption of no substitutability between labor and capital in production. In that context, the only way to increase output in the short run is by increasing the workweek of capital. Hours beyond the standard workweek generate additional disutility. In such a model, a permanent increase in labor-augmenting technology is shown to generate a short-run decline in hours. The intuition is simple, and in the final analysis not much different from other modifications proposed. While output increases in the short run (due to increased investment opportunities), that increase is not sufficient to compensate for the fact that any quantity of output can now be produced with less employment (per shift) and a shorter workweek.

Rotemberg (2003) develops a version of the RBC model in which technological change diffuses much more slowly than implied by conventional specifications found in the RBC literature. The rate at which technology is adopted is calibrated on the basis of the micro studies on the speed of diffusion. Rotemberg shows that when the smooth technology process is embedded in the RBC model, it generates small short-run fluctuations in output and employment, which are largely unrelated to the cyclical variations associated with a detrended measured of employment and output. In particular, a positive innovation to technology that diffuses very slowly generates a very large wealth effect (relative to the size of the innovation), which in turn leads households to increase their consumption of leisure. As a result, both hours and output experience a short-run decline in response to a technology shock of a typical size before they gradually increase above their initial levels. Because those responses are so smooth, they imply very small movements at cyclical frequencies. It follows that technology shocks with such characteristics will account only for a small fraction of observed cyclical fluctuations in output and hours.

Collard and Dellas (2002) emphasize an additional mechanism, specific to an open economy, through which technology shocks may induce short-run negative comovements between output and labor input even in the absence of nominal rigidities. They analyze a two-country RBC model with imperfect substitutability between domestic and foreign consumption goods. If that substitutability is sufficiently low, a positive technology shock in the home country triggers a large deterioration in its terms of trade (i.e., a large decline in the price of domestic goods relative to foreign goods). That change in relative prices may induce households to increase their consumption of leisure at any given product wage, thus contracting labor supply and lowering hours. The quantitative analysis of a calibrated version of their model suggests that while technology shocks may be a nonnegligible source of output fluctuations, its role is likely to be very small as a driving force behind hours fluctuations.

The papers discussed in this section provide examples of model economies that can account for the evidence regarding the effects of technology shocks without relying on any nominal frictions. On the basis of that evidence, it is not possible to sort out the relative role played by nominal and real frictions in accounting for the evidence. The reason is simple: there is no clear mapping between the estimated coefficients in a structural VAR and the underlying structural parameters that determine the degree of those frictions. As a result, estimated VARs cannot serve as the basis of the sort of counterfactual simulations that would allow us to uncover the implied effects of technology shocks if either nominal or real frictions were not present. Such counterfactual exercises require the use of an estimated structural model. In the next section, we turn our attention to one such model.

5. Technology Shocks and the Business Cycle in an Estimated DSGE Model

In this section, we try to sort out the merits of the two types of explanations discussed above by estimating and analyzing a framework that incorporates both types of frictions and that is sufficiently rich to be taken to the data. The features that we incorporate include habit formation in consumption, staggered price- and wage-setting à la Calvo, flexible indexation of wages and prices to lagged inflation, and a monetary policy rule of the Taylor type with interest rate smoothing.

Several examples of estimated general equilibrium models can be found in the literature. Our framework is most closely related to the one used in Rabanal (2003), with two main differences. First, we allow for a unit root in the technology process in a way consistent with the assumptions underlying the identification strategy pursued in Section 2. Second, we ignore the cost channel mechanism allowed in Rabanal (2003), in light of the evidence in that paper suggesting an insignificant role for that mechanism.

We estimate the parameters of the model using Bayesian methods and focus our analysis on the implications of the estimated model regarding the effects of technology shocks and the contribution of the latter to the business cycle. The use of a structural estimated model allows us to determine, by means of counterfactual simulations, the role played by different factors in accounting for the estimated effects of technology shocks. Last but not least, the estimated model gives us an indication of the nature of the shocks that have played a dominant role as a source of postwar business cycles.

The use of Bayesian methods to estimate DSGE models has increased over recent years, in a variety of contexts.[36] Fernández-Villaverde and Rubio-Ramírez (2004) show that parameter estimation is consistent in the Bayesian framework even under model misspecification. Smets and Wouters (2003a, 2003b) estimate a model with capital accumulation, and both nominal and real rigidities for the European area and the United States. Lubik and Schorfheide (2003b) use the Bayesian framework to estimate a small-scale model allowing for indeterminacy. Rabanal (2003) estimates a general equilibrium model for the United States and the European area in search for cost channel effects of monetary policy.[37]

Next we summarize the set of equilibrium conditions of the model.[38] The demand side of the model is represented by the Euler-like equation:

$$b\Delta y_t = E_t\{\Delta y_{t+1}\} - (1-b)(r_t - E_t\{\pi_{t+1}\}) + (1-\rho_g)(1-b)g_t \tag{9}$$

which modifies equation (5) above by allowing for some external habit formation (indexed by parameter b) and introducing a preference shock $\{g_t\}$ that follows an AR(1) process with coefficient ρ_g. Underlying equation (9) is an assumption that preferences are separable between consumption and hours, and logarithmic in the quasidifference of consumption to preserve the balanced growth path property.[39] Aggregate output and hours are related by the simple log-linear production function:

$$y_t = a_t + n_t$$

Using a tilde to denote variables normalized by current productivity (to induce lack of movement), we have:

$$\tilde{y}_t = n_t \tag{10}$$

Log-linearization of the optimal price-setting condition around the zero inflation steady state yields an equation describing the dynamics of inflation as a function of the deviations of the average (log) markup from its steady-state level, which we denote by μ_t^p:[40]

$$\pi_t = \gamma_b \pi_{t-1} + \gamma_f E_t\{\pi_{t+1}\} - \kappa_p(\mu_t^p - u_t) \tag{11}$$

where $\gamma_b = \eta_p/(1+\beta\eta_p)$, $\gamma_f = \beta/(1+\beta\eta_p)$, $\kappa_p = (1-\beta\theta_p)(1-\theta_p)/\theta_p(1+\eta_p\beta)$, θ_p is the probability of not adjusting prices in any given period, and $\eta_p \in [0,1]$ is the degree of price indexation to lagged inflation. Notice that $\mu_t^p = -\log(W_t/P_tA_t) \equiv -\tilde{\omega}_t$ is the price markup, where $\tilde{\omega}_t = \omega_t - a_t$ is the real wage per efficiency unit. Variable u_t denotes exogenous variations in the desired price markup.

Log-linearization of the optimal wage-setting condition yields the following equation for the dynamics of the (normalized) real wage:

$$\tilde{\omega}_t = \frac{1}{1+\beta}\tilde{\omega}_{t-1} + \frac{\beta}{1+\beta}E_t\{\tilde{\omega}_{t+1}\} - \frac{1}{1+\beta}\Delta a_t + \frac{\beta}{1+\beta}E_t\{\Delta a_{t+1}\}$$

$$+ \frac{\eta_w}{1+\beta}\pi_{t-1} - \frac{(1+\beta\eta_w)}{1+\beta}\pi_t + \frac{\beta}{1+\beta}E_t\{\pi_{t+1}\} - \frac{\kappa_w}{1+\beta}(\mu_t^w - v_t) \quad (12)$$

where θ_w denotes the fraction of workers that do not re-optimize their wage, $\eta_w \in [0,1]$ is the degree of wage indexation to lagged inflation, and $\kappa_w \equiv (1-\theta_w)(1-\beta\theta_w)/\theta_w(1+\varepsilon_w\varphi)$, and ε_w is the wage elasticity of labor demand in the steady state. Also notice that $\mu_t^w \equiv \tilde{\omega}_t - ((1/(1-b))\tilde{y}_t - (b/(1-b))\tilde{y}_{t-1} - g_t + (b/(1-b))\Delta a_t + \varphi n_t)$ is the wage markup. Variable v_t denotes exogenous variations in the desired wage markup.

Finally, we close the model by assuming that the monetary authority adjusts interest rates in response to changes in inflation and output growth according to the rule:

$$r_t = \phi_r r_{t-1} + (1-\phi_r)\phi_\pi \pi_t + (1-\phi_r)\phi_y \Delta y_t + z_t \quad (13)$$

where z_t is an exogenous monetary shock.[41]

The exogenous driving variables are assumed to evolve as follows:

$$a_t = a_{t-1} + \varepsilon_t^a$$

$$g_t = \rho_g g_{t-1} + \varepsilon_t^g$$

$$u_t = \rho_u u_{t-1} + \varepsilon_t^u$$

$$v_t = \rho_v v_{t-1} + \varepsilon_t^v$$

$$z_t = \varepsilon_t^z$$

Notice that while we do not observe $\tilde{\omega}_t$ and $\tilde{y}_t$, the two variables are related as follows:

$$\omega_t - y_t = \tilde{\omega}_t - \tilde{y}_t$$

and $\omega_t - y_t$ is an observable variable, which should be stationary in equilibrium. In the next section, we explain how to write the likelihood function in terms of the five observable variables: output growth, inflation, the nominal interest rate, hours, and the real wage-output ratio.

5.1 *Parameter Estimation*

5.1.1 Data

We estimate the model laid out in the previous section using U.S. quarterly time series for five variables: real output, inflation, real wages, hours, and interest rates. The sample period is 1948:1 to 2002:4. For consistency with the analysis in Section 2, we use the same series for output and hours. Our measure of nominal wages is the compensation per hour in the nonfarm business sector (LXNFC), and the measure for the price level is the nonfarm business sector deflator (LXNFI). Finally, we use the quarterly average daily readings of the 3-month T-bill (FTB3) as the relevant nominal interest rate. To render the series stationary, we detrend hours and the real wage-output ratio using a quadratic trend. We treat inflation, output growth, and the nominal interest rate as stationary, and express them in deviations from their sample mean.

As is well known from Bayes's rule, the posterior distribution of the parameters is proportional to the product of the prior distribution of the parameters and the likelihood function of the data. Until recently, only well-known and standard distributions could be used. The advent of fast computer processors and Markov Chain Monte Carlo (MCMC) methods has removed this restriction, and a more general class of models and distributions can be used.[42] To implement the Bayesian estimation method, we need to be able to evaluate numerically the prior and the likelihood function. Then we use the Metropolis-Hastings algorithm to obtain random draws from the posterior distribution, from which we obtain the relevant moments of the posterior distribution of the parameters.

5.1.2 The Likelihood Function

Let ψ denote the vector of parameters that describe preferences, technology, the monetary policy rule, and the shocks of the model; d_t be the vector of endogenous variables (observable or not); z_t be the vector of shocks; and ε_t be the vector of innovations. The system of equilibrium conditions and the process for the exogenous shocks can be written as a second-order difference equation:

$$A(\psi)E_t\{d_{t+1}\} = B(\psi)d_t + C(\psi)d_{t-1} + D(\psi)z_t$$

$$z_t = N(\psi)z_{t-1} + \varepsilon_t$$

$$E(\varepsilon_t\varepsilon_t') = \Sigma(\psi)$$

We use standard solution methods for linear models with rational expectations (see, for example, Uhlig, 1999) to write the law of motion in state-space form and the Kalman filter, as in Hamilton (1994), to evaluate the likelihood of the five observable variables $x_t = [r_t, \pi_t, \omega_t - y_t, n_t, \Delta y_t]'$. We denote by $L(\{x_t\}_{t=1}^T \mid \psi)$ the likelihood function of $\{x_t\}_{t=1}^T$.

5.1.3 Priors

In this section, we denote by $\Pi(\psi)$ the prior distribution of the parameters. We present the list of the structural parameters and its associated prior distributions in the first three columns of Table 4. Most of the priors involve uniform distributions for the parameters, which simply restrict the support. We use uniform distributions for the parameter that explains habit formation, for the probabilities of the Calvo lotteries, and for the indexation parameters. The prior for all these parameters has support between 0 and 1, except the probabilities of the Calvo lottery, which are allowed to take values up to 0.9; i.e., we are ruling out average price and wage durations of more than 10 quarters.

We try to supplement as much prior information as possible for the model's exogenous shocks. The AR(1) coefficients have uniform prior distributions between 0 and 0.97. Gamma distributions for the standard deviations of the shocks are assumed (to guarantee nonnegativity). We select their hyperparameters to match available information for the prior mean standard deviation of the innovations, while allowing reasonable uncertainty in these parameters. For instance, for the monetary policy rule, we choose the means of the inflation and output growth coefficients to match the ones proposed by Taylor.[43] For the monetary policy shock, we use the standard deviation that comes from running an OLS regression for the Taylor rule equation.

In addition, we fix some parameters. We set the discount factor at $\beta = 0.99$. The elasticities of product and labor demand are set to 6 (implying steady-state markups of 20%). These values are pretty conventional in the literature.

Table 4
Prior and posterior distributions

Parameter	Prior distribution			Posterior distribution	
		Mean	Standard deviation	Mean	Standard deviation
b	Uniform$(0, 1)$	0.50	0.289	0.42	0.04
φ	Normal$(1, 0.25)$	1.00	0.25	0.80	0.11
θ_p	Uniform$(0, 0.9)$	0.45	0.259	0.53	0.03
θ_w	Uniform$(0, 0.9)$	0.45	0.259	0.05	0.02
η_p	Uniform$(0, 1)$	0.50	0.289	0.02	0.02
η_w	Uniform$(0, 1)$	0.50	0.289	0.42	0.28
ρ_r	Uniform$(0, 0.97)$	0.485	0.284	0.69	0.04
ϕ_y	Normal$(0.5, 0.125)$	0.50	0.13	0.26	0.06
ϕ_π	Normal$(1.5, 0.25)$	1.50	0.25	1.35	0.13
ρ_g	Uniform$(0, 0.97)$	0.485	0.284	0.93	0.02
ρ_u	Uniform$(0, 0.97)$	0.485	0.284	0.95	0.02
ρ_v	Uniform$(0, 0.97)$	0.485	0.284	0.91	0.01
σ_z	Gamma$(25, 0.0001)$	0.0025	0.0005	0.003	0.0001
σ_a	Gamma$(25, 0.0004)$	0.01	0.002	0.009	0.001
σ_g	Gamma$(16, 0.00125)$	0.02	0.005	0.025	0.0024
σ_u	Gamma$(4, 0.0025)$	0.01	0.005	0.011	0.001
σ_v	Gamma$(4, 0.0025)$	0.01	0.005	0.012	0.001

5.1.4 Drawing from the Posterior

From Bayes's rule, we obtain the posterior distribution of the parameters as follows:

$$p(\psi \mid \{x_t\}_{t=1}^{T}) \propto L(\{x_t\}_{t=1}^{T} \mid \psi)\Pi(\psi)$$

The posterior density function is proportional to the product of the likelihood function and the prior joint density function of ψ. Given our priors and the likelihood functions implied by the state-space solution to the model, we are not able to obtain a closed-form solution for the posterior distributions. However, we are able to evaluate both expressions numerically. We follow Fernández-Villaverde and Rubio-Ramírez (2004) and Lubik and Schorfheide (2003a) and use the random walk Metropolis-Hastings algorithm to obtain a random draw of size 500,000 from $p(\psi \mid \{x_t\}_{t=1}^{T}, m)$. We use the draw to estimate the moments of the posterior distribution and to obtain impulse responses and second moments of the endogenous variables.

5.2 *Main Findings*

5.2.1 Parameter Estimates and Second Moments

The last two columns of Table 4 report the mean and standard deviation of the posterior distributions for all the parameters. Notice that the habit formation parameter is estimated to be 0.42, a value somewhat smaller than that suggested by Christiano, Eichenbaum, and Evans (2003) or Smets and Wouters (2003b). The parameter that measures the elasticity of the marginal disutility of hours, φ, is estimated to be 0.80, which is close to values usually obtained or calibrated in the literature.

The average duration of price contracts implied by the point estimate of the price stickiness parameter lies slightly above two quarters. We view this estimate as a moderate amount of price stickiness in the economy. Perhaps most surprising is the low degree of wage stickiness uncovered by our estimation method. Such an implausible low estimate may suggest that the Calvo model is not the best formalism to characterize wage dynamics.[44]

The price indexation coefficient is estimated at a low value, 0.04, suggesting that the pure forward-looking model is a good approximation for inflation dynamics, once we allow for autoregressive price markup shocks. On the other hand, indexation in wage setting is more important, with a posterior mean of 0.42. The coefficients of the interest rate rule suggest a high degree of interest rate smoothing, 0.69, a small response of the interest rate to output growth fluctuations, and a coefficient of the response of the interest rate to inflation of 1.33, which corresponds to a lean-against-the-wind monetary policy. The estimated processes for the shocks of the model suggest that all of them are highly autocorrelated, with parameters between 0.95 for the price markup shock and 0.91 for the wage markup shock.[45]

Table 5 displays some selected posterior second moments implied by the model estimates and compares them to the data.[46] The first two columns present the standard deviation of the observed variables, and their counterparts implied by the estimated model. We can see that the model does a very good job in replicating the standard deviations of output, inflation, and the nominal interest rate. The model also does well in mimicking the unconditional correlation between the growth rates of hours and output: in the data, it is 0.75; in the model, it is 0.72. However, it overestimates the standard deviation of hours (3.11% in

Table 5
Second moments of estimated DSGE model

	Standard deviations (%)			Contribution to variance technology shocks
	Data	Model	Technology component	
Original data				
Output growth	1.36	1.27	0.60	22.3%
Inflation	0.72	0.73	0.18	6.0%
Interest rate	0.72	0.67	0.04	0.3%
Hours	3.11	4.60	0.42	0.8%
Real wage/output	3.69	4.44	0.13	0.1%
Correlation between (dy, dn)	0.75	0.72	−0.49	
Bandpass filtered data				
Output	2.04	2.04	0.87	18.2%
Hours	1.69	1.69	0.26	2.3%
Correlation between (y, n)	0.88	0.88	−0.14	

the data and 4.6% in the model) and to a lesser extent the real wage–output ratio (3.69% in the data, 4.44% in the model).

5.2.2 The Effects of Technology Shocks

Next, we turn our attention to the estimated model's predictions regarding the effects of technology shocks.[47] Figure 7 displays the posterior impulse responses to a permanent technology shock of a size normalized to one standard deviation.[48] We can observe that the model replicates the VAR-based evidence fairly well, in spite of the differences in the approach. In particular, the estimated model implies a persistent decline in hours in response to a positive technology shock, and a gradual adjustment of output to a permanently higher plateau. It takes about four quarters for output to reach its new steady-state level. Hours drop on impact, by about 0.4 percentage points, and converge monotonically to their initial level afterward.[49]

The third column of Table 5 reports the second moments of the observed variables conditional on technology shocks being the only driving force. The fourth column shows the fraction of the variance of each variable accounted for by the technology shock.[50] We can see that technology shocks do not play a major role in explaining the variability of the five observed variables. They explain 22% of the variability of output growth and 6% of the variability of inflation. For the rest of

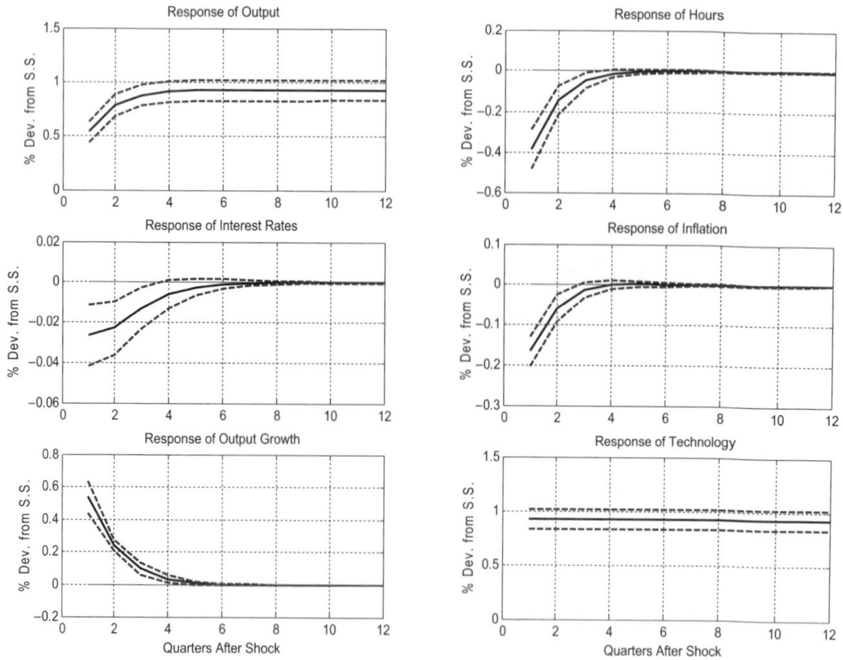

Figure 7
Posterior impulse responses to a technology shock: model based estimates

variables, including hours, they explain an insignificant amount of overall volatility. A key result emerges when we simulate the model with technology shocks only: we obtain a correlation between $(\Delta y_t, \Delta n_t)$ of -0.49, which contrasts with the high positive correlation between the same variables observed in the data.

The last three rows of Table 5 report statistics based on bandpass filtered data. In this case, the series of output growth and hours generated by the estimated model (when all shocks other than technology are turned off) are used to obtain the (log) levels of hours and output, on which the bandpass filter is applied. Once again, we find that technology shocks can account for only a small fraction of the variance of the business-cycle component of output and hours. The conditional correlation between those two variables falls to -0.14, from a value of 0.88 for the actual filtered series.

The previous findings are illustrated in Figure 8, which displays the business-cycle components of log output and log hours associated with technology shocks, according to our estimated model. It is apparent

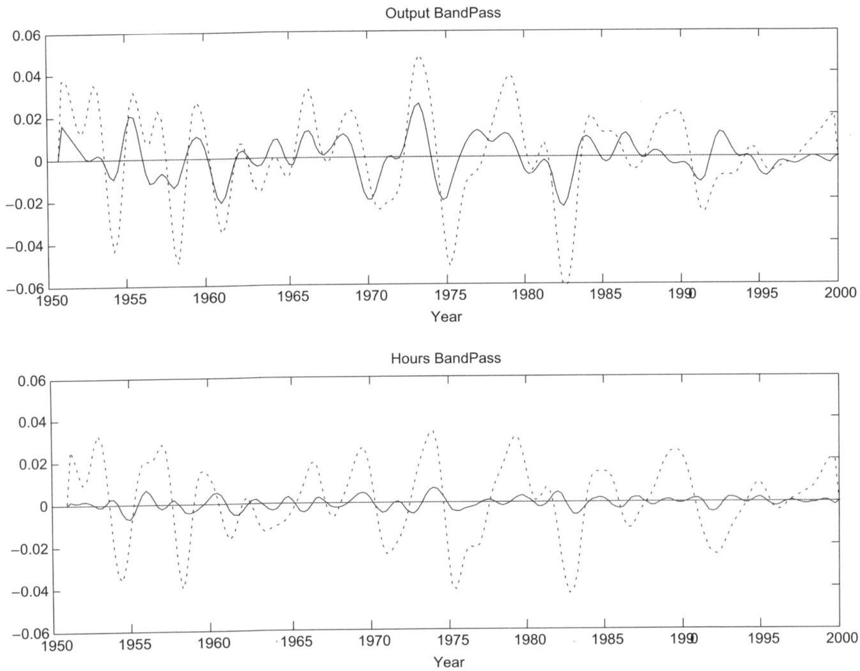

Figure 8
The role of technology shocks in U.S. postwar fluctuations: model-based estimates
Note: Solid line: technology component (BP-filtered); dashed line: U.S. data (BP-filtered).

that technology shocks explain only a minor fraction of output fluctuations. This is even more dramatic when we look at fluctuations in hours, in a way consistent with most of the VAR findings. Similar qualitative findings are found in Altig et al. (2003), Ireland (2004), and Smets and Wouters (2003b), using slightly different models and/or estimation methods.

5.2.3 What Are the Main Sources of Economic Fluctuations?

Which shocks play a more important role in explaining fluctuations in our observed variables? In Table 6, we report the contribution of each shock to the total variance of each variable implied by our model estimates. The shock that explains most of the variance of all variables in our framework is the preference shock, which we can interpret more broadly as a (real) demand shock. It explains above 70% of the variance of hours, the real wage-output ratio, and the nominal interest rate. The preference shock also explains 57% of the variance of output

Table 6
Variance decomposition from estimated DSGE model

	Shocks				
	Monetary	Technology	Preference	Price markup	Wage markup
Output growth	4.8%	22.3%	57.1%	8.0%	7.1%
Inflation	27.1%	6.1%	36.3%	13.7%	14.7%
Nominal rate	5.0%	0.4%	72.3%	9.8%	11.8%
Hours	0.4%	0.8%	70.0%	17.6%	9.6%
Wage – output	0.1%	0.1%	73.6%	12.0%	12.8%

and 36% of the variance of inflation. On the other hand, the monetary shock explains only approximately 5% of output growth and the nominal interest rate, and is an important determinant of inflation variability, contributing to 27% of total volatility. Price and wage markup shocks both have some importance in explaining the volatility of all variables, with contributions to the variance that range from 7% to 17%. Overall, the picture that emerges from Table 6 is that preference shocks are key for explaining the volatility of all variables. The monetary and technology shocks have some importance in the sense that they explain about 20% of the variance in one of the variables (output growth in the case of technology, inflation in the case of monetary shocks), but their contribution to the remaining variables is very small. The price and wage markup shocks explain a small fraction of variability in all variables.

5.2.4 Structural Explanations for the Estimated Effects of Technology Shocks

Finally, we examine which features of the model are driving the negative comovement between hours and output in response to technology shocks. In Table 7, we present the correlation between the business-cycle components of output and hours that arises under several counterfactual scenarios. For each scenario, we shut down some of the rigidities of the model and simulate it again while keeping the same value for the remaining parameter estimates.

Three features of the model stand out as natural candidates to explain the negative correlation between output and hours: sticky prices, sticky wages, and habit formation. When we shut down each of those, we find that the remaining rigidities still induce a large and negative

Table 7
Technology-driven fluctuations output and hours: correlations implied by alternative model specifications (BP-filtered data)

Original	−0.14
Flexible wages	−0.16
Flexible prices	−0.18
No habit formation	−0.29
Flexible prices and wages	−0.21
No frictions (RBC)	0.22
Inflation targeting	−0.15

conditional correlation. For instance, in the second row of the table, we can see that assuming flexible wages ($\theta_w = \eta_w = 0$) delivers basically the same correlations. This result is not surprising given that nominal wage rigidities do not appear to be important in turn given the parameter estimates. When we assume flexible prices but keep sticky wages and habit formation, things do not change much either.

A particular scenario would seem to be of special interest: one with flexible prices and wages, and habit formation. In that case, once again, a similar pattern of correlations emerges. A similar result is obtained by Smets and Wouters (2003b), who interpret it as evidence favorable to some of the real explanations found in the literature. Yet when we turn off habit formation in our estimated model but keep nominal rigidities operative, we find a qualitatively similar result: the conditional and unconditional correlations between hours and output have the same pattern of signs as that observed in the data. It is only when we shut down all rigidities (nominal and real) that we obtain a positive correlation between hours and output, both conditionally and unconditionally, and in a way consistent with the predictions of the basic RBC model.

Finally, we consider a calibration in which the central bank responds exclusively to inflation changes but not to output. Some authors have argued that the negative comovement of output and hours may be a consequence of an attempt by the monetary authority to overstabilize output. Our results suggest that this cannot be an overriding factor: when we set the coefficient on output growth equal to zero (but keeping both habit formation and nominal rigidities operative), we still obtain a negative conditional correlation between hours and output.

In light of the previous findings, we conclude that both real rigidities (habit formation, in our model) and nominal rigidities (mostly sticky prices) appear to be relevant factors in accounting for the evidence on the effects of technology shocks. By way of contrast, *both* nominal and real rigidities seem to be required to account for the empirical effects of monetary policy shocks (see, for example, Christiano, Eichenbaum, and Evans, 1999, or the dynamics of inflation, for example, Galí and Gertler, 1999).

6. Conclusion

In the present paper, we have reviewed recent research efforts that seek to identify and estimate the role of technology as a source of economic fluctuations in ways that go beyond the simple unconditional second-moment matching exercises found in the early RBC literature. The number of qualifications and caveats of any empirical exercise that seeks to provide an answer to the above questions is never small. As is often the case in empirical research in economics, the evidence does not speak with a single voice, even when similar methods and data sets are used. Those caveats notwithstanding, the bulk of the evidence reported in the present paper raises serious doubts about the importance of changes in aggregate technology as a significant (or, even more, a dominant) force behind business cycles, in contrast with the original claims of the RBC literature. Instead, it points to demand factors as the main force behind the strong positive comovement between output and labor input measures that is the hallmark of the business cycle.

7. Addendum: A Response to Ellen McGrattan

In her comments to the present paper, Ellen McGrattan (2004) dismisses the evidence on the effects of technology shocks based on structural VARs (SVARs) that rely on long-run identifying restrictions. The purpose of this addendum is to explain why we think McGrattan's analysis and conclusions are misleading. Since some of her argument and the evidence she provides is based on her recent working paper with Chari and Kehoe, our discussion often refers directly to their paper (Chari, Kehoe, and McGrattan, 2004a).

Our main point is easy to summarize. McGrattan and Chari, Kehoe, and McGrattan (CKM) study a number of model economies, all of which predict that hours should rise in response to a positive technology shock. Yet when they estimate an SVAR on data generated by those models, the resulting impulse responses show a decline in hours in response to such a shock (with one exception, to be discussed below).

McGrattan presents her findings and those in CKM as an illustration of a general flaw with SVARs. But we find that conclusion unwarranted. What McGrattan and CKM really show is that a *misidentified* and/or *misspecified* SVAR often leads to incorrect inference. As McGrattan herself acknowledges, in her example of a standard RBC model (as well as in all but one of the examples in CKM), the assumptions underlying the data-generating model are inconsistent with the identifying assumption in the VAR: either technology is stationary, or nontechnology shocks have a permanent effect on productivity, or the order of integration of hours is wrong.[51] In those cases, the finding of incorrect inference is neither surprising nor novel since it restates points that have already been made in the literature.[52] That conclusion should be contrasted with that of Erceg, Guerrieri, and Gust (2004), who show that when the SVAR is correctly specified and the identifying restrictions are satisfied by the underlying data-generating models, the estimated responses to technology shocks match (at least qualitatively) the theoretical ones.

We think that, when properly used, SVARs provide an extremely useful guide for developing business-cycle theories. Evidence on the effects of particular shocks that is shown to be robust to a variety of plausible identification schemes should not be ignored when developing and refining DSGE models that will be used for policy analysis. On the one hand, that requirement imposes a stronger discipline on model builders than just matching the patterns of *unconditional* second moments of some time series of interest, the approach traditionally favored by RBC economists. On the other hand, it allows one to assess the relevance of alternative specifications without knowledge of all the driving forces impinging on the economy.[53]

Another finding in CKM that may seem striking to many readers is that their business accounting framework produces a rise in hours in response to a positive technology shock, in contrast with the evidence summarized in Section 2 of the present paper. Below, we conjecture that such a result hinges critically on treating the conventional Solow residual as an appropriate measure of technology, in contrast to the wealth of evidence suggesting the presence of significant procyclical error in that measure of technology. By way of contrast, most of the SVAR-based findings on the effects of technology shocks overviewed in the present paper rely on identifying assumptions that are much weaker than those required for the Solow residual to be a suitable measure of technology.

Next, we elaborate on the previous points as well as on other issues raised by McGrattan's comment. First, we try to shed some light on why the estimated SVARs do not recover the model-generated impulse responses. Second, we provide a conjecture about why CKM's estimated model would predict an increase in hours in response to a positive technology shock, even if the opposite were true. Finally, we comment on CKM's proposed alternative to SVARs.

7.1 *Why Does the SVAR Evidence Fail to Match the McGrattan and CKM Models' Predictions?*

The reason why the SVAR estimates reported by McGrattan fail to recover the joint response of output and hours implied by her RBC model should not be viewed as reflecting an inherent flaw in the SVAR approach. Instead, it is most likely a consequence of misspecification and misidentification of the SVAR used.

First, and most flagrantly, the geometric growth specification of technology assumed in the McGrattan exercise implies that technology shocks will have only temporary effects on labor productivity. A maintained assumption in Galí (1999) and in Section 2.1 above is the existence of a unit root in the technology process, underlying the observed unit root in productivity. It is clear that if a researcher holds an inherent belief in the stationarity of technology, she will not want to use that empirical approach to estimate the effects of technology shocks. We find the notion that technology shocks don't have permanent effects hard to believe, though we cannot offer any proof (and though we have provided suggestive evidence along those lines in Section 3.1). In any event, we find it useful to point out that the literature contains several examples, reviewed in Section 2, that do not rely on the unit root assumption and that yield results similar to Galí (1999).[54]

In principle, CKM appear to overcome the previous misidentification problem by using as a data-generating mechanism an RBC model that assumes a unit root in technology. They consider two versions of that model (preferred and baseline), which we discuss in turn. Their preferred specification fails to satisfy the identifying restriction of the VAR in another important dimension: because of the *endogeneity* of technology in their model (reflected in the nonzero off-diagonal terms in the process describing the driving forces), shocks that are non-technological in nature are going to have an effect on the level of technology and hence on productivity. As a result, the identification underlying the SVAR will be incorrect, and inference will be distorted.

The two misidentification problems just discussed should not affect the CKM baseline specification because in the latter, technology is assumed to follow an *exogenous* random walk process. Yet when we look at the properties of that model, we uncover a *misspecification* problem in the VAR used. In a nutshell, and as is the case for most RBC models found in the literature, CKM's baseline model implies that hours worked follow a stationary process, though they estimate the SVAR using first-differenced hours. The potential problems associated with that misspecification were originally pointed out by CEV (2003) and have been discussed extensively in Section 3 of the present paper.[55]

CKM provide one example (the exception we were referring to above) in which the estimated SVAR satisfies both the key long-run identifying restriction (technology is exogenous and contains a unit root) and is correctly specified (hours are introduced in levels). In that case, and not surprisingly, the SVAR makes a correct inference: hours are estimated to rise in response to a technology shock, as the model predicts. While CKM acknowledge that fact, they instead focus on the finding that the estimated impulse response shows a nonnegligible bias. This is an interesting point, but it is not central to the controversy regarding the effects of technology shocks: the latter has focused all along on the estimated *sign* of the comovement of output and hours, not on the size of the responses. Nor is it novel: it is one of the two main findings in Erceg, Guerrieri, and Gust (2003), who already point out and analyze the role played by the slow adjustment of capital in generating that downward bias.

Neither McGrattan nor CKM emphasize Erceg, Guerrieri, and Gust's (EGG's) second main finding, which is highly relevant for their purposes: using both a standard RBC model and a new Keynesian model with staggered wage and price setting as data-generating mechanisms, they conclude that the estimated responses to a technology shock, using the same SVAR approach as in Galí (1999), look like the true responses to that shock in both models, at least from a qualitative viewpoint (leading to a rise in hours in the former case, and to a drop in the latter, in a way consistent with the models' predictions).

7.2 *Why Does the CKM Accounting Framework Predict a Rise in Hours?*

The framework used by McGrattan in Section 2.2 of her comment is unlikely to be recognized by most macroeconomists as a standard RBC model, the title of the subsection notwithstanding. Instead, it consists of a version of the business-cycle *accounting* framework originally developed in Chari et al. (2004b). That framework consists of a standard RBC model with four driving forces (or wedges, in their terminology). One of those driving forces, which enters the production function as a conventional productivity parameter, is interpreted as a technology shock. Two other driving forces are broadly interpreted as a labor market and an investment wedge. The fourth is government spending. After assuming functional forms for preferences and technology as well as a conventional calibration of the associated parameters conventional in the RBC literature, CKM estimate a VAR model for the four driving forces using time series for output, hours, investment, and government consumption.

Let us put aside some of the issues regarding the suitability of SVARs discussed in the previous section to turn to a different question: Why does the estimated CKM accounting framework predict an increase in hours in response to a positive technology shock? The interest of the question may be puzzling to some readers; after all, the CKM model looks like a standard RBC model augmented with many shocks. But that description is not accurate in a subtle, but important dimension: the disturbances/wedges in the CKM accounting framework are not orthogonal to each other, having instead a rich dynamic structure. Thus, nothing prevents, at least in principle, some of the nontechnology wedges from responding to a technology shock in such a way as to generate a negative comovement between output and hours in response to that shock. After all, the increase in markups following a positive technology shock is precisely the mechanism through which a model with nominal rigidities can generate a decline in hours.

Here, we can only speculate on the sources of the sign of the response of hours predicted by the CKM model. But a cursory look at the structure of the model, and the approach to uncovering its shocks, points to a very likely candidate for that finding: the CKM measure of the technology parameter corresponds to the gap between (log) GDP and a weighted average of (log) capital and (log) hours, with the weights based on average income shares. In other words, the CKM measure of technology corresponds, for all practical purposes, to the conventional Solow (1957) residual. In adopting that approach to identification of technology, CKM are brushing aside two decades of research pointing to the multiple shortcomings of the Solow residual as a measure of short-run variations to technology, from Hall (1988) to BFK (1999). In the absence of any adjustments for market power, variable utilization of inputs, and other considerations, the Solow residual, as an index of technological change, is known to have a large (and highly procyclical) measurement error.

To illustrate this, consider an economy with a constant technology (and no capital) in which output and (measured) hours are linked according to the following reduced-form equilibrium relationship:

$$y_t = \alpha n_t$$

CKM's index of technology z_t would have been computed, using the Solow formula as:

$$z_t = y_t - s n_t$$

where s is the average labor income share. Under Solow's original assumptions, $s = \alpha$. But the existing literature provides a number of compelling reasons why in practice we will almost surely have $\alpha > s$. It follows that CKM's technology index can be written as:

$$z_t = (\alpha - s) n_t$$

thus implying a mechanical positive correlation between measured technology and hours.

The previous example is admittedly overstylized, but we think it illustrates the point clearly. Thus, it should come as no surprise if the estimated responses of the different wedges to innovations in that error-ridden measure of technology were to be highly biased and may indeed resemble the responses to a demand disturbance. In fact, the use of VARs based on either long-run restrictions (as in Galí, 1999) or purified Solow residuals (as in BFK, 1999) as well as the approach to model calibration in Burnside and Eichenbaum (1996) was largely motivated by that observation.

7.3 *Some Agreement*

We cannot conclude this addendum without expressing our agreement with CKM's proposed alternative approach to the identification and estimation of technology (and other shocks), based on the specification of a "state representation and a set of identifying assumptions that nests the class of models of interest" and that can be "conveniently estimated with Kalman filtering" techniques. But this is precisely the approach that we have pursued in Section 5 of the present paper, following the footsteps of a number authors referred to in that section (including the second author of the present paper).

In her comment, McGrattan criticizes the particular model that we choose to implement that approach (which she refers to as the triple-sticky model) on the grounds that it abstracts from capital accumulation. But our goal was not to develop a fully-fledged model, encompassing all relevant aspects of the economy, just to provide an illustration of a potentially fruitful approach to analyzing the role of different frictions in shaping the estimated effects of technology shocks. Other authors have provided a similar analysis using a richer structure that includes endogenous capital accumulation, among many other features. The models used in that literature allow (but do not impose) all sorts of frictions in a highly flexible way, and nest the standard RBC model as a particular case. Most important for our purposes here, some of those papers (see, for example, Smets and Wouters, 2003b) have analyzed explicitly the effects of technology shocks implied by their estimated models. In a way consistent with our findings above, those effects have been shown to imply a negative response of hours to a positive technology shock. McGrattan reports no comparable evidence for her triple-sticky model with investment, though we conjecture that the latter would imply a similar response.

Notes

Prepared for the nineteenth NBER Annual Conference on Macroeconomics. We are thankful to Susanto Basu, Olivier Blanchard, Yongsung Chang, John Fernald, Albert Marcet, Barbara Rossi, Julio Rotemberg, Juan Rubio-Ramirez, Robert Solow, Jaume Ventura, Lutz Weinke, the editors (Mark Gertler and Ken Rogoff), and discussants (Ellen McGrattan and Valerie Ramey) for useful comments. We have also benefited from comments by participants in seminars at the CREI-UPF Macro Workshop, MIT Macro Faculty Lunch, and Duke. Anton Nakov provided excellent research assistance. We are grateful to Craig Burnside, Ellen McGrattan, Harald Uhlig, Jonas Fisher, and Susanto Basu for help with the data. Galí acknowledges financial support from DURSI (Generalitat de Catalunya), CREA (Barcelona Economics), Fundación Ramón Areces, and the Ministerio de Ciencia y Tecnología (SEC2002-03816). This paper should not be reported as representing the views of the International Monetary Fund (IMF). The views expressed are those of the authors and do not necessarily reflect the views of the IMF or IMF policy.

1. Prescott (1996a).

2. See Blanchard and Quah (1989) and Galí (1999) for details.

3. It is precisely this feature that differentiates the approach to identification in Galí (1999) from that in Blanchard and Quah (1989). The latter authors used restrictions on long-run effects on output, as opposed to labor productivity. In the presence of a unit root in labor input, that could lead to the mislabeling as technology shocks of any disturbances that was behind the unit root in labor input.

4. With four lags, the corresponding *t*-statistics are −2.5 and and −7.08, the level and first-difference, respectively.

5. That distribution is obtained by means of a Montecarlo simulation based on 500 drawings from the distribution of the reduced-form VAR distribution.

6. Notice that the distribution of the impact effect on hours assigns a zero probability to an increase in that variable.

7. See, e.g., King et al. (1988a) and Campbell (1994).

8. See also Francis and Ramey (2003a), among others, for estimates using higher dimensional VARs.

9. Blanchard (1989, p. 1158).

10. See the comment on Shea's paper by Galí (1998) for a more detailed discussion of that point.

11. The latter evidence contrasts with their analysis of long-term U.S. data, in which the results vary significantly across samples and appear to depend on the specification used (more below).

12. An analogous but somewhat more detailed analysis can be found in Francis and Ramey (2003a).

13. Of course, that was also the traditional view regarding technological change, but one that was challenged by the RBC school.

14. Exceptions include stochastic versions of endogenous growth models, as in King et al. (1988b). In those models, any transitory shock can in principle have a permanent effect on the level of capital or disembodied technology and, as a result, on labor productivity.

15. We are grateful to Craig Burnside and Ellen McGrattan for providing the data.

16. A similar conclusion is obtained by Fisher (2003) using a related approach in the context of the multiple technology shock model described below.

17. In particular, we use their fully corrected series from their 1999 paper When revising the present paper, BFK told us of an updated version of their technology series, extending the sample period through to 1996 and incorporating some methodological changes. The results obtained with the updated series were almost identical to the ones reported below.

18. That odds ratio increases substantially when an *F*-statistic associated with a covariates ADF test is incorporated as part of the encompassing analysis.

19. With the exception of their bivariate model under a level specification, CEV also find the contribution of technology shocks to the variance of output and hours at business cycles to be small (below 20%). In their bivariate, level specification model, that contribution is as high as 66 and 33%, respectively.

20. Given the previous observations, one wonders how an identical prior for both specifications could be assumed, as CEV do when computing the odds ratio.

21. Unfortunately, CEV do not include any statistic associated with the null of no trend in hours in their encompassing analysis. While it is certainly possible that one can get a t statistic as high as 8.13 on the time-squared term with a 13% frequency when the true model contains no trend (as their Montercarlo analysis suggests), it must surely be the case that such a frequency is much higher when the true model contains the quadratic trend as estimated in the data!

22. In fact, total hours was the series used originally in Galí (1999).

23. The finding of a slight short run decline in output was obtained in BFK (1999).

24. Pesavento and Rossi (2003) propose an agnostic procedure to estimate the effects of a technology shock that does not require taking a stance on the order of integration of hours. They find that a positive technology shock has a negative effect on hours on impact.

25. We thank Jonas Fisher for kindly providing the data on real investment price.

26. See the discussion in McGrattan (1999); Dotsey (2002); and Galí, López-Salido, and Vallés (2003), among others.

27. This would be consistent with any model in which velocity is constant in equilibrium. See Galí (1999) for an example of such an economy.

28. Such a reduced-form relationship would naturally arise as an equilibrium condition of a simple RBC model with productivity as the only state variable.

29. The absence of another state variable (say, capital stock or other disturbances) implies a perfect correlation between the natural levels of output and employment, in contrast with existing RBC models in the literature, where that correlation is positive and very high, but not one.

30. Throughout we assume that the condition $\kappa(\phi_\pi - 1) + (1 - \beta)\phi_y > 0$ is satisfied. As shown by Bullard and Mitra (2002), that condition is necessary to guarantee a unique equilibrium.

31. This corresponds to the impact elasticity with respect to productivity and ignores the subsequent adjustment of capital (which is very small). The source is Table 3 in Campbell (1994), with an appropriate adjustment to correct for his (labor-augmenting) specification of technology in the production function (we need to divide Campbell's number by two-thirds).

32. A similar result can be uncovered in an unpublished paper by McGrattan (1999). Unfortunately, the author did not seem to notice that finding (or, at least, she did not discuss it explicitly).

33. The analysis in Galí, López-Salido, and Vallés (2003) has been extended by Francis, Owyang, and Theodorou (2004) to other G7 countries. They uncover substantial differences across countries in the joint response of employment, prices, and interest rates to technology shocks, and argue that some of those differences can be grounded in differences in the underlying interest rate rules.

34. A less favorable assessment is found in Chang and Hong (2003), who conduct a similar exercise using four-digit U.S. manufacturing industries, and rely on evidence of sectoral nominal rigidities based on the work of Bils and Klenow (2002).

35. See Lettau and Uhlig (2000) for a detailed analysis of the properties of an RBC model with habit formation. As pointed out by Francis and Ramey, Lettau and Uhlig seem to dismiss the assumption of habits on the grounds that it yields "counterfactual cyclical behavior."

36. However, the existing literature on estimating general equiilibrium models using Bayesian methods assumes that all shocks are stationary, even when highly correlated. A novelty of this paper is that we introduce a permanent technology shock. Ireland (2004) estimates a general equilibrium model with permanent technology shocks, using maximum likelihood.

37. A somewhat different estimation strategy is the one followed by Christiano, Eichenbaum, and Evans (2003); Altig et al. (2003); and Boivin and Giannoni (2003), who estimate general equilibrium models by matching a model's implied impulse-response functions to the estimated ones.

38. Details can be found in an appendix available from the authors upon request.

39. Specifically, every household j maximizes the following utility function:

$$E_0 \sum_{t=0}^{\infty} \beta^t \left[G_t \log(C_t^j - bC_{t-1}) - \frac{(N_t^j)^{1+\varphi}}{1+\varphi} \right]$$

subject to a usual budget constraint. The preference shock evolves, expressed in logs, as: $g_t = (1-\rho_g)\bar{G} + \rho_g g_{t-1} + \varepsilon_t^g$

40. See Smets and Wouters (2003a) for a derivation of the price- and wage-setting equations.

41. Following Erceg and Levin (2003), we assume that the Federal Reserve reacts to output growth rather than the output gap. An advantage of following such a rule, as Orphanides and Williams (2002) stress, is that mismeasurement of the level of potential output does not affect the conduct of monetary policy (as opposed to using some measure of detrended output to estimate the output gap).

42. See Fernández-Villaverde and Rubio-Ramírez (2004).

43. If a random draw of the parameters is such that the model does not deliver a unique and stable solution, we assign a zero likelihood value, which implies that the posterior density will be zero as well. See Lubik and Schorfheide (2003b) for an estimated DSGE model allowing for indeterminacy.

44. Rabanal (2003) finds a similar result for an estimated DSGE model that is only slightly different from the one used here.

45. We have also conducted some subsample stability analyses, splitting the sample into pre-Volcker years and the Volcker–Greenspan era. While there were some small differences in estimated parameters across samples, none of the main conclusions of this section were affected.

46. These second moments where obtained using a sample of 10,000 draws from the 500,000 that were previously obtained with the Metropolis-Hastings algorithm.

47. A related analysis has been carried out independently by Smets and Wouters (2003b), albeit in the context of a slightly different DSGE model.

48. The posterior mean and standard deviations are based on the same sample that was used to obtain the second moments.

49. A similar pattern of responses of output and hours to a technology shock can be found in Smets and Wouters (2003b).

50. We use the method of Ingram, Kocherlakota, and Savin (1994) to recover the structural shocks. This method is a particular case of using the Kalman filter to recover the structural shocks. We assume that the economy is at its steady-state value in the first observation, rather than assuming a diffuse prior. By construction, the full set of shocks replicate the features of the model perfectly.

51. In the one case where the VAR is identified correctly, it yields the correct qualitative responses, though with some quantitative bias resulting from the inability to capture the true dynamics with a low-order VAR. This result has been shown in Erceg, Guerrieri, and Gust (2004).

52. See Cooley and Dwyer (1998) and Christiano et al. (2003), among others.

53. See Christiano et al. (2003) for an illustration of the usefulness of that approach.

54. See, for example, BFK (1999), Francis et al. (2003), and Pesavento and Rossi (2004).

55. CKM's discussion of that problem is somewhat obscured by their reference to "the insufficient number of lags in the VAR" as opposed to just stating that hours are overdifferenced. See also Marcet (2004) for a more general discussion of the consequences (or lack thereof) of overdifferencing.

References

Altig, David, Lawrence J. Christiano, Martin Eichenbaum, and Jesper Linde. (2003). Monetary policy and the dynamic effects of technology shocks. Northwestern University. Mimeo.

Basu, Susanto, John Fernald, and Miles Kimball. (1999). Are technology improvements contractionary? Mimeo.

Basu, Susanto, and Miles Kimball. (1997). Cyclical productivity with unobserved input variation. NBER Working Paper No. 5915.

Baxter, Marianne, and Robert G. King. (1999). Measuring business cycles: Approximate band-pass filters for economic time series. *The Review of Economics and Statistics* 81(4):575–593.

Bils, Mark, and Peter J. Klenow. (2002). Some evidence on the importance of sticky prices. NBER Working Paper No. 9069.

Blanchard, Olivier J. (1989). A traditional interpretation of macroeconomic fluctuations. *American Economic Review* 79(5):1146–1164.

Blanchard, Olivier J., and Danny Quah. (1989). The dynamic effects of aggregate demand and supply disturbances. *American Economic Review* 79(4):654–673.

Blanchard, Olivier, Robert Solow, and B. A. Wilson. (1995). Productivity and unemployment. Massachusetts Institute of Technology. Mimeo.

Boivin, Jean, and Marc Giannoni. (2003). Has monetary policy become more effective? NBER Working Paper No. 9459.

Bullard, James, and Kaushik Mitra. (2002). Learning about monetary policy rules. *Journal of Monetary Economics* 49(6):1105–1130.

Burnside, Craig, and Martin Eichenbaum. (1996). Factor hoarding and the propagation of business cycle shocks. *American Economic Review* 86(5):1154–1174.

Burnside, Craig, Martin Eichenbaum, and Sergio Rebelo. (1995). Capital utilization and returns to scale. *NBER Macroeconomics Annual 1995* 10:67–110.

Calvo, Guillermo. (1983). Staggered prices in a utility maximizing framework. *Journal of Monetary Economics* 12:383–398.

Campbell, John Y. (1994). Inspecting the mechanism: An analytical approach to the stochastic growth model. *Journal of Monetary Economics* 33(3):463–506.

Carlsson, Mikael. (2000). Measures of technology and the short-run responses to technology shocks: Is the RBC model consistent with Swedish manufacturing data? Uppsala University. Mimeo.

Chang, Yongsung, and Jay H. Hong. (2003). On the employment effects of technology: Evidence from U.S. manufacturing for 1958–1996. University of Philadelphia. Mimeo.

Christiano, Larry, Martin Eichenbaum, and Charles Evans. (2003). Nominal rigidities and the dynamic effects of a shock to a monetary policy. *Journal of Political Economy*, forthcoming.

Christiano, Lawrence, Martin Eichenbaum, and Robert Vigfusson. (2003). What happens after a technology shock? NBER Working Paper No. 9819. Mimeo.

Collard, Fabrice, and Harris Dellas. (2002). Technology shocks and employment. Université de Toulouse. Mimeo.

Cooley, Thomas F., and Mark Dwyer. (1998). Business cycle analysis without much theory: A look at structural VARs. *Journal of Econometrics* 83(1):57–88.

Cooley, Thomas F., and Edward C. Prescott. (1995). Economic growth and business cycles. In *Frontiers of Business Cycle Research*, T. F. Cooley (ed.). Princeton, NJ: Princeton University Press.

Cummins, Jason, and Gianluca Violante. (2002). Investment-specific technical change in the United States (1947–2000). *Review of Economic Dynamics* 5(2):243–284.

Dotsey, Michael. (2002). Structure from shocks. *Economic Quarterly* 88(4):1–13.

Erceg, Christopher, Luca Guerrieri, and Christopher Gust. (2003). Can long run restrictions identify technology shocks? Federal Reserve Board. Mimeo.

Erceg, Christopher J., Luca Guerrieri, and Christopher Gust. (2004). Can long run restrictions identify technology shocks? Federal Reserve Board. Mimeo.

Erceg, Christopher J., and Andrew Levin. (2003). Imperfect credibility and inflation persistence. *Journal of Monetary Economics* 50(4):915–944.

Fernald, John. (2004). Trend breaks, long run restrictions, and the contractionary effects of a technology shock. Federal Reserve Bank of Chicago. Mimeo.

Fernández-Villaverde, Jesús, and Juan F. Rubio-Ramírez. (2004). Comparing dynamic equilibrium economies to data: A Bayesian approach. *Journal of Econometrics*, forthcoming.

Fisher, Jonas. (2003). Technology shocks matter. Federal Reserve Bank of Chicago. Mimeo.

Francis, Neville. (2001). Sectoral technology shocks revisited. Lehigh University. Mimeo.

Francis, Neville R., Michael T. Owyang, and Athena T. Thedorou. (2003). The use of long run restrictions for the identification of technology shocks. *The Federal Reserve Bank of St. Louis Review*, November–December:53–66.

Francis, Neville, and Valerie Ramey. (2003a). Is the technology-driven real business cycle hypothesis dead? Shocks and aggregate fluctuations revisited. University of California, San Diego. Mimeo.

Francis, Neville, and Valerie Ramey. (2003b). The source of historical economic fluctuations: An analysis using long-run restrictions. University of California San Diego. Mimeo.

Franco, Francesco, and Thomas Philippon. (2004). Industry and aggregate dynamics. MIT. Mimeo.

Galí, Jordi. (1998). Comment on 'What do technology shocks do?' *NBER Macroeconomics Annual 1998* 13:310–316.

Galí, Jordi. (1999). Technology, employment, and the business cycle: Do technology shocks explain aggregate fluctuations? *American Economic Review* 89(1):249–271.

Galí, Jordi. (2003). New perspectives on monetary policy, inflation, and the business cycle. In *Advances in Economics and Econometrics*, vol. III, M. Dewatripont, L. Hansen, and S. Turnovsky (eds.). Cambridge: Cambridge University Press.

Galí, Jordi. (2004). On the role of technology shocks as a source of business cycles: Some new evidence. *Journal of the European Economic Association*, forthcoming.

Galí, Jordi, and Mark Gertler. (1999). Inflation dynamics: A structural econometric analysis. *Journal of Monetary Economics* 44(2):195–222.

Galí, Jordi, J. David López-Salido, and Javier Vallés. (2003). Technology shocks and monetary policy: Assessing the Fed's performance. *Journal of Monetary Economics* 50(4):723–743.

Gordon, Robert J. (2000). *The Measurement of Durable Goods Prices*. Chicago: University of Chicago Press.

Greenwood, Jeremy, Zvi Hercowitz, and Gregory W. Huffman. (1988). Investment, capacity utilization, and the real business cycle. *American Economic Review* 78(3):402–417.

Greenwood, Jeremy, Zvi Hercowitz, and Per Krusell. (1997). The role of investment-specific technological change in the business cycle. *European Economic Review* 44(1):91–116.

Greenwood, Jeremy, Zvi Hercowitz, and Per Krusell. (2000). The role of investment-specific technical change in the business cycle. *European Economic Review* (44):91–115.

Hall, Robert E. (1988). The relation between price and marginal cost in U.S. industry. *Journal of Political Economy* (96):921–947.

Hamilton, James. (1994). *Time Series Analysis*. Princeton, NJ: Princeton University Press.

Hoover, Kevin D., and Stephen J. Perez. (1994). Post hoc ergo procter once more: An evaluation of 'Does monetary policy matter?' in the spirit of James Tobin. *Journal of Monetary Economics* 34(1):47–74.

Ingram, Beth, Narayana Kocherlakota, and N. E. Savin. (1994). Explaining business cycles: A multiple-shock approach. *Journal of Monetary Economics* 34(3, December 1994):415–428.

Ireland, Peter. (2004). Technology shocks in the new Keynesian model. Boston College. Mimeo.

Jones, J. B. (2002). Has fiscal policy helped stabilize the U.S. economy? *Journal of Monetary Economics* 49(4):709–746.

Kiley, Michael T. (1997). Labor productivity in U.S. manufacturing: Does sectoral comovement reflect technology shocks? Federal Reserve Board. Unpublished Manuscript.

King, Robert G., Charles I. Plosser, and Sergio T. Rebelo. (1988a). Production, growth, and business cycles: I. The basic neoclassical model. *Journal of Monetary Economics* 21(2/3):195–232.

King, Robert G., Charles I. Plosser, and Sergio T. Rebelo. (1988b). Production, growth, and business cycles: II. New directions. *Journal of Monetary Economics* 21(2/3):309–343.

King, Robert G., and Sergio T. Rebelo. (1999). Resuscitating real business cycles. In *Handbook of Macroeconomics*, Volume 1B, J. B. Taylor and M. Woodford (eds.), pp. 928–1002. Also published as NBER Working Paper No. 7534.

Kwiatkowski, D., P. C. B. Phillips, P. Schmidt, and Y. Shin. (1992). Testing the null hypothesis of stationarity against the alternative of a unit root. *Journal of Econometrics* 54:159–178.

Lettau, Martin, and Harald Uhlig. (2000). Can habit formation be reconciled with business cycle facts? *Review of Economic Dynamics* 3(1):79–99.

Lubik, T., and F. Schorfheide. (2003a). Testing for indeterminacy: An application to U.S. monetary policy. *American Economic Review* 94(1):190–217.

Lubik, T., and F. Schorfheide. (2003b). Do central banks respond to exchange rates? A structural investigation? Philadelphia: University of Pennsylvania. Unpublished.

Marcet, Albert. (2004). Overdifferencing VARs is OK. University Pompei Fabra. Mimeo.

Marchetti, Domenico J., and Francesco Nucci. (2004). Price stickiness and the contractionary effects of technology shocks. *European Economic Review*, forthcoming.

McGrattan, Ellen. (1994). The macroeconomic effects of distortionary taxation. *Journal of Monetary Economics* 33:573–601.

McGrattan, Ellen. (1999). Predicting the effects of Federal Reserve policy in a sticky-price model. Federal Reserve Bank of Minneapolis. Working Paper No. 598.

McGrattan, Ellen. (2004). Comment. *NBER Macroeconomics Annual 2004* 19:289–308.

Orphanides, Athanasios, and John Williams. (2002). Robust monetary policy rules with unknown natural rates. *Brookings Papers on Economic Activity* 2002:63–118.

Pesavento, Elena, and Barbara Rossi. (2004). Do technology shocks drive hours up or down: A little evidence from an agnostic procedure. Duke University. Unpublished Manuscript.

Prescott, Edward C. (1986a). Response to a skeptic. *Quarterly Review* 10:28–33.

Prescott, Edward C. (1986b). Theory ahead of business cycle measurement. *Quarterly Review* 10:9–22.

Rabanal, Pau. (2003). The cost channel of monetary policy: Further evidence for the United States and the Euro area. IMF Working Paper No. 03/149.

Ramey, Valerie. (2005). Comment. *NBER Macroeconomics Annual 2004* 19:309–314.

Ramey, Valerie, and Matthew D. Shapiro. (1998). Costly capital reallocation and the effects of government spending. *Carnegie–Rochester Conference Series on Public Policy* 48:145–194.

Romer, Christina, and David Romer. (1989). Does monetary policy matter? A test in the spirit of Friedman and Schwartz. *NBER Macroeconomics Annual 1998* 13:63–129.

Rotemberg, Julio J. (2003). Stochastic technical progress, smooth trends, and nearly distinct business cycles. *American Economic Review* 93(5):1543–1559.

Rotemberg, Julio, and Michael Woodford. (1999). Interest rate rules in an estimated sticky price model. In *Monetary Policy Rules*, J. B. Taylor (ed.). Chicago: University of Chicago Press.

Shea, John. (1998). What do technology shocks do? *NBER Macroeconomics Annual* 275–310.

Smets, Frank, and Raf Wouters. (2003a). An estimated stochastic dynamic general equilibrium model of the Euro area. *Journal of the European Economic Association* 1(5):1123–1175.

Smets, Frank, and Raf Wouters. (2003b). Shocks and frictions in U.S. business cycles: A Bayesian DSGE approach. European Central Bank. Unpublished Manuscript.

Solow, Robert. (1957). Technical change and the aggregate production function. *Review of Economics and Statistics* 39:312–320.

Stock, James, and Mark W. Watson. (1999). Business cycle fluctuations in U.S. macroeconomic time series. In *Handbook of Macroeconomics*, Volume 1A, J. B. Taylor and M. Woodford (eds.), pp. 3–64. Also published as NBER Working Paper No. 6528.

Taylor, John B. (1993). Discretion versus policy rules in practice. *Carnegie-Rochester Series on Public Policy* 39:195–214.

Uhlig, Harald. (1999). A toolkit for analyzing nonlinear dynamic stochastic models easily. In *Computational Methods for the Study of Dynamic Economies*, Ramon Marimon and Andrew Scott (eds.). Oxford: Oxford University Press.

Uhlig, Harald. (2004). Do technology shocks lead to a fall in total hours worked? *Journal of the European Economic Association*, forthcoming.

Wen, Yi. (2001). Technology, employment, and the business cycle: Do technology shocks explain aggregate fluctuations? A comment. Cornell University Working Paper No. 01-19.

Comment

Ellen R. McGrattan
Federal Reserve Bank of Minneapolis and University of Minnesota

1. Introduction

An important task of macroeconomists is the development of models that account for specific features of the business cycle. All policymakers would agree that having reliable models to analyze the effects of policy is useful. In taking on the important endeavor of developing reliable models, I applaud Galí and Rabanal (GR). I do, however, dispute some of their key findings.

GR survey research in the structural vector autoregression (SVAR) literature emphasizing the role of technology for the business cycle. (See the many references in Section 2.2 of GR.) The findings of this literature are used to dismiss a line of business-cycle research beginning with Kydland and Prescott's (1982) real business cycle (RBC) model. The claim is that the data clearly show that RBC models are inconsistent in crucial ways with the observed behavior of the U.S. economy in the postwar period. This claim amounts to asserting that no RBC model can produce time series for key macro aggregates—namely, productivity and hours—that have similar patterns to those in U.S. data. The SVAR literature arrives at this claim by estimating empirical impulse responses and noting that the responses are different from the theoretical impulse responses in most RBC models.

In these comments, I argue that the claim of the SVAR literature is incorrect. I do this by estimating a standard RBC model with maximum likelihood for U.S. data. My estimation procedure ensures that the model can account for the patterns of productivity and hours in the data. With this RBC model, I then show that the SVAR procedure is easily misled. I simulate time series for the model (many times), apply the SVAR procedure, and estimate empirical impulse responses. I show that these empirical impulse responses look very similar to those estimated in the literature. Thus, given data simulated from my model, the SVAR procedure would wrongly conclude that the data were *not* simulated from a real business cycle model.

The problem with trying to use the SVAR procedure to make broad claims about a class of models, like the entire class of RBC models, is the following: most RBC models do not satisfy the narrow set of identifying assumptions typically made in the SVAR literature. My estimated RBC model is no exception. Hence, the SVAR procedure is misspecified with respect to most of the models it tries to shed light on.

On this point, I think there is some agreement between GR and myself.[1] The SVAR procedure is not useful for evaluating models or classes of models that do not satisfy the SVAR's precise identifying assumptions. I conclude from this that since we do not know the assumptions a priori, SVARs are not a useful guide to developing new models. Since we do not know the identifying assumptions a priori, the SVAR cannot robustly identify how the economy responds to shocks, like technology or monetary shocks. SVARs are potentially useful but only for classes of models that satisfy all of the identifying assumptions. In every application of which I am aware, the class of models that satisfy the (explicit or implicit) identifying assumptions of the SVAR procedure is an extremely small subset of the class of interesting models.

The false rejection of the RBC model motivates the second part of GR's study, a study of business cycles using a model with sticky prices. Like many other studies in the sticky-price literature, GR do not include investment in their model. I introduce investment into a version of their model and analyze its predictions for business cycles. I find that technology shocks, monetary shocks, and government consumption shocks are of little importance in the sticky-price model. This explains why GR find that preference shocks and shocks to the degree of monopoly power play such a large role for aggregate fluctuations.

2. The Death Knell for RBC Theory

Galí and Rabanal first review the SVAR literature that considers the fit of real business cycle models and the role of technology shocks for business cycles. They ask, How well does the RBC model fit postwar U.S. data? The answer they give is, Not so well. According to evidence from the SVARs, hours fall in response to technology shocks, and the contribution of technology shocks to the business cycle is small. In standard RBC models, the opposite is true. Francis and Ramey (2002), who have contributed to the SVAR literature that GR review, summarize the findings of this literature by saying that "the original technology-driven real business hypothesis does appear to be dead."

2.1 *Applying Blanchard and Quah*

Let me start by summarizing how researchers in the SVAR literature reach the conclusion that RBC theory is not consistent with U.S. data. It is a direct application of Blanchard and Quah (1989). They estimate a vector autoregression (VAR) using data on labor productivity and hours, invert it to get a moving average (MA) representation, and impose certain structural assumptions about the shocks hitting the economy. They then argue that the empirical impulse responses from the structural MA are very different from the theoretical impulse responses of a standard RBC model. They also show that the contribution of technology shocks to output fluctuations is empirically small, a prediction at odds with standard RBC theories.

To be more precise, let X_t be a two-dimensional vector containing the change in the log of labor productivity and the change in the log of hours. The first step is to estimate a vector autoregression by regressing X_t on a certain number of lags. GR choose four. They invert this VAR to get the corresponding Wold moving average:

$$X_t = v_t + B_1 v_{t-1} + B_2 v_{t-2} + \cdots \tag{1}$$

where v_t is the residual from the VAR and $Ev_t v_t' = \Omega$. Mechanically, it is easy to recursively compute the B coefficients having estimates of the VAR coefficients. An estimate of the matrix Ω is easily constructed from the VAR residuals.

One more step is needed to derive the structural MA. The goal is to work with an MA process that has interpretable shocks, namely, a shock they call a "technology" shock and a shock they call a "demand" shock. In particular, the structural MA they use is:

$$X_t = C_0 e_t + C_1 e_{t-1} + C_2 e_{t-2} + \cdots \tag{2}$$

where $Ee_t e_t' = \Sigma$, $e_t = C_0^{-1} v_t$, and $C_j = B_j C_0$ for $j \geq 1$. The first element of e_t is the technology shock, and the second element is the demand shock.

We need identifying restrictions to determine the seven parameters in C_0 and Σ. Seven restrictions typically used in the SVAR literature that GR review are as follows. Three come from equating

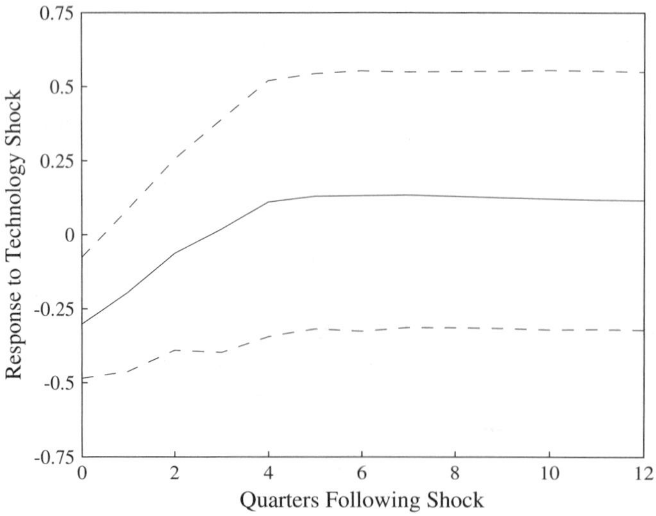

Figure 1
SVAR impulse response of U.S. total hours to technology
Dashed lines mark upper and lower values of the 95% confidence band for bootstrapped standard errors.

variance-covariance matrices ($C_0 \Sigma C_0' = \Omega$). Three come from assuming that the shocks are orthogonal ($\Sigma = I$). The last comes from the assumption that demand shocks have no long-run effect on labor productivity ($\sum_j C_j(1,2) = 0$).

With these restrictions imposed, I can compute the empirical impulse responses. Since I want to compare models to the national accounts, I am actually going to work, not with the nonfarm business sector as GR do, but with gross domestic product (GDP) and total hours.[2] In Figure 1, I show the response of total hours to a one-time, 1% innovation in technology (that is, a 1% increase in the first element of e_0). I also plot the 95% confidence bands computed using the method described by Runkle (1987). Using the aggregate series for productivity and hours is not a problem for GR since I reach the same conclusions as they do. In particular, Figure 1 shows that hours fall on impact in response to a rise in technology. In standard RBC models, hours rise on impact in response.

A second statistic emphasized in the literature is the contribution of technology to the variance of logged output and hours, which is computed after these series are filtered with a bandpass filter. With data from the nonfarm business sector, GR find that only 7% of output fluctuations are due to technology and 5% of hours fluctuations. For my example with GDP and total hours, I find that 14% of output fluctuations are due to technology and 9% of hours fluctuations. Thus, like GR, I find that the SVAR predicts that technology plays a small role in the business cycle.

2.2 *A Standard RBC Model*

I am going to evaluate the SVAR findings using a standard RBC model. In particular, I work with a version of the model I used in McGrattan (1994), with parameters estimated by maximum likelihood for U.S. data. I simulate many time series from that model, and I apply the SVAR procedure to the artificial data. This exercise allows me to compare the SVAR statistics to their theoretical counterparts. I also determine if the SVAR recovers the technology shocks that I feed into the model.

The model economy is a standard growth model with households, firms, and a government. The representative household with N_t members in period t chooses per-capita consumption c, per-capita investment x, and the labor input l to solve the following maximization problem:

$$\max_{\{c_t, x_t, l_t\}} E\sum_{t=0}^{\infty} \beta^t [c_t(1-l_t)^{\psi})^{1-\sigma} - 1]/(1-\sigma)N_t$$

subject to $c_t + (1 + \tau_{xt})x_t = r_t k_t + (1 - \tau_{lt})w_t l_t + T_t$, $N_{t+1}k_{t+1} = [(1-\delta)k_t + x_t]N_t$, and $c_t, x_t \geq 0$ in all states and taking initial capital k_0 and processes for the rental rate r, wage rate w, the tax rates τ_x and τ_l, and transfers T_t as given. I assume that N_t grows at rate γ_n.

The representative firm solves a simple static problem at t:

$$\max_{\{K_t, L_t\}} K_t^{\theta}(Z_t L_t)^{1-\theta} - r_t K_t - w_t L_t \tag{3}$$

where θ is the share of capital in production, capital letters denote economy aggregates, and Z_t is the level of technology that varies stochastically around a constant growth trend. In particular, I assume that $Z_t = (1+\gamma_z)^t z_t$, where γ_z is the trend growth rate and z_t is stochastic. Total factor productivity in this economy is $Z_t^{1-\theta}$.

The government sets rates of taxes and transfers so that it can finance a stochastic sequence of per-capita purchases g_t and satisfy its budget constraint:

$$N_t g_t + N_t T_t = N_t[\tau_{lt} w_t l_t + \tau_{xt} x_t]$$

each period. In equilibrium, the following conditions must hold:

$$N_t(c_t + x_t + g_t) = Y_t = K_t^{\theta}(Z_t L_t)^{1-\theta}$$
$$N_t k_t = K_t \tag{4}$$
$$N_t l_t = L_t.$$

The model has four exogenous shocks, namely, total factor productivity, a tax on labor, a tax on investment, and government spending. The process governing these shocks is:

$$s_{t+1} = P_0 + P s_t + Q\varepsilon_{t+1} \tag{5}$$

where $s_t = [\log z_t, \tau_{lt}, \tau_{xt}, \log g_t - t \log(1 + \gamma_z)]$. I compute maximum likelihood estimates for P_0, P, and Q using data on U.S. output, investment, hours, and government spending for the period 1959:1–2003:4.[3] These estimates are reported in Table 1.

2.3 *The Model Predictions*

Given estimates for the parameters, I compute an equilibrium for the model economy that implies decision rules for c_t, x_t, l_t, and k_{t+1} in terms of the state variables $k_t, z_t, \tau_{lt}, \tau_{xt}$, and g_t (once I have detrended all variables that grow over time).

I can use these decision rules to compute impulse responses and contributions to the output spectrum for each of the four shocks. Because P and Q are not diagonal, a specification soundly rejected by a likelihood ratio test, estimates of the theoretical impulse responses and the contributions to the spectrum depend on how I decompose QQ' (or how I order s, keeping Q lower triangular). For the estimated parameters in Table 1, $d \log l_t / d \log \varepsilon_{z,t}$ is positive for all decompositions, where $\varepsilon_{z,t}$ is the first element of ε_t. In terms of the contributions to the output spectrum, technology shocks are important no matter how I assign covariances. The contribution, averaged across all possible assignments, is over 35%. If I compute the contributions for all examples with z first in s and Q lower triangular, I find that the average contribution of technology to the output spectrum is 70%. Thus, as most RBC models predict, hours rise in response to a technology shock, and technology shocks are important contributors to the business cycle.

Table 1
Parameters of vector AR(1) stochastic process for the model*

$$P = \begin{bmatrix} .769 & .0471 & .432 & -.0419 \\ (.0239) & (.0959) & (.0756) & (.0570) \\ -.0233 & .994 & .0417 & -.00452 \\ (.0601) & (.0133) & (.120) & (.0128) \\ -.101 & .0253 & 1.18 & -.0180 \\ (.0186) & (.0445) & (.00780) & (.0224) \\ -.0306 & .0423 & -.00160 & .997 \\ (.0712) & (.0257) & (.136) & (.0212) \end{bmatrix}$$

$$Q = \begin{bmatrix} .0108 & 0 & 0 & 0 \\ (.00113) & & & \\ -.00257 & .00623 & 0 & 0 \\ (.00120) & (.00135) & & \\ .00371 & .000888 & .00196 & 0 \\ (.00101) & (.00102) & (.00165) & \\ -.00501 & .00505 & .0148 & .00000202 \\ (.00214) & (.00266) & (.00102) & (.0610) \end{bmatrix}$$

$$\text{Mean}(s_t) = [-.122(.0306), .235(.0172), .218(.0201), -1.710(.0384)]$$

*Estimated using maximum likelihood with data on output, labor, investment, and government consumption. Numbers in parentheses are standard errors.

Given the empirical findings of the SVAR, GR and others they survey conclude that RBC models such as the one I just described are simply not consistent with U.S. data.

2.4 *The Death Knell for the SVAR Procedure?*

I now describe an obvious check on the SVAR methodology. I act as the data-generating process and let the SVAR user be the detective. This is a game I play when I teach students at the University of Minnesota. I give the students data for an economy of my own making and they have to tell me what is driving fluctuations in that economy.

With my RBC model, I draw 1000 random sequences of length 180 for the ε vector in equation (5). I use decision functions to compute 1000 sequences for productivity and hours. I then apply the SVAR procedure to each model simulation to get impulse responses. The result is displayed in Figure 2, which shows the mean responses (with a solid line). The dashed lines mark the upper and lower value of the interval containing 95% of the responses. They are obtained by eliminating the top 2.5% and the bottom 2.5% for each impulse response coefficient.

Figure 2 shows that for most of the simulations, and on average, a researcher using the SVAR procedure would infer that hours fall in re-

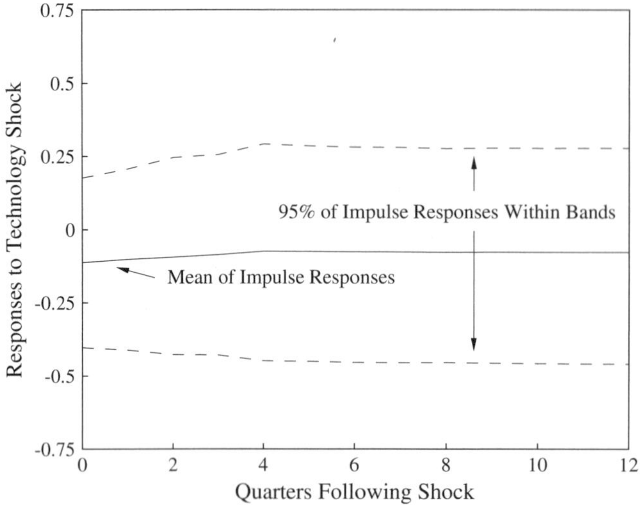

Figure 2
SVAR impulse response of model hours to technology

sponse to a positive technology shock. This is the same inference I would make for the U.S. data using this procedure. (See Figure 1.) If I compute the contribution of technology to the variance of logged output and hours (after applying a bandpass filter), I find that a researcher using the SVAR procedure would infer that the fractions are 26.7% and 6%, respectively. Recall that when I apply the SVAR to U.S. data, the contributions of technology to output and hours fluctuations are 14% and 9%, respectively. Because hours fall in response to a positive technology shock and because the contribution of technology to the business cycle is smaller than RBC theory predicts, an SVAR user would conclude that the data could not have come from an RBC model. But the data did come from an RBC model.

Figure 2 should not be surprising because the parameters of the model are maximum likelihood estimates for the U.S. data. It simply reflects the fact that my RBC model can produce time series for the key macro aggregates that have similar patterns to those in the U.S. data. In fact, I could think of the U.S. data as one draw of time series from the model because I can choose the sequence of four shocks in ε_t to match exactly the observed sequences for output, investment, labor, and government consumption. Unless the U.S. data were unlikely given my probability model, I should get SVAR results similar to those reported in Figure 1. It turns out that they are not unlikely.

In the exercise leading up to Figure 2, I treated tax rates as unobserved. These tax rates can be interpreted as summarizing all distortions to factors of production. However, one could do the same exercise with measures of a key component of these distortions, namely, income taxes on labor and capital. In McGrattan (1994), I use data from the U.S. Internal Revenue Service and the U.S. national accounts to construct estimates for taxes on capital and labor. I estimate the parameters of the model with tax rates observed and show that the model produces time series for key macro aggregates that have similar patterns to those in the U.S. data. A good fit between U.S. data and the model time series implies an empirical impulse response like that in Figure 1 if I apply the SVAR procedure to simulated time series of the model.

What if I compare the technology implied by the SVAR procedure to the log of total factor productivity implied by the model? Technology backed out using the SVAR is the cumulative sum of the first element of e_t in equation (2). The log of technology implied by the model is $\log Z_t$ in equation (4) computed with U.S. data for Y, K, and L. In

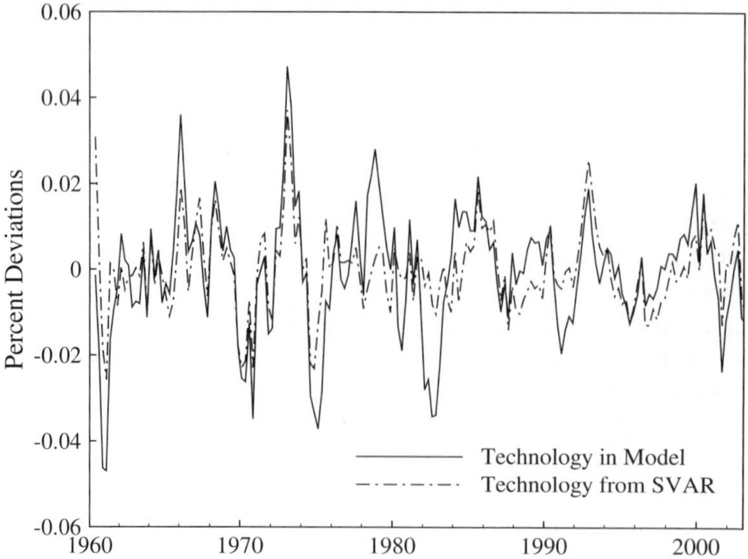

Figure 3
Technology shocks from the model and those predicted by the SVAR

Figure 3, I plot the two series after applying the Hodrick-Prescott filter. The figure shows that the SVAR does not back out the true technology.

In fact, the realization of the SVAR technology has very different properties than its theoretical counterpart. It is hardly correlated with GDP and negatively correlated with total hours. The correlations with GDP and hours are 0.42 and −0.04, respectively. The true technology is highly correlated with GDP and positively correlated with total hours. The correlations with GDP and hours are 0.84 and 0.43, respectively.

2.5 *Why Does the SVAR Get It So Wrong?*

The literature that directly or indirectly critiques the SVAR approach gives us many possible answers to this question.[4] The problem could be mistaken assumptions about the dimension of the shock vector. It could be mistaken assumptions about the orthogonality of the shocks. It could be mistaken assumptions about whether growth trends are deterministic or stochastic. It could be mistaken assumptions about the long-run implications of nontechnology shocks. Maybe data samples are too short. Perhaps four lags in the VAR are not enough. It could be a more subtle problem, like the lack of invertibility of the RBC model's theoretical MA. In fact, for the example above, which is based on a standard RBC model and an SVAR procedure that has been applied many times, the answer is: all of the above.

SVARs are held up as useful tools that reveal "facts" about the data without having to get into the messy details of economic theories. Typically these "facts" are then used to point researchers in the direction of a promising class of models and away from models that are not consistent with them. If the identifying assumptions of the SVAR are relevant for only a tiny subset of models within a class of models, then claims should be made in the context of the tiny subset.

Chari, Kehoe, and McGrattan (2004) extend the analysis I have done here and show that mistaken inferences are large even if my RBC model is restricted to satisfy the key identifying assumptions laid out in Section 2.1. That is, we restrict the model to have only two orthogonal shocks: the technology shock Z_t and the tax rate τ_{lt} (or "demand shock"), with a unit root in Z_t and an autoregressive process for τ_{lt}. We show that auxiliary assumptions that SVAR researchers make are not innocuous. For the technology-driven SVAR analyzed by GR and many others, an important assumption is the number of lags in the VAR. If capital accumulation is a central component of the model, we show that hundreds of lags are needed to detect the true impulse responses. The sample we have, on the other hand, is only 180 periods long. This is an important finding since the model being studied is the growth model, the workhorse of applied macroeconomic research. Perhaps this finding is the death knell for SVAR analysis.

At the risk of adding insult to injury, I want to also note that the RBC model of Section 2.2 encompasses the statistical model generated by the SVAR. That is, if the data come from this RBC model, we can account for the prediction of the SVAR that hours fall on impact when there is a positive technology shock. On the other hand, the SVAR model does not encompass the RBC model since it cannot be used to make predictions about many of the statistics of interest to business-cycle researchers, such as the relative variance of investment to output.

Let me summarize what I have learned from these exercises. We should not view the empirical impulse responses from an SVAR as something we want our theoretical impulse responses to reproduce. SVAR users can and should do the same diagnostic checks as Chari, Kehoe, and McGrattan (2004). The analysis has to be done within the context of a theoretical model or a class of theoretical models. Of course, this brings us full circle: once we construct a theoretical model, there is no reason to use an SVAR.

3. A Triple-Sticky Model Versus U.S. Facts

The second part of Galí and Rabanal's paper considers life after RBC models (which was the original title of the paper). They describe a model that, at least for some parameterizations, is consistent with the VAR evidence laid out in the first part of their paper. This model, which I call the triple-sticky model, has sticky prices, sticky wages, and habit persistence (sticky consumption). They estimate the model and report the contributions of different shocks to aggregate fluctuations. From that, they conclude that demand factors—not technological factors—are key for business cycles.

3.1 A Forgotten Lesson from RBC Theory

Before discussing the triple-sticky business-cycle model, I should review an important lesson from the RBC literature. GR's triple-sticky model includes lots of frictions, but it excludes the key component in modern business-cycle models: investment.

One important lesson from previous business-cycle research is that the main impact of technology on the cycle is through investment, not through hours. By leaving out investment, GR are minimizing the role that technology would have. For this reason, I bring investment back in.

3.2 A Triple-Sticky Model with Investment

The model I work with has many of the same elements as those in Chari, Kehoe, and McGrattan (2000, 2002) and McGrattan (1999). To compare my results to those of GR, I also allow for habit persistence in consumer preferences and preference shocks.

3.3 Effects of Monetary Shocks

One of the main results in GR is that demand shocks are the main force for the business cycle. Given the choice of model used by GR, it is natural to ask if money is an important demand shock. Nominal rigidities let money shocks have real effects, and habit persistence extends the effects.

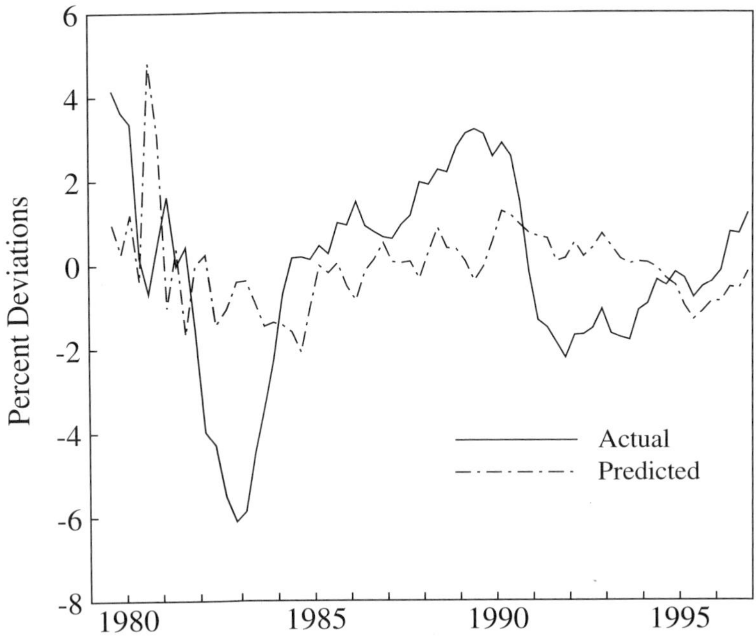

Figure 4
GDP relative to trend

To investigate the role of money, I compare time series from data (after detrending or demeaning) with time series from my triple-sticky model. I set parameters to be consistent with GR's model wherever possible and otherwise use standard estimates from the business-cycle literature. In Figures 4 and 5, I show simulations of the model hit only by shocks to the Taylor rule in equation (13) in the appendix (see Section 5). For the sequence of shocks, I use innovations from Clarida, Galí, and Gertler's (2000) estimated Taylor rule. The figures confirm the finding of GR that monetary shocks in these models play only a small role. Even if I do not add habit persistence, the model predictions are far too smooth relative to the fluctuations in the data.

If I include plausible shocks to technology and government spending, the match between actual and predicted improves slightly.[5] But inflation in the model is still much smoother than in the data. Thus, any missing demand shocks must fill in the gap between actual and predicted inflation, which was particularly large in the 1970s and early 1980s.

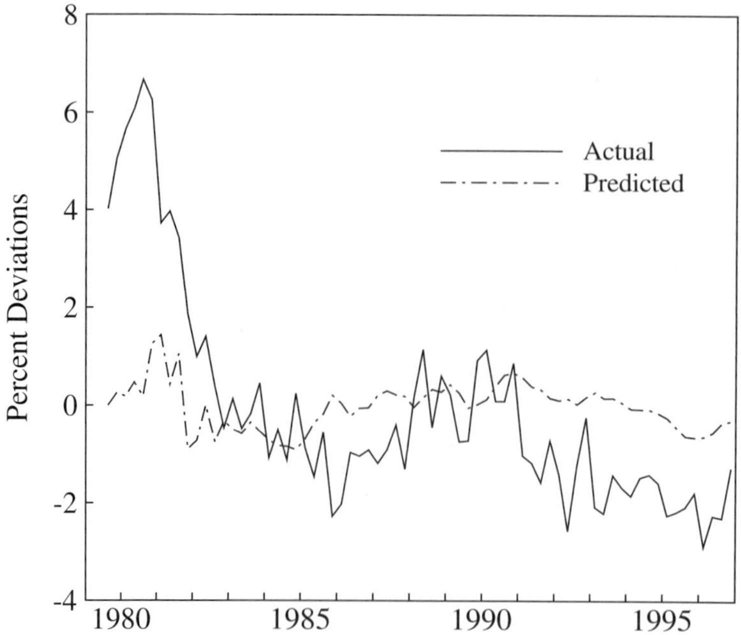

Figure 5
Inflation relative to its mean

3.4 What Are the Demand Shocks?

If it is not money, government spending, or technology, what drives business-cycle fluctuations? The answers for GR are preference shocks and shocks to the degree of monopoly power. For GR, these unobserved demand shocks account for 80% of the variance in hours, 72% of the variance in output, and 65% of the variance in inflation. As I find with my triple-sticky model, observed factors account for a very small fraction of the business cycle.

This is reminiscent of the finding of Rotemberg and Woodford (1997). To generate U.S.-like business cycles, Rotemberg and Woodford need large and variable shocks to preferences and to a variable called aggregate demand appearing in the resource constraint. In the appendix to their paper, they report that standard deviations of the shocks to preferences are 13.7%. This is large relative to the standard deviation of logged output, which is only 2.1%.

The fluctuations of aggregate demand shocks, which are shocks to the resource constraint and enter additively with consumption, are even larger. The standard deviation is 29.5%, 14 times that of logged output. Plotting the aggregate demand shocks yields a picture that looks a lot like inflation. This is not surprising since there is a large gap between actual and predicted inflation without the unobserved shocks.

In summary, given my calculations and those of Rotemberg and Woodford (1997), I was not surprised that GR find they need a large role for unobserved preference shocks and shocks to the degree of monopoly power. I am not convinced that this is progress. It seems to me that we are simply replacing an old black box ("technology shocks") with a new black box ("demand shocks").

4. Conclusion

GR have written a thought-provoking paper claiming that RBC models are not consistent with U.S. data. I have shown that the SVAR methodology they use fails a simple diagnostic test. When given data from an RBC model, the SVAR procedure tells us that the data could not have come from an RBC model.

I have analyzed a version of GR's triple-sticky model, extending it to include investment. Like GR, I find that the model does a poor job generating U.S.-like business cycles with only technology and monetary shocks. The fit of GR's model to U.S. data, therefore, requires the inclusion of large unobserved shocks to preferences and to the degree of monopoly power.

Finally, I should note that the RBC literature has moved far beyond Kydland and Prescott (1982). Current research is modeling sources of variation in total factor productivity in large part as arising from variations in government policies, not from variations in the stock of blueprints.[6] This work came about partly in response to claims that total factor productivity in Kydland and Prescott (1982) was an exogenous black box. I encourage GR to consider these recent studies before shifting the black box from technology to demand.

5. Appendix

This appendix provides details of the triple-sticky model I simulate. For details on computation, see McGrattan (2004).

In each period t, the model economy experiences one of finitely many events s_t. I denote by $s^t = (s_0, \ldots, s_t)$ the history of events up through and including period t. The probability, as of period zero, of any particular history s^t is $\pi(s^t)$. The initial realization s_0 is given.

There are producers of final goods and intermediate goods. Final goods producers behave competitively and solve a static profit-maximization problem. In each period, producers choose inputs $y(i)$ for $i \in [0,1]$ and output y to maximize profits:

$$\max Py - \int_0^1 P(i)y(i)\,di \qquad \text{subject to } y = \left(\int_0^1 y(i)^\theta\,di\right)^{1/\theta} \tag{6}$$

where y is the final good, P is the price of the final good, $y(i)$ are intermediate goods, and $P(i)$ are the prices of the intermediate goods. The demand for intermediate goods, which I use later, is given by $y(i) = [P/P(i)]^{1/(1-\theta)}y$.

Consider next the problem faced by intermediate goods producers. Intermediate goods producers are monopolistically competitive. They set prices for their goods, but they must hold them fixed for N periods. I assume that price setting is done in a staggered fashion so that $1/N$ of the firms are setting in a particular period. I compute a symmetric equilibrium, so I assume that all firms $i \in [0, 1/N]$ behave the same way, all firms $i \in [1/N, 2/N]$ behave the same way, and so on.

More specifically, the problem solved by the intermediate goods producers setting prices is to choose sequences of prices $P(i)$, capital stocks $k(i)$, investments $x(i)$, and labor inputs $l(i,j)$, $j = 1, \ldots, \mathcal{N}$ to maximize:

$$\sum_{\tau=0}^{\infty}\sum_{s^\tau}\tilde{Q}(s^\tau)\left[P(i,s^\tau)y(i,s^\tau) - \int W(j,s^{\tau-1})l(i,j,s^\tau)\,dj - P(s^\tau)x(i,s^\tau)\right] \tag{7}$$

subject to the input demand, the production technology:

$$y(i,s^t) = k(i,s^{t-1})^\alpha (A(s^t)L^d(i,s^t))^{1-\alpha} \tag{8}$$

the constraint on labor:

$$L^d(i,s^t) \le \left[\int l(i,j,s^t)^v\,dj\right]^{1/v} \tag{9}$$

the law of motion for capital used in producing good i:

$$k(i,s^t) = (1-\delta)k(i,s^{t-1}) + x(i,s^t) - \phi\left(\frac{x(i,s^t)}{k(i,s^{t-1})}\right)k(i,s^{t-1}) \tag{10}$$

and the following constraints on prices:

$$P(i,s^{t-1}) = P(i,s^t) = \cdots P(i,s^{t+N-1})$$
$$P(i,s^{t+N}) = P(i,s^{t+N+1}) = \cdots P(i,s^{t+2N-1}) \tag{11}$$

and so on, where $\tilde{Q}(s^\tau)$ is the τth period Arrow-Debreu price (that is, a product of the one-period $Q(s^t|s^{t-1})$'s).

Consider next the problem faced by consumers of final goods who are wage setters. One can think of the economy organized into a continuum of unions indexed by j. Each union j consists of all the consumers in the economy with labor of type j. This union realizes that it faces a downward-sloping demand curve for its type of labor. It sets nominal wages for $\mathcal{N}$ periods at $t, t+\mathcal{N}, t+2\mathcal{N}$, and so on. Thus, it faces constraints:

$$W(j,s^{t-1}) = W(j,s^t) = \cdots = W(j,s^{t+\mathcal{N}-1})$$
$$W(j,s^{t+\mathcal{N}}) = W(j,s^{t+\mathcal{N}+1}) = \cdots = W(j,s^{t+2\mathcal{N}-1})$$

and so on, in addition to the ones I describe below.

The problem solved by a consumer of type j is to maximize utility:

$$\max \sum_{t=0}^{\infty} \sum_{s^t} \beta^t \pi(s^t) U(c(j,s^t), c(j,s^{t-1}), L^s(j,s^t), M^d(j,s^t)/P(s^t); \varphi_t)$$

which allows for habit persistence and preference shocks (φ), subject to the sequence of budget constraints, the definition of labor supply, and the labor demands of the firms:

$$P(s^t)c(j,s^t) + M^d(j,s^t) + \sum_{s_{t+1}} Q(s^{t+1}|s^t)B(j,s^{t+1})$$
$$\leq W(j,s^{t-1})L^s(j,s^t) + M^d(j,s^{t-1}) + B(j,s^t) + \Pi(s^t) + T(s^t) \tag{12}$$

$$L^s(j,s^t) = \int l(i,j,s^t)\,di$$

$$l(i,j,s^t) = \left(\frac{\overline{W}(s^t)}{W(j,s^{t-1})}\right)^{1/(1-v)} L^d(i,s^t)$$

for all i.

There are also borrowing constraints $B(s^{t+1}) \geq -P(s^t)\bar{b}$. M and B are consumers' holdings of money and contingent claims, Q is the price of the claims, $W(j,s^{t-1})$ is the nominal wage chosen by one cohort of consumers, Π are profits, and T are government transfers. The consumer agrees to supply whatever is demanded at that wage chosen.

The government in this world behaves so that the nominal interest rate set by the Federal Reserve is given by

$$\begin{aligned} r(s^t) = a'[&r(s^{t-1}), r(s^{t-2}), r(s^{t-3}), E_t \log(P(s^{t+1})/P(s^t)), \\ &\log(P(s^t)/P(s^{t-1})), \log(P(s^{t-1})/P(s^{t-2})), \log(P(s^{t-2})/P(s^{t-3})), \\ &\log y(s^t), \log y(s^{t-1}), \log y(s^{t-2})] + \text{constant} + \varepsilon_{r,t}. \end{aligned} \tag{13}$$

The government also spends $g(s^t)$, and thus, the economywide resource constraint is:

$$y(s^t) = \int_0^1 c(j, s^t)\, dj + \int_0^1 x(i, s^t)\, di + g(s^t). \tag{14}$$

For the simulations in Figures 4 and 5, I set $N = 4$, $\mathcal{N} = 2$, $U(c, c_{-1}, l, m) = \log(c - .42c_{-1}) - l^{1.8}/1.8 + .0076m^{-1.56}/(-1.56)$, $\theta = .9$, $v = .87$, $\alpha = 1/3$, $\beta = .97^{1/4}$, $Eg(s^t) = .6$, $\delta = 1 - .92^{1/4}$, and $\phi(x/k) = 10(x/k - \delta)^2$. The Taylor rule in equation (13) is that estimated by Clarida, Galí, and Gertler (2000).

Notes

This discussion was prepared for the 2004 *NBER Macroeconomics Annual*. I received very helpful comments from my colleagues at the Federal Reserve Bank of Minneapolis. Data, codes, and notes used in this project are available at my Web site (minneapolisfed.org/research). The views expressed herein are those of the author and not necessarily those of the Federal Reserve Bank of Minneapolis or the Federal Reserve System.

1. See Section 7, where Galí and Rabanal note that "a *misidentified* and/or *misspecified* SVAR often leads to incorrect inference.... In those cases, the finding of incorrect inference is neither surprising nor novel since it restates points that have already been made in the literature."

2. See McGrattan (2004) for data sources.

3. I fixed parameters of utility and technology as follows: $\psi = 2.24$, $\sigma = 1$, $\beta = .9722$, $\theta = .35$, $\delta = .0464$, $\gamma_n = 1.5\%$, and $\gamma_z = 1.6\%$. These values are standard in the literature. I also restrict measurement errors in observed data to be very small. See McGrattan (2004) for further details.

4. See, for example, Sims (1971, 1972), Hansen and Sargent (1991), Lippi and Reichlin (1993), Faust and Leeper (1997), Cooley and Dwyer (1998), Erceg et al. (2004), and Uhlig (2004).

5. This is also demonstrated in my earlier work: McGrattan (1999).

6. See, for example, Parente and Prescott (2000), Lagos (2003), and Schmitz (2004).

References

Blanchard, Olivier J., and Danny Quah. (1989). The dynamic effects of aggregate demand and supply disturbances. *American Economic Review* 79:655–673.

Chari, V. V., Patrick J. Kehoe, and Ellen R. McGrattan. (2000). Sticky price models of the business cycle: Can the contract multiplier solve the persistence problem? *Econometrica* 68:1151–1179.

Chari, V. V., Patrick J. Kehoe, and Ellen R. McGrattan. (2002). Can sticky price models generate volatile and persistent real exchange rates? *Review of Economic Studies* 69:533–563.

Chari, V. V., Patrick J. Kehoe, and Ellen R. McGrattan. (2004). Are structural VARs useful guides for developing business cycle theories? Federal Reserve Bank of Minneapolis. Working Paper No. 631.

Clarida, Richard, Jordi Galí, and Mark Gertler. (2000). Monetary policy rules and macroeconomic stability: Evidence and some theory. *Quarterly Journal of Economics* 115:147–180.

Cooley, Thomas F., and Mark Dwyer. (1998). Business cycle analysis without much theory: A look at structural VARs. *Journal of Econometrics* 83:57–88.

Erceg, Christopher, Luca Guerrieri, and Christopher Gust. (2004). Can long-run restrictions identify technology shocks? Board of Governors of the Federal Reserve System. International Finance Discussion Paper No. 792.

Faust, Jon, and Eric Leeper. (1997). When do long-run identifying restrictions give reliable results? *Journal of Business and Economic Statistics* 15:345–353.

Francis, Neville, and Valerie A. Ramey. (2002). Is the technology-driven real business cycle hypothesis dead? NBER Working Paper No. 8726.

Hansen, Lars Peter, and Thomas J. Sargent. (1991). Two difficulties in interpreting vector autoregressions. In *Rational Expectations Econometrics, Underground Classics in Economics*. Oxford: Westview Press, pp. 77–119.

Kydland, Finn E., and Edward C. Prescott. (1982). Time to build and aggregate fluctuations. *Econometrica* 50:1345–1370.

Lagos, Ricardo. (2003). A model of TFP. Federal Reserve Bank of Minneapolis. Mimeo.

Lippi, Marco, and Lucrezia Reichlin. (1993). The dynamic effects of aggregate demand and supply disturbances: Comment. *American Economic Review* 83:644–652.

McGrattan, Ellen R. (1994). The macroeconomic effects of distortionary taxation. *Journal of Monetary Economics* 33:573–601.

McGrattan, Ellen R. (1999). Predicting the effects of Federal Reserve policy in a sticky price model: An analytical approach. Federal Reserve Bank of Minneapolis. Working Paper No. 598.

McGrattan, Ellen R. (2004). Technical appendix: Comment on Galí and Rabanal. Federal Reserve Bank of Minneapolis. Mimeo.

Parente, Stephen L., and Edward C. Prescott. (2000). *Barriers to Riches*. Cambridge, MA: MIT Press.

Rotemberg, Julio J., and Michael Woodford. (1997). An optimization-based econometric framework for the evaluation of monetary policy. *NBER Macroeconomics Annual*. Cambridge, MA: MIT Press, pp. 297–346.

Runkle, David E. (1987). Vector autoregressions and reality. *Journal of Business and Economic Statistics* 5:437–442.

Schmitz, James A., Jr. (2004). What determines labor productivity? Lessons from the dramatic recovery of the U.S. and Canadian iron-ore industries since their early 1980s crisis. Federal Reserve Bank of Minneapolis. Staff Report No. 286.

Sims, Christopher. (1971). Distributed lag estimation when the parameter space is explicitly infinite-dimensional. *Annals of Mathematical Statistics* 42:1622–1636.

Sims, Christopher. (1972). The role of approximate prior restrictions in distributed lag estimation. *Journal of the American Statistical Association* 67:169–175.

Uhlig, Harald. (2004). What are the effects of monetary policy on output? Results from an agnostic identification procedure. Humbolt University. Mimeo.

Comment

Valerie Ramey
University of California-San Diego and NBER

1. Introduction

Jordi Galí and Pau Rabanal's paper presents a comprehensive review and synthesis of a rapidly growing literature on the role of technology shocks in business-cycle fluctuations. The paper is a must read for anyone who wishes to understand this literature. In addition to reviewing and consolidating the evidence, Galí and Rabanal specify and estimate the parameters of a model with both real and nominal rigidities to determine which features of the model are important for matching key aspects of the data.

The issues discussed in this paper are central to macroeconomics. Four separate questions are raised by this paper:

- Does a positive technology shock lead hours to rise in the data?
- Do technology shocks account for an important part of the variance of output and hours at business-cycle frequencies?
- What does the evidence on technology shocks imply about the relevance of real versus nominal rigidities?
- What are the main sources of economic fluctuations?

Much of the paper can be characterized as reviewing the results from the literature with respect to these questions, and then adding some new results. Thus, I will organize my discussion around these four questions.

2. Does a Positive Technology Shock Lead Hours to Rise in the Data?

Galí and Rabanal give a thorough review of the literature on this point. The main source of controversy concerns how labor input is specified in the empirical model. It should be noted that the identification restriction does not *require* labor to have a unit root, but it appears that results can be sensitive to the way in which labor input is included.

Galí and Rabanal perform a great service by combining in one place many possible specifications for labor input. The results presented in their Tables 1 and 2 show that in 11 of 12 possible specifications, a positive technology shock leads labor input to decline. It is only when hours per capita (defined as nonfarm hours divided by the population age 16 and older) are assumed to be stationary that labor input is predicted to increase.

Is this measure of hours per capita stationary? As Figure 6 of the paper shows, this hours per-capita series displays some important low-frequency movements. How important are these low-frequency movements? Very important. If we ignore the low-frequency movements in hours and we continue to assume that labor productivity and output have a unit root, we must then revamp the stylized facts of business cycles. While the correlation of hours growth with output growth is 0.7, the correlation of the level of hours with output growth is −0.017, contrary to the notion of positive comovement of hours and output. Ignoring the low-frequency movements also means that we should revise the business-cycle peak and trough dates. For example, relative to the mean of the entire series, 2002 was more of a boom year in employment than either the 1973 peak or the 1980 peak.

As Galí and Rabanal's review of the literature indicates, there are numerous other reasons why one should not assume that this measure of hours per capita is stationary. First, even Christiano, Eichenbaum and Vigfusson (2003) find that standard Augmented Dickey-Fuller, Hansen, and Kwiatowski, Phillips, Schmidt, and Shin tests support a unit root in the series that extends back to 1947. Second, Francis and Ramey (2003) show that nonstationary hours is consistent with standard Real Business Cycle theory. Third, Francis and Ramey (2003) suggest that the specification with hours in levels is underidentified. While the specification with hours in differences produces a technology shock that is not Granger-caused by variables such as oil shocks and the federal funds rate, the specification with stationary hours produces a technology shock that is Granger-caused by these variables. Moreover, the specification with hours in levels implies that the *nontechnology* shock has a highly persistent effect on labor productivity, a result that is contrary to the key identifying assumption.

Fernald (2004) explains the source of the problem with the specification with hours in levels. He shows two statistically significant breaks in the mean growth of labor productivity that coincide with some of the key low-frequency movements of hours per capita. While the first difference specification is robust to these breaks, the stationary hours specification is not. Including these breaks in the hours in levels specifications produces a negative response of hours to technology shocks, consistent with the other specifications.

In summary, Galí and Rabanal are correct in their contention that the weight of evidence supports the result that positive technology shocks lead to a decline in hours.

3. Do Technology Shocks Account for an Important Part of the Variance of Output and Hours at Business-Cycle Frequencies?

Even those who cling to specifications with stationary hours find that neutral technology shocks are not an important source of fluctuations. Recent work, however, suggests that we should be looking at another type of technology shock: investment-specific technological change shocks, abbreviated as I-shocks. Using a calibrated dynamic general equilibrium (DGE) model, Greenwood, Hercowitz, and Krusell (2000) find that I-shocks can account for 30% of the variance of output. Using longrun restrictions, Fisher (2003) finds that I-shocks account for more than 50% of the variance of output in the data.

These results on the importance of I-shocks are not without controversy, however. Galí and Rabanal analyze the sensitivity of Fisher's results to his assumption of stationary hours per capita. When hours are in first differences, I-shocks still have a positive effect on hours. However, the conclusions regarding variance change. When hours are in first-differences, I-shocks contribute only 20% of the variance of output and hours.

The evidence compiled so far suggests that these types of shocks are more promising candidates than neutral technology shocks. How important they are remains to be seen.

4. What Does the Evidence on Technology Shocks Imply About the Relevance of Real Versus Nominal Rigidities?

My reading of the evidence with respect to this question is "not much," at least at the aggregate level. As shown by Francis and Ramey (2003),

Rotemberg (2003), and Lindé (2003), RBC models with real rigidities, such as slow technology diffusion or adjustment costs on investment, can produce a negative effect of technology on hours. Similarly, work by King and Wolman (1996) and Basu (1998) as well as this paper has shown that certain parameterizations of sticky price models can reproduce the results as well. All models, with real or nominal rigidities, produce a decline in hours through the same intertemporal substitution mechanism: real wages do not rise much initially, so individuals expect future wages to be higher and hence they work less today.

Galí and Rabanal's estimated model supports the notion that it is difficult to distinguish the importance of real versus nominal rigidities based on aggregate data. They present and estimate a model with habit formation in consumption, sticky wage and price setting, and a Taylor rule. For simplicity, they assume constant returns to labor and no capital. In a very informative exercise, they shut down each of the rigidities one by one and examine the ability of the model to reproduce the business-cycle correlations. Either the real rigidity alone or the nominal rigidities alone can reproduce the patterns in the data.

5. What Are the Main Sources of Economic Fluctuations?

The estimates of Galí and Rabanal's model implies a central role for preference shocks. They find that preference shocks explain 57% of output growth and 70% of hours growth. On the other hand, technology shocks explain 22% of output growth and 0.8% of hours. Monetary shocks account for only 5% of output growth and 0.4% of hours.

To what extent should we believe this variance decomposition? At this point, I am led to the following conclusion.

6. Conclusion: It's Déjà Vu All Over Again

After reading Galí and Rabanal's comprehensive review of the literature and the new results they present, I am struck by the similarity of the current debate to one that began almost 20 years ago. The papers in the earlier debate produced widely varying results about the importance of technology shocks. This lack of unanimity led some observers to comment on the uncertainty concerning the source of shocks.

Consider the following series of quotes from that debate that are now echoed in the present debate:

• Prescott, 1986:

[T]echnology shocks account for more than half the fluctuations in the postwar period, with a best point estimate near 75%.

• Shapiro and Watson, 1988:

Technological change accounts for roughly one-third of output variation.

[P]ermanent shocks in labor (supply) account for at least 40 percent of output variation at all horizons. . . .

Hours now fall sharply in response to shock to technology. . . .

• Blanchard and Quah, 1989:

Demand disturbances make a substantial contribution to output fluctuations at short and medium-term horizons; however, the data do not allow us to quantify this contribution with great precision.

"Favorable" supply disturbances may initially increase unemployment.

• Eichenbaum, 1991:

What the data are actually telling us is that, while technology shocks almost certainly play some role in generating the business cycle, there is simply an enormous amount of uncertainty about just what percent of aggregate fluctuations they actually do account for. The answer could be 70% . . . , but the data contain almost no evidence against either the view that the answer is really 5% or that the answer is really 200%.

• Cochrane, 1994:

I conclude that none of these popular candidates accounts for the bulk of economic fluctuations.

If this view is correct, we will forever remain ignorant of the fundamental causes of economic fluctuations.

• Hall, 1997:

The prime driving force in fluctuations turns out to be shifts in the marginal rate of substitution between goods and work.

The two key sets of questions in the study of business cycles are: (1) What are the impulses? and (2) What are the propagation mechanisms? The last 10 years of research has focussed more on the second question. Current-generation DGE models now capture key aspects of the data such as the effect of monetary shocks and the hump-shaped responses of output to shocks. Thus, we now have a better mouse trap. On the other hand, we are lacking in consensus about which shocks are important, just as we were 20 years ago. Thus, it is clear that we need continued research on the nature of the impulses, in the hope that we can find some plausible mice to run through our mouse traps!

References

Basu, Susanto. (1998). Technology and business cycles: How well do standard models explain the facts? In *Beyond Shocks: What Causes Business Cycles?* Jeffrey Fuhrer and Scott Schuh (eds.). Federal Reserve Bank of Boston. Conference Series No. 42.

Blanchard, Olivier J., and Danny Quah. (1989). The dynamic effects of aggregate demand and supply disturbances. *American Economic Review* 79:655–673.

Christiano, Lawrence, Martin Eichenbaum, and Robert Vigfusson. (2003). What happens after a technology shock? NBER working paper 9819.

Cochrane, John H. (1994). Shocks. *Carnegie-Rochester Conference Series on Public Policy* 41:295–364.

Eichenbaum, Martin. (1991). Real business cycle theory: Wisdom or whimsy? *Journal of Economic Dynamics and Control* 15:607–626.

Fernald, John. (2004). Trend breaks, long-run restrictions, and the contractionary effects of technology shocks. Federal Reserve Bank of Chicago. Manuscript.

Fisher, Jonas. (2003). Technology shocks matter. Federal Reserve Bank of Chicago. Manuscript.

Francis, Neville, and Valerie A. Ramey. (2003). Is the technology-driven real business cycle hypothesis dead? Shocks and aggregate fluctuations revisited. *Journal of Monetary Economics*, forthcoming.

Greenwood, Jeremy, Zvi Hercowitz, and Per Krusell. (2000). The role of investment-specific technological change in the business cycle. *European Economic Review* 44(1):91–115.

Hall, Robert E. (1997). Macroeconomic fluctuations and the allocation of time. *Journal of Labor Economics* 15:S223–S250.

King, Robert G., and Alexander Wolman. (1996). Inflation targeting in a St. Louis Model of the 21st century. *Federal Reserve Bank of St. Louis Review* 78:83–107.

Lindé, Jesper. (2003). The effects of permanent technology shocks on labor productivity and hours in the RBC model. Sveriges Riksbank Stockholm, Sweden. Unpublished Manuscript.

Prescott, Edward C. (1986). Theory ahead of business cycle measurement. *Quarterly Review* 10:9–22.

Rotemberg, Julio J. (2003). Stochastic technical progress, smooth trends, and nearly distinct business cycles. *American Economic Review* 93:1543–1559.

Shapiro, Matthew D., and Mark Watson. (1988). Sources of business cycle fluctuations. *NBER Macroeconomics Annual 1988*. Vol. 3, pp. 111–148.

Discussion

Some of the discussants were concerned about the details of McGrattan's model in the discussion and wondered about the possible source of differences with the authors' framework. Galí interpreted McGrattan's results as implying that the identifying restrictions of their vector autoregression (VAR) were incorrect, and then he wondered about the source of the unit root on hours per worker if it was not technology shocks. Harald Uhlig stated that if technology shocks were the only source of permanent movements in labor productivity, then the identification strategy of Galí and Rabanal had to be right. On the other hand, if there were other permanent shocks that also influenced labor productivity, then the identification was wrong. According to Uhlig, McGrattan's model had to have other permanent shocks other than productivity and suggested that maybe one could be the investment wedge shock. Matthew Shapiro commented that there were a variety of variables that were not mean-reverting fast enough to fit McGrattan's growth model well. According to Shapiro, the natural rate of unemployment, the real interest rate, and hours per worker were all variables with low-frequency movements that could not be explained by technology or by demand shocks and might be driven by preference shocks or tax wedges.

Galí mentioned a recent paper by Christopher Erceg, Luca Guerrieri, and Christopher Gust in which they did the exercise McGrattan proposed, but they used a real business cycle model and a new Keynesian–type model, where the model and the driving forces were specified so that the identifying restrictions were correct. They used the model to determine to what extent the estimation procedure of Galí and Rabanal captured well the predictions of the two models. Their conclusions, he said, were that indeed it captured it well. Éva Nagypál commented that according to her, the conclusions of the paper by Erceg et al. were that when one was using a VAR with 45 years of quarterly data and one was trying to identify productivity shocks using long-run restrictions, then the Montecarlo simulation showed that one was going to have a hard time making definite projections on the sign on the response of hours and that to do so, one would need data for 300 years.

Galí responded to McGrattan's comment that economists who once claimed technology shocks as important were not doing so any more and instead were looking at other issues, such as the sources of changes in total factor productivity. Galí said that although these were very interesting exercises, he did not see their usefulness when trying to explain business-cycle fluctuations. He also addressed her point that their environment ignored investment and said that the reason behind it was to simplify the model. He added that extended versions of their framework, such as in recent papers by Pau Rabanal or Frank Smets and Raf Wouters, found similar results on the role of technology shocks as a source of fluctuations.

On McGrattan's remark that money did not seem to be important in their model, he commented that he did not believe that many people claimed that monetary policy shocks were an important source of economic fluctuation. However, this did not mean, he added, that monetary policy was not important, but that central banks did not act in erratic ways. Frederic Mishkin seconded Galí's view and said that what was important in terms of successful monetary policy was its systematic part and that reasonable models implied that these shocks were an important source of fluctuations.

Galí agreed with Valerie Ramey about the idea of not taking a dogmatic stand concerning the behavior of hours. According to him, the data seemed to show hours and hours per worker as nonstationary and there were many factors, such as demographic factors used in recent work by Robert Shimer, that could account for this nonstationarity. Harald Uhlig was concerned about the use of first differences of hours in the VAR. He noted that the paper by Lawrence Christiano, Martin Eichenbaum, and Robert Vigfusson showed that one could explain the difference results in terms of the level specification but not the other way around, and hence it was more difficult to explain their results away than just saying that hours worked were nonstationary.

Uhlig also questioned the authors about the sign of the response of measured productivity and if it was procyclical as in the data. Galí replied that their model could not account for procyclical productivity in response to demand shocks or other shocks since by construction they had a simple technology that was constant returns to labor. He added that it would be easy to extend the framework by allowing for unobserved changes in effort, as he did in his *American Economic Review* paper.

Some of the discussants were concerned with the large variety of models and shocks used to explain similar events and commented on the need to set some common ground to compare results. David Backus asked if there were some common shocks about which all economists could agree and that could be used as a common starting point. Lucrezia Reichlin sugested the use of only two shocks, one of which would be a large nonneutral shock on output that one should not necessarily interpret as a technology shock due to the difficulties of forecasting output on long horizons. Susanto Basu suggested the use of the same type of short-run model regardless of the source of shock and to avoid adding frictions depending on whether one was studying technological, monetary, or fiscal shocks, as was done in the paper by David Altig, Lawrence Christiano, Martin Eichenbaum, and Jesper Lindé.

Robert Gordon commented on Figure 1 of the paper and noted the different relationship between hours worked and output in the last two jobless recoveries, 1991–1992 and 2001–2003. He thought that there was a genuine change in behavior and that one could not explain what was happening in the last two years using the experience of the previous twenty or thirty years.

Jesús Fernández-Villaverde stated that some of the models in the literature had been unfair to the neoclasical growth model and with its predictions. He noted that most of the exercises were conducted after detrending output, but the neoclassical model was able to explain a recession at the beginning of the century and a greater recession in the 1930s as a consequence of a change in the growth of technology. He also thought that one should remember the distinction between temporary changes and changes in the trend when trying to identify technology shocks. John Fernald responded to Villaverde and said that hours worked fall if one conditions on the regime shift, so he did not think that it was a growth trend change that drove any of the results in the paper by Galí and Rabanal. Galí added to Fernald's point that although one could modify the technology process to account for the sort of evidence emphasized in the paper, that would not help the model account for business cycles since those were characterized by a positive correlation between output and hours.

Exotic Preferences for Macroeconomists

David K. Backus, Bryan R. Routledge, and Stanley E. Zin
New York University and NBER; Carnegie Mellon University; and Carnegie Mellon University and NBER

1. Introduction

Applied economists (including ourselves) are generally content to study theoretical agents whose preferences are additive over time and across states of nature. One version goes like this: Time is discrete, with dates $t = 0, 1, 2, \ldots$. At each $t > 0$, an event z_t is drawn from a finite set $\mathscr{Z}$, following an initial event z_0. The t-period history of events is denoted by $z^t = (z_0, z_1, \ldots, z_t)$ and the set of possible t-histories by $\mathscr{Z}^t$. The evolution of events and histories is conveniently illustrated by an event tree, as in Figure 1, with each branch representing an event and each node a history or state. Environments like this, involving time and uncertainty, are the foundation of most of modern macroeconomics and finance. A typical agent in such a setting has preferences over payoffs $c(z^t)$ for each possible history. A general set of preferences might be represented by a utility function $U(\{c(z^t)\})$. More common, however, is to impose the additive expected utility structure

$$U(\{c(z^t)\}) = \sum_{t=0}^{\infty} \beta^t \sum_{z^t \in \mathscr{Z}^t} p(z^t) u[c(z^t)] = E_0 \sum_{t=0}^{\infty} \beta^t u(c_t), \tag{1}$$

where $0 < \beta < 1$, $p(z^t)$ is the probability of history z^t, and u is a period/state utility function. These preferences are remarkably parsimonious: behavior over time and across states depends solely on the discount factor β, the probabilities p, and the function u.

Although equation (1) remains the norm throughout economics, there has been extraordinary theoretical progress over the last fifty years (and particularly the last twenty-five) in developing alternatives. Some of these alternatives were developed to account for the anomalous predictions of expected utility in experimental work. Others arose from advances in the pure theory of intertemporal choice. Whatever

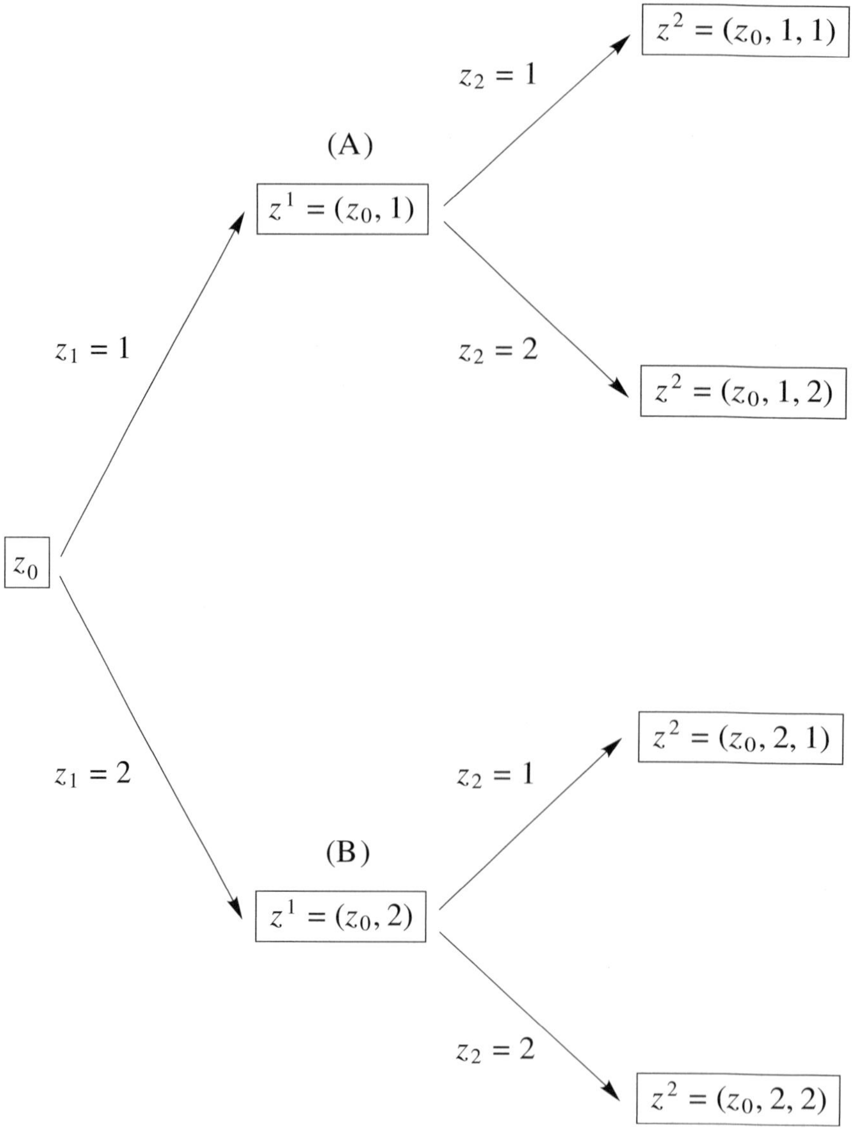

Figure 1
A representative event tree. This event tree illustrates how uncertainty might evolve through time. Time moves from left to right, starting at date $t = 0$. At each date t, an event z_t occurs. In this example, z_t is drawn from the two-element set $\mathscr{Z} = \{1, 2\}$. Each node is marked by a box and can be identified from the path of events that leads to it, which we refer to as a history and denote by $z^t \equiv (z_0, z_1, \ldots, z_t)$, starting with an arbitrary initial node z_0. Thus the upper right node follows two up branches, $z_1 = 1$ and $z_2 = 1$, and is denoted $z^2 = (z_0, 1, 1)$. The set $\mathscr{Z}^2$ of all possible 2-period histories is therefore $\{(z_0, 1, 1), (z_0, 1, 2), (z_0, 2, 1), (z_0, 2, 2)\}$, illustrated by the far right "column" of nodes.

their origin, they offer greater flexibility along several dimensions, often with only a modest increase in analytical difficulty.

What follows is a user's guide, intended to serve as an introduction and instruction manual for economists studying problems in which the structure of preferences may play an important role. Our goal is to describe exotic preferences to mainstream economists: preferences over time, preferences across states or histories, and (especially) combinations of the two. We take an overtly practical approach, downplaying or ignoring altogether the many technical issues that arise in specifying preferences in dynamic stochastic settings, including their axiomatic foundations. (References are provided in the appendix for those who are interested.) We generally assume without comment that preferences can be represented by increasing, (weakly) concave functions, with enough smoothness and boundary conditions to generate interior solutions to optimizations. We focus instead on applications, using tractable functional forms to revisit some classic problems: consumption and saving, portfolio choice, asset pricing, and Pareto optimal allocations. In most cases, we use utility functions that are homogeneous of degree 1 (hence invariant to scale) with constant elasticities (think power utility). These functions are the workhorses of macroeconomics and finance, so little is lost by restricting ourselves in this way.

You might well ask: Why bother? Indeed, we will not be surprised if most economists continue to use (1) most of the time. Exotic preferences, however, have a number of potential advantages that we believe will lead to much wider application than we've seen to date. One is more flexible functional forms for approximating features of data—the equity premium, for example. Another is the ability to ask questions that have no counterpart in the additive model. How should we make decisions if we don't know the probability model that generates the data? Can preferences be dynamically inconsistent? If they are, how do we make decisions? What is the appropriate welfare criterion? Can we think of some choices as tempting us away from better ones? Each of these advantages raises further questions: Are exotic preferences observationally equivalent to additive preferences? If not, how do we identify their parameters? Are they an excuse for free parameters? Do we even care whether behavior is derived from preferences?

These questions run through a series of nonadditive preference models. In Section 2, we discuss time preference in a deterministic setting, comparing Koopmans's time aggregator to the traditional time-additive structure. In Section 3, we describe alternatives to expected utility in a static setting, using a certainty-equivalent function to summarize preference toward risk. We argue that the Chew–Dekel class extends expected utility in useful directions without sacrificing analytical and empirical convenience. In Section 4, we put time and risk preference together in a Kreps–Porteus aggregator, which leads to a useful separation between time and risk preference. Dynamic extensions of Chew–Dekel preferences follow the well-worn path of Epstein and Zin. In Section 5, we consider risk-sensitive and robust control, whose application to economics is associated with the work of Hansen and Sargent. Section 6 is devoted to ambiguity, in which agents face uncertainty over probabilities as well as states. We describe Gilboa and Schmeidler's max-min utility for static settings and Epstein and Schneider's recursive extension to dynamic settings. In Section 7, we turn to hyperbolic discounting and provide an interpretation based on Gul and Pesendorfer's temptation preferences. The final section is devoted to a broader discussion of the role and value of exotic preferences in economics.

A word on notation and terminology: We typically denote parameters by Greek letters and functions and variables by Latin letters. We denote derivatives with subscripts; thus, V_2 refers to the derivative of V with respect to its second argument. In a stationary dynamic programming problem, J is a value function and a prime ($'$) distinguishes a future value from a current value. The abbreviation *iid* means "independent and identically distributed," and NID(x, y) means "normally and independently distributed with mean x and variance y."

2. Time

Time preference is a natural starting point for macroeconomists since so much of our subject is concerned with dynamics. Suppose there is no risk and (for this paragraph only) c_t is one-dimensional. Preferences might then be characterized by a general utility function $U(\{c_t\})$. A common measure of time preference in this setting is the marginal rate of substitution between consumption at two consecutive dates (c_t and c_{t+1}, say) along a constant consumption path ($c_t = c$ for all t). If the marginal rate of substitution is

$$\text{MRS}_{t,t+1} = \frac{\partial U / \partial c_{t+1}}{\partial U / \partial c_t},$$

then time preference is captured by the discount factor

$$\beta(c) \equiv \text{MRS}_{t,t+1}(c).$$

(Picture the slope, $-1/\beta$, of an indifference curve along the 45-degree line.) If $\beta(c)$ is less than 1, the agent is said to be impatient: she requires more than one unit of consumption at $t+1$ to induce her to give up one unit at t. For the traditional time-additive utility function,

$$U(\{c_t\}) = \sum_{t=0}^{\infty} \beta^t u(c_t), \tag{2}$$

$\beta(c) = \beta < 1$ regardless of the value of c, so impatience is built in and constant. The rest of this section is concerned with preferences in which the discount factor can vary with the level of consumption.

2.1 *Koopmans's Time Aggregator*

Koopmans (1960) derives a class of stationary recursive preferences by imposing conditions on a general utility function U for a multidimensional consumption vector c. Our approach and terminology follow Johnsen and Donaldson (1985). Preferences at all dates come from the same date-zero utility function U. As a result, they are dynamically consistent by construction: preferences over consumption streams starting at any future date t are consistent with U. Following Koopmans, let ${}_tc \equiv (c_t, c_{t+1}, \ldots)$ be an infinite consumption sequence starting at t. Then we might write utility from date $t = 0$ on as

$$U({}_0c) = U(c_0, {}_1c).$$

Koopmans's first condition is *history-independence*: preferences over sequences ${}_tc$ do not depend on consumption at dates prior to t. Without this condition, an agent making sequential decisions would need to keep track of the history of consumption choices to be able to make future choices consistent with U. The marginal rate of substitution between consumption at two arbitrary dates could depend, in general, on consumption at all dates past, present, and future. History-independence rules out dependence on the past. With it, the utility function can be expressed in the form

$$U({}_0c) = V[c_0, U_1({}_1c)]$$

for some *time aggregator* V. As a result, choices over ${}_1c$ do not depend on c_0. (Note, for example, that marginal rates of substitution between elements of ${}_1c$ do not depend on c_0.) Koopmans's second condition is *future independence*: preferences over c_t do not depend on ${}_{t+1}c$. (In

Koopmans's terminology, the first and second conditions together imply that preferences over the present (c_t) and future $({}_{t+1}c)$ are *independent*.) This is trivially true if c_t is a scalar, but a restriction on preferences otherwise. The two conditions together imply that utility can be written

$$U({}_0c) = V[u(c_0), U_1({}_1c)]$$

for some functions V and u, which defines u as a composite commodity for consumption at a specific date. Koopmans's third condition is that preferences are stationary (the same at all dates). The three conditions together imply that utility can be written in the stationary recursive form

$$U({}_tc) = V[u(c_t), U({}_{t+1}c)] \tag{3}$$

for all dates t. This is a generalization of the traditional utility function (2), where (evidently) $V(u, U) = u + \beta U$ or the equivalent. As in traditional utility theory, preferences are unchanged when we apply a monotonic transformation to U: if $\hat{U} = f(U)$ for f increasing, then we replace the aggregator V with $\hat{V}(u, \hat{U}) = f(V[u, f^{-1}(\hat{U})])$.

In the Koopmans class of preferences represented by equation (3), time preference is a property of the time aggregator V. Consider our measure of time preference for the composite commodity u. If U_t and u_t represent $U({}_tc)$ and $u(c_t)$, respectively, then

$$U_t = V(u_t, U_{t+1}) = V[u_t, V(u_{t+1}, U_{t+2})].$$

The marginal rate of substitution between u_t and u_{t+1} is therefore

$$\mathrm{MRS}_{t,t+1} = \frac{V_2(u_t, U_{t+1})V_1(u_{t+1}, U_{t+2})}{V_1(u_t, U_{t+1})}.$$

A constant consumption path with period utility u is defined by $U = V(u, U)$, implying $U = g(u) = V[u, g(u)]$ for some function g. (Koopmans calls g the *correspondence function*.) The discount factor is therefore $\beta(u) = V_2[u, g(u)]$. You might verify for yourself that V_2 is invariant to increasing transformations of U.

In modern applications, we generally work in reverse order: we specify a period utility function u and a time aggregator V and use them to characterize the overall utility function U. Any U constructed this way defines preferences that are dynamically consistent, history independent, future independent, and stationary. In contrast to time-additive preferences, discounting depends on the level of utility u.

To get a sense of how this works, consider the behavior of V_2. If preferences are increasing in consumption, u must be increasing in c and V must be increasing in both arguments. If we consider sequences with constant consumption, U must be increasing in u, so that

$$g_1(u) = V_1[u, g(u)] + V_2[u, g(u)]g_1(u) = \frac{V_1[u, g(u)]}{1 - V_2[u, g(u)]} > 0.$$

Since $V_1 > 0$, $0 < V_2[u, g(u)] < 1$, the discount factor is between zero and one and depends (in general) on u. Many economists impose an additional condition of *increasing marginal impatience*: $V_2[u, g(u)]$ is decreasing in u, or

$$V_{21}[u, g(u)] + V_{22}[u, g(u)]g_1(u) = V_{21}[u, g(u)] + V_{22}[u, g(u)]\frac{V_1[u, g(u)]}{1 - V_2[u, g(u)]} < 0.$$

In applications, this condition is typically used to generate stability of steady states.

Two variants of Koopmans's structure have been widely used by macroeconomists. One was proposed by Uzawa (1968), who suggested a continuous-time version of

$$V(u, U) = u + \beta(u)U.$$

(In his model, $\beta(u) = \exp[-\delta(u)]$.) Since $V_{21} = 0$, increasing marginal impatience is simply $\beta_1(u) < 0$ [or $\delta_1(u) > 0$]. Another is used by Epstein and Hynes (1983), Lucas and Stokey (1984), and Shi (1994), who generalize Koopmans by omitting the future independence condition. The resulting aggregator is $V(c, U)$, rather than $V(u, U)$, which allows choice over c to depend on U. If c is a scalar, this is equivalent to (3) [set $u(c) = c$], but otherwise need not be. An example is

$$V(c, U) = u(c) + \beta(c)U,$$

where there is no particular relationship between the functions u and β.

2.2 *Examples*

Example 1 (growth and fiscal policy) In the traditional growth model, Koopmans preferences can change both the steady state and the short-run dynamics. Suppose the period utility function is $u(c)$ and the time aggregator is $V(u,U') = u + \beta(u)U'$, with u increasing and concave and $\beta_1(u) < 0$. Gross output y is produced with capital k using an increasing concave technology f. The resource constraint is $y = f(k) = c + k' + g$, where c is consumption, k' is tomorrow's capital stock, and g is government purchases (constant). The Bellman equation is

$$J(k) = \max_{k'} u[f(k) - k' - g] + \beta(u[f(k) - k' - g])J(k').$$

The first-order and envelope conditions are

$$u_1(c)\{1 + \beta_1[u(c)]J(k')\} = \beta[u(c)]J_1(k')$$

$$J_1(k) = u_1(c)f_1(k)\{1 + \beta_1[u(c)]J(k')\},$$

which together imply $J_1(k) = \beta[u(c)]J_1(k')f_1(k)$. In a steady state, $1 = \beta(u[f(k) - k - g])f_1(k)$.

One clear difference from the traditional model is the role of preferences in determining the steady state. With constant β, the steady-state capital stock solves $\beta f_1(k) = 1$; u is irrelevant. With recursive preferences, the steady state solves $\beta(u[f(k) - k - g])f_1(k) = 1$, which depends on u through its impact on β. Consider the impact of an increase in g. With traditional preferences, the steady-state capital stock doesn't change, so any increase in g is balanced by an equal decrease in c. With recursive preferences and increasing marginal impatience, an increase in g reduces current utility and therefore raises the discount factor. The initial drop in c is therefore larger than in the traditional case. In the resulting steady state, the increase in g leads to an increase in k and a decline in c that is smaller than the increase in g. The magnitude of the decline depends on β_1, the sensitivity of the discount factor to current utility. [Adapted from Dolmas and Wynne (1998).]

Example 2 (optimal allocations) Time preference affects the optimal allocation of consumption among agents over time. Consider an economy with a constant aggregate endowment y of a single good, to be divided between two agents with Koopmans preferences, represented here by the aggregators V (the first agent) and W (the second). A Pareto optimal allocation is summarized by the Bellman equation:

$$J(w) = \max_{c,w'} V[y - c, J(w')]$$

subject to

$$W(c, w') \geq w.$$

Note that both consumption c and promised utility w pertain to the second agent. If λ is the Lagrange multiplier on the constraint, the first-order and envelope conditions are

$$V_1[y-c, J(w')] = \lambda W_1(c, w')$$

$$V_2[y-c, J(w')]J_1(w') + \lambda W_2(c, w') = 0$$

$$J_1(w) = -\lambda.$$

If agents' preferences are additive with the same discount factor β, then the second and third equations imply $J_1(w')/J_1(w) = W_2(c, w')/V_2[y-c, J(w')] = \beta/\beta = 1$: an optimal allocation places the same weight $\lambda = -J_1(w)$ on the second agent's utility at all dates and promised utility w is constant. If preferences are additive and $\beta_2 > \beta_1$ (the second agent is more patient), then $J_1(w')/J_1(w) = \beta_2/\beta_1 > 1$: an optimal allocation increases the weight over time on the second, more patient agent and raises her promised utility ($w' > w$). In the more general Koopmans setting, the dynamics depend on the time aggregators V and W. The allocation converges to a steady state if both aggregators exhibit increasing marginal impatience and future utility is a normal good. [Adapted from Lucas and Stokey (1984).]

Example 3 (long-run properties of a small open economy) Small open economies with perfect capital mobility raise difficulties with the existence of a steady state that can be resolved by endogenizing the discount factor. We represent preferences over sequences of consumption c and leisure $1-n$ with a period utility function $u(c, 1-n)$ and a time aggregator $V(c, 1-n, U) = u(c, 1-n) + \beta(c, 1-n)U$. Let output be produced with labor using the linear technology $y = \theta n$, where θ is a productivity parameter. The economy's resource constraint is $y = c + x$, where x is net exports. The agent can borrow and lend in international capital markets at gross interest rate r, giving rise to the budget constraint $a' = r(a + x) = r(a + \theta n - c)$. The Bellman equation is

$$J(a) = \max_{c,n}\ u(c, 1-n) + \beta(c, 1-n)J[r(a + \theta n - c)].$$

The first-order and envelope conditions are

$$u_1 + \beta_1 J(a') = \beta J_1(a')$$

$$u_2 + \beta_2 J(a') = \beta J_1(a')\theta$$

$$J_1(a) = \beta J_1(a')r.$$

The last equation tells us that in a steady state, $\beta(c, 1-n)r = 1$. With constant discounting, there is no steady state, but with more general discounting schemes the form of discounting determines the steady state and its response to changes in the environment. Here, the long-run impact of a change in (say) θ (the wage) depends on the form of β. Suppose β is a function of n only. Then the steady-state condition $\beta(1-n)r = 1$ determines n independently of θ! More generally, the long-run impact on n of a change in θ depends on the form of the discount function $\beta(c, 1-n)$. [Adapted from Epstein and Hynes (1983), Mendoza (1991), Obstfeld (1981), Schmitt-Grohé and Uribe (2002), and Shi (1994).]

Example 4 (dynamically inconsistent preferences) Suppose preferences as of date t are given by:

$$U_t({}_tc) = u(c_t) + \delta\beta u(c_{t+1}) + \delta\beta^2 u(c_{t+2}) + \delta\beta^3 u(c_{t+3}) + \cdots$$

with $0 < \delta \leq 1$. When $\delta = 1$, this reduces to the time-additive utility function (2). Otherwise, we discount utility in periods $t+1, t+2, t+3, \ldots$ by $\delta\beta, \delta\beta^2, \delta\beta^3, \ldots$. A little effort should convince you that these preferences cannot be put into stationary recursive form. In fact, they are dynamically inconsistent in the sense that preferences over (say) (c_{t+1}, c_{t+2}) at date t are different from preferences at $t+1$. (Note, for example, the marginal rates of substitution between c_{t+1} and c_{t+2} at t and $t+1$.) This structure is ruled out by Koopmans, who begins with the presumption of a consistent set of preferences. We'll return to this example in Section 7. [Adapted from Harris and Laibson (2003) and Phelps and Pollack (1968).]

3. Risk

Our next topic is risk, which we consider initially in a static setting. Our theoretical agent makes choices that have risky consequences or payoffs and has preferences over those consequences and their probabilities. To be specific, let us say that the state z is drawn with probability $p(z)$ from the finite set $\mathscr{Z} = \{1, 2, \ldots, Z\}$. Consequences ($c$, say) depend on the state. Having read Debreu's *Theory of Value* or the like, we might guess that with the appropriate technical conditions, the agent's preferences can be represented by a utility function of state-contingent consequences (consumption):

$$U(\{c(z)\}) = U[c(1), c(2), \ldots, c(Z)].$$

At this level of generality, there is no mention of probabilities, although we can well imagine that the probabilities of the various states will show up somehow in U, as they do in equation (1). In this section, we regard the probabilities as known, which you might think of as an assumption of risk or rational expectations. We consider unknown probabilities (ambiguity) in Sections 5 and 6.

We prefer to work with a different (but equivalent) representation of preferences. Suppose, for the time being, that c is a scalar; very little of the theory depends on this, but it streamlines the presentation. We define the *certainty equivalent* of a set of consequences as a certain consequence μ that gives the same level of utility:

$$U(\mu, \mu, \ldots, \mu) = U[c(1), c(2), \ldots, c(Z)].$$

If U is increasing in all its arguments, we can solve this for the certainty-equivalent function $\mu(\{c(z)\})$. Clearly μ represents the same preferences as U, but we find its form particularly useful. For one thing, it expresses utility in payoff (consumption) units. For another, it summarizes behavior toward risk directly: since the certainty equivalent of a sure thing is itself, the impact of risk is simply the difference between the certainty equivalent and expected consumption.

The traditional approach to preferences in this setting is expected utility, which takes the form:

$$U(\{c(z)\}) = \sum_z p(z)u[c(z)] = Eu(c)$$

or

$$\mu(\{c(z)\}) = u^{-1}\left(\sum_z p(z)u[c(z)]\right) = u^{-1}[Eu(c)],$$

a special case of (1). Preferences of this form are used in virtually all macroeconomic theory, but decades of experimental research have documented numerous difficulties with it. Among them: people seem more averse to bad outcomes than expected utility implies. See, for example, the summaries in Kreps (1988, Chapter 14) and Starmer (2000). We suggest the broader Chew–Dekel class of risk preferences, which allows us to account for some of the empirical anomalies of expected utility without giving up its analytical tractability.

3.1 *The Chew–Dekel Risk Aggregator*

Chew (1983, 1989) and Dekel (1986) derive a class of risk preferences that generalizes expected utility, yet leads to first-order conditions that are linear in probabilities, hence easily solved and amenable to econometric analysis. In the Chew–Dekel class, the certainty equivalent function μ for a set of payoffs and probabilities $\{c(z), p(z)\}$ is defined implicitly by a *risk aggregator* M satisfying

$$\mu = \sum_z p(z) M[c(z), \mu]. \tag{4}$$

This is Epstein and Zin's (1989) equation (3.10) with $M \equiv F + \mu$. Chew (1983, 1989) and Dekel (1986, Section 2) show that such preferences satisfy a weaker condition than the notorious independence axiom that underlies expected utility. We assume M has the following properties: (i) $M(m, m) = m$ (sure things are their own certainty equivalents), (ii) M is increasing in its first argument (first-order stochastic dominance), (iii) M is concave in its first argument (risk aversion), and (iv) $M(kc, km) = kM(c, m)$ for $k > 0$ (linear homogeneity). Most of the analytical convenience of the Chew–Dekel class follows from the linearity of equation (4) in probabilities.

In the examples that follow, we focus our attention on the following tractable members of the Chew–Dekel class:

• *Expected utility.* A version with constant relative risk aversion is implied by

$$M(c, m) = c^\alpha m^{1-\alpha}/\alpha + m(1 - 1/\alpha).$$

If $\alpha \leq 1$, M satisfies the conditions outlined above. Applying (4), we find

$$\mu = \left(\sum_z p(z) c(z)^\alpha \right)^{1/\alpha},$$

the usual expected utility with a power utility function.

• *Weighted utility.* Chew (1983) suggests a relatively easy way to generalize expected utility given (4): weight the probabilities by a function of outcomes. A constant-elasticity version follows from

$$M(c, m) = (c/m)^\gamma c^\alpha m^{1-\alpha}/\alpha + m[1 - (c/m)^\gamma/\alpha].$$

For M to be increasing and concave in c in a neighborhood of m, the parameters must satisfy either (a) $0 < \gamma < 1$ and $\alpha + \gamma < 0$ or (b) $\gamma < 0$ and $0 < \alpha + \gamma < 1$. Note that (a) implies $\alpha < 0$, (b) implies $\alpha > 0$, and both imply $\alpha + 2\gamma < 1$. The associated certainty equivalent function satisfies

$$\mu^\alpha = \frac{\sum_z p(z)c(z)^{\gamma+\alpha}}{\sum_x p(x)c(x)^\gamma} = \sum_z \hat{p}(z)c(z)^\alpha,$$

where

$$\hat{p}(z) = \frac{p(z)c(z)^\gamma}{\sum_x p(x)c(x)^\gamma}.$$

This version highlights the impact of bad outcomes: they get greater weight than with expected utility if $\gamma < 0$, less weight otherwise.

• *Disappointment aversion.* Gul (1991) proposes another model that increases sensitivity to bad events (disappointments). Preferences are defined by the risk aggregator

$$M(c,m) = \begin{cases} c^\alpha m^{1-\alpha}/\alpha + m(1 - 1/\alpha) & c \geq m \\ c^\alpha m^{1-\alpha}/\alpha + m(1 - 1/\alpha) + \delta(c^\alpha m^{1-\alpha} - m)/\alpha & c < m \end{cases}$$

with $\delta \geq 0$. When $\delta = 0$, this reduces to expected utility. Otherwise, disappointment aversion places additional weight on outcomes worse than the certainty equivalent. The certainty equivalent function satisfies

$$\mu^\alpha = \sum_z p(z)c(z)^\alpha + \delta \sum_z p(z)I[c(z) < \mu][c(z)^\alpha - \mu^\alpha] = \sum_z \hat{p}(z)c(z)^\alpha,$$

where $I(x)$ is an indicator function that equals 1 if x is true and 0 otherwise and

$$\hat{p}(z) = \left(\frac{1 + \delta I[c(z) < \mu]}{1 + \delta \sum_x p(x)I[c(x) < \mu]}\right)p(z).$$

It differs from weighted utility in scaling up the probabilities of all bad events by the same factor, and scaling down the probabilities of good events by a complementary factor, with good and bad defined as better and worse, respectively, than the certainty equivalent. All three expressions highlight the recursive nature of the risk aggregator M: we need to know the certainty equivalent to know which states are bad so that we can compute the certainty equivalent (and so on).

Each of these models is described in Epstein and Zin (2001). Other tractable preferences include semiweighted utility (Epstein and Zin, 2001), generalized disappointment aversion (Routledge and Zin, 2003), and rank-dependent preferences (Epstein and Zin, 1990). All but the last one are members of the Chew–Dekel class.

One source of intuition about these preferences is their state-space indifference curves, examples of which are pictured in Figure 2. For

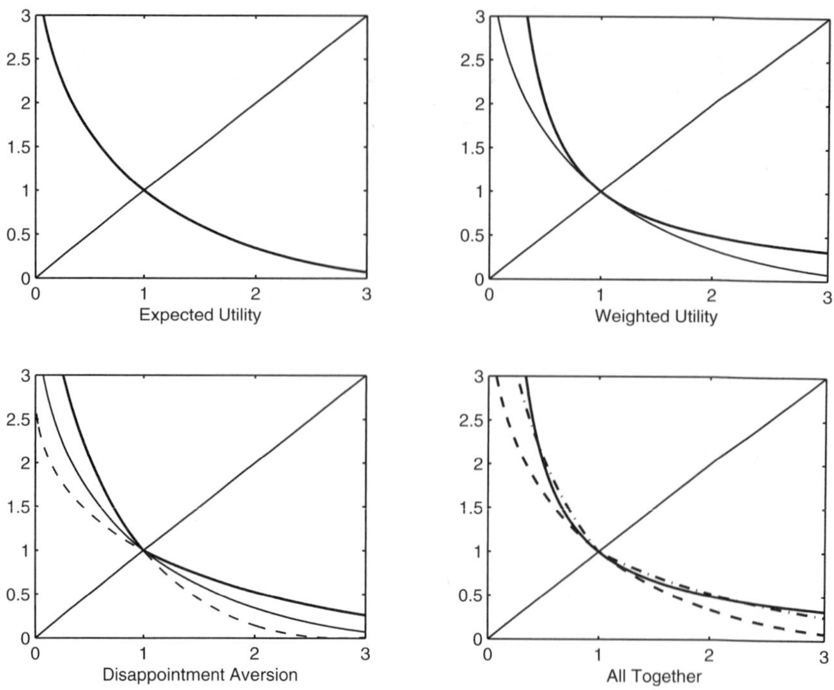

Figure 2
State-space indifference curves with Chew–Dekel preferences. The figure contains indifference curves for three members of the Chew–Dekel class of risk preferences. In each case, the axes are consumption in state 1 and state 2 and states are equally likely. The risk preferences are expected utility (upper left, $\alpha = 0.5$), weighted utility (upper right, bold line, $\gamma = -0.25$), and disappointment aversion (lower left, bold line, $\delta = 0.5$). For weighted utility and disappointment aversion, expected utility is pictured with a lighter line for comparison. For disappointment aversion, the indifference curve is the upper envelope of two indifference curves, each based on a different set of transformed probabilities. The extensions of these two curves are shown as dashed lines. The lower right figure has all three together: expected utility (dashed line), weighted utility (solid line), and disappointment aversion (dash-dotted line). Note that disappointment aversion is more sharply convex than weighted utility near the 45-degree line (the effect of first-order risk aversion), but less convex far away from it.

the purpose of illustration, suppose there are two equally likely states ($Z = 2,\ p(1) = p(2) = 1/2$). The 45-degree line represents certainty [$c(1) = c(2)$]. Since preferences are linear homogeneous, the unit indifference curve ($\mu = 1$) completely characterizes preferences. For expected utility, the unit indifference curve is

$$\mu(\text{EU}) = [0.5c(1)^{\alpha} + 0.5c(2)^{\alpha}]^{1/\alpha} = 1.$$

This is the usual convex arc with a slope of -1 (the odds ratio) at the 45-degree line. As we decrease α, the arc becomes more convex. For weighted utility, the unit indifference curve is

$$\mu(\text{WU}) = \left[\frac{c(1)^{\gamma+\alpha} + c(2)^{\gamma+\alpha}}{c(1)^{\gamma} + c(2)^{\gamma}}\right]^{1/\alpha} = 1.$$

Drawn for the same value of α and a modest negative value of γ, it is more convex than expected utility, suggesting greater risk aversion. With disappointment aversion, the equation governing the indifference curve depends on whether $c(1)$ is larger or smaller than $c(2)$. If it's smaller (so that $z = 1$ is the bad state), the indifference curve is

$$\mu(\text{DA}) = \left[\left(\frac{1+\delta}{2+\delta}\right)c(1)^{\alpha} + \left(\frac{1}{2+\delta}\right)c(2)^{\alpha}\right]^{1/\alpha} = 1.$$

If it's larger, we switch the two states around. To express this more compactly, define sets of transformed probabilities, $\hat{p}_1 = [(1+\delta)/(2+\delta), 1/(2+\delta)]$ (when $z = 1$ is the bad state) and $\hat{p}_2 = [1/(2+\delta), (1+\delta)/(2+\delta)]$ (when $z = 2$ is the bad state). Then the indifference curve can be expressed as

$$\left[\min_i \sum_z \hat{p}_i(z)c(z)^{\alpha}\right]^{1/\alpha} = 1.$$

We'll see something similar in Section 6. For now, note that the indifference curve is the upper envelope of two curves based on different sets of probabilities. The envelope is denoted by a solid line, and the extensions of the two curves by dashed lines. The result is an indifference curve with a kink at the 45-degree line, where the bad state switches. (As we cross from below, the bad state switches from 2 to 1.)

Another source of intuition is the sensitivity of certainty equivalents to small risks. For the two-state case discussed above, consider the certainty equivalent of the outcome $c(1) = 1 - \sigma$ and $c(2) = 1 + \sigma$ for small $\sigma > 0$, thereby defining the certainty equivalent as a function of σ. How much does a small increase in σ reduce μ? For expected utility, a second-order Taylor series expansion of $\mu(\sigma)$ around $\sigma = 0$ is

$$\mu(\text{EU}) \approx 1 - (1-\alpha)\frac{\sigma^2}{2}.$$

This familiar bit of mathematics suggests $1-\alpha$ as a measure of risk aversion. For weighted utility, a similar approximation yields

$$\mu(\text{WU}) \approx 1 - (1-\alpha-2\gamma)\frac{\sigma^2}{2},$$

which suggests $1-\alpha-2\gamma$ as a measure of risk aversion. Note that neither expected utility nor weighted utility has a linear term: agents with these preferences are effectively indifferent to very small risks. For disappointment aversion, however, the Taylor series expansion is

$$\mu(\text{DA}) \approx 1 - \left(\frac{\delta}{2+\delta}\right)\sigma - (1-\alpha)\left(\frac{4+4\delta}{4+4\delta+\delta^2}\right)\frac{\sigma^2}{2}.$$

The linear term tells us that disappointment aversion exhibits *first-order risk aversion*, a consequence of the kink in the indifference curve.

3.2 Examples

Example 5 (certainty equivalents for log-normal risks) We illustrate the behavior of Chew–Dekel preferences in an environment in which the impact of risk on utility is particularly transparent. Define the risk premium on a risky consumption distribution by $rp \equiv \log[E(c)/\mu(c)]$, the logarithmic difference between consumption's expectation and its certainty equivalent. Suppose consumption is log-normal: $\log c(z) = \kappa_1 + \kappa_2^{1/2} z$, with z distributed $\text{N}(0,1)$. Recall that if $\log x \sim \text{N}(a,b)$, then $\log E(x) = a + b/2$ ["Ito's lemma," equation (42) of Appendix 9.2]. Since $\log c \sim \text{N}(\kappa_1, \kappa_2)$, expected consumption is $\exp(\kappa_1 + \kappa_2/2)$. Similarly, the certainty equivalent for expected utility is $\mu = \exp(\kappa_1 + \alpha\kappa_2/2)$ and the risk premium is $rp = (1-\alpha)\kappa_2/2$. The proportionality factor $(1-\alpha)$ is the traditional coefficient of relative risk aversion. Weighted utility is not quite kosher in this context (M is concave only in the neighborhood of μ), but the example nevertheless gives us a sense of its properties. Using similar methods, we find that the certainty equivalent is $\mu = \exp(\kappa_1 + (\alpha + 2\gamma)\kappa_2/2)$ and the risk

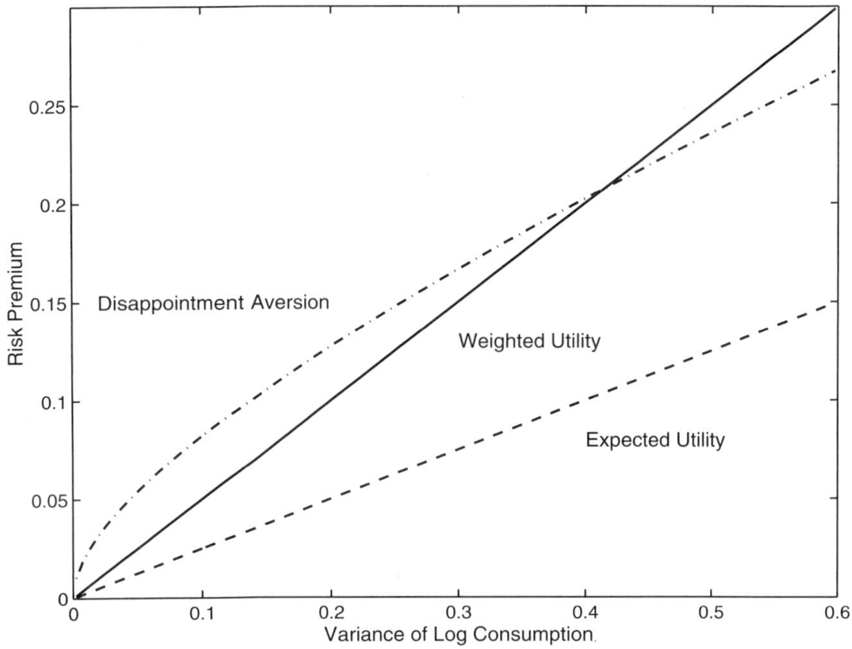

Figure 3
Risk and risk premiums with Chew–Dekel preferences. The figure illustrates the relation between risk and risk premiums discussed in Example 5 for three members of the Chew–Dekel class of risk preferences. The preferences are: expected utility (dashed line), weighted utility (solid line), and disappointment aversion (dash-dotted line). The point is the nonlinearity of disappointment aversion: the ratio of the risk premium to risk is greater for small risks than large ones. Parameter values are the same as Figure 2.

premium is $rp = (1 - \alpha - 2\gamma)\kappa_2/2$. Note that the risk premium is the same as expected utility with parameter $\alpha' = \alpha + 2\gamma$. This equivalence of expected utility and weighted utility doesn't extend to other distributions, but it suggests that we might find some difficulty distinguishing between the two in practice. For disappointment aversion, we find the certainty equivalent using mathematics much like that underlying the Black–Scholes formula:

$$\mu^\alpha = e^{\alpha\kappa_1 + \alpha^2\kappa_2/2} + \delta\left[e^{\alpha\kappa_1+\alpha^2\kappa_2/2}\Phi\left(\frac{\log\mu - \kappa_1 - \alpha\kappa_2}{\kappa_2^{1/2}}\right) - \Phi\left(\frac{\log\mu - \kappa_1}{\kappa_2^{1/2}}\right)\right],$$

where Φ is the standard normal distribution function [see equation (41) in Appendix 9.2]. Apparently the risk premium is no longer proportional to κ_2. We show this in Figure 3, where we graph rp against κ_2 for all three preferences using the same parameter values as Figure 2

($\alpha = \delta = 0.5$, $\gamma = -0.25$). As you might expect, disappointment aversion implies proportionately greater aversion to small risks than large ones; in this respect, it is qualitatively different from expected utility and weighted utility. Routledge and Zin's (2003) generalized disappointment aversion does the reverse: it generates greater aversion to large risks. Different sensitivity to large and small risks provides a possible method to distinguish such preferences from expected utility.

Example 6 (portfolio choice with Chew–Dekel preferences) One strength of the Chew–Dekel class is that it leads to first-order conditions that are easily solved and used in econometric work. Consider an agent with initial net assets a_0 who invests fractions w in a risky asset with (gross) return $r(z)$ in state z and $1 - w$ in a risk-free asset with return r_0. For an arbitrary choice of w, consumption in state z is $c(z) = a_0[r_0 + w(r(z) - r_0)]$. The portfolio choice problem might then be written as

$$\max_w \mu[a_0\{r_0 + w(r(z) - r_0)\}] = a_0 \max_w \mu[r_0 + w(r(z) - r_0)],$$

the second equality stemming from the linear homogeneity of μ. The direct approach to this problem is to choose w to maximize μ, and in some cases we'll do that. For the general Chew–Dekel class, however, we may not have an explicit expression for the certainty equivalent function. In those cases, we use equation (4):

$$\max_w \mu[\{r_0 + w(r(z) - r_0)\}] = \max_w \sum_z p(z) M[r_0 + w(r(z) - r_0), \mu^*],$$

where μ^* is the maximized value of the certainty equivalent function. The problem on the righthand side has first-order condition

$$\sum_z p(z) M_1[r_0 + w(r(z) - r_0), \mu^*][r(z) - r_0]$$

$$= E[M_1(r_0 + w(r - r_0), \mu^*)(r - r_0)] = 0. \tag{5}$$

(There are M_2 terms, too, but you might verify for yourself that they can be eliminated.) We find the optimal portfolio by solving the first-order condition and (4) simultaneously for w and μ^*. The same conditions can also be used in econometric work to estimate preference parameters.

To see how you might use (5) to determine w, consider a numerical example with two equally likely states and returns $r_0 = 1.01$, $r(1) = 0.90$, and $r(2) = 1.24$ (the "equity premium" is 6%). With expected utility, the first-order condition is

$$(\mu^*)^{\alpha-1}(1-\beta)\sum_z p(z)(r_0 + w[r(z) - r_0])^{\alpha-1}[r(z) - r_0] = 0.$$

Note that μ^* drops out and we can solve for w independently. For $\alpha = 0.5$, the solution is $w = 4.791$, which implies $\mu^* = 1.154$. The result is the dual of the equity premium puzzle: with modest risk aversion, the observed equity premium induces a huge long position in the risky asset, financed by borrowing. With disappointment aversion, the first-order condition is

$$(1+\delta)p(1)(r_0 + w[r(1) - r_0])^{\alpha-1}[r(1) - r_0] \\ + p(2)(r_0 + w[r(2) - r_0])^{\alpha-1}[r(2) - r_0] = 0,$$

since $z = 1$ is the bad state. For $\delta = 0.5$, $w = 2.147$ and $\mu^* = 1.037$. [Adapted from Epstein and Zin (1989, 2001).]

Example 7 (portfolio choice with rank-dependent preferences) Rank-dependent preferences are an interesting alternative to the Chew–Dekel class. We rank states so that the payoffs $c(z)$ are increasing in z and define the certainty equivalent function by

$$\mu = u^{-1}\left(\sum_z (g[P(z)] - g[P(z-1)])u[c(z)]\right) = u^{-1}\left(\sum_z \hat{p}(z)u[c(z)]\right),$$

where g is an increasing function satisfying $g(0) = 0$ and $g(1) = 1$, $P(z) = \sum_{u=1}^{z} p(u)$ is the cumulative distribution function, and $\hat{p}(z) = g[P(z)] - g[P(z-1)]$ is a transformed probability. If $g(p) = p$, this is simply expected utility. If g is concave, these preferences exhibit risk aversion even if u is linear. However, since μ is nonlinear in probabilities, it cannot be expressed in Chew–Dekel form. At the end of this section, we discuss the difficulties this raises for econometric estimation. In the portfolio choice problem, the first-order condition is

$$\sum_z \hat{p}(z)u_1[c(z)][r(z) - r_0] = 0, \tag{6}$$

which is readily solved if we know the probabilities. [Adapted from Epstein and Zin (1990) and Yaari (1987).]

Example 8 (risk sharing) Consider a Pareto problem with two agents who divide a given risky aggregate endowment $y(z)$. If their certainty equivalent functions are identical and homogeneous of degree 1, each agent consumes the same fraction of the aggregate endowment in all states. The problem is more interesting if the agents have different preferences. Let us say that two agents, indexed by i, have certainty equivalent functions $\mu^i[c^i(z)]$. A Pareto optimal allocation solves: choose $\{c^1(z), c^2(z)\}$ to maximize μ^1 subject to $c^1(z) + c^2(z) \leq y(z)$ and $\mu^2 \geq \bar{\mu}$ for some number $\bar{\mu}$. If λ is the Lagrange multiplier on the second constraint, the first-order conditions have the form

$$\frac{\partial \mu^1}{\partial c^1(z)} = \lambda \frac{\partial \mu^2}{\partial c^2(z)}.$$

With Chew–Dekel risk preferences, the derivatives have the form:

$$\begin{aligned}\frac{\partial \mu^i}{\partial c^i(z)} &= p(z) M_1^i[c^i(z), \mu^i] + \sum_x p(x) M_2^i[c^i(x), \mu^i] \frac{\partial \mu^i}{\partial c^i(z)} \\ &= p(z) M_1^i[c^i(z), \mu^i] \bigg/ \left(1 - \sum_x p(x) M_2^i[c^i(x), \mu^i]\right).\end{aligned}$$

This expression is not particularly user-friendly, but in principle we can solve it numerically for specific functional forms. With expected (power) utility, an optimal allocation solves

$$[\mu^1]^{1-\alpha_1}[y(z) - c^2(z)]^{\alpha_1 - 1} = \lambda [\mu^2]^{1-\alpha_2} c^2(z)^{\alpha_2 - 1},$$

which implies allocation rules that we can express in the form $c^i = s^i(y)y$. If we substitute into the optimality condition and differentiate, we find $ds^1/dy > 0$ if $\alpha_1 > \alpha_2$: the less risk averse agent absorbs a disproportionate share of the risk.

3.3 *Discussion: Moment Conditions for Preference Parameters*

One of the most useful features of Chew–Dekel preferences is how easily they can be used in econometric work. Since the risk aggregator (4) is linear in probabilities, we can apply method of moments estimators directly to first-order conditions.

In a typical method of moments estimator, a vector-valued function f of data x and a vector of parameters θ of equal dimension satisfies the *moment conditions*

$$Ef(x, \theta_0) = 0, \tag{7}$$

where $\theta = \theta_0$ is the parameter vector that generated the data. A method of moments estimator θ_T for a sample of size T replaces the population mean with the sample mean:

$$T^{-1} \sum_{t=1}^{T} f(x_t, \theta_T) = 0.$$

Under reasonably general conditions, a law of large numbers implies that the sample mean converges to the population mean and θ_T converges to θ_0. When the environment permits a central limit theorem, we can also derive an asymptotic normal distribution for θ_T. If the number of moment conditions (the dimension of f) is greater than the number of parameters (the dimension of θ), we can apply a generalized method of moments estimator with similar properties (see Hansen, 1982.)

The portfolio-choice problem with Chew–Dekel preferences has exactly this form if the number of preference parameters is no greater than the number of risky assets. For each risky asset i, there is a moment condition,

$$f_i(x, \theta) = M_1(c, \mu^*)(r_i - r_0),$$

analogous to equation (5). In the static case, we also need to estimate μ^*, which we do using equation (4) as an additional moment condition. [In a dynamic setting, a homothetic time aggregator allows us to replace μ^* with a function of consumption growth; see equation (13).]

Outside the Chew–Dekel class, estimation is a more complex activity. First-order conditions are no longer linear in probabilities and do not lead to moment conditions in the form of equation (7). To estimate, say, equation (6) for rank-dependent preferences, we need a different estimation strategy. One possibility is a simulated method of moments estimator, which involves something like the following: (i) conjecture a probability distribution and parameter values; (ii) given these values, solve the portfolio problem for decision rules; (iii) calculate (perhaps through simulation) moments of the decision rule and compare them to moments observed in the data; (iv) if the two sets of moments are sufficiently close, stop; otherwise, modify parameter values and return to step (i). All of this can be done, but it highlights the econometric convenience of Chew–Dekel risk preferences.

4. Time and Risk

We are now in a position to describe nonadditive preferences in a dynamic stochastic environment like that illustrated by Figure 1. You might guess that the process of specifying preferences over time and states of nature is simply a combination of the two. In fact, the combination raises additional issues that are not readily apparent. We touch on some of them here; others come up in the next two sections.

4.1 *Recursive Preferences*

Consider the structure of preferences in a dynamic stochastic environment. In the tradition of Kreps and Porteus (1978), Johnsen and Donaldson (1985), and Epstein and Zin (1989), we represent a class of recursive preferences by

$$U_t = V[u_t, \mu_t(U_{t+1})], \tag{8}$$

where U_t is shorthand for utility starting at some date-t history z^t, U_{t+1} refers to utilities for histories $z^{t+1} = (z^t, z_{t+1})$ stemming from z^t, u_t is date-t utility, V is a time aggregator, and μ_t is a certainty-equivalent function based on the conditional probabilities $p(z_{t+1}|z^t)$. This structure is suggested by Kreps and Porteus (1978) for expected utility certainty equivalent functions. Epstein and Zin (1989) extend their work to stationary infinite-horizon settings and propose the more general Chew–Dekel class of risk preferences. As in Section 2, such preferences are dynamically consistent, history independent, future independent, and stationary. They are also *conditionally independent* in the sense of Johnsen and Donaldson (1985): preferences over choices at any history at date t ($\bar{z}^t$, for example) do not depend on other histories that may have (but did not) occur ($z^t \neq \bar{z}^t$). You can see this in Figure 1: if we are now at the node marked (A), then preferences do not depend on consumption at nodes stemming from (B) denoting histories that can no longer occur.

If equation (8) seems obvious, think again. If you hadn't read the previous paragraph or its sources, you might just as easily propose

$$U_t = \mu_t[V(u_t, U_{t+1})],$$

another seemingly natural combination of time and risk preference. This combination, however, has a serious flaw: it implies dynamically inconsistent preferences unless it reduces to equation (1). See Kreps and Porteus (1978) and Epstein and Zin (1989, Section 4). File away for later the idea that the combination of time and risk preference can raise subtle dynamic consistency issues.

We refer to the combination of the recursive structure (8) and an expected utility certainty equivalent as Kreps–Porteus preferences. A popular parametric example consists of the constant elasticity aggregator,

$$V[u, \mu(U)] = [(1-\beta)u^{\rho} + \beta\mu(U)^{\rho}]^{1/\rho}, \tag{9}$$

and the power certainty equivalent,

$$\mu(U) = [E(U^{\alpha})]^{1/\alpha}, \tag{10}$$

with $\rho, \alpha < 1$. Equations (9) and (10) are homogeneous of degree 1 with constant discount factor β. This is more restrictive than the aggregators we considered in Section 2, but linear homogeneity rules out more general discounting schemes: it implies that indifference curves have the same slope along any ray from the origin, so their slope along the 45-degree line must be the same, too. If U is constant, the weights $(1-\beta)$ and β define $U = u$ as the (steady-state) level of utility. It is common to refer to $1-\alpha$ as the coefficient of relative risk aversion and $1/(1-\rho)$ as the intertemporal elasticity of substitution. If $\rho = \alpha$, the model is equivalent to one satisfying equation (1), and intertemporal substitution is the inverse of risk aversion. More generally, the Kreps–Porteus structure allows us to specify risk aversion and intertemporal substitution independently. Further, a Kreps–Porteus agent prefers early resolution of risk if $\alpha < \rho$; see Epstein and Zin (1989, Section 4). This separation of risk aversion and intertemporal substitution has proved to be not only a useful empirical generalization but an important source of intuition about the properties of dynamic models.

We can generate further flexibility by combining (8) with a Chew–Dekel risk aggregator (4), thereby introducing Chew–Dekel risk preferences to dynamic environments. We refer to this combination as Epstein–Zin preferences.

4.2 *Examples*

Example 9 (Weil's model of precautionary saving) We say that consumption-saving models generate *precautionary saving* if risk decreases consumption as a function of current assets. In the canonical consumption problem with additive preferences, income risk has this effect if the period utility function u has constant $k \equiv u_{111}u_1/(u_{11})^2 > 0$. See, for example, Ljungqvist and Sargent (2000, pp. 390–393). Both power utility and exponential utility satisfy this condition. With power utility $[u(c) = c^\alpha/\alpha]$, $k = (\alpha - 2)(\alpha - 1)$, which is positive for $\alpha < 1$ and therefore implies precautionary saving. (In the next section, we look at quadratic utility, which effectively sets $\alpha = 2$, implying $k = 0$ and no precautionary saving.) Similarly, with exponential utility $[u(c) = -\exp(-\alpha c)]$, $k = 1 > 0$. With Kreps–Porteus preferences, we can address a somewhat different question: does precautionary saving depend on intertemporal substitution, risk aversion, or both? To answer this question, consider the problem characterized by the Bellman equation

$$J(a) = \max_c \{(1-\beta)c^\rho + \beta\mu[J(a')]^\rho\}^{1/\rho}$$

subject to the budget constraint $a' = r(a - c) + y'$, where $\mu(x) = -\alpha^{-1} \log E \exp(-\alpha x)$ and $\{y_t\} \sim \text{NID}(\kappa_1, \kappa_2)$. The exponential certainty equivalent μ is not homogeneous of degree 1, but it is analytically convenient for problems with additive risk. The parameters satisfy $\rho \le 1$, $\alpha \ge 0$, $r > 1$, and $\beta^{1/(1-\rho)} r^{\rho/(1-\rho)} < 1$. Of particular interest are ρ, which governs intertemporal substitution, and α, which governs risk aversion.

The value function in this example is linear with parameters that can be determined by the time-honored guess-and-verify method. We guess (we've seen this problem before) $J(a) = A + Ba$ for parameters (A, B) to be determined. The certainty equivalent of future utility is

$$\mu[J(a')] = \mu[A + Br(a-c) + By'] = A + Br(a-c) + B\kappa_1 - \alpha B^2\kappa_2/2, \quad (11)$$

which follows from equation (42) of Appendix 9.2. The first-order and envelope conditions are

$$0 = J(a)^{1-\rho}[(1-\beta)c^{\rho-1} - \beta\mu^{\rho-1}Br]$$

$$J_1(a) = B = J(a)^{1-\rho}\beta\mu^{\rho-1}Br,$$

which imply

$$\mu = (\beta r)^{1/(1-\rho)} J(a) = (\beta r)^{1/(1-\rho)}(A + Ba)$$

$$c = [(1-\beta)/B]^{1/(1-\rho)} J(a) = [(1-\beta)/B]^{1/(1-\rho)}(A + Ba).$$

The latter tells us that the decision rule is linear, too. If we substitute both equations into (11), we find that the parameters of the value function must be:

$$A = (r-1)^{-1}(\kappa_1 - B\alpha\kappa_2/2)B$$

$$B = \left[\frac{(1-\beta)^{1/(1-\rho)}}{1-\beta^{1/(1-\rho)}r^{\rho/(1-\rho)}}\right]^{(1-\rho)/\rho}.$$

They imply the decision rule

$$c = (1-\beta^{1/(1-\rho)}r^{\rho/(1-\rho)})(a + (r-1)^{-1}[\kappa_1 - B\alpha\kappa_2/2]).$$

The last term is the impact of risk. Apparently a necessary condition for precautionary saving is $\alpha > 0$, so the parameter controlling precautionary saving is risk aversion. [Adapted from Weil (1993).]

Example 10 (Merton–Samuelson portfolio model) Our next example illustrates the relation between consumption and portfolio decisions in iid environments. The model is similar to the previous example, and we use it to address a similar issue: the impact of asset return risk on consumption. At each date t, a theoretical agent faces the following budget constraint:

$$a_{t+1} = (a_t - c_t)\sum_i w_{it}r_{it+1},$$

where w_{it} is the share of post-consumption wealth invested in asset i and r_{it+1} is its return. Returns $\{r_{it+1}\}$ are iid over time. Preferences are characterized by the constant elasticity time aggregator (9) and an arbitrary linearly homogeneous certainty equivalent function. The Bellman equation is

$$J(a) = \max_{c,w}\{(1-\beta)c^\rho + \beta\mu[J(a')]^\rho\}^{1/\rho},$$

subject to

$$a' = (a-c)\sum_i w_i r_i' = (a-c)r_p'$$

and $\sum_i w_i = 1$, where r_p is the portfolio return. Since the time and risk aggregators are linear homogeneous, so is the value function, and the problem decomposes into separate portfolio and consumption problems. The portfolio problem is:

$$\max_w \ \mu[J(a')] = (a-c)\ \max_w \ \mu[J(r_p')].$$

Since returns are iid, the portfolio problem is the same at all dates and can be solved using methods outlined in the previous section. Given a solution μ^* to the portfolio problem, the consumption problem is:

$$J(a) = \max_{c}\{(1-\beta)c^{\rho} + \beta[(a-c)\mu^*]^{\rho}\}^{1/\rho}.$$

The first-order condition implies the decision rule $c = [A/(1+A)]a$, where

$$A = [(1-\beta)/\beta]^{1/(1-\rho)}(\mu^*)^{-\rho/(1-\rho)}.$$

The impact of risk is mediated by μ^* and involves the familiar balance of income and substitution effects. If $\rho < 0$, the intertemporal elasticity of substitution is less than 1 and smaller μ^* (larger risk premium) is associated with lower consumption (the income effect). If $\rho > 0$, the opposite happens. In contrast to the previous example, the governing parameter is ρ; the impact of risk parameters is imbedded in μ^*. Note, too, that the impact on consumption of a change in μ^* can generally be offset by a change in β that leaves A unchanged. This leads to an identification issue that we discuss at greater length in the next example. Farmer and Gertler use a similar result to motivate setting $\alpha = 1$ (risk neutrality) in the Kreps–Porteus preference model, which leads to linear decision rules even with risk to income, asset returns, and length of life. [Adapted from Epstein and Zin (1989), Farmer (1990), Gertler (1999), and Weil (1990).]

Example 11 (asset pricing) The central example of this section is an exploration of time and risk preference in the traditional exchange economy of asset pricing. Preferences are governed by the constant elasticity time aggregator (9) and the Chew–Dekel risk aggregator (4). We characterize asset returns for general recursive preferences and discuss the identification of time and risk preference parameters. We break the argument into a series of steps.

Step (i) (consumption and portfolio choice). Consider a stationary Markov environment with states z and conditional probabilities $p(z'|z)$. A dynamic consumption/portfolio problem for this environment is characterized by the Bellman equation

$$J(a,z) = \max_{c,w}\{(1-\beta)c^{\rho} + \beta\mu[J(a',z')]^{\rho}\}^{1/\rho},$$

subject to the budget constraint $a' = (a-c)\sum_i w_i r_i(z,z') = (a-c)\cdot \sum_i w_i r_i' = (a-c)r_p'$, where r_p is the portfolio return. The budget constraint and linear homogeneity of the time and risk aggregators imply linear homogeneity of the value function: $J(a,z) = aL(z)$ for some scaled value function L. The scaled Bellman equation is

$$L(z) = \max_{b,w}\{(1-\beta)b^{\rho} + \beta(1-b)^{\rho}\mu[L(z')r_p(z,z')]^{\rho}\}^{1/\rho},$$

where $b \equiv c/a$. Note that $L(z)$ is the marginal utility of wealth in state z.

As in the previous example, the problem divides into separate portfolio and consumption decisions. The portfolio decision solves: choose $\{w_i\}$ to maximize $\mu[L(z')r_p(z,z')]$. The mechanics are similar to Example 6. The portfolio first-order conditions are

$$\sum_{z'} p(z'|z)M_1[L(z')r_p(z,z'),\mu]L(z')[r_i(z,z') - r_j(z,z')] = 0 \tag{12}$$

for any two assets i and j. Given a maximized μ, the consumption decision solves: choose b to maximize L. The intertemporal first-order condition is

$$(1-\beta)b^{\rho-1} = \beta(1-b)^{\rho-1}\mu^{\rho}. \tag{13}$$

If we solve for μ and substitute into the (scaled) Bellman equation, we find

$$\begin{aligned} \mu &= [(1-\beta)/\beta]^{1/\rho}[b/(1-b)]^{(\rho-1)/\rho} \\ L &= (1-\beta)^{1/\rho}b^{(\rho-1)/\rho}. \end{aligned} \tag{14}$$

The first-order condition (13) and the value function (14) allow us to express the relation between consumption and returns in almost familiar form. Since μ is linear homogeneous, the first-order condition implies $\mu(x'r'_p) = 1$ for

$$x' = L'/\mu = [\beta(c'/c)^{\rho-1}(r'_p)^{1-\rho}]^{1/\rho}.$$

The last equality follows from $(c'/c) = (b'/b)(1-b)r'_p$, a consequence of the budget constraint and the definition of b. The intertemporal first-order condition can therefore be expressed as

$$\mu(x'r'_p) = \mu([\beta(c'/c)^{\rho-1}r'_p]^{1/\rho}) = 1, \tag{15}$$

a generalization of the tangency condition for an optimum (set the marginal rate of substitution equal to the price ratio). Similar logic leads us to express the portfolio first-order conditions (12) as

$$E[M_1(x'r'_p, 1)x'(r'_i - r'_j)] = 0.$$

If we multiply by the portfolio weight w_j and sum over j, we find

$$E[M_1(x'r'_p, 1)x'r'_i] = E[M_1(x'r'_p, 1)x'r'_p]. \tag{16}$$

Euler's theorem for homogeneous functions allows us to express the right side as

$$E[M_1(x'r'_p, 1)x'r'_p] = 1 - EM_2(x'r'_p, 1).$$

Whether this is helpful depends on M. [Adapted from Epstein and Zin (1989).]

Step (ii) (equilibrium). Now shift focus to an exchange economy in which output growth follows a stationary Markov process: $g' = y'/y = g(z')$. In equilibrium, consumption equals output and the optimal portfolio is a claim to the stream of future output. We denote the price of this claim by q and the price-output ratio by $Q = q/y$. Its return is therefore

$$r'_p = (q' + y')/q = (Q'y' + y')/(Qy) = g'(Q' + 1)/Q. \tag{17}$$

With linear homogeneous preferences, the equilibrium price-output ratio is a stationary function of the current state, $Q(z)$. Asset pricing then consists of these steps: (a) substitute (17) into (15) and solve for Q:

$$\mu([\beta(g')^\rho(Q' + 1)]^{1/\rho}) = Q^{1/\rho};$$

(b) compute the portfolio return r_p from equation (17); and (c) use (16) to derive returns on other assets.

Step (iii) (the iid case). If the economy is iid, we cannot generally identify separate time and risk parameters. Time and risk parameters are intertwined in (16), but suppose we were somehow able to estimate the risk parameters. How might we estimate the time preference parameters β and ρ from observations of r_p (returns) and b (the consumption-wealth ratio)? Formally, equations (13) and (14) imply the intertemporal optimality condition

$$(1 - b)^{1-\rho} = \beta\mu(r'_p)^\rho.$$

If r_p is iid, μ and b are constant. With no variation in μ or b, the optimality condition cannot tell us both ρ and β: for any value of ρ, we can satisfy the condition by adjusting the discount factor β. The only limit to this is the restriction $\beta < 1$. Evidently a necessary condition for identifying separate time and risk parameters is that risk varies over time.

The issue doesn't arise with additive preferences, which tie time preference to risk preference. [Adapted from Kocherlakota (1990) and Wang (1993).]

Step (iv) (extensions). With Kreps–Porteus preferences and non-iid returns, the model does somewhat better in accounting for asset returns. Nevertheless, it fails to provide an entirely persuasive account of observed relations between asset returns and aggregate consumption. Roughly speaking, the same holds for more general risk preference specifications, although the combination of exotic preferences and time-varying risk shows promise. [See Bansal and Yaron (2004); Epstein and Zin (1991); Lettau, Ludvigson, and Wachter (2003); Routledge and Zin (2003); Tallarini (2000); and Weil (1989).]

Example 12 (risk sharing) With additive preferences and equal discount factors, Pareto problems generate constant weights on agents' utilities over time and across states of nature, even if period/state utility functions differ. With Kreps–Porteus preferences, differences in risk aversion lead to systematic drift in the weights. To be concrete, suppose states z follow a Markov chain with conditional probabilities $p(z'|z)$. Aggregate output is $y(z)$. Agents have the same aggregator, $V(c, \mu) = (c^\rho + \beta\mu^\rho)/\rho$, but different certainty equivalent functions,

$$\mu^i[x(z')] = \left(\sum_{z'} p(z'|z)x(z')^{\alpha_i}\right)^{1/\alpha_i}$$

for state-dependent utility x. The Bellman equation for the Pareto problem is

$$J(w, z) = \max_{c, \{w_{z'}\}} ((y(z) - c)^\rho + \beta\mu^1[J(w_{z'}, z')]^\rho)/\rho$$

subject to

$$(c^\rho + \beta\mu^2[w_{z'}]^\rho)/\rho \geq w.$$

Here, c and $w_{z'}$ refer to consumption and promised future utility of the second agent. The first-order and envelope conditions imply

$$(y(z) - c)^{\rho-1} = \lambda c^{\rho-1}$$

$$(\mu^1)^{\rho-\alpha_1} J(w_{z'}, z')^{\alpha_1-1} J_1(w_{z'}, z') = J_1(w, z)(\mu^2_{z'})^{\rho-\alpha_2} w_{z'}^{\alpha_2-1}$$

$$J_1(w, z) = -\lambda.$$

The first equation leads to the familiar allocation rule $c = [1 + \lambda^{1/(\rho-1)}]^{-1} y(z)$. If $\alpha_1 \neq \alpha_2$, the weight λ will generally vary over time. [Adapted from Anderson (2004) and Kan (1995).]

Example 13 (habits, disappointment aversion, and conditional independence) Habits and disappointment aversion both assess utility by comparing consumption to a benchmark. With disappointment aversion, the benchmark is the certainty equivalent. With habits, the benchmark is a function of past consumption. Despite this apparent similarity, there are a number of differences between them. One is timing: the habit is known and fixed when current decisions are made, while the certainty equivalent generally depends on those decisions. Another is that disappointment aversion places restrictions on the benchmark that have no obvious analog in the habit model. A third is that habits take us outside the narrowly defined class of recursive preferences summarized by equation (8): they violate the assumption of conditional independence. Why? Because preferences at any node in the event tree depend on past consumption through the habit, which in turn depends on nodes that can no longer be reached. In Figure 1, for example, decisions at node (A) depend on the habit, which was chosen at (say) the initial node z_0 and therefore depends on anything that could have happened from there on, including (B) and its successors. The solution, of course, is to define preferences conditional on a habit state variable and proceed in the natural way.

4.3 *Discussion: Distinguishing Time and Risk Preference*

The defining feature of this class of preferences is the separation of time preference (summarized by the aggregator V) and risk preference (summarized by the certainty equivalent function μ). In the functional forms used in this section, time preference is characterized by a discount factor and an intertemporal substitution parameter. Risk preference is characterized by risk aversion and possibly other parameters indicated by the Chew–Dekel risk aggregator. Therefore, we have added one or more parameters to the conventional additive utility function (1). Examples suggest that the additional parameters may be helpful in explaining precautionary saving, asset returns, and the intertemporal allocation of risk.

A critical question in applications is whether these additional parameters can be identified and estimated from a single time series realization of all the relevant variables. If so, we can use the methods outlined in the previous section: apply a method of moments estimator to the first-order conditions of the problem of interest. Identification hinges on the nature of risk. If risk is iid, we cannot identify separate time and risk parameters. This is clear in examples, but the logic is both straightforward and general: we need variation over time to identify time preference. A more formal statement is given by Wang (1993).

5. Risk-Sensitive and Robust Control

Risk-sensitive and robust control emerged in the engineering literature in the 1970s and were brought to economics and developed further by Hansen and Sargent, their many coauthors, and others. The most popular version of risk-sensitive control is based on Kreps–Porteus preferences with an exponential certainty equivalent function. Robust control considers a new issue: decision making when the agent does not know the probability model generating the data. The agent considers instead a range of models and makes decisions that maximize utility given the worst possible model. The same issue is addressed from a different perspective in the next section. Much of this work deals with linear-quadratic-guassian (LQG) problems, but the ideas are applicable more generally. We start by describing risk-sensitive and robust control in a static scalar LQG setting, where the insights are less cluttered by algebra. We go on to consider dynamic LQG problems, robust control problems outside the LQG universe, and challenges of estimating—and distinguishing between—models based on risk-sensitive and robust control.

5.1 *Static Control*

Many of the ideas behind risk-sensitive and robust control can be illustrated with a static, scalar example. We consider traditional optimal control, risk-sensitive control, and robust control as variants of the same underlying problem. The striking result is the equivalence of optimal decisions made under risk-sensitive and robust control.

In our example, an agent maximizes some variant of a quadratic return function,

$$u(v, x) = -[Qv^2 + Rx^2],$$

subject to the linear constraint,

$$x = Ax_0 + Bv + C(w + \varepsilon), \tag{18}$$

where v is a control variable chosen by the agent, x is a state variable that is controlled indirectly through v, x_0 is a fixed initial value, $(Q, R) > 0$ are preference parameters, (A, B, C) are nonzero parameters describing the determination of x, $\varepsilon \sim \mathrm{N}(0, 1)$ is noise, and w is a distortion of the model that we'll describe in greater detail when we get to robust control. The problem sets up a trade-off between the cost (Qv^2) and potential benefit (Rx^2) of nonzero values of v. If you've seen LQG control problems before, most of this should look familiar.

Optimal control. In this problem and the next one, we set $w = 0$, thereby ruling out distortions. The control problem is: choose v to maximize Eu given the constraint (18). Since

$$Eu = -[Qv^2 + R(Ax_0 + Bv)^2] - RC^2, \tag{19}$$

the objective functions with and without noise differ only by a constant. Noise therefore has no impact on the optimal choice of v. For both problems, the optimal v is

$$v = -(Q + B^2R)^{-1}(ABR)x_0.$$

This solution serves as a basis of comparison for the next two.

Risk-sensitive control. Continuing with $w = 0$, we consider an alternative approach that brings risk into the problem in a meaningful way: we maximize an exponential certainty equivalent of u,

$$\mu(u) = -\alpha^{-1} \log E \exp(-\alpha u),$$

where $\alpha \geq 0$ is a risk aversion parameter. (This is more natural in a dynamic setting, where we would compute the certainty equivalent of future utility à la Kreps and Porteus.) We find $\mu(u)$ by applying formula (43) of Appendix 9.2:

$$\mu(u) = -(1/2) \log(1 - 2\alpha RC^2) \\ - [Qv^2 + [R/(1 - 2\alpha RC^2)](Ax_0 + Bv)^2] \tag{20}$$

as long as $1 - 2\alpha RC^2 > 0$. This condition places an upper bound on the risk aversion parameter α. Without it, the agent can be so sensitive to risk that her objective function is negative infinity regardless of the control. The first term on the right side of (20) does not depend on v or x, so it has no effect on the choice of v. The important difference from (19) is the last term: the coefficient of $(Ax_0 + Bv)^2$ is larger than R, making the agent more willing to tolerate nonzero values of v to bring x close to zero. The optimal v is

$$v = -(Q + B^2 R - \alpha QRC^2)^{-1}(ABR)x_0.$$

If $\alpha = 0$ (risk neutrality) or $C = 0$ (no noise), this is the same as the optimal control solution. If $\alpha > 0$ and $C \neq 0$, the optimal choice of v is larger in absolute value because risk aversion increases the benefit of driving x to zero.

Robust control. Our third approach is conceptually different. We bring back the distortion w and tell the following story: We are playing a game against a malevolent nature, who chooses w to minimize our objective function. If our objective were to maximize Eu, then w would be infinite and our objective function would be minus infinity regardless of what we do. Therefore, let us add a penalty (to nature) of θw^2, making our objective function

$$\min_w \; Eu + \theta w^2.$$

The parameter $\theta > 0$ has the effect of limiting how much nature distorts the model, with small values of θ implying weaker limits on nature. The minimization implies

$$w = (\theta - RC^2)^{-1} R(Ax_0 + Bv),$$

making the robust control objective function

$$\min_w \; Eu + \theta w^2 = -[Qv^2 + [R/(1 - \theta^{-1}RC^2)](Ax_0 + Bv)^2] - RC^2. \tag{21}$$

The remarkable result: if we set $\theta^{-1} = 2\alpha$, the robust control objective differs from the risk-sensitive control objective (20) only by a constant, so it leads to the same choice of v. As in risk-sensitive control, the choice of v is larger in absolute value, in this case to offset the impact of w. There is, once again, a limit on the parameter: where α was bounded above, θ is bounded below. An infinite value of θ reproduces the optimal control objective function and solution.

An additional result applies to the example: risk-sensitive and robust control are observationally equivalent to the traditional control problem with suitably adjusted R. That is, if we replace R in equation (19) with

$$\hat{R} = R/(1 - 2\alpha RC^2) = R + 2\alpha R^2C^2/(1 - 2\alpha RC^2) > R, \tag{22}$$

then the optimal control problem is equivalent to risk-sensitive control, which we've seen is equivalent to robust control. If Q and R are functions of more basic parameters, it may not be possible to adjust R in this way, but the exercise points to the qualitative impact on the control: be more aggressive. This result need not survive beyond the scalar case, but it's suggestive.

Although risk-sensitive and robust control lead to the same decision, they are based on different preferences and give the decision different interpretations. With risk-sensitive control, we are concerned with risk for traditional reasons, and the parameter α measures risk aversion. With robust control, we are concerned with model uncertainty (possible nonzero values of w). To deal with it, we make decisions that maximize given the worst possible specification error. The parameter θ controls how bad the error can be.

Entropy constraints. One of the most interesting developments in robust control is a procedure for setting θ: namely, choose θ to limit the magnitude of model specification error, with specification error measured by *entropy*. We define the entropy of transformed probabilities $\hat{p}$ relative to reference probabilities p by

$$I(\hat{p}; p) \equiv \sum_z \hat{p}(z) \log[\hat{p}(z)/p(z)] = \hat{E} \log(\hat{p}/p), \tag{23}$$

where the expectation is understood to be based on $\hat{p}$. Note that $I(\hat{p}; p)$ is nonnegative and equals zero when $\hat{p} = p$. Since the likelihood is the probability density function expressed as a function of parameters, entropy can be viewed as the expected difference in log-likelihoods between the reference and transformed models, with the expectation based on the latter.

In a robust control problem, we can limit the amount of specification error faced by an agent by imposing an upper bound on I: consider (say) only transformations $\hat{p}$ such that $I(\hat{p}; p) \leq I_0$ for some positive number I_0. This *entropy constraint* takes a particularly convenient form in the normal case. Let $\hat{p}$ be the density of x implied by equation (18) and p the density with $w = 0$:

$$\begin{aligned}
\hat{p}(x) &= (2\pi C^2)^{-1/2} \exp[-(x - Ax_0 - Bv - Cw)^2/2C^2] \\
&= (2\pi C^2)^{-1/2} \exp[-\varepsilon^2/2] \\
p(x) &= (2\pi C^2)^{-1/2} \exp[-(x - Ax_0 - Bv)^2/2C^2] \\
&= (2\pi C^2)^{-1/2} \exp[-(w + \varepsilon)^2/2].
\end{aligned}$$

Relative entropy is

$$I(\hat{p}; p) = \hat{E}(w^2/2 + w\varepsilon) = w^2/2.$$

If we add the constraint $w^2/2 \leq I_0$ to the optimal control objective (19), the new objective is

$$\min_w \; -[Qv^2 + R(Ax_0 + Bv + Cw)^2] - RC^2 + \theta(w^2 - 2I_0),$$

where θ is the Lagrange multiplier on the constraint. The only difference from the robust control problem we discussed earlier is that θ is determined by I_0. Low values of I_0 (tighter constraints) are associated with high values of θ, so the lower bound on θ is associated with an upper bound on I_0.

Example 14 (Kydland and Prescott's inflation game) A popular macroeconomic policy game goes like this: the government chooses inflation q to maximize the quadratic return function,

$$u(q, y) = -[q^2 + Ry^2],$$

subject to the Phillips curve,

$$y = y_0 + B(q - q^e) + C(w + \varepsilon),$$

where y is the deviation of output from its social optimum, q^e is expected inflation, (R, B, C) are positive parameters, y_0 is the noninflationary level of output, and $\varepsilon \sim \mathrm{N}(0, 1)$. We assume $y_0 < 0$, which imparts an inflationary bias to the economy.

This problem is similar to our example, with one twist: we assume q^e is chosen by private agents to equal the value of q they expect the government to choose (another definition of rational expectations) but taken as given by the government (and nature). Agents know the model, so they end up setting $q^e = q$. A robust control version of this problem leads to the optimization:

$$\max_q \min_w \; -E(q^2 + R[y_0 + B(p - p^e) + C(w + \varepsilon)]^2) + \theta w^2.$$

Note that we can do the min and max in any order (the min-max theorem). We do both at the same time, which generates the first-order conditions

$$q + RB[y_0 + B(q - q^e) + Cw] = 0$$

$$-\theta w + RC[y_0 + B(q - q^e) + Cw] = 0.$$

Applying the rational expectations condition $q^e = q$ leads to

$$q = -\left(\frac{RB}{1-\theta^{-1}RC^2}\right)y_0, \qquad w = \left(\frac{\theta^{-1}RC}{1-\theta^{-1}RC^2}\right)y_0.$$

Take $\theta^{-1} = 0$ as the benchmark. Then $q = -RBy_0 > 0$ (the inflationary bias we mentioned earlier) and $w = 0$ (no distortions). For smaller values of $\theta > RC^2$, inflation is higher. Why? Because negative values of w effectively lower the noninflationary level of output (it becomes $y_0 + Cw$), leading the government to tolerate more inflation. As θ approaches its lower bound of RC^2, inflation approaches infinity. If we treat this as a constraint problem with entropy bound $w^2/2 \le I_0$, then $w = -(2I_0)^{1/2}$ (recall that $w < 0$) and the Lagrange multiplier θ is related to I_0 by

$$\theta = RC^2 - RCy_0/(2I_0)^{1/2}.$$

The lower bound on θ corresponds to an upper bound on I_0. All of this is predicated on private agents understanding the government's decision problem, including the value of θ. [Adapted from Hansen and Sargent (2004, Chapter 5) and Kydland and Prescott (1977).]

Example 15 (entropy with three states) With three states, the constraint $I(\hat{p}; p) \le I_0$ is two-dimensional since the probability of the third state can be computed from the other two. Figure 4 illustrates the constraint for the reference probabilities $p(1) = p(2) = p(3) = 1/3$ (the point marked $+$) and $I_0 = 0.1$. The boundary of the constraint set is the egg shape. By varying I_0, we vary the size of the constraint set. Chew–Dekel preferences can be viewed from the same perspective. Disappointment aversion, for example, is a one-dimensional class of distortions. If the first state is the only one worse than the certainty equivalent, the transformed probabilities are $\hat{p}(1) = (1+\delta)p(1)/[1+\delta p(1)]$, $\hat{p}(2) = p(2)/[1+\delta p(1)]$, and $\hat{p}(3) = p(3)/[1+\delta p(1)]$. Their entropy is

$$I(\delta) = \log[1+\delta p(1)] - p(1)\log(1+\delta),$$

a positive increasing function of $\delta \ge 0$. By varying δ subject to the constraint $I(\delta) \le I_0$, we produce the line shown in the figure. (It hits the boundary at $\delta = 1.5$.) The interpretation of disappointment aversion, however, is different: in the theory of Section 3, the line represents different preferences, not model uncertainty.

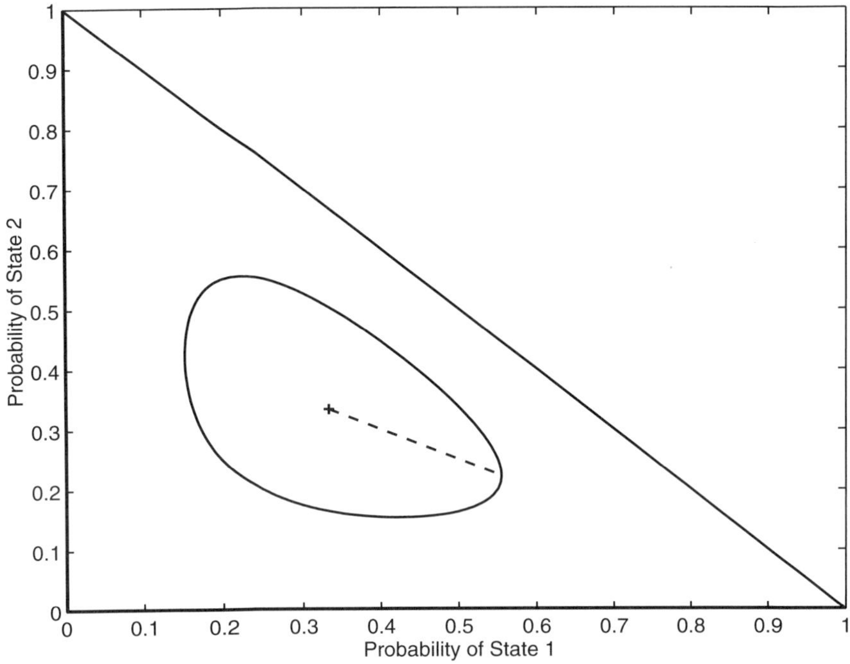

Figure 4
Transformed probabilities: Entropy and disappointment aversion. The figure illustrates two sets of transformed probabilities described in Example 15: one set generated by an entropy constraint and the other by disappointment aversion. The bold triangle is the three-state probability simplex. The "+" in the middle represents the reference probabilities: $p(1) = p(2) = p(3) = 1/3$. The area inside the egg-shaped contour represents transformed probabilities with entropy less than 0.1. The dashed line represents probabilities implied by disappointment aversion with δ between 0 to 1.5.

5.2 *Dynamic Control*

Similar issues and equations arise in dynamic settings. The traditional linear-quadratic control problem starts with the quadratic return function,

$$u(v_t, x_t) = -(v_t^\top Q v_t + x_t^\top R x_t + 2x_t^\top S v_t),$$

where v is the control and x is the state. Both are vectors, and (Q, R, S) are matrices of suitable dimension. The state evolves according to the law of motion

$$x_{t+1} = Ax_t + Bv_t + C(w_t + \varepsilon_{t+1}), \tag{24}$$

where w is a distortion (zero in some applications) and $\{\varepsilon_t\} \sim \mathrm{NID}(0, I)$ is random noise. We use these inputs to describe optimal, risk-sensitive, and robust control problems. As in the static example, the central result is the equivalence of decisions made under risk-sensitive and robust control. We skip quickly over the more torturous algebraic steps, which are available in the sources listed in Appendix 9.1.

Optimal control. We maximize the objective function:

$$E_0 \sum_{t=0}^{\infty} \beta^t u(v_t, x_t)$$

subject to (24) and $w_t = 0$. From long experience, we know that the value function takes the form

$$J(x) = -x^\top P x - q \tag{25}$$

for a positive semidefinite symmetric matrix P and a scalar q. The Bellman equation is

$$\begin{aligned} -x^\top P x - q = \max_v \{ & -(v^\top Q v + x^\top R x + 2x^\top S v) \\ & - \beta E[(Ax + Bv + C\varepsilon')^\top P(Ax + Bv + C\varepsilon') + q]\}. \end{aligned} \tag{26}$$

Solving the maximization in (26) leads to the Riccati equation

$$P = R + \beta A^\top P A - (\beta A^\top P B + S)(Q + \beta B^\top P B)^{-1}(\beta B^\top P A + S^\top). \tag{27}$$

Given a solution for P, the optimal control is $v = -Fx$, where

$$F = (Q + \beta B^\top P B)^{-1}(\beta B^\top P A + S^\top). \tag{28}$$

As in the static scalar case, risk is irrelevant: the control rule (28) does not depend on C. You can solve such problems numerically by iterating on the Riccati equation: make an initial guess of P (we use I), plug it into the right side of (27) to generate the next estimate of P, and repeat until successive values are sufficiently close together. See Anderson, Hansen, McGrattan, and Sargent (1996) for algebraic details, conditions guaranteeing convergence, and superior computational methods (the doubling algorithm, for example).

Risk-sensitive control. Risk-sensitive control arose independently but can be regarded as an application of Kreps–Porteus preferences using an exponential certainty equivalent. The exponential certainty equivalent introduces risk into decisions without destroying the quadratic structure of the value function. The Bellman equation is

$$J(x) = \max_v \{u(v, x) + \beta\mu[J(x')]\},$$

where the maximization is subject to $x' = Ax + Bv + C\varepsilon'$ and $\mu(J) = -\alpha^{-1} \log E \exp(-\alpha J)$. If the value function has the quadratic form of (25), the multivariate analog to (43) gives us

$$\mu[J(Ax + Bv + C\varepsilon')] = -(1/2) \log|I - 2\alpha C^\top PC| + (Ax + Bv)^\top \hat{P}(Ax + Bv),$$

where

$$\hat{P} = P + 2\alpha PC(I - 2\alpha C^\top PC)^{-1}C^\top P \tag{29}$$

as long as $|I - 2\alpha C^\top PC| > 0$. Each of these pieces has a counterpart in the static case. The inequality again places an upper bound on the risk aversion parameter α; for larger values, the integral implied by the expectation diverges. Equation (29) corresponds to (22); in both equations, risk sensitivity increases the agent's aversion to nonzero values of the state variable. Substituting $\hat{P}$ into the Bellman equation and maximizing leads to a variant of the Riccati equation,

$$P = R + \beta A^\top \hat{P} A - (\beta A^\top \hat{P} B + S)(Q + \beta B^\top \hat{P} B)^{-1}(\beta B^\top \hat{P} A + S^\top), \tag{30}$$

and associated control matrix,

$$F = (Q + \beta B^\top \hat{P} B)^{-1}(\beta B^\top \hat{P} A + S^\top).$$

A direct (if inefficient) solution technique is to iterate on equations (29) and (30) simultaneously. We describe another method shortly.

Robust control. As in our static example, the idea behind robust control is that a malevolent nature chooses distortions w that reduce our utility. A recursive version has the Bellman equation:

$$J(x) = \max_v \min_w \{u(v, x) + \beta(\theta w^\top w + EJ(x'))\}$$

subject to the law of motion $x' = Ax + Bv + C(w + \varepsilon')$. The value function again takes the form of equation (25), so the Bellman equation can be expressed as

$$-x^\top Px - q = \max_v \min_w \{-(v^\top Qv + x^\top Rx + 2v^\top Sx) + \beta\theta w^\top w - \beta E([Ax + Bv + C(w + \varepsilon')]^\top P(Ax + Bv + C\varepsilon') + p)\}. \tag{31}$$

The minimization leads to

$$w = (\theta I - C^\top PC)^{-1} C^\top P(Ax + Bv)$$

and

$$\theta w^\top w - (Ax + Bv + Cw)^\top P(Ax + Bv + Cw) = (Ax + Bv)^\top \hat{P}(Ax + Bv),$$

where

$$\hat{P} = P + \theta^{-1} PC(I - \theta^{-1} C^\top PC)^{-1} C^\top P. \tag{32}$$

Comparing (32) with (29), we see that risk-sensitive and robust control lead to similar objective functions and produce identical decision rules if $\theta^{-1} = 2\alpha$.

A different representation of the problem leads to a solution that fits exactly into the traditional optimal control framework and is therefore amenable to traditional computational methods. The min-max theorem suggests that we can compute the solutions for v and w simultaneously. With this in mind, define:

$$\hat{v} = \begin{bmatrix} v_t \\ w_t \end{bmatrix}, \qquad \hat{Q} = \begin{bmatrix} Q & 0 \\ 0 & -\beta\theta I \end{bmatrix}, \qquad \hat{S} = [S \quad 0], \qquad \hat{B} = [B \quad C].$$

Then the problem is one of optimal control and can be solved using the Riccati equation (27) applied to $(\hat{Q}, R, \hat{S}, A, \hat{B})$. The optimal controls are $v = -F_1 x$ and $w = -F_2 x$, where the F_i come from partitioning F. A doubling algorithm applied to this problem provides an efficient computational technique for robust and risk-sensitive control problems.

Entropy constraints. As in the static case, dynamic robust control problems can be derived using an entropy constraint. Hansen and Sargent (2004, Chapter 6) suggest

$$\sum_{t=0}^{\infty} \beta^t w_t^\top w_t / 2 \leq I_0.$$

Discounting is convenient here, but is not a direct outcome of a multiperiod entropy calculation. They argue that discounting allows distortions to continue to play a role in the solution; without it, the problem tends to drive I_t and w_t to zero with time. A recursive version of the constraint is

$$I_{t+1} = \beta^{-1}(w_t^\top w_t - I_t).$$

A recursive robust constraint problem is based on an expanded state vector, (x, I), and the law of motion for I above. As in the static case, the result is a theory of the Lagrange multiplier θ. Conversely, the solution to a traditional robust control problem with given θ can be used to compute the implied value of I_0. The recursive version highlights an interesting feature of this problem: nature not only minimizes at a point in time, but also allocates entropy over time in the way that has the greatest adverse impact on the agent.

Example 16 (robust precautionary saving) Consider a linear-quadratic version of the precautionary saving problem. A theoretical agent has quadratic utility, $u(c_t) = (c_t - \gamma)^2$, and maximizes the expected discounted sum of utility subject to a budget constraint and an autoregressive income processs:

$$a_{t+1} = r(a_t - c_t) + y_{t+1}$$

$$y_{t+1} = (1 - \varphi)\bar{y} + \varphi y_t + \sigma\varepsilon_{t+1},$$

where $\{\varepsilon_t\} \sim \text{NID}(0, 1)$. We express this as a linear-quadratic control problem using c_t as the control and $(1, a_t, y_t)$ as the state. The relevant matrices are

$$\begin{bmatrix} Q & S^\top \\ S & R \end{bmatrix} = \begin{bmatrix} 1 & -\gamma & 0 & 0 \\ -\gamma & \gamma^2 & 0 & 0 \\ 0 & 0 & 0 & 0 \\ 0 & 0 & 0 & 0 \end{bmatrix},$$

$$A = \begin{bmatrix} 1 & 0 & 0 \\ (1-\varphi)\bar{y} & r & \varphi \\ (1-\varphi)\bar{y} & 0 & \varphi \end{bmatrix}, \qquad B = \begin{bmatrix} 0 \\ -r \\ 0 \end{bmatrix}, \qquad C = \begin{bmatrix} 0 \\ \sigma \\ \sigma \end{bmatrix}.$$

We set $\beta = 0.95$, $r = 1/\beta$, $\gamma = 2$, $\bar{y} = 1$, $\varphi = 0.8$, and $\sigma = 0.25$. For the optimal control problem, the decision rule is

$$c_t = 0.7917 + 0.0500a_t + 0.1583y_t.$$

For the robust control problem with $\theta = 2$ (or the risk-sensitive control problem with $\alpha = 1/2\theta = 0.25$), the decision rule is

$$c_t = 0.7547 + 0.0515a_t + 0.1632y_t.$$

The impact of robustness is to reduce the intercept (precautionary saving) and increase the responsiveness to a and y. Why? The anticipated distortion is

$$w_t = -0.1557 + 0.0064a_t + 0.0204y_t,$$

making the actual and distorted dynamics

$$A = \begin{bmatrix} 1 & 0 & 0 \\ 0.2 & 1.0526 & 0.8 \\ 0.2 & 0 & 0.8 \end{bmatrix},$$

$$A - CF_2 = \begin{bmatrix} 1 & 0 & 0 \\ -0.1247 & 1.0661 & 0.8425 \\ -0.1247 & 0.0134 & 0.8425 \end{bmatrix}.$$

The distorted dynamics are pessimistic (the income intercept changes from 0.2 to −0.1247) and more persistent (the maximal eigenvalue increases from 1.0526 to 1.1086). The latter calls for more aggressive responses to movements in a and y. [Adapted from Hansen, Sargent, and Tallarini (1999) and Hansen, Sargent, and Wang (2002).]

5.3 *Beyond LQG*

You might conjecture (as we did) that the equivalence of risk-sensitive and robust control hinges critically on the linear-quadratic-gaussian structure. It doesn't. The critical functional forms are the exponential certainty equivalent and the entropy constraint. With these two ingredients, the objective functions of risk-sensitive and robust control are the same.

We demonstrate the equivalence of risk-sensitive and robust control objective functions in a finite-state setting where the math is relatively simple. Consider an environment with conditional probabilities $p(z'|z)$. Since z is immaterial in what follows, we ignore it from now on. In a typical dynamic programming problem, the Bellman equation includes the term $EJ = \sum_{z'} p(z')J(z')$. A robust control problem has a similar term based on transformed probabilities $\hat{p}(z')$ whose values are limited by an entropy penalty:

$$\hat{J} = \min_{\{\hat{p}(z')\}} \sum_{z'} \hat{p}(z')J(z') + \theta\left\{\sum_{z'} \hat{p}(z') \log[\hat{p}(z')/p(z')]\right\}$$
$$+ \lambda\left(\sum_{z'} \hat{p}(z') - 1\right).$$

If $\hat{p}(z') = p(z')$, this is simply EJ. The new elements are the minimization with respect to $\hat{p}$ (the defining feature of robust control), the entropy penalty on the choice of $\hat{p}$ (the standard functional form), and the constraint that the transformed probabilities sum to 1. For each $\hat{p}(z')$, the first-order condition for the minimization is

$$J(z') + \theta\{\log[\hat{p}(z')/p(z')] + 1\} + \lambda = 0. \tag{33}$$

If we multiply by $\hat{p}(z')$ and sum over z', we get $\hat{J} + \theta + \lambda = 0$, which we use to eliminate λ below. Each first-order condition implies

$$\hat{p}(z') = p(z')e^{-[J(z')+\theta+\lambda]/\theta} = p(z')e^{-J(z')/\theta+\hat{J}/\theta}.$$

If we sum over z' and take logs, we get

$$\hat{J} = -\theta \log\left(\sum_{z'} p(z') \exp[-J(z')/\theta]\right),$$

our old friend the exponential certainty equivalent with risk aversion parameter $\alpha = \theta^{-1}$. If we place $\hat{J}$ in its Bellman equation context, we've shown that robust control is equivalent (even outside the LQG class) to maximizing Kreps–Porteus utility with an exponential certainty equivalent. The log in the entropy constraint of robust control reappears in the exponential certainty equivalent. An open question is whether there's a similar relationship between Kreps–Porteus preferences with (say) a power certainty equivalent and a powerlike alternative to the entropy constraint.

5.4 *Discussion: Interpreting Parameters*

Risk-sensitive and robust control raise a number of estimation issues, some we've seen and some we haven't. Risk-sensitive control is based on a special case of Kreps–Porteus preferences and therefore leads to the same identification issues we faced in the previous section: we need variation over time in the conditional distribution of next period's state to distinguish time and risk parameters.

Robust control raises new issues. Risk-sensitive and robust control lead to the same decision rules, so we might regard them as equivalent. But they're based on different preferences and therefore lead to different interpretations of parameters. While risk-sensitive control suggests a risk-averse agent, robust control suggests an agent who is uncertain about the model that generated the data. In practice, the two can be quite different. One difference is plausibility: we may find an agent with substantial model uncertainty (small θ) more plausible than one with enormous risk aversion (large α). Similarly, if we find that a model estimated for Argentina suggests greater risk aversion than one estimated for the United States, we might prefer to attribute the difference to model uncertainty. Hansen and Sargent (2004, Chapter 8) have developed a methodology for calibrating model uncertainty (error detection probabilities) that gives the robust-control interpretation some depth. Another difference crops up in comparisons across policy regimes: the two models can differ substantially if we consider policy experiments that change the amount of model uncertainty.

6. Ambiguity

In Sections 3 and 4, agents know the probabilities they face, and with enough regularity and repetition, an econometrician can estimate them. Here we consider preferences when the consequences of our choices are uncertain or ambiguous. It's not difficult to think of such situations: what are the odds that China revalues this year by more than 10%, that the equity premium is less than 3%, or that productivity shocks account for more than half of the variance of U.S. output growth? We might infer probabilities from history or market prices, but it's a stretch to say that we know (or can find out) these probabilities, even though they may affect some of our decisions. One line of attack on this issue was suggested by Savage (1954): that people maximize expected utility using personal or subjective probabilities. In this case, we retain the analytical tractability of expected utility but lose the empirical convenience of preferences based on the same probabilities that generate outcomes (rational expectations). Another line of attack generalizes Savage: preferences are characterized by multiple probability distributions, or priors. We refer to such preferences as capturing ambiguity and ambiguity aversion, and explore two examples: Gilboa and Schmeidler's (1989) max-min expected utility for static environments and Epstein and Schneider's (2003) recursive multiple priors extension to dynamic environments. The central issues are dynamic consistency (something we need to address in dynamic settings) and identification (how do we distinguish agents with ambiguous preferences from those with expected utility?).

6.1 Static Ambiguity

Ambiguity has a long history and an equally long list of terminology. Different varieties have been referred to as Knightian uncertainty, Choquet expected utility, and expected utility with nonadditive (subjective) probabilities. Each of these terms refers to essentially the same preferences. Gilboa and Schmeidler (1989) provide a simple representation and an axiomatic basis for a preference model in which an agent entertains multiple probability models or priors. If the set of priors is Π, preferences are represented by the utility function

$$U(\{c(z)\}) = \min_{\pi \in \Pi} \sum_z \pi(z) u[c(z)] = \min_{\pi \in \Pi} E_\pi u(c). \tag{34}$$

Gilboa and Schmeidler refer to such preferences as max-min because agents maximize a utility function that has been minimized with respect to the probabilities π. We denote probabilities by π, rather than p, as a reminder that they are preference parameters. The defining feature is Π, which characterizes both ambiguity and ambiguity aversion. If Π has a single element, (34) reduces to Savage's subjective expected utility.

Gilboa and Schmeidler's max-min preferences incorporate aversion to ambiguity: agents dislike consequences with unknown odds. Consider an agent choosing among mutually exclusive assets in a three-state world. State 1 is pure risk: it occurs with probability $1/3$. State 2 is ambiguous: it occurs with probability $1/3 - \gamma$, with $-1/6 \leq \gamma \leq 1/6$. State 3 is also ambiguous and occurs with probability $1/3 + \gamma$. The agent's probability distributions over γ define Π. We use the distributions $\pi_\gamma(\gamma = g) = 1$ for $-1/6 \leq g \leq 1/6$, which imply $(1/3, 1/3 - g, 1/3 + g)$ as elements of Π. These distributions over γ are *dogmatic* in the sense that each places probability 1 on a particular value. The approach also allows nondogmatic priors, such as $\pi_\gamma(\gamma = -1/6) = \pi_\gamma(\gamma = 1/6) = 1/2$. In this setting, consider the agent's valuation of three assets: A pays 1 in state 1, nothing otherwise; B pays 1 in state 2; and C pays 1 in state 3. How much is each asset worth on its own to a max-min agent? To emphasize the difference between risk and ambiguity, let $u(c) = c$. Using (34), we find that asset A is worth $1/3$ and assets B and C are each worth $1/6$. The agent is apparently averse to ambiguity in the sense that the ambiguous assets, B and C, are worth less than the unambiguous asset, A. In contrast, an expected utility agent would never value both B and C less than A.

Example 17 (portfolio choice and nonparticipation) We illustrate the impact of ambiguity on behavior with an ambiguous version of Example 6. An agent has max-min preferences with $u(c) = c^\alpha/\alpha$ and $\alpha = 0.5$. She invests fraction w of initial wealth a_0 in a risky asset with returns

$[r(1) = \kappa_1 - \sigma,\ r(2) = \kappa_1 + \sigma$, with $\sigma = 0.17]$ and fraction $1 - w$ in a risk-free asset with return $r_0 = 1.01$ in both states. Previously we assumed the states were equally likely: $\pi(1) = \pi(2) = 1/2$. Here we let $\pi(1)$ take on any value in the interval $[0.4, 0.6]$ and set $\pi(2) = 1 - \pi(1)$. Two versions of this example illustrate different features of max-min preferences.

• Version 1: First-order risk aversion generates a nonparticipation result. With expected utility, agents are approximately neutral to fair bets. In a portfolio context, this means they'll buy a positive amount of an asset whose expected return is higher than the risk-free rate, and sell it short if the expected return is lower. They choose $w = 0$ only if the expected return is the same. With multiple priors, the agent chooses $w = 0$ for a range of values of κ_1 around the risk-free rate (the nonparticipation result). If we buy, state 1 is the worst state and the min sets $\pi(1) = 0.6$. To buy a positive amount of the risky asset, the first-order condition must be increasing at $w = 0$:

$$0.6(r_0)^{\alpha-1}(\kappa_1 - \sigma - r_0) + 0.4(r_0)^{\alpha-1}(\kappa_1 + \sigma - r_0) \geq 0,$$

which implies $\kappa_1 - r_0 \geq 0.2\sigma$ or $\kappa_1 \geq 1.01 + 0.2(0.17) = 1.044$. If we sell, state 2 is the worst and the min sets $\pi(2) = 0.6$. The analogous first-order condition must be decreasing:

$$0.4(r_0)^{\alpha-1}(\kappa_1 - \sigma - r_0) + 0.6(r_0)^{\alpha-1}(\kappa_1 + \sigma - r_0) \leq 0,$$

which implies $\kappa_1 \leq r_0 - 0.2\sigma = 0.976$. For $0.976 \leq \kappa_1 \leq 1.044$, the agent neither buys nor sells.

• Version 2: Let $\kappa_1 = 1.07$. Then the mean return is high enough to induce the agent to buy the risky asset and state 1 is the worst. The optimal portfolio is $w = 2.147$. In this two-state example, the result is identical to disappointment aversion with $\delta = 0.5$. With more states, this need not be the case.

[Adapted from Dow and Werlang (1992) and Routledge and Zin (2001).]

6.2 *Dynamic Ambiguity*

Epstein and Schneider (2003) extend max-min preferences to dynamic settings, providing an axiomatic basis for

$$U_t = u_t + \beta \min_{\pi \in \Pi_t} E_\pi U_{t+1}, \qquad (35)$$

where U_t is shorthand for utility starting at some date-t history z^t, u_t is utility at z^t, U_{t+1} refers to utilities starting with histories $z^{t+1} = (z^t, z_{t+1})$ stemming from z^t, Π_t is a set of one-period conditional probabilities $\pi(z_{t+1}|z^t)$, and E_π denotes the expectation computed from the prior π. Hayashi (2003) generalizes (35) to nonlinear time aggregators: $U_t = V(u_t, \min_{\pi \in \Pi_t} E_\pi U_{t+1})$.

As in Section 4, the combination of time and risk raises a question of dynamic consistency: can (35) be reconciled with some reasonable specification of date-zero max-min preferences? The answer is yes, but the argument is subtle. Consider the dilation example suggested by Seidenfeld and Wasserman (1993). The starting point is the event tree in Figure 1, to which we add ambiguous probabilities. (We suggest you write them on the tree.) Date-one probabilities are $\pi(z_1 = 1) = \pi(z_1 = 2) = 1/2$; they are not ambiguous. Date-two (conditional) probabilities depend on z_1 and an autocorrelation parameter ρ, for which the agent has dogmatic priors on the values $+1$ and -1. Listed from top to bottom in the figure, the conditional probabilities of the four date-two branches are $\pi(z_2 = 1 \,|\, z_1 = 1) = \pi(z_2 = 2 \,|\, z_1 = 2) = (1+\rho)/2$ and $\pi(z_2 = 2 \,|\, z_1 = 1) = \pi(z_2 = 1 \,|\, z_1 = 2) = (1-\rho)/2$. In words: the probabilities depend on whether z_1 and z_2 are the same or different and whether ρ is $+1$ or -1.

With these probabilities, consider the value of an asset that pays 1 if $z_2 = 1$, 0 otherwise. For convenience, let $u(c) = c$ and set $\beta = 1$. If the recursive and date-zero valuations of the asset differ, preferences are dynamically inconsistent. Consider recursive valuation. At node (A) in Figure 1, the value is $(1+\rho)/2$. Minimizing with respect to ρ, as suggested by (35), implies $\rho = -1$ and a value of 0. Similarly, the value at node (B) is also 0, this time based on $\rho = 1$. The value at date zero is therefore 0 as well; there is no ambiguity, so the value is $(1/2)(0) + (1/2)(0) = 0$. Now consider a (naive) date-zero problem based on the two-period probabilities of the four possible two-period paths: $(1+\rho)/4$, $(1-\rho)/4$, $(1-\rho)/4$, and $(1+\rho)/4$. Ambiguity in these probabilities is again represented by ρ. Since the asset pays 1 if the first or third path occurs, its date-zero value is $(1+\rho)/4 + (1-\rho)/4 = 1/2$, which is not ambiguous. The date-zero value (1/2) is clearly greater than the recursive value (0), so preferences are dynamically inconsistent. The computational point: our recursive valuation allows ρ to differ across date-one nodes, while our date-zero valuation does not. The conceptual point: giving the agent access to date-one information increases the amount of information but also increases the amount of ambiguity, which reduces the value of the asset.

Any resolution of this dynamic inconsistency problem must modify either recursive or date-zero preferences. Epstein and Schneider propose the latter. They show that if we expand the set of date-zero probabilities in the right way, they lead to the same preferences as (35). In general, preferences depend on probabilities over complete paths, which in our example you might associate with the four terminal nodes in Figure 1. Epstein and Schneider's rectangularity condition tells us to compute the set of probabilities recursively, one period at a time, starting at the end. At each step, we compute a set of probabilities for paths given our current history. In our example, the main effect of this approach is to eliminate any connection between the values of ρ at the two date-one nodes. The resulting date-zero probabilities take the form $(1+\rho_1)/4$, $(1-\rho_1)/4$, $(1-\rho_2)/4$, and $(1+\rho_2)/4$. The value of the asset is therefore $(1+\rho_1)/4+(1-\rho_2)/4 = 1/2+(\rho_1-\rho_2)/4$. If we minimize with respect to both ρ_1 and ρ_2, we set $\rho_1=-1$ and $\rho_2=+1$ and the value is zero, the same value we computed recursively. In short, expanding the date-zero set of probabilities in this way reconciles date-zero and recursive valuations and resolves the dynamic inconsistency problem.

A related example illustrates the Epstein–Schneider approach in a somewhat more complex environment that allows comparison to an alternative based on entropy constraints. The setting remains the event tree in Figure 1. Date-one probabilities are $\pi(z_1=1)=(1+\delta)/2$ and $\pi(z_1=2)=(1-\delta)/2$, with a dogmatic prior for any δ in the interval $[-\bar{\delta},\bar{\delta}]$ and $0\le\bar{\delta}<1$. Date-two probabilities remain $(1+\rho)/2$, $(1-\rho)/2$, $(1-\rho)/2$, and $(1+\rho)/2$, but we restrict ρ to the interval $[-\bar{\rho},\bar{\rho}]$ for $0\le\bar{\rho}\le1$. An asset has date-two payoffs of (from top to bottom in the tree) $1+\varepsilon,\varepsilon,1$, and 0, where $\varepsilon\ge0$. The Seidenfeld–Wasserman example is a special case with $\bar{\delta}=\varepsilon=0$ and $\bar{\rho}=1$. The addition of ε to the payoffs introduces a concern for first-period ambiguity. Consider four approaches to the problem of valuing the asset:

- *Naive date-zero approach.* The four branches have date-zero probabilities of $[(1+\delta)(1+\rho)/4,(1+\delta)(1-\rho)/4,(1-\delta)(1-\rho)/4,(1-\delta)(1+\rho)/4]$. Conditional on δ and ρ, the asset is worth $(1+\varepsilon+\delta+\delta\rho)/2$. If we minimize with respect to both δ and ρ, the value is $(1+\varepsilon+\bar{\delta}\varepsilon-\bar{\delta}\bar{\rho})/2$. If $\bar{\delta}=\bar{\rho}=1/2$ and $\varepsilon=1$, the value is $9/8$.

- *Recursive approach.* We work our way through the tree, starting at the end and applying (35) as we go. At node (A), the value of the asset is $(1-\rho)/2$. If we minimize with respect to ρ, the value is

$\min_\rho(1+\rho)/2+\varepsilon=(1-\bar{\rho})/2+\varepsilon$ (set $\rho=-\bar{\rho}$). At (B), the value is $\min_\rho(1-\rho)/2=(1-\bar{\rho})/2$ (set $\rho=\bar{\rho}$). At the initial node, the value is $(1-\bar{\rho})/2+(1+\delta)\varepsilon/2$. Minimizing with respect to δ gives us $(1-\bar{\rho})/2+(1-\bar{\delta})\varepsilon/2=[1-\bar{\rho}+(1-\bar{\delta})\varepsilon]/2$ (set $\delta=-\bar{\delta}$). This is smaller than the date-zero valuation, which implicitly forced us to choose the same value of ρ at (A) and (B). If $\bar{\delta}=\bar{\rho}=1/2$ and $\varepsilon=1$, the value is $1/2$.

• *Rectangular approach (sophisticated date-zero).* As in the dilation example, we allow ρ to differ between the two date-one nodes, giving us two-period probabilities of $[(1+\delta)(1+\rho_1)/4, (1+\delta)(1-\rho_1)/4, (1-\delta)(1-\rho_2)/4, (1-\delta)(1+\rho_2)/4]$. Conditional on δ, ρ_1, and ρ_2, the asset is worth $(1+\delta)(1+\rho_1)(1+\varepsilon)/4+(1+\delta)(1-\rho_1)\varepsilon/4+(1-\delta)(1-\rho_2)/4$. Minimizing with respect to the parameters gives us the same value as the recursive approach.

• *Entropy approach.* In this context, entropy is simply a way of describing the set Π: an entropy constraint places limits on (δ,ρ_1,ρ_2) that correspond to limits on the conditional probabilities at each node. We compute entropy at each node from equation (23) using $(1/2,1/2)$ as the reference probabilities. The date-one entropy of probabilities following the initial node is

$$I_1(\delta)=(1/2)[(1+\delta)\log(1+\delta)+(1-\delta)\log(1-\delta)].$$

Note that $I_1(0)=0$, $I_1(\delta)=I_1(-\delta)\geq 0$, and $dI_1/d\delta=(1/2)\log[(1+\delta)/(1-\delta)]$. Similarly, the date-two entropy for the node following $z_1=i$ is

$$I_{2i}(\rho_i)=(1/2)[(1+\rho_i)\log(1+\rho_i)+(1-\rho_i)\log(1-\rho_i)],$$

which has the same functional form as I_1. The overall two-period entropy constraint is

$$I_1(\delta)+[(1+\delta)/2]I_{21}(\rho_1)+[(1-\delta)/2]I_{22}(\rho_2)\leq\bar{I} \tag{36}$$

for some number $\bar{I}>0$ (a preference parameter). Our problem is to chose (δ,ρ_1,ρ_2) to minimize the value of the asset subject to the entropy constraint. What's new is the ability to shift ambiguity across periods implicit in the trade-off between first- and second-period entropy.

We solve this problem recursively. To do this, it's helpful to break the constraint into pieces: $I_1(\delta)\leq\bar{I}_1$ and, for each i, $I_{2i}(\rho_i)\leq\bar{I}_2\equiv\bar{I}-\bar{I}_1$. They are equivalent to the single entropy constraint (36) if the multipliers on the individual constraints are equal. In the first period, we choose not only the value of δ that satisfies the date-one entropy constraint but how much entropy to use now ($\bar{I}_1$) and how much to save for the second period ($\bar{I}_2 = \bar{I} - \bar{I}_1$). The solution is the allocation of entropy that equates the multipliers. Given a choice $\bar{I}_1$, we solve the date-two problems. At node A, the entropy-constrained valuation problem is to choose ρ_1 to minimize $\varepsilon + (1+\rho_1)/2$ subject to the entropy constraint $I_{21}(\rho_1) \le \bar{I}_2$. If θ is the multiplier on the constraint, the first-order condition is

$$1/2 + (\theta/2) \log[(1+\rho_1)/(1-\rho_1)] = 0.$$

As with rectangularity, we set $\rho_1 < 0$ to reduce the probability of the good state ($z_2 = 1$). We're going to reverse-engineer this and determine the constraint associated with setting $\rho_1 = -1/2$, the number we used earlier. With this value, entropy is $\bar{I}_2 = 0.1308$ and the first-order condition implies $\theta = 0.9102$. The value of the asset at this node is therefore $\varepsilon + 1/4$. At node B, if $\bar{I}_2 = 0.1308$ a similar calculation implies $\rho_2 = 1/2$, $\theta = 0.9102$, and an asset value of $1/4$. Note, in particular, that ρ is set differently at the two nodes, just as it is under rectangularity. At the initial node, we now have the problem of choosing δ to minimize $[(1+\delta)/2](\varepsilon + 1/4) + [(1-\delta)/2](1/4) = 1/4 + [(1+\delta)/2]\varepsilon$ subject to the entropy constraint $I_1(\delta) \le \bar{I}_1$. The first-order condition is

$$\varepsilon/2 + (\theta/2) \log[(1+\delta)/(1-\delta)] = 0.$$

If $\varepsilon = 1$ and $\bar{I} = 0.2616$, the solution includes $\delta = 1/2$, $\bar{I}_1 = 0.1308$, and $\theta = 0.9102$. As with rectangularity, the value is $1/2$. However, for other values of ε entropy will be reallocated between the two periods in the way that has the largest adverse impact on utility. If $0 \le \varepsilon < 1$, the risk between nodes (A) and (B) is relatively small and entropy will be shifted from period one to period two, increasing $|\rho_i|$ and decreasing $|\delta|$. If $\varepsilon > 1$, first-period risk is more important and entropy will be shifted from period two to period one, with the opposite effect. This reallocation of ambiguity has no counterpart with rectangularity, where the range of probabilities (and associated parameters) is unrelated to other aspects of the problem (the payoffs, for example, represented here by ε).

We have, then, four approaches to the same problem, each of which has arguments in its favor. The naive date-zero approach, which is in the spirit of Chamberlain's (2000) econometric application, allows less impact of ambiguity than the other approaches but does so in a way that remains consistent with a version of date-zero max-min preferences. It does place some importance, however, on the choice of date zero: if we reoptimize in the future, we would typically compute different decisions. The recursive approach, without rectangularity, might be justified as a game among agents at different dates. The same idea has been widely used in other contexts (the next section, for example). The rectangular approach is a clever way to reconcile date-zero and recursive approaches and leads to a natural recursive extension of Gilboa–Schmeidler. One puzzling consequence is that it can induce ambiguity in events that have none to begin with. (Recall the joint probability of the first and third paths in the dilation example, which is 1/2 regardless of ρ.) The apparent puzzle is resolved if we realize that the date-zero rectangular set does not represent date-zero ambiguity; it represents the date-zero probabilities needed to anticipate preferences over future ambiguity. Epstein and Schneider (2003, p 16) put it this way: "[T]here is an important conceptual distinction between the set of probability laws that the decision maker views as possible ... and the set of priors that is part of the representation of preference." Finally, the entropy approach allows the min to operate not only within a period but across periods, as entropy and ambiguity are allocated over time to have the greatest impact. This violates conditional independence for reasons similar to habits (Example 13) but seems consistent with the spirit of pessimism captured by the min in (34).

Example 18 (precautionary saving) Ambiguity generates precautionary saving through pessimism: pessimistic forecasts of future income reduce current consumption and raise current saving. The magnitude depends on the degree of ambiguity. We illustrate the result with a two-period example that shares several features with its robust control counterpart (Example 16). The endowment is y_0 at date zero and $y_1 \sim \mathrm{N}(\kappa_1 + \gamma, \kappa_2)$ at date one. The parameter γ governs ambiguity: $\gamma^2 \leq g^2$ for some positive number g. An agent has utility function

$$U = u(c_0) + \beta \min_{\gamma} Eu(c_1)$$

with $u(c) = -\exp(-\alpha c)$. The budget constraint is $c_1 = y_1 + r(y_0 - c_0)$. If we substitute this into the objective function and compute the expectation, we find

$$U = -\exp(-\alpha c_0) - \beta \min_{\gamma} \exp[-\alpha r(y_0 - c_0) - \alpha(\kappa_1 + \gamma) + \alpha^2\kappa_2/2].$$

The minimization implies $\gamma = -g$ (pessimism). The first-order condition for c_0 then implies

$$c_0 = \log(\beta r)/[\alpha(r-1)] + (ry_0 + \kappa_1)/(1+r) - \alpha\kappa_2/[2(1+r)] - g/(1+r).$$

Here the second term is permanent income, the third is risk and risk aversion, and the fourth the impact of ambiguity. [Adapted from Miao (2003).]

Example 19 (sharing ambiguity) If agents have identical homothetic preferences, optimal allocations are proportional: the ratio of date-state consumption by one agent is proportional to that of every other agent. In stationary settings, we often say (with some abuse of the language) that consumptions are perfectly correlated. Observations of individuals and countries, however, exhibit lower correlations, suggesting a risk-sharing puzzle. One line attack on this puzzle is to let agents have different preferences. In international economics, for example, we might let the two countries consume different goods. A variation on this theme is to let preferences differ in their degree of ambiguity. In particular, suppose agents have less ambiguity over their own endowment than over other agents' endowments. A symmetric two-period, two-agent example shows how this might work. Agent i has utility function

$$U^i = \log c_0^i + \beta \min_{\pi^i \in \Pi^i} \sum_z \pi^i(z) \log c_1^i(z),$$

for $i = 1, 2$. In period zero, each is endowed with one unit of the common good. In period one, there are four states (z) with the following endowments (y^i) and probabilities (π^i):

z	y^1	y^2	π^1	π^2	c^1	c^2
1	2	2	$1/4 - \gamma_1$	$1/4 - \gamma_2$	2	2
2	2	1	$1/4 + \gamma_1$	$1/4 - \gamma_2$	9/4	3/4
3	1	2	$1/4 - \gamma_1$	$1/4 + \gamma_2$	3/4	9/4
4	1	1	$1/4 + \gamma_1$	$1/4 + \gamma_2$	1	1

Each set Π^i is constructed from dogmatic priors over values for γ_i between $-1/8$ and $1/8$. Note that each agent is ambiguous about the other agent's endowment, but not her own. Without ambiguity ($\gamma_i = 0$), the symmetric optimal allocation consists of one-half the aggregate endowment in all states: perfect correlation across the date-one states. With ambiguity, agent i chooses the value of γ_i that minimizes her utility, $\gamma_i = 1/8$. Since agent 1 applies a lower probability (1/8) to state 3 than agent 2 (3/8), she gets a proportionally smaller share of the aggregate endowment in that state. The resulting allocations are listed in the table and show imperfect correlation across agents. The amount of ambiguity in this case is so large that in states 2 and 3 the agent with the larger endowment consumes even more than her endowment. A simple decentralization makes the same point. Suppose agents at date zero trade claims to the endowments of the two countries. How much would each invest in her own endowment, and how much in the other agent's endowment? If w is agent 1's investment in her own endowment, it satisfies

$$wy^1(z) + (1 - w)y^2(z) = c^1(z)$$

for all states z. The solution in this case is $w = 5/4$: agent 1 exhibits extreme home bias in her portfolio. [Adapted from Alonso (2004) and Epstein (2001).]

6.3 *Discussion: Detecting Ambiguity*

Preferences based on subjective probabilities capture interesting features of behavior that other preferences cannot, but they raise challenging issues for quantitative applications. Consider subjective expected utility. If we allow the probabilities that enter preferences (π) to differ from those that generate the data (p), we can "explain" many things that are otherwise puzzling. The equity premium, for example, could result from agents placing lower probability on high-return states than the data-generating process. It is precisely the lack of predictive content in such explanations that led us to rational expectations ($\pi = p$) in Sections 3 and 4.

Ambiguity provides a justification for systematically pessimistic probabilities—they're the minimizing choice from a larger set—but raises two new issues. One is how to specify the larger set of probabilities or models. Hansen and Sargent (2004) propose choosing models that have similar log-likelihood functions, much as we do in hypothesis tests. Differences between such models are presumably difficult to detect in finite data sets. Epstein and Schneider (2004) suggest nonstationary ambiguous models that are indistinguishable from a reference model, even in infinite samples. The other issue is observational equivalence: robust control and recursive multiple priors generate behavior that could have been generated by an expected utility agent, and possibly by a Kreps–Porteus agent as well. In some cases, the agent seems implausible, but in others it does not. Distinguishing between ambiguous and expected utility agents remains an active area of current research. The most ambitious example to date is Epstein and Schneider (2004), who note that ambiguous news has an unusual asymmetric affect on asset prices since bad news affects the minimizing probability distribution but good news does not.

7. Inconsistency and Temptation

Economists often tell stories about the hazards of temptation and the benefits of reducing our choice sets to avoid it. We eat too much junk food, we overconsume addictive substances, and we save too little. To counter these tendencies, we may put ourselves in situations where the range of choices limits our ability to make bad decisions. We go to restaurants that serve only healthy food, support laws that discourage or prohibit addictive substances, and sequester our wealth in housing and 401(k) accounts that are less easily used to finance current consumption. The outstanding questions are why we make such choices, what the relevant welfare criterion should be, and how we might detect the impact of temptation on observed decisions.

7.1 *Inconsistent Preferences*

The traditional approach was outlined in Example 4: dynamically inconsistent preferences. This line of research is motivated by experimental studies, which suggest that subjects discount the immediate future more rapidly than the distant future. Common practice is to approximate this pattern of discounting with the quasi-geometric or quasi-hyperbolic scheme: $1, \delta\beta, \delta\beta^2, \delta\beta^3$, and so on, with $0 < \beta < 1$ and $0 < \delta \leq 1$. The critical parameter is δ: if $\delta < 1$, the discount factor between dates $t = 0$ and $t = 1$ (namely, $\delta\beta$) is less than the discount factor between dates $t = 1$ and $t = 2$ (β).

Let us say, then, that an agent's utility from date t on is

$$\begin{aligned} U_t &= E_t[u(c_t) + \delta\beta u(c_{t+1}) + \delta\beta^2 u(c_{t+2}) + \delta\beta^3 u(c_{t+3}) + \cdots] \\ &= u(c_t) + \delta\beta E_t \sum_{j=0}^{\infty} \beta^j u(c_{t+j+1}). \end{aligned}$$

The only difference from Example 4 is the introduction of uncertainty implicit in the conditional expectation E_t. The dynamic inconsistency of these preferences suggests two questions: With competing preferences across dates, what does such an agent do? And what preferences should we use for welfare analysis? We need an answer to the first question to derive the behavioral implications of inconsistent preferences, and an answer to the second to evaluate the benefits of policies that limit choice.

The consensus answer to the first question has become: treat the problem as a game with the agent at each date acting as a separate player. Each such player makes choices that maximize her utility, given the actions of other players (herself at other dates). There are many games like this, corresponding to different strategy spaces. We look at stationary Markov perfect equilibria, in which agents' decisions are stationary functions of the current state for some natural definition of the state. Consider the classical consumption problem with budget constraint $a_{t+1} = r_{t+1}(a_t - c_t) + y_{t+1}$, where y and r are iid positive random variables, and a borrowing constraint $a \geq \underline{a}$ that we will ignore. Our objective is a stationary decision rule $c_t = h(a_t)$ that solves the game. With constant discounting ($\delta = 1$), the problem is the solution to the dynamic programming problem summarized by the Bellman equation,

$$J(a) = \max_c \ u(c) + \beta E J[r'(a-c) + y'].$$

Under standard conditions, J exists and is unique, continuous, concave, and differentiable. Given such a J, the maximization leads to a continuous stationary decision rule $c = h(a)$.

The equilibrium of a game can be qualitatively different. A stationary decision rule can be derived with a future value function

$$J(a) = u(c^*) + \beta E J[r'(a-c^*) + y'], \tag{37}$$

where

$$c^* = \arg\max_c \ u(c) + \delta\beta E J[r'(a-c) + y']. \tag{38}$$

Note the difference: when $\delta < 1$, the relation that generates J is different from that generating the choice of c. As a result, the decision rule need not be unique or continuous; see Harris and Laibson (2001), Krusell and Smith (2004), and Morris and Postlewaite (1997). For all of these reasons, there can be no general observational equivalence result between constant and quasi-geometric discounting. Nevertheless, the solutions are similar in some common examples.

Example 20 (consumption and saving) Consider the classical saving problem with log utility ($u(c) = \log c$), budget constraint $a_{t+1} =$

$r_{t+1}(a_t - c_t)$ (no labor income), and log-normal return ($\{\log r_t\} \sim \text{NID}(\mu, \sigma^2)$). With quasi-geometric discounting, we compute the stationary decision rule from:

$$J(a) = \log c^* + \beta EJ[r'(a - c^*)]$$

$$c^* = \arg\max_c \log c + \delta\beta EJ[r'(a - c)].$$

We find the solution by guessing that the value function has the form $J(a) = A + B \log a$. The first-order condition from the maximization implies $c = (1 + \delta\beta B)^{-1} a$. Substituting into the recursion for J, we find $B = (1 - \beta)^{-1}$ and

$$c = \left(\frac{1 - \beta}{1 - \beta + \delta\beta}\right) a = h(a).$$

Compare this decision rule with two others:

• *Constant discounting.* The decision rule with constant discounting is $c = (1 - \beta)a$ (set $\delta = 1$). Note that with quasi-geometric discounting the agent consumes more, but not as much more as an agent with constant discount factor $\beta\delta$. The latter is the result of strategic interactions between agents. The data-t agent would like to save a fraction $\delta\beta$ of her assets at date t, and a larger fraction β at future dates $t + n > t$. She knows, however, that future agents will make the same calculation and choose saving rates less than β. To induce future agents to consume more (absolutely, not as a fraction of wealth), she saves more than $\delta\beta$ today. Note, too, that her consumption behavior is observationally equivalent to an agent with constant discount factor

$$\hat{\beta} = \frac{\delta\beta}{1 - \beta + \delta\beta} < \beta.$$

A similar result holds for power utility and suggests that, despite the difficulties noted earlier, constant and quasi-geometric discounting may be difficult to distinguish in practice.

• *Commitment.* Suppose the date-t agent can choose decision rules for future agents. Since the agent's discount factor between any future dates $t + n > t$ and $t + n + 1$ is β, she chooses the decision rules $c_t = (1 - \delta\beta)a_t$ for date t and $c_{t+n} = (1 - \beta)a_{t+n}$ for all future dates $t + n > t$. This allocation maximizes the utility of the date-t agent, so in that sense commitment (limiting our future choice sets) is good. But it's not clear that date-t preferences are the appropriate welfare criterion.

[Adapted from Barro (1999); İmrohoğlu, İmrohoğlu, and Joines (2003); and Phelps and Pollack (1968).]

Example 21 (asset pricing) A similar example can be used to illustrate the role of quasi-geometric discounting on asset prices. The first step is to derive the appropriate Euler equation for equations (37) and (38). Define the current value function by

$$L(a) = \max_{c} \ u(c) + \delta\beta EJ[r'(a-c) + y']. \tag{39}$$

The first-order and envelope conditions are

$$u_1(c) = \delta\beta E[J_1(a')r']$$

$$L_1(a) = \delta\beta E[J_1(a')r'],$$

implying the familiar $L_1(a) = u_1(c)$. In the constant discounting case, $J(a) = L(a)$ and we're almost done. With quasi-geometric discounting, we need another method to express J_1 in terms of u_1. If we multiply (37) by δ and subtract from (39), we can relate J to L and u: $\delta J(a) = L(a) - (1-\delta)u(c)$. Differentiating yields

$$\delta J_1(a) = L_1(a) - (1-\delta)u_1(c)h_1(a).$$

If we multiply by β and substitute into the first-order condition, we get the Euler equation,

$$u(c_t) = E_t\{\beta[1-(1-\delta)h_1(a_{t+1})]u_1(c_{t+1})r_{t+1}\}.$$

This relation is a curious object: it depends not only on the current agent's decision problem, but (through h) on the strategic interactions among agents. The primary result is to decrease the effective discount factor, and raise mean asset returns, relative to the standard model. [Adapted from Harris and Laibson (2003); Krusell, Kuruşçu, and Smith (2002); and Luttmer and Mariotti (2003).]

7.2 *Temptation*

Many of us have been in situations in which we felt we had too many choices. (Zabar's Delicatessen and Beer World have that effect on us.) In traditional decision theory, this statement is nonsense: extra choices are at best neutral because you can always decide not to use them. Gul and Pesendorfer (2001) give the phrase meaning: they develop preferences in which adding inferior choices (temptations) can leave you worse off. Among its features: utility can depend on the set of choices, as well as the action taken; temptation (in the sense of inferior choices) can reduce utility; and commitment (in the sense of restricting the choice set) can increase utility. We describe their theory in a static setting, then go on to explore dynamic extensions, including some that resemble quasi-geometric discounting.

Let us compare two sets of choices, A and B. In traditional decision theory, the utility of a set of possible choices is the utility of its best element. If the best element of A is at least as good as the best element of B, then we would say A is weakly preferred to B: $A \succeq B$ in standard notation. Suppose we allow choice over the potentially larger set $A \cup B$. The traditional approach would tell us that this cannot have an impact on our decision or utility: if $A \succeq B$, then we are indifferent between A and $A \cup B$. Gul and Pesendorfer suggest a *set betweenness* condition that allows inferior choices to affect our preference ordering:

$$A \succeq B \qquad \text{implies} \qquad A \succeq A \cup B \succeq B.$$

The traditional answer is one extreme (namely, $A \sim A \cup B$), but set betweenness also allows inferior choices B to reduce our utility ($A \succ A \cup B$). We say in such cases that B is a temptation.

Adding set betweenness to an otherwise traditional theory, Gul and Pesendorfer show that preferences can be represented by a utility function of the form:

$$u(A) = \max_{c \in A}[v(c) + w(c)] - \max_{c \in A} w(c). \tag{40}$$

Note that preferences are defined for the choice set A; we have abandoned the traditional separation between preferences and opportunities. To see how this works, compare the choices $c^* = \arg\max_{c \in A} \cdot [v(c) + w(c)]$ and $c^{**} = \arg\max_{c \in A} w(c)$ for some choice set A. If $c^* = c^{**}$, then v and w agree on A and preferences are effectively governed by v (the w terms cancel). If not, then w acts as a temptation function.

Example 22 (consumption and saving) A clever use of temptations reproduces quasi-geometric discounting. Let

$$v(c_1, c_2) = u(c_1) + \beta u(c_2)$$

$$w(c_1, c_2) = \gamma[u(c_1) + \delta\beta u(c_2)],$$

with $0 < \delta < 1$ and $\gamma \geq 0$ (intensity of temptation). The budget constraint has two parts: $c_1 + k_2 = rk_1$ and $c_2 = rk_2$, with k_1 given, which defines A. The agent solves

$$\max_{c_1, c_2 \in A} [(1+\gamma)u(c_1) + (1+\gamma\delta)\beta u(c_2)] - \max_{c_1, c_2 \in A} \gamma[u(c_1) + \delta\beta u(c_2)].$$

The first max delivers the first-order condition:

$$1 = \left(\frac{1+\gamma\delta}{1+\gamma}\right)\beta\frac{u_1(c_2)}{u_1(c_1)}r.$$

The difference from the standard model lies in the first term. The two extremes are $\gamma = 0$ (which gives us the standard no-temptation model) and $\gamma = \infty$ (which gives us an irresistible temptation and the quasi-geometric discount factor $\delta\beta$). Since the term is decreasing in γ, greater temptation raises first-period consumption. [Adapted from Krusell, Kuruşçu, and Smith (2001).]

Gul and Pesendorfer (2002, 2004) and Krusell, Kuruşçu, and Smith (2001) have extended the temptation approach to quasi-geometric discounting to infinite-horizon settings. We illustrate the idea with a nonstochastic version of the consumption problem. Krusell, Kuruşçu, and Smith suggest an approach summarized by the "Bellman equation"

$$J(a) = \max_c \{u(c) + \beta J[r(a-c)] + L[r(a-c)]\} - \max_c L[r(a-c)],$$

where

$$L(a) = \gamma\{u(c^*) + \delta\beta L[r(a-c^*)]\}$$

serves as a temptation function and $c^* = \arg\max_c u(c) + \beta J[r(a-c)] + L[r(a-c)]$. Gul and Pesendorfer suggest the special case $\delta = 0$. The Krusell–Kuruşçu–Smith version reproduces the first-order conditions and decision rules generated by the Markov perfect equilibrium for quasi-geometic discounting. The Gul–Pesendorfer version avoids some of the mathematical oddities associated with the former. Each suggests an answer to the welfare question.

7.3 *Discussion: Detecting Inconsistency and Temptation*

The difficulty of estimating the parameters of models based on quasi-geometric discounting is that the decision rules often look like those from traditional models with constant discounting. In some cases, they're identical. One way to distinguish between them is to look for evidence of commitment. Agents with inconsistent preferences or temptations will typically be willing to pay something to restrict their future choice sets. In models with constant discounting, there is no such incentive, so commitment devices provide a natural way to tell the two approaches apart. Laibson, Repetto, and Tobacman (1998, 2004) apply this logic and find that the combination of illiquid asset positions (pensions, 401(k) accounts) and high-interest liabilities (credit card debt) generates sharp differences between the two models and precise estimates of the discount parameters ($\delta = 0.70$, $\beta = 0.96$, annual). With constant discounting, borrowing at high rates and investing at (on average) lower rates are incompatible.

The focus on commitment devices seems right to us, both for quasi-geometric discounting and for temptations more generally. There are some outstanding questions, however, most of them noted by Kocherlakota (2001). One is whether tax-sheltered savings have other explanations (lower taxes, for example). If 401(k) plans were a pure commitment device, we might expect people to pay more for them and receive less, but this doesn't seem to be the case: sheltered and unsheltered investment vehicles have pretty much the same returns. Similarly, if commitment is valuable, why would an agent hold both liquid (uncommitted) and illiquid (committed) assets? The former would seem to undercut the bite of the latter. Finally, what is the likely market response to the conflicting demands of commitment and temptation? Will the market supply commitment devices or ways to avoid them? Is credit card debt designed to satisfy agents' desire to undo past commitments? Does it lower welfare? Perhaps future work will resolve these questions.

8. Questions, Answers, and Final Thoughts

We have described a wide range of exotic preferences and applied them to a number of classic macroeconomic problems. Are there any general lessons we might draw from this effort? We organize a discussion around specific questions.

8.1 Why Model Preferences Rather Than Behavior?

Preferences play two critical roles in economic models. The first is that they provide, in principle, an unchanging feature of a model in which agents can be confronted with a wide range of different environments, institutions, or policies. For each environment, we derive behavior (decision rules) from the same preferences. If we modeled behavior directly, we would also have to model how it adjusted to changing circumstances. The second role of preferences is to evaluate the welfare effects of changing policies or circumstances. Without preferences, it's not clear how we should distinguish good policies from bad. In our view, this is a major accomplishment of the temptation interpretation of quasi-geometric discounting: it suggests a clear welfare criterion.

8.2 *Are Exotic Preferences Simply an Excuse for Free Parameters?*

Theoretical economists think nothing of modifying the environments faced by their agents. Aggregate and individual risk, length of life, information structures, enforcement technologies, and productivity shocks are all fair game. However, many economists seem to believe that modifying preferences is cheating—that we will be able to explain anything (and hence nothing) if we allow ourselves enough freedom over preferences. We would argue instead that we have restricted ourselves to an extremely limited model of preferences for no better reasons than habit and convenience. Many of the weaknesses of expected utility, for example, have been obvious since the 1950s. We now have the tools to move beyond additive preferences in several directions. Why not use them?

Equally important, the axiomatic foundations that underlie the preferences described above impose a great deal of discipline on their structure. We have let these foundations go largely without mention, but they nevertheless restrict the kinds of flexibility we've considered. Chew–Dekel risk preferences, for example, are more flexible than expected utility, but they are far less flexible than general preferences over state-contingent claims. One consequence: exotic preferences have led to some progress on the many empirical puzzles that plague macroeconomics and finance, but they have yet to resolve them.

Some exotic preferences make greater—or at least novel—demands on the data than we are used to. Kreps–Porteus and Epstein–Zin preferences, for example, require time-dependence of risk to identify separate time and risk preference parameters. Robust control comes with an entropy toolkit for setting plausible values of the robustness parameter, but comparisons across environments may be needed to distinguish robust from risk-sensitive control. Applications of temptation preferences to problems with quasi-geometric discounting rely heavily (entirely?) on observed implications of commitment devices, about which there is some difference of opinion. In short, exotic preferences raise new empirical issues that deserve open and honest debate. We see no reason, however, to rule out departures from additive utility before we start.

8.3 *Are Exotic Preferences Behavioral?*

Many of the preferences we've described were motivated by discrepancies between observed behavior and the predictions of the additive preference model. In that sense, they have a behaviorial basis. They are also well-defined neoclassical preference orderings. For that reason, we think our approach falls more naturally into neoclassical economics than into the behavioral sciences.

We regard this as both a strength and a weakness. On the one hand, the strong theoretical foundations for exotic preferences allow us to use all the tools of neoclassical economics, particularly optimization and welfare analysis. On the other hand, these tools ignore aspects of human behavior stressed in other social sciences, particularly sociology and social psychology. Kreps (2000) and (especially) Simon (1959) are among the many economists who have argued that something of this sort is needed to account for some aspects of behavior. We have some sympathy for this argument, but it's not what we've done in this paper.

8.4 *Are There Interesting Preferences We've Missed?*

If you've gotten this far, you may feel that we can't possibly have left anything out. But it's not true. We barely scratched the surface of robust control, ambiguity, hyperbolic discounting, and temptation. If you'd like to know more, you might start with the papers listed in Appendix 9.1. We also ignored some lines of work altogether. Among them are:

• *Incomplete preferences.* Some of the leading decision theorists suggest that the most troubling axiom underlying expected utility is not the infamous independence axiom but the more common assumption of completeness: that all possible choices can be compared. Schmeidler (1989), for example, argues that the critical role of the independence axiom is to extend preferences from choices that seem obvious to those that do not—that it delivers completeness. For this and other reasons, there is a long history of work on incomplete preferences. Notable applications in macroeconomics and finance include Bewley (1986) and Kraus and Sagi (2002, 2004).

• *Flexibility, commitment, and self-control.* Kreps (1979) describes environments in which agents prefer to maintain flexibility over future choices, just as agents with temptations prefer commitment. Amador, Werning, and Angeletos (2003) characterize optimal allocation rules when you put the two together. Ameriks, Caplin, Leahy, and Tyler (2004) quantify self-control with survey evidence and relate it to individual financial decisions. Benhabib and Bisin (2004) take a cognitive approach to a similar problem in which agents choose between automatic processes, which are subject to temptations, and control processes, which are not.

• *Social utility.* Experimental research suggests that preferences often depend on comparisons with others; see, for example, Blount (1995) and Rabin (1998). Abel (1990) and Galí (1994) present well-known applications to asset pricing.

• *Other psychological approaches.* Bénabou and Tirole (2002) model self-confidence. Bernheim and Rangel (2002) build a cognitive model and apply it to addiction. Brunnermeier and Parker (2003) propose a model of subjective beliefs in which agents balance the utility benefits of optimism and the utility cost of inferior decisions. Caplin and Leahy (2001) introduce anxiety into an otherwise standard dynamic choice frame work and explore its implications for portfolio choice and the equity premium.

We find all of this work interesting, but leave a serious assessment of it to others.

8.5 *Have We Wasted Your Time (and Ours)?*

It's too late, of course, but you might ask yourself whether this has been worth the effort. To paraphrase Monty Python, "Have we deliberately wasted your time?" We hope not. We would guess that additive preferences will continue to be the industry standard in macroeconomics, finance, and other fields. Their tight structure leads to strong and clear predictions, which is generally a virtue. But we would also guess that exotic preferences will become more common, particularly in quantitative work. Who knows? They may even lose their claim to being "exotic."

We think several varieties of exotic preferences have already proved themselves. Applications of Kreps–Porteus and Epstein–Zin preferences to asset pricing, precautionary saving, and risk-sharing are good examples. While these preferences have not solved all of our problems, they have become a frequent source of insight. Their ease of use in econometric work is another point in their favor.

The preferences described in the last three sections are closer to the current frontiers of research, but we are optimistic that they, too, will lead to deeper understanding of economic behavior. Certainly robust control, recursive multiple priors, and temptation are significant additions to our repertoire. They also raise new questions about identification and estimation. Multiple priors is a good example. When the probabilities affecting an agent's preferences are not characterized simply by the probabilities generating the data, we need to parameterize the agent's uncertainty and describe how it evolves through time. We also need to explore ways to distinguish such agents from those with expected utility or Kreps–Porteus preferences. Temptation is another. As a profession, we need to clarify the features of data that identify the parameters of temptation functions, as well as the kinds of temptations that are most useful in applied work. None of these tasks is simple, but we think the progress of the last decade gives us reason to hope for more.

Let's get to work!

9. Appendixes

9.1 *Reader's Guide*

We have intentionally favored application over theory, but if you'd like to know more about the theoretical underpinnings of exotic preferences, we recommend the following:

Section 2. Koopmans (1960) is the classic reference. Koopmans (1986) lays out the relevant theory of independent preferences. Lucas and Stokey (1984) approach the problem from what now seems like a more natural direction: they start with an aggregator function, while Koopmans derives one. Epstein and Hynes (1983) propose a convenient functional form and work through an extensive set of examples.

Section 3. Kreps (1988) is far and away the best reference we've seen for the theory underlying the various approaches to expected utility. Starmer (2000) gives a less technical overview of the theory and discusses both empirical anomalies and modifications of the theory designed to deal with them. Brandenburger (2002) describes some quite different approaches to probability assessments that have been used in game theory.

Section 4. Our two favorite theory references on dynamic choice in risky environments are Kreps and Porteus (1978) and Johnsen and Donaldson (1985). Epstein and Zin (1989) describe the technical issues involved in specifying stationary recursive preferences and explain the roles of the parameters of the constant elasticity version.

Section 5. Our primary reference is Hansen and Sargent's (2004) monograph on robust control; we recommend Chapters 2 (overview), 5 (static robust control), 6 (dynamic robust control), and 9 and 17 (entropy constraints). Whittle (1990) is an introduction to linear-quadratic robust control for engineers. Hansen and Sargent (1997) introduce risk-sensitive control in Chapters 9 and 15. Gianonni (2002), Maenhout (2004), Onatski and Williams (2003), and Van Nieuwerburgh (2001) are interesting applications.

Section 6. The essential references are Gilboa and Schmeidler (1989) and Epstein and Schneider (2003). Among the other papers we have found useful are Ahn (2003); Casadesus-Masanell, Klibanoff, and Ozdenoren (2000); Chamberlain (2000); Epstein and Schneider (2002, 2004); Gilboa and Schmeidler (1993); Hayashi (2003); Klibanoff, Marinacci, and Mukerji (2003); Sagi (2003); Schmeidler (1989); and Wang (2003).

Section 7. The relevant theory is summarized in Gul and Pesendorfer (2004); Harris and Laibson (2003); and Krusell, Kuruşçu, and Smith (2001). DeJong and Ripoll (2003); Esteban, Miyagawa, and Shum (2004); and Krusell, Kuruşçu, and Smith (2002) are interesting applications.

9.2 *Integral Formulas*

A number of our examples lead to normal-exponential integrals, most commonly as expectations of log-normal random variables or exponential certainty equivalents of normal random variables. The following definitions and formulas are used in the paper.

Standard normal density and distribution functions. If $x \sim \mathrm{N}(0,1)$, its density is $f(x) = (2\pi)^{-1/2}e^{-x^2/2}$. Note that f is symmetric: $f(x) = f(-x)$. The distribution function is $\Phi(x) \equiv \int_{-\infty}^{x} f(u)\,du$. By symmetry, $\int_x^{\infty} f(u)\,du = 1 - \Phi(x) = \Phi(-x)$.

Integrals of "$e^{a+bx}f(x)$." We come across integrals of this form in Section 3, when we compute certainty equivalents for log-normal risks, and Section 4, when we consider the exponential certainty equivalent of a linear value function (Weil's model of precautionary saving). Evaluation follows from a change of variables. Consider the integral:

$$\int_{-\infty}^{x^*} e^{a+bx}f(x)\,dx = (2\pi)^{-1/2}\int_{-\infty}^{x^*} e^{a+bx-x^2/2}\,dx.$$

We solve this by completing the square: expressing the exponent as $a + bx - x^2/2 = d - y^2/2$, where d is a scalar and $y = fx - g$ is a linear transformation of x. We find $y = x - b$ ($f = 1, g = b$) and $d = a + b^2/2$, so the integral is

$$\begin{aligned}(2\pi)^{-1/2}\int_{-\infty}^{x^*} e^{a+bx-x^2/2}\,dx &= e^{a+b^2/2}\int_{-\infty}^{x^*-b} f(y)\,dy \\ &= e^{a+b^2/2}\Phi(x^* - b). \qquad (41)\end{aligned}$$

A common special case has an infinite upper limit of integration:

$$E(e^{a+bx}) = (2\pi)^{-1/2}\int_{-\infty}^{\infty} e^{a+bx-x^2/2}\,dx = e^{a+b^2/2}. \qquad (42)$$

As an example, let $\log y = \mu + \sigma x$; then $Ey = E(e^{\log y}) = E(e^{\mu+\sigma x}) = e^{\mu+\sigma^2/2}$.

Integrals of "$e^{a+bx+cx^2}f(x)$." Integrals like this arise in Section 5 in risk-sensitive control with a quadratic objective. Consider

$$\int_{-\infty}^{\infty} e^{a+bx+cx^2}f(x)\,dx = (2\pi)^{-1/2}\int_{-\infty}^{\infty} e^{a+bx-(1-2c)x^2/2}\,dx.$$

We assume $1 - 2c > 0$; otherwise the integral diverges. We solve by the same method: express the exponent as $a + bx - (1-2c)x^2/2 = d - y^2/2$ for some $y = fx - g$. We find $f = (1-2c)^{1/2}$, $g = b/(1-2c)^{1/2}$, and $d = a + b^2/(1-2c)$, so that $y = (1-2c)^{1/2}x - b/(1-2c)^{1/2}$. The integral becomes

$$\begin{aligned}\int_{-\infty}^{\infty} e^{a+bx+cx^2}f(x)\,dx &= (1-2c)^{-1/2}e^{a+b^2/[2(1-2c)]}\int_{-\infty}^{\infty} f(y)\,dy \\ &= (1-2c)^{-1/2}e^{a+b^2/[2(1-2c)]}. \qquad (43)\end{aligned}$$

Note

We are unusually grateful to the many people who made suggestions and answered questions while we worked through this enormous body of work. Deserving special mention are Mark Gertler, Lars Hansen, Tom Sargent, Rob Shimer, Tony Smith, Iván Werning, Noah Williams, and especially Martin Schneider. We also thank Pierre Collin-Dusfresne, Kfir Eliaz, Larry Epstein, Anjela Kniazeva, Per Krusell, David Laibson, John Leahy, Tom Tallarini, Stijn Van Nieuwerburgh, and seminar participants at Carnegie Mellon University and New York University.

References

Abel, Andrew B. (1990). Asset pricing under habit formation and keeping up with the Joneses. *American Economic Review (Papers and Proceedings)* 80:38–42.

Ahn, David. (2003). Ambiguity without a state space. Unpublished Manuscript. September.

Alonso, Irasema. (2004). Ambiguity in a two-country world. Unpublished Manuscript. March.

Amador, Manuel, Iván Werning, and George-Marios Angeletos. (2003). Commitment vs. flexibility. NBER Working Paper No. 10151. December.

Ameriks, John, Andrew Caplin, John Leahy, and Tom Tyler. (2004). Measuring self control. NBER Working Paper No. 10514. May.

Anderson, Evan W. (2004). The dynamics of risk-sensitive allocations. Unpublished Manuscript. February.

Anderson, Evan W., Lars Peter Hansen, Ellen R. McGrattan, and Thomas J. Sargent. (1996). Mechanics of forming and estimating dynamic linear economies. In *Handbook of Computational Economics* (Volume 1), H. Amman, D. A. Kendrick, and J. Rust (eds.). Amsterdam: Elsevier.

Bansal, Ravi, and Amir Yaron. (2004). Risks for the long run: A potential resolution of asset pricing puzzles. *Journal of Finance* 59:1481–1509.

Barro, Robert J. (1999). Ramsey meets Laibson in the neoclassical growth model. *Quarterly Journal of Economics* 114:1125–1152.

Bénabou, Roland, and Jean Tirole. (2002). Self-confidence and personal motivation. *Quarterly Journal of Economics* 115:871–915.

Benhabib, Jess, and Alberto Bisin. (2004). Modeling internal commitment mechanisms and self-control: A neuroeconomics approach to consumption-saving decisions. Unpublished Manuscript. February.

Bernheim, B. Douglas, and Antonio Rangel. (2002). Addiction and cue-conditioned cognitive processes. NBER Working Paper No. 9329. November.

Bewley, Truman F. (1986). Knightian decision theory: Part I. Cowles Foundation Discussion Paper No. 807. November.

Blount, Sally. (1995). When social outcomes aren't fair. *Organizational Behavior and Human Decision Processes* 63(August):131–144.

Brandenburger, Adam. (2002). The power of paradox. Unpublished Manuscript. December.

Brunnermeier, Markus K., and Jonathan A. Parker. (2003). Optimal expectations. Unpublished Manuscript. June.

Caplin, Andrew, and John Leahy. (2001). Psychological expected utility theory and anticipatory feelings. *Quarterly Journal of Economics* 116:55–79.

Casadesus-Masanell, Ramon, Peter Klibanoff, and Emre Ozdenoren. (2000). Maxmin expected utility over Savage acts with a set of priors. *Journal of Economic Theory* 92:35–65.

Chamberlain, Gary. (2000). Econometric applications of maxmin expected utility. *Journal of Applied Econometrics* 15:625–644.

Chew, Soo Hong. (1983). A generalization of the quasi-linear mean with applications to the measurement of inequality and decision theory resolving the Allais paradox. *Econometrica* 51:1065–1092.

Chew, Soo Hong. (1989). Axiomatic utility theories with the betweenness property. *Annals of Operations Research* 19:273–298.

DeJong, David, and Marla Ripoll. (2003). Self-control preferences and the volatility of stock prices. Unpublished Manuscript. April.

Dekel, Eddie. (1986). An axiomatic characterization of preferences uncer uncertainty: Weakening the independence axiom. *Journal of Economic Theory* 40:304–318.

Dolmas, Jim, and Mark A. Wynne. (1998). Elastic capital supply and the effects of fiscal policy. *Economic Inquiry* 36:553–574.

Dow, James, and Sérgio Ribeiro da Costa Werlang. (1992). Uncertainty aversion, risk aversion, and the optimal choice of portfolio. *Econometrica* 60:197–204.

Epstein, Larry G. (2001). Sharing ambiguity. *American Economic Review (Papers and Proceedings)* 91:45–50.

Epstein, Larry G., and J. Allan Hynes. (1983). The rate of time preference and dynamic economic analysis. *Journal of Political Economy* 91:611–635.

Epstein, Larry G., and Martin Schneider. (2002). Learning under ambiguity. Unpublished Manuscript. September.

Epstein, Larry G., and Martin Schneider. (2003). Recursive multiple-priors. *Journal of Economic Theory* 113:1–31.

Epstein, Larry G., and Martin Schneider. (2004). Ambiguity, information quality, and asset pricing. Unpublished Manuscript. May.

Epstein, Larry G., and Stanley E. Zin. (1989). Substitution, risk aversion, and the temporal behavior of consumption and asset returns: A theoretical framework. *Econometrica* 57:937–969.

Epstein, Larry G., and Stanley E. Zin. (1990). "First-order" risk aversion and the equity premium puzzle. *Journal of Monetary Economics* 26:387–407.

Epstein, Larry G., and Stanley E. Zin. (1991). Substitution, risk aversion, and the temporal behavior of consumption and asset returns: An empirical analysis. *Journal of Political Economy* 99:263–286.

Epstein, Larry G., and Stanley E. Zin. (2001). The independence axiom and asset returns. *Journal of Empirical Finance* 8:537–572.

Esteban, Susanna, Eiichi Miyagawa, and Matthew Shum. (2004). Nonlinear pricing with self-control preferences. Unpublished Manuscript. March.

Farmer, Roger E. A. (1990). Rince preferences. *Quarterly Journal of Economics* 105:43–60.

Galí, Jordi. (1994). Keeping up with the Joneses: Consumption externalities, portfolio choice, and asset prices. *Journal of Money, Credit, and Banking* 26:1–8.

Gertler, Mark. (1999). Government debt and social security in a life-cycle economy. *Carnegie-Rochester Conference Series on Public Policy* 50:61–110.

Giannoni, Marc P. (2002). Does model uncertainty justify caution? Robust optimal monetary policy in a forward-looking model. *Macroeconomic Dynamics* 6:111–144.

Gilboa, Itzhak, and David Schmeidler. (1989). Maxmin expected utility with non-unique priors. *Journal of Mathematical Economics* 18:141–153.

Gilboa, Itzhak, and David Schmeidler. (1993). Updating ambiguous beliefs. *Journal of Economic Theory* 59:33–49.

Gul, Faruk. (1991). A theory of disappointment aversion. *Econometrica* 59:667–686.

Gul, Faruk, and Wolfgang Pesendorfer. (2001). Temptation and self-control. *Econometrica* 69:1403–1435.

Gul, Faruk, and Wolfgang Pesendorfer. (2002). Self-control and the theory of consumption. Unpublished Manuscript. November. Forthcoming *Econometrica.*

Gul, Faruk, and Wolfgang Pesendorfer. (2004). Self-control, revealed preference, and consumption choice. *Review of Economic Dynamics* 7:243–264.

Hansen, Lars Peter. (1982). Large sample properties of generalized method of moments estimators. *Econometrica* 50:1029–1054.

Hansen, Lars Peter, and Thomas J. Sargent. (1997). "Recursive models of dynamic linear economies." Unpublished Manuscript. December.

Hansen, Lars Peter, and Thomas J. Sargent. (2004). "Misspecification in recursive macroeconomic theory." Unpublished Manuscript. January.

Hansen, Lars Peter, Thomas J. Sargent, and Thomas Tallarini. (1999). Robust permanent income and pricing. *Review of Economic Studies* 66:873–907.

Hansen, Lars Peter, Thomas J. Sargent, and Neng E. Wang. (2002). Robust permanent income and pricing with filtering. *Macroeconomic Dynamics* 6:40–84.

Harris, Christopher, and David Laibson. (2001). Dynamic choices of hyperbolic consumers. *Econometrica* 69:935–957.

Harris, Christopher, and David Laibson. (2003). Hyperbolic discounting and consumption. *Advances in Economics and Econometrics*. Cambridge UK: Cambridge University Press.

Hayashi, Takashi. (2003). Intertemporal substitution, risk aversion, and ambiguity aversion. Unpublished Manuscript. December.

İmrohoğlu, Ayşe, Selahattin İmrohoğlu, and Douglas H. Joines. (2003). Time-inconsistent preferences and social security. *Quarterly Journal of Economics* 118:745–784.

Johnsen, Thore H., and John B. Donaldson. (1985). The structure of intertemporal preferences under uncertainty and time consistent plans. *Econometrica* 53:1451–1458.

Kan, Rui. (1995). Structure of Pareto optima when agents have stochastic recursive preferences. *Journal of Economic Theory* 64:626–631.

Klibanoff, Peter, Massimo Marinacci, and Sujoy Mukerji. (2003). A smooth model of decision making under ambiguity. Unpublished Manuscript. April.

Kocherlakota, Narayana R. (1990). Disentangling the coefficient of relative risk aversion from the elasticity of intertemporal substitution. *Journal of Finance* 45:175–190.

Kocherlakota, Naryana R. (2001). Looking for evidence of time-inconsistent preferences in asset-market data. *Federal Reserve Bank of Minneapolis Quarterly Review* 25(Summer):13–24.

Koopmans, Tjalling C. (1960). Stationary ordinal utility and impatience. *Econometrica* 28:287–309.

Koopmans, Tjalling C. (1986). Representation of preference orderings with independent components of consumption, and Representation of preference orderings over time. In *Decision and Organization* (2d ed.), C. B. McGuire and Roy Radner (eds.). Minneapolis, MN: University of Minnesota Press.

Kraus, Alan, and Jacob S. Sagi. (2002). Intertemporal preference for flexibility and risky choice. Unpublished Manuscript. November.

Kraus, Alan, and Jacob S. Sagi. (2004). Asset pricing with unforseen contingencies. Unpublished Manuscript. March.

Kreps, David M. (1979). A representation theorem for "preference for flexibility." *Econometrica* 47:565–578.

Kreps, David M. (1988). *Notes on the Theory of Choice*. Boulder, CO: Westview Press.

Kreps, David M. (2000). Beliefs and tastes: Confessions of an economist. Remarks made at the AAU Centennial Meeting. October.

Kreps, David M., and Evan L. Porteus. (1978). Temporal resolution of uncertainty and dynamic choice theory. *Econometrica* 46:185–200.

Krusell, Per, Bruhanettin Kuruşçu, and Anthony A. Smith. (2001). Temptation and taxation. Unpublished Manuscript. June.

Krusell, Per, Bruhanettin Kuruşçu, and Anthony A. Smith. (2002). Time orientation and asset prices. *Journal of Monetary Economics* 49:107–135.

Krusell, Per, and Anthony A. Smith. (2004). Consumption-saving decisions with quasi-geometric discounting. *Econometrica* 71:365–375.

Kydland, Finn E., and Edward C. Prescott. (1977). Rules rather than discretion: The inconsistency of optimal plans. *Journal of Political Economy* 85:473–492.

Laibson, David, Andrea Repetto, and Jeremy Tobacman. (1998). Self-control and saving for retirement. *Brookings Papers on Economic Activity* (1):91–196.

Laibson, David, Andrea Repetto, and Jeremy Tobacman. (2004). Estimating discount functions from lifecycle consumption choices. Unpublished Manuscript. January.

Lettau, Martin, Sydney C. Ludvigson, and Jessica A. Wachter. (2003). The declining equity premium: What role does macroeconomic risk play? Unpublished Manuscript. September.

Ljungqvist, Lars, and Thomas J. Sargent. (2000). *Recursive Macroeconomic Theory*. Cambridge MA: MIT Press.

Lucas, Robert E., and Nancy L. Stokey. (1984). Optimal growth with many consumers. *Journal of Economic Theory* 32:139–171.

Luttmer, Erzo, and Thomas Mariotti. (2003). Subjective discounting in an exchange economy. *Journal of Political Economy* 111:959–989.

Maenhout, Pascal J. (2004). Robust portfolio rules and asset pricing. *Review of Financial Studies*, forthcoming.

Mendoza, Enrique G. (1991). Real business cycles in a small open economy. *American Economic Review* 81:797–818.

Miao, Jianjun. (2003). Consumption and saving under Knightian uncertainty. Unpublished Manuscript. December.

Morris, Stephen, and Andrew Postlewaite. (1997). Observational implications of nonexponential discounting. Unpublished Manuscript. November.

Obstfeld, Maurice. (1981). Macroeconomic policy, exchange rate dynamics, and optimal asset accumulation. *Journal of Political Economy* 89:1142–1161.

Onatski, Alexei, and Noah Williams. (2003). Modeling model uncertainty. Unpublished Manuscript. April.

Phelps, E. S., and R. A. Pollack. (1968). On second-best national saving and game-equilibrium growth. *Review of Economic Studies* 35:185–199.

Rabin, Matthew. (1998). Economics and psychology. *Journal of Economic Literature* 36:11–46.

Routledge, Bryan R., and Stanley E. Zin. (2001). Model uncertainty and liquidity. NBER Working Paper No. 8683. December.

Routledge, Bryan R., and Stanley E. Zin. (2003). Generalized disappointment aversion and asset prices. NBER Working Paper No. 10107. November.

Sagi, Jacob S. (2003). Anchored preference relations. Unpublished Manuscript. August.

Savage, L. J. (1954). *The Foundations of Statistics*. New York: Wiley.

Schmeidler, David. (1989). Subjective probability and expected utility without additivity. *Econometrica* 57:571–587.

Schmitt-Grohé, Stephanie, and Martín Uribe. (2002). Closing small open economy models. *Journal of International Economics* 61:163–185.

Seidenfeld, Teddy, and Larry Wasserman. (1993). Dilation for sets of probabilities. *Annals of Statistics* 21:1139–1154.

Shi, Shouyong. (1994). Weakly nonseparable preferences and distortionary taxes in a small open economy. *International Economic Review* 35:411–428.

Simon, Herbert A. (1959). Theories of decision-making in economic and behavioral science. *American Economic Review* 49:253–283.

Starmer, Chris. (2000). Developments in non-expected utility theory. *Journal of Economic Literature* 38:332–382.

Tallarini, Thomas D. (2000). Risk-sensitive real business cycles. *Journal of Monetary Economics* 45:507–532.

Uzawa, H. (1968). Time preference, the consumption function, and optimum asset holdings. In *Value, Capital, and Growth: Papers in Honour of Sir John Hicks*, J. N. Wolfe (ed.). Chicago IL: Aldine Publishing Company.

Van Nieuwerburgh, Stijn. (2001). Robustness and optimal contracts. Unpublished Manuscript. July.

Wang, Susheng. (1993). The local recoverability of risk aversion and intertemporal substitution. *Journal of Economic Theory* 59:333–363.

Wang, Tan. (2003). Conditional preferences and updating. *Journal of Economic Theory* 108:286–321.

Weil, Philippe. (1989). The equity premium puzzle and the risk-free rate puzzle. *Journal of Monetary Economics* 24:401–421.

Weil, Philippe. (1990). Nonexpected utility in economics. *Quarterly Journal of Economics* 105:29–42.

Weil, Philippe. (1993). Precautionary savings and the permanent income hypothesis. *Review of Economic Studies* 60:367–383.

Whittle, Peter. (1990). *Risk-Sensitive Optimal Control*. New York: Wiley.

Yaari, Menachem E. (1987). The dual theory of choice under risk. *Econometrica* 55:95–115.

Comment

Lars Peter Hansen
University of Chicago and
NBER

1. Introduction

Backus, Routlege and Zin (which I will henceforth refer to as BRZ) have assembled an ambitious catalog and discussion of nonstandard, or *exotic*, specifications of preferences. BRZ include illustrations of how some of these specifications have been used in macroeconomic applications. Collecting the myriad of specifications in a single location is an excellent contribution. It will help to expand the overall accessibility and value of this research.

In my limited remarks, I will not review all of their discussion, but I will develop some themes a bit more and perhaps add a different but complementary perspective on some of the literature. Also, my discussion will feature some contributions not mentioned in the BRZ reader's guide. Most of my discussion will focus on environments in which it is hard or impossible to distinguish seemingly different relaxations of expected utility. While BRZ emphasize more distinctions, I will use some examples to feature similarities across specifications. Much of my discussion will exploit continuous-time limits with Brownian motion information structures to display some revealing limiting cases. In particular, I will draw on contributions not mentioned in the BRZ reader's guide by Duffie and Epstein (1992); Geoffard (1996); Dumas, Uppal, and Wang (2000); Petersen, James, and Dupuis (2000); Anderson, Hansen, and Sargent (2003); and Hansen, Sargent, Turmuhambetova, and Williams (2004) along with some of the papers cited by BRZ.

As a precursor to understanding the new implications of exotic preferences, we explore how seemingly different motivations for altering preferences give rise to similar implications and in some circumstances the same implications. BRZ have separate sections entitled *time* (Section 2), *time and risk* (Section 4), *risk sensitive and robust control* (Section

5), and *ambiguity* (Section 6). In what follows, I will review some existing characterizations in the literature to display a tighter connection than what might be evident from reading their paper.

2. Endogenous Discounting

I begin with a continuous-time version of the discussion in the BRZ treatment of *time* (Section 2 of their paper). An important relaxation of discounted utility is the recursive formulation of preferences suggested by Koopmans (1960), Uzawa (1968), and others. These are preferences that allow for endogenous discounting. A convenient generalization of these preferences is one in which the discount rate is a choice variable subject to a utility penalty, as in the *variational utility* specification of Geoffard (1996).

Consider preferences for consumption defined over an interval of time $[0, T]$ with undiscounted continuation value U_t that satisfies:

$$\begin{aligned} \lambda_t U_t &= E_t \int_t^T \lambda_s F(c_s, v_s)\, ds \\ \lambda_t &= \exp\left(\int_0^t -v_\tau\, d\tau\right) \end{aligned} \tag{1}$$

where $\{c_t : 0 \leq t \leq T\}$ is an admissible consumption process and $\{v_t : 0 \leq t \leq T\}$ is an admissible subjective discount rate process.[1] Then λ_t is a discount factor constructed from current and past discount rates. The notation E_t is used to denote the expectation operator conditioned on date t information. Equation (1) determines the continuation values for a consumption profile for each point in time. In particular, the date zero utility function is given by:

$$U_0 = E_0 \int_0^T \lambda_s F(c_s, v_s)\, ds$$

The function F gives the instantaneous contribution to utility, and it can depend on the subjective rate of discount v_s for reasons that will become clear.

So far we have specified the discounting in a flexible way, but stipulating the subjective discount rates must still be determined.[2] To convert this decision problem into an endogenous discount factor model, we follow Geoffard (1996) by determining the discount rate via minimization. This gives rise to a nondegenerate solution because of our choice to enter v as an argument in the function F. To support this minimization, the function $F(c, v)$ is presumed to be convex in v. Given the recursive structure to these preferences, v solves the continuous-time Bellman equation:

$$V(c_t, U_t) \doteq \inf_v [F(c_t, v) - vU_t] \tag{2}$$

The first-order conditions for minimizing v are:

$$F_v(c_t, v_t) = U_t$$

which implicitly defines the discount rate v_t as a function of the current consumption c_t and the current continuation value U_t.

This minimization also implies a forward utility recursion in U_t by specifying its drift:

$$\lim_{\varepsilon \downarrow 0} \frac{E_t U_{t+\varepsilon} - U_t}{\varepsilon} = -V(c_t, U_t)$$

This limit depicts a Koopmans (1960)–style aggregator in continuous-time with uncertainty. Koopmans (1960) defined an implied discount factor via a differentiation. The analogous implicit discount rate is given by the derivative:

$$v = -V_U(c, U)$$

consistent with representation (1).

So far we have seen how a minimum discount rate formulation implies an aggregator of the type suggested by Koopmans (1960) and others. As emphasized by Geoffard (1996), we may also go in the other direction. Given a specification for V, the drift for the continuation value, we may construct a Geoffard (1996)–style aggregator. This is accomplished by building a function F from the function V. The construction (2) of V formally is the Legendre transform of F. This transform has an inverse given by the algorithm:

$$F(c, v) = \sup_U [V(c, U) + vU] \tag{3}$$

Example 2.1 The implied discount rate is constant and equal to δ when:

$$V(c, U) = u(c) - \delta U$$

Taking the inverse Legendre transform, it follows that:

$$F(c,v) = \sup_U [u(c) - \delta U + vU]$$

$$= \begin{cases} u(c) & \text{if } v = \delta \\ +\infty & \text{if } v \neq \delta \end{cases}$$

This specification of V and F gives rise to the familiar discounted utility model.

Of course, the treatment of *exotic* preferences leads us to explore other specifications outside the confines of this example. These include preferences for which v is no longer constant.

In economies with multiple consumers, a convenient device to characterize and solve for equilibria is to compute the solutions to resource allocation problems with a social objective given by the weighted sum of the individual utility functions (Negishi, 1960). As reviewed by BRZ, Lucas and Stokey (1984) develop and apply an intertemporal counterpart to this device to study economies in which consumers have recursive utility. For a continuous time specification, Dumas, Uppal, and Wang (2000) use Geoffard's formulation of preferences to characterize efficient resource allocations. This approach also uses Negishi/Pareto weights and discount rate minimization. Specifically Dumas, Uppal, and Wang (2000) use a social objective:

$$\begin{aligned} &\inf_{\{v^i_\tau : \tau \geq t\}} \sum_i E_t \int_t^T \lambda^i_s F^i(c^i_s, v^i_s)\, ds \\ &\frac{d\lambda^i_t}{dt} = -v^i_t \lambda^i_t \end{aligned} \tag{4}$$

where the Negishi weights are the date zero initial conditions for λ^i_0 and i denotes individuals.

Thus far, we have produced two ways to represent endogenous discount factor formulations of preferences. BRZ study the Koopmans (1960) specification in which $V(c,u)$ is specified and a discount rate is defined as $-V_U(c,U)$. In the Geoffard (1996) characterization, $V(c,U)$ is the outcome of a problem in which discounted utility is minimized by choice of a discount rate process. The resulting function is concave in U. As we will see, however, the case in which V is convex in U is of particular interest to us. An analogous development to that given by Geoffard (1996) applies in which discounted utility is maximized by choice of the discount rate process instead of minimized.

3. Risk Adjustments in Continuation Values

Consider next a specification of preferences due to Kreps and Porteus (1978) and Epstein and Zin (1989). (BRZ refer to these as *Kreps–Porteus preferences* but certainly Epstein and Zin played a prominent role in demonstrating their value.) In discrete time, these preferences can be depicted recursively using a recursion with a risk-adjustment to the continuation value of the form:

$$U_t^* = u(c_t) + \beta h^{-1} E_t h(U_{t+1}^*) \tag{5}$$

As proposed by Kreps and Porteus (1978), the function h is increasing and is used to relax the assumption that compound intertemporal lotteries for utility can be reduced in a simple manner. When the function h is concave, it enhances risk aversion without altering intertemporal substitution (see Epstein and Zin, 1989).

Again it is convenient to explore a continuous-time counterpart. To formulate such a limit, scale the current period contribution by ε, where ε is the length of the time interval between observations, and parameterize the discount factor β as $\exp(-\delta\varepsilon)$, where δ is the instantaneous subjective rate of discount. The local version of the risk adjustment is:

$$\lim_{\varepsilon \downarrow 0} \frac{E_t h(U_{t+\varepsilon}^*) - h(U_t^*)}{\varepsilon} = -h'(U_t^*)[u(c_t) - \delta U_t^*] \tag{6}$$

The lefthand side can be defined for a Brownian motion information structure and for some other information structures that include jumps.

Under a Brownian motion information structure, the local evolution for the continuation value can be depicted as:

$$dU_t^* = \mu_t^* \, dt + \sigma_t^* \cdot dB_t \tag{7}$$

where $\{B_t\}$ is multivariate standard Brownian motion. Thus, μ_t^* is the local mean of the continuation value and $|\sigma_t^*|^2$ is the local variance:

$$\mu_t^* = \lim_{\varepsilon \downarrow 0} \frac{E_t U_{t+\varepsilon}^* - U_t^*}{\varepsilon}$$

$$|\sigma_t^*|^2 = \lim_{\varepsilon \downarrow 0} \frac{E_t (U_{t+\varepsilon}^* - U_t^*)^2}{\varepsilon}$$

By Ito's Lemma, we may compute the local mean of $h(U_t^*)$:

$$\frac{E_t h(U^*_{t+\varepsilon}) - h(U^*_t)}{\varepsilon} = h'(U^*_t)\mu^*_t + \frac{1}{2}h''(U^*_t)|\sigma^*_t|^2$$

Substituting this formula into the lefthand side of equation (6) and solving for μ^*_t gives:

$$\mu^*_t = \delta U^*_t - u(c_t) - \frac{h''(U^*_t)}{2h'(U^*_t)}|\sigma^*_t|^2 \tag{8}$$

Notice that the risk-adjustment to the value function adds a variance contribution to the continuation value recursion scaled by what Duffie and Epstein (1992) refer to as the *variance multiplier*, given by:

$$\frac{h''(U^*_t)}{h'(U^*_t)}$$

When h is strictly increasing and concave, this multiplier is negative. The use of h as a risk adjustment of the continuation value gives rise to concern about variation in the continuation value. Both the local mean and the local variance are present in this recursion.

As Duffie and Epstein (1992) emphasize, we can transform the utility index and eliminate the explicit variance contribution. Applying such a transformation gives an explicit link between the Kreps and Porteus (1978) specification and the Koopmans (1960) specification. To demonstrate this, transform the continuation value via $U_t = h(U^*_t)$. This results in the formula:

$$\lim_{\varepsilon \downarrow 0} \frac{E_t U_{t+\varepsilon} - U_t}{\varepsilon} = -V(c_t, U_t)$$

where

$$V(c, U) = h'[h^{-1}(U)][u(c) - \delta h^{-1}(U)]$$

The Geoffard (1996) specification with discount rate minimization can be deduced by solving for the inverse Legendre transform in equation (3). The implied endogenous discount rate is:

$$-V_U(c, U) = \delta - \frac{h''[h^{-1}(U)]}{h'[h^{-1}(U)]}[u(c) - \delta h^{-1}(U)]$$

Consider two examples. The first has been used extensively in the literature linking asset prices and macroeconomics aggregates including consumption.

Example 3.1 *Consider the case in which*

$$u(c) = \frac{c^{1-\varrho}}{1-\varrho} \qquad \text{and} \qquad h(U^*) = \frac{[(1-\varrho)U^*]^{(1-\gamma)/(1-\varrho)}}{1-\gamma}$$

where $\varrho > 0$ *and* $\gamma > 0$. *We assume that* $\varrho \neq 1$ *and* $\gamma \neq 1$ *because the complementary cases require some special treatment. This specification is equivalent to the specification given in equations (9) and (10) of BRZ.*[3] *Then:*

$$V(c, U) = [(1-\gamma)U]^{(\varrho-\gamma)/(1-\gamma)}\left(\frac{c^{1-\varrho}}{1-\varrho}\right) - \delta\left(\frac{1-\gamma}{1-\varrho}\right)U$$

with implied endogenous discount rate:

$$v = \frac{1-\gamma}{1-\varrho}\delta + \frac{(\gamma-\varrho)}{(1-\varrho)}\left[\frac{u(c)}{h^{-1}(U)}\right]$$

Notice that the implied endogenous discount rate simplifies, as it should, to be δ *when* $\varrho = \gamma$. *The dependent component of the discount rate depends on the discrepancy between* ϱ *and* γ *and on the ratio of the current period utility to the continuation value without the risk adjustment:*

$$U^* = h^{-1}(U)$$

At the end of Section 2, we posed an efficient resource allocation problem (4) with heterogenous consumers. In the heterogeneous consumer economy with common preferences of the form given in Example 3.1, the consumption allocation rules as a function of aggregate consumption are invariant over time. The homogeneity discussed in Duffie and Epstein (1992) and by BRZ implies that the ratio of current period utility to the continuation value will be the same for all consumers, implying in turn that the endogenous discount rates will be also. With preference heterogeneity, this ceases to be true, as illustrated by Dumas, Uppal, and Wang (2000).

We will use the next example to relate to the literature on robustness in decisionmaking. It has been used by Tallarini (1998) in the study of business cycles and by Anderson (2004) to study resource allocation with heterogeneous consumers.

Example 3.2 *Consider the case in which* $h(U^*) = -\theta \exp(-U^*/\theta)$ *for* $\theta > 0$. *Notice that the transformed continuation utility is negative. A simple calculation results in:*

$$V(c, U) = -\frac{U}{\theta}\left[u(c) + \delta\theta \log\left(-\frac{U}{\theta}\right)\right]$$

which is convex in U. The maximizing v of the Legendre transform (2) is:

$$v = \delta + \frac{1}{\theta}\left[u(c) + \delta\theta \log\left(-\frac{U}{\theta}\right)\right]$$

and the minimizing U of the inverse Legendre transform (3) is:

$$U = -\theta \exp\left[\frac{\theta v - \theta\delta - u(c)}{\delta\theta}\right]$$

Consequently:

$$F(c, v) = -\delta\theta \exp\left[\frac{\theta v - \theta\delta - u(c)}{\delta\theta}\right]$$

which is concave in v.

So far, we have focused on what BRZ call Kreps–Porteus preferences. BRZ also discuss what they call Epstein–Zin preferences, which are dynamic recursive extensions to specifications of Chew (1983) and Dekel (1986). Duffie and Epstein (1992) show, however, how to construct a corresponding variance multiplier for versions of these preferences that are sufficiently smooth and how to construct a corresponding risk-adjustment function h for Brownian motion information structures (see page 365 of Duffie and Epstein, 1992).

This equivalence does not extend to all of the recursive preference structures described by BRZ. This analysis has not included, for instance, dynamic versions of preferences that display first-order risk aversion.[4] BRZ discuss such preferences and some of their interesting implications.

Let me review what has been established so far. By taking a continuous-time limit for a Brownian motion information structure, a risk-adjustment in the continuation value for a consumption profile is equivalent to an endogenous discounting formulation. We can view this endogenous discounting as a continuous-time version of a Koopmans (1960)–style recursion or as a specification in which discount rates are the solution to an optimization problem, as in Geoffard (1996). These three different starting points can be used to motivate the same set of preferences. Thus, we produced examples in which some of the preference specifications in Sections 2 and 4 of BRZ are formally the same.

Next, we consider a fourth specification.

4. Robustness and Entropy

Geoffard (1996) motivates discount rate minimization as follows:

> [T]he future evolution of relevant variables (sales volumes, asset default rates or prepayment rates, *etc.*) is very important to the valuation of a firm's debt. A probability distribution on the future of these variables may be difficult to define. Instead, it may be more intuitive to assume that these variables remain within some confidence interval, and to define the value of the debt as the value in the worst case, *i.e.* when the evolution of the relevant state variables is systematically adverse.

It is not obvious that Geoffard's formalization is designed for a robustness adjustment of this type. In what follows a conservative assessment made by exploring alternative probability structures instead leads to a formulation where the discounted utility is maximized by choice of discount rates and not minimized because the implied $V(c, U)$ is convex in U. In this section we will exploit a well-known close relationship between *risk sensitivity* and a particular form of *robustness* from control theory, starting with Jacobson (1973). A discussion of the linear-quadratic version of risk-sensitive and robust control theory is featured in Section 5 of BRZ. The close link is present in much more general circumstances, as I now illustrate.

Instead of recursion (5), consider a specification in which beliefs are distorted subject to penalization:

$$U_t^* = \min_{q_{t+1} \geq 0, E_t q_{t+1} = 1} u(c_t) + \beta E_t(U_{t+1}^* q_{t+1}) + \beta \theta E_t[(\log q_{t+1}) q_{t+1}] \tag{9}$$

The random variable q_{t+1} distorts the conditional probability distribution for date $t + 1$ events conditioned on date t information. We have added a penalization term to limit the severity of the probability distortion. This penalization is based on a discrepancy measure between the implied probability distributions called conditional relative entropy. Minimizing with respect to q_{t+1} in this specification produces a version of recursion (5), with h given by the risk-sensitive specification of Example 3.2. It gives rise to the exponential tilting because the penalized worst-case q_{t+1} is:

$$q_{t+1} \propto \exp\left(-\frac{U_{t+1}^*}{\theta}\right)$$

Probabilities are distorted less when the continuation value is high and more when this value is low. By making the θ large, the solution to this problem approximates that of the recursion of the standard form of time-separable preferences. Given this dual interpretation, robustness can look like risk aversion in decisionmaking and in prices that clear security markets. This dual interpretation is applicable in discrete and continuous time. For a continuous time analysis, see Hansen, Sargent, Turmuhambetova, and Williams (2004) and Skiadas (2003).

Preferences of this sort are supported by worst-case distributions. Blackwell and Girshick (1954) organize statistical theory around the theory of two-player zero-sum games. This framework can be applied in this environment as well. In a decision problem, we would be led to solve a max-min problem. Whenever we can exchange the order of minimization and maximization, we can produce a worst-case distribution for the underlying shocks under which the action is obtained by a simple maximization. Thus, we can produce ex post a shock specification under which the decision process is optimal and solves a standard dynamic programming problem. It is common in Bayesian decision theory to ask what prior justifies a particular rule as being optimal. We use the same logic to produce a (penalized) worst-case specification of shocks that justifies a robust decision rule as being optimal against a correctly specified model.

This poses an interesting challenge to a rational expectations econometrician studying a representative agent model. If the worst-case model of shock evolution is statistically close to that of the original model, then an econometrician will have difficulty distinguishing *exotic preferences* from a possibly more complex specification of shock evolution. See Anderson, Hansen, and Sargent (2003) for a formal discussion of the link between statistical discrimination and robustness and Hansen, Sargent, Turmuhambetova, and Williams (2004) for a discussion and characterization of the implied worst-case models for a Brownian motion information structure. In the case of a decision problem with a diffusion specification for the state evolution, the worst-case model replaces the Brownian motion shocks with a Brownian motion distorted by a nonzero drift.

In the case of Brownian motion information structures, Maenhout (2004) has shown the robust interpretation for a more general class of recursive utility models by allowing for a more general specification of the penalization. Following Maenhout (2004), we allow θ to depend on the continuation value U_t^*.

In discrete time, we distorted probabilities using a positive random variable q_{t+1} with conditional expectation equal to unity. The product of such random variables:

$$z_{t+1} = \prod_{j=1}^{t+1} q_j$$

is a discrete time martingale. In continuous time, we use nonnegative martingales with unit expectations to depict probability distortions. For a Brownian motion information structure, the local evolution of a nonnegative martingale can be represented as:

$$dz_t = z_t g_t \cdot dW_t$$

where g_t dictates how the martingale increment is related to the increment in the multivariate Brownian motion $\{W_t : t \geq 0\}$. In continuous time, the counterpart to $E_t(q_{t+1} \log q_{t+1})$ is the quadratic penalty $|g_t|^2/2$, and our minimization will entail a choice of the random vector g_t.

In accordance with Ito's formula, the local mean of the distorted expectation of the continuation value process $\{U_t^* : t \geq 0\}$ is:

$$\lim_{\varepsilon \downarrow 0} \frac{E_t z_{t+\varepsilon} U_{t+\varepsilon}^* - z_t U_t^*}{\varepsilon} = z_t \mu_t^* + z_t \sigma_t^* g_t$$

where the continuation value process evolves according to equation (7). The continuous-time counterpart to equation (9) is:

$$z_t \mu_t^* = \min_{g_t} -z_t \sigma_t^* g_t - z_t u(c_t) + z_t \delta U_t^* - z_t \theta(U_t^*) \frac{|g_t|^2}{2}$$

with the minimizing value of g_t given by:

$$g_t = -\frac{\sigma_t^*}{\theta(U_t^*)}$$

Substituting for this choice of g_t, the local mean for the continuation value must satisfy:

$$\mu_t^* = -u(c_t) + \delta U_t^* + \frac{|\sigma_t^*|^2}{2\theta(U_t^*)}$$

(provided of course that z_t is not zero). By setting θ to be:

$$\theta(U^*) = -\frac{h'(U^*)}{h''(U^*)}$$

we reproduce equation (8) and hence obtain the more general link among utility recursions for h increasing and concave. This link, however, has been established only for a continuous-time economy with a Brownian motion information structure for a general specification of h.

The penalization approach can nest other specifications not included by the utility recursions I discussed in Sections 2 and 3. For instance, the concern about misspecification might be concentrated on a proper subset of the shock processes (the Brownian motions).

To summarize, we have now added a concern about model specification to our list of *exotic preferences* with comparable implications when information is approximated by a Brownian motion information structure. When there is a well-defined worst-case model, an econometrician might have trouble distinguishing these preferences from a specification with a more complex but statistically similar evolution for the underlying economic shocks.

5. Uncertainty Aversion

The preferences built in Section 4 were constructed using a penalty based on conditional relative entropy. Complementary axiomatic treatments of this penalty approach to preferences have been given by Wang (2003) and Maccheroni, Marinacci, and Rustichini (2004).

Formulation (9) used θ as a penalty parameter, but θ can also be the Lagrange multiplier on an intertemporal constraint (see Petersen, James, and Dupuis, 2000, and Hansen, Sargent, Turmuhambetova, and Williams, 2004). This interpretation of θ as a Lagrange multiplier links our previous formulation of robustness to decision making when an extensive family of probability models are explored subject to an intertemporal entropy constraint. While the implied preferences differ, the interpretation of θ as a Lagrange multiplier gives a connection between the decision rules from the robust decision problem described at the outset of Section 4 and the multiple priors model discussed in Section 6 of BRZ. Thus, we have added another possible interpretation to the risk-sensitive recursive utility model. Although the Lagrange multiplier interpretation is deduced from a date zero vantage point, Hansen, Sargent, Turmuhambetova, and Williams (2004) describe multiple ways in which such preferences can look recursive.

Of course, there are a variety of other ways in which multiple models can be introduced into a decision problem. BRZ explore some aspects of dynamic consistency as it relates to decision problems with multiple probability models. A clear statement of this issue and its ramifications requires much more than the limited space BRZ had to address it. As a consequence, I found this component of the paper less illuminating than other components.

A treatment of dynamic consistency with multiple probability models either from the vantage point of robustness or ambiguity is made most interesting by the explicit study of environments in which learning about a parameter or a hidden state through signals is featured. Control problems are forward-looking and are commonly solved using a backward induction method such as dynamic programming. Predicting unknown states or estimating parameters is inherently backward-looking. It uses historical data to make a current period prediction or estimate. In contrast to dynamic programming, recursive prediction iterates going forward. This difference between control and prediction is the source of tension when multiple probability models are entertained. Recursive formulations often ask that you back away from the search for a single coherent worst-case probability model over observed signals and hidden states or parameters. The connection to Bayesian decision theory that I mentioned previously is often broken. In my view, a pedagogically useful treatment of this issue has yet to be written, but it requires a separate paper.

6. Conclusion

We have shown how divergent motivations for generalizing preferences sometimes end up with the same implications. So what? There are at least three reasons I can think of why an economic researcher should be interested in these alternative interpretations. One reason is to understand how we might calibrate or estimate the new preference parameters. The different motivations might lead us to think differently about what is a reasonable parameter setting. For instance, what might appear to be endogenous discounting could instead reflect an aversion to risk when a decision maker cares about the intertemporal composition of risk. What might look like an extreme amount of risk aversion could instead reflect the desire of the decision maker to accommodate model misspecification.

Second, we should understand better the new testable implications that might emerge as a result of our exploring nonstandard preferences. Under what auxiliary assumptions are there interesting testable implications? My remarks point to some situations when testing will be challenging or fruitless.

Finally, we should understand better when preference parameters can be transported from one environment to another. This understanding is at least implicitly required when we explore hypothetical changes in macroeconomic policies.

It would be nice to see a follow-up paper that treated systematically (1) the best sources of information for the new parameters, (2) the observable implications, and (3) the policy consequences.

Notes

Conversations with Jose Mazoy, Monika Piazzesi, and Grace Tsiang were valuable in the preparation of these remarks.

1. We may define formally the notion of *admissible* by restricting the consumption and discount rate processes to be progressively measurable given a prespecified filtration.

2. Geoffard (1996) does not include uncertainty in his analysis, but as Dumas, Uppal, and Wang (2000) argue, this is a straightforward extension.

3. This equivalence follows by letting $\rho = 1 - \varrho$ and $\alpha = 1 - \gamma$ and transforming the utility index.

4. See Duffie and Epstein (1992), page 361, for a more complete discussion about what is excluded under the Brownian information structure by their variance multiplier formulation.

References

Anderson, E. (2004). The dynamics of risk-sensitive allocations. University of North Carolina. Unpublished Manuscript.

Anderson, E., L. Hansen, and T. Sargent. (2003). A quartet of semigroups for model specification, robustness, prices of risk, and model detection. *Journal of the European Economic Association* 1(1):68–123.

Blackwell, D., and M. A. Girshick. (1954). *Theory of Games and Statistical Decisions*. New York: Wiley Publications in Statistics.

Chew, S. H. (1983). A generalization of the quasi-linear mean with applications to the measurement of inequality and decision theory resolving the Allais paradox. *Econometrica* 51:1065–1092.

Dekel, E. (1986). An axiomatic characterization of preference under uncertainty: Weakening the independence axiom. *Journal of Economic Theory* 40:304–318.

Duffie, D., and L. G. Epstein. (1992). Stochastic differential utility. *Econometrica* 60(2):353–394.

Dumas, B., R. Uppal, and T. Wang. (2000). *Journal of Economic Theory* 93:240–259.

Epstein, L., and S. Zin. (1989). Substitution, risk aversion and the temporal behavior of consumption and asset returns: A theoretical framework. *Econometrica* 57:937–969.

Geoffard, P. Y. (1996). Discounting and optimizing: Capital accumulation problems as variational minmax problems. *Journal of Economic Theory* 69:53–70.

Hansen, L. P., T. J. Sargent, G. A. Turmuhambetova, and N. Williams. (2004). Robust control, min-max expected utility, and model misspecification. University of Chicago. Unpublished Manuscript.

Jacobson, D. H. (1973). Optimal stochastic linear systems with exponential performance criteria and their relation to deterministic differential games. *IEEE Transactions for Automatic Control* AC-18:1124–1131.

Koopmans, T. J. (1960). Stationary ordinal utility and impatience. *Econometrica* 28:287–309.

Kreps, D. M., and E. L. Porteus. (1978). Temporal resolution of uncertainty and dynamic choice. *Econometrica* 46:185–200.

Lucas, R. E., and N. L. Stokey. (1984). Optimal growth with many consumers. *Journal of Economic Theory* 32:139–171.

Maccheroni, F., M. Marinacci, and A. Rustichini. (2004). Variational representation of preferences under ambiguity. University of Minnesota. Unpublished Manuscript.

Maenhout, P. J. (2004). Robust portfolio rules and asset pricing. *Review of Financial Studies* 17:951–983.

Negishi, T. (1960). Welfare eeconomics and existence of an equilibrium for a competitive economy. *Metroeconomica* 12:92–97.

Petersen, I. R., M. R. James, and P. Dupuis. (2000). Minimax optimal control of stochastic uncertain systems with relative entropy constraints. *IEEE Transactions on Automatic Control* 45:398–412.

Skiadas, C. (2003). Robust control and recursive utility. *Finance and Stochastics* 7:475–489.

Tallarini, T. (1998). Risk sensitive business cyles. *Journal of Monetary Economics* 43:507–532.

Uzawa, H. (1968). Time prefernce, the consumption function, and optimum asset holdings. In *Value, Capital, and Growth: Papers in Honor of Sir John Hicks*, J. N. Wolfe (ed.). Edinburgh: Edinburgh University.

Wang, T. (2003). A class of multi-prior preferences. University of British Columbia. Unpublished Manuscript.

Comment

Ivan Werning
MIT, NBER, and Universidad Torcuato di Tella

1. Introduction

This paper provides a practical and user-friendly overview of preference specifications outside the very dear, but perhaps too pervasive, additively separable expected-utility framework.[1] The paper's stated intention is for choice-theorists to reach out to macroeconomists, offering a road map to a selection of exotic preference specifications accumulated through years of progress.

The paper succeeds at its main objective: any macroeconomist wishing greater preference flexibility should consult this paper. Given the intended audience and space limitations, the authors make some excellent choices, such as sacrificing axiomatic foundations and emphasizing examples with homogeneity assumptions.

I would have welcomed more space devoted to the difficult question regarding how useful the overall exotic preference strategy may be for macroeconomics, or more competitive comparisons across exotic preference that could help clarify which specifications might be most fruitful. Perhaps it is too early to make these calls, but with so many offered options more guidance would be have been very welcome.

Review papers are to some extent comments on a literature. So for the rest of my commentary, instead of layering a comment over another, I will attempt to add to the discussion by expanding on some general themes that lurk in the background of the paper. My discussion revolves around three ideas. I will first discuss why exotic aspects of preferences may be of great importance by reviewing some normative implications. I then use observational equivalence results to illustrate the empirical challenges faced in identifying exotic aspects of preferences. I conclude by discussing a few examples of exotic alternatives that macroeconomists have taken to altering preferences.

2. Exotic Welfare Calculations

Exotic preferences often have their most interesting implications for counterfactual situations, common in normative analyses, where the observational equivalence issues discussed below do not apply. These normative implications underscore why identifying exotic aspects of preferences may be important.

Indeed, in the case of intertemporal preferences with temptations or time inconsistencies one can argue that normative implications have been at center stage. In the case of preferences for risk, an interesting example of great relevance for macroeconomists is provided by the welfare costs of business-cycles calculations pioneered by Lucas (1987).[2] This exercise requires only specifying a preference relation for a representative agent and two consumption processes, one with and one without business cycles. As a measure of the cost of business cycles one computes the proportional increase in the first consumption process required to make the representative agent indifferent to the second process.

The exercise is attractive for its simplicity; it is renowned and influential for its outcome. Lucas performed the exercise using additive expected-utility and obtained small costs, on the order of 0.1% of consumption, for the removal of *all* consumption risk around a deterministic linear trend. Several authors have explored whether such low welfare costs may be an artifact of simplifying assumptions, especially regarding preferences. One reason for concern is that the equity-premium puzzle (Mehra and Prescott, 1985) shows that additive expected-utility preferences underestimate the required compensation for equity return risk we've historically observed. Thus, it may also be ill-suited for evaluating the compensation required for aggregate consumption risk.

Preferences that arguably do a better job matching asset price data do lead to larger welfare cost calculations. For example, Obstfeld (1994) and Tallerini (2000) explore the welfare costs of aggregate consumption risk with the non-expected recursive iso-elastic preferences used by Epstein and Zin (1989). They show that the costs can be two orders of magnitude larger if one increases the risk-aversion parameter to match the historical equity premium. Dolmas (1998) uses certainty-equivalence functions that display first-order risk aversion and reaches similar conclusions.[3]

3. Exotic Data

The example above illustrates that exotic preferences may significantly affect important welfare calculations. Motivated by their relevance one is ready to face the challenge of selecting a specification and choosing its parameters. This identification problem is often quite difficult, and the paper gives several clues why.

The paper contains many examples where exotic preferences do not lead to exotic behavior, or where different exotic specifications lead to similar behavior. Extreme instances are provided by observational equivalence results: situations where identical behavior is obtained for more than one parameter specification.

Theoretically, one can view observational equivalence, for a particular economic situation, as a convenient way of isolating the role *not* played by the extra degrees of freedom introduced by exotic specifications. The new parameters affect behavior that is in some sense orthogonal to an initial subset of behavior, that for which the observational equivalence result holds.

Empirically, observational equivalence results illustrate the more general challenge of identifying the additional new parameters that exotic preferences may introduce, or selecting among alternative preference specifications.[4] Since observational equivalence results are situation specific, enriching or changing the environment and data available may deliver enough additional information to identify preference parameters. However, this comes at the cost of increasing the data and modeling requirements.

To illustrate these issues consider hyperbolic discounting preferences. In standard consumption-saving situations, where no illiquid asset is available, observational equivalence results are pervasive and holds for all specifications for which closed form solutions are available in the case with standard geometric discounting.[5] Various combinations of the two discount parameters, β and δ, deliver exactly the same behavior. This suggests that, in general, with income and consumption data alone it will be very difficult to identify these preference parameters separately.

To see how changing the environment can aid identification consider a hyperbolic consumer facing stochastic i.i.d. labor income with two risk-free assets, liquid and illiquid.[6] Suppose the illiquid asset requires a lag in liquidation so that it cannot be used for immediate consumption. This effectively impose a cash-in-advance constraint so that consumption is bounded by the sum of labor income and wealth held in the liquid asset. The liquid and illiquid asset may have different rates of return.

Total savings continue to depend on both discount factors and various combinations of β and δ imply the same total savings. Thus, observation of total saving behavior itself does not provide enough information to identify both discount factors separately. However, the portfolio choice between liquid and illiquid assets can provide additional information. In general, this information can help disentangle the discount factors β and δ. Indeed, with sufficient knowledge of other primitives observation of the demand for liquid and illiquid assets identifies β and δ.[7]

The challenge is that the relative demand for liquidity depends on many other primitives aside from the discount factors, such as the degree of risk aversion and intertemporal substitution, the distribution of income shocks, the return to both assets or more general characteristics of the assets. For instance, suppose we observe high relative demand for an illiquid asset such as housing. It is difficult to discern whether this is evidence of hyperbolic discounting or of relatively high expected returns or other desired characteristics of the illiquid housing asset. Without knowledge of these primitives identification of β and δ becomes difficult.

The lesson is more general than this hyperbolic example. The paper offers many other cases of observational equivalence, or situations with near observational equivalence, and the resulting problems of identification. For example, the authors explain why it may be difficult to tell apart expected utility from weighted utility, or robust control from risk-sensitive preferences.

Each of these situations certainly pose specific challenges, but meeting these challenges will require richer, exotic data. Moreover, one needs to consider richer modeling situations to place these preferences into and this in itself can bring additional parameters to be identified. These considerations explain why identifying new parameters introduced by exotic preferences may be extremely challenging, but certainly not impossible.

4. Exotic Alternatives: Complements or Substitutes?

The typical economic model consists, at a minimum, of a specification of the following triplet: preferences, technology, and market arrangements. An alternative to exotic preferences is to consider non standard or exotic technology and/or market arrangements. The latter is possibly the road most heavily traveled by macroeconomists.

As an example consider models with incomplete markets. One interesting application of these models is to explore and enrich the business-cycle cost calculations discussed above. Lucas's representative agent calculation implicitly assumes complete markets, but without them, small aggregate movements in consumption may hide much more dramatic fluctuations for a subset of individuals. Using a calibrated incomplete markets model, Krusell and Smith (2002) show that the welfare costs may vary greatly across individuals; indeed, while business cycles may make poorer agents lose significantly, around 3% of consumption, it may actually make richer agents *gain* a comparable amount.

Constantinides and Duffie (1996) construct an incomplete markets model that is observationally equivalent for asset pricing and aggregate consumption data to representative agent models with higher risk aversion. In their setting, modifying preferences or the market environment is a substitute for each other.

On the other hand, household income and consumption data have been approached with models combining richer preferences *and* market arrangements, such as borrowing and other financial constraints. Thus, in some cases, exotic preferences may indeed complement other modeling approaches.

Notes

1. I follow the authors in using the term *exotic* for anything outside this more standard model.

2. See Lucas (2003) for an updated critical review of the literature.

3. Most contributions compute the benefit of a removal of all aggregate consumption risk, i.e. the process without business cycles is deterministic. This is probably unrealistic, and Alvarez and Jermann (2000) show that it can make a huge difference. They find huge gains for the removal of all uncertainty but only moderate ones for the removal of uncertainty at business-cycle frequencies.

4. While exact observational equivalence results usually rely on specific functional form assumptions, they are often symptomatic of more general near observational equivalence results that make parameter estimation extremely difficult.

5. These include, for the income fluctuations problem with i.i.d. labor income and constant interest rate the exponential, constant absolute risk aversion (CARA) and quadratic utility functions. With deterministic labor income one can add the iso-elastic, constant relative risk aversion (CRRA) utility function, see Example 21 in the paper.

6. I have characterized the model described here with exponential-CARA utility quite sharply.

7. This is related to the strategy pursued recently by Liabson, Repeto and Tobacman (2004).

References

Alvarez, Fernando, and Urban Jermann. (2000). Using asset prices to measure the costs of business cycles. NBER Working Paper No. 7978. October.

Constantinides, George M., and Darrell Duffie. (1996). Asset pricing with heterogenous consumers. *Journal of Political Economy* 104:219–240.

Dolmas, James. (1998). Risk-preferences and the welfare costs of business cycles. *Review of Economic Dynamics* 1(3):646–676.

Epstein, Larry G., and Stanley E. Zin. (1989). Substitution, risk aversion, and the temporal behavior of consumption growth and asset returns I: A theoretical framework. *Econometrica* 57(4): 937–969.

Krusell, Per, and Anthony A. Smith, Jr. (2002). Revisiting the welfare effects of eliminating business cycles. Mimeo. Princeton University.

Laibson, David, Andrea Repeto, and Jeremy Tobacman. (2004). Estimating discount functions from lifecycle consumption choices. Mimeo. Harvard University.

Lucas, Robert E., Jr. (1987). *Models of Business Cycles*. New York: Basil Blackwell.

Lucas, Robert E., Jr. (2003). Macroeconomic Priorities. *American Economic Review* 93(1):1–14.

Mehra, Rajnish, and Edward C. Prescott. (1985). The equity premium: A puzzle. *Journal of Monetary Economics* 15(2):145–161.

Obstfeld, Maurice. (1994). Evaluating risky consumption paths: The role of intertemporal substitutability. *European Economic Review* 38(7):1471–1486.

Tallerini, Thomas D., Jr. (2000). Risk-sensitive real business cycles. *Journal of Monetary Economics* 45(3):507–532.

Discussion

In response to the discussants, especially to Lars Hansen, Stanley Zin agreed with the three main points that Hansen emphasized: empirical implementation, identification of new parameters, and policy relevance. He noted how some authors, such as José-Victor Rios-Rull or Edward Prescott, believed that when one deviates from the standard utility framework, one could obtain any result one wanted, but their paper proved that this was not correct and that it was, in fact, very easy to get nothing at all. The challenging issue, he pointed out, was to understand what these preference models were doing and not doing, and he referred to Ivan Werning's last example, where different frictions delivered different responses from the model. Zin mentioned that the use of these less standard preferences was not incompatible with the use of tools, such as calibration of parameters or moment matching, that economists utilized in expected utility models. Related to policy relevance, he noted that another contribution of the paper was to delineate where Pareto comparisons of different policies could and could not be done since these comparisons required explicit utility functions and not only behavioral decision outcomes.

Several participants commented on Ivan Werning's model with liquid and illiquid assets. David Laibson made some observations on the identification of the hyperbolic model and on the challenge proposed by Zin of using standard tools with these nontraditional preferences. He noted that in one of his recent papers, he and his co-authors developed a model, similar to the one presented by Werning, where they were able to obtain very precise estimates of the short-run discount parameter, β, of around $\frac{2}{3}$ and of the long-run discount parameter, δ, of about 4%. Robert Shimer talked about the empirical implications of time-inconsistent preferences. In particular, he mentioned a paper by Narayana Kocherlakota published in 2001 in the *Federal Reserve Bank of*

Minneapolis Quarterly Review, where he considered an equilibrium asset-pricing model with liquid and illiquid assets. Kocherlakota found that the model delivered some counterfactual results, such as a premium on the illiquid asset and the fact that, in equilibrium, agents fully specialized in one type of asset without mixing assets.

Fumio Hayashi noted another important empirical fact (besides the asset-price puzzle already mentioned): the comovement of consumption and income. He suggested that the preferences proposed by Hansen in his discussion, which had Pareto weights and were time invariant, might be able to explain this puzzle.

Mark Gertler commented that a related approach to using exotic preferences to explain the equity premium and its time variation was to use external habit formation, such as in the models of John Campbell and John Cochrane or Andrew Abel, and questioned the authors about using exotic preferences as opposed to habit formation. Zin replied to Gertler that in the case of context-dependent preferences like the ones he mentioned, it was hard to think of Pareto comparisons of policies since policy changes that alter the economy also modified the individuals, since these context-dependent preferences were specific to the environment.

Marjorie Flavin noted that the expected utility framework had been criticized for being overly restrictive, and she believed that some of the overly restrictive results were usually the consequence of additional assumptions, such as costlessly adjustable consumption goods. She mentioned that in her recent work, she had developed models that retained the expected utility framework but included nondurable consumption and housing, subject to substantial adjustment costs, and she was able to obtain state dependence of risk aversion, path dependence of risk aversion, and the possibility of disentangling risk aversion from the elasticity of intertemporal substitution.

Finally, Kenneth Rogoff criticized the discussants for their harsh critique of the motivation of the paper because he believed that the type of work the authors had done was not possible two decades ago. In this respect, he noted the large implementation lags between the time when utility functions were thought of and when they could actually be implemented in economic problems.

The Business Cycle and the Life Cycle

Paul Gomme, Richard Rogerson, Peter Rupert, and Randall Wright
University of Iowa and Federal Reserve Bank of Cleveland; Arizona State University and NBER; University of Western Ontario and Federal Reserve Bank of Cleveland; and University of Pennsylvania and NBER

1. Introduction

The representative household model is the workhorse of modern business-cycle theory. One can understand this from several perspectives. First, from an empirical perspective, the business cycle is defined in terms of time series variation in the per-capita values for several key aggregate variables. By construction, the representative agent model is a model of per-capita values. Second, from a conceptual perspective, the process of understanding is facilitated by first analyzing economic forces in simple settings, and abstracting from heterogeneity helps to maintain simplicity in the model. Third, from a technical perspective, the appropriate theoretical framework in modern business-cycle theory is dynamic stochastic general equilibrium theory, and the assumption of a representative agent greatly reduces the burden of such analysis, both computationally and theoretically.

These factors suggest that representative agent models are a useful starting point for analyzing the economic forces that shape aggregate fluctuations. However, the thesis of this paper is that our understanding of labor market fluctuations (in particular) will be enhanced by moving beyond the representative agent model. The essence of our argument follows from a simple empirical finding. As we document, the magnitude of business-cycle fluctuations in hours of market work varies quite significantly across subgroups in the population. We believe that understanding why some groups fluctuate more than others should be relevant for understanding why the aggregate fluctuates as much as it does. Consider two scenarios. In the first, suppose that for reasonable parameterizations, a given model is *unable* to account for a sizable fraction of observed fluctuations in aggregate hours. In assessing which modifications to the theory may be most relevant, it would be important to know if the problem was that the model systematically underaccounts for fluctuations in hours across all groups, or if the problem is that it cannot account for the magnitude of fluctuations experienced by some specific groups. In the second scenario, suppose that for reasonable parameterizations, a given model is *able* to account for the bulk of aggregate fluctuations in hours. While this is useful information, we would obviously be more confident that the economic forces captured in this model are indeed the relevant ones if they were also able to account for the patterns of fluctuations across various groups.

In this paper, we pursue a disaggregated analysis of fluctuations in market work by considering one specific dimension of heterogeneity—age. Specifically, we document how cyclical fluctuations in hours of market work vary over the life cycle, and then assess the predictions of a life-cycle version of the growth model for the observations. Our analysis yields a simple but striking finding. The main discrepancy between the model and the data lies in the inability of the model to account for fluctuations in hours for individuals over the first half of their life cycle; it can account for most of the fluctuations for individuals aged 45–64 without resorting to extreme labor supply elasticities. This suggests that in looking for alternative theories to account for aggregate labor market fluctuations, attention should be directed toward features that specifically affect individuals during the first half of their lives. Although the goal of this paper is not to present alternatives to the benchmark life-cycle growth model, one is led to think about the options: e.g., to ask whether search frictions, say, as opposed to sticky wage models or other candidates, may be more relevant in terms of affecting workers differently at different stages of the life cycle.[1] In this sense, our goal is to raise some issues without trying to resolve everything here.

While heterogeneity has received a lot of recent attention in macroeconomics, it is important to distinguish our emphasis from that of others. A recurring issue in many studies is whether introducing a particular type of heterogeneity, often in connection with some other feature, will influence the properties of the *aggregate* time series. In these studies, the emphasis remains on the properties of the aggregate variables and not on the behavior of disaggregated series. One example of this is Krusell and Smith (1998), who ask whether a model with idiosyncratic income shocks and incomplete markets would produce different aggregate responses to technology shocks. Another example is Rios-Rull (1996), who studies a similar model to the one used here, but whose main objective is to see if aggregate fluctuations are different in an overlapping generations model than in the standard infinitely lived agent model. Both of these studies concluded that the properties of aggregate fluctuations were not much affected. In contrast, our goal is to ask whether allowing for heterogeneity provides more insight into the details of a particular shock and propagation mechanism by explicitly focusing on the implications of the model for fluctuations at the disaggregated level.[2]

Though our work is related to several papers in the literature, two papers are particularly relevant. The first is Clark and Summers (1981), who documented that cyclical fluctuations in employment vary across demographic groups, and the second is Rios-Rull (1996), who examined fluctuations in a life-cycle economy. Our empirical work extends Clark and Summers along several important dimensions. Specifically, we analyze additional dimensions of heterogeneity, use more conventional methods to define cyclical components, examine both the intensive and extensive margins, and perform additional robustness checks. While our results for fluctuations by age are similar to theirs, we find differences along other dimensions. Our theoretical work also extends the work of Rios-Rull along several dimensions. Specifically, we consider a different class of preferences, our model allows for home production and life-cycle preference shifters, and we assume a different market structure. Most important, however, we carry out a detailed analysis of the role that various factors play in shaping the volatility of hours over the life cycle.

Although we do not pursue it here, we believe that the life-cycle model developed and analyzed in this work is of independent interest in other contexts as well. For example, it would allow one to study how fluctuations in cohort size affect economic outcomes. Shimer (1998), for example, argued empirically that fluctuations in cohort size had a large impact on fluctuations in aggregate unemployment.

The rest of the paper is organized as follows. In Section 2, we describe a standard representative household (infinitely lived agent) model and examine its predictions concerning fluctuations in aggregate hours. Section 3 documents the extent to which the cyclical variation in hours varies with several household characteristics. Section 4 presents and calibrates our version of the growth model populated by overlapping generations. Section 5 presents the results of the model concerning business-cycle fluctuations, with a particular focus on its implications for fluctuations in hours by age. Section 6 is devoted to discussing the factors that give rise to the observed pattern of fluctuations. Section 7 presents some international evidence on fluctuations in hours worked by age, and Section 8 concludes.

2. A Representative Agent Model

For purposes of comparison, it is instructive to start with a representative agent model of the sort that serves as one of the benchmark models of business-cycle analysis. Rather than formulating the model in its most general form, we restrict attention to a specification with commonly used functional forms. We add two features relative to the simplest possible specification: household production and a government sector. We include household production because previous work has shown that models with household production do a much better job of accounting for several aspects of business cycles, particularly for hours of market work.[3] We include a government sector because taxes are an important element in calibrating home and market capital stocks.

2.1 *Model*

There is an infinitely lived representative household with preferences:

$$\sum_{t=0}^{\infty} \beta^t \left[\log C_t - \frac{\omega}{\gamma} H_t^{\gamma} \right]$$

where $\beta \in (0, 1)$ is the discount factor, C_t is a constant elasticity of substitution (CES) aggregator of market and home consumption in period t, and H_t is total time spent working in the market and at home in period t. That is,

$$C_t = [\psi C_{mt}^{\xi} + (1 - \psi) C_{nt}^{\xi}]^{1/\xi}$$

$$H_t = H_{mt} + H_{nt}$$

where C_{mt} and C_{nt} are market and home consumption, respectively, and H_{mt} and H_{nt} are market and home work, respectively. The agent is endowed with one unit of time each period and K_0 units of capital at

$t = 0$. The parameters $\gamma \geq 1$ and $\xi \leq 1$ play a key role in influencing the business-cycle predictions of the model since γ determines the substitutability in hours worked across time, and $\xi \leq 1$ determines the extent of substitutability between home and market goods. As a result, these parameters dictate the amount of intertemporal and intratemporal substitution in hours of market work.

We choose the utility function $\log C - (\omega/\gamma)H_t^\gamma$ to facilitate comparison with the large literature in labor economics that tries to estimate γ. The standard life-cycle labor literature (without home production) typically assumes separability in the sense that $U(C_t, H_t) = u(C_t) + v(H_t)$. In a deterministic setting, this means that the first-order condition for h_t can be written as:

$$v'(H_t) = -w_t\lambda$$

where λ is the Lagrange multiplier on the lifetime budget constraint and w_t is the wage in period t. Due to separability, this condition does not include C_t, so one can take the equation to the data without having to observe consumption. If $v(H) = -(\omega/\gamma)H^\gamma$, then (after taking logs and rearranging) we have:

$$\log(H_t) = \alpha_0 + \frac{1}{\gamma - 1}\log(w_t)$$

where α_0 can incorporate a constant, a time trend, and an error term, depending on assumptions. From this, one can estimate the elasticity $1/(\gamma - 1)$ and recover the structural parameter γ.[4]

The above analysis does not require specifying $u(C)$. It is well-known in macro, however, that balanced growth requires either $U(C, H) = C^\sigma v(H)$ or $U(C, H) = \log(C) + v(H)$ for some function $v(H)$. Hence, assuming separability so that we can apply the labor supply results, we are led to:

$$U(C, H) = \log(C) + v(H)$$

for some function $v(H)$. Although in principle any function $v(H)$ satisfying the usual regularity conditions would do, we will adopt the common specification $v(H) = -(\omega/\gamma)H^\gamma$.

Incorporating home production into the analysis now merely requires reinterpreting C and H as composites of market and home consumption and of market and home work: $C = C(C_M, C_H)$ and $H = H(H_M, H_H)$. Here, we follow much of the previous literature by assuming $C = [\psi C_m^\xi + (1 - \psi)C_n^\xi]^{1/\xi}$, so that we can appeal to existing estimates of the parameter ξ, and $H = H_m + H_n$, which means hours worked in the market and home are perfect substitutes. The last thing to say about preference is that, although there will be a government in the model, we assume that agents derive no utility from government consumption.[5]

In terms of technology, there is a production function:

$$Y_{mt} = z_t K_{mt}^{\theta}[(1+g)^t H_{mt}]^{1-\theta}$$

where Y_{mt} is market output in period t; K_{mt} and H_{mt} are capital and labor services, respectively, used in market production in period t; z_t is a technology shock; and g represents the constant rate of labor augmenting technological change. We assume that z_t follows the process:

$$\log z_{t+1} = \rho \log z_t + \varepsilon_{t+1}$$

where ε_t is an independently and identically distributed (iid) random variable that is normally distributed with mean μ_m and variance σ_m^2. The period t realization of ε is observed before any decisions are made. Market output produced in period t can be used either as market consumption C_{mt}, government consumption G_t, or investment I_t:

$$C_{mt} + G_t + I_t = Y_{mt}$$

There is also a production function for home produced goods:

$$Y_{nt} = K_{nt}^{\eta}[(1+g)^t H_{nt}]^{1-\eta}$$

where Y_{nt} is household production in period t; K_{nt} and H_{nt} are capital and labor services, respectively, used in home production in period t; and g again represents the constant rate of labor augmenting technological change. We assume the same rate of technological change in the two production functions, as is required for balanced growth. Although we assume the home production function is Cobb–Douglas, following Greenwood and Hercowitz (1991), some authors have argued that departures from Cobb–Douglas are crucial for understanding certain issues, including the pattern of investments in home and market capital. The estimates in McGrattan et al. (1997) imply the home production function is significantly different from Cobb–Douglas (the model actually allows both market and home production functions to be CES, but the estimates implied only the latter is significantly different from Cobb–Douglas). For the issues on which we focus, however, this does not matter much, so we use Cobb–Douglas for simplicity. We also abstract from shocks to the home production function since they will not play any role in the subsequent analysis.[6]

One asymmetry between market and home production is that the only use of home-produced output is as home consumption, i.e.:

$$C_{nt} = Y_{nt}$$

That is, although capital is used in home production, it is produced only in the market sector. Capital accumulation is given by:

$$K_{mt+1} = (1 - \delta_m)K_{mt} + I_{mt}$$

$$K_{nt+1} = (1 - \delta_n)K_{nt} + I_{nt}$$

where I_{mt} and I_{nt} are investment in market and home capital, respectively, in period t, and both are constrained to be nonnegative, while $\delta_m \in (0, 1)$ and $\delta_n \in (0, 1)$ are depreciation rates. Aggregate investment in period t is the sum of investment in home and market capital:[7]

$$I_t = I_{mt} + I_{nt}$$

It is well known that empirically plausible tax rates can have big effects in this model. Since we will be choosing some parameter values by calibrating to steady-state values, it is important to incorporate taxes into the specification. Given that our primary reason for doing so is to facilitate calibration, however, we assume constant tax rates. In particular, we assume that market labor income is taxed at the constant rate τ_h, and capital income is taxed at the constant rate τ_k. The government uses tax revenues to finance spending G_t, which we assume is a constant ratio of market output. The government faces a period-by-period budget constraint, with lump-sum transfers τ_t serving to achieve budget balance.

2.2 *Parameterization*

Calibration of parameter values for this model is fairly standard. Because of this, and also because we will go into detail on the calibration of the overlapping generations model later in the paper, we do not provide details here and simply report the parameter values in Table 1. Note that we set a period to be a year in this paper. While it is more common in infinitely lived agent models to use a quarter rather than a year, the basic properties of the model are not affected by this choice. We will be using an annual model once we introduce overlapping

Table 1
Parameters for infinitely-lived household calibration

β	θ	η	δ_m	δ_n	g	ρ	σ_ε	τ_h	τ_k
.954	.30	.27	.065	.057	.018	.806	.0139	.25	.50

generations because the data on hours worked by age is at annual frequency. Not shown in Table 1 is that we assume government spending relative to market output to be .20.

There are also four utility parameters not listed in Table 1: the elasticity parameters γ and ξ, and the coefficients giving weights on market versus home consumption and on hours versus total consumption, ψ and ω. The standard procedure for determining values for these parameters is to set ω and ψ so that the steady-state values of H_m and H_n are equal to some target values taken from the data, typically $H_m = \frac{1}{3}$ and $H_n = \frac{1}{4}$, and to set γ and ξ in accord with the empirical literature because they cannot be pinned down easily by steady-state considerations. It is well known that the values of the two elasticity parameters γ and ξ matter a lot for the cyclical properties of hours. There is also considerable controversy over these parameters, and estimates can vary a lot depending on which group one looks at (e.g., males versus females), which features are incorporated (e.g., skill accumulation, home production), and which margins one considers (e.g., the intensive versus the extensive margin). Hence, we will present results for a wide range of values for γ and ξ, without necessarily taking a stand on any particular value.

2.3 *Results*

It is well known that models of this sort can mimic the broad features of cyclical fluctuations in the U.S. economy, although the magnitude of fluctuations in market hours has received considerable attention since the model does less well on this (see Hansen and Wright, 1992). In particular, we will emphasize the relative standard deviation of market hours to market output.[8] In the data, the relevant number is .80, which is the standard deviation of market hours based on current population survey (CPS) data over the period 1962–2000, relative to the standard deviation of output over this same period. The standard deviation of hours is 1.79 and the standard deviation of output is 2.23, where these numbers are annual and correspond to data that has been

Table 2
Standard deviation of market hours relative to output

	$\gamma = 1$	$\gamma = 2$	$\gamma = 2.5$	$\gamma = 3.0$	$\gamma = 4$	$\gamma = 11$
$\xi = 0$	.66	.48	.45	.43	.40	.35
$\xi = .2$	.67	.50	.47	.45	.43	.38
$\xi = .4$	.68	.53	.51	.49	.47	.44
$\xi = .5$	.69	.56	.54	.52	.50	.47
$\xi = .6$	.71	.59	.57	.56	.54	.52
$\xi = .8$	.78	.71	.70	.69	.69	.68

Hodrick–Prescott (HP)-filtered with a smoothing parameter of 100. We note that our output measure excludes the service flow from housing since we treat this as a nonmarket service.

Given the calibration strategy discussed above, Table 2 reports values for the standard deviation of market work relative to market output (both HP-filtered) that come from simulating the model. We generate samples that are 39 periods in length, the same as our data, and average over 1000 runs. Table 2 reports the results for values of γ ranging from 1 to 11, which corresponds to elasticities ranging from infinite to .1, and values of ξ ranging from 0 to .8, which corresponds to elasticities ranging from 1 to 5. As can be seen, and as is fairly well known, the model can account for most of the fluctuations in market hours if (and only if) the elasticities are sufficiently large. Perhaps somewhat less well known is that it is not sufficient to know the value of the intertemporal elasticity parameter γ to assess the model on this dimension since even if γ is set to 11, the model would still be able to account for the bulk of the observed fluctuations if the value of ξ were sufficiently high.[9]

There is considerable debate over the appropriate value of γ for the representative household, and even less is known about the parameter ξ. This notwithstanding, just to fix ideas, suppose we use values in the upper part of the plausible range, in particular, $\gamma = 2.5$ and $\xi = .5$, corresponding to elasticities of $\frac{2}{3}$ and 2, respectively. The implied relative standard deviation of hours is equal to .54, roughly two-thirds of what we observe in the data. This suggests that although the model accounts for a substantial fraction of the volatility in market hours, there is also a sizable fraction that it misses.

One is then naturally led to consider modifications to the model to better match the behavior of market hours. Many such modifications have been proposed in the literature, including alternative specifications of preferences (e.g., Kydland and Prescott, 1982), search frictions (e.g., Merz, 1995; Andolfatto, 1996; and Den Haan, Ramey, and Watson, 2000), informational asymmetries (e.g., Gomme, 1999, and Alexopoulos, 2004), restrictions on working hours (e.g., Rogerson, 1988, and Hansen, 1985), alternative formulations of technology (e.g., Kydland and Prescott, 1988), and alternative wage-setting mechanisms (e.g., Danthine and Donaldson, 1995). What we want to argue in the remainder of this paper is that if we are looking for ways to isolate the key empirical deficiencies of equilibrium macro models like the one described above, we ought to consider a lower level of aggregation. In the next section, we document a wide range in variability of market hours over the business cycle across subgroups. In view of this, it seems interesting to ask whether the mechanism implicit in the model underaccounts for fluctuations across all subgroups, or if perhaps it does account for the fluctuations of some groups but not others. Put somewhat differently, if we are trying to understand the causes of fluctuations in hours of work over the business cycle, it seems reasonable that understanding why some groups fluctuate much more than other groups would be a key piece of information.

3. Beyond Aggregate Data

In this section, we document differences in the magnitude of cyclical fluctuations in market hours across groups in the population. In particular, we disaggregate by age, education, marital status, gender, and industry of employment.

3.1 Fluctuations by Age

Using data from the March Supplement of the CPS for the period 1962–2000, we compute aggregate market hours per capita for the entire population aged 16 and above, and market hours per capita by age for seven age groups: 16–19, 20–24, 25–34, 35–44, 45–54, 55–64, and 65+. The standard procedure for defining the business-cycle component of an aggregate series is the percentage deviation from a suitably defined trend, defined here using the HP filter. To extract the component of fluctuations in aggregate hours that is accounted for by each age group, we use a two-step procedure described in the appendix (Section 9). The results are in Table 3.

Table 3
Relative cyclical fluctuations of hours by age group

	16–19	20–24	25–34	35–44	45–54	55–64	65+
σ_h/σ_{Y_m}	2.23	1.23	.86	.64	.57	.59	1.26
% of H_m	4	11	26	25	20	12	2
% of σ_{H_m}	11	16	28	19	14	9	3

Table 4
Fluctuations of sectoral hours relative to GDP

Sector	Agr	Min	Cons	Mfg	Trans	Wh/Re Tr	FIRE	Serv
σ_h/σ_{Y_m}	1.44	1.69	2.17	1.24	.75	.80	.55	.57

The first row shows fluctuations in the hours of each age group relative to output. The second row indicates the fraction of average hours worked by each age group over the entire sample period. The third row indicates the fraction of fluctuations accounted for by each age group. Several interesting patterns emerge. First, note that the pattern of fluctuations across age groups is U-shaped: fluctuations are highest for young and old workers, and are lowest for middle-aged workers. Related to this, the second and third rows indicate the extent to which cyclical fluctuations in hours are disproportionately accounted for by fluctuations in the hours of work of younger workers. Workers aged 16–24 account for only 15% of total market hours, but more than 25% of fluctuations in market hours. Conversely, prime-age workers, between the ages of 35 and 54, account for 45% of total market hours but for only 33% of fluctuations in market hours.[10]

One may be concerned that the patterns displayed above are not due to age effects per se but are really an artifact of a situation in which workers of different ages work at different jobs, with some jobs being more cyclically volatile than others. To explore this possibility, we examine the role that the age distribution of hours worked across one-digit industries may play in shaping fluctuations by age group. Table 4 shows the relative volatility of hours of work across one-digit sectors. As is well known, hours in some sectors fluctuate much more over the business cycle. In particular, goods-producing sectors display more volatility than do service sectors. Table 5 indicates the distribution of hours worked by each age group across each of these eight sectors.

Table 5
Sectoral distribution of hours by age

	16–19	20–24	25–34	35–44	45–54	55–64	65+
Agr	5.17	2.99	2.91	3.20	3.81	.01	12.89
Min	.45	.92	1.08	1.06	.98	.90	.43
Cons	4.59	6.26	6.81	6.56	5.87	5.91	3.66
Mfg	15.78	22.34	23.82	24.23	24.78	25.07	11.04
Trans	2.97	5.94	7.86	8.62	8.35	7.70	3.59
Wh/Re Tr	44.30	26.10	19.52	17.98	18.30	20.43	22.47
FIRE	4.43	7.13	6.93	6.38	6.21	6.52	7.55
Ser	22.32	28.33	31.08	31.97	31.70	33.46	38.37

Table 6
Relative fluctuations induced by sectoral composition

Age	16–19	20–24	25–34	35–44	45–54	55–64	65+
$\sigma_{h_m}/\sigma_{Y_m}$	.81	.83	.84	.84	.84	.81	.79

Table 5 reveals that there are indeed some sharp differences across age groups in how their hours of work are distributed across sectors. For example, the distribution of hours in the manufacturing sector is increasing in age up until 65. Hours of work of teenagers are heavily skewed toward the wholesale and retail trade sector. Mining, construction, and transportation and public utilities all display an inverted U-shape across age groups, whereas wholesale and retail trade displays a U-shape across age groups. Given that each age group has a distinctive pattern of hours across sectors and that fluctuations vary across sectors, we can ask how fluctuations would vary by age if the only source of differences by age were the sectoral distribution of hours. The answer is given in Table 6, where we take a weighted average of the sectoral relative volatilities for each group using the age distribution of hours across sectors as weights.

Two observations emerge from this exercise. First, the size of the effects induced by differences in sectoral composition across age groups is small—the range of values goes only from .79 to .84. We conclude from this finding that abstracting from sectoral composition effects is a reasonable thing to do. Second, to the extent that sectoral composition effects do matter, they actually generate an inverted U for the pattern of volatility across age, the opposite of what we see in the data. It follows that the pattern in Table 3 would be even more pronounced if we controlled for sectoral composition.

Given previous research on the importance of the intensive and extensive margins of labor hours adjustment, it is also of interest to see if there is any systematic difference across groups in the importance of the two margins. However, analysis revealed this not to be the case. We found that the percentage of total fluctuations accounted for by the extensive margin varied within the relatively narrow range of 68–72%.

To close this subsection, recall the discussion of the infinitely lived representative agent model in the previous section. We suggested that an empirically plausible parameterization generates relative fluctuations in hours of work equal to .54. Recall also the first row of Table 3, which showed the relative volatility of hours by age. Looking at this row with the number .54 in mind raises a key issue. One interpretation of these findings is that the previous model is actually successful in accounting for the fluctuations of hours of prime-age individuals, and that its main shortcoming is accounting for the fluctuations in hours of younger workers. Of course, this interpretation is not warranted in the infinitely lived representative agent framework; we need to consider a model in which agents differ by age. We pursue exactly this in the remaining sections of this paper. Before we do so, however, we think it is also of interest to examine the heterogeneity in hours fluctuations along some additional dimensions.

3.2 *Fluctuations by Education*

Here, we repeat the previous analysis, but this time we split the population by education. Because we do not model fluctuations by educational attainment in our theoretical analysis below, we do not carry out as extensive an analysis of this case as we did for age. Also, due to data issues, we restrict our attention to the years 1974–2000. And because measuring educational attainment for young workers is difficult, we restrict our attention to individuals age 25 or greater. For each year, using the March CPS, we compute hours per person for individuals in four educational groups: (1) those with less than high school, (2) those with exactly high school, (3) those with some college but no college degree, and (4) those with at least a college degree. Again, we extract the component of fluctuations in aggregate hours accounted for by each of these groups.

Table 7
Hours fluctuations by education, 1974–2000

	<HS	HS	SC	C
$\sigma_{h_m}/\sigma_{Y_m}$	1.20	.84	.67	.23

Table 8
Hours fluctuations by gender, 1962–2000

	Males	Females
$\sigma_{h_m}/\sigma_{Y_m}$	.87	.73

The results are reported in Table 7, which raises a similar issue to the one in the previous subsection: is it possible that the model does a good job of explaining fluctuations for those with, say, at least some college education, and that the model's shortcomings are entirely to do with the fluctuations in the other groups? Although we will not address this question explicitly in this paper, we believe that understanding the sources of these differences in volatility across education groups may also help us better understand the fluctuations in the aggregate data.

3.3 *Fluctuations by Gender and Marital Status*

In the model that we study below, we will continue to take the unit of analysis to be a household, and we will assume the sole dimension along which households differ is age. In particular, we will abstract from differences in household size, and we will abstract from the issue of time allocations across household members in multimember households. We still think it is interesting, however, to examine the extent to which fluctuations in market hours differ along the dimensions of marital status and gender (if for no other reason, this helps in assessing the extent to which our abstractions are warranted). Using the same procedure as above, we extract the component of aggregate hours fluctuations that is accounted for first by men and women, and then by married and unmarried individuals. For these series, the data cover the period 1962–2000.

Table 8 reports relative fluctuations for men and women. Somewhat surprisingly, men display larger cyclical fluctuations than do women. One may suspect that part of this difference is accounted for by sec-

Table 9
Hours fluctuations by gender and sector ($\sigma_{h_m}/\sigma_{Y_m}$), 1962–2000

	Agr	Min	Cons	Mfg	Tran	Wh/ Re Tr	FIRE	Ser
Males	1.49	1.64	1.99	1.09	.72	.70	.61	.63
Females	1.46	2.28	1.51	1.27	.68	.83	.47	.52

Table 10
Relative standard deviation of hours by age and gender ($\sigma_{h_m}/\sigma_{Y_m}$), 1962–2000

	16–19	20–24	25–34	35–44	45–54	55–64	65+
Male	2.60	1.52	.96	.64	.60	.73	1.16
Female	2.01	1.00	.75	.69	.55	.45	1.50

Table 11
Standard deviation of hours by marital status and age, 1962–2000

	16–19	20–24	25–34	35–44	45–54	55–64	65+
Married	1.98	1.03	.79	.61	.52	.61	1.19
Not Married	2.35	1.36	1.07	.80	.87	.61	1.47

toral composition patterns. Table 9 shows that this is indeed a factor. This table shows that in several sectors, notably manufacturing and wholesale and retail trade, males display less volatility than do females.

It is also of interest to examine how the variability across the life cycle varies by gender. In Table 10, we report relative variability by age, using the same procedure as before. Table 10 shows the pattern of volatility over the life cycle is U-shaped for both males and females, though the timing of the trough is different across the groups—for men, the volatility begins to increase in the 55–64 group, whereas for women, it does not increase until the 65+ group. Quantitatively there are some differences—for younger workers, the volatility of hours is somewhat less for females, while for individuals aged 35–44, the volatility is somewhat higher for females. Taken together, we interpret these findings with respect to gender as supporting our decision to abstract from the within-family decision in the analysis that follows.[11]

Table 11 reports the results disaggregated by marital status, where we note that fluctuations here are at the individual level and not at the household level. Fluctuations for single individuals are significantly larger than they are for married individuals. It is important to keep in mind that among prime-age individuals, the majority are married, so that for these individuals, the aggregate numbers look very similar to those of the married group. For younger groups, however, the reverse is true. Here again, note that the basic pattern is U-shaped for both groups, with the exception of the observation for the 45–54 group that is not married. For this group, however, the majority of fluctuations in hours are not correlated with movements in aggregate hours, so this number does not necessarily reflect the overall fluctuations for this group. We conclude from Table 11 that there are indeed differences across married and unmarried individuals. If we interpret our model as applying to married households, it follows that the target levels of volatility are somewhat lower as a result.

4. A Life-Cycle Model

In the remainder of the paper, we focus on the nature of fluctuations by age. The obvious way to incorporate this type of heterogeneity into the model is to move from the infinitely lived representative agent framework to the overlapping generations framework. The goal will be to retain the basic structure of the infinitely lived household model as much as possible, while introducing life-cycle considerations. To maintain simplicity, some of these considerations will be captured in somewhat of a reduced form manner—for example, rather than explicitly modeling fertility, we will simply assume that preference parameters change systematically over the life cycle.

4.1 Model

In each period, a representative T-period lived household is born. We abstract from population growth and assume that length of life is deterministic, although one could extend things on these dimensions at some cost in terms of simplicity. In our quantitative analysis, we interpret a period to be a year and set $T = 55$, and we think of a household beginning economic decisionmaking at age 20 and continuing until 75. We impose exogenously that agents retire at age T_R. Agents have preferences over lifetime profiles of consumption and work. For a generic variable s, we will use s_t^a to denote the value of s for an agent of age a in period t, and we use lowercase (uppercase) letters to represent choices at the individual (aggregate) level. Hence, for an agent born in period t, preferences are given by:

$$\sum_{a=0}^{T-1} \beta^a U(c_{m,t+a}^{a+1}, c_{n,t+a}^{a+1}, h_{m,t+a}^{a+1}, h_{n,t+a}^{a+1}, \psi^a, \omega^a)$$

where c_m^a is market consumption, c_n^a is household consumption, h_m^a is market work, and h_n^a is home work at age a, while ψ^a and ω^a are life-cycle preference shifters.[12]

We make the same assumption regarding functional forms as earlier. In particular, the period utility function $U(c_m^a, c_n^a, h_m^a, h_n^a, \psi^a, \omega^a)$ is of the form:

$$U = [\psi^a (c_m^a)^{\xi} + (1-\psi^a)(c_n^a)^{\xi}]^{1/\xi} - \frac{\omega^a}{\gamma}(h_m^a + h_n^a)^{\gamma}$$

Each household is endowed with one unit of time in each period of life, which can again be allocated among three uses: working in the market, working at home, and enjoying leisure. As in the previous model, agents derive no utility from government consumption.

An important empirical regularity is that wages exhibit significant changes over the life cycle. We incorporate this feature by assuming that the efficiency units corresponding to a given amount of time spent working changes with age. In particular, each unit of time spent in market work at age a yields e^a efficiency units of market labor input.[13] We could also assume that each unit of time spent in home work at age a yields e_n^a efficiency units of household labor input. However, given the life-cycle preference shifter ψ^a, there is really nothing to be gained by this, so we assume e_n^a does not vary with a.[14]

As before, we assume that home-produced goods are nontraded and can be used only as consumption. Hence, for a household of age a at time t, we have:

$$c_{nt}^a = (k_{nt}^a)^{\eta}[(1+g)^t h_{nt}^a]^{1-\eta}$$

where k_{nt}^a is the stock of home capital for a household of age a in period t, h_{nt}^a is time spent in home production by a household of age a in period t, and we assume that the rate of technological progress is the same in both production functions to have balanced growth.

The laws of motion for individual stocks of capital satisfy:

$$k_{mt+1}^{a+1} = (1-\delta_m)k_{mt}^a + i_{mt}^a$$

$$k_{nt+1}^{a+1} = (1-\delta_n)k_{nt}^a + i_{nt}^a$$

while the aggregate laws of motion for the capital stocks are given by:

$$K_{mt+1} = (1 - \delta_m)K_{mt} + I_{mt}$$

$$K_{nt+1} = (1 - \delta_n)K_{nt} + I_{nt}$$

We assume that each household begins economic life with an endowment of home capital k_{n0}; that is, $k^1_{nt} = k_{n0}$ for all t. Without this endowment, agents would have no home capital in the first period of their life, which gives rise to big differences in the time allocated to home work in the first and all other periods of life. For internal consistency, we assume that this endowment of home capital is transferred from the age T cohort to the newborn cohort each period; i.e., we require that individuals make choices such that $k^{T+1}_{tn} = k_{n0}$. Aside from this, we assume no links between the generations.

As above, the government consumes G and finances expenditures via proportional taxes τ_h and τ_k that do not vary over time, balancing the budget every period by adjusting the lump-sum transfer τ_t. Given that the total mass of households alive at any date is T, and letting w_t and r_t denote the wage per efficiency unit of labor and the rental rate of market capital, respectively, this implies:

$$\tau_t = (\tau_h w_t E_{mt} + \tau_k r_t K_{mt} - G_t)/T$$

where E_{mt} is the aggregate supply of labor measured in efficiency units.

Individual budget constraints are given by:

$$c^i_{mt} + i^i_{mt} + i^i_{nt} = (1 - \tau_h)w_t e^a h^a_{mt} + (1 - \tau_k)r_t k^a_{mt} + \tau_t$$

We require that k^a_{nt} is always nonnegative. By contrast, although aggregate market capital cannot be negative, we assume that individuals may hold negative market capital k^a_{mt} as a way to borrow. We do not place any explicit restriction on the extent to which individuals can borrow, but we do require that everyone have zero holdings of market capital at the time of death, $k^{T+1}_{mt} = 0$. In a deterministic model, these restrictions implicitly generate a maximum feasible debt at each age. In a stochastic model, the situation is more complicated, but in practice, we found that this issue is irrelevant in the quantitative analysis since the shocks are not that large. Hence, we impose no explicit restrictions on holdings of market capital.

The market technology is given by:

$$Y_{mt} = z_t K^{\theta}_{mt}[(1 + g)^t E_{mt}]^{1-\theta}$$

where K_{mt} is the input of market capital, E_{mt} is the input of market labor measured in efficiency units, g is the constant rate of labor augmenting technological progress, and z_t is an aggregate shock that follows exactly the same process as in the representative agent model. Aggregate efficiency units of market labor are given by:

$$E_{mt} = \sum_{a=1}^{T} e^a h_{mt}^a$$

Market output in period t has four uses: private market consumption C_{mt}, government consumption G_t, investment in market capital I_{mt}, and investment in home capital I_{nt}. Hence feasibility requires:

$$C_{mt} + G_t + I_{mt} + I_{nt} \leq Y_{mt}$$

where

$$C_{mt} = \sum_{a=1}^{T} c_{mt}^a, \qquad I_{mt} = \sum_{a=1}^{T} i_{mt}^a, \qquad \text{and} \qquad I_{nt} = \sum_{a=1}^{T} i_{nt}^a$$

We abstract from any form of public social security and do not allow markets for risk sharing. Note that in this model, all shocks are aggregate shocks, which induce changes in wages and rental rates, but all individuals face the same wage per efficiency unit of labor. In principle, once one allows for heterogeneity, there is the possibility of the shocks affecting individuals differently even if they are perfectly correlated. It is possible, for example, that fluctuations in market hours differ across groups because the size of the shocks differ across groups. Our formulation implicitly rules this out since we think this provides the most natural baseline for comparison with the standard representative agent model.

4.2 *Equilibrium and Computation*

Our solution concept is recursive competitive equilibrium. The aggregate state of the economy at t will be the the technology shock, plus μ_{mt} and μ_{nt}, which denote the distributions of market and home capital across agents indexed by age at t. We denote the aggregate state by S_t. For a given agent, the individual state is given by their age and their two capital stocks. We denote an individual state vector by s_t. In a recursive competitive equilibrium, prices at t are time invariant functions of the aggregate state variable; i.e., $w_t = W(S_t)$, and $r_t = R(S_t)$. Since our notion of equilibrium is standard, in the interests of space, we do not provide a formal definition.[15]

In equilibrium, individual decision rules depend on the entire state vector, including the two distributions μ_{mt} and μ_{nt}. Solving for these decision rules would be prohibitively costly in terms of computational time unless they are restricted to being linear; see Rios-Rull (1996). We therefore adopt the following procedure to solve for equilibrium numerically. We linearize the households' first-order conditions, the firms' first-order conditions, and the equilibrium conditions around the model's steady state, and then we use a Schur algorithm to solve for the linearized decision rules; see Klein (2000) for details.

4.3 *Calibration*

We use the model to interpret the choices of households between ages 20 and 74. Thus, we set a period length to be one year and set $T = 55$ and $T_R = 45$, implying that agents retire at 65. We now turn to the choice of parameter values for our benchmark specification. We emphasize that these choices are only for a benchmark, and that we have carried out sensitivity analyses to explore the implications of alternative values for several parameters. Given that we have a home production model, there is an important decision regarding the division of activity between the home and market. Typically, housing services are treated as a component of market consumption. This does not fit well with a model that describes market output as the result of combining market hours with market capital. We treat housing as a form of home capital, and so in our treatment of the data, we subtract the flow of housing services from market activity. Because the data on market hours fluctuations by age is for the period 1962–2000, we restrict attention to this period for all of our measurement.[16]

As is standard, we follow the procedure of requiring that parameter values are such that the model's deterministic steady state matches the time series averages for several aggregate variables. There are various specific procedures that one may adopt to carry this out. We have experimented with several and found that it made little difference to our conclusions. For our benchmark case, we do the following. The capital share parameter for the market production function is set to $\theta = .3$ to match the capital share of market income in the data. The capital share parameter for the home production function η is set to generate the same ratio of home investment to market output as in the data. The ratio of home investment to gross domestic product (GDP) in the data is .1248, and the resulting value is $\eta = .21$. The two depreciation rates are picked on the basis of estimated depreciation by the Bureau of Economic Analysis (BEA). This implies $\delta_m = .0654$ and $\delta_n = .0568$.

We use a standard procedure to pick values for the stochastic process for the market technology shock. In particular, we construct a series for the Solow residual over the period 1954–2000 using annual data and then estimate an $AR(1)$ process assuming a polynomial time trend.[17] This leads us to $\rho_m = .8953$ and $\sigma_m = .0153$. The trend growth rate g is set to a value of .0184. For the government sector, we choose G so that government spending on goods and services is always equal to .20 of market output, which is roughly the average ratio of government spending to output over the period 1962–2000. We set $\tau_h = .25$ and $\tau_k = .5$.

This leaves household parameters. There are three sets of such parameters: preference parameters that are constant over the life cycle (β, ξ, and γ), the efficiency units profile e^a, and the profiles for the preference shifters ψ^a and ω^a. We choose the discount factor so that households, on average, have investment in market capital that amounts to the share .1203 of market output. The implied value for β is .9563.[18] For ξ, which determines substitutability between home and market goods and given the empirical results in Rupert et al. (1995) and McGrattan et al. (1997), a reasonable range is between .4 and .5; we set $\xi = .45$.[19] For γ, which determines the degree of intertemporal substitution in hours of work, there are a variety of estimates to consider, for both men and women, with estimates for the latter usually being greater. In our sensitivity analysis, we explore many values for γ, but as a benchmark, we set $\gamma = 2.5$, which we think is a reasonable compromise between the range of estimates for men and women. This is the estimate obtained by Rupert et al. (2000) using life-cycle data for males in a model that explicitly allowed for time spent in home work as well as market work. As they point out, this estimate is larger than those often found for males, but this is explained by the fact that neglecting home work leads to a negative bias in previous estimation procedures.

We choose the efficiency units profile for market work for the household by matching data on male wages over the life cycle. In particular, we use cross-section data from the March CPS for the years 1975–1981 and then use the fitted values from a regression on a constant, age and

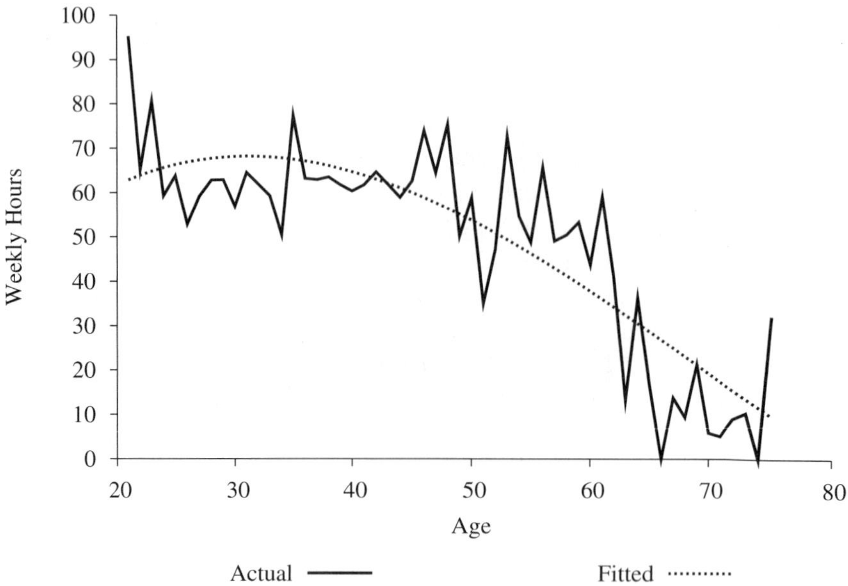

Figure 1
Household profile for market hours

age squared.[20] The parameters ψ^a and ω^a, which dictate the relative weights on market versus home consumption and on consumption relative to work, are important because they influence the absolute amount of time spent working and the relative amount of time spent on market and home work. Thus, we choose these parameters to match the profile of time spent on home and market work, given the other parameters. We obtain life-cycle profiles of time spent on market and home work for married couple households from the Time Use Study. In particular, we use data from the Michigan Time Use Longitudinal Panel Study for the years 1975–1981. We use data on market and home hours for married households and use the fitted values from a regression on a constant, age, age squared, and age cubed. Figure 1 shows the life-cycle profile for market hours that we use in the calibration, and Figure 2 shows the life-cycle profile for home hours. Figure 3 shows the calibrated profile for ψ over the life cycle, and Figure 4 shows the profile of ω over the life cycle.[21]

As can be seen, the calibrated profile for ψ has a U-shape, increasing during the middle part of the life cycle, whereas the profile for ω is increasing over time. This profile has a large jump at retirement age

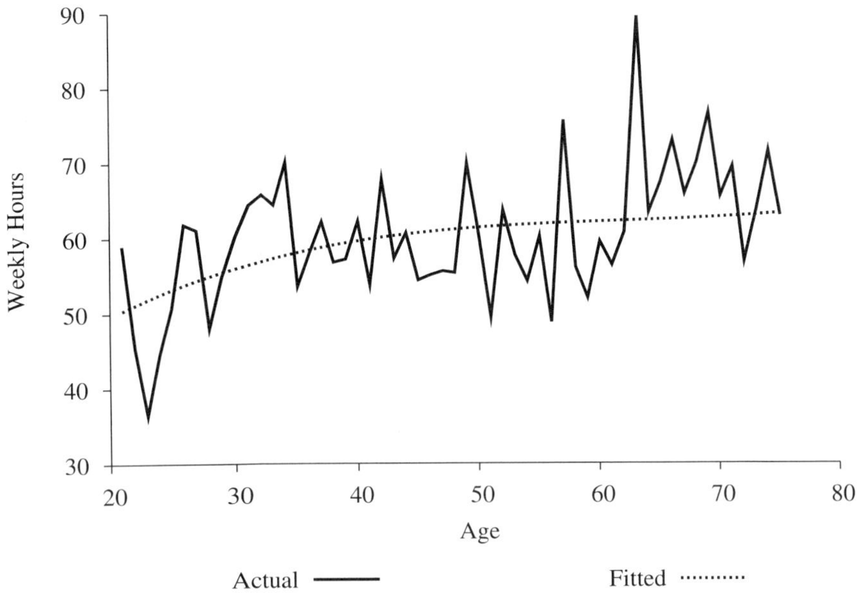

Figure 2
Household profile for home hours

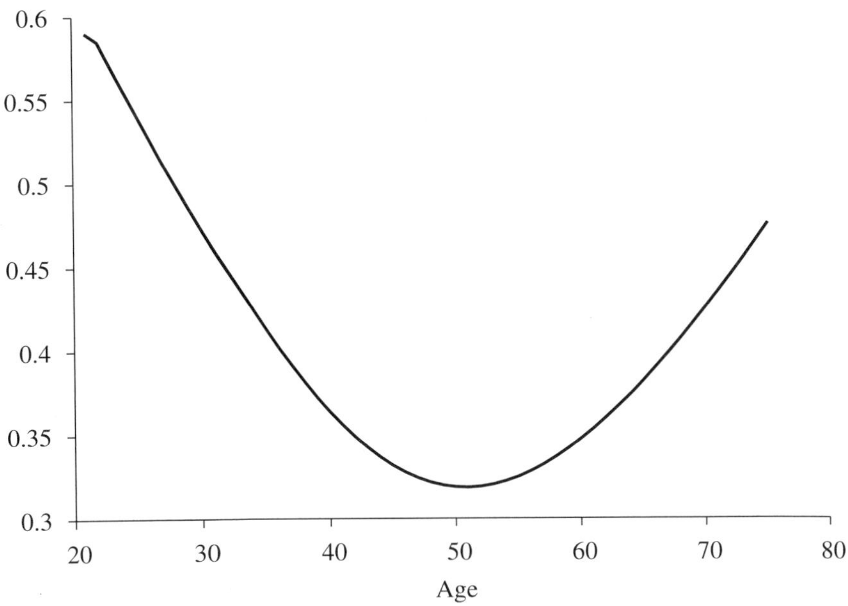

Figure 3
Calibrated profile for ψ

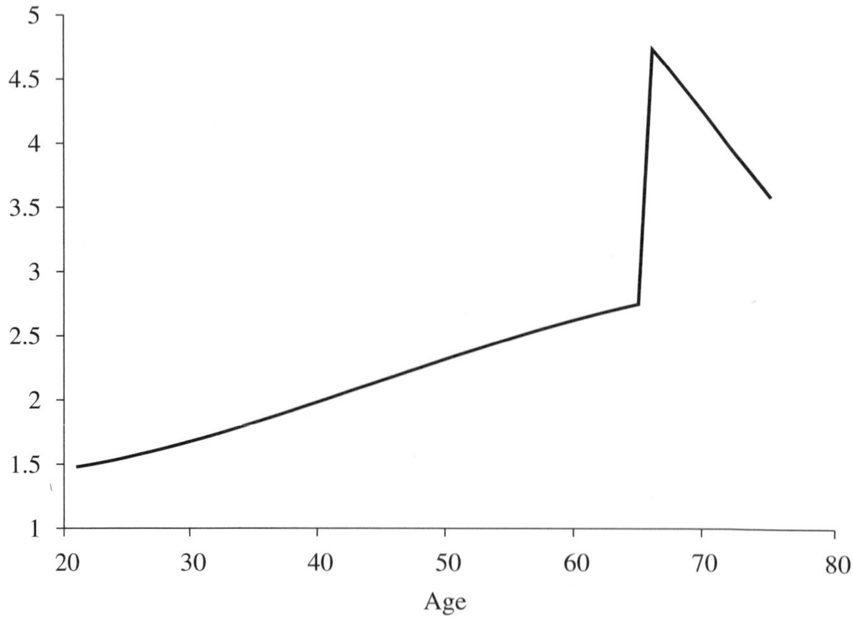

Figure 4
Calibrated profile for ω

since we require the first-order condition for total work to hold on either side of retirement. Perhaps not surprisingly, the calibration then requires that the disutility of working increases rather sharply at retirement. To understand the shape of the ω profile, note that in the steady-state equilibrium of this model, the standard first-order conditions for market hours at each point of the life cycle with positive market hours implies a relationship between total hours (market plus home) at each period relative to hours in the first period; relative efficiency units at each point relative to the first period; and the value of γ, the parameter that determines the intertemporal elasticity. Our calibrated hours series implies a series for total hours that is hump-shaped, similar to the efficiency units profile. The profile for ω is increasing over time because with $\gamma = 2.5$, the data on total hours and efficiency units can be reconciled only with an increasing profile for ω. Given the series for total hours, the series for ψ effectively justifies the split of total hours between home and market work over the life cycle.

Last, we need to assign a value to the endowment of home capital that a household receives when they begin economic life. We set this

Table 12
Parameters for benchmark calibration

β	θ	η	δ_m	δ_n	g	ρ	σ_m	τ_h	τ_k	γ	ξ
.967	.30	.21	.065	.057	.018	.895	.0153	.25	.50	2.5	.45

Table 13
Properties of aggregate fluctuations

variable (x)	σ_x	σ_x/σ_{Y_m}	$corr(x_t, x_{t-1})$	$corr(x_t, Y_{mt})$
A. U.S. data, 1962–2000				
Y_m	2.23	1.00	.54	1.00
Y_{mp}	2.36	1.06	.52	.99
C_m	1.37	.61	.65	.91
I	5.68	2.55	.56	.89
H_{mE}	1.95	.87	.58	.86
H_{mH}	1.79	.80	.55	.75
Y_{mp}/H_{mE}	1.14	.51	.34	.47
B. Model				
Y_m	2.25	1.00	.52	1.00
C_m	1.12	.50	.56	.97
I	4.99	2.22	.51	.99
H_m	1.05	.47	.54	.98
Y_m/H_m	1.23	.55	.51	.99

to .2 in our benchmark since with this value, we did not need any large departures from the profiles for the ω^a and ψ^a to match the life-cycle hours profiles. This condition is obviously somewhat weak; however, we found that this parameter does not matter for the model's business-cycle properties. This completes the calibration. Table 12 summarizes the key parameter values for our benchmark economy.

5. Results

In this section, we present the results for our benchmark model. As is standard, we simulate the model for 39 years, starting from the deterministic steady state, and compute sample statistics from the equilibrium time series. We then repeat this 1000 times and average across the trials. Panel A of Table 13 shows the standard set of aggregate business-cycle statistics for the U.S. economy, and Panel B shows the same set of statistics for our benchmark model.

A few remarks on the data are in order. The measure of output that we use in Panel A is GDP per capita, less the imputed value of owner-occupied housing services. As discussed earlier, subtracting the value of owner-occupied housing services is consistent with viewing this as a nonmarket service that derives from the stock of home capital. We also report a measure of private GDP. Although our model has a government sector, by assumption in our model, the government sector fluctuates as much as the private sector and is perfectly correlated with fluctuations in the private sector. In reality, although the government sector does fluctuate about as much as the private sector, the two series are virtually uncorrelated. Our measure of consumption is spending on consumer nondurables and services (net of the imputed service flow for owner-occupied housing). Spending on consumer durables is counted as investment in home capital and hence is included in the investment category. Because our model abstracts from inventories, our investment series excludes this component. We report two hours series—one from the household series and one from the establishment series. The productivity series reported is for productivity in the private sector and is derived from using the data on private GDP and the hours series from the establishment series.

The relationship between the model statistics and their real-world counterparts is fairly typical for this literature, so we do not devote much space to it here. Note, however, that if one calibrates to annual data, then Solow residuals are large enough to account for virtually all fluctuations in market output, whereas in a quarterly model, the typical result is that the model accounts for roughly two-thirds of output fluctuations.[22]

Our focus here is on the ability of the model to account for fluctuations in hours, and as we can see from the above tables, the model can account for only about 60% of relative fluctuations in market hours. Also, consistent with the findings of Rios-Rull (1996), note that the volatility of aggregate hours in the overlapping generations model is very similar to that of the infinitely lived representative agent model. The relative standard deviation of hours here is .47, whereas it is .52 in the infinitely lived representative agent model, with the same values for labor supply elasticities. However, note that in the infinitely lived representative agent model, all labor services were equally productive, so that the variability of labor services in efficiency units was the same as the variability of labor services as measured by units of time. This is not the case in the calibrated overlapping generations model. If we

Table 14
Relative standard deviation of market hours by age group

Age group	Data	Model	Model/data
16–19	2.23	—	—
20–24	1.23	.39	.32
25–34	.86	.35	.41
35–44	.64	.35	.54
45–54	.57	.46	.81
55–64	.59	.97	1.64
65+	1.26	—	—
Aggregate	.80	.47	.59

compute the standard deviation of efficiency units of labor input instead, we obtain a value of .50 for the relative volatility. We conclude that the ability of the two models to account for aggregate labor market fluctuations is basically the same.

Since these aggregate statistics have been studied extensively in this context, we do not wish to devote any additional space to them here. Rather, we wish to look more carefully at the model's implications for market hours fluctuations by different age groups. Table 14 presents some summary statistics. The first column shows the standard deviations of hours fluctuations by age group, using the detrending procedure described earlier. As can be seen, these fluctuations exhibit a U-shaped pattern over the life cycle, with prime-age individuals exhibiting the smallest fluctuations.

A striking pattern emerges. In particular, the model's ability to account for fluctuations in hours increases as we consider older age groups. Although the magnitude of fluctuations exhibits a U-shaped profile over the life cycle in both the data and the model, this shape is much more pronounced in the data. In the model, the profile is effectively flat over the first part of the life cycle and increasing thereafter. We also note that in the model, the high variability of the age group 55–64 is due to the individuals in the 60–64 age group. If one considers the age group 55–59, the model predicts a relative standard deviation of roughly .73, which is much closer to the actual data. A simple message emerges from Table 14. Although the various income and substitution effects present in this model are sufficient to account for only about 60% of all fluctuations in hours, the extent of the shortcoming varies dramatically across age groups. We conclude that whatever the key additional mechanisms might be to help account for hours fluctuations, these mechanisms must be very nonuniform across age groups, as evidenced by the last column in Table 14.

A key property of these results that we want to emphasize is the pattern of volatility over the life cycle. We will explore the economic factors behind this shape more fully in the next section. But before doing so, we want to emphasize that this pattern is very robust with regard to our calibration strategy. In particular, this pattern is basically independent of the elasticity parameters. Changing the elasticity parameters basically generates parallel shifts in the curve that shows volatility over the life cycle.

6. Understanding the Life-Cycle Pattern of Volatility

In this section, we try to shed some light on why the life-cycle profile of fluctuations takes on the shape that it does. Note that in the model, all shocks are aggregate in the sense that all individuals face exactly the same shock processes. The differing responses of individuals over the business cycle are purely the result of individuals responding differently to common shocks. There are two different aspects to heterogeneity in the model. The first is that individuals are of different ages and hence at any point in time the agents that are alive have different planning horizons. In our model, this is also associated with different weights on home and market consumption, different weights on consumption and time spent working, and different productivities in market work. All of these differences represent heterogeneity in the *exogenous* component of an individual's state vector. The second source of heterogeneity is in the *endogenous* component of an individual's state vector. Optimal decisionmaking implies that, on average, individuals of different ages will have accumulated different amounts of capital. Individuals with different amounts of capital will potentially respond differently to the same shock. In seeking to understand the pattern of hours volatility over the life cycle predicted by the model, it will be useful to acknowledge these two different sources of heterogeneity.

To learn about the role that various features play in shaping the resulting profile of hours volatility over the life cycle, we find it instructive to compare outcomes across models in which specific model features are varied. If we do this type of analysis in the context of the full general-equilibrium model that we studied earlier, a difficulty emerges since with any change in model features we will potentially generate different parameters from a given calibration procedure. The equilibrium properties of the stochastic wage and rental rate processes may also vary. This makes it more difficult to assess the role of the various changes. This would also be true even if we did not redo the calibration with the new model feature present.

Because of this, in this section, we have chosen to focus on a comparison of decision theoretic cases in which we take a given stochastic process for wage (or rental) rates, solve individual decision problems with different features, and then compare the outcomes. We feel that this is a useful way to isolate the manner in which changes in features of the individual decision problem lead to changes in the volatility of hours for a given exogenous stochastic process for wages (or rental rates).

6.1 *Case I: The Pure Effect of the Time Horizon*

We begin by focusing on the pure effects of differences in the time horizon; i.e., we are interested in how the time horizon affects the response of an individual to a given shock, holding all other factors constant, such as the stock of capital owned by the individual, or the individual's productivity in market work. We will do this in two contexts, one in which there is no retirement, and the other in which there is retirement since it is of separate interest to understand the role of retirement. In this section, we present results for the case of no retirement. For simplicity, we abstract from home production in these exercises. Hence, we consider an individual with a period utility function given by:

$$\log(c_t) - \frac{\omega}{\gamma} h_t^\gamma$$

We consider an individual with constant efficiency in market work and who begins life with zero assets. The individual works for T periods and then dies. We assume that the individual faces stochastic processes for wage and rental rates that approximate those in the benchmark equilibrium above, except that we assume that the mean rental rate of capital is such that the return to capital exactly offsets the effect of discounting. In each exercise, we allow for only one stochastic process, holding the other price constant. We do this analysis for various values of T. In each case, we simulate the decision problem and compute the variability of hours at each stage of the life cycle. One appealing feature of this specification is that the individual has no life-cycle motive for capital accumulation, so that in the absence of shocks the individual would not accumulate any capital—he or she would simply work the same amount each period and then consume their income.

All results reported below are for the case of $\gamma = 2.5$. We assume that wage and rental rate stochastic processes follow AR(1) processes with a persistence parameter of .75. Average hours of work in the no-shock case are equal to .33, and average wages are equal to .96. The standard deviations in the tables below are based on the raw series and are not HP-filtered since we are not comparing these to actual data.

Comparing the volatility of, say, those in years 1–5 of life across cases with different T provides a way to assess the role of the time horizon in shaping the magnitude of the response. Intuitively, in this model, the key mechanism through which changes in wages and capital rental rates influence hours of market work is through intertemporal substitution. The shorter the horizon, the less scope there is for intertemporal substitution. In fact, in the extreme case of a one-period context, the intertemporal substitution effect vanishes. Table 15 shows the results of this exercise. As in the previous analysis, we interpret our individuals as starting life at age 20.

Reading down the columns of the table, one sees the various life-cycle profiles of volatility. Two patterns emerge. First, for a given life cycle, volatility decreases as the household ages. Second, holding age of the household fixed, volatility increases as we increase the number of periods remaining. The two patterns are strongly related. In fact, the table reveals that the volatility in hours is effectively determined by how many periods remain in the household's planning horizon:

Table 15
Effect of planning horizon: wage shocks, no retirement

Age interval	$T = 5$	$T = 15$	$T = 25$	$T = 35$	$T = 45$	$T = 55$
20–24	.026	.115	.179	.223	.252	.272
25–29		.087	.161	.214	.249	.272
30–34		.044	.129	.193	.235	.264
35–39			.087	.163	.215	.249
40–44			.042	.128	.190	.232
45–49				.087	.162	.213
50–54				.042	.128	.190
55–59					.087	.162
60–64					.042	.128
65–70						.087
71–75						.042

holding the number of periods remaining fixed, it is basically irrelevant how old the household is. The decreasing pattern is consistent with the intuition that we expressed earlier—as the horizon becomes shorter, there is less opportunity for intertemporal substitution. Or put somewhat differently, as the horizon becomes shorter, the shocks appear to be more permanent, and with balanced growth preferences, individuals do not change hours of market work in response to a permanent shock to wages (if they have no additional income). Recall that, given our earlier comment, capital holdings do not vary systematically with age in the deterministic version of this problem.

The table also allows us to assess the quantitative significance of the time horizon effect. The table indicates that once the number of years remaining is around 30, the effect of further increasing the number of periods remaining is relatively small. However, comparing the volatility at different points in the life cycle, we see that the associated effects are very large. Specifically, consider the final column of the table, which corresponds to a planning horizon of 55 years. Volatility in the first five years of working life is more than six times as large as volatility in the final five years of working life, and about one-third larger than volatility during the middle five years of working life.

We have done this same exercise using the stochastic process for rental rates on capital rather than the stochastic process on wage rates. The patterns are virtually identical, though the volatility is about half as much on average. Since there is little additional information, we do not present the results for this case.

6.2 *The Effect of Retirement*

Next, we consider the same situation except that we add retirement. In particular, we consider an individual who works for 45 periods and then retires for T_R periods, where we vary T_R. The results are shown in Table 16. As before, each column depicts the life-cycle pattern of volatility for a given length of retirement. The first column in Table 16 is identical to the second to last column in Table 15—both correspond to a case in which the worker works for 45 years and then dies. A striking new pattern appears. With the prospect of retirement, volatility no longer decreases monotonically over the life cycle. In fact, once T_R exceeds zero, we see that the highest volatility always occurs in the final five years of working life, which is just the opposite of what we found in the case without retirement. Looking at the results more

Table 16
Effect of retirement: wage shocks

Age	$T_R = 0$	$T_R = 10$	$T_R = 15$	$T_R = 20$
20–24	.252	.253	.253	.255
25–29	.249	.254	.256	.260
30–34	.235	.247	.252	.256
35–39	.215	.235	.242	.249
40–44	.190	.225	.236	.246
45–49	.162	.219	.235	.249
50–54	.128	.222	.247	.266
55–59	.087	.256	.291	.316
60–64	.042	.390	.427	.451

carefully, we see volatility is not monotone as we read down the columns. Loosely speaking, the pattern is for volatility to be roughly constant over the first 15 or so years of working life, then to decrease somewhat prior to increasing over the final ten or fifteen years of working life. The overall pattern is roughly U-shaped.

Why does the final five years of working life now have the highest level of volatility? The reason is once again intuitive. The presence of retirement extends the worker's planning horizon beyond the final period in which he or she works. If a worker in the final year of working life realizes a positive wage shock in the no-retirement case, he or she will increase current-period consumption by the same amount by which labor income increases. And with balanced growth path preferences, this results in no increase in hours of work. In contrast, a worker with a large number of periods left will not increase current consumption by the full amount by which current labor income increases since he or she will save some of it to supplement consumption when wages are low sometime in the future. When we add a retirement period, a worker in the final period of working life will spread any increased income across all retirement periods, so that current consumption increases by only a fraction of the increase in current labor income. If the same individual were to have additional working periods after the current period, he or she would shift less income forward since in the face of a persistent positive shock to wages, he or she would plan on working more, not just this period but also in future periods. This lessens the incentive to work more this period and explains why the response is even larger for someone facing retirement. Put somewhat differently, if a worker is in the final period of working life prior to retirement and experiences a positive persistent shock to wages, the fact that he or she will retire next period makes the shock seem more transitory than it really is, and intertemporal substitution is larger in response to less persistent shocks. Of course, this effect is present not only in the final period prior to retirement but also in earlier periods, which is why we see that volatility will increase not only in the final five years of working life but also earlier.

Intuitively, the model without retirement predicts a monotone decreasing pattern for volatility over the life cycle, whereas the argument just made suggests that retirement gives rise to an increasing pattern for volatility over the life cycle. The size of these effects are not uniform over the life cycle, so when they are combined, we see that one dominates over the early part of the life cycle and the other dominates over the latter part, giving rise to the rough U-shaped pattern.

It is also important to note the quantitative importance of retirement. As just remarked, the pattern of volatility over the life cycle is roughly U-shaped. However, going from the first five periods to the middle five periods, the decrease in volatility is only about 10%, whereas in going from the middle five years to the final five years, the volatility of hours almost doubles. This quantitative pattern is reminiscent of what we found in our benchmark simulations. While the model does generate a U-shaped pattern, the lefthand side of the U is in fact almost flat.

The key message from this exercise is that adding retirement is likely to have a large effect both qualitatively and quantitatively on the nature of volatility over the life cycle. However, it should also be noted that once the retirement period reaches ten years, the resulting profile of volatility over the life cycle is in fact relatively constant in the face of additional increases in the retirement period.

Though we do not deal with the case of endogenous retirement, it is worth noting that in such a context, one would probably expect the sharp increase in volatility just prior to retirement to be mitigated somewhat. An individual who realizes a positive wage shock at age 65 would potentially postpone retirement to take further advantage of the increased earnings opportunities rather than focusing all of the increased hours in one period. Conversely, the fact that individuals become eligible for social security benefits at age 62 could cause individuals to have much larger responses to negative shocks if a persistent negative shock leads them to opt for early retirement.

Table 17
Effect of life-cycle earnings: wage shocks, no retirement

	Standard deviation of hours		
Age	No peak	Peak = 2	Peak = 3
20–24	.272	.293	.303
25–29	.272	.252	.245
30–34	.264	.212	.191
35–39	.249	.175	.143
40–44	.232	.149	.112
45–49	.213	.146	.118
50–54	.190	.169	.162
55–59	.162	.186	.203
60–64	.128	.196	.243
65–69	.087	.211	.285
70–74	.042	.220	.323

6.3 *The Effect of Life-Cycle Changes in Wages*

We now ask how the presence of changes in wages over the life cycle influences the pattern of volatility over the life cycle. To better isolate the role of this factor, we consider a somewhat stylized version in which wages over the life cycle are represented by a symmetric triangle. In the benchmark case considered above, efficiency units were always equal to one. We now consider cases where the peak efficiency units are 2 and 3. Table 17 presents the results. For this exercise, we assume that the worker works for 55 periods and then dies.

As noted earlier, the life-cycle profile of volatility in the first column is decreasing. As we move from the first column to the second column, we see that the amount of volatility is decreased in the middle of the life cycle and is increased at the two edges of the life cycle. Note that the decrease is largest for the periods in which efficiency units are greatest. Why does this happen? We believe there is a simple intuitive explanation for this. There are two perspectives from which one can view the mechanics of intertemporal substitution in this model. One perspective is that when an individual engages in intertemporal substitution, he or she is effectively substituting production of income today for production of income at some future date; i.e., he or she is choosing to produce income when it is most efficient to do so. The other perspective is that the individual is trading off leisure today for leisure in the future. We argue that both of these perspectives lead us to expect volatility of hours of work to be lower during periods of high efficiency units.

We begin with the first perspective. If one is considering trading off production of income in two periods in which efficiency units differ, then the trade-off in hours will not necessarily be one-for-one. In particular, the change in hours from the lower-productivity period must be greater to compensate for the change in hours from the higher-productivity period. This suggests that intertemporal substitution in this context will necessarily lead to lower changes in hours in the high-productivity period and higher changes in hours in the low-productivity period, as we see in Table 17. Next, consider the second perspective. If leisure is lower in the period with high efficiency units, then at the margin, leisure is more valuable in these periods. It follows that if the individual is trading off leisure in the different periods, then it takes more leisure in the low-efficiency unit periods to compensate for one unit of leisure in the high-efficiency units period. Again, this suggests that hours should be less volatile in the high-efficiency unit periods.

The results in Table 17 also reflect another factor that is mechanical in nature. To see this, note that if we change the profile of hours over the life cycle in the absence of shocks but keep the absolute magnitude of fluctuations in hours worked over the life cycle constant, then it would actually appear that percentage fluctuations in hours worked were lower during periods in which efficiency units are higher. To assess the magnitude of this mechanical effect, we have also computed standard deviations of the business-cycle component of hours worked by age by using actual hours rather than the log of hours. When we did this, we found a U-shaped pattern of volatility that was of roughly the same quantitative magnitude as in Table 17, so we conclude that this mechanical channel is not driving the results. The potential size of this effect can also be gauged by noting that the variation in hours worked over the life cycle is not that large.

As with the previous factors, it is important to assess the quantitative magnitude of the effect associated with the life-cycle pattern of efficiency units. The case of peak efficiency units equal to two is of roughly the appropriate order of magnitude in terms of reality. As can be seen, this effect decreases volatility of hours in the middle of the life cycle by about one-third, and increases the volatility of older workers quite substantially.

In this subsection, we have focused on life-cycle changes in wages. However, we note that if there were life-cycle changes in the value of leisure, we would get similar effects. In particular, if leisure is valued differently at different points, then intertemporal tradeoffs are altered. Given the similarity to the effects just analyzed, we do not present any results for this particular specification. But it should be noted that our benchmark calibration does entail a changing value of leisure over the life cycle.

6.4 *Discussion*

The objective of this section was to investigate the role that various factors play in producing the life-cycle profile of volatility generated by our calibrated model. We have shown that three factors seem to be quantitatively significant. First, the finite time horizon matters. Second, the existence of a retirement period matters. And third, the variation of parameters over the life cycle to mimic life-cycle patterns in wages and hours of work also matter. Based on this analysis, we feel that the basic finding regarding volatility of hours over the life cycle is a robust property of the benchmark model with a reasonable parameterization. This is not to claim that our results are robust to all changes in various model features. For example, as mentioned earlier, it is possible that having an endogenous retirement decision in the context of a realistic social security program may influence the nature of fluctuations for older individuals.

What is the relative importance of the three factors just described? To provide an answer to this question, we redid our general-equilibrium calibration exercise keeping everything the same except that we imposed no change in parameters over the life cycle. In particular, we assumed that the efficiency unit profile is constant, as are the profiles for the preference shifters. We then examined the business-cycle properties of this model. The main finding is the following. Volatility of hours worked increases monotonically over the life cycle. The relative volatility of the youngest group is roughly the same as in the benchmark calibration, while the volatility of the oldest group is about two-thirds as volatile as in the benchmark calibration. The main impact of the parameters that vary over the life cycle is to depress volatility during the middle years and increase volatility in later years. It remains true in this exercise that the model's ability to account for the pattern of volatility over the life cycle is increasing in age. We conclude from this that our key quantitative finding is largely due to the finite horizon and retirement aspects.

7. International Evidence

Earlier in the paper, we presented evidence pertaining to properties of labor market fluctuations in the United States. It is of interest to ask to what extent these patterns are also found in other countries. This may well help us think about what factors are generating these patterns. In particular, given that labor market policies and regulations differ quite widely across economies, if these factors are playing a central role, we would expect to see quite different patterns across countries.

Data limitations prevent us from exactly repeating our earlier analysis using data that is available from international statistical agencies such as the Organization for Economic Cooperation and Development (OECD). One would have to go directly to country-level data sets to extract equivalent information. However, data that is available from the OECD does allow us to compare fluctuations in employment to population ratios by age groups for several countries. The time period for which this data is available does vary from country to country, but Table 18 presents summary statistics for several countries for which there is sufficient data.[23] In this table, we report standard deviations relative to the age group 45–54.

In all countries but one, we observe that volatility is highest for individuals in the 15–24 group, and that it decreases until we reach the age group 45–54, though for two countries, the volatility increases slightly going from the 35–44 age group to the 45–54 age group. For most countries, relative volatility increases as we move to the oldest group,

Table 18
International evidence

	15–24	25–34	35–44	45–54	55–64
Australia (1963–2001)	1.78	1.19	1.14	1.00	7.71
France (1968–2001)	3.06	2.36	1.21	1.00	4.20
Germany (1970–2001)	1.68	1.29	1.03	1.00	1.02
Ireland (1961–2001)	2.60	1.24	.96	1.00	.86
Norway (1972–2001)	2.20	1.33	.97	1.00	.84
Portugal (1974–2001)	3.94	1.65	1.16	1.00	1.60
Spain (1972–2001)	2.74	1.79	1.09	1.00	.98
Sweden (1963–2001)	4.24	2.22	1.54	1.00	1.53

though for two countries, the change is minimal and for two others, there is a relatively sizable decrease. A more complete assessment of the cross-country data is beyond the scope of this paper, but based on this first look at the data, we conclude that the life-cycle pattern of volatility that we documented for the United States is a robust stylized fact for a broad cross-section of countries.

8. Summary and Directions for Future Research

The motivation for this paper consisted of two simple observations. The first motivating observation is that for what many would view as reasonable parameterizations, the standard infinitely lived representative agent household business-cycle model cannot account for the magnitude of fluctuations in aggregate hours of market work over the cycle. According to our benchmark specification and our metric, this model can account for about 60% of observed fluctuations. This observation has lead many researchers to modify the model in ways to produce greater fluctuations in hours of work for the representative household. The second motivating observation is that fluctuations in hours of market work over the business cycle vary quite dramatically across subgroups in the population. We documented this heterogeneity along two specific dimensions: age and education.

Taken together, this suggests to us a clear direction for research that has been largely ignored. If some groups experience much larger cyclical fluctuations in hours of work than do other groups, this should presumably provide substantial insight into the factors that account for these fluctuations. Or put somewhat differently, if a model produces average fluctuations that are too small, but there is substantial heterogeneity in the magnitude of fluctuations, a natural question to ask is, Which groups are not fluctuating enough? Is the shortfall of fluctuations uniform across all groups, or is it concentrated in a few select groups? The answer to this question should influence the nature of modifications that researchers choose to explore.

This paper has taken a first step in this line of research. We analyzed business-cycle fluctuations in a model in which households differ in age, and we used it to explore the implications of standard shocks and economic forces for the pattern of fluctuations in hours by age. The finding is quite striking. As in the standard model, average hours of market work do not fluctuate enough. But significantly, the main shortfall in fluctuations is accounted for by the behavior of young individuals. Taken at face value, this suggests that whatever modifications one believes are empirically relevant for generating larger fluctuations in average hours, these modifications should be such that they interact with age in a very nonneutral manner.

It is beyond the scope of this paper to explore what these modifications might be. One plausible feature is some sort of search friction. One aspect of labor market behavior that varies with age is that younger workers are more likely to be in the process of searching for a career. Aggregate shocks may interact with this process in a distinctive manner.

Another plausible modification could involve human capital accumulation since the nature of human capital accumulation varies over the life cycle. While our model implies that human capital accumulation varies over the life cycle, it implicitly assumed that human capital accumulation at any age occurred at the same rate independently of how an individual allocates his or her time among market work, home work, and leisure. It seems very reasonable to consider modifications of the human capital accumulation process. In this vein, the work of Imai and Keane (2004) is relevant since they argue that allowing for endogenous human capital accumulation greatly increases the estimated labor supply elasticities.

Finally, one qualification that was mentioned earlier also bears repeating. In a model that allows for heterogeneous agents, one must also allow for the possibility that differences in volatilities might also reflect the fact that these agents face different shocks. Even if the shocks are perfectly correlated, the magnitudes of the shocks could vary.

Although our analysis focused solely on the age dimension, the empirical work that we summarized also suggests that a fuller treatment will consider age and human capital accumulation jointly in the business-cycle context. It will be important to assess the key economic forces that alter the way in which individuals who differ in age and human capital respond to common shocks.[24] More generally, the analysis carried out suggests a research agenda in which macroeconomists take seriously the patterns of hours fluctuations at disaggregated levels to better assess the economy's impulse and propagation mechanisms.

9. Appendix

In this appendix, we outline in detail the procedure that we used to produce the statistics reported in Table 3. As stated in the paper, our

Table 19
Cyclical fluctuations of hours by age group

	16–19	20–24	25–34	35–44	45–54	55–64	65+
σ	6.91	3.38	2.19	1.61	1.55	1.92	5.13

data source is the CPS March Supplement for the years 1962–2000. We use the question on total number of hours of market work in the preceding week to compute average hours per person for all individuals age 16 and over as well as for each of the seven age groups listed in the paper. We use these numbers as our estimates of hours of work per person in the aggregate and by age for each year in the sample, giving us an annual data set for each series.

We define the cyclical component of aggregate hours per person by applying the Hodrick–Prescott (HP) filter to the log of aggregate hours and applying a smoothing parameter of 100. This series has a standard deviation of 1.99.

Our basic goal is to determine how changes in aggregate hours per person are accounted for by changes in hours per person of each age group. The first step we take is to apply the Hodrick–Prescott filter to each age-specific series. Doing this produces the values in Table 19. These values display the U-shaped pattern that figured prominently in the analysis in the paper. However, these values are not necessarily the best measures of fluctuations by age for our purposes. There are two issues. First, in going from aggregate data to age-specific data, the survey sample sizes are reduced considerably and there is the possibility of additional noise in the data. Given our detrending procedure this noise will likely show up as cyclical fluctuations. Second, there may be some nonbusiness cycle shocks that affect relative hours across age groups that we do not want to interpret as representing business-cycle shocks. Table 20 presents cross-correlations for the various age-specific cyclical components with each other and the aggregate component.

As expected, one sees that each of the age-specific series is highly correlated with the aggregate, with the exception of the over-65 age group. This group also accounts for very few hours worked. In fact, the basic pattern is that the greater the age-specific hours worked, the greater is the correlation with the aggregate. All of the cross-correlations between age groups are also fairly positive. However, the basic pattern suggests that measurement error and/or some age-specific shocks may be a factor.

Table 20
Contemporaneous correlations across age groups, HP filtered data

	16–19	20–24	25–34	35–44	45–54	55–64	65+	Agg
16–19	1.00							
20–24	.81	1.00						
25–34	.81	.92	1.00					
35–44	.70	.84	.92	1.00				
45–54	.59	.77	.82	.86	1.00			
55–64	.44	.50	.62	.71	.79	1.00		
65+	.34	.19	.31	.41	.39	.53	1.00	
Agg	.80	.89	.96	.96	.90	.74	.43	1.00

Table 21
Standard deviations by age group, HP filtered data

	16–19	20–24	25–34	35–44	45–54	55–64	65+
Raw	6.91	3.38	2.19	1.61	1.55	1.92	5.13
Adjusted	5.67	3.04	2.12	1.58	1.41	1.46	3.11

Hence, the second step in our two-step procedure is to remove the component due to measurement error and/or idiosyncratic shocks. To do this, we take each age-specific series for HP residuals and find the component that is correlated with changes in aggregate hours. We regress each age-specific series on a constant, and current and lagged aggregate hours, and then use the predicted values as our measure of the cyclical component of each series. We experimented with additional lags but found that it made no difference. In fact, except for the groups aged 55 and above, the effect of adding one lag of aggregate hours was very small. Table 21 shows the effect that this has on the measure of volatility for each group.

The first row repeats the standard deviations of the deviations from the HP trend, and the second row presents the values produced by our second step. As can be seen, the changes are relatively small for prime-age individuals, but they are sizable for the youngest and oldest individuals. We should emphasize that for the points that we make in our analysis, the raw data would actually make our case somewhat stronger, so this process of adjustment is not to make our case stronger. As evidence that our adjustment serves its purpose, we note that if one uses the raw data and computes the weighted average of age-specific standard deviations using age-specific hours as weights, then the resulting series has a standard deviation that is more than 10% larger than the aggregate series, but when we do the same calculation using our adjusted series, we obtain the same standard deviation as for the aggregate series. In this sense, we feel that we have isolated the age-specific components of the aggregate fluctuations.

There is one final adjustment that we make for all data reported in the text. This adjustment is irrelevant for purposes of comparing standard deviations across hours series, but it is relevant for comparing volatility of hours with a series such as GDP. Ideally, we would have computed the annual value for aggregate average hours per person by averaging the monthly values for each year. Because we do not have the monthly values for all years, we are unable to do this. Intuitively we would expect that using only the values for March rather than all months would lead to greater variance in the series. To estimate the extent of this effect, we carried out a similar exercise using establishment hours. In particular, for this series, we asked how the standard deviation of the cyclical component changes when we use only the March data as our annual estimate rather than averaging over all twelve months. We find that the standard deviation is larger by 10% in the case in which only March is used. To retain comparability with other annual series for which we use all observations, in what follows we will make a 10% adjustment to the standard deviation of all of our hours series based on using only March data. Note that this has no impact on any comparisons of relative volatility across hours series—it is relevant only when comparing the volatility of an hours series to some other series, such as GDP.

Notes

The authors thank Mark Gertler, Paul Klein, Éva Nagypál, Ken Rogoff, Robert Shimer, and conference participants for useful comments. Rogerson and Wright thank the National Science Foundation for financial support.

1. For example, if one was thinking that the main shortcoming of the model was the absence of rigidities in real wages, one would have to argue that this feature is more important for young workers than it is for prime-age workers.

2. Researchers have previously suggested that trying to understand fluctuations at a more disaggregate level would be useful; an example is Gertler and Gilchrist (1994), who argue that the differences in behavior of large and small manufacturing firms provide additional information about the nature and propagation of aggregate shocks.

3. Some of the standard references on home production in macroeconomics include Benhabib, Rogerson, and Wright (1991); Greenwood and Hercowitz (1991); Greenwood,

Rogerson, and Wright (1995); McGrattan, Rogerson, and Wright (1997); Baxter and Jermann (1999); and Gomme, Kydland, and Rupert (2001).

4. Standard references in the labor supply literature include, for example, MaCurdy (1981), Altonji (1986), and Pencaval (1986). See Mulligan (1998) for estimates based on other sources.

5. We could also assume that individuals do derive utility from government consumption but that it is separable with respect to the other arguments, which accords with results in the literature, like Christiano and Eichenbaum (1992) and McGrattan et al. (1997).

6. For some other issues, however, shocks to the home technology are crucial; for example, Benhabib, Rogerson, and Wright (1991) show how such shocks can generate a reasonable contemporaneous correlation between productivity and hours, and Hall (1997) finds that home-sector shocks are actually a significant source of aggregate fluctuations.

7. Alternatively, one could assume that installed home and market capital can be costlessly transformed into each other, as in Benhabib et al. (1991). For the issues on which we focus here, this would not make much of a difference.

8. In assessing the magnitude of fluctuations in hours, two normalizations have been used in the literature—one normalizes relative to fluctuations in output, while the other normalizes relative to fluctuations in average labor productivity. For our purposes, this choice does not matter because the benchmark specification accounts for roughly two-thirds of fluctuations by either metric. Hence, we will simply report the relative volatility of hours to output.

9. Our choice of metric for assessing the magnitude of fluctuations in hours was made in the context of an analysis that emphasizes technology shocks. For a model driven by monetary shocks, this may not be a good metric. Nonetheless, we believe the basic point—that one should consider implications for disaggregated data—to be relevant for all business-cycle models.

10. Using slightly different methods, this basic observation has previously been noted by Clark and Summers (1981). See also Blanchard and Diamond (1990) and Keane and Prasad (1996).

11. There are some attempts to model within-household time allocation explicitly over the business cycle; see, for example, Cho and Rogerson (1988).

12. The role of these shifters will become clear subsequently, but loosely speaking, ψ^a allows a household's relative desire for home versus market consumption to change systematically over the life cycle, and ω^a allows a household's value of consumption relative to leisure to change over the life cycle.

13. We are assuming the life-cycle profile of efficiency units is not affected by decisions taken by the individual, such as investment in human capital; this is similar to much of the labor supply literature, but there are exceptions, including Shaw (1989); Chang, Gomes, and Schorfheide (2002); Imai and Keane (2004) and Olivetti (2001).

14. The issue is that events such as having children and buying a home tend to affect the time allocated to home production. One can view these changes as affecting the efficiency of time spent in home production or as affecting one's preferences for home consumption. This choice is not likely to matter for our results. One thing that might be more interesting is to make the timing of these events endogenous, but this is beyond the scope of the current project.

15. While we will not get into them at all, we note that there are important issues concerning the existence of recursive competitive equilibria in overlapping generations models with incomplete markets. See Kubler and Polemarchakis (2004) for a discussion and some related results.

16. The one exception is in the case of determining the stochastic process for the Solow residual since we think it is important to use as much data as possible to obtain more precise estimates of this process.

17. Specifically, we use data on private GDP as the output measure, market capital as the capital input, and data from the Establishment Survey on hours in private establishments as the labor input.

18. We could have chosen β to target a particular rate of return to capital. Our choice implies an after-tax rate of return of approximately 7%. Targeting a lower value would generate a much larger investment share. Ultimately, there is some tension between the various statistics that we ask the model to match. Matching a lower rate of return and a reasonable investment share would require a higher capital share.

19. Related evidence is contained in work by Aguiar and Hurst (2003), who document substantial substitution between expenditures and time in the production of food consumption in response to variation in the opportunity cost of time.

20. It would be more appropriate to use a weighted average of male and female wages over the life cycle. Given the selection issues that are more significant in estimating wages for women and the secular changes in women's wages and hours of work, we chose to use men's wages as a proxy.

21. As a side issue, we note that for a given profile of efficiency units e^a and elasticity parameters ξ and γ, one can always find values of the ψ^a and ω^a profile such that observed life-cycle hours are consistent with optimization. This should make one leery of studies that claim to identify the value of γ from life-cycle data on wages and hours worked since one cannot make this inference without knowing the values of the preference shifters, and they are clearly unobservable.

22. This point is not new—Plosser (1989) found the same result in his model. Note, however, that although Rios-Rull (1996) was an annual model, he also found that his model could account for roughly two-thirds of observed fluctuations in output. The reason for this apparent discrepancy is that he effectively used the Solow residuals computed using quarterly data. In particular, he computed Solow residuals using quarterly data and then aggregated the quarterly process to get an annual process.

23. The data are annual and the numbers in the table are based on standard deviations of cyclical components as defined by the HP filter. Unlike in the earlier tables, we have made no additional adjustments.

24. An early attempt to understand differences in fluctuations in hours of market work across different skill groups is Kydland (1984).

References

Aguiar, M., and E. Hurst. (2003). Consumption vs. expenditure. NBER Working Paper No. 10307.

Alexopoulos, M. (2004). Unemployment and the business cycle. *Journal of Monetary Economics* 51:277–298.

Altonji, J. (1986). Intertemporal substitution in labor supply: Evidence from micro data. *Journal of Political Economy* 94:S176–S215.

Andolfatto, D. (1996). Business cycles and labor market search. *American Economic Review* 86:112–132.

Baxter, M., and U. Jermann. (1999). Household production and the excess sensitivity of consumption to current income. *American Economic Review* 89:902–920.

Benhabib, J., R. Rogerson, and R. Wright. (1991). Homework in macroeconomics: Household production and aggregate fluctuations. *Journal of Political Economy* 99:1166–1187.

Blanchard, O., and P. Diamond. (1990). The cyclical behavior of the gross flows of U.S. workers. *Brookings Papers on Economic Activity* 2:85–143.

Chang, Y., Gomes, J., and F. Schorfheide. (2002). Learning-by-doing as a propagation mechanism. *American Economic Review* 92:1498–1520.

Cho, J. O., and R. Rogerson. (1988). Family labor supply and aggregate fluctuations. *Journal of Monetary Economics* 21:233–246.

Christiano, L., and M. Eichenbaum. (1992). Current real business cycle theory and aggregate labor market fluctuations. *American Economic Review* 82:430–450.

Clark, K., and L. Summers. (1981). Demographic differences in cyclical employment variation. *Journal of Human Resources* 16:61–79.

Danthine, J. P., and J. Donaldson. (1995). Non-Walrasian economies. In *Frontiers in Business Cycle Theory*, T. F. Cooley (ed.). Princeton, NJ: Princeton University Press.

Den Haan, W., G. Ramey, and J. Watson. (2000). Job destruction and propagation of shocks. *American Economic Review* 90:482–498.

Gertler, M., and S. Gilchrist. (1994). Monetary policy, business cycles and the behavior of small manufacturing firms. *Quarterly Journal of Economics* 109:309–340.

Gomme, P. (1999). Shirking, unemployment and aggregate fluctuations. *International Economic Review* 40:3–21.

Gomme, P., F. Kydland, and P. Rupert. (2001). Home production meets time to build. *Journal of Political Economy* 109:1115–1131.

Greenwood, J., and Z. Hercowitz. (1991). The allocation of capital and time over the business cycle. *Journal of Political Economy* 99:1188–1214.

Greenwood, J., R. Rogerson, and R. Wright. (1995). Household production in real business cycle theory. In *Frontiers in Business Cycle Theory*, T. F. Cooley (ed.). Princeton, NJ: Princeton University Press.

Hall, R. (1997). Macroeconomic fluctuations and the allocation of time. *Journal of Labor Economics* 15:S223–S250.

Hansen, G. (1985). Indivisible labor and the business cycle. *Journal of Monetary Economics* 16:309–327.

Hansen, G. D., and R. Wright. (1992). The labor market real business cycle theory. *Federal Reserve Bank of Minneapolis Quarterly Review* 16:2–12.

Imai, S., and M. Keane. (2004). Intertemporal labor supply and human capital accumulation. *International Economic Review* 45:601–641.

Keane, M., and E. Prasad. (1996). The employment and wage effects of oil price shocks: A sectoral analysis. *Review of Economics and Statistics* 78:389–400.

Klein, P. (2000). Using the generalized schur form to solve a multivariate linear rational expectations model. *Journal of Economic Dynamics and Control* 24:1405–1423.

Krusell, P., and A. Smith. (1998). Income and wealth heterogeneity in the macroeconomy. *Journal of Political Economy* 106:867–896.

Kubler, F., and H. Polemarchakis. (2004). Stationary Markov equilibria for overlapping generations. *Economic Theory*, forthcoming.

Kydland, F. (1984). Labor force heterogeneity and the business cycle. *Carnegie-Rochester Series on Public Policy* 21:173–208.

Kydland, F., and E. Prescott. (1982). Time to build and aggregate fluctuations. *Econometrica* 50:1345–1370.

Kydland, F., and E. Prescott. (1988). The workweek of capital and its implications. *Journal of Monetary Economics* 21:343–360.

MaCurdy, T. (1981). An empirical model of labor supply in a life cycle setting. *Journal of Political Economy* 89:1059–1085.

McGrattan, E., R. Rogerson, and R. Wright. (1997). An equilibrium model of the business cycle with household production and fiscal policy. *International Economic Review* 38:267–290.

Merz, M. (1995). Search in the labor market and the real business cycle. *Journal of Monetary Economics* 36:269–300.

Mulligan, C. (1998). Substitution over time: Another look at the evidence. In *NBER Macroeconomics Annual*, Ben S. Bernanke and Julio J. Rotemberg (eds.). Cambridge, MA: MIT Press.

Olivetti, C. (2001). Changes in women's hours of work: The effect of changing returns to experience. Boston University. Mimeo.

Pencavel, J. (1986). Labor supply of men. In *Handbook of Labor Economics*, O. Ashenfelter and R. Layard (eds.). Amsterdam: North Holland.

Plosser, C. (1989). Understanding real business cycles. *Journal of Economic Perspectives* 3:51–78.

Rios-Rull, V. (1996). Life-cycle economies and aggregate fluctuations. *Review of Economic Studies* 63:465–489.

Rogerson, R. (1988). Indivisible labor, lotteries and equilibrium. *Journal of Monetary Economics* 21:1–16.

Rupert, P., R. Rogerson, and R. Wright. (1995). Using panel data to estimate substitution elasticities in household production models. *Economic Theory* 6:179–193.

Rupert, P., R. Rogerson, and R. Wright. (2000). Homework in labor economics: Household production and intertemporal substitution. *Journal of Monetary Economics* 46:557–579.

Shaw, K. (1989). Life-cycle labor supply with human capital accumulation. *International Economic Review* 30:431–456.

Shimer, R. (1998). Why is the US unemployment rate so much lower? In *NBER Macroeconomics Annual*, Ben S. Bernanke and Julio J. Rotemberg (eds.). Cambridge, MA: MIT Press.

Comment

Éva Nagypál
Northwestern University

1. Introduction

It has been well known for at least the past two decades that the neoclassical growth model with aggregate shocks, notwithstanding its surprising success in explaining many aggregate phenomena, performs poorly when it comes to explaining business-cycle fluctuations in the labor market.

The work of Gomme, Rogerson, Rupert, and Wright (GRRW) builds on the premise that the understanding of labor market fluctuations over the business cycle is enhanced by moving beyond standard representative agent models. In particular, they propose to analyze models with heterogeneous agents and to study their implications, not only for the aggregate time series, but also for cyclical variation across heterogeneous groups of agents. There are at least two reasons why this is a promising approach to take. First, the empirical evidence shows that different demographic groups exhibit substantially different labor market fluctuations over the business cycle. Second, the heterogeneous impact of business-cycle shocks is an important testing ground for theories of fluctuations that aim to improve the ability of business-cycle models to explain labor market phenomena. Many such theories have been proposed in the literature, so offering additional ways to test the empirical validity of these alternatives is much needed.

For these reasons, I applaud the premise of the paper—the emphasis on heterogeneity in understanding labor market fluctuations—since it sets the stage for further exploration of some crucial questions in the study of labor markets over the business cycle. It also provides a good overview of the relevant empirical and theoretical results. In particular, the empirical results of the paper show that the findings of Clark and Summers (1981) regarding the demographic differences in cyclical volatility extend to the recessions of the last two decades, while the theoretical part of the paper shows that extending the model studied by Rios-Rull (1996) to include home production and incomplete markets does not significantly alter its implications for the life-cycle pattern of cyclical volatility.

The aim of my discussion is, first, to highlight the most important empirical phenomenon regarding the life-cycle pattern of business-cycle volatility that a theoretical model should aim to explain; second, to clarify why the theoretical approach taken by GRRW fails to explain this phenomenon; and, finally, to push the premise of the paper further and offer an alternative explanation of this phenomenon. Correspondingly, my discussion is organized to deliver three main points.

First, I argue that the difference in the cyclical volatility of hours between prime-age and old workers is second-order in comparison to the substantial difference in the cyclical volatility of hours between young and prime-age workers. Hence, the very high cyclical variation in the hours of young workers is by far the most important empirical phenomenon that a model that sets out to explain the life-cycle variation in business-cycle volatility should aim to tackle. This means that the authors' focus on the U-shape of cyclical volatility over the life cycle is somewhat misplaced since what is quantitatively relevant is the high cyclical volatility at a young, and not an old, age. Second, I argue that the model studied by GRRW explains only a small fraction of the high business-cycle volatility of hours of the young compared to that of prime-age workers. I explore which of the mechanisms in the GRRW model work in the right direction to explain the higher business-cycle volatility of the hours of the young and which do not. I argue that several of the mechanisms built into the model have no potential to explain the high relative volatility at a young age, and highlight the one mechanism that does. Finally, I suggest that an additional promising mechanism to explain the high cyclical volatility of young workers is the increase in the amount of specific human capital or experience with age. I propose an alternative model with such a mechanism and show that it helps to explain qualitatively why the hours of young workers respond more to business-cycle shocks.

2. Empirical Evidence on Labor Market Fluctuations over the Life Cycle

To empirically motivate their study, the authors present measures of cyclical volatility for different demographic groups. Since heterogeneity by age is the driving force in the theoretical model studied by GRRW, I restrict my discussion to the results regarding age. It is worth noting, however, that there is also substantial variation in cyclical volatility of hours by education group, a fact that has frequently been noted empirically but that has not received much attention in theoretical work (for an exception, see my earlier work in Nagypál, 2004).

The authors use the March Current Population Survey to construct average hours worked by demographic group for each year between 1962 and 2000. Then, as a measure of cyclical volatility in hours worked by group, they use the standard deviation of the projection of the group-specific Hodrick-Prescott (HP)-filtered log weekly hours series onto the aggregate HP-filtered log weekly hours series.[1] The measure thus constructed does not have well-established statistical properties and possibly expects more from the available annual data than they might be able to deliver. This is because, in the annual hours data between 1962 and 2000, there are only four distinguishable downturns, i.e., four episodes during which aggregate hours declined, each episode roughly corresponding to a period of recession. This is due to the fact that, even though there were five recessions between 1962 and 2000, the twin recessions of the early 1980s are not distinguishable using annual data. Hence, as a robustness check, I construct a less demanding measure of cyclical volatility. I use the same dataset, but extend it to 2003 to have information on the most recent downturn, which started in 2001. For each downturn,[2] I calculate the share of total hours worked by each age group in the peak year preceding it:

$$s_{i,r} = \frac{H_{i,r}^{p}}{H_{r}^{p}} \tag{1}$$

where H_r^p is the aggregate number of hours worked in the peak year in recession r, and $H_{i,r}^p$ is the total number of hours worked in the same year by group i. I compare this to the share of each age group in the drop in total hours between the peak and the trough year:

$$d_{i,r} = \frac{H_{i,r}^{t} - H_{i,r}^{p}}{H_{r}^{t} - H_{r}^{p}} \tag{2}$$

where H_r^t is the aggregate number of hours worked in the trough year in recession r, and $H_{i,r}^t$ is the total number of hours worked in the same year by group i. In Figure 1, I plot $s_{i,r}$ and $d_{i,r}$ by age group averaged over the five downturns in the data.[3] If there were no difference in the

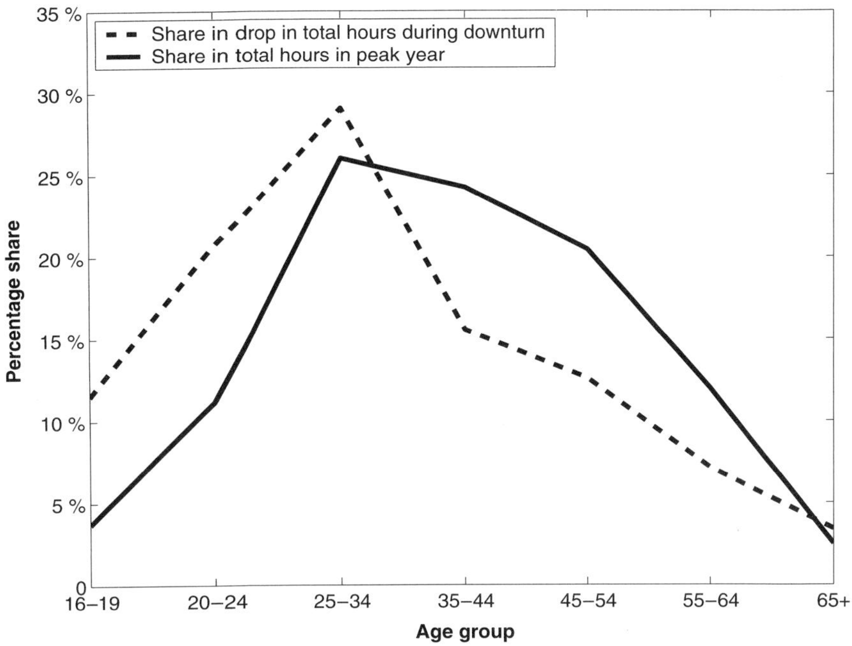

Figure 1
Share of different age groups in total hours in the peak year and in the drop in total hours during the subsequent downturn averaged over the downturns in the data between 1962 and 2003

cyclical volatility of hours across age groups, we would expect hours worked by each age group to shrink by the same extent in a downturn, and we would therefore expect the share in total hours in the peak year, $s_{i,r}$, to be the same as the share in the drop during the downturn, $d_{i,r}$. Instead, what we see is that the share of younger workers in the drop in hours during a downturn is much larger than their share in total hours. This implies that workers in their early thirties and younger bear a disproportionate share of the contraction in total hours. It is this phenomenon that is by far the most important one quantitatively.

How does this measure relate to the one reported by GRRW? Note that $d_{i,r}/s_{i,r}$ is a measure comparable to that used by GRRW, except for a scaling factor. The measure $d_{i,r}/s_{i,r}$, in fact, exhibits a very similar pattern to the measure used by GRRW, both of them having a U-shape. It is clear from Figure 1, however, that the increase at an older age of the relative volatility is exclusively due to workers above the age of 65, who account for a very small share of total hours in the data and who are excluded from the theoretical model of GRRW. Emphasizing the U-shape therefore detracts from the essence of the empirical finding, which is that young workers bear a disproportionate burden in downturns.

With the focus placed so heavily on young workers, it is useful to ask whether it is the extensive or the intensive margin that accounts for the bulk of the drop in their hours during a downturn. To do this, I decompose the drop $d_{i,r}$ into its extensive and intensive margin components, and find that, for all age groups, between 69% and 80% of the drop in hours during a downturn is due to the extensive margin, i.e., to the fact that fewer workers are employed, as opposed to workers working fewer hours. This number is somewhat higher than the one reported by GRRW based on a different measure, but it shares the feature that it does not show substantial variation with age.

3. The GRRW Model

In the theoretical part of the paper, the authors set out to study the life-cycle version of the neoclassical growth model with technology shocks, variable labor, home production, and incomplete markets to understand the extent to which the above facts can be explained by such a model.

It is instructive to consider the different channels in the model that give rise to differences among the age groups in labor-market responses to aggregate shocks. The first two channels, the *time-horizon channel* and the *time-to-retirement channel*, are studied in detail in Sections 6.1 and 6.2 of the paper, so I will review them only briefly.

The *time-horizon channel* is present because, as agents get older, they have fewer and fewer periods of consumption (of leisure and of consumption goods) remaining. This means that a given innovation in the present discounted value of income due to an aggregate shock induces a larger and larger increase in the consumption of all goods for the remainder periods, including the consumption of leisure in the current period. In other words, the income effect on leisure of an increase in wages is higher as agents get older, which in turn implies a lower response in labor supply to aggregate shocks as agents age. This channel works in the right direction, at least qualitatively, to explain the larger labor-supply response of young workers, as is demonstrated in Section 6.1.

Let us next turn to the *time-to-retirement channel*.[4] This channel introduces an increasing lifetime profile of labor-supply response to persistent business-cycle shocks. This is due to the fact that, for young workers, an innovation in the aggregate productivity process induces a large income effect on the consumption of leisure due to the persistence of the shock, *and* to the fact that young workers have many periods over which they can expect to have a higher wage. This large income effect means that the labor-supply response to higher wages is muted for young workers. For workers closer to retirement, the same innovation in the aggregate productivity process induces a smaller income effect on the consumption of leisure because they have fewer periods over which they can expect to have a higher wage. So despite the fact that the shock is persistent, older workers respond to it as if it were temporary. Older workers thus respond to the same shock by increasing their hours more than young workers.

The third channel, and the one the authors emphasize the most, is the *life-cycle profile of productivity and preferences channel* (or the *life-cycle-profile channel*). This is present in the GRRW model because the authors assume that the efficiency units of working, the disutility from labor, and the weight placed on the consumption of home goods all change deterministically over the life cycle. One can show that this channel works by influencing the life-cycle profile of three quantities: the ratio of labor income to market consumption, the ratio of home to market consumption, and the ratio of home to market hours.[5] The ratio of labor income to market consumption matters because it determines the extent of the income effect of a change in the market wage. When labor income is large compared to market consumption (as in Section 6.3, during middle age), the income effect on the consumption of leisure of a temporary wage increase is large, and the labor supply response to this temporary wage increase is therefore small. The ratio of home to market consumption matters because it determines the strength of the income *versus* substitution effect of a temporary change in the market wage. A temporary change in the market wage has only an income effect on the consumption of the market good, but has an income and a substitution effect on the consumption of the home good. Finally, the ratio of home to market hours matters because it determines the extent to which market hours respond to a wage change for a given change in total and in home hours. The deterministic preference and productivity shifters play a role in determining the labor-supply response of the different age groups only to the extent that they influence these three ratios.

These three ratios, though, are observable directly. In particular, it is well known from the empirical consumption literature that household labor income and market consumption profiles are fairly similar, implying that their ratio is roughly constant over the life cycle. The ratio of home to market consumption is more difficult since the authors do not report this measure, but presumably it is closely related to the ratio of home to market hours. The ratio of home to market hours, in turn, can be backed out from the calibration exercise of GRRW since they use both market and home hours to calibrate the deterministic preference and productivity shifters. Since the ratio of home to market hours is strictly increasing with age in the GRRW calibration, one can show that the life-cycle profile channel introduces an increasing volatility of market hours with age in the GRRW calibration. Just as the time-to-retirement channel, the life-cycle-profile channel works in the wrong direction, at least given the values to which GRRW calibrate.[6]

Finally, the last channel is the *asset-holding channel*. The GRRW model features incomplete markets, and younger workers have lower asset positions than older workers, on average: all workers start their life with no market capital and a fixed amount of home capital, and workers accumulate assets over time for the period of retirement at the end of life. The low asset position of young workers means that, holding all else equal, they work more and consume less for precautionary reasons. Hence, a positive innovation in their income will lead to a higher effect on leisure and thus a lower labor supply response compared to agents with higher asset levels.[7] This means that increasing asset levels over the working life implies increasing labor supply response to aggregate shocks in the model, so this channel also works in the wrong direction.

To summarize, in terms of explaining the high cyclical volatility of the hours of young workers compared to prime-age workers, the asset-market and the time-to-retirement channels always work in the wrong direction, the life-cycle-profile channel most likely works in the wrong direction given the calibration of GRRW of the home to market share of hours, and the time-horizon channel is the only one that works in the right direction. Given these observations, it is not surprising that the quantitative results of GRRW confirm that the model cannot explain the high cyclical volatility of the hours of young workers.

Table 1
Cyclical volatility of hours of different age groups relative to age 35–44 in the Rios-Rull and GRRW models, and in the data

Age group	Rios-Rull (1996)*	GRRW (2004)	Data reported by GRRW
20–24	1.21	1.11	1.92
25–34	1	1	1.34
35–44	1	1	1
45–54	1.72	1.31	0.89
55–64	1.72	2.77	0.92

*In Rios-Rull (1996), age group 25–34 is not distinguished from age group 35–44, and age group 45–54 is not distinguished from age group 55–64.

In terms of the quantitative results, it is worth noting that three of the above four channels are already present in the model studied by Rios-Rull (1996). Since he studies a complete-markets version of the GRRW model without home production, the asset-market channel is not present in his model, while the life-cycle-profile channel has a more limited role. Since both of these channels work in the wrong direction, it is not surprising that the results of GRRW are, if anything, less successful at explaining the high cyclical volatility of the hours of young workers. Table 1 compares the results of GRRW and those of Rios-Rull by calculating the cyclical volatility of hours for each age group relative to the age group 35–44. We can see that the two sets of results are rather similar, implying that the additional channels are quantitatively not very important.[8]

4. Accumulation of Human Capital over the Life Cycle

To explain the life-cycle pattern of cyclical volatility more successfully, one needs to explore additional channels through which differences in age groups arise. This is an issue I take up in this section by exploring one additional channel, the *human-capital channel*, and examine whether it works in the right direction, at least qualitatively.

Differences in human capital are often emphasized in labor economics as one of the major differences between young and old workers. There are, of course, different measures of human capital, the two most prominent ones being education and experience. At first glance, it might seem that differences in education could explain some of the differences in the life-cycle profile. Younger workers (at least under a certain age) might have somewhat less education and, as is documented

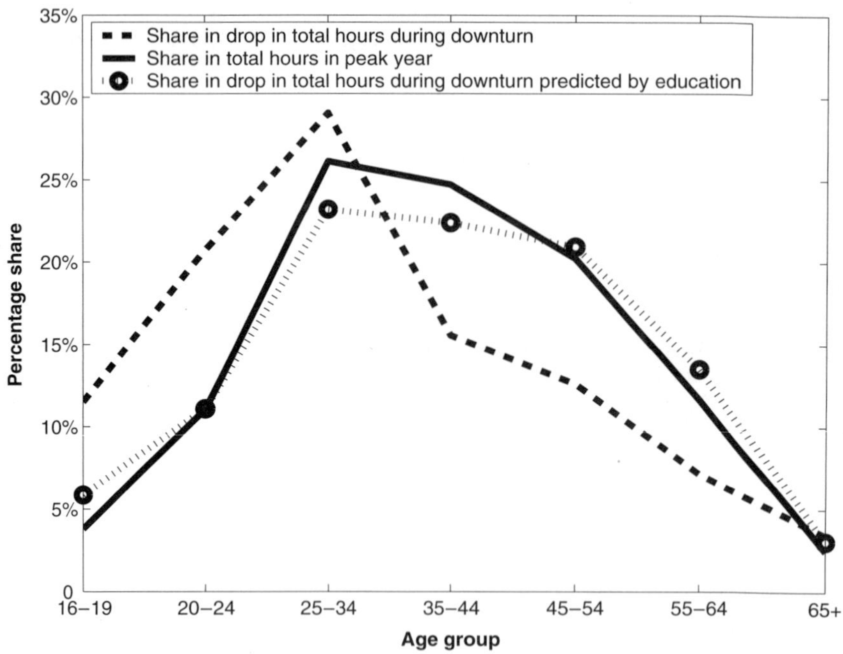

Figure 2
Share of different age groups in the drop in total hours during a downturn predicted by education variation

in the paper, there is significant variation in the response of hours to business-cycle shocks by education. It turns out, though, that if the only variation allowed across the age groups was in education, this would not be enough to explain the differential business-cycle responses. To show this, I plot in Figure 2, for each of the different age groups plotted in Figure 1, the share in total hours in the peak year and the share in the drop in total hours during the downturn, together with the share in the drop in total hours during a downturn that would be predicted solely by a different educational composition of the age groups. We see that it is only for teenagers that conditioning on education works in the right direction. The reason for this is the secular increase in educational attainment over the period of study, which means that workers in their late twenties and thirties tend to have more education, and thus a lower predicted business-cycle response, than workers in their forties and fifties.

Another, more promising variation in human capital across age groups is in specific human capital, or experience. Younger workers

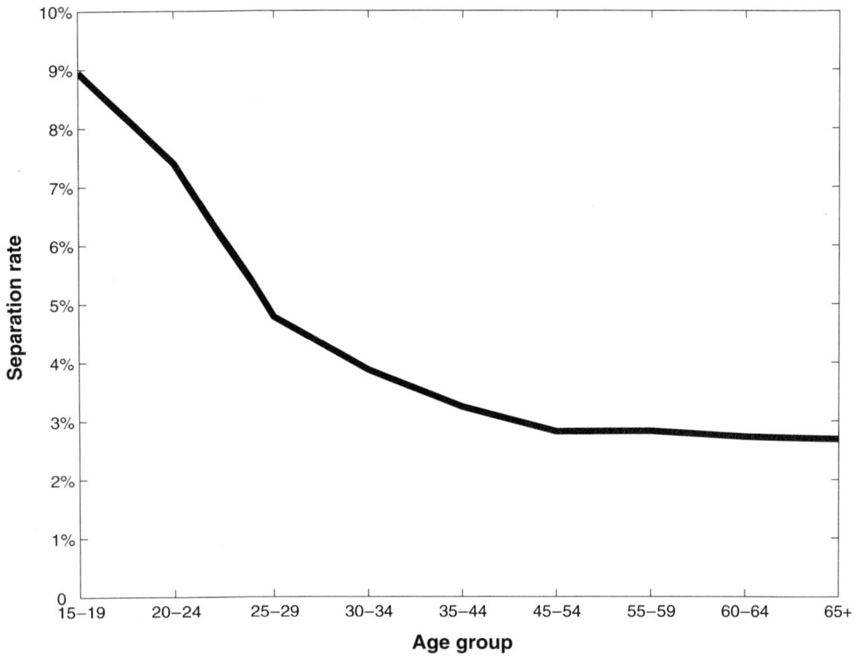

Figure 3
Monthly separation rate by age conditional on staying in the labor force

have less experience and lower tenure, on average, than their older counterparts. This experience includes knowledge about a particular firm, industry, or occupation, but it also includes knowledge about the worker's own ability or fit.

One way to demonstrate this lower level of specific human capital is to look at labor-market mobility by age. Figure 3 plots the monthly separation rate by age, conditional on staying in the labor force, using data from the Basic Monthly CPS between 1994 and 2003. It is clear that younger workers have much higher mobility levels than older workers do, even when conditioning on remaining in the labor force, i.e., disregarding the fact that younger workers are more likely to move in and out of the labor force.

4.1 *Looking for a Good Match when Young*

In this section, I sketch a model that relies on differences in a particular notion of specific human capital—differences in the knowledge about own ability/fit—to explain the higher response of young workers to business-cycle shocks.[9] Its primary goal is to demonstrate, at least qualitatively, that differential amounts of specific human capital is a promising mechanism to consider. To keep the discussion simple, I abstract from the other channels considered in the GRRW model: the agents in the model are infinitely lived (no time-horizon channel), face no retirement (no time-to-retirement channel), have the same potential productivity regardless of age (no life-cycle-profile channel), and are risk-neutral (no asset-market channel since there is no precautionary savings motive).

4.1.1 The Environment

Consider the following extension of the model of Mortensen and Pissarides (1994). There is a unit mass of workers of two types, half of them *round* and half of them *square*.[10] Workers are risk-neutral and discount future income at rate r. New workers are born and enter the labor market at rate σ, which is also the Poisson arrival rate of death, so that the size of the population remains constant over time. Newly born workers start out unemployed and do not know their type, although they know that they have probability one-half of being round and probability one-half of being square.

There are two labor markets: one for round people and one for square people. If a round person is matched in the round market, she produces px; if a square person is matched in the round market, she produces φpx, where $\varphi < 1$. Here, p is aggregate productivity, while x is the idiosyncratic productivity of the match, the evolution of which is discussed below. If a square person is matched in the square market, she produces px; if a round person is matched in the square market, she produces φpx. Unemployed workers enjoy a flow utility of b.

There is a large measure of potential firms who are risk-neutral and have the same discount rate r. These firms can open a vacancy in either market and keep the vacancy open at a flow cost of c. Firms with a vacancy do not see, prior to matching, whether a worker is round or square. There is a single matching function in each market with the usual properties. Once a worker and a firm are matched, the type of the worker is revealed. The idiosyncratic productivity x takes on its highest value of 1 when the worker and the firm match. While matched, new realizations of x arrive at rate δ and are drawn from distribution F: $[0, 1] \to [0, 1]$. A worker and a firm can separate at any point in time and will generally choose to do so when the idiosyncratic productivity is low. Finally, wages are determined by Nash bargaining.

4.1.2 Equilibrium

It is straightforward to show that, in the steady-state equilibrium of this model for a given level of aggregate productivity, half of new workers are lucky and enter the market where they are well matched (i.e., they enter the market of their own type). They learn their type during their first employment spell and never switch from that market again. The other half of new workers are unlucky and enter the market where they are badly matched. They go through one employment spell, learn their type and the fact that they are better matched in the other market, switch to the market where they are well matched, and stay there until they die. It can also be shown that there is a distinct reservation productivity of a match depending on whether the worker is well-matched or not: $R_{well} < R_{badly}$. In other words, matches that find out that they are badly matched do not end their relationship immediately since they find it beneficial to take advantage of their high idiosyncratic productivity. They are more stringent, however, about the level of idiosyncratic productivity required to continue the relationship since they know that the worker will be better matched in the other market once the relationship dissolves.

4.1.3 Comparative Statics

It is well known that, due to the high job finding rate that these type of models are generally calibrated to, analyzing a full dynamic stochastic version of the model with an explicit stochastic process for aggregate productivity gives results similar to analyzing the comparative static responses to changes in aggregate productivity. For the sake of simplicity then, I resort to the latter. It is easy to show that, just as in the standard Mortensen–Pissarides model, a decrease in the aggregate productivity p gives rise to an increase in the reservation productivities. For a uniform distribution, the increase in the reservation productivity is higher for badly matched workers than it is for well-matched workers. Hence, the impact of a negative shock is larger on the destruction margin for badly matched workers than for well-matched workers. Since badly matched workers are disproportionately young, this means that the impact of a negative shock is larger on young workers. The mechanism of the model thus works in the right direction for explaining the larger response of the hours of the young to aggregate shocks.

4.1.4 Simulation Results

To demonstrate the above claim, I simulate the above economy and study the response of the hours of the different age groups to aggregate shocks. In particular, I use the following approximations. I assume that aggregate productivity follows a two-state Markov process. Instead of trying to determine the history-dependent optimal policies of the workers, I approximate their optimal policies by the steady-state optimal policies corresponding to the two levels of aggregate productivity.[11]

In Figure 4, I report statistics that correspond to the statistics constructed using the actual data in Figure 1. In particular, I report the share in total hours in the peak year and the share in the drop in total hours during the downturn for each age group. As can be seen, this

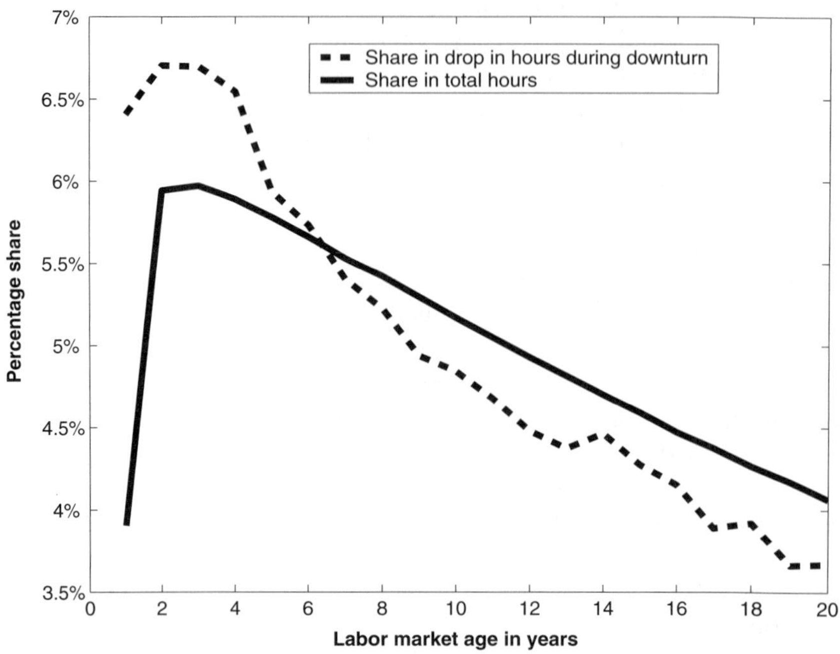

Figure 4
Model simulated share by age in total hours compared to model simulated share in drop in total hours during downturns

model can qualitatively generate the main pattern in the data, namely, that young workers are more responsive to business-cycle shocks than are older workers. In other words, in the model, the burden of a downturn falls disproportionately on the young, just as in the data.

Since the model is one that features bilaterally efficient separations, it is not possible to distinguish between quits and layoffs. The results regarding cyclical variation can be understood, however, both from the firm's and from the worker's perspective. From the firm's perspective, during a boom, a firm is willing to employ even relatively unproductive and relatively poorly matched workers. During a recession, however, a firm becomes more stringent, and separates from workers who are relatively unproductive or are relatively poorly matched. Being relatively unproductive is a risk that all workers face, while the risk of being poorly matched falls on young workers. Hence, young workers face larger risk of separation during a recession. From a worker's perspective, during a boom, she is willing to work even in relatively unproductive jobs and in relatively poor matches since the opportunity cost of searching for a more productive job or a better match is high. During a recession, however, the opportunity cost of searching for a better match becomes lower. If a worker is relatively unproductive or badly matched, she separates and starts looking for a more productive match. Again, being badly matched is a risk that only young workers face; hence, they have larger separation rates in a recession.

5. Conclusion

The work of GRRW directs attention to a new and very exciting avenue of research regarding the heterogeneous labor-market impact of business-cycle shocks. They focus on heterogeneity in age, which, together with education, seems to be the most important dimension along which workers differ in their response to business-cycle shocks. While much work remains to be done, the work of GRRW demonstrates some of the mechanisms that could result in differing business-cycle responses across the life cycle.

Understanding demographic heterogeneity over the business cycle is relevant for several reasons. As the authors point out, the heterogeneous impact of business-cycle shocks is an important testing ground for theories of fluctuations. There are other reasons beyond methodological ones. For example, political-economy considerations implied by demographic heterogeneity could be crucial for understanding stabilization policies. Also, labor-market heterogeneity could have important consequences for economists' understanding of the cost of business cycles. In particular, if business-cycle shocks have larger and potentially lasting effects on the labor-market performance of young workers, this could significantly increase macroeconomists' estimates of the costs of business cycles. Overall, demographic heterogeneity in the labor-market response to aggregate shocks is something that is long overdue in arriving on the research agenda of macro-labor economists.

Notes

1. See the appendix in Section 9 of their paper for a more detailed explanation of the measure used and a motivation for its use.

2. The five downturns distinguishable in the annual data are 1970 to 1971, 1974 to 1975, 1981 to 1983, 1990 to 1991, and 2001 to 2002, corresponding to the recessions beginning in December 1969, November 1973, January 1980, July 1990, and March 2001, respectively.

3. Plotting them separately for each downturn gives very similar patterns.

4. The cleanest way to disentangle this channel from the time-horizon channel is to consider an infinitely lived agent who can work only for the first T_R periods of her life and is then forced to retire and receive a fixed endowment in all subsequent periods. The numerical exercise in Section 6.2 of the paper maintains the assumption of finite lives, meaning that the results are influenced both by the time-horizon and the time-to-retirement channel.

5. This can be established more formally by log-linearizing the optimality conditions characterizing the decision problem of the worker around the steady state, which I omit for the sake of brevity, but which is available on request.

6. In light of the importance of the ratio of home to market hours, one could question the calibration exercise: it calibrates to married households only, which presumably biases the hours figures substantially for young households. Young people also spend a large fraction of their time in education, something that does not appear in the model or the calibration.

7. This channel is present in the variable labor version of the Krusell and Smith (1998) model presented in the appendix of their paper.

8. This comparison is made somewhat more difficult because Rios-Rull (1996) treated workers between 45 and 64 as one age group, while GRRW break them into two age groups. The primary effect of this difference is to make the impact of the time to retirement channel even more clear.

9. A more detailed exposition is available on request.

10. There is no conceptual difficulty in extending the model to more than two types.

11. In the standard Mortensen–Pissarides model, all decision variables are forward-looking, and market tightness can adjust instantaneously, so it turns out that the optimal policies simply depend on the current aggregate state. In the variant of the model consid-

ered here, this is no longer true because the distribution of well-matched and badly matched workers enters the state space of the firms.

References

Clark, K., and L. Summers. (1981). Demographic differences in cyclical employment variation. *Journal of Human Resources* 16:61–79.

Krusell, P., and A. Smith. (1998). Income and wealth heterogeneity in the macroeconomy. *Journal of Political Economy* 106(5):867–896.

Mortensen, D. T., and C. A. Pissarides. (1994). Job creation and job destruction in the theory of unemployment. *Review of Economic Studies* 61:397–415.

Nagypál, E. (2004). Unemployment differentials by skill: An explanation based on learning capital. Northwestern University. Working Paper.

Rios-Rull, V. (1996). Life-cycle economies and aggregate fluctuations. *Review of Economic Studies* 63:465–489.

Comment

Robert Shimer
University of Chicago and
NBER

1. Introduction

This is an ambitious paper. The authors extend the standard real business-cycle model in two directions. First, they allow for both market production and home production, as in Benhabib, Rogerson, and Wright (1991). Second, they allow for overlapping generations of finitely lived agents, as in Rios-Rull (1996). They then compute the aggregate implications of the overlapping generations model for cyclical fluctuations, focusing on the relative volatility of market hours (the number of hours that the representative agent spends working in the market sector) and market output (the output that she produces in the market sector). The main question they ask is, Can this generalization of the real business cycle model explain the observed differentials in the cyclical fluctuations in hours across age groups in the United States? I will use most of my discussion to address this question, but an initial digression is useful.

2. Representative Agent Model

The representative agent model which the authors develop in Section 2 performs remarkably well. Depending on the intertemporal elasticity of labor supply $1/(\gamma - 1)$ and the elasticity of substitution between home and market goods $1/(1 - \xi)$, the authors can easily match the relative volatility of market hours and market output (see their Table 2).[1] Therefore, a critical question is, Which values of these parameters are reasonable?

A well-established microeconomics literature starting with MaCurdy (1981) concludes from the life-cycle behavior of wages and hours worked in the market that an appropriate value for γ is close to infinity, at least for men, but recent work has questioned that finding. For example, Keane and Imai (2004) argue that MaCurdy and followers neglect an important component of the compensation of younger workers, human capital accumulated at work. After correcting for this, they find that the intertemporal elasticity is close to 4; i.e., γ is approximately 1.25. More to the point of this paper, Rupert, Rogerson, and Wright (2000) conclude that hours worked at home is an important omitted variable in MaCurdy-type regressions and show that including home work raises the estimated value of γ considerably. Both of these arguments seem quite convincing, and so values of γ not much larger than 1 are plausible.

There is much less evidence on the parameter ξ, that is, on the elasticity of substitution between home and market goods, although this parameter is also critical to the performance of the model. If home and market goods are strong complements, a decrease in market productivity induces workers to reduce the time they spend producing the complementary home goods, further reducing the cyclical fluctuations in market hours. The introduction of home goods amplifies the cyclical fluctuations in market hours only if the elasticity of substitution exceeds 1. So what is a reasonable value of ξ? To my knowledge, only two papers have tackled this question. McGrattan, Rogerson, and Wright (1997) pin down ξ using macro data and show that the model requires a high elasticity of substitution $1/(1-\xi)$ to match the behavior of important aggregate variables, including market hours and consumption and home capital. But this is analogous to saying that we know that the intertemporal elasticity of substitution is high because we observe that market hours fluctuate a lot over the business cycle. It does not provide independent evidence on the empirical relevance of the particular model. One wants to use microeconomic evidence to calibrate macroeconomic models.

Rupert, Rogerson, and Wright (1995) provide the best such evidence, but their estimates are imprecise. They start by estimating a fairly complicated home production model, allowing for the possibility that home and market goods are imperfect substitutes, home and market hours are imperfect substitutes, and the production of home goods is a concave function of home hours. Perhaps not surprisingly, their estimates of this very general model are imprecise. Despite this, their point estimates suggest that the elasticity of substitution between home and market goods is economically indistinguishable from one for single men and married couples, although it is larger for single women. This would seem to be a significant blow for the usefulness of the home production model in thinking about macroeconomics. But in footnote 13 in their paper, Rupert et al. impose that home and market hours are perfect substitutes and restrict the curvature of the home production function exogenously. They show that the estimates of ξ for married couples range between 0.2 and 0.3, somewhat less than the numbers that Gomme, Rogerson, Rupert, and Wright use in the current paper, but still significantly larger than zero. Based on this evidence, or lack of evidence, I think it is fair to say that the jury is still out on the true value of ξ, a viewpoint that seems to contrast with that of the authors.

3. Life-Cycle Model: Cyclical Fluctuations

The heart of this paper is the analysis of the behavior of employment volatility conditional on a worker's age. The authors use data from the March Current Population Survey (CPS) from 1962 to 2000 to document that the cyclical volatility of market hours is almost four times as high for teenagers as it is for prime-age workers.[2] This volatility decreases monotonically until approximately age 50, but is twice as high for workers over age 65 compared to workers age 45 to 64. I've constructed a similar measure using times series for age-contingent employment-population ratios, constructed by the Bureau of Labor Statistics (BLS) from the basic (monthly) CPS from 1948 to 2003. The results are remarkably similar to those in the paper. It is also worth noting that the relative volatility of different age groups is extremely stable over time.

Looking at this data and at the behavior of the aggregate model, the obvious hypothesis is that the aggregate model can satisfactorily explain the behavior of prime-age workers but does a poor job of explaining the behavior of younger and older workers. Of course, to test this hypothesis, it is necessary to write down a model in which workers of different ages interact. The overlapping generations model in Sections 4 and 5 is an obvious benchmark.

How well does the model perform? The authors claim that "the model's ability to account for fluctuations in [market] hours increases as we consider older age groups." At some level this is correct. In fact, the model predicts more hours volatility for workers age 55 to 64 than there is in the data. But this conclusion is misleading. The model ignores teenagers, the group with the greatest fluctuations in market hours. It imposes mandatory retirement at age 65, and so it cannot hope to match the high volatility of market hours for the oldest workers. And for the age ranges that are considered in the model, the standard deviation of market hours is basically a decreasing function of age in the data and an increasing function of age in the model (Table 14). A more accurate conclusion is that the life-cycle model can explain virtually none of the age pattern of fluctuations in hours. If anything, the life-cycle model predicts the opposite of what is observed in the data.

It is not particularly surprising that the life-cycle model predicts little of the variation in the observed fluctuations in hours. As my discussion of the aggregate model should have made clear, there are two important determinants of the volatility of market hours: the intertemporal elasticity of labor supply $1/(\gamma - 1)$ and the elasticity of substitution between home and market goods $1/(1 - \xi)$. Although the authors allow different age workers to have different preferences over market goods, home goods, and leisure, and they allow different age workers to be endowed with labor that is more or less productive, they do not allow either of the elasticities to vary with age. I suppose this puts discipline on the theoretical exercise, but in light of the results, the obvious reconciliation between the model and data is to allow for the possibility that younger workers have a more elastic labor supply or are more willing to substitute between market and home goods than are prime-age workers.

Of course, one would like some direct microeconomic evidence in support of this hypothesis. It seems impossible to measure age variation in the intertemporal elasticity of labor supply using MaCurdy's (1981) methodology, so this might be untestable. But the authors could have easily extended Rupert, Rogerson, and Wright (1995) to examine how the elasticity of substitution between home and market goods varies with age. Introspection suggests to me that as people age and have children, they become less willing to substitute between any goods, in particular market and home goods, a pattern that may help to reconcile the model and data.[3] Conversely, if the data do not show differential elasticities of substitution, I would again use the authors' words against them: "In looking for alternative theories to better account for aggregate labor market fluctuations, attention should be directed toward features that specifically affect individuals during the first half of their life." If the elasticity of substitution is the same over the life cycle, attention is best diverted away from home production models.

4. Life-Cycle Model: Secular Trends

There are some very interesting facts lurking in the shadows of this paper, in the secular trends in market hours. Although the number of hours worked per adult has not shown any trend in the United States during the past 55 years,[4] this is not true for particular age groups. Figure 1 shows that in 1948, the employment-population ratio for people over age 65 stood at over 26%. This fell steadily until around 1990, reaching as low as 10% before increasing slightly in the last fifteen years. The decline for older men has been even more dramatic. The same data indicate the opposite pattern for workers age 20 to 54, a secular increase in employment due to a sharp increase in women's increased labor force participation partially offset by a moderate decline in employment for prime-age men. Of course, this is not news to at least one of these authors, who has written: "the number of average weekly hours of market work per person in the United States since World War II ... has been roughly constant; for various groups, however, it has shifted dramatically from males to females, from older people to younger people, and from single- to married-person households" (McGrattan and Rogerson, 1998).

Why does this matter for Gomme, Rogerson, Rupert, and Wright? I am not simply saying that they should have written about secular trends instead of business-cycle fluctuations because the trends are more interesting than the cycle. In fact, it is conceivable that the same forces that explain the differential cyclical fluctuations in employment are also important for understanding the differential secular trends. But the secular trends raise a major concern: How does one calibrate such a model? The authors write "as is standard, we follow the procedure of requiring that parameter values are such that the model's deterministic steady state matches the time series averages for several aggregate variables." But if the aggregate variables are trending over time, does that mean that the calibrated parameters must also trend over time? It seems they must, which casts doubt on the discipline of the calibration exercise.

Conversely, the secular trends contain a lot of information that the authors ignore. McGrattan and Rogerson (1998) claim that changes in

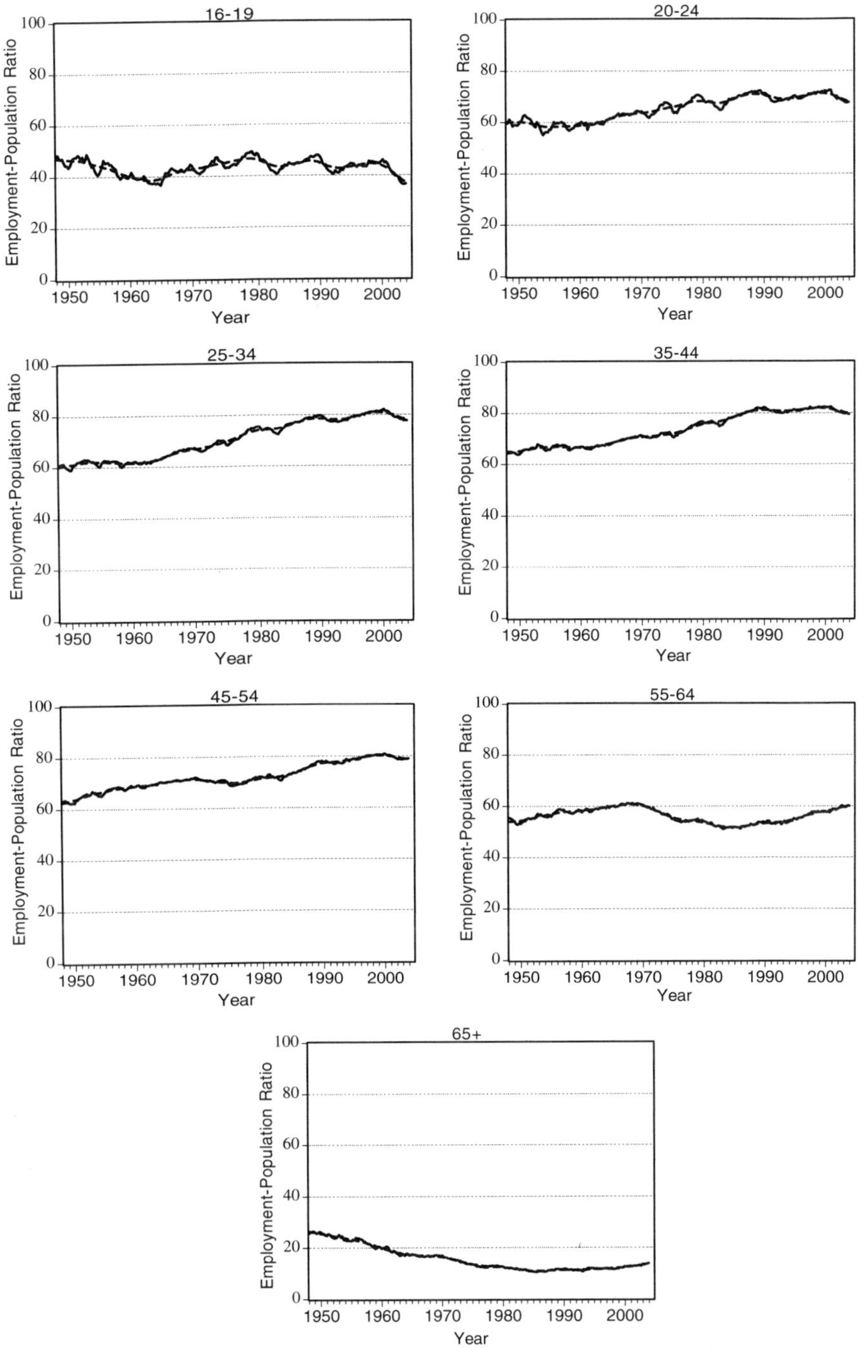

Figure 1
Employment-population ratio as a function of age, 1948–2003
The dashed line is an HP filter with smoothing parameter 1600 on quarterly data. The data were constructed by the Bureau of Labor Statistics from the CPS.

social security benefits, in fertility rates, and in family structure are critical for understanding secular changes in the employment-population ratio. In light of these changes, should we be surprised that the cross-sectional pattern of volatility is so stable over time? For example, if the cross-sectional pattern of volatility is due to different elasticities of substitution, then why did changes in fertility and family structure not alter the age-conditional elasticity of substitution and therefore rearrange the cross-sectional pattern of volatility? In other words, why is cyclical volatility so stable over time, even in the presence of the changes that induced large secular shifts in employment? Unfortunately, the paper does not answer this question.

5. Conclusion

Let me conclude by saying what I think we learn from this exercise. First, the authors make a convincing case that any model that purports to explain employment fluctuations must be able to explain why employment fluctuates more for younger workers and workers over the age of 65 than it does for prime-age workers. Second, they carefully describe and solve one particular model that, based on this criterion, cannot explain employment fluctuations: the real business-cycle model extended to allow for home production and overlapping generations. The next step is to explain what type of model can explain the cross-sectional pattern of employment fluctuations. That is an interesting and important question that I suspect will continue to occupy researchers' attention for many years.

Notes

1. The authors do not ask whether the model can explain the absolute volatility of the variables. Presumably the answer depends on whether cyclical fluctuations in the Solow residual represent a primitive technology shock.

2. The authors measure the volatility of hours as the standard deviation of the detrended hours series for a particular age group projected on the detrended hours series for the overall population.

3. Of course, this only makes the high volatility of hours for older workers more puzzling. Explaining this first requires a serious model of the retirement decision.

4. I measure the employment-population ratio using the basic CPS and average hours worked for production workers using the Current Employment Statistics (CES). The product of these two numbers is a rough measure of average hours per person. Between 1964 (the first year when hours data are available) and 1983, the average person worked

21.1 hours per week. Over the next 20-year period, this increased to 21.5 hours per week. There is no evidence of a secular trend in this variable.

References

Benhabib, Jess, Richard Rogerson, and Randall Wright. (1991). Homework in macroeconomics. *Journal of Political Economy* 99:1166–1187.

Keane, Michael, and Susumu Imai. (2004). Intertemporal lbor supply and human capital accumulation. *International Economic Review* 45:601–641.

MaCurdy, Thomas. (1981). An empirical model of labor supply in a life cycle setting. *Journal of Political Economy* 89:1059–1085.

McGrattan, Ellen, and Richard Rogerson. (1998). Changes in hours worked since 1950. *Federal Reserve Bank of Minneapolis Quarterly Review* 22:2–19.

McGrattan, Ellen, Richard Rogerson, and Randall Wright. (1997). An equilibrium model of the business cycle with household production and fiscal policy. *International Economic Review* 38:267–290.

Rios-Rull, Victor. (1996). Life-cycle economies and aggregate fluctuations. *Review of Economic Studies* 63:465–489.

Rupert, Peter, Richard Rogerson, and Randall Wright. (1995). Using panel data to estimate substitution elasticities in household production models. *Economic Theory* 6:179–193.

Rupert, Peter, Richard Rogerson, and Randall Wright. (2000). Homework in labor economics: Household production and intertemporal substitution. *Journal of Monetary Economics* 46:557–579.

Discussion

In response to the discussants' question about the objective and value added of the exercise presented in the paper, Richard Rogerson said that their work was rather a robustness exercise on some previous work, such as the one conducted by José-Víctor Ríos-Rull, and attempted a deeper analysis into what types of changes over the life cycle could account for the changes in volatility over the life cycle. Rogerson explained that Ríos-Rull's work was centered on whether aggregate fluctuations properties looked different in a life-cycle model than in an infinitely lived representative agent model, and looked at what happens to volatility over the life cycle but did not look into why it behaved the way it did. Rogerson said that in their work, they concluded that for reasonable parametrizations it was impossible to get the life-cycle pattern and that although they did not expect to obtain it, it was important to understand why. The fact that they obtained something that was flat over the life cycle meant that there was a failure of the model to generate the life cycle and this had very important implications concerning the type of modifications these models needed.

A number of participants expressed opinions regarding the relevance of incorporating frictions into the analysis. First, Rogerson responded to Éva Nagypál's comments by saying that even if their model did not include frictions, the way they were looking at the data might allow more precise identification of frictions and their effects on different age groups. John Leahy said that even if Rogerson had dismissed wage frictions as a potential explanation for their findings, maybe it would be interesting to look at seniority rules in firing decisions and what happened if that friction occurred. He wondered what the effects would be on decisions of who gets fired and who does not, or what types of jobs people got through the life cycle. Rogerson responded that they did not consider wage variability per se to be very important for explaining long-term relationships and they did not expect the wage to reflect the marginal value of production. Dave Backus said that what was useful about frictions was to use the same friction to explain more than one thing and suggested looking at the work of Romer and Gerome, which tried to explain consumption heterogeneity by age. In that work, young people who did not have a cushion of assets were pressed by the borrowing constraint and were more responsive on the consumption side; Backus wondered if this might have a similar effect on hours worked and be relevant to the authors' work. On this topic of the borrowing constraint, Éva Nagypál believed that it went the wrong way. Intuitively, she said, one might think that young workers, because of this constraint, had less opportunity to decrease their hours in a recession, but if one included durables and other kinds of goods, then the direction would be reversed. David Laibson believed that nominal wage rigidity mechanisms affected new workers more than those with more seniority because of the lack of joint surplus. He believed that high-frequency variations for new/young workers, the kind of dynamics shown in the data, would be appearing more and more often.

There were several interventions dealing with the differences along the life span. Steve Davis believed that the previous explanations were not enough because this was not just a cyclical phenomenon and suggested looking at the elasticity of the substitution parameter between market- and home-produced goods as a function of age. Rogerson admitted that in passing from an infinitely lived agent to the life cycle, they maintained the assumption of constant elasticities over the entire life span. He said that many of the labor supply elasticities came from estimations of prime-age individuals. Taking that into consideration, their model worked well for prime-age individuals but not for the wage history. Alessandra Fogli suggested looking at different family arrangements to understand different elasticities at different ages. Younger and older workers might rely more heavily on their prime-age relatives who were less elastic. Rogerson said that in their overlapping generations model, they considered workers starting at age 20 and did not consider the 16 to 19 group precisely for the reasons mentioned by Fogli. The household structure in their model was based on a married couple, and people aged 16–19 were not considered to be in that kind of structure. He said that an open-ended question might be to what extent 16- to 19-year-olds were in different family structures and if that produced different outcomes.

Mark Gertler brought attention to the fact that the authors were trying to address alternative explanations for a possible life-cycle pattern of volatility and this was innovative work. He also said that originally he had thought that the pattern found by the authors responded to the fact that most young workers could be in manufacturing. However, the authors' analysis showed that this did not seem to be the case and that the life-cycle pattern did exist for other sets of factors, such as sex or education. Gertler also agreed with Robert Shimer on the importance of the effect of demographics on volatility. He wondered if demographics could have a first-order effect on volatility the way that Shimer's work showed it did for the equilibrium unemployment rate. Gertler thought that getting at this would involve having effects and that it would need a structural model showing that demographics would have an aggregate effect on volatility. Rogerson responded by saying that Shimer mentioned the secular decline and that although it seemed interesting, it was difficult to incorporate it into their model because there was no consensus about what drives those secular trends. However, it would be possible to conduct an analysis like the one suggested by Shimer in terms of looking at two different pictures of the life-cycle profile, one for the 1950s and one for the 1990s. This could be a way to calibrate the model in two different ways and to see if there were different results. However, Rogerson believed the result would be similar to the one they had obtained and that it would be flat over the life cycle. He raised a deeper question, though, about the interactions between trends and cycles. He thought that sometimes there was confusion about what was a cycle and what was a trend and that such confusion could exaggerate fluctuations in some groups versus others.

Harald Uhlig was intrigued with the difference between the numbers for quarterly data and yearly data, which are what the authors used. He said that it was possible to use the Hodrick-Prescott (HP) smoothing parameter equal to 100, but if they really wanted to replicate what was done with quarterly data, they would have to use a parameter of 7. He thought that since they were using the parameter of 100, maybe they were missing things that were happening at lower frequencies. He suggested that maybe hours fluctuate more quickly at higher frequencies, while unemployment fluctuates more at lower frequencies.

Finally, Jordi Galí expressed his reservations regarding the initial motivation given by the authors in terms of the inability of a standard representative-household model to generate sufficient volatility of hours with respect to output or productivity. He believed this was because the authors had chosen a model exclusively driven by technology shocks. With a model that allowed for sources of fluctuations other than technology shocks, there would be more volatility in hours than in either output or productivity. Rogerson acknowledged that their motivation came from a particular type of model and that other models would produce greater fluctuations.